651
A

Office practice

GENERAL OFFICE PROCEDURES

FRED C. ARCHER
Professor of Business Education
Shippensburg State College
Shippensburg, Pennsylvania

RAYMOND F. BRECKER
Assistant Superintendent for Financial
and Business Management
Buffalo City School District
Buffalo, New York

JEFFREY R. STEWART, JR.
Professor of Business Education
Virginia Polytechnic Institute and State University
Blacksburg, Virginia

GENERAL OFFICE PROCEDURES

FOURTH EDITION

Gregg and Community College Division/McGraw-Hill Book Company
New York St. Louis Dallas San Francisco Düsseldorf Johannesburg
Kuala Lumpur London Mexico Montreal New Delhi Panama
Paris São Paulo Singapore Sydney Tokyo Toronto

ACKNOWLEDGMENTS

The authors wish to express their gratitude to the many teachers who offered suggestions for this revision. They also are indebted to many business organizations for supplying information and reviewing sections of the manuscript. These include:

Allied Chemical Corporation; American Telephone & Telegraph Company; Chambersburg Trust Co.; Dauphin Deposit Trust Company; H. C. Gabler, Inc.; Gestetner Corporation; Horn's Motor Express, Inc.; International Business Machines Corporation; Parker Distributors; Penn-Central Railroad; Pennsylvania Bureau of Employment Security; People's National Bank, Shippensburg, Pa.; Smead Manufacturing Company; South Penn Motor Club, Chambersburg, Pa.; 3M Company; United Parcel Service; United States Postal Service; The United Telephone Company of Pennsylvania; Western Union International, Inc.; Western Union Telegraph Company; T. B. Wood's Sons Company.

Our thanks to the following for photographs appearing on unit-opening pages:

Unit 1, p. 1, McGraw-Hill, Inc.; Unit 2, p. 33, Mobil Oil Corporation; Unit 3, p. 69, The Babcock & Wilcox Company; Unit 4, p. 82, American Telephone & Telegraph Company; Unit 5, p. 121, American Management Association; Unit 6, p. 158, International Business Machines Corporation; Unit 7, p. 207, Pfizer Inc.; Unit 8, p. 261, Irving Trust Company; Unit 9, p. 293, The Babcock & Wilcox Company; Unit 10, p. 329, Metropolitan Life Insurance Co.; Unit 11, p. 342, Pfizer Inc.; Unit 12, p. 366, American Management Association; Unit 13, p. 383, The Chase Manhattan Bank, photo by Van Vachniewicz; Unit 14, p. 411, Allied Chemical Corporation; Unit 15, p. 425, American Management Association; Unit 16, p. 441, Allied Chemical Corporation; Unit 17, p. 463, Exxon Corporation; Unit 18, p. 481, Victor Comptometer Corp.; Unit 19, p. 497, Allied Chemical Corporation.

Designer	Barbara Bert
Sponsoring Editor	Margaret Halmy
Editing Manager	Elizabeth Huffman
Editor	Janice Johnson
Production Supervisor	Gary Whitcraft

GENERAL OFFICE PROCEDURES, Fourth Edition

Library of Congress Cataloging in Publication Data

Archer, Fred Coleman, date.
    General office procedures.

    First–3d editions published under title: General office practice.
      1. Office practice. I. Brecker, Raymond Franklin, date, joint author. II. Stewart, Jeffrey Robert, date, joint author. III. Title.
HF5547.5.A75 1975   651   74-2135
ISBN 0-07-002161-9

PREFACE

Offices in business, government, and industry offer an extraordinary number and variety of opportunities for immediate employment. The expansion of office staffs plus the replacement of workers in various clerical positions results in a pressing demand for hundreds of thousands of new typists, general office clerks, file clerks, payroll clerks, messengers, and other vitally important employees each year. Thus the main objective of *General Office Procedures, Fourth Edition,* is to help high school students qualify for the entry-level office jobs most frequently and most widely available today.

IMPORTANT FEATURES

This fourth edition of *General Office Procedures* retains the features that led to the widespread popularity and success of the previous editions. However. this edition has been changed in ways that will enhance its usefulness not only as the basic textbook in a regular office procedures course but also as an invaluable reference in office block programs, cooperative education programs, simulation-based classes, and so on.

The text material is organized into 19 units, which are subdivided into 44 sections. The following discussion highlights the significant features of these units and sections.

Career Information

Units 1 and 2, which consist of Sections 1 through 5, provide students with helpful information about a variety of office jobs and paths of career advancement. The discussion of these topics, as well as all others throughout the program, reflects the numerous gains that have been made, and are continuing to be made, in equal employment and career advancement opportunity for all. Among these gains, of course, is the recent and continuing change in employment attitudes and practices with regard to the job roles of men and women. A larger and ever-increasing number of supervisory and managerial positions are opening up to qualified women as well as men. Similarly, jobs traditionally held by women are now being made available to men.

In Unit 19, at the end of the text, the students will learn how to get the job they want—how to locate job openings, prepare for interviews, complete résumés, and so on.

General Office Skills

The main purpose of Units 3 through 12 is to help students acquire the necessary knowledge and the skills related to such basic office activities as these: handling mail, typing, filing, duplicating, and business writing. Although the responsibilities associated with these office functions are often assigned to a number of specialized office workers, many office employees must perform some or all of these duties as a part of their regular job assignments.

Office Systems and Procedures

In Units 13 through 18, students study principles, techniques, and procedures related to cash control, sales, inventory and stock control, shipping, purchasing, and payroll systems in a modern business. They learn the duties of various jobs within the context of a total business operation.

Student Activities

The fourth edition of *General Office Procedures* offers a variety of student activities so that students gain the complete mastery of the principles and procedures needed to obtain and succeed in a job in a modern office. These activities include Reviewing Your Reading questions as well as Office Assignments projects at the end of each section. Also, Business Cases and Problems — including various kinds of human relations problems occurring in an office — appear at the end of each unit.

So that they can be used with greater convenience and flexibility, the mathematics, grammar, and punctuation skill-builders that appeared at the end of each chapter in the previous edition now appear in the Appendix at the end of the text. Students may use all these materials as part of a comprehensive skill-development program, or they may work on only certain skill-builders as the need arises.

SUPPORTING MATERIALS

The *Workbook for General Office Procedures, Fourth Edition*, provides worksheets and business forms for all the office assignments appearing at the end of each section of the textbook. In addition, it includes a number of bonus projects to afford the students additional applications of the skills and knowledge they have acquired.

A new edition of the *Model Office Practice Set* and other specialized practice sets are also available. Each of these completely self-contained programs reinforces and enriches the textbook presentation of principles and procedures related to various office activities.

The *Teacher's Manual and Key* presents numerous suggestions for organizing and teaching the course and provides the solutions to all the textbook and workbook exercises. It also contains a series of objective tests correlated with the textbook. The tests may be adapted or reproduced without charge for classroom use.

Fred C. Archer
Raymond F. Brecker
Jeffrey R. Stewart, Jr.

CONTENTS

UNIT 1
THE OFFICE IN TODAY'S BUSINESS

The Modern Office

You can get a good idea of how important office workers are to business from the fact that they make up more than one-sixth of the total working population of the country! This adds up to more than 14 million office jobs.

It makes office workers the second largest occupational group in the United States. And if you are thinking of office work as a career, you'll be interested in knowing the prediction that an additional 3¾ million office workers will be needed by the end of the 1970s. This amounts to an extraordinary 26 percent increase.

A company of any size is made up of many parts, or departments, which must work together smoothly and efficiently. Every part is supported by the activities of office workers. Indeed, the office staff is appreciatively described as the backbone of a business organization.

WHAT DO OFFICE WORKERS DO?

Office workers perform the following two indispensable services for an organization:

1 They help company executives, department managers, supervisors, and fellow workers meet their responsibilities.
2 They expedite the day-to-day operations of the company.

WHAT KIND OF SUPPORT DOES MANAGEMENT NEED?

If a business is to be successful and to make a profit, it must be organized and operated by its managers so that it runs smoothly and efficiently. In order to do this, the managers call on trained office personnel to help them meet their responsibilities in each of the four vital areas of business management: *communication, control, production,* and *coordination.* Let's look at the important role of office workers in each of these areas.

Communication

A manager who assigns a task to an employee must make sure that all directions are transmitted to the employee quickly, accurately, and completely. The manager uses office communication systems to save valuable time in transmitting these directions. Instead of interrupting a worker on the job to explain what needs to be done, the manager dictates the instructions either to a secretary or into a dictating machine. The letter, bulletin, or memorandum is transcribed, put in finished form, and sent to the worker. By putting the directions in writing, the manager not only saves time but also makes the instructions clear, so that the worker will neither misunderstand nor forget them.

Control

Once work is assigned, a manager relies on the office staff to follow up on the assignment and to check on its progress. Frequent reports of work completed by every department are received. By reading these reports, the manager can keep a close check on company operations without having to leave the office. When corrective action needs to be taken, the manager promptly issues new instructions, which the office staff processes, distributes, and acts upon.

Production

A visit to an automobile assembly plant is a thrilling experience. A new car takes shape before your eyes with unbelievable speed and precision. But what you cannot see and, perhaps, not even realize is the amount of work done by the office staff in order to keep the production line running. The split-second timing whereby each piece, each tool, and each worker is in the right place at the right time depends upon the orderly flow of materials and instructions, which are controlled through the office.

Coordination

Coordination depends upon teamwork. One of management's hardest tasks is to see that the separate parts of an organization work together harmoniously. A sales force, for example, may work hard to boost sales. In anticipation of increased business, the shipping room hires extra help. That's good planning. But if the factory force fails to produce enough stock to take care of the increased sales orders, the extra efforts of the other two groups are wasted.

To avoid this kind of situation, a manager, through the use of communication and duplicating services, informs the office staff about any new plan of operation. And, in turn, the manager expects the office staff to report on the progress of their operations. Reports prepared by the office staff show how every work unit is contributing to the total work effort. Through close and frequent communication between manager and office staff, a manager can detect problems in company operations quickly, deal with them before they become serious, and concentrate on the supervision of a well-coordinated, smooth-running operation.

HOW DOES THE OFFICE EXPEDITE OPERATIONS?

Each company generally has a number of standard operations that are handled systematically by the office staff. The work gets done swiftly and efficiently because it is performed step by step, according to careful instructions. The most common routine in a typical office is the handling of a sales order, a process which involves many people from many different departments. Just how many different people and departments it involves will surprise you when you look at the chart on page 5 illustrating the flow of work from the time a customer places an order, either in person or by mail, to the time a messenger delivers the final report on the completed order to the manager.

All business procedures are defined by individual tasks or functions. Look at the variety of tasks involved in the processing of a typical sales order.

Directing customers and *routing* orders to the place where they will receive proper attention.

Computing carefully and accurately.

Verifying or double-checking details and calculations to make sure they are correct.

Filling out or preparing accurately orders, invoices, and other papers, which instruct other workers what to do.

Sending and dispatching papers and goods in order to get them on their way to the customer as quickly as possible.

Entering and posting information on permanent, original records to note what a customer owes.

Filing data for future reference and *finding* it again.

Preparing reports, *duplicating* them, and *distributing* copies to key personnel.

HOW DO YOU GET ASSIGNED TO A PARTICULAR JOB?

Your special talents, skills, and training matched up against the job openings in a company at a given time determine what specific unit and job you'll be assigned to. Now is the time for you to take advantage of the many options you have in planning a career. And you can do this only if you get to know all you can about the wide range of office careers that exist. They fall into eight general categories: business data processing; computing and accounting; filing and related occupations; information and message distribution; materials support; stenographic, secretarial, and related occupations; typing and related occupations; and miscellaneous clerical occupations. You'll find through discussion and research that within these categories there are many different individual jobs.

Don't be concerned if you find it hard to make a specific job choice right away. The business world is bound to be new and strange to you, but it can be most interesting! As you learn more about individual office jobs, you'll find it easier to focus on a job you want.

Take the time to explore. Ask questions. Talk to people you meet about the kind of work they do, and ask them how they feel about it. If you can arrange it, visit some business offices and look around. You may even get a chance to help out in some clerical capacity during vacation periods. However, whatever you do, try to get a close view of some of the jobs in the area of work that interests you.

Don't stop there. Look into some of the areas you may never have considered before. There will never be a better time to widen your career horizons. Who knows what you may discover?

PROCESSING A SALES ORDER

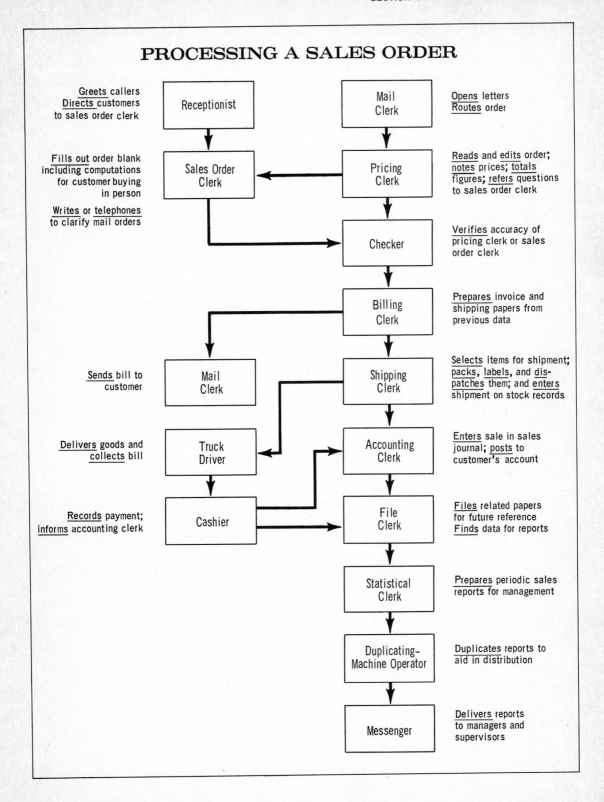

Greets callers
Directs customers
to sales order clerk

Receptionist

**Mail
Clerk**

Opens letters
Routes order

Fills out order blank
including computations
for customer buying
in person

Writes or telephones
to clarify mail orders

**Sales Order
Clerk**

**Pricing
Clerk**

Reads and edits order;
notes prices; totals
figures; refers questions
to sales order clerk

Checker

Verifies accuracy of
pricing clerk or sales
order clerk

**Billing
Clerk**

Prepares invoice and
shipping papers from
previous data

Sends bill to
customer

**Mail
Clerk**

**Shipping
Clerk**

Selects items for shipment;
packs, labels, and dis-
patches them; and enters
shipment on stock records

Delivers goods and
collects bill

**Truck
Driver**

**Accounting
Clerk**

Enters sale in sales
journal; posts to
customer's account

Records payment;
informs accounting clerk

Cashier

**File
Clerk**

Files related papers
for future reference
Finds data for reports

**Statistical
Clerk**

Prepares periodic sales
reports for management

**Duplicating–
Machine Operator**

Duplicates reports to
aid in distribution

Messenger

Delivers reports
to managers and
supervisors

REVIEWING YOUR READING

1 Why should you consider office work as a career?

2 How do office operations help the manager to communicate with the organization and control its work?

3 What does *coordination* mean? Do you think it might be difficult to achieve?

4 Describe the clerical duties involved in processing a sales order.

5 List the eight categories of clerical occupations open to beginning office workers.

6 How can you benefit from learning more about individual office jobs?

OFFICE ASSIGNMENTS

1 The office helps management to communicate and to control. Here is an interoffice memorandum issued by a personnel director in a large company. Read it carefully; then answer these questions: **(a)** What specific instructions are given? **(b)** How will this manager ever know if the order was obeyed?

Interoffice | *Memorandum* | BIRCH COMPANY

TO   All Employees

SUBJECT Application for Special
         Training Courses

FROM   F. A. Clark

DATE   September 5, 19--

All requests for special training courses must reach this office in writing not later than ten days prior to the start of the course. Use Form 69--Application for Special Training--for this purpose, and complete it in triplicate.

Each applicant will submit all three copies of Form 69 to his unit supervisor. In turn, the supervisor will indicate approval or reason for denial of the request in the space provided at the bottom of the form. The original, or the first copy, of all requests will be forwarded to the Education and Training Section, the second copy will be sent to me, and the third copy will be retained by the supervisor for future reference.

                                FAC

2 Here is a sales invoice that has just been prepared by the billing clerk in a manufacturing company. Assume that your firm processes a sales invoice in

the same way as illustrated on page 5. Identify each of the remaining steps in the processing of this order and the job title of the person involved in each step. If you are using the workbook, insert the job title of the person in the blank space provided.

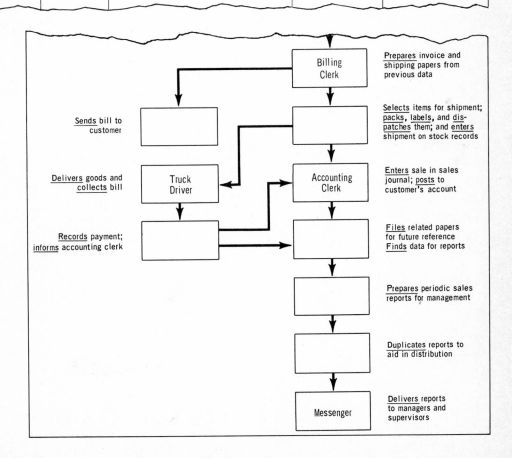

B. J. Dawson Company
1100 Torrence Street
Waco, Texas 76705

Invoice No. **A-2503**

Date	March 16, 19--
Terms	2/10, n/30
Order No. or Date	S 854
Shipped Via	Prepaid/Lombardy Truck

Sold To General Machinery Company
Box 2001 South Station
Newark, New Jersey 07014

Ship To Liberty Textile Company
380 Verona Avenue
Green Pond, South Carolina 29446

Quantity	Stock No.	Description	Unit Price	Amount
1	001	Grinding Wheel	129.00	129.00
1	002	Buffer	44.00	44.00
		Total		173.00

Billing Clerk — Prepares invoice and shipping papers from previous data

Sends bill to customer

Selects items for shipment; packs, labels, and dispatches them; and enters shipment on stock records

Delivers goods and collects bill

Truck Driver

Accounting Clerk — Enters sale in sales journal; posts to customer's account

Records payment; informs accounting clerk

Files related papers for future reference
Finds data for reports

Prepares periodic sales reports for management

Duplicates reports to aid in distribution

Messenger — Delivers reports to managers and supervisors

3 Parson Distributors has just received the order and remittance illustrated below from a customer, Dan P. Bordon. How does this order form simplify the work of the mail clerk, pricing clerk, billing clerk, and cashier? The correct answer for the mail clerk is supplied as an example.

Example: Mail clerk: The distinctive design of the form immediately identifies the item as an order, which can be routed to the pricing clerk right away.

PARSON DISTRIBUTORS
998 Olmstead Avenue
Bronx, New York 10473

FIRST NAME: D A N   LAST NAME: B O R D O N
STREET ADDRESS: 1 0 1   N O B E Y   D R I V E
CITY: A K R O N   STATE: O H   ZIP CODE: 4 4 3 0 6

SHIP VIA: PLEASE CHECK ONE   U.P.S. ☐   REA ☐   P.P. ☑   AIR MAIL ☐   TRUCK COLLECT ☐

DATE 4 / 30 /19--

PLEASE USE CATALOG NUMBERS AND GIVE COMPLETE DESCRIPTIONS

PAGE NO.	QUANTITY	CATALOG NUMBER	IMPORTANT: STATE MAKE, MODEL, COLOR, SIZE, ETC.	UNIT PRICE	TOTAL AMOUNT
2	1	0314/0923	50-lb. TEST LINE	1.99	1 99
5	1	0716/1358	RODDY BR 10' ROD	20.95	20 95
8	1	0918/5165	COLD WEATHER BAG	23.95	23 95

TOTAL FOR GOODS	46	89
TAX*		
SHIPPING & INSURANCE	1	55
TOTAL CASH PRICE	48	44
AMT. ENCLOSED	48	44

* NEW YORK STATE RESIDENTS ONLY. ADD APPLICABLE SALES TAX

Dan P. Bordon   No. 396

Pay
To The   April 30, 19--   56-651 / 412
Order Of *Parson Distributors* ———————— $48 44/100

Forty-eight and 44/100 ———————————————— Dollars

People's Bank of Akron
Akron, Ohio 44308

Dan P. Bordon

⑆0412⑆0651⑆ 255⑆026⑈

2 Where Office Jobs Are

Office work is a fast-growing field. More office workers are needed every year as replacements for workers who change jobs or leave the job market and as additional staff to meet the public's increased demand for products and services. As you can see in the chart below, the majority of office jobs fall into 13 classifications.

Perhaps you already have an idea as to what career you want to pursue. If you haven't, however, you now have the opportunity to examine what the job prospects are in certain areas of office work, the training required, and the opportunities for advancement.

OCCUPATIONS OF OFFICE WORKERS

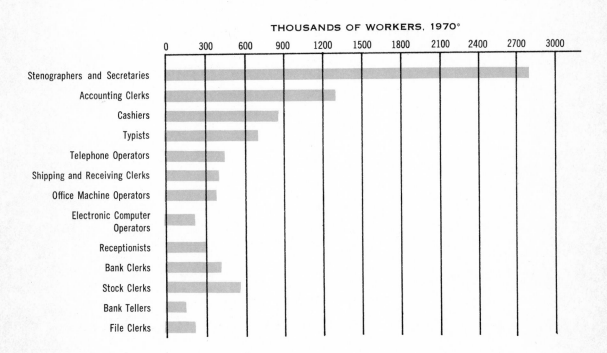

THOUSANDS OF WORKERS, 1970*

OCCUPATIONAL OUTLOOK HANDBOOK, 1972–1973, Department of Labor.

*Estimated.

STENOGRAPHERS AND SECRETARIES

Stenographers take dictation in shorthand of correspondence and reports and transcribe dictated material, using a typewriter. They perform a variety of

A skilled secretary contributes greatly to efficient business management.

Courtesy General Telephone & Electronics Corporation

clerical duties, except when they work in a stenographic pool, and may also transcribe material from sound recordings. Secretaries schedule appointments, give information to callers, take dictation, and otherwise relieve officials of clerical work and minor administrative and business details, such as reading and routing incoming mail.

Number Needed

Employed in 1970 2,800,000
Number of job openings annually:
      Replacements........ 155,000
      New positions 82,000
      Total 237,000
New positions 1970 to 1980 adding to total employed 820,000
Total number of people employed in this category by 1980 3,620,000

Where Employed

Although stenographers and secretaries are employed in organizations of every size and type, more than half of them work for service industries, such as finance, insurance, and real estate, and for government organizations. Many technical stenographers and secretaries work for professionals such as physicians and attorneys. A few stenographers are self-employed either as public stenographers, who take dictation and transcribe for anyone on a fee basis, or as reporting stenographers, who cover hearings, meetings, conventions, and similar special events. Stenographic and secretarial jobs for men tend to be concentrated in public administration, education, and manufacturing. It's interesting to note that many of the stenographers who specialize in court reporting are men.

Training Required

A good basic education and technical training in shorthand, typing, and business English is needed. Also it would be helpful for the applicant to know how to handle mail, to file, and to operate some business machines. Graduation from high school is essential for practically all positions. Some employers prefer a background of academic high school subjects supplemented by technical training taken after graduation.

Advancement Opportunities

Capable and well-trained stenographers and secretaries have good opportunities for advancement. Many stenographers advance to better-paying positions as secretaries; some who develop great speed in taking dictation become reporting stenographers. Both secretaries and stenographers may be promoted to jobs such as administrative assistant, office supervisor, executive secretary, or more responsible positions requiring specialized knowledge of the employer's industry or business.

ACCOUNTING CLERKS

These office workers perform a variety of duties that have to do with calculating, typing, and posting (the recording of transactions on specific accounts). They may type vouchers, invoices, statements, payrolls, and reports. An adding machine is often used for some aspects of the work.

Number Needed

Employed in 1970 1,340,000
Number of job openings annually:
    Replacements........ 58,000
    New positions 20,000
    Total 78,000
New positions 1970 to 1980 adding to total employed 200,000
Total number of people employed in this category by 1980 1,540,000

Where Employed

Jobs, in general, are found in banks, insurance companies, manufacturing firms, service organizations, and retail stores.

Training Required

Most employers prefer high school graduates who have taken business mathematics and accounting. Some prefer applicants who have completed junior college. It is helpful to know how to type and to use office machines. Many companies cooperate with business schools and high schools in work-study programs, which give students practical part-time work experience that can be helpful in obtaining employment after graduation. Other companies offer new accounting clerks on-the-job training.

Advancement Opportunities

Beginning accounting clerks usually start by recording simple accounting transactions and then advance to more responsible assignments, such as preparing income statements and operating complex accounting machines. Some are promoted to supervisors. Those who complete college accounting and qualify as skilled professionals in fiscal matters can function on a management level.

CASHIERS

Cashiers receive funds from customers and employees and issue checks or pay out money when authorized to do so. They prepare bank deposits and deposit slips, post data to accounts, balance incoming and outgoing funds, and compile reports dealing with the collection of money, the outflow of money, and the bank reconciliation statements. They operate equipment such as typewriters and calculating, accounting, and checkwriting machines.

Number Needed

Employed in 1970 847,000
Number of job openings annually:
      Replacements........ 38,000
      New positions 31,000
      Total 69,000
New positions 1970 to 1980 adding to total employed 310,000
Total number of people employed in this category by 1980 1,157,000

Where Employed

Grocery, drug, and other retail stores continue to be the main source of employment for nearly three-fourths of the nation's cashiers. A large number of cashiers also are employed in restaurants and theaters. Cashier positions are found in small towns, in large cities, and in shopping centers in heavily populated suburban areas.

Training Required

Requirements vary. Some employers want persons who have special business skills or experience in typing or selling. Other employers fill cashier jobs by promoting clerk-typists in offices, bag boys in supermarkets, and other qualified personnel already employed by the firm. Competent cashiers need to have an aptitude for working with figures, finger dexterity, and good eye-hand coordination. Accuracy is important. And since they, in general, deal directly with the public, it is important that cashiers be tactful, courteous, and neat in appearance.

Advancement Opportunities

Opportunities for promotion are likely to be limited, especially in small firms. However, cashiers have a particularly good chance to learn a great deal about their employer's business. The position, therefore, can serve as a stepping-stone to a more responsible office job or possibly to some type of managerial position. For example, in chain stores and in other large retailing enterprises, cashiers can be promoted to department or store managers.

TYPISTS

The work of typists is varied. Typists generally type letters, reports, stencils, forms, or other straight-copy material from rough draft or corrected copy. They also may be expected to verify totals on report forms, requisitions, or bills. Many operate duplicating machines.

Number Needed

Employed in 1970 700,000
Number of job openings annually:
    Replacements 42,000
    New positions 21,000
    Total 63,000
New positions 1970 to 1980 adding to total employed 210,000
Total number of people employed in this category by 1980 910,000

Where Employed

Jobs are available in almost all types of private and public enterprises, particularly in manufacturing firms, banks, insurance companies, and federal, state, and local government agencies. In addition, hundreds of thousands of workers in other kinds of clerical occupations use typing skills in connection with their main job assignments.

Training Required

Applicants are generally asked to take a typing test and are expected to have a minimum typing speed of 40 to 50 words a minute. It is important that they know how to spell well, have a reasonably wide vocabulary, and have a knowledge of punctuation and grammar. Employers generally prefer that they be high school graduates and consider it an extra advantage if they have had some business training and are familiar with the operation of such office equipment as duplicating and adding machines.

Advancement Opportunities

A typist may be promoted from junior to senior typist or to another clerical position involving greater responsibility and higher pay. Typists who know shorthand may be promoted to stenographer or secretary.

TELEPHONE OPERATORS

These workers operate cord or cordless switchboards to relay incoming and outgoing calls. They may supply information to callers, record messages, and keep records of calls placed and the toll charges. Many perform clerical duties, such as typing, proofreading, and sorting mail. Some operate a system of bells or buzzers to call individuals in a business to the phone when they are in the building but away from their phone.

Number Needed

Employed in 1970 430,000
Number of job openings annually:
     Replacements 21,000
     New positions 6,900
     Total 27,900
New positions 1970 to 1980 adding to total employed 69,000
Total number of people employed in this category by 1980 499,000

These skilled operators connect callers to countries all over the world.

Courtesy American Telephone & Telegraph Company

Where Employed

Three-fifths of the operators employed work as central office operators in telephone companies, and the remainder work as PBX operators in a variety of establishments, particularly in manufacturing plants, hospitals, schools, and department stores. Jobs tend to be concentrated in heavily populated areas such as New York, Chicago, and Los Angeles, but a good number of jobs can be found in most cities.

Training Required

Employers prefer that applicants have at least a high school education. Courses in typing, English, and business mathematics and a familiarity with office procedures can be very helpful, because many jobs combine handling telephone calls with other office work.

Advancement Opportunities

A central office operator may be promoted to central office supervisor and eventually to chief operator or to some other office position within the telephone company. The same is true for a PBX operator in a large firm. Opportunities in small businesses are more limited.

SHIPPING AND RECEIVING CLERKS

Shipping clerks prepare merchandise for shipment. This includes counting and comparing items to be shipped against the order, assembling containers, packing, addressing, and moving shipments to their destination points. Receiving clerks accept goods, unpack and examine them, verify the completeness of the order against other shipping records, and route goods to departments.

Number Needed

Employed in 1970 380,000
Number of job openings annually:
     Replacements 7,600
     New positions 7,800
     Total 15,400
New positions 1970 to 1980 adding to total employed 78,000
Total number of people employed in this category by 1980 458,000

Where Employed

Two-thirds of the positions are found in manufacturing firms. A large number are in wholesale houses and retail stores. In general, jobs are concentrated in metropolitan areas.

Training Required

Employers prefer to hire high school graduates for beginning jobs in shipping and receiving departments. An important asset is the ability to write legibly. Courses in business mathematics and typing and a familiarity with office procedures can be very helpful.

Advancement Opportunities

The job offers an ambitious person an excellent opportunity to learn about the company's products and markets. Some clerks, particularly those who get further training or take courses in transportation, can advance to warehouse manager, industrial traffic manager, or purchasing agent.

OFFICE MACHINE OPERATORS

Workers in this category operate calculating machines; keep accounts; and prepare statements, bills, and invoices. They use machines to copy and record data, to analyze records of transactions, and to prepare summaries and reports.

Number Needed

Employed in 1970 350,000
Number of job openings annually:
     Replacements 15,000
     New positions 10,000
     Total 25,000
New positions 1970 to 1980 adding to total employed 100,000
Total number of people employed in this category by 1980 450,000

Where Employed

Jobs are found chiefly in firms having a large volume of recordkeeping activities and paper work. Firms such as these would be manufacturing companies, banks, insurance companies, government agencies, and wholesale and retail firms. Positions are also found in *service centers*, which are agencies that own an assortment of office machines and contract to do tasks such as preparing monthly bills and mailing circulars for firms that do not have such equipment.

Training Required

Graduation from high school or business school is the minimum educational requirement for all but the most routine office machine operator jobs. Specialized training is usually necessary to handle such machines as electronic calculators and some kinds of tabulating and duplicating equipment. Beginning positions require that applicants have a general knowledge of office equipment. It is helpful if applicants have studied business mathematics and typing. In some cases it is also helpful if they know how to operate more than one type of machine, since a variety of tasks are likely to be assigned.

Advancement Opportunities

A person may be promoted from a beginning, simple machine job to a more complex or related clerical job. In such cases employers often provide the additional training required. In firms with large clerical staffs, office machine operators can advance to positions where they are responsible for training beginners and checking on the accuracy of their work or to supervisory jobs where they are section or department heads. In this area employers frequently follow a promotion-from-within policy, taking into consideration seniority and proven ability.

ELECTRONIC COMPUTER OPERATORS

These trained workers monitor and control electronic digital computers, which process business, scientific, engineering, or other data, according to operating instructions. Electronic computer operators may set control switches on equipment, select and load input and output units with materials, or supervise operators of peripheral equipment.

Number Needed

Employed in 1970 200,000
Number of job openings annually:
     Replacements 1,600
     New positions 18,800
     Total 20,400
New positions 1970 to 1980 adding to total employed 188,000
Total number of people employed in this category by 1980 388,000

Where Employed

Jobs are mainly in government agencies, insurance companies, banks, wholesale and retail businesses, transportation and public utility companies, and large manufacturing firms. Many electronic computer operators are employed in service centers that process data for other firms.

Training Required

The minimum educational requirement for computer operators is a high school diploma. If they have not had specialized training or previous experience in related work, applicants for peripheral equipment operator jobs in the federal government are required to have a high school diploma, since they are regarded as assistants to computer operators. As assistants they operate electronic or

By using a computerized system, this employee can tell in seconds where a railroad car is, where it is going, and what it is carrying.

Courtesy Union Pacific Railroad

electromechanical data processing equipment. Console operators should have a high school education and some work experience. They use the console portion of the computer to control the machine manually, to correct errors, and to check on the status of circuits and the contents of storage. College training is preferred in some instances, although console operators may qualify for appointment on the basis of their previous experience and their general aptitude for computer work.

Advancement Opportunities

Computer operators may be assigned to more complex equipment as they gain experience and eventually can become supervisors or be promoted to jobs which combine supervisory duties and console operation. With further study and experience, they can qualify as programmers.

RECEPTIONISTS

Receptionists receive clients or customers coming into the office, determine the purpose of their visits, direct callers to their destination, and record the visitors' names, time of their calls, nature of business, and persons called upon.

Number Needed

Employed in 1970 300,000
Number of job openings annually:
     Replacements 17,000
     New positions 13,000
     Total 30,000
New positions 1970 to 1980 adding to total employed 130,000
Total number of people employed in this category by 1980 430,000

Where Employed

Although jobs for receptionists exist in practically all kinds of establishments, over half of the positions are found in the offices of physicians, attorneys, and other professionals. Other receptionists are employed in hospitals, educational institutions, banks, insurance companies, real estate offices, manufacturing concerns, and beauty shops. At the last count about one out of every four receptionists was employed as a part-time worker who spent fewer than 35 hours a week on the job. Many men who are employed as receptionists are found in medical services, hospitals, manufacturing companies, and banking and credit agencies.

Training Required

Employers seldom specify any formal educational requirements beyond that of a high school diploma, but as many as one out of every five receptionists has had some college training. It is an advantage to have had courses in business English, typing, and elementary accounting. It is also helpful to know how to operate an office telephone switchboard, although many times this skill is learned on the job.

Advancement Opportunities

While opportunities for promotion are somewhat limited, experience as a receptionist plus business training can lead to a better-paying position, such as secretary or administrative assistant.

BANK CLERKS

These clerks compute service charges, file checks, photograph records, operate various office machines, sell traveler's checks and savings bonds, and open new accounts.

Number Needed

Employed in 1970 400,000
Number of job openings annually:
    Replacements 20,000
    New positions 9,500
    Total 29,500
New positions 1970 to 1980 adding to total employed 95,000
Total number of people employed in this category by 1980 495,000

Where Employed

Jobs are found in banking institutions.

Training Required

Applicants can qualify for beginning clerical jobs in a bank if they have a high school diploma. It is also helpful if they have had courses in accounting, typing, business mathematics, and office machine operation.

Advancement Opportunities

Bank clerks can advance to positions where they supervise other clerks, to tellers, to credit analysts, and eventually to senior supervisors. Outstanding workers who have had college training or who have taken specialized courses in banking have the opportunity to advance to bank officer positions. Excellent courses are offered by the American Institute of Banking and other institutions to help employees learn more about their field and prepare for their advancement.

STOCK CLERKS

Stock clerks receive, store, and issue equipment, material, supplies, merchandise, foodstuffs, or tools; and they compile stock records in a stockroom, warehouse, or storage yard.

Number Needed

Employed in 1970 500,000
Number of job openings annually:
      Replacements 23,000
      New positions .... (Negligible)
      Total 23,000
New positions 1970 to 1980 adding to total employed .... (Negligible)
Total number of people employed in this category by 1980 500,000

Where Employed

Most stock clerks work in manufacturing companies and in the wholesale and retail trades, but large numbers are also employed in mail-order houses, airlines, government agencies, hospitals, transportation companies, and other establishments that keep large inventories of items on hand. Most jobs are found in metropolitan areas where there are factories, warehouses, and stores.

Training Required

Although there are no specific educational requirements, most employers prefer to hire high school graduates. In considering applicants, they look for proficiency in business English, business mathematics, typing, and filing.

Advancement Opportunities

These often depend on the size of the establishment. In a small firm the stock clerk may advance to a position as salesclerk or become an assistant buyer or purchasing agent. In a larger organization the stock clerk may have a chance to advance to a more responsible stock clerk position, such as invoice clerk, stock control clerk, or merchandise supply clerk. With further study and a knowledge of marketing, the stock clerk can advance to the position of supervisor or manager of the stockroom.

BANK TELLERS

Tellers receive and pay out money and keep records of money and papers involved in various bank transactions.

Number Needed

Employed in 1970 150,000
Number of job openings annually:
      Replacements   9,000
      New positions .... _6,000_
      Total 15,000
New positions 1970 to 1980 adding to total employed .... _60,000_
Total number of people employed in this category by 1980 210,000

Where Employed

Every bank, no matter how small, has at least one teller who receives and pays out money and records these transactions. In very small banks one teller may handle many different kinds of transactions; in larger banks one bank teller is responsible for one kind of transaction.

Courtesy Bowery Savings Bank

Meeting the public daily is an important part of a bank teller's job.

Training Required

Banks prefer to hire high school graduates who are trained or experienced in clerical work. They look for candidates who are mature, neat, tactful, and courteous, because tellers deal primarily with the public. Since tellers handle large sums of money, the bank protects itself against theft by requiring that tellers be bonded. This means that an insurance company investigates the applicant and, after ascertaining his honesty and stability, agrees to assume the risk of insuring the bank against any theft committed by that applicant.

Advancement Opportunities

A competent teller who has gained some experience in a large bank may advance to head teller. With college or specialized training offered by the banking industry, tellers may eventually become bank officers.

FILE CLERKS

These workers file correspondence, cards, invoices, receipts, and other records in alphabetic or numeric order or according to subject matter. They read incoming material and sort and file papers according to the filing system in use. More advanced file clerks search for and investigate information contained in the files, insert additional data on file records, make up reports, and keep files up to date.

Number Needed

Employed in 1970 170,000
Number of job openings annually:
      Replacements   15,300
      New positions .... (Negligible)
      Total   15,300
New positions 1970 to 1980 adding to total employed .... (Negligible)
Total number of people employed in this category by 1980 170,000

Where Employed

Three-fourths of these jobs in 1970 were found in finance, insurance, real estate, and manufacturing establishments. In addition, hundreds of thousands of workers in other kinds of clerical occupations also do filing in connection with their work.

Training Required

Most employers prefer to hire high school graduates. It is quite useful to have had business courses in recordkeeping or accounting, in clerical or office procedures, in general business, and particularly in typing.

Advancement Opportunities

As they become more experienced, file clerks move on to do more difficult filing work or to supervise other file clerks. With additional training the file clerk can advance to such clerical positions as information clerk or office machine operator—and eventually, if interested and ambitious, on to managerial positions.

THE ADVANTAGES OF OFFICE WORK

It is very revealing to review the significant advantages of office work. Go over them carefully when you make your first career decision.

Salaries Are Good

Average salaries in clerical occupations have risen steadily, and from all indications they will continue to rise.

Many Industries Are Expanding

Many companies employing a large clerical staff are planning to expand their operations in the next few years. Some expect their businesses to grow faster than the overall rate of employment growth. This will create a need for workers and equipment and result in a great volume of paper work—and paper work is where the office worker comes in. Moreover, the additional complications involved in managing larger and more diverse enterprises will mean even greater job opportunities for capable workers.

Work Is Steady

Office work usually means steady employment. There is always a need for trained office personnel, even when other jobs are scarce or are phased out. Surveys indicate a very low unemployment rate for clerical and sales workers.

Jobs Are Everywhere

Wherever there is an establishment of any kind—business, educational, professional, industrial—there is an office job. This means that whether you live at present in a small town or in a large city or move to another location, you'll always find businesses which employ office workers.

Office Work Is Pleasant

Modern construction, furnishings, and equipment make most offices pleasant places in which to work. Many jobs offer a seven-hour day. You have opportunities to meet, talk, and work with people of diverse talents, backgrounds, and interests. Your work can be varied and interesting, and modern machines will help you speed the flow of work. It is an environment that invites you to grow as you begin to deal with situations that challenge your initiative.

Positions Are Open to All

Office workers with a wide range of skills are needed, and positions are open to qualified men and women of all ages, races, and creeds—married or single.

Civil Service and Military Opportunities Are Available

The federal government is the largest employer of clerical workers and has on its payroll about 20 percent of the nation's total number of clerical workers. By taking an examination, you can obtain a federal civil service rating, which enables you to apply for openings in federal agencies in any part of the country. Sometimes it is possible to take civil service tests while you are still in school so that you can move right into a position after graduation. The salaries, opportunities, and benefits offered in the federal civil service compare favorably with jobs in private enterprise.

Men and women who are skilled office technicians are always in demand for positions in the Armed Forces, where they generally have a better chance of getting a job that makes use of their skills in some administrative capacity. Increased responsibility in the Armed Forces can mean better working and living conditions, higher rank, and more personal privileges. This experience can perhaps be an asset when they return to civilian life and look for a job.

Around-the-Clock Schedules Are Available

Office work is no longer a 9 a.m. to 5 p.m. operation. Around-the-clock schedules have been introduced so that maximum use can be made of expensive, automated equipment that would otherwise stand idle two-thirds of the day. The current flexibility in work hours provides excellent employment opportunities for students, housewives, and many people who work part-time for added income. Schedules now include three or more shifts in a single day, double shifts from 9 a.m. to 5 p.m. and from 5 to 12 p.m., or overlapping shifts in critical departments where extra help is needed during the busiest hours. For example, the first shift in a mail room may start at 7 a.m. so that incoming mail can be delivered early to the regular office staff. The second shift may start at 3 p.m. and stay until 10 p.m. to make sure that all the work completed during that day is processed.

Part-Time and Temporary Jobs Are Always Available

There may be times when you want to work but are unable either to fit a full-time job into your schedule or to undertake a permanent job. What you can do, however, is accept a part-time or temporary job. There are lots of them in office work; in fact, there are so many that certain private employment agencies specialize in this type of placement. If you have office skills, you can usually find part-time or temporary work with business firms that need extra help when their work load becomes too heavy or when vacations or absences leave gaps in their staff. Part-time jobs are also available in institutions with long service hours, such as libraries and hospitals.

New Services Create Job Opportunities

Many firms have certain specialized office work performed by outside companies, or service centers. By doing this, firms save on office space, avoid having to buy expensive office equipment, operate with fewer personnel, and obtain the services of experts at moderate cost. Service centers offer many job opportunities for trained office workers in the areas of accounting, duplicating, computing, form letter reproduction, mailing list maintenance and addressing, mail pickup, telephone answering, and messenger work.

Jobs Are Tailored to Temperament

Do you like to work where there are many people, or do you prefer to work on your own? Do you like a fresh problem every day, or do you like repetitive work? Thanks to the great diversity of office jobs you can almost write your own ticket.

OFFICE ORGANIZATION PLANS

Because offices are the control centers of all businesses, they need to be organized, supervised, staffed, and equipped in accordance with a plan designed to promote maximum operating efficiency. Which plan a company uses depends on the company's size, the nature of its business, and the number of office workers it employs. For instance, a small retail shop with few records to keep requires only a small clerical staff. But a large insurance company with thousands of detailed records to keep needs a larger clerical staff. Any firm, however large or small, follows an organization plan that helps it operate most effectively.

The Small Office Plan

In a small office where all the standard clerical tasks have to be performed by a limited staff, each staff member takes on a number of varied responsibilities. A small-town appliance store may have an owner-manager, a salesclerk, an accounting clerk, and a clerk-stenographer. Each member, in addition to specific duties, takes turns waiting on customers and answering the telephone. The owner-manager probably orders the stock, assists with sales, answers letters, and supervises the work of the entire staff. The salesclerk helps customers with their problems and takes their orders. When necessary, the salesperson assists and substitutes for the manager during absences. The accounting clerk keeps all financial records, handles the cash, keeps track of stock balances, takes inventory, and, when needed, assists the others. The clerk-stenographer types letters and orders, answers the telephone (often giving sales information), and assists the accounting clerk with reports. Teamwork is vitally important in a small office.

There are many such offices in every city and town, and you may find that you prefer working in a smaller enterprise because you like the idea of having a variety of duties and seeing firsthand the complete workings of a business. Generally, in this type of atmosphere you enjoy the extra benefit of having more flexible working hours and perhaps less commuting time.

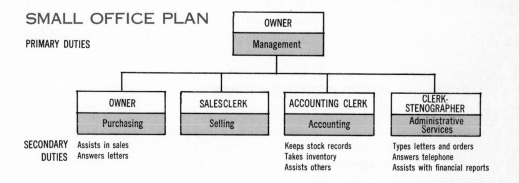

The Departmentalized Office Plan

With this plan an organization is broken down into different departments which operate as self-contained units. Each department office has its own mail clerk, telephone operators, messengers, and receptionist. A sales department, for example, will have its own order clerks, file clerks, billing clerks, and secretaries and stenographers to take care of correspondence. The department will

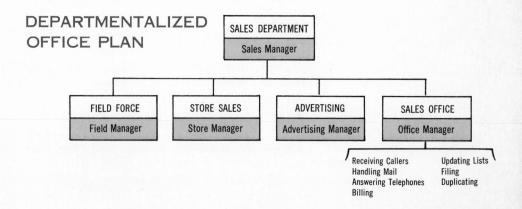

be organized to handle every office activity pertaining to sales from the actual sale of the item to the processing of the invoice for the sale. Such an arrangement enables the sales department manager to observe all sales operations and have direct control over his phase of business.

The Centralized Office Plan

Clerical activities that are frequently centralized in large office operations include handling mail, duplicating, correspondence, payroll, reception, and messenger work. Businesses sometimes centralize activities common to many departments because this arrangement is less expensive and complicated than running separate office activities for each department. Suppose you were a company manager and were in a hurry to find out as much as you could about a certain customer. You'd have to go to the sales department for sales information, the credit department for credit information, and perhaps the accounting

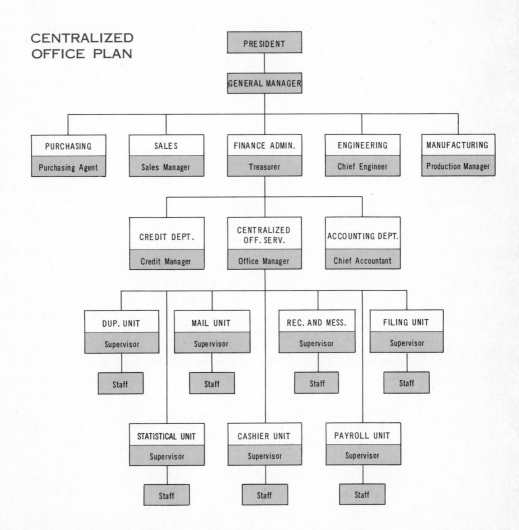

CENTRALIZED
OFFICE PLAN

department and the shipping department for more information. Obviously, it would take you a great deal of time to gather this information from the various departments, and in your haste you could overlook important data in one of the departments.

Therefore, some firms use the centralized office plan in which a company maintains a central office for many of its activities. All phone calls are routed through a central office. All accounting is handled centrally. All the records concerning a particular person or subject are collected and contained in one filing center.

The Tailor-Made Office Plan

Since office activities vary with the size and nature of the business, it is sometimes necessary to structure office operations in order to meet a firm's special needs. For example, a small, nationally known sporting goods mail-order house in the eastern part of the country found it necessary to organize its operations so that clerical work could be done in its warehouse, in its front office, and in its executive offices. The mail-order business involves thousands of customers and requires paper work which is unique to that business.

OFFICE WORK AS A DOOR OPENER

It's good business for an employer to move you up the promotion ladder as you prove your ability. A promotion means that you have done satisfactory work, have grown in the job, and have shown yourself ready to assume greater responsibilities. It generally means a greater challenge as well as a welcome increase in salary. Promotion from within the company is profitable for your employer because he benefits from the skills you have developed during your employment.

From a clerical job you may be promoted to unit supervisor. In this position you would be responsible for the work of a small group of clerks involved in a particular type of office activity, such as duplicating, handling mail, or filing. You would take your orders from the office manager, set up the rules governing your unit's operations, and assign work to the persons employed in your group.

With further experience and training you might qualify for the position of office manager or manager of administrative services. Here you would be responsible for all office systems and procedures in your department or company. You would receive general orders and policies from the general manager and would be expected to plan procedures and improve on the performance of your staff.

If the future in office work looks bright—and it certainly should—remember that how far you go in your chosen career will depend in large measure on your ability and training. The days of the marginally trained office worker are numbered. In fact, it is predicted that the new generation of office workers will be the best-educated and most highly skilled in history.

Right now you have a chance to train for a clerical occupation that offers attractive career possibilities and job opportunities in industries with good growth prospects. Why not get started now?

REVIEWING YOUR READING

1 Is the immediate availability of beginning job openings the only factor to consider in making career plans? Explain.
2 List some of the special advantages, aside from salary, that make office work a desirable career.
3 Why is superior training such an important asset in getting ahead in the office of the future?
4 How can an office position serve as a stepping-stone to advancement?

OFFICE ASSIGNMENTS

1 Study the list of job classifications on pages 9–23. Select three jobs that interest you, and rank them in order of your preference. Explain why you might be qualified for these jobs.
2 Using the data on pages 9–23, prepare a comparative chart showing the number employed in each of the 13 classifications in 1970, the annual replacements, the new positions available each year, and the estimated total number of people that will be employed in each classification by 1980. Use the format suggested below.

Occupation	Employed in 1970	Annual Replacements	New Positions Available Annually	Estimated Number Employed by 1980
Stenographer/ Secretary	2,800,000	155,000	82,000	3,620,000

3 Using the data from the chart prepared in Office Assignment 2 and the format below, prepare a chart showing the total ten-year increase in jobs in each of the 13 classifications.

Occupation	Actual 1970	Estimated 1980	Estimated Increase
Stenographer/ Secretary	2,800,000	3,620,000	820,000

4 Reread the training requirements for the 13 job classifications, and for each classification identify the business subjects or skills specifically mentioned as

required or desirable for beginning workers. Then prepare a chart to keep for future reference. Use the format suggested below.

	Shorthand	Typing	Business English	Handling Mail	Filing	Office Machines	Business Math	Accounting	Work-Study	Selling
Stenographers and Secretaries	X	X	X	X	X	X				
Accounting Clerks		X					X	X	X	X
Cashiers										
Typists										
Telephone Operators										
Shipping and Receiving Clerks										
Office Machine Operators										
Electronic Computer Operators										
Receptionists										
Bank Clerks										
Stock Clerks										
Bank Tellers										
File Clerks										

5 Refer to the above chart, and do the following:

a Underscore the names of the subjects that are included in your business training program.

b Put a check mark in front of the name of the subject that you find especially interesting.

c Draw a circle around the names of the subjects in which you need further study or extra help.

d Double underscore the titles of those occupations for which your training will qualify you for employment.

6 Study the advancement possibilities of the 13 classifications discussed. Then:

a List the jobs for which advancement limitations are mentioned, and explain the nature of the limitations.

b Suggest how each limitation might be overcome by an ambitious and capable worker.

7 Clerical workers are needed in virtually every enterprise, but the largest number of them are employed in the fields of manufacturing, public utilities,

finance, insurance, and real estate. How many of these types of businesses are in your area? For each group list the names and addresses of five firms located in your area.

8 Study the organization chart appearing on page 27, and then answer the following questions:

 a To whom does the office manager report?

 b Does the chief engineer outrank the chief accountant?

 c Who prepares the payroll for the Credit Department?

 d If you were a posting machine operator in the Accounting Department, to whom would you report?

 e Who files the purchasing agent's correspondence?

 f Who escorts visitors to the president's office?

 g If you worked in the Credit Department, through what channels would you go to notify the Sales Department that you could not approve credit on a new order?

 h Who prepares the financial statements for the business?

 i If the general manager wants to know the amount of the next payroll, whom does he ask?

 j An employee in the Cashier Unit wants to transfer to the Purchasing Department. Who must approve the request?

UNIT 1

BUSINESS CASES AND PROBLEMS

In the Boss's Shoes **1** Your supervisor insists that all work must be checked and double-checked to ensure accuracy. Some of the details are so simple that you think checking them is a waste of time. Should you tell the supervisor what you think, or should you rely on your own judgment and verify only the "important" items?

2 Joe Tolin, applying for his first job, asks the interviewer about the advancement possibilities within the company. "Mr. Tolin," she replies, "they are unlimited." "Great!" says Joe. "But specifically, where will I be if I stay with this firm for 20 years?" Her answer is that each person's progress depends upon his talent, his performance, available openings, business conditions, and other factors. "For all those reasons," she says, "there is no way to guarantee advancement to a specific job." Joe feels that her answer is evasive and that the prospects for "unlimited" advancement are neither certain nor clear.

Is the interviewer trying to dodge the issue? Would you expect her to be more definite in her statements at this time?

Your Human Relations   1   You are very pleased with your job assignment in the sales order office. In fact, you frequently and enthusiastically boast that the sales department is the most important department in the company. Do you think that the workers in the production department would agree with you? Why might they think that their department is as important as yours? Which department is really the most vital?

2   During her high school days Helene Huerra found it easier to work on her studies alone. By working alone, she felt she avoided distractions; she worked faster and received excellent grades. However, on her first office job assignment she discovers that she is to be part of a "team" operation in the billing section of the sales order department. She feels that her productivity will be limited by the slower performance of her co-workers and that her superior ability will therefore go unrecognized. Most of all she feels she would prefer to work by herself at her own pace. What can she do?

What Would You Do If . . . ?   1   You are interested in a career in office work but are not ready at this time to select a specific job title as your ultimate objective.

2   You apply for a job as a junior accountant but are told that beginners are hired only as junior accounting clerks.

What Does This Mean?   1   The office is a service unit.

2   Some office machine operators are employed in service centers.

Business in Your Area   1   Consult references in your school or public library in order to answer the following questions: **(a)** What are the major industries in your area? **(b)** Approximately how many office workers are employed in your city or county?

2   Think of an office job which might interest you. **(a)** How many new workers in this specific job category are needed annually? **(b)** Can most newly trained persons expect to find openings in this job category? **(c)** What happens when there are too many applicants for a job? **(d)** What happens when there aren't enough applicants to fill positions available in a job category?

UNIT 2
EVALUATING YOURSELF FOR OFFICE WORK

3 The Fundamental Skills and Knowledge Needed

The spelling drills, the English tests, and the penmanship you practice can be a bore sometimes, and you may wonder how these activities relate to business. But as you find out more about what takes place in an office, you will realize that these exercises help you to build essential fundamental skills that are basic to all clerical work. You must have these skills to get a job, to keep it, and to do it well.

THE BASIC SKILLS

The following are the job skills that are basic to all office jobs. You must perfect these abilities so that you can perform your job effectively.

Ability to Communicate

Someone estimated that business adds 300 billion pieces of paper to its files every year. This massive collection of paper includes just about every type of written communication. But if this volume sounds impressive, think of the countless *oral* communications required to keep the wheels of business turning smoothly. Modern business simply could not function without effective written and oral communications.

Your effectiveness as a communicator depends upon your ability to read, write, speak, and listen well. You must be able to read with both speed and comprehension so that you can summarize quickly and accurately the written messages from your boss, your co-workers, and the public. You must be able to convey your own thoughts clearly.

You must also learn how to listen carefully so that you can grasp instructions the first time, without having to ask that they be repeated. Active listening is an art. It requires that you concentrate on what is being said so that you absorb and retain the message.

The Methodical Use of Notes

A typical business office is a busy place. You can't rely on your memory alone to keep track of what you are told, what you did, or what you are expected to do. Jotting down instructions, ideas, and other information will aid recall later on. A reputation for being both right and efficient is bound to increase your chance for advancement.

Spelling Proficiency

Written business messages involve the use of words, terms, and expressions in a great variety of combinations. You need to know how to spell words correctly so that your message will not be misinterpreted. For instance, it makes a big difference whether you write *dew, do,* or *due.* Errors of this kind harm the reputation of a business. A customer who is inconvenienced by a mistake may transfer his business to a more reliable company.

Figure Know-How

Figures furnish the important data from which many letters, reports, and statements are prepared. Figures must be accurate if sound decisions are to be based on them. Your figures can't be "almost right."

Most jobs that involve working with figures are not really difficult. Doing these jobs well is a matter of understanding basic arithmetic, developing habits of care and concentration, and checking your work thoroughly. Many companies have figures double-checked by a second person to minimize the chances of error. Modern machines, of course, speed up calculations, but you can use the machines more effectively to solve a given problem if you understand the arithmetic involved. Also, sometimes a machine is not around to help with on-the-spot figuring, and a knowledge of math comes in handy to make a quick estimate or to decide if a set of figures "looks right."

Legible Handwriting

The days of flowery penmanship are past, but you still must have good legible handwriting for clerical work. Notations have to be made and read, some figures have to be posted by hand, and forms have to be filled out in longhand. A poorly written word, letter, or figure can have serious consequences if the faulty writing causes another person to make an error in quoting a price or recording a date. It's not enough that *you* understand what you have written; others also must be able to read what you've written without hesitation. You will find that you can improve your penmanship considerably by paying careful attention to letter shapes.

SPECIFIC JOB SKILLS

Office employees are assigned to specialized jobs, according to their individual talents and skills. The kind of job you will be assigned will depend upon your interests, the specific skills you acquire in school, and how well you have mastered those skills. Few office jobs require only a single skill; some 87 percent of office jobs involve two or more skills.

Typing

Records and correspondence are typed in most businesses. Though handwriting can be pleasing to the eye, typewritten communications make a better appearance and are much easier to read. Also, someone who types can turn out more work in less time: a person can write 25 to 50 words a minute with a pen, but a good typist can type at twice that rate. Typing, therefore, must be considered a fundamental skill needed for all clerical occupations, including those related to the new computer technology, such as card punching and computer console operation, magnetic tape or card typewriter assignments, and machine transcription.

Shorthand

The ability to take dictation or to make notes of meetings and of special instructions in shorthand is particularly useful to clerical workers interested in using their work as a stepping-stone to more important positions. Shorthand can open many doors to opportunity: you can be promoted from clerk to stenographer, from stenographer to secretary, and from secretary to a number of executive positions.

Recordkeeping and Accounting

If you want to work as a cashier, a payroll clerk, or an accounting clerk, you need to know how to keep accurate financial records. And understanding the principles of accounting will help you to grasp better the overall financial picture of your company as you are promoted to positions of increasing responsibility.

Filing

Nearly every office has letters, reports, memorandums, and instructions that need to be filed. You should know how to put papers away systematically so that they can be found quickly and easily when needed. New employees are frequently given filing assignments in order to help them become acquainted quickly with customers' names and company documents and routines. If you are trained in filing procedures, you will find your work easier on a new job.

Office Machine Operation

Businessmen rely on time-saving machines, such as adding machines, calculators, posting machines, duplicating equipment, and automated equipment of all kinds, to help speed office operations. Training in machine operation while you are in school will give you still another advantage when you apply for a position. Your supervisor will certainly recognize and appreciate your ability to choose the right machine for a given assignment and to use that machine effectively.

LEARNING WHAT KINDS OF JOBS THERE ARE

You are bound to be happier and more successful in your work if you know where you are going in life. The occupational information on pages 9–23

Copiers are among the most useful of office machines; they can reproduce documents in seconds.

Courtesy SCM Corporation

may help you decide on your chosen career. Weigh both the short- and long-range employment opportunities in the area of office work that interests you. Once you pick your entrance job, keep yourself informed about the lines of promotions, transfers, and new openings that the job offers. If you learn as much as you can about the occupation you want to pursue while you're still in school, you can make the right moves and progress steadily toward the goals you set for yourself.

LEARNING WHAT BUSINESS IS ALL ABOUT

The luckiest person in the world is one who enjoys his work. You'll enjoy it more, and do it better, if you know what your company does, how it is organized, and how your work fits into the company's overall operations. Get to know thoroughly, if you can, the business systems and routines used by your employer. Know exactly what you're expected to do. Of course, you will pick up a great deal of business information on the job, but you will catch on much faster if you have had instruction in business and office systems.

CULTIVATING GOOD PERSONAL QUALITIES

In addition to your education, skills, and training, your future employer will be interested in your personal qualities. When he offers you a job, he will expect you to have the following qualities.

Ability to Work With Others

When people work together to serve others, they must be able to work well with each member of their unit. The success of most office assignments depends upon the cooperation of co-workers.

Courtesy Xerox Corporation

Warmth and courtesy make any office a congenial place in which to work.

As a new employee, you'll welcome help and cooperation from your co-workers. And your co-workers will expect help and cooperation from you, when necessary. Deeds of friendliness and concern for the interests of others will help you win the acceptance of your fellow workers. Work becomes more pleasant when there is an atmosphere of mutual helpfulness and respect.

Judgment

The man or woman who heads a department or runs a business can't be everyone at once. He assigns certain important duties to others so that he will have sufficient time to devote to making major decisions. He wants workers upon whom he can rely and who will use the same careful judgment that he would use—judgment based on first gathering all the facts, studying them carefully, and then, with the firm's interests in mind, deciding upon the best course of action to follow.

Energy and Ambition

It is a tested axiom that business cannot stand still. If it does not move ahead and prosper, it will slip behind in the competitive race of the free enterprise system. Employers look for young people who will enjoy and help maintain this swift and demanding pace. A willingness to work with energy and a readiness to assume new responsibilities are important traits to develop if you expect to go places in your chosen career. And your efforts not only help business but also help you develop. A capable person reaching for the top rung of the ladder must prove her abilities by performing well on the job all the time. Doing superior work in a beginning job is looked on as being a significant clue as to what you might do later with more important assignments.

Growth Potential

You may gain your employer's regard by showing a willingness to assume more responsibility, but how can you convince him that you can handle it? Tryouts can be costly for an employer. What you must do is demonstrate that you have "grow power." Once you land your first job, start on a program of self-improvement. This may mean joining thousands of other young people who are taking advanced studies at high schools or training centers. Then when you ask for more responsibility (or when it is thrust upon you), you will have "grown" enough to take these new duties in stride. Education does pay off in dollars and cents.

Imagination and Resourcefulness

Business values highly those workers who are capable of offering new ideas and suggestions in order to improve office operations. Young people who acquire a wide knowledge of job details can make valuable money-saving and time-saving suggestions. To the imaginative person a work project is not merely something that must get done, it is something that might be done better. Bonuses and promotions are frequently awarded workers who help to improve the firm's efficiency. The resourceful person—the person with practical ideas—is particularly valuable in a rapidly changing job situation, because she can be counted on to think on her feet and to adjust quickly to new conditions.

Ability to Work Under Pressure

When you walk into a store to make a purchase, you expect prompt service. The store, in turn, demands fast service from the manufacturer, and the manufacturer must move swiftly to replenish his own stock. The office, too, feels its share of pressure. Operations must be run according to definite schedules in order to meet deadlines. That's why an office needs people who can adjust their pace to the varying demands of the company. When a business enters its seasonal rush, the adaptable person works under pressure, understands that it is temporary, and contributes that extra push needed to get the work done. She realizes that almost any job requires occasional extra effort, and she carries her share of additional duties without sacrificing quality or pride in workmanship.

Dependability

A superior employee carries out instructions without constant supervision. He knows that the flow of office work must be kept moving if orders are to be filled promptly and customers' inquiries handled properly. He knows what he has to do and the importance of getting it done on time. That kind of depend-

The success of mailings to customers and prospects depends on up-to-date lists that can be run off quickly.

Courtesy Babcock & Wilcox Company (photo by Gerry D. Mack)

able performance from each staff member is the backbone of a good, steady, winning team—the kind you can be on if you put your full share of effort and talent into each job you do.

Ability to Concentrate

Just as home is a place where you live, and school is a place where you study, the office is a place where you work. When you accept a position, you agree to work a certain number of hours a day and to concentrate on your job while you are there; your employer agrees to pay you a certain salary. It's a contract made in good faith between you and your employer. He figures his costs on the amount of work he estimates you can do; you figure your budget on the basis of the salary you expect to be paid.

Neatness and Orderliness

You will be a productive and accurate worker if you organize your desk well, plan your work carefully, select your tools and equipment wisely, and take care of your supplies properly. An employer wants employees with orderly work habits, because he knows that such habits yield better results for the company. He knows also that a neat and orderly office gives visitors a positive impression of the company. Many firms even try to make the office a showplace for sales promotion purposes. This is why you must do your share to keep your work area and the office looking their best.

Punctuality

Customers expect reliable and prompt service. To meet their demands, office people must be punctual and be on hand regularly in order to complete their share of the work on time. If you aim for an office career, you should expect to report to work every business day of the year, unless you are ill or have a serious emergency.

Good Health

If you have average health and stamina, you can meet the physical demands of office work. Most office work is done sitting down, although a certain amount of standing and walking is required. Opportunities in office work are increasing for the physically handicapped. Good hearing and vision are essential, but, of course, eyeglasses and hearing aids may be worn. You must have a good speaking voice for positions such as telephone operator, receptionist, sales-clerk, and secretary. Messengers and shipping and receiving clerks need to be strong enough to lift, carry, push, and pull packages and boxes.

REVIEWING YOUR READING

1   List the basic *skills* required in office work, and explain why they are important.
2   Explain why the ability to type is regarded as a specific job skill for most office workers today.
3   When making a business decision, why should one always consider the best interests of the firm first?

OFFICE ASSIGNMENTS

1   Spelling is a very important qualification for office workers to have. On a separate sheet complete the correct spelling of each word below by supplying the missing letters.

a exten__ion	**g** defend__nt	**m** pamp__let	**s** accept__nce
b dev__ce	**h** co__rel__tion	**n** invar__bly	**t** feas__ble
c pers__vere	**i** syst__m	**o** subst__ute	**u** num__rous
d e__asp__rate	**j** subsid__ry	**p** questio__aire	**v** li__bil__ty
e servic__ble	**k** __rrears	**q** stren__then	**w** maint__nance
f l__sure	**l** fa__simile	**r** promi__ory	**x** con__ede

2   Clerical work involves figuring and checking. Suppose a personnel interviewer asked you to take the following short test to give him an indication of your mastery of basic mathematics. Could you make the grade?

Add.

a	**b**	**c**	**d**	**e**
698	1.071	$6 \frac{1}{4}$	$10.81	$ 629.16
2,841	.27	$18 \frac{1}{2}$	2.35	84.95
565	18.59	$4 \frac{3}{8}$	15.03	266.34
1,472	6.1	$2 \frac{3}{4}$	26.47	1,107.19

Subtract.

	a	b	c	d	e
	698	$24.99	$16.56	14 ⅝	14.079
	− 247	− 18.01	− 8.69	− 2 ¾	− 2.1018

Multiply.

	a	b	c	d	e
	29	436	646	$12.10	1.6141
	× 17	× 28	× 164	× 480	× 1.078

Divide.

a $168 \div 12$ **b** $275 \div 25$ **c** $2,880 \div 16$ **d** $2,740 \div 15$ **e** $18.90 \div 4.5$

Compute the interest.

a $100 at 12 percent for 60 days
b $350 at 12 percent for 45 days
c $660 at 12 percent for 6 days
d $1,600 at 8 percent for 15 days

Compute the discount.

	Cost	Rate of Discount	Discount
a	$25.00	20%	_____
b	32.00	15%	_____
c	42.60	16 ⅔%	_____
d	64.88	12 ½%	_____
e	128.75	10%	_____

Find the profit or loss.

	Selling Price	Cost	Profit or Loss
a	$ 69.25	$ 14.64	_____
b	239.18	118.43	_____
c	469.18	124.49	_____
d	565.14	685.11	_____
e	328.07	29.88	_____

3 Study the illustration below. Then copy the paragraph in good cursive style. Compare your finished work with the sample, and practice your cursive writing to improve your weak points.

Cursive writing can be done more speedily and is generally used for writing longer messages and for completing the more lengthy details on business forms and records.

Aa Bb Cc Dd Ee Ff Gg Hh Ii Jj Kk Ll Mm Nn Oo Pp Qq Rr Ss Tt Uu Vv Ww Xx Yy Zz   1 2 3 4 5 6 7 8 9 0

4 In Unit 1, Section 2, Office Assignment 1, you were asked to select three job titles that interested you the most. For any one of these jobs, identify the **(a)** basic skills required to do the work, **(b)** personal qualities required, and **(c)** machine operating skills required.

SECTION 4 Getting Along With People

One of the most exciting aspects of working in the business world is that you can meet new people, all kinds of people. Knowing them will in time expand your horizons, just as their knowing you will expand theirs. Each of the men and women you will be meeting is an individual, as unique as you are. Each is different in background, personality, physical makeup, intelligence, abilities, and attitudes. The better you get to know them, the closer you will feel to them. This doesn't mean that you should pry into their personal affairs, but it does mean that you should try to know something about their likes and dislikes, their aspirations, their special interests, and their reactions to a variety of situations. An investment of this kind in people takes time and effort, but in a career and in a lifetime, this investment will pay off again and again. Actually, no single talent that you have will bring you success unless you can get along with people.

HOW TO MAKE PEOPLE REACT FAVORABLY TOWARD YOU

Starting with the assumption that everyone *is* an individual, you can make a great stride toward achieving good human relations if you try to put into practice some elementary rules.

Recognize the Importance of Others

Everyone likes to feel that he is needed and that he is important. When your classmates count on you for help in giving a school dance or when someone turns to you for your opinion on a particular question, doesn't it make you feel good? Of course it does. Even people who pretend that they don't care about being recognized are pleased when they are complimented for their efforts. And how do you feel about the person who commends you for a job well done? Certainly you appreciate him; we all appreciate a person who can look beyond the "circle of his own halo" and see the good things in other people. Are you this type of person? Do you compliment others for a job well done? Do you do it as often as you should?

Respect the Ideas of Others

Whether you work out a new play for Saturday's big football game or have an idea for a news feature, you like to find your associates willing to listen to and to try out your plan. And whether it is accepted or not, you at least want the satisfaction of being able to present your ideas.

But how do you feel when it is your turn to be a listener? For instance, when a friend of yours suggests a few changes in your plan, are you willing to listen to his ideas and weigh them honestly? Are you big enough to admit that your friend's plan might be as good as, if not better than, yours? It's not easy to admit this, but if you learn to accept criticism and evaluate opinions objectively, you'll earn the respect and admiration of others.

Respect the Ambition of Others

As a new employee you will be eager to get ahead as quickly as you can. Just remember, though, you don't have the exclusive rights to advancement. Your co-workers may also want the job you're aiming for. Who should get it? The more qualified person, of course.

By respecting the other fellow's ambitions and obeying the rules of the game, everyone gets a fair chance to win—including you. In any prosperous business there are plenty of opportunities and rewards for all.

Do Your Full Share

"Mary is a very capable girl, but she thinks only of herself." Would this kind of reputation help you to make friends on the new job? Of course not.

Office work has to be teamwork, because the success of a business depends upon cooperation between each worker and each work unit. An invoice typist

Courtesy Allied Chemical Company

Everyone benefits from the exchange of ideas and the interaction of people at work.

in a billing department can work efficiently only if the sales order data has been carefully compiled for her by a sales order clerk in the sales department. The office supply clerk keeps the typist stocked with invoice forms, carbon paper, and erasers; and the supervisor is readily available to answer questions. The invoice checker verifies the accuracy of typed work and passes it along promptly for further processing. You will be doing more for your human relations if you work *with* the members of your team. When you do, you will be pleased to find that the team works with you too. This kind of cooperation makes office work more productive and life more friendly and pleasant.

Meet Others Halfway

"I think your idea is good. Let's try it that way and see if it works better than my way." That kind of give-and-take attitude is the mark of a mature person who understands that you can't always have your own way and that many times two heads are better than one. This approach is essential in getting along with people; and remember, you cannot get along without them. Don't be afraid to make the first move toward compromise—the results can surprise you, and your co-workers will respect you as the kind of person with whom they can deal.

Practice Office Etiquette

Etiquette is plain good manners coupled with your personal brand of consideration for others. Etiquette is reflected every day in the countless things that you do and say. "Politeness," someone once said, "is like a cushion. It helps to ease the bump."

Make Introductions Meaningful

When you are introduced to your new colleagues, greet them with a friendly smile and a gracious "How do you do, Mr. Jones." Saying the person's name helps you to remember it later. Besides, everyone likes to hear his own name.

When your turn comes to make an introduction, introduce people promptly and smoothly, so that they will feel at ease. Present the man to the woman, the younger to the older, the lower in rank to the higher. For instance, you would say, "Mrs. Brown, may I present John Smith," or more informally, "Mrs. Brown, I'd like you to meet John Smith." Your thoughtfulness in adding some piece of information about the person to help launch a conversation will be very much appreciated. For example, "Mr. Jones, this is Roger Clark, head of the accounting department," or "Mr. Jones, this is Mr. Clark, head of the accounting department."

Greet People Warmly

A cheerful "Good morning" is a welcome greeting and an indication of your friendly disposition. Co-workers, customers, and visitors all appreciate a personal greeting before getting down to business. And you'll help public relations more by spending a few moments in pleasant conversation with a departing visitor than by giving him a quick brush-off.

Be Friendly But Not Personal

Genuine friendliness in the office contributes to a pleasant atmosphere and harmonious working conditions. However, be considerate. Don't bore or embarrass others with long recitals of your personal troubles or achievements. Avoid, if you can, serious personal entanglements that could interfere with your work or with your chances of promotion. It's a rule well worth remembering because entanglements are difficult to get out of, once you become involved in them.

Use Names or Titles Appropriately

At school people tend to be informal and address each other by their first names. In many offices this informal manner is acceptable when dealing with persons of the same age and rank within the department. However, superiors in the office and people outside the company are usually addressed as "Mr.," "Miss," "Mrs.," or "Ms." In fact, some firms insist that all employees, regardless of age or position, use formal address. Find out your firm's preference about names and titles, and guide yourself accordingly.

Be a Team Player

As part of the office team you are counted on to support the honest efforts of team members and to share their problems. Don't seek personal advantage at the expense of the group. Avoid arguments and petty bickering while on the

Courtesy General Telephone & Electronics Corporation

A cheerful response to a request for some facts or figures is always appreciated.

job. Remember that a gossip usually has no real friends. Don't carry tales about your fellow workers. Avoid criticizing what they do, and respect their right to privacy about their personal lives.

Keep Confidences

A company is like a family. When you have worked for a time as a member of the company family, you gain access to all kinds of information, some of which may be confidential. Keep that confidence. Don't make public anything that is not intended for general information, and refuse firmly an outsider or even a fellow employee who asks for information to which he has no right. If you have any doubts about what to do in a case like this, discuss the matter with your supervisor.

Be Thoughtful

The "please" and "thank you," the unexpected anniversary card, the birthday greeting, and the timely message of sympathy are all examples of little touches that win you the high regard of others. A helping hand or a thoughtful gesture shows, far more effectively than words, that you are a considerate person.

Be Deserving of Respect

Winning the acceptance and respect of your fellow workers isn't always easy. In order to do this, you'll have to put into practice the suggestions presented here and those you'll learn through experience. Keep working at it. And remember, getting off to a good start puts you on the first rung of a career ladder, which is made up of people and people-made problems. How far you will go in your job depends in large measure upon your skill in human relations.

Be Polite Under Stress

When many people work together closely every day, tempers can sometimes wear very thin. Be careful when you are under pressure; an insignificant thoughtless word or action can cause a great deal of unpleasantness. Many an argument has started at the time clock, the coffee cart line, the cafeteria line, the bus stop line, or the parking lot entrance or exit because someone was too aggressive, pushing ahead of others. Keep cool and wait your turn. You'll find that at the end of the day you'll be much more relaxed.

Observe Food Etiquette

Sometimes large offices have a cafeteria that offers money-saving employee lunches. Of course, good table manners apply in the cafeteria just as they apply in your home or in a restaurant. Everyone is expected to do his part to keep the lunch line moving and to share tables with other workers. Trays and

Courtesy Allied Chemical Corporation

Company lunchrooms offer attractively priced meals in congenial settings.

dishes are generally "bussed," chairs are replaced under the table, and the area is left tidy.

But lunch isn't the only occasion for eating in the office. Depending upon company rules, some late-rising employees may bring into the office a hasty breakfast of coffee and pastry, which they will eat just before they start to work. There are also offices that have coffee breaks at midmorning and at midafternoon, when you can buy a beverage and a light snack.

You may at times bring a sandwich from home or at busy times have something sent to your desk from the cafeteria or an outside restaurant. Watch out where you place the food (hopefully not on papers and documents), how you discard the trash (preferably in a covered garbage can with a plastic liner inside), and how you handle the reusable utensils (which should be carefully washed, dried, and stored inconspicuously in a clean cabinet or drawer). You have to be your own waiter or waitress, busboy, and dishwasher. If you're not careful about how you handle food in the office, your desk will soon be a mess, work will be spoiled, furniture and rugs will be stained, and your area will be invaded by insects and pests.

Help New Employees

Once you learn the ropes, you may be asked to help a new employee. In fact, don't wait to be asked if you can help him without neglecting your own duties. Remember how you felt when you first began work. Put the new employee at ease, show him what supplies he needs to get started, and be sure to introduce him to the other workers in his department. Then check from time to time to see how he is progressing. He will always remember your friendly interest.

WHAT AN EMPLOYER LOOKS FOR

The modern executive works under the unrelenting pressure of competition. To minimize the risk and danger of failure, he works out plans and routines for each step of his operation. Then he picks the best staff he can find to help him operate his business successfully. Interviews, references, investigations, tests, and many other devices help him to screen job applicants.

After being hired, a new worker is generally observed during a probationary period. This is a time when the employer watches the new worker carefully and looks for the qualities that he considers important in a desirable employee, including the ability to adjust well and get along with other people.

Employers report that workers lose more jobs because of personality deficiencies than for any other reason. Why? Because major personality hang-ups affect others and create some very difficult problems on a job. Even small irritations have a way of snowballing into troublesome proportions. Most employers are tolerant of the minor shortcomings of their staff members and are particularly tolerant of the shortcomings of new employees. However, there is a practical dollars-and-cents limit to their patience, which is why employers seek the traits below to supplement technical skills.

Consideration

The know-it-all person can soon discourage the friendly help of others. If you were a boss, how would you feel about keeping a clerk who constantly found fault with everyone's work except her own, complained continually, and even sometimes took into her own hands matters that did not concern her? Such behavior on the part of an individual can hurt office morale, lose good employees and customers who may be offended, and contribute to general office inefficiency.

Promptness

Arriving ten minutes late in the morning or back from lunch hardly sounds like something about which to get concerned. But if you multiply ten minutes a morning by the number of working days in a year, you will discover that you have missed the equivalent of an entire week of work. If you were the boss, how would you feel about paying an employee for a week of work in which no work was accomplished? And that's for just *one* employee!

Good Attendance

Excessive employee absence is a serious problem for the businessman. American industry actually loses over 12 billion dollars a year in benefit payments to absent employees. However, the benefit payments are only part of the cost; the loss caused by delay in company operations is incalculable. The employee who reports for work on time but cannot be found at his work station when he is wanted is wasting his employer's money. An employee who is absent from work repeatedly delays the work of others and seriously limits his own chances to advance. Because of his negligence, the employee is ultimately dismissed.

Initiative

No boss wants to hound his workers to see that schedules are kept or that jobs are done properly. He simply can't spare the time to inspect the work of every employee or to stop what he is doing to settle petty disputes. He wants to feel that he can depend upon his workers to carry their share of responsibility and rely on them to handle any minor problems. He counts on suggestions and ideas from his working force to improve business operations and has no interest in the employee who is just "putting in his time" on a job. That kind of a person can retard operations because of his disinterest and lack of initiative.

Care

Office machinery and equipment cost a great deal of money. Fifteen hundred dollars hardly covers the basic desk, chair, typewriter, file cabinets, and simple gadgets that are required to equip a worker in a typical typing job. In fact, some specialized machines cost thousands of dollars each. You can understand why a businessman wants his property cared for and protected. The office supplies used—and wasted—can add up to a great deal of money in a year. Your boss wants you to use only what you need and to be careful not to waste materials.

Your employer is also interested in care and pride in workmanship. Any craftsman will tell you that your work becomes more interesting and meaningful when you take pride in it. Poor work that has to be discarded or redone is a waste of time. Shoddy, careless work satisfies neither you nor the person who receives it. There is great satisfaction in knowing that others respect your skill and feel that if the work comes from you, it is almost certain to be right. The

Office workers handle mechanical equipment worth thousands of dollars.

Courtesy American Telephone & Telegraph Company

key is care — care in following instructions and observing routines, care in writing clearly so that mistakes are avoided, care in checking calculations so that books balance, care in turning out letters that look so professional that they sustain the confidence customers have in the company.

Good Attitude

The hard truth is that there is no such thing as a free lunch. Someone has to pay for it. When an employee takes on a job, he takes on his share of the work. If he does less than his share, someone else must carry an extra load. If it turns out that you have no interest in your job or in the future it holds for you, you owe it to yourself, even more than to your employer, to leave.

Loyalty

You and your boss share a very real interest in making a success of the business. That success assures you of a permanent job and a future career; it offers your boss a livelihood in a business that represents his life's work. Both of you have a stake in it. When the going gets rough, an employer, even without asking, has a right to expect you to support him and give a little extra help in a crisis. In turn, you have a right to expect him to back you up in a tight spot. The relationship is a mutual one, and it works best when you have confidence in the products and policies of the company you work for and when your employer has confidence in you.

Patience

If one could get to the top overnight, *everyone* would be there. It takes time and work to achieve success and recognition. Match your ambition with effort and energy.

Regard for Privileges

Everyone has personal responsibilities to which he must attend. Sometimes you can only take care of these personal matters during the day, and when that happens, most employers are willing to give you time off for the emergency. But no employee can expect his employer to let him take time out of work again and again for personal affairs. Today almost all retail and service businesses — banks, stores, beauty shops and barber shops, ticket offices, and even doctors, dentists, and lawyers — have some evening and weekend hours so that you can attend to your affairs after business hours.

Good Adjustment

Many young graduates from small towns and rural areas migrate to cities in search of jobs in large modern offices. In addition to finding jobs, they face the big task of locating a room or an apartment, getting settled, and dealing with a budget perhaps for the first time. Most of these young people have never lived away from home before. At home they had families who took care of them. Now, however, they are suddenly preparing meals, cleaning house, washing, ironing, and shopping. With all these extra things to think about, in addition to starting a new job, new workers can become very tired. And if they don't eat properly or are filled with anxieties about their new situation, they will not be effective workers. Usually all they need is a little time to adjust gradually. Since most people manage before too long, employers try to be as understanding as possible. But sometimes it is best to find your first or second job in your home town. Whatever you do, be realistic. Examine the situation, and be quite sure that you can live away from home at the same time you begin a new job.

THE VALUE OF A PERSONALITY CHECKUP

A strong ego and feelings of personal worth that one obtains from concrete accomplishments are fine things to have. The more positive your feelings are about yourself, the more possible it is to examine your shortcomings and to take steps to remedy them. Self-evaluation, however, is difficult. To help you in your analysis, you may want to use a rating device such as the one on pages 53–55 (also shown in your workbook). It is one of many kinds of more formal tests and measuring devices used by guidance counselors, placement directors, and psychologists to evaluate personality. Take it and don't be surprised if it reveals some things about yourself you never suspected.

HOW CAN YOU IMPROVE?

Once you know what your shortcomings are, you can begin to remedy them. Fortunately, there are many ways you can help yourself.

Be Open-Minded

Don't be self-destructive. Everyone has strengths and weaknesses. Simply recognize that there are specific areas of your personality that need improvement.

Be Cooperative

Ratings by counselors or by groups are meant to help you, so be as helpful as you can. Tell them everything that you feel they should know in a frank and straightforward manner.

Have Confidence

Most good personalities don't just happen; they are shaped by conscious effort. Be confident that you can be helped with your individual problems as others have been helped with theirs.

WHAT DOES YOUR PERSONALITY CHECKUP SHOW?

	Yes	Some-times	No

Relationship With Others

Are you:

1 Friendly toward others?
2 Willing to do something for others without being asked?
3 On time for appointments with others?
4 Loyal to your friends?
5 Willing to accept responsibility?
6 Willing to share your belongings with others?

Do you:

7 Try not to hurt the feelings of others?
8 Do your share of work for family and school groups?
9 Try to resolve arguments?
10 Think ahead about the result of your actions?
11 Try not to take advantage of the good nature of others?
12 Choose language appropriate to the occasion?
13 Use prudence in your choice of friends?

Attitude Toward the Rights of Others

Do you:

14 Treat new employees with kindness?
15 Respect property belonging to others?
16 Respect the good name of others?
17 Share your good fortune with others?
18 Treat others respectfully and courteously?
19 Cooperate with the particular group of which
you are a member?

Initiative and Leadership

Do you:

20 Get a job done without having to be reminded?
21 Start projects for the good of the group?
22 Assume leadership of group activities?
23 Solve problems immediately rather than put them off?
24 Do what needs to be done rather than wait to be told?
25 Initiate new activities yourself?
26 Accept an office in clubs of which you are a member?
27 Refuse to give up in the face of obstacles?
28 Set and usually achieve high standards and worthy goals?
29 Have confidence in the fact that you can do a good job?

Health Habits

Do you:

30 Keep clothing neat and clean?
31 Avoid too many snacks between meals?
32 Keep your weight within the limits right for you?

WHAT DOES YOUR PERSONALITY CHECKUP SHOW? (Continued)

	Yes	Some-times	No

Do you:

33 Brush your teeth regularly and see a dentist at regular intervals?

34 Take a bath regularly?

35 Wash your hands before meals?

36 Get adequate exercise to keep physically fit?

37 Keep fingernails clean and well manicured?

38 Get the proper amount of rest, sunshine, and fresh air?

Personal Habits and Attitudes

Do you:

39 Talk in a moderate tone of voice when in a group?

40 Keep to a minimum the amount of borrowing you do?

41 Talk with others without monopolizing conversation?

42 Find that you can take criticism, as well as give it?

43 Make your word one that can be depended on?

44 Consider the feelings of others?

45 Refrain from forcing your opinions on others?

46 Respect others' opinions when they differ from yours?

47 Have a drive and desire to succeed?

Social and Recreational Skills

Do you:

48 Enjoy group activities?

49 Participate in outdoor and indoor sports in season?

50 Drive with regard to safety?

51 Feel you can address a group without being self-conscious?

52 Have hobbies others share?

53 Enjoy playing or listening to music?

54 Swim and have training in lifesaving and first aid?

Mental Alertness

Do you:

55 Pay careful attention to instructions?

56 Learn from mistakes?

57 Understand and follow instructions exactly?

58 Investigate problems more deeply than you are required?

59 Use judgment to distinguish the unimportant from the important?

60 React affirmatively to suggestions for improvement?

61 Contribute to groups of which you are a member?

62 Consider all facts and facets of a problem before attempting to solve it?

63 Consider the consequences of your actions?

64 Readily adapt yourself to meet new situations?

WHAT DOES YOUR PERSONALITY CHECKUP SHOW? (Continued)

	Yes	Some-times	No

Personal Appearance

Do you:

65	Have a ready smile?	___	___	___
66	Keep your hair well groomed?	___	___	___
67	Watch diet to prevent skin disorders?	___	___	___
68	Use a deodorant to prevent body odor?	___	___	___
69	Avoid use of excessive makeup?	___	___	___
70	Dress according to the situation?	___	___	___
71	Keep clothing well pressed at all times?	___	___	___
72	Keep shoes well shined or cleaned?	___	___	___
73	Sit, stand, and walk with good posture?	___	___	___

Production Ability

Do you:

74	Tackle tasks with energy?	___	___	___
75	Remain cheerful even though a task is somewhat unpleasant?	___	___	___
76	Get instructions straight before starting a job?	___	___	___
77	Organize work efficiently before starting a task?	___	___	___
78	Work at a steady pace without frequent stops for rest?	___	___	___
79	Work up to your capabilities?	___	___	___
80	Never sacrifice quality for quantity?	___	___	___
81	Profit by your mistakes and improve as you repeat tasks?	___	___	___
82	Keep waste and wasted effort to a minimum?	___	___	___
83	Tackle a job the right way rather than the wrong way?	___	___	___

Dependability

Do you:

84	Require a minimum of supervision to complete assigned tasks?	___	___	___
85	Finish your assignments in the time required and on time?	___	___	___
86	Use moderation when taking advantage of privileges granted?	___	___	___
87	Keep periods of absence from work to a minimum?	___	___	___
88	Do more work than you are required to do in an emergency?	___	___	___
89	Complete assigned tasks in spite of difficulties and obstacles?	___	___	___
90	Choose the course of action that is honest and morally right?	___	___	___
91	Willingly admit your own mistakes and not blame others for them?	___	___	___
92	Ask when something seems to be wrong?	___	___	___
93	Keep engagements once they are made?	___	___	___

Seek Advice

Knowing what your deficiencies are is just the first step. Seek whatever advice you can about corrective measures. Your parents, friends, teachers, counselors, or clergy may be able to offer valuable suggestions. There is also a considerable amount of information on personality development in magazines, pamphlets, and books. Ask your teacher or librarian to help you find good references.

Take Action

Reading or being told how to correct your problem is not enough. Once you know what to do, practice it until the correct routine becomes a habit.

Check Your Progress

You'll enjoy measuring your progress. Periodically have your personality reviewed by someone who not only knows you but also knows what you are trying to do. Such a person can help you judge the progress you've made and can help to pinpoint special areas that need improvement.

REVIEWING YOUR READING

1 Explain five rules suggested for making friends and getting along with people.
2 Give examples of office situations in which good manners are of great importance.
3 Major personality faults can create difficult problems on the job. Cite some examples, and explain why these faults cause troubles.
4 Explain why there is a practical limit to the boss's patience with the personal shortcomings of his employees.
5 What makes frank self-evaluation so difficult?
6 What is the advantage of knowing your weak points?

OFFICE ASSIGNMENTS

1 Analyze the following office situations. Then write a paragraph explaining how you would act, demonstrating good human relations in each case.

   a Your work is up to date, but if you do more, the additional work will help your supervisor to achieve a better efficiency rating for the department.
   b A beginner seems to be having difficulty with his work. It is not your duty to help him, but you are aware of several errors he has made.
   c A co-worker is being reprimanded for an error you made. He is willingly taking the blame for you.

d A fellow employee is asked to work overtime. You know that he will have to break an important engagement. You have very little urgent work to do.

e One of the office employees does not seem to be accepted by the group, yet he seems to be a friendly, willing, and cooperative worker.

2 Study the following example of manuscript writing. Then copy the paragraph in good manuscript style. Compare your finished work with the sample, and practice to improve your weak points.

Manuscript writing is generally used where absolute legibility is needed, such as in writing the name and address on an order blank, mailing label, or heading of an important business record.

Aa Bb Cc Dd Ee Ff Gg Hh Ii Jj Kk Ll Mm
Nn Oo Pp Qq Rr Ss Tt Uu Vv Ww Xx Yy Zz
1234567890

3 Are you a well-adjusted person who can easily work with others and fit into an office situation?

a Rate yourself by filling in the personality checkup in your workbook; or if you are not using a workbook, refer to the checkup on pages 53–55 of the text, and write your answers on a separate sheet of paper.

b Explain what you can do to change each "Sometimes" or "No" item to a "Yes."

4 Accuracy in verifying or checking business information is one of the most important qualities of the successful office worker. Compare each pair of numbers to determine whether they are identical or different in any way. Then on a separate sheet of paper, copy the two columns of figures on page 58 and list your answers in a third column. Use a ruler or another object with a straight edge to focus your vision on one set of figures at a time. If the two numbers are identical, place a check mark in the Answer column. If the two

numbers are different, place an X in the Answer column, draw a line through the number in Column 2, and rewrite the number to agree with the one in Column 1.

	Column 1	Column 2	Answer
Example:	4327	4327	✔
Example:	1121	~~1211~~ 1121	X
1	4091	4091	
2	3566	3655	
3	7887	7878	
4	1020	1020	
5	6413	6418	
6	35536	35536	
7	89906	89096	
8	74411	744111	
9	62200	62200	
10	34309	34309	
11	772881	778211	
12	450967	450947	
13	328804	823304	
14	471111	471111	
15	900733	907333	
16	4778216	4778216	
17	3655201	3565201	
18	8989988	8989988	
19	2332147	2332147	
20	4300419	4300019	
21	82330194	82230194	
22	10007432	10007432	
23	21479886	21497886	
24	34776520	34776520	
25	19491990	19499190	
26	727071227	727071227	
27	649287624	649287624	
28	147300126	147301126	
29	899889798	899887898	
30	472610000	47261000	
31	3193169738	3193167938	
32	4200765532	4200765532	
33	5155151551	51551551551	
34	2873233202	2873233202	
35	1482007147	1482007147	
36	60067667767	60067667767	
37	43856728196	43856928196	
38	84332383283	84332383283	

5 A rating scale used by an employer for appraisal at the end of the probationary period shows the following evaluation of a worker's personal factors. Would you retain this employee? If not, why not? If so, would you regard her as a good or a passable employee? How does the evaluation on the rating scale below differ from the one you might obtain from the rating scale on page 60?

TRAINEE EVALUATION RECORD

10/27/--
Date

Henrietta Taylor
Trainee's Name

Accounting Clerk
Current Training Program

RATINGS
E—Excellent
S—Satisfactory
NI—Needs Improvement

I—Improved
NC—No Change
SD—Slowed Down

TRAINEE CHARACTERISTICS	CURRENT PERFORMANCE			PERFORMANCE PROGRESS		
	E	S	NI	I	NC	SD
1. KNOWLEDGE OF JOB. Understands what has to be done and knows how to do it. Follows directions carefully and uses the proper materials.			✓			
2. QUALITY OF WORK. Turns out work that meets business standards of accuracy and neatness.			✓			
3. QUANTITY OF WORK. Works steadily and turns out a quantity of work that meets business standards of production.			✓			
4. DEPENDABILITY. Is present and on time each day. Can be counted on to stick with a job until it is done.			✓			
5. WORK ORGANIZATION. Thinks through each training assignment and assembles the needed materials before starting. Handles the work in order of priority.			✓			
6. JUDGMENT IN SEEKING HELP. Knows when to ask questions on training procedures so as to avoid making mistakes or wasting time. Also knows when to seek in-service training to build needed skills.			✓			
7. ATTITUDE. Is enthusiastic about mastering the job. Accepts constructive criticism gracefully. Works smoothly and cooperatively with fellow trainees. Is friendly and helpful to visitors.			✓			
8. APPEARANCE OF WORK STATION. Training materials, supplies, and equipment are kept in good order while work is in progress. Everything is left in good condition or put neatly away at the end of each training session.		✓				
9. PERSONAL APPEARANCE. Always looks clean and neat. Meets business standards of grooming.		✓				
10. PERSONAL CHARACTERISTICS. Is honest in all his dealings with others and respects their rights and property. Can be trusted with confidential information. Expresses himself clearly and tactfully.		✓				
11. IN-SERVICE TRAINING. Carries out the special skill-building exercises assigned to improve job performance.		✓				
12. GROUP ACTIVITIES. Works well with others on special group projects.		✓				
13. ADMINISTRATIVE JOB ASSIGNMENTS. Helps by carrying out the various administrative jobs that are assigned from time to time.		✓				

EMPLOYEE EVALUATION FORM

Use this form to evaluate each employee. For each factor, select the group of words which best describes your judgment of the employee and circle the appropriate point value. When you have rated the employee on all factors, add the points and record the total score.

NAME _Gerald Harris_   DATE _10/28/--_   TOTAL POINTS _79_
DEPARTMENT _Purchasing_   JOB TITLE _Purchasing Clerk_

1. KNOWLEDGE OF JOB: Consider extent of person's knowledge of *present* job. Does he know what to do and why? Is he on the alert to increase his knowledge?	Has an exceptionally thorough knowledge of work **10**	Has good knowledge of work ✓ **8**	Requires considerable coaching **6**	Has inadequate knowledge of work **4**
2. QUALITY OF WORK: Consider ability to turn out work which meets high quality standards. Consider accuracy and neatness of work, regardless of volume. How frequent and serious are errors?	Highest quality **15**	Well done ✓ **12**	Passable **9**	Poor **6**
3. QUANTITY OF WORK: Consider the volume of work produced under normal conditions. Does he produce the volume he should on each task? Does he meet the quantity standards you have set for job?	Large volume **15**	Good volume **12**	Slightly below average volume **9** ✓	Unsatisfactory volume **6**
4. ATTENDANCE AND PUNCTUALITY: Consider frequency of absences as well as lateness.	Record is excellent ✓ **10**	Occasionally absent or late **8**	Frequently absent or late **6**	Undependable; absent or late without notice **4**
5. ATTITUDE: Consider attitude toward work, company, and associates, and willingness to work with and for others. Does he "pitch in" when needed? Work smoothly with others? Make an effort to understand and observe company policies? Is he willing to do the less desirable tasks?	Unusually fine attitude **10**	Good attitude ✓ **8**	Passable **6**	Poor attitude **4**
6. JUDGMENT: Consider ability to make decisions and to utilize working time to best advantage. Does he plan logically to get work done in best possible manner? Are all facts obtained before making decisions? Does he know when to seek advice? In unusual situations, does he act wisely?	Justifies utmost confidence **10**	Applies himself well; needs little supervision ✓ **8**	Needs frequent checking **6**	Cannot be relied upon; needs constant supervision **4**
7. RELIABILITY: Consider ability to get work out under pressure, and to follow job through to completion. Can he be depended upon to complete assignments satisfactorily and on schedule? Is he willing to dig in to meet peak loads? Does he retain his composure under pressure?	Can always be counted upon **15**	Generally can be counted on ✓ **12**	Unpredictable under pressure **9**	"Cracks up" under pressure **6**
8. FLEXIBILITY-ADAPTABILITY: Consider the speed with which he learns and the amount of instruction required to teach him new duties. Does he adapt easily to new conditions? Does he learn fast and is he confident of his ability to learn? Is he willing to try new ideas?	Learns fast **10**	Learns reasonably fast ✓ **8**	Slow to learn **6**	Unable to learn **4**
9. PERSONAL CHARACTERISTICS: Consider Appearance, Personality, Integrity, "Housekeeping". Is his honesty and integrity beyond reproach? Is he capable of properly representing the company over the phone or directly with the public? Does he dress suitably for the job? Is general impression one of neatness and cleanliness? Does he keep his desk or work area orderly?	Decidedly favorable **5**	Good ✓ **4**	Passable **3**	Generally unsatisfactory **2**

5 The Importance of How You Look

Whether you greet customers and visitors or just see associates on the job, how you look is important. A clean, well-groomed, attractive appearance reflects your personal pride in yourself and strongly implies that you have equal pride in your work.

It takes careful advance planning to make the most of your appearance. Fashions, it is true, have changed somewhat, but the office is still not the place for extreme styles or party clothes. There is an appropriate way to dress for business, and you have a broad range of styles from which to choose.

PHYSICAL CHARACTERISTICS THAT IDENTIFY YOU

Many factors affect your physical appearance, and it's important that you know what they are so that you can always look and feel your best.

Posture

Learn to stand and walk tall and erect. When you do, you look more attractive, whether you are a man or a woman; your clothes look and fit better; you don't tire so quickly; and you enjoy better health.

Weight

Snacks are tempting, but they can cause you to gain weight before you realize it. To look trim and alert, keep your weight within the normal limits of your height and bone structure.

Energy Reserve

There's lots to do while you're at work. It takes energy to keep operations moving on schedule, and you can't work effectively if you're exhausted. A balanced diet and eight to ten hours of sleep each night are what most young people need to perform efficiently.

Body Hygiene

Everyone perspires, some more, some less. Although office work generally doesn't involve a lot of physical exertion, normal activity, plus the tension generated by a new job or new projects, can cause you to perspire. Perspiration is easy enough to control with a daily bath and a deodorant, and cleanliness is appreciated by all in an office where people work together in close quarters.

Hair Grooming

Well-groomed hair, tastefully styled, is always attractive. Extreme hairstyles for either men or women should be avoided. Hair should be shampooed and trimmed regularly, if it is always to look its best.

Cosmetics

Makeup is an art that clever women cultivate. No matter how much makeup they use, they always try to look natural. Use makeup to look fresh and attractive, not overdone. Touch up your face and hair in the ladies' room rather than at your desk. This is good office etiquette, and a good way to keep your makeup tricks to yourself!

Shaving

Men are expected to look their best too. And why not? This means that you should shave every morning. If you have a heavy beard, you might want to keep an electric shaver at the office, so that you can shave before a meeting scheduled late in the afternoon or early evening.

Beards, Mustaches, and Sideburns

Office rules about these vary, but keep whatever you sport—beard, mustache, or sideburns—trimmed elegantly.

Teeth

Brush your teeth after every meal, if it is at all possible. If you can't, at least rinse out your mouth after you have eaten. Your breath will feel fresher.

Hands

It's important that you keep your hands clean because of the large amount of paper handled in the office. Typewritten work or records that have smudges or fingerprint marks on them have to be done over. Use a cloth or absorbent tissue to wipe your hands when they become damp with perspiration or soiled from dust or ink. You'll avoid broken fingernails if you trim them to a medium length. Have a routine for regularly cleaning your nails. It can be a disaster if you suddenly point a dirt-rimmed finger at something you're showing the boss! And of course, having clean nails is good hygiene.

THE IMPACT OF HOW YOU DRESS

What you wear to the office depends a great deal on *where* you work, *what* you do, and *with whom* you come in contact during your working hours.

Appropriate Clothing

Your clothes should suit your job. The best rule is to observe the local customs. Large offices in cities in the Northeast tend to be more conservative than those in the West and South. Businesses in large cities can be less flexible about dress than those in smaller communities. New businesses or those with younger managers are apt to be more easygoing about standards of dress than older firms. Some businesses are more traditional about dress than others. Bank employees, for example, are required to dress more conservatively than employees in up-to-the-minute retail establishments.

To avoid any embarrassment or disappointment, find out what clothing styles are acceptable in the industry or office where you plan to work. How?

☐ Ask a reliable friend or relative who works in a business office or who visits offices frequently.

☐ Observe for yourself how people are dressed as they wait at the bus stop en route to work each morning.

☐ Note the styles being worn in the offices that you may visit on field trips or when paying bills.

☐ Study job advertisements or recruiting literature that may show people at work.

☐ Obtain a copy of a firm's employee newspaper or magazine, and note how the people are dressed in the pictures.

☐ Observe how people are dressed when they emerge from their office at lunch or at closing time.

☐ Ask your guidance counselor or placement officer for suggestions.

☐ If you are still in doubt, dress on the conservative side for a while until you know your company's preferences.

The Right Accessories

By simply adding a scarf, a belt, a collar, or some jewelry, you can give a dozen different looks to a basic dress. But be selective in choosing accessories; don't overdo it. The simple look is usually the most elegant. In order to learn how to choose the right accessories, think of them as doing for your outfit what the right musical accompaniment does for a singer—it simply enhances a good performance.

Emergency Apparel

It's a great idea to keep reserve accessories and supplies at the office for emergencies. Extra hosiery, handkerchiefs, scarves, and gloves in a desk drawer can come in very handy. A pocket-size raincoat can be most welcome when an unexpected downpour occurs at lunchtime or closing time. For men an extra handkerchief or an extra clean shirt and tie can be useful to freshen up for an unexpected evening appointment or an after-hours training session.

THE "LOOK" COUNTS WHEN YOU'RE ON A JOB

There's no single fashion that's the right one, but there is a way of presenting yourself that makes a statement about who and what you are and how you feel about yourself.

1 and 5, courtesy Sears, Roebuck and Co.; 2 and 4, courtesy Vidal Sassoon's International Division for Men; 3, courtesy Allied Chemical Corporation; 6, courtesy Simplicity Pattern Co., Inc.

7, courtesy Mademoiselle Magazine (Copyright 1973, The Conde Nast Publications, Inc.); 8, courtesy American Telephone & Telegraph Company; 9, courtesy National Hairdressers and Cosmetologists Association, Inc.; 10 and 12, courtesy John H. Breck, Inc.; 11, courtesy Burlington Industries, Inc.; 13, 14, and 15, courtesy Sears, Roebuck and Co.

Outerwear

If your job is in a part of the country which enjoys cold weather, you'll want the kind of outerwear that will keep you from catching cold. In addition to warm wools and pile-lined cottons, there are handsome new, lightweight synthetics, many of which are water-resistant. Natural fibers, too, can be given a water-resistant treatment when the garment is sent to the cleaners.

Clothing Maintenance

If you rotate your wardrobe, your clothes will last longer and you'll not tire of them so easily. Brush your dress, suit, or skirt, and hang up your clothes after each time you wear them. Do a weekly wardrobe inspection for minor repair jobs—loose buttons, torn pockets, frayed cuffs, open seams, sagging hems. To look really well dressed, make sure everything you wear is clean and well pressed. Keep your hosiery and handkerchiefs laundered, and wear a fresh change of underclothing each day. Clean gloves, an orderly handbag, and a tie without spots are all important details which contribute to an overall good-looking picture. A well-pressed suit can't keep you from looking messy if your shirt is soiled and your socks are faded. A clean blouse still looks sloppy if your skirt is wrinkled and your stockings have runs. For that alert, sparkling look, pay attention to *all* the details. People tend to have more confidence in a person who looks neat and well-groomed.

Clothes Sense

Before you buy an article of clothing for office wear, ask yourself these questions:

- ☐ Is it something I want and can afford?
- ☐ Does this style suit me?
- ☐ Is it appropriate for office wear?
- ☐ Does it fit?
- ☐ Is it comfortable?
- ☐ Is it well made?
- ☐ Is the fabric of good quality? Can it be cared for easily?
- ☐ Does the color look well on me?
- ☐ Will it combine with other clothing I already own?
- ☐ Does the price represent a good buy?

If you can answer "yes" to the above questions, if you read advertisements carefully, if you shop around before making your final purchase, and if you really want to make a good appearance, you will develop "clothes sense." Clothes sense means knowing what to wear and when to wear it. If you know how to buy clothes, you'll never spend the money you earn foolishly. If you know how to wear clothes, you'll have the confidence and comfort that go with a good appearance, and you will be free to do your best work.

HOW TO PREPARE YOURSELF FOR THE JOB YOU WANT

Now that you have read about the important skills, knowledge, and personal qualities that employers look for in office workers, take another look at the beginning office jobs listed on pages 9–23 and think about positions for which you would be qualified. You'll benefit more from your school training if you establish your goals early: you can obtain good advice from your teachers on the best plan of training required for the job you want.

Once you have a goal and an organized plan of study, you'll be able more easily to choose the courses you need. You can tie in your classroom instruction with specific problems about the work that interests you. You may even be able to get a part-time or summer job to see what office work is really like.

But the outcome of all of your training depends on you. Apply yourself to get the most from the training your school has to offer so that you will face your job interview with the confidence which comes from knowing that you have had the best preparation for the work to be done. You can stand ready to prove that you have what it takes to meet today's business standards.

REVIEWING YOUR READING

1 How can the beginning office worker determine what styles of dress are acceptable in offices today?
2 Outline the considerations to be weighed in purchasing clothing for the office.

OFFICE ASSIGNMENT

List the components of a complete wardrobe (dress, blouse, suit, jacket, accessories) that would be appropriate for you to wear in an office in your community during **(a)** the winter months and **(b)** the summer months. Next to each item indicate the color, style, and other important characteristics, such as durability and ease of maintenance. In a third column, list the approximate retail price of each item, and then total the prices to find out how much the entire wardrobe would cost.

UNIT 2

BUSINESS CASES AND PROBLEMS

In the Boss's Shoes   1   Jill applied for a transfer from the duplicating unit to the reception desk. She told the interviewer in the personnel office that she wanted a more varied job assignment. She also mentioned that the receptionist job would give her a chance to wear fancier clothes and to meet people. The interviewer then asked her what she meant by fancy clothes. Jill was surprised by this line of questioning. In fact, she thought that what she wore to the office was her own business and almost said so.

Did Jill have the right to be indignant? Did the interviewer have any justification for his questions? Was he prying into her personal business?

2   Your boss has been seriously considering a promotion for Roberta, a young accounting clerk, because she works very quickly and accurately. However, he is hesitant about promoting her, because Roberta seems to be impatient in her dealings with other employees. The boss has dropped a few hints about this to Roberta, but she hasn't changed her manner. In fact, she brushes off the hints as a huge joke. What more can your boss do to help Roberta without assuming a dictatorial attitude?

Your Human Relations   **1**   "I want to work for your company because all my friends work here. I think it will be fun."

Can you socialize extensively on the job without affecting your business efficiency? Explain.

2   "But that isn't the way we did it when I worked at X company."

Why would X company's method not necessarily apply to Y company's? How do you think this remark will be received by a supervisor who has explained a job to a new worker? If the new worker really knows a better method, how and when should he present it?

What Would You Do If . . . ?   You have tried to be friendly and considerate in order to get acquainted with workers at the office, but a few of them still seem to be cold and standoffish.

What Does This Mean?   **1**   You must have a combination of skills in order to perform clerical work efficiently.

2   To get along with a person, you must learn to understand him.

Business in Your Area   **1**   What skill qualifications do local want ads mention most often for beginning clerical workers?

2   What personal qualifications are mentioned most often in the ads?

3   Which employers in your community require that beginning office workers successfully complete a probationary period before they receive a regular clerical assignment? What factors are considered in the employee evaluation at the end of the probationary period? What employee behavior is noted most frequently by employers at this time?

UNIT 3
RECEPTION AND MESSENGER WORK

Meeting the Public

As a receptionist you do far more than receive callers and announce them. Your response to and attitude toward visitors, your voice, and your appearance project an image that creates good or ill will for your company and its products. Few jobs bring you face-to-face with more people, all of whom are different and require the kind of individual attention that only a sensitive person like you can give.

GREETING VISITORS

Every receptionist develops a style of his or her own, and in time you will too. You'll come to recognize frequent callers and greet them by name, and they will respond to your recognition of them with pleasure. You'll find it useful to keep in mind and to review often the following guidelines on how to be a topnotch receptionist.

Be Friendly

Greet the visitor with a cheerful smile and a cordial word. When you say, "Good morning, may I help you?" look and sound as if you, a representative of the company, are sincerely glad to see him.

Be Attentive

Remember that everyone likes personal attention and consideration. When a visitor arrives, stop your other work and give him your undivided attention, even though you may be very busy with other tasks and quite pressed for time. The caller should receive priority and be made to feel that you have been waiting just for him to arrive.

Size Up the Caller

Experienced receptionists have a knack of getting at least a partial impression of the visitor even before he states his business. Look for telltale clues which reveal his mood, his manner, his importance, and his probable mission.

Use the Right Approach

A quick appraisal of the caller's disposition helps you to decide on the best tentative opening. An irate visitor may need soothing treatment, while an aggressive caller may warrant another method.

Ask Necessary Questions

Opening lines are very useful in establishing a good feeling and help you to find out what you need to know in order to serve the caller. If the visitor fails to communicate the reason for his call, don't hesitate to ask him questions such as the following:

☐ "Whom do you wish to see?"
☐ "Whom do you represent?"
☐ "What is the nature of your business?"
☐ "Do you have an appointment?"

These are all reasonable inquiries, and the visitor will understand that you are asking these questions in order to help him.

If a caller does not know whom he should see, your questions will identify the object of his visit, so that you can direct the caller to the proper person in the company. Questions such as the following will provide helpful leads for you:

☐ "May I help you?"
☐ "What do you wish to find out?"
☐ "Have you been here before?"
☐ "Have you any correspondence from us about this?"

Be Noncommittal

Some visitors deliberately fish for information.

☐ "Is Mr. Benson in?"
☐ "When is a good time to see him?"
☐ "Where does Mr. Hunter usually have lunch?"
☐ "Where do you buy your company stationery?"

You should respond to these types of questions—even though they may be innocent—with a polite but firm "I really can't say."

Put the Caller at Ease

Invite callers to be seated while you are making further arrangements for them. It's a good idea to seat them far enough away from your telephone so that you can speak freely without being overheard. See that they are comfortable, and point out the place for them to put their hats, coats, and parcels. If possible, have magazines and newspapers on hand to help them pass the time while they are waiting, and be sure there is sufficient light for them to read.

ANNOUNCING VISITORS

Since you cannot leave the reception desk unattended at any time during business hours, you must use the telephone to announce the arrival of a guest.

Without leaving her desk, this receptionist can communicate with people through as many as 60 telephone outlets.

Courtesy American Telephone & Telegraph Company

Telephone the secretary of the person that the caller wishes to see. Relay what you have learned about the caller, such as his name, title, firm, and purpose of his visit. Many receptionists announce visitors by telephone like this: "Mr. Lang, service representative for the Royal Machinery Corporation, wishes to see Mr. Benson about the renewal of the service contract." You give full information about the caller without revealing whether the company official is in, out, or busy at the time.

If a prior appointment was made, the secretary at the other end of the phone will probably issue instructions to you at once. If not, she will consult her boss and relay the decision to you. Most business people try to be obliging and hospitable, but there will be times when you will be asked to turn down a visitor's request or direct him to someone else. Executives need to use their time to the best advantage and, naturally, they must honor previous commitments first. There are just so many people they can see in the course of a day and still accomplish everything else that they have to do.

HANDLING VISITORS

As you learn to size up visitors and to greet them easily, you will find that they fall into two groups: those with whom you can deal routinely and those who present special problems.

Routine Situations

After you have announced their presence, you can use one of six courses of action with visitors who have routine inquiries.

Caller is to be admitted After you receive instructions to admit the visitor, you may press a buzzer on your desk to signal a messenger or escort. When he or she appears, give him all the necessary instructions, including the name of the company official and the number of the room to which the visitor is to be escorted. Then explain to the visitor, "Mr. Lang, Mr. Benson will see you now. Your escort will show you the way."

In a small firm the boss's office may be adjacent to the reception area. In this case you can escort and announce the visitor yourself without going more than a few feet from your desk.

Caller is asked to wait Notify the visitor at once if you have been told to ask him to wait. This reassures him that he will be admitted, and he can feel relaxed about using the waiting time to good advantage.

Don't forget him. If you are supposed to receive a signal in 20 minutes and don't, follow up by telephoning the secretary of the executive to remind her that the caller is still waiting. In the small office, call the boss directly. The interruption may help to terminate a prolonged conference.

Caller cannot wait The caller may have a busy schedule and may not be able to wait for a long period of time. If he chooses to leave, invite him to make an appointment for some other day. Whether he accepts your invitation or not, notify the executive's office that the caller has left.

Caller is to be redirected The executive may be too busy to see the visitor in person. However, he may wish to find out what the man wants or what he has to sell. In this case you may be told to refer the caller to another executive or an assistant. You can do this graciously by saying: "Mr. Benson can't see you today, but he has arranged for Mr. Johnson to talk to you instead. Your escort will take you to his office right away."

Caller is denied admittance Don't feel embarrassed if you are told that Mr. Benson does not wish to see the visitor. Be direct, but tactful, and tell the caller, "I'm sorry, but Mr. Benson is not interested." The seasoned caller will not take personal offense to this and will understand that this is merely part of your job. Probably he has been turned away from other places many times before—it is one of the hard facts of his business.

Caller is denied admittance temporarily If you have been informed that Mr. Benson cannot see the caller today but would consider making an appointment for some future time, say: "Mr. Benson can't see you today. However, he would be glad to see you at another time, if you care to make an appointment." If the caller proposes a date and time, relay the information to Mr. Benson's secretary and have her confirm the appointment before the visitor departs.

Special Problems

A good receptionist learns to handle unusual situations as well as routine ones. In a busy office you may encounter any of the following.

Complainants   Persons who present themselves at the reception desk and who are obviously very much disturbed about poor service or faulty products should be given the quickest attention possible. The sooner you pass them along to the proper department for prompt assistance, the less chance there is for them to create a disturbance in the reception room. It also goes without saying that the sooner their troubles receive attention, the sooner they will be satisfied. Meanwhile, reassuring but noncommittal remarks such as the following will hold off the complainant until his problem can be placed in the proper hands for appraisal and adjustment:

☐ "I will have someone look into it at once."
☐ "Our service department will know just what the trouble is."
☐ "The company stands behind all its products."

Messages for the visitor   In this day of long-distance commuting, business visitors who travel back and forth in a single day between major cities, such as New York and Chicago, may not have a hotel or other contact address where

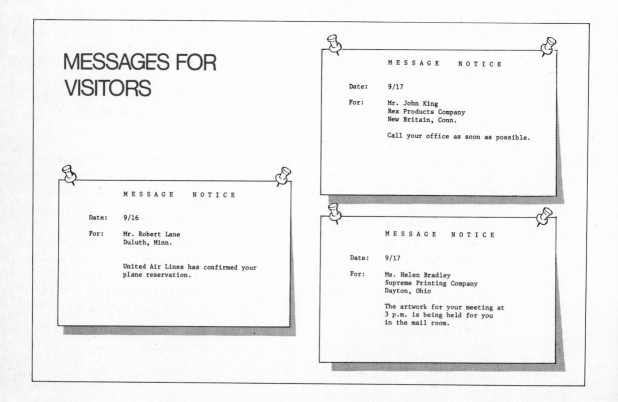

MESSAGES FOR VISITORS

MESSAGE NOTICE

Date: 9/17

For: Mr. John King
Rex Products Company
New Britain, Conn.

Call your office as soon as possible.

MESSAGE NOTICE

Date: 9/16

For: Mr. Robert Lane
Duluth, Minn.

United Air Lines has confirmed your
plane reservation.

MESSAGE NOTICE

Date: 9/17

For: Ms. Helen Bradley
Supreme Printing Company
Dayton, Ohio

The artwork for your meeting at
3 p.m. is being held for you
in the mail room.

Log of Callers						
DATE	NAME	FIRM	TIME OF ARRIVAL	TIME ESCORTED TO DESTINATION	REFERRED TO	TIME OF DEPARTURE
May 8	Leroy Winston	Insulation, Inc.	9:05 a.m.	9:15 a.m.	Dan Holmes	9:30 a.m.
8	Francis Patruno	Travel Digest	10:15 a.m.	10:20 a.m.	Angela Rossi	10:45 a.m.
8	Leila Sutton	Trim Mfg. Co.	10:40 a.m.	10:52 a.m.	Dan Holmes	11:10 a.m.
8	Henry Billard	Printing, Inc.	11:25 a.m.	11:30 a.m.	Marty Sentler	12:05 p.m.

they can receive messages. A receptionist may be asked to hold messages for such visitors who are expected to arrive or may relay messages to persons who may be waiting for them when they are delayed. Such messages can be highly important to the visitor, and you must take precautions against these messages being lost or overlooked. Although systems to guard against this happening vary, most systems involve noting the receipt of the message in a record book and posting a notice (such as the addressee's name) on a "message board" in each reception area. In addition, a carbon or photocopy of the message is attached to the current page of the log of callers, so that the visitor can plainly see the message when he registers. As a further precaution a copy of the message can be left with the secretary of the executive that the visitor is coming to see.

Charity drives   Representatives of charitable organizations will occasionally present themselves at your desk to ask if they may solicit contributions from the employees. It is customary to refer such persons to the personnel department. Most companies do not allow outsiders to solicit directly from individual employees, regardless of how worthy the cause may be.

Job applicants   Applicants for positions with the company are generally referred to the personnel department. It's best not to offer information about vacancies, hiring policies, or other company practices unless you are instructed to do so.

Disorderly persons   Once in a very great while an objectionable person will appear at the reception desk. Don't become flustered. Go through the regular routine of greeting the caller, and ignore any odd mannerisms or coarse remarks. At the same time use your buzzer or telephone to summon your supervisor or other help by a prearranged signal. The unwelcome caller will then be escorted from the premises.

Tour visitors   As a part of a public relations program, some large organizations maintain their buildings and grounds as showplaces, which are open to the public. Visitor-tourists are escorted around the premises by specially trained guides. In general, the tours follow a planned route and fixed schedule. The receptionist usually directs such visitors to a special waiting room where a tour supervisor schedules them to be included in the next group.

Friends and relatives   Standard reception procedures are usually modified when the boss's relatives and close friends call. Sometimes these persons are even allowed to walk directly into the inner offices unannounced. As a receptionist you should find out how each executive wants his special guests handled and learn the names of those persons who are included in the "special" category. If in doubt, treat the caller as a regular business visitor; you may be protecting the executive from an unwelcome intrusion.

Emergencies   You will undoubtedly encounter some emergencies if you are a receptionist working near the door through which visitors, executives, and perhaps employees come and go. Fortunately, most emergencies are minor — the forgotten briefcase; the lost eyeglasses; the mislaid name, address, or telephone number. However, when a visitor becomes ill or when an accident occurs near the lobby area, you must keep calm and act efficiently in summoning the help needed. Large organizations have standard procedures for handling all types of emergencies, and, in general, you use the telephone to summon the assistance required. If you are a receptionist in a medium-size or small concern, you may also function as the switchboard operator, and it may be your responsibility to keep emergency numbers handy at all times and to call the medical service and the police or fire departments, when needed. Once you have summoned aid, notify your boss as quickly as possible about the action you have taken.

SECURITY PRECAUTIONS

In recent years business offices have been severely victimized by thieves, vandals, and other unwelcome intruders. Some offices have employed reception procedures that have been redesigned in order to serve as a part of a system of defense against such persons.

For example, the visitor may be screened through several reception areas. The first reception area may be situated just inside the front door in the main lobby (usually staffed by men, possibly uniformed guards). The visitor is asked to identify himself and explain the purpose of his visit (see Ask Necessary Questions, page 71). When the receptionist receives instructions to admit the visitor, she records or *logs* the visitor's name and other information as illustrated on page 75, issues a pass or visitor's badge, and calls an escort. While waiting for the escort, the visitor is invited to check his outer clothing, and parcels that he wishes to carry inside with him are inspected and marked for identification.

The escort then conducts the visitor to a second reception area serving the floor, unit, or division he plans to visit. The second receptionist also logs the visitor, notifies the person or office that is expecting the caller, and if he is to be admitted, summons an escort. When the meeting is concluded, the executive or his secretary calls for an escort, and the whole process is reversed in a formal checkout procedure. At no time is a visitor permitted beyond the front door without clearance and registration. At no time is the visitor left alone on the premises. Finally, the checkout process accounts for all visitors who were admitted during visiting hours.

RECEPTION RECORDS AND OTHER DUTIES

In addition to the log of callers, many receptionists maintain a register in which messages and parcels received are recorded. You may also keep a file for business cards and other data to help you direct frequent callers more efficiently. A manual is usually provided to instruct and guide you in general company policies and special reception procedures. Telephone books, public and company directories, and employee rosters are common reception room equipment.

In addition to their main duty of greeting and directing callers, some receptionists have other office duties such as operating the switchboard, assembling reports, typing form letters, sorting and filing papers, or checking mailing lists. They also serve as valuable general utility workers who ease the work load of other units during peak periods.

MESSENGER DUTIES

A messenger contributes a great deal to the impression outsiders get of a company. If you are hired as a messenger, you'll have a number of responsibilities.

Visitor Escort

☐ Answer the summons promptly.
☐ Listen to the receptionist's instructions.
☐ Greet the caller with a smile, and act as if you are truly eager to serve him.
☐ Ask the visitor to follow you, and then escort him to his destination.
☐ See that the visitor reaches the proper place quickly and safely.
☐ Help him carry any heavy or bulky bags, packages, or equipment.
☐ Keep the visitor away from work areas where his presence may involve physical danger or disrupt routine.
☐ Introduce the visitor to the secretary. She will then relieve you as escort and introduce the visitor to her boss.
☐ If no secretary is on duty, introduce the visitor to the boss yourself by saying, "Mr. Benson, this is Mr. Lang of the Royal Machinery Company."
☐ Once you have completed the introduction, watch for some signal or instructions from the boss or secretary. You may be needed to obtain files, papers, or materials; you may be asked to stand by to escort the visitor to another unit; or if the visit is a brief one, you may be needed in a few minutes to show the visitor the way out.

☐ When you are thanked and dismissed by the boss or his secretary, return to your work station for a new assignment.

Inside Errands

Some visitors delivering special messages or parcels are allowed to go only as far as the reception desk. In large offices the receptionist signals for a company messenger, who makes the delivery to the proper unit. If you are the company messenger, act promptly so that the message or parcel is delivered to the appropriate place as swiftly as possible. It may be a very urgent matter. Consult the company directory if you don't know the person to whom the item is addressed. The directory usually lists the name, division, location, and extension number of all company personnel.

Outside Errands

Messengers often perform important errands outside the office. An executive may request that airline tickets be picked up immediately; an engineer may ask to have drawings rushed to the blueprint shop; an order clerk sending a package by air express may want to have it taken to the airport to speed up delivery.

When you are assigned to do an outside errand, take these few preliminary steps to save time and prevent mistakes:

☐ Dress for the weather.
☐ Have plenty of carfare.
☐ Carry personal identification.
☐ Get full written instructions before you start.
☐ Consult maps or directories if you are not sure how to get to your destination.
☐ Place the message or parcel in a safe place, preferably in a dispatch case or bag.

Once you get started, keep these pointers in mind:

☐ Travel by the fastest and shortest route.
☐ Always avoid crowds and disturbances.
☐ Don't loiter along the way.
☐ If you need to stop and get directions, ask a police officer, a bus driver, or an elevator starter rather than just anyone.
☐ If you are seriously delayed en route or if you cannot complete the delivery exactly as instructed, telephone your unit supervisor from where you are for further instructions.
☐ When you get to your destination, find the person you are looking for by consulting the lobby directory, elevator starter, or main floor receptionist if there is one.
☐ Get a receipt for your delivery.
☐ Telephone the supervisor of the messenger unit before you start your return journey. He may want you to do another errand on your way back.

Messengers sometimes keep records on 5- by 3-inch cards of addresses of places to which they make frequent deliveries. They keep handy data on these cards, such as the fastest routes, bus numbers, and transfer points.

General Utility Worker

Messengers, like receptionists, frequently have spare time during the working day and are often called upon to help out with special assignments. You may be assigned to the mail unit if it is shorthanded or the duplicating unit if it is bogged down with extra work.

A messenger job has been the starting point of many highly successful business careers. The varied experience you can get as a messenger teaches you a great deal about the procedures and operations of the company. As you go about your daily work, you come into close contact with supervisors and executives; you have a good chance to demonstrate your diligence, judgment, common sense, and dependability to people who may be impressed enough with your efforts to consider you for further training and promotion. Look on it as an opportunity, and make the most of it.

REVIEWING YOUR READING

1 Demonstrate or explain how a receptionist should handle a caller who does not know whom he should see.
2 Demonstrate or explain how a visitor can be announced by telephone without revealing information to him.
3 What special treatment should be given to messages for visitors? Explain why an efficient procedure is so important.
4 What records are usually kept by a receptionist? Why?
5 Demonstrate or outline the duties of a messenger escorting a visitor.

OFFICE ASSIGNMENTS

1 Complete the following conversation between a receptionist and a caller who has asked to see the president of your company. Make it realistic.

Caller approaches the reception desk and is greeted by the receptionist.
Receptionist says:
Caller responds, asking to see the president:
Receptionist asks about an appointment:
Caller explains that he has a complaint and that he has been a steady customer for twenty years:
Receptionist asks the nature of the complaint:
Caller explains that his statement of account has not been corrected for three months because of the company's failure to record a payment:

Receptionist expresses regret for the nuisance. Explains that a new central-ized accounting system has been installed and that there was some delay in getting everything in full operation. Suggests that the caller see Mr. X, the supervisor of the accounts receivable section:

Caller agrees to see Mr. X:

Receptionist thanks the caller and calls a messenger to escort the caller to the proper destination:

2   A messenger assigned to run an errand outside the office should get com-plete instructions before he starts out. Your supervisor has just said to you, "Hurry over to the ticket office, and pick up some tickets for Mr. Harris." Assuming that you are rather new on the job, what questions should you ask so that you can complete the errand correctly?

3   In the log of callers in your workbook, record the time the following callers arrived, the time they were escorted to their destination, and the time of their departure on Monday, September 24, 19—. If you are not using the workbook, prepare a form similar to that shown on page 75 of this text.

10:10 a.m.: John L. King, salesman, Rex Products Company, requested to see Mr. Lowe, Purchasing Department. No appointment. Escorted to Mr. Lowe at 10:13 a.m. Departed at 11:00 a.m.

10:17 a.m.: C. Richard Poole, attorney, to see Mr. Link, vice president. No appointment. Mr. Link out. Made appointment for 2:30 p.m., September 27, through Mr. Link's secretary. Departed at 10:20 a.m.

10:24 a.m.: Miss Marian Coleman, job applicant. Referred to Personnel Department. Departed at 10:50 a.m.

10:43 a.m.: Frank A. Bates, designer, to see Mr. Allison, Advertising Department, by appointment. Escorted to Mr. Allison's office at 10:45 a.m. Departed at 12 noon.

4   Assume that you are on duty at the receptionist's desk and have just sum-moned a messenger to escort Mr. Rogers, representing the Kingston Desk Company, to see Mr. Blake, one of your firm's executives.

a   How would you introduce the messenger to the visitor?
b   What instructions would you give to the messenger, and how would you say them?
c   Now assume that you are the messenger. How would you introduce Mr. Rogers to Mr. Blake's secretary, Miss Greene?

5   As a receptionist for the Emperor Glass Manufacturing Company, you must be sure to issue a numbered identification badge to each visitor and obtain each visitor's badge when he leaves. When a number of badges become lost because they are not returned, you decide to redesign the log of callers in some way so as to control the badges. Working from the illus-tration on page 75 as a start, redesign the form so that you are able to control the issuance and collection of the identification badges.

UNIT 3

BUSINESS CASES AND PROBLEMS

In the Boss's Shoes   When a caller is announced and the boss says, "Tell him I'm out," the receptionist has to use tact and diplomacy with the caller so that his feelings won't be hurt. Why doesn't the boss see everybody and make the receptionist's job more pleasant? Or why doesn't the boss turn away unwanted callers himself and not expect the receptionist to assume this difficult duty?

Your Human Relations   A caller has arrived late for an appointment. The manager who was expecting him had to leave to keep another engagement. You were told to refer the caller to the manager's assistant. The caller refuses to talk to the assistant but says that he wants to see the president to tell him about the shabby treatment he is receiving. The president is in his office, and it is apparent that the caller knows it. Should you attempt to reason with the caller? If so, how? Or should you arrange for him to see the president at once? Explain how you would handle this situation.

What Would You Do If . . . ?   As a receptionist you have been told by your employer that he absolutely does not want to see any salesmen that day. After lunch, a local high school student arrives to ask your boss if he would like to buy an advertisement in the school yearbook again this year.

What Does This Mean?   Experienced receptionists look for telltale clues to the visitor's mood, manner, importance, and probable mission.

Business in Your Area   1   What kinds of offices employ receptionists in your community?

2   Do you know any receptionists who are employed full-time in your community? Do you know any who are employed part-time?

3   What other duties do receptionists perform in addition to receiving callers?

UNIT 4

TELEPHONE CALLS AND TELEGRAMS

SECTION 7 Telephone Communications

Because telephones are so common now, it's easy to forget the tremendous impact telephone communications have had on the business world. Today, a businessman can communicate with almost anyone, anywhere, and at any time.

THE TELEPHONE IN BUSINESS

The telephone is invaluable in helping to make direct, fast contact with customers in order to complete urgent business. A salesman can talk directly to a customer, give him the necessary information, work out terms immediately, and confirm shipping dates at once.

After he makes the sale, the salesman can telephone instructions regarding the production and shipment of the goods. Additional calls verify the completion of the order and give shipping information to the buyer.

Although face-to-face conversations are important in many business affairs, telephone contact, in certain instances, is more efficient. A telephone call can reach an executive directly, whereas a personal visit may involve making a special appointment and perhaps waiting some time in the reception room. The telephone encourages brevity and inhibits small talk, which is more likely to occur in face-to-face conversations. Over the phone an executive can conclude his business promptly and have time for other matters.

OPERATING PROCEDURES

Telephone procedures have been devised in order to use telephone equipment to its fullest advantage and yet to overcome its limitations. These procedures are observed in order to save valuable time for the busy people at both ends of the line and also to cut operating and service costs—important considerations inasmuch as over 500 million calls are made in a single day. The personal courtesies you use over the telephone are the same ones usually practiced by people when they greet one another face-to-face. It is important that you use these courtesies, precisely because you do not see the person at the other end of the line. For the same reason be sure to speak distinctly and include information that might be obvious if you were speaking face-to-face.

FINDING TELEPHONE NUMBERS

A local telephone number usually consists of seven digits, like 555-2879. There are still a few places where two letters and five digits are used, but these will soon be changed. Record numbers that you call frequently in a desk reference book or card file or any other convenient form. Add new numbers to the list from time to time, as needed. You can generally get these additional telephone numbers from letterheads, invoices, calling cards, address files, advertisements, and other business papers. If these handy sources fail, you can quickly find the desired number in the telephone directory. Note the illustration below from the Yellow Pages, where firms are listed alphabetically by industry. In order to find newly listed and out-of-town numbers, call the telephone company's directory assistance operator, who will be glad to help you.

Restaurants		Restaurants—(Cont'd)	
A. LA GOURMET		**ASTI KITCHEN ITALIANO**	
649-78W9	238-3444	102LexoxRd	649-3042
AD & GILL RESTRNT		**ATLANTIC REST**	
WestSt&6Av	922-4080	689SeaviewDr	258-6470
ABERLY SWISS CHALET		**ATLANTIC VIEW COFFEE SHOP**	
2WUnionDr	447-8624	232Front	332-2701
ACT 2		**AVIAN RESTRNT INC**	
31MidtownAv	343-2754	62-62W9Rd	306-5043
Ad Man Restaurant Inc		**BACK STAGE KITCHENS**	
268FoyRd	711-0861	249AtlanticAve	602-9033
ADAMS CAFTRIA INC		Bailey Bar & Grill	
1033N1Ct	659-7031	86WKentRd	605-9033
ADANOS BELL		**BALL'S RESTRNT INC**	
659BroomRd	222-8735	56WPix	204-3993
AESOP CAFE		**BARKIN**	
60N8Av	246-8421	64NPackerRd	697-3000
AGUIDO RESTRNT		**BARRETTE FRENCH CAFE**	
649RecordAve	294-3046	2839WBond	284-9032
Ahmed's Bazaar Restrnt		Bass & Pheasant Cafe	
291WCarton	214-3026	3W4Ct	886-5732
AIDA			

Courtesy New York Telephone Company

MAKING LOCAL CALLS

The procedure to follow for making an outgoing local call from your office work station depends upon the telephone equipment in use.

Calls Without Direct Dial Extension Service

Suppose you want to reach Mr. Wilson at 555-3268. When you lift your receiver, your company switchboard attendant responds by saying, "Your call, please." Then you say, "May I have an outside line, please?" She connects you with an idle trunk line. A dial tone is your signal to dial the desired number from your own telephone. The rotary dial unit has ten finger holes. To dial 555-3268, find the finger hole for 5, insert your finger, move the plate clockwise as far as the finger stop, and then release your finger. Proceed with the second 5, and continue to dial the remaining digits in the telephone number. (Be sure to distinguish between the letter *O* and the numeral zero and between the letter *I* and the numeral one.) Automatic relays in the central telephone office complete your connection with the other party.

When your call goes through the switchboard of the firm you are calling, the switchboard attendant may answer with: "Good afternoon. Mailing Machine Repair Company." Then you say, "May I speak to Mr. Wilson, scale department, please?"

Calls With Direct Dial Extension Service

This type of equipment allows you to place your own outside call. When you lift the handset, you hear a dial tone indicating that the telephone equipment is ready to accept your call. The first step is to dial 9, which connects you with an outside line. When you hear the second dial tone, you can dial 555-3268.

SPEEDING UP CALLS

Keep your calls brief and to the point in order to save yourself time and the company money. When Mr. Wilson answers his telephone, he is likely to say, "Scale department, Henry Wilson." You answer: "Good afternoon, Mr. Wilson. This is George Jackson of Parson Distributors. Is our scale ready to be picked up? Our truck will be in the neighborhood of your plant in about an hour."

If Mr. Wilson says, "Yes, Mr. Jackson, it is ready and waiting," you may close with, "Thank you. Our man will be there very shortly to pick it up. Goodbye." Your call is completed, and you hang up your handset.

DIRECT-DISTANCE DIALING

Most telephones are now equipped for direct-distance dialing (DDD) service. This means that you can dial your long-distance calls to many locations in the United States and Canada without the assistance of the telephone company's operator. All you do is consult the area code index in your telephone directory and then proceed to dial. You dial the area code along with the regular telephone number. If you are calling 555-3268 in Salina, Kansas, from a telephone in a distant city, you dial 913-555-3268. (In some states the number 1 precedes the area code, as for example, 1-913-555-3268.) From your direct dial extension office telephone you first dial 9 for an outside line and then the long-distance number you are calling, 913-555-3268. Automatic devices time the call and compute and add the charges to your monthly bill. The charges vary, according to the time of the day the call is made, the length of the call, and the distance.

© New York Telephone Company 1973

area codes for some cities

place	area code	place	area code	place	area code	place	area code	place
ALABAMA		GEORGIA		LOUISIANA		MICHIGAN (Cont'd)		NEW JERSEY
All points	205	Athens	404	Baton Rouge	504	Detroit	313	Asbury Park
		Atlanta	404	New Orleans	504	Flint	313	Atlantic City
ALASKA		Augusta	404	Shreveport	318	Grand Rapids	616	Barnegat
All points	907	Columbus	404			Jackson	517	Bayonne
		Gainesville	404			Kalamazoo	616	Bloomfield
ARIZONA		Macon	912	MAINE		Lansing	517	Bound Brook
All points	602	Marietta	404	All points	207	Marquette	906	Bridgeton
		Rome	404			Midland	517	Burlington
ARKANSAS		Savannah	912	MARYLAND		Niles	616	Camden
All points	501			All points	301	Pontiac	313	Ca

Accuracy in dialing is particularly important with direct-distance dialing. When you do get a wrong number, notify the telephone company operator immediately so that your company will not be charged for the call. Avoid making errors and save time by noting the telephone number and its area code prefix in a reference book or card file.

To get out-of-town information, dial the area code of the city you want, then dial 555-1212.

A DDD call is considered to be a *station-to-station* call. This means that you will speak to anyone who answers your call; the charges for the call begin as soon as someone picks up the receiver.

If you wish to talk to a specific person, you use *person-to-person* service. In many areas you first dial 0 (operator) and then dial the DDD number as before. To speak to Mr. William Cunningham in Salina, Kansas, you dial 0-913-555-3268. The operator intercepts the call, and then you, the caller, say, "I wish to speak to Mr. William Cunningham, please." In other areas you dial the long-distance operator and have her place the call. When the telephone is answered at the other end of the line, the telephone company operator asks for the person requested. Although person-to-person service is more expensive than station-to-station, the charges for a person-to-person call do not begin until the person requested responds. If he is not there to answer the call, no charge is made.

REPRESENTATIVE LONG-DISTANCE RATES FOR 3-MINUTE CALLS

St. Louis to:	Customer Dialed Station-to-Station				Operator-Handled		Person-to-Person	
	Day	Evening	Weekend	Night	Day	Evening, Weekend, and Night	Day	Evening, Weekend, and Night
Chicago	$ .85	$ .55	$ .50	$ .20	$1.05	$ .95	$1.60	$1.60
Each addnl. min.	.25	.15	.15	.15	.25	.20	.25	.20
Denver	1.15	.65	.50	.20	1.45	1.10	2.40	2.40
Each addnl. min.	.35	.20	.15	.15	.35	.25	.35	.25
New York	1.15	.65	.50	.20	1.45	1.10	2.40	2.40
Each addnl. min.	.35	.20	.15	.15	.35	.25	.35	.25
Pittsburgh	1.05	.60	.50	.20	1.35	1.05	2.15	2.15
Each addnl. min.	.32	.20	.15	.15	.32	.20	.32	.20
Seattle	1.35	.75	.65	.25	1.70	1.30	3.10	3.10
Each addnl. min.	.42	.25	.20	.20	.42	.25	.42	.25

Day rates: 8 a.m. to 5 p.m., Monday through Friday.
Evening rates: 5 p.m. to 11 p.m., Sunday through Friday.
Weekend rates: 8 a.m. to 11 p.m., Saturday; 8 a.m. to 5 p.m. Sunday.
Night rates: 11 p.m. to 8 a.m. daily. (These rates are based on one minute.)
SOURCE: American Telephone & Telegraph Company, January 1, 1974.

TOUCH-TONE TELEPHONE

The latest telephone equipment features Touch-Tone dialing. A 10- or 12-button arrangement replaces the rotary dial mechanism. Push the buttons in the same order that you read the letters and numbers in the telephone number you are calling. The soft musical tones you hear tell you that your call is going through. All other procedures pertaining to outgoing calls are the same as the procedures used with standard equipment.

RECEIVING CALLS

Procedures for handling incoming business calls vary with the equipment in use. In some cases the calls are received at a switchboard and then routed to the proper extension by the switchboard attendant. In an increasing number of cases, an incoming call is received directly at the extension telephone on the desk of the person called.

Calls Through the Switchboard

The switchboard attendant serves as a receptionist for the invisible clients who visit by telephone. As a switchboard attendant, you respond to the signal of an incoming call with a cheery greeting, such as "Good morning, Parson Distributors." The first few words are the same as the personal greeting you give to friends everywhere. The mention of the company name reassures the person calling that the connection is a correct one. It is the same as saying: "We heard your ring. You have reached Parson Distributors. What can we do for you?" but instead you use only four words to say it all.

When the caller hears the greeting of the Parson Distributors' switchboard attendant, he will probably ask for the person he wants to reach by saying, "May I speak to Mr. Jackson in the mail unit, please?" The switchboard attendant acknowledges the request with a "Thank you." She then routes the call to Mr. Jackson's telephone. The correct response for Mr. Jackson is, "Mail unit, George Jackson," which identifies the unit and the person answering the phone. It is the same as saying: "Your call has been connected with the mail unit. This is George Jackson speaking. May I help you?" Once again, a few well-chosen words can get across a whole message.

Direct Inward Dialing

If your office is equipped for direct inward dialing (DID), you will be the first person to answer your telephone when it rings. Your responses to calls should be prompt, preferably within ten seconds of the first ring, and include your company name as well as the name of your unit and personal identification. You say, "Parson Distributors, mail unit, George Jackson." Your response tells the caller that he has reached the right firm, the right unit, and the right person.

COMPLETING A CALL

When a caller hears you identify yourself, he tells you who he is and explains the reason for his call. For instance, he may say: "Good morning, Mr. Jackson. This is Wilson of the Mailing Machine Repair Company. It will cost about $25 to fix the scale that you sent to our repair shop yesterday. Shall we go ahead?"

If you can answer him right away, do so as briefly as possible. "Good morning, Mr. Wilson. Yes, your estimate sounds very reasonable. Go ahead with the repairs. When may we expect to have the scale returned?" Once the conversation is finished, close pleasantly with a "Thank you for calling" or "It was nice to hear from you." Then say "Goodbye" to indicate that you have said all that you intend to say and are about to hang up.

Sometimes, of course, you can't make a quick decision. When that happens, make a note about the basic facts of the conversation so that you can consult a file or confer with someone else. If this cannot be done quickly, say, "If you will excuse me a moment, I'll check on that right away." If the checking will take time, it is more efficient and considerate to say: "It may take several minutes to give you an answer. Would you rather have me call you back?"

If Mr. Wilson decides to wait, show your thoughtfulness with an occasional progress report such as: "I have just received the file. It should take only another moment or two now." When you return to the telephone with your answer, remember to comment on the caller's patience: "Thank you for waiting, Mr. Wilson. I've received authorization for the repairs. Please go ahead."

Occasionally, you will not have the knowledge or authority to answer the question raised by the caller. In this case refer him to the proper person by saying: "Mr. Roberts of the purchasing department is the only person who can authorize the work. His extension is 3169. Please hold on. I'll ask the operator to transfer your call." Then, depending on the telephone equipment being used in your office, call or flash your switchboard attendant and say to her: "Please transfer this call to Mr. Roberts, purchasing department, extension 3169. Thank you." Wait for the attendant to acknowledge your request; then hang up. With more modern equipment you press the switch hook of your telephone, listen for a dial tone, and then dial extension 3169 to make the transfer. When the person called answers, announce the call by saying, "Mr. Roberts, Mr. Wilson of the Mailing Machine Repair Company would like to speak to you." Depress the switch hook to connect the caller, and then hang up.

ANSWERING ANOTHER TELEPHONE

When the telephone rings for one of your co-workers or for your boss and he is not at his desk, answer the call as quickly as possible. This speeds up service for the person who is calling. When you answer the call, say, "Mr. Edwards' office, George Jackson."

This assures the caller that he has been connected to the proper office and tells him who you are. He may then say: "This is Carl Davis of Davis and Blane. May I speak to Mr. Edwards, please?"

Your reply at this point may be: "Mr. Edwards is not in his office at present. May I help you?" By saying this, you can offer the caller immediate assistance, if needed, or give him the opportunity to leave a message. If you have the authority to provide him with the information he wants, give it to him, and make a note to tell Mr. Edwards about it when he comes back.

However, if Mr. Davis requests something beyond your knowledge or authority, you may refer him to someone else, as you previously referred Mr. Wilson to Mr. Roberts. If the matter proves to be something that can be answered only by Mr. Edwards, say: "I'm sorry, but that's a matter for Mr. Edwards' personal attention. I am expecting him to return very shortly. May I have him call you back?"

Be sure to get the caller's name, firm, and telephone number, including the area code and, if necessary, the extension number. Note these essential facts on a telephone memorandum pad similar to the one shown here. Spell the name, and repeat the number. Then say: "Thank you for calling, Mr. Davis. I'll give the message to Mr. Edwards as soon as he comes in." Then hang up. Place the written message in a conspicuous place where Mr. Edwards will be sure to find it. Some employers prefer to have their messages taped to the telephone base, so that they will not blow off the desk or get buried under other papers.

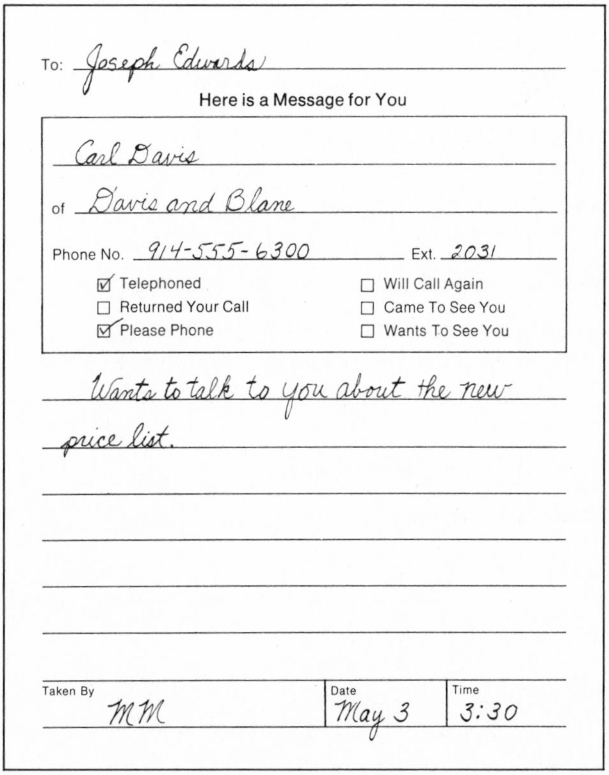

To: _Joseph Edwards_

Here is a Message for You

Carl Davis

of _Davis and Blane_

Phone No. _914-555-6300_   Ext. _2031_

☑ Telephoned   ☐ Will Call Again
☐ Returned Your Call   ☐ Came To See You
☑ Please Phone   ☐ Wants To See You

Wants to talk to you about the new
price list.

Taken By	Date	Time
M M	May 3	3:30

INTEROFFICE CALLS

The same dial telephone equipment that you use to call persons outside your firm can be used to call co-workers at other telephone extensions in your office. All you have to do is dial the number of the extension you want. Most extension numbers consist of four digits, such as 3268. Consult the company telephone directory for a complete listing of extension numbers arranged alphabetically by the person's name or by other groupings. You answer an interoffice call the same way you answer an outside call.

TELEPHONE COURTESY

"Please" and "thank you" are expressions that have the same priceless value over the telephone as they have in face-to-face contact. Such courtesies are verbal cushions, which ease many situations and indicate sincere consideration for the other fellow. In the following list you will find some valuable courtesy pointers that enhance your telephone personality:

☐ Greet the caller pleasantly. Sound as though you are glad to hear her voice.
☐ Smile as you talk. Your voice will sound more friendly, and your facial and throat muscles will be much more relaxed.
☐ Use the customer's name.
☐ Try to visualize the person. Speak to her—not at the telephone.
☐ Be attentive. The person at the other end of the line will appreciate your listening politely and attentively. Apply the same rules of courtesy in telephone conversation that you would apply in face-to-face conversation. For instance, you would not turn away abruptly from a person to whom you were speaking face-to-face.
☐ Take time to be helpful. It's better to spend seconds keeping a customer happy than to spend months trying to regain his goodwill. Apologize for errors or delays. Maybe things won't always go right, but you can always be courteous. Be sincere; an artificial apology is worse than none at all.
☐ Let the caller hang up first. That's good manners.

You'll enjoy the favorable results of your telephone courtesy, and you'll find that you are actually working more efficiently. Experience proves that saying the right thing at the right time saves words and time.

TELEPHONE EFFICIENCY

The most modern technical developments can't speed up telephone service if your phone is in use. To get maximum value from your phone, keep it free, so that you can accept incoming calls and make outgoing calls. This kind of telephone efficiency comes from observing the following rules:

☐ Don't tie up the line with long and frequent personal calls during business hours. None of the expensive automatic equipment previously described can complete the next call until you release the line.

☐ Keep your business calls brief. Long conversations tie up the line and delay other communications.

☐ Use letters, notes, and notations on photocopies and carbon copies for less urgent communications within the company.

☐ Inquire about company policy before placing long-distance business calls or accepting collect calls.

☐ When you leave your desk, arrange for someone in your office to answer the telephone in your absence, so that communication with the person calling is assured.

☐ Tell people where you are going when you leave your desk. Keep track of where your boss is at all times, so that calls can be transferred without delay. Repeated and returned calls are a waste of time and money.

☐ If you are involved in a complicated assignment, arrange for someone to answer your telephone and take messages for you until you are free. If no one is available to answer the telephone for you, answer it yourself but ask the caller if you may return the call later when you have finished the urgent work at hand.

☐ If you telephone someone and he is not at his desk, find out *when* and *where* you can return the call, so that you don't have to call repeatedly.

☐ Keep a writing pad and pencil handy to make notes about your telephone conversations. On a busy day you may have dozens of calls and will find it hard to remember all the facts of the conversations.

☐ When you have a poor connection or reach a wrong number for no apparent reason or are disconnected, ask the telephone company operator for help. It will save time and expense.

☐ If it is your job to intercept calls on your boss's line, remember to announce the caller to your boss when you put the call through. If the caller does not give you his name, ask for it by saying, "May I say who is calling, please?" or "May I tell her who is calling?" Knowing the caller's name and business helps your boss to respond more intelligently.

☐ Keep emergency numbers handy. You never know when you will need them in a hurry.

☐ Delay and consolidate into one call low-priority messages and reports to the same person. This procedure means fewer calls, less dialing, and most important of all, fewer interruptions for both parties.

☐ If you are expecting a call, be at your desk to receive it. If you cannot be at your desk all the time and cannot have someone take the call for you, tell the caller *when* to call.

☐ If you are alone in the office, you may have the problem of handling two calls at once. Suppose you are talking on the telephone to one customer and a second telephone rings. Without being rude, interrupt the conversation at the first opportunity and say: "Will you please excuse me for a moment? I'm alone in the office, and another telephone is ringing. I'll not be a minute." If the first caller agrees, answer the second call as quickly as you can. Find out who is calling and say: "May I call you back in a couple of minutes, please? I'm here alone and have another call." When the second caller agrees, ask for his number, thank him, hang up, and return to the first caller. Renew the conversation with a considerate "Thank you for waiting."

REVIEWING YOUR READING

1 Demonstrate or discuss the use of the telephone directory for finding the number of the person or firm that you are trying to reach.
2 Demonstrate or explain how to place an outgoing local call **(a)** without direct dial extension service and **(b)** with direct dial extension service.
3 Demonstrate or explain how to place a long-distance call using direct-distance dialing for **(a)** station-to-station and **(b)** person-to-person service.
4 Demonstrate or discuss how to receive an incoming call that **(a)** travels through the company switchboard to your extension or **(b)** goes directly to your extension on direct inward dialing equipment.
5 Demonstrate or explain the special techniques for answering another person's telephone.
6 Prepare a script for a two-part skit to demonstrate as many of the telephone courtesy pointers mentioned in the text as possible.

OFFICE ASSIGNMENTS

1 Using the Yellow Pages section of the local telephone directory, see how quickly you can locate and list a telephone number for as many of the following types of businesses as possible:

a	A florist	**i**	A jeweler
b	An architect	**j**	An optician
c	A real estate firm	**k**	A driveway contractor
d	A shoe repair shop	**l**	A barber
e	A bookstore	**m**	A certified public accountant
f	A business school	**n**	A taxi company
g	A hospital	**o**	A stockbroker
h	A fire insurance agency	**p**	A statistical service

2 Refer to your local telephone directory, and make a list of emergency telephone numbers that you would use for ready reference at work, at school, or at home.
3 Some concerns observe periodically the handling of incoming calls in order to render better service to their customers. Copy and complete the rating sheet on page 93, or use the form in your workbook. For a rating of "good" in each of the grading factors, quote what you would say or explain what you would do in the How to Handle column.

Example: Answering Time: Respond within ten seconds of the first ring.

```
┌──────────────────────────────────────────────────┐
│      TELEPHONE TRAINING OBSERVATION RECORD         │
│ Extension _555-4125_ Employee's Name _H. Davies_   │
│ Customer's Name and Address _Precision Tool Company_│
│ _60 Brent Avenue, Flint, Michigan 48506_           │
│ Date __5/10/-__      Time __11:30 a.m.__            │
└──────────────────────────────────────────────────┘
```

Grading Factors	Good	Fair	How to Handle
Answering time	✓		
Proper identification (firm, name)	✓		
Handling waiting intervals	✓		
Handling transfers	✓		
Courtesy	✓		
Service	✓		
Speech—good grammar	✓		
Choice of words	✓		
Voice	✓		
Knowledge of job	✓		

Number of times customer's name was used: _3_

Manner and attitude (alert, efficient, <u>courteous</u>, friendly, <u>cooperative</u>, mechanical, indifferent).

Essential information obtained (<u>name</u>, <u>address</u>, <u>telephone number</u>).

RATED BY: _J. L. Russo_

4 Complete a telephone message memorandum based on the following conversation, which took place at 10:35 a.m. Use the form in your workbook, or copy the form shown on page 89.

You: Mr. Rowe's office, Miss Ames speaking.
Outside Caller: This is the First National Bank. May I speak to Mr. Rowe, please?
You: Mr. Rowe is not in his office right now. May I help you?
Outside Caller: Thank you just the same. Please have him call me.
You: Yes, I'll do that.

a What blank spaces were you unable to fill out?
b What additional questions should you have asked to make a follow-up call easier?

5 Organizing your thoughts in advance will help you to keep your call brief. Suppose you were about to call the local stationery store to find out when they were going to ship an order that you placed a couple of weeks ago. What data would you need to assemble in advance to make an intelligent inquiry?

6 Suppose you answer telephone inquiries for a travel agency. A Mr. Jones inquires about schedules, fares, and hotel accommodations. You find the required information in various timetables and directories while the caller waits on the line. Mr. Jones then says that he'll call back and hangs up. The next day his wife calls to say, "Go ahead with the arrangements." Since you responded to many inquiries yesterday, all you can say is, "What arrangements?" How could notes and efficient questioning have saved time and prevented this embarrassing situation?

8 Telephone Equipment and Special Services

In order to handle the increasing volume of calls that are made every day, the makers of telephone equipment have developed a great deal of new and improved apparatus. They have also devised new services, so that their customers can make greater use of the equipment available. You will find it useful and interesting to become familiar with the most common telephone equipment and services.

SWITCHBOARD EQUIPMENT

A skilled switchboard attendant can be an important asset to the company, because she contributes greatly to the efficiency of office operations and to good customer relations. Telephone companies provide educational materials and on-the-job training for new switchboard attendants, so that they can develop their skills. If you are assigned to switchboard work and if there is no one available in the office to teach you how to operate the equipment, get your boss's permission to call the local telephone company business office. An instructor will work side by side with you at the switchboard until you learn the operating procedures. There is no charge to you or to your employer for the instruction, because the telephone company is glad to help you become an efficient switchboard attendant.

Cord PBX Switchboard

Large firms with heavy telephone activity normally use the cord PBX (private branch exchange) switchboard because it can service many outside trunk lines and inside extension telephones.

The board of a cord switchboard looks like a table with an upright backboard. This backboard has circuit holes, called *jacks*, which are connected to inside extension lines and outside trunk lines, and lamp signals for each extension telephone and for each trunk line to the outside. The table section has a series of coordinated groups of controls. Each control group, from the rear to the front, consists of two connecting cords, two cord lamps, two ringing keys, and a lever, or talking key. The operator is also equipped with a plug-in headset, consisting of a mouthpiece and an earphone. This device frees both her hands so that she can operate the controls while she talks and listens.

Dial PBX Switchboard

In an office requiring fewer than 50 telephones, the work of the switchboard attendant is greatly reduced by the dial PBX switchboard. Incoming calls are completed by the touch of a button. Executives make outside calls by dialing directly from their own desk telephones.

Both photos courtesy American Telephone & Telegraph Company

The cord PBX meets the needs of companies that have a large volume of telephone activity.

Push buttons make this dial PBX switchboard easy for the attendant to operate.

Key PBX Switchboard

The key PBX switchboard, a cordless unit designed for use when telephone traffic is light, is a small cabinet that can be placed on a desk or table top. It is found in many professional offices, schools, and small businesses. The unit contains several rows of keys and lamp signals. To operate it, the PBX attendant presses keys instead of moving cords to establish a connecting line or call circuit. Only a limited number of calls can be handled at one time.

BUTTON TELEPHONE SERVICE

Packaging of products is commonplace today, but the handsome packaging of telephones is a new and exciting development. Button telephones are not only efficient but also excellent examples of good industrial design.

Courtesy American Telephone & Telegraph Company

Multi-Button Telephone

The typical telephone desk set, with which you are familiar, is used only for answering or for making one call at a time. The multi-button unit shown here has six buttons below the dial and can originate and receive calls on four inside or outside lines. Note the HOLD and INT (intercom) buttons. Here is how you operate it:

1   When an incoming call rings on a line, the button connected to that line flashes.

2　To answer the call, depress the flashing line button and lift the handset.

3　To make a call, depress the unlighted button of a line which is not in use, lift the handset, wait for the dial tone, and then dial the desired number.

4　To hold a call on one line and return a call on another line, depress the HOLD button. To terminate the second call and return to the first call, depress the button of the line which you have been holding.

5　Although it is not shown here, some phones have a SIG button which sounds a bell or buzzer on another telephone. Your supervisor might use it to signal you to come into his office.

6　The INT button provides a direct line to one or more telephones in the office. If your supervisor wants to talk to you, he presses the SIG button to signal you to answer the phone and then depresses the INT button to make the connection to talk to you.

Call Director

The Call Director is a further development of the button telephone. The compact desk-top unit can be used to a greater capacity and is more flexible than the regular desk telephone but is not as cumbersome as switchboard equipment. These units are available in 18-button or 30-button models. The lines are arranged to fit the particular needs of a business. For example, an 18-button system might consist of 1 to 6 outside line buttons but not more than 17 inside lines or extensions, plus 1 hold button. Here is how you work it.

Answering an incoming call　When a flashing line button and a coordinated ring indicate an incoming call:

1　Depress the flashing line button.
2　Pick up the handset.
3　Answer with a greeting, your company's name, and your name.

Courtesy American Telephone & Telegraph Company

This 30-button Call Director, like the 18-button one, fills a gap between a regular desk telephone and a large switchboard.

If you answer the call in the capacity of secretary or receptionist and the caller wishes to speak to your supervisor:

1 Depress the HOLD button.
2 Depress the intercom button.
3 Signal your supervisor to pick up the phone by pressing the signal buzzer.
4 When he answers, tell him who is calling.
5 If he wishes to take the call, he presses the button of the line on which his incoming call is being held.

Making an outside call   When you are making the call and make your own connection:

1 Push an unlighted button connected with an outside line.
2 Use the line when the button light goes on and when you hear a dial tone.

Making an interoffice call   When you want to make the connection yourself:

1 Depress the DL INT (Dial Intercom) button and dial the extension number or
2 Depress the DL INT button and then depress the extension button.

Special features   There are optional features that give added versatility to the Call Director:

1 An Add-On Button permits another person associated with the DL INT system to participate in an outside call on your boss's line.
2 Groups of up to six specially wired extension telephones can be summoned simultaneously by an intercom conference dial code or an intercom conference button. This device permits the persons on these extensions to conduct a telephone conference.
3 When the extension that you call is busy, all you need do is hold the line, and a Camp-On feature monitors your call until the extension is available and then puts your call through.

SPECIAL TELEPHONE EQUIPMENT

It is more than likely that your experience with telephones has, up to now, been limited to the conventional equipment found in homes, public centers, and small offices. But there are many ingeniously designed units, such as those described here, that greatly extend the usefulness of the phone.

Automatic Call Distributor

When the volume of telephone traffic swamps several switchboards, as in airline ticket offices, brokerage houses, and telephone-order selling operations, the switchboard can be cleverly relieved of the overwhelming burden of calls through the use of an automatic call distributor. With this device the calls do not go through the switchboard at all. Instead, customers call a nonswitchboard number, and the automatic call distributor feeds the calls to attendants in the order in which the calls are received. When all the attendants are busy, the waiting calls are stored and released as an attendant becomes available.

Answering Service

Keeping a telephone covered during office hours is a relatively simple matter of scheduling personnel. However, professional men, service companies, and others may need telephone coverage 24 hours of every day. The Bell 100-A Automatic Answering Service answers the telephone and gives the caller a recorded message. Also, other equipment answers the telephone, gives your message, records a message from the caller, and plays the caller's message back to you. Home and business telephones are also answered by live attendants employed by many private telephone answering service bureaus (TAS). This is the kind of service that your family doctor probably uses because handling his messages requires quick judgment and varied responses.

Speakerphone

This is a unit used in conjunction with a desk telephone or Call Director. It permits two-way communication without requiring the worker to hold the handset and enables him to have both hands free for writing or handling paper. The Speakerphone is also used as a conference telephone. Because its volume is adjustable, a group in an office can take part in a telephone discussion in which all members of the group can hear and be heard.

Mobile Telephone

This is a service that makes it possible to communicate with mobile units, such as ships, trucks, buses, trains, utility crews, outdoor workers, and emergency vehicles. It is used in automobiles by salesmen, doctors, and traveling executives who need to report periodically to their offices and want to be available to accept important calls wherever they may be. Calls to mobile units can be made by dialing the seven-digit number, if known, or dialing O and asking for the Mobile Service Operator.

Personal Signaler

Ordinarily communications cannot be completed if the person called is not at his telephone. Messages frequently have to wait until the absent person returns. But many busy executives are constantly on the move inspecting their plants or visiting their customers or suppliers. Messengers, also on the move from place to place, must keep in contact with their home offices. The Bellboy unit helps these persons to keep in touch. Here is how it works:

1 The executive puts a Bellboy unit in his pocket whenever he is going to be away from his regular telephone.

2 When his associates wish to contact him, they merely dial his Bellboy number, just as they would dial any telephone number.

3 This immediately sends out the executive's own Bellboy signal from radio transmitters located throughout the coverage area.

4 The signal is picked up at once by his Bellboy unit only.

5 He then calls his base of operations from any convenient telephone and receives his message.

SPECIAL SERVICES

Even though you may not be called on in your office to operate telephone equipment, it is worthwhile to know about the many special services that telephone companies make available. There may be occasions when you can save your employer time and money by calling his attention to one or more of them.

Conference Calls

With many scattered branch offices under his control, your boss may find it too time-consuming to make a separate long-distance telephone call to each branch office every time some new and urgent development arises. Furthermore, speaking with each branch manager separately on a typical two-way hookup prevents your boss from being able to combine the opinions of all his branch managers at one time. The conference call is the ideal answer to this problem because it allows several people to be connected on one line at the same time. One call conveys the information to all and makes possible the exchange of ideas among the members of the group.

When you are arranging for a conference call through the telephone company operator, be sure to allow for differences in time zones. Suppose a telephone conference asking regional managers to report to the president of the company at the home office in Topeka, Kansas, is scheduled for 10 a.m. This time will be 11 a.m. in the Newark, New Jersey, office; 10 a.m. in the New Orleans office; 9 a.m. in the Denver office; and 8 a.m. in the Seattle and San Francisco offices.

Foreign Exchange Service (FX)

A firm doing business with customers in towns some distances away can make it easy and inexpensive for these customers to order by telephone. Under the Foreign Exchange Service, the firm is assigned a local number in a distant city where its customers are located. That number is listed in the local directory of that city. For the price of a local call a customer can call the number and be connected directly with the firm's home office in another part of the country. The same procedure is followed in any city in which the firm wishes to be listed.

Tie Line Service (TL)

Firms that have many plants and offices all over the country need to make lots of telephone calls in order to keep their operations running smoothly. If each

AREA CODES AND STANDARD TIME ZONES

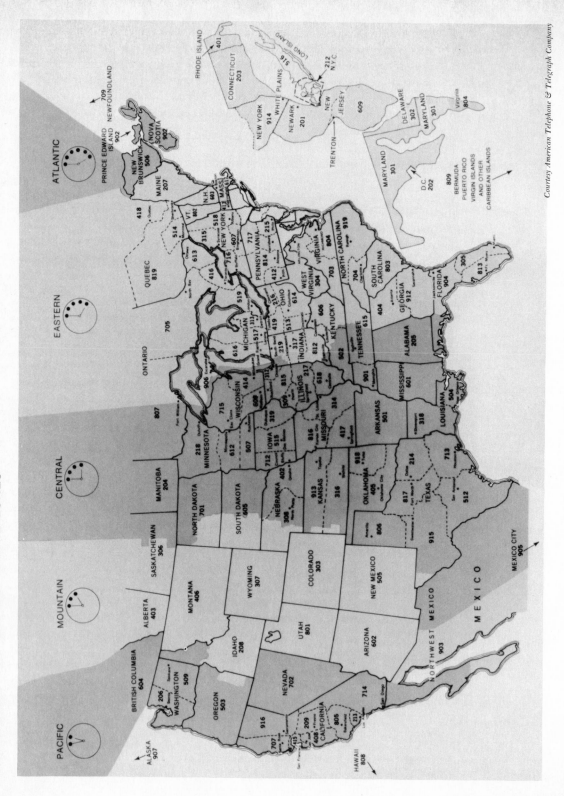

Courtesy American Telephone & Telegraph Company

of those calls were a regular long-distance toll call, the expense would be enormous. Such firms arrange for direct and private tie lines to run between the various offices. Calls are made back and forth as if they were being made between local extensions. For a flat monthly rate, an unlimited number of calls are permitted.

Wide Area Telephone Service (WATS and INWATS)

WATS is another service for customers who make many long-distance calls. INWATS is for customers who receive many long-distance calls. The customer obtains a special access line that is connected to the nationwide dialing network. Each access line is arranged at the customer's option for either incoming or outgoing calls, but not for both over the same line. Also, the customer selects those areas of the country he wishes his service to cover—WATS or INWATS service can cover the entire country except Alaska and Hawaii. For calls within a state, WATS and INWATS access lines are also available in most states. Charges are not based on individual calls. The customer may choose full-time service 24 hours a day, or for a lower monthly rate he may choose what is called measured-time service and buy ten hours of conversation a month, with additional use charged by the hour.

Collect Calls

Sometimes a salesman may have to call his home office from a public telephone or from a client's office where it may not be convenient at that time to pay for telephone service. He will dial 0 for operator and then dial the desired number, 913-555-3268. In some cities the long-distance operator intercepts the call, and he asks her to reverse the charges. In other areas the salesman will dial the long-distance operator and give her the information. When you, the switchboard attendant, receive the call at your board, you are asked if the company will accept the charges.Your employer will give you instructions about what to do in such cases. If you inform the outside operator that your company will accept the charges, the expense of the call will be added to your firm's monthly bill.

Credit Card Calls

With a telephone company credit card all you need to do is to dial the operator (0) and the number, 913-555-3268. The operator asks for your credit card number and charges the call to your account.

Night Rate Calls

Reduced rates are in effect for station-to-station, long-distance calls from 5 p.m. to 8 a.m. on weekdays and all day Saturday and Sunday. There are no reduced rates for person-to-person calls.

Overseas Telephone Calls

Telephone users in the United States can be connected with 97 percent of all the telephone users in the world. Your long-distance operator can dial connections direct to Hawaii, Alaska, and Puerto Rico. She will route your other call requests to overseas call centers. The overseas operator asks for the usual information—the person to whom you wish to speak, his address, and the time of day most convenient for the connection. Station-to-station service is available to several countries, but most overseas service is on a person-to-person basis. Charges vary according to the length of the call, the distance, the hour of the day, and the day of the week on which the call is made. Many telephone exchanges are now equipped with international direct-distance dialing (IDDD), whereby an individual can dial overseas calls directly. In order to do this, the caller dials a series of codes, which stand for IDDD and the country and city he is calling, along with the regular telephone number.

STATION-TO-STATION OVERSEAS RATES FROM PENNSYLVANIA

	Day Rates		Night Rates (After 5 p.m. Monday through Saturday and all day Sunday.)	
	Initial 3 Minutes	Additional Minutes	Initial 3 Minutes	Additional Minutes
England	$ 5.40	$1.80	$4.05	$1.35
Italy	6.75	2.25	5.10	1.70
Israel	9.00	3.00	6.75	2.25
Japan	9.00	3.00	6.75*	2.25*
Kenya	13.50	2.70	. . .	. . .

*Sundays only.

REVIEWING YOUR READING

1 Explain why switchboards are made in various sizes. How can a new clerical worker learn how to operate the type of switchboard used in his or her office?
2 Demonstrate or explain how the multi-button telephone provides more flexibility in business use than the typical no-button instrument?
3 Demonstrate or explain how the Call Director is operated for handling **(a)** incoming calls, **(b)** outside calls, and **(c)** interoffice calls.
4 Demonstrate or explain how collect and credit card calls are placed.
5 Consult your local telephone directory or your operator to find out how to place an overseas telephone call.

OFFICE ASSIGNMENTS

1   Practice saying the following sentences aloud to improve your speech habits. Pronounce every word clearly and distinctly. Then have a classmate listen to you, and ask him to make a note of the words that he feels need your special attention.

   a   For distinct enunciation, every word, every syllable, and every sound must be given its proper form and value.
   b   Think of the mouth chamber as a mold in which the correct form must be given to every sound.
   c   Move your lips noticeably.
   d   Your teeth should never be kept closed while you are talking.
   e   As your voice is the most direct expression of your innermost self, you should do full justice to yourself and use your voice to its fullest advantage.
   f   You may know what you are saying, but others won't unless you make your meaning clear to them.
   g   Through practice we can learn to speak more rapidly but still distinctly.
   h   Good speech is within the reach of everyone who practices it.
   i   The courtesy of a smile apparent in face-to-face conversation can be conveyed by telephone only through a smiling voice.

2   Get two copies of the local telephone directory, and team up with a classmate. Both of you are to make a list of ten names from the white pages of the directory. Then exchange lists, and race each other to locate the telephone number for each of the ten names. Check each other's work. A number reported incorrectly disqualifies you from winning.

3   Refer to page 86 of the text showing time periods during which various long-distance rates apply.

   a   When do you need the operator to make a station-to-station call?
   b   Why can't you make collect calls at station-to-station rates?
   c   Why do person-to-person calls fall into a separate and higher rate category?
   d   When would be the least expensive time during the regular work week for a traveling salesman to call his family long-distance about nonurgent personal matters? What would be the least expensive service?
   e   What long-distance telephone service would you use to reach your boss, an insurance agent, who will be making brief calls on a number of clients in a distant city today (Tuesday) during the afternoon and early evening?
   f   If you are delayed in traveling home and want to call your family, but not collect, when would be the least expensive time to make your long-distance call and what would be the least expensive service?

4   Persons who place long-distance calls are frequently expected to keep a record of them in order to be certain they are not overcharged on their

telephone bills. Here is a typical monthly record. Enter the following items in the special form provided in your workbook. If you are not using the workbook, copy the form below.

Date

Jan.	3	Called	K. Ryan	New York, NY	212-619-4896
	4	Called	H. Lewis	Hagerstown, MD	301-908-6921
	7	Collect call from	R. Cavalier	Washington, DC	202-812-1343
	12	Called	J. Schmidt	Blacksburg, VA	703-718-4233
	13	Collect call from	L. Barnes	Nyack, NY	914-407-2233
	17	Called	H. Gibb	Hockessin, DE	302-917-5969
	26	Called	D. Burkhart	St. Louis, MO	314-719-3447
	27	Called	T. Robinson	San Francisco, CA	415-508-5030
	28	Called	K. Oyler	El Paso, TX	915-717-4800
	29	Called	J. Carmody	Spokane, WA	509-706-6670
	30	Called	J. Singer	Philadelphia, PA	215-909-2914
	31	Called	D. Fogarty	Lincoln, NE	402-409-0922

EXTENSION 555-2879
RECORD OF LONG-DISTANCE CALLS
January, 19—

Date	Outgoing Call	Incoming Collect Call	Person	Place	Number

5   When a person-to-person, long-distance call to your boss cannot be completed because he is out of the office, the caller may request the outside operator to ask you to have your boss return the call. The operator will then say: "Please have Mr. Davis call Mr. Harry Baker when he returns. Ask for Operator 6 in Topeka, Kansas, and refer to 913-555-3200." Using the form in the workbook or a copy of the form on page 89, prepare the message you will leave on your boss's desk. Assume that this call was placed at 10:15 a.m. Use the current date. Should you ask the operator for any additional information to complete the form?

SECTION 9 Telegraph Communications

Often in business there is a need to send someone an urgent message that can be stated in very few words. The brevity of the message may not warrant the minimum person-to-person rate of a telephone call, but the importance of the message may make even the fastest mail service too slow to use. The gap can be filled by commercial telegraph service, which enables a person to transmit written communications economically and quickly.

The telegram may be used for a variety of tasks:

Expediting or tracing shipments.
Announcing price and style changes.
Issuing instructions to branch offices and field staffs.
Quoting prices or making offers.
Accepting offers.
Notifying customers about special sales.
Acknowledging orders and confirming shipping dates.
Reporting on daily operations.
Replenishing stocks that have fallen below safe levels.
Collecting delinquent accounts.

DOMESTIC SERVICES

A sender may choose any one of a variety of ways to send a message via Western Union. The class of service that he chooses plus the manner in which he elects to have his message delivered determines the price.

Telegrams

The telegram is the fastest class of service. The initial charge is based on the first 15 words. Charges for additional words are on a per word basis. Telegrams are accepted for immediate transmission and delivery, but a certain amount of time must be allowed for handling. If the company or person to whom the message is being sent has a telephone, the message will be telephoned to him shortly after it is received by the telegraph office. For a fee a copy of the message can be mailed to the addressee. If the sender has specified that he prefers the telegram to be delivered by messenger service, delivery will take a little longer. There is also a higher charge for this service. Telegrams may be telephoned in by the sender, placed in person at any Western Union office or agency of Western Union, or sent via TWX or Telex (specially installed equipment described later on in this section).

⊔⊔⊔ western union				Telegram	
NO. WDS.–CL. OF SVC.	PD. OR COLL.	CASH NO.	CHARGE TO THE ACCOUNT OF	☐ OVER NIGHT TELEGRAM	
			Sender	UNLESS BOX ABOVE IS CHECKED THIS MESSAGE WILL BE SENT AS A TELEGRAM	

Send the following message, subject to the terms on back hereof, which are hereby agreed to

May 12, ___ 19 ──

TO   Harry S. French
            Foster Cosmetics Corporation
STREET & NO. 18 Leland Avenue
CITY & STATE San Francisco, California

CARE OF OR APT. NO.
TELEPHONE 415-555-6725
ZIP CODE 94134

All proof due May 15. Return with revised price list.

Gregory Phillips
Howard Publications

SENDER'S TEL. NO. 609-555-5533   NAME & ADDRESS Howard Publications
111 Center Street
Princeton, New Jersey 08540

Courtesy Western Union Telegraph Company

Overnight Telegrams

The overnight telegram may be sent any time of the day up until 12 midnight for delivery the following day. The initial rate is based on a minimum of 100 words. Charges for additional words are at a reduced rate. You can save as much as $3 on this kind of telegram if you indicate that it can be delivered by nonmessenger means—telephone, Western Union tie line, Telex, or TWX.

Mailgrams

The Mailgram is a new service, developed jointly by Western Union and the Postal Service. It is faster than regular mail but, of course, not as fast as a telegram. Mailgram service costs less than a telegram, however, and is used primarily when a message is long or when the same message is being sent to many different people or when it is desirable to use a type of communication which will receive more attention than just a letter. Rates are based on a minimum charge for the first 100 words and half the minimum charge for each additional 100 words.

To send a Mailgram, you write your message on a Mailgram form, which you obtain from a local Western Union office or from a Western Union service representative office. You can deliver the form to them by hand or you can telephone in the message. The address and phone number are generally listed in your local telephone directory under *Western Union Telegraph Co.* (Sometimes it is followed by the phrase *to send Telegrams, Mailgrams, or International Messages.*) A Mailgram may also be sent from your office via Telex or TWX to a Western Union office, which will forward it to the post office of destination for delivery the next day.

Courtesy Western Union Telegraph Company

THE WESTERN UNION TELEGRAPH COMPANY

TABLES OF RATES, TOLLS, AND CHARGES FOR MESSAGES BETWEEN WESTERN UNION POINTS IN THE UNITED STATES

BASIC TELEGRAM RATES

For Delivery by Tieline or by Telephone	TELEGRAMS			OVERNIGHT TELEGRAMS	
	FOR 15 WORDS OR LESS	FOR EACH ADD'L WORD		FOR 100 WORDS OR LESS	FOR EACH ADD'L WORD OVER 100 WORDS
		16-50 WORDS	OVER 50 WORDS		
	$3.75*	$.12	$.08	$3.00*	$.03

TABLE OF TOLLS FOR TELEGRAMS AND OVERNIGHT TELEGRAMS

TELEGRAMS								OVERNIGHT TELEGRAMS							
NO. OF WORDS	*CHARGE	NO. OF WORDS	*CHARGE	NO. OF WORDS	*CHARGE	NO. OF WORDS	*CHARGE	NO. OF WORDS	*CHARGE	NO. OF WORDS	*CHARGE	NO. OF WORDS	*CHARGE	NO. OF WORDS	*CHARGE
1-15	$ 3.75		$		$		$	1-100	$ 3.00		$		$		$
16	3.87	46	7.47	76	10.03	106	12.43	101	3.03	131	3.93	161	4.83	191	5.73
17	3.99	47	7.59	77	10.11	107	12.51	102	3.06	132	3.96	162	4.86	192	5.76
18	4.11	48	7.71	78	10.19	108	12.59	103	3.09	133	3.99	163	4.89	193	5.79
19	4.23	49	7.83	79	10.27	109	12.67	104	3.12	134	4.02	164	4.92	194	5.82
20	4.35	50	7.95	80	10.35	110	12.75	105	3.15	135	4.05	165	4.95	195	5.85
21	4.47	51	8.03	81	10.43	111	12.83	106	3.18	136	4.08	166	4.98	196	5.88
22	4.59	52	8.11	82	10.51	112	12.91	107	3.21	137	4.11	167	5.01	197	5.91
23	4.71	53	8.19	83	10.59	113	12.99	108	3.24	138	4.14	168	5.04	198	5.94
24	4.83	54	8.27	84	10.67	114	13.07	109	3.27	139	4.17	169	5.07	199	5.97
25	4.95	55	8.35	85	10.75	115	13.15	110	3.30	140	4.20	170	5.10	200	6.00
26	5.07	56	8.43	86	10.83	116	13.23	111	3.33	141	4.23	171	5.13	201	6.03
27	5.19	57	8.51	87	10.91	117	13.31	112	3.36	142	4.26	172	5.16	202	6.06
28	5.31	58	8.59	88	10.99	118	13.39	113	3.39	143	4.29	173	5.19	203	6.09
29	5.43	59	8.67	89	11.07	119	13.47	114	3.42	144	4.32	174	5.22	204	6.12
30	5.55	60	8.75	90	11.15	120	13.55	115	3.45	145	4.35	175	5.25	205	6.15
31	5.67	61	8.83	91	11.23	121	13.63	116	3.48	146	4.38	176	5.28	206	6.18
32	5.79	62	8.91	92	11.31	122	13.71	117	3.51	147	4.41	177	5.31	207	6.21
33	5.91	63	8.99	93	11.39	123	13.79	118	3.54	148	4.44	178	5.34	208	6.24
34	6.03	64	9.07	94	11.47	124	13.87	119	3.57	149	4.47	179	5.37	209	6.27
35	6.15	65	9.15	95	11.55	125	13.95	120	3.60	150	4.50	180	5.40	210	6.30
36	6.27	66	9.23	96	11.63	126	14.03	121	3.63	151	4.53	181	5.43	211	6.33
37	6.39	67	9.31	97	11.71	127	14.11	122	3.66	152	4.56	182	5.46	212	6.36
38	6.51	68	9.39	98	11.79	128	14.19	123	3.69	153	4.59	183	5.49	213	6.39
39	6.63	69	9.47	99	11.87	129	14.27	124	3.72	154	4.62	184	5.52	214	6.42
40	6.75	70	9.55	100	11.95	130	14.35	125	3.75	155	4.65	185	5.55	215	6.45
41	6.87	71	9.63	101	12.03	Each		126	3.78	156	4.68	186	5.58	Each	
42	6.99	72	9.71	102	12.11	Word		127	3.81	157	4.71	187	5.61	Word	
43	7.11	73	9.79	103	12.19	Over	8¢	128	3.84	158	4.74	188	5.64	Over	3¢
44	7.23	74	9.87	104	12.27	130		129	3.87	159	4.77	189	5.67	215	
45	7.35	75	9.95	105	12.35	Words		130	3.90	160	4.80	190	5.70		

* For messenger delivery within established delivery limits of telegraph offices, add $3.00 per message.

```
MGMNYAC NYK
1-029073A094 04/06/--
ICS IPMTBZU MTWN
20202995 MGM TDMT UPPER SADDLE RIVER NJER 100 04-06 0220P EST
ZIP 10022
```

WU Mailgram

```
JOSEPH M. ARNARY
CENTURY HOME PRODUCTS COMPANY
499 MADISON AVENUE
NEW YORK, N.Y. 10022
```

```
WATCH FOR OUR NEW BOOKLET, "HOW TO MAKE FRIENDS, MONEY (OR BOTH)
WITH MAILGRAMS," WHICH WE ARE SENDING YOU TODAY.  IT WILL GIVE YOU
VALUABLE INFORMATION ON HOW TO BUILD GOODWILL AND INCREASE
PROFITS BY USING MAILGRAMS WHICH COMBINE THE SPEED AND ATTENTION-
GETTING FEATURES OF TELEGRAMS WITH THE ECONOMY OF MAIL.

    WESTERN UNION TELEGRAPH CO
    ONE LAKE STREET
    UPPER SADDLE RIVER NJER 07458


1431 EST

MGMNYAC NYK
```

Courtesy Western Union Telegraph Company

Once you place your Mailgram message, it is relayed electronically by computer to a post office serving the destination area, where it is put into a distinctive blue and white envelope and delivered with the regular mail. There is no separate charge for delivery.

Money by Telegram

Money can be transmitted by telegraph to many points in the United States. There is an additional charge for any message accompanying it. You, the sender, purchase and pay for (or by prearrangement, charge) a money order at a Western Union office or at one of their service representative offices (sometimes referred to as an accepting agency). The person to whom you are sending the money receives payment from the office in his locality. The charge made for the money order and for the telegram is based on the amount of money being sent and the number of words in the message. For purposes of identification the receiver of the money may be asked to answer a test question supplied by the sender, such as the receiver's birth date or the names of certain members of his family.

MONEY ORDER CHARGES
(Not Including Tolls for Supplementary Messages)

AMOUNT OF ORDER	MONEY ORDER CHARGE+		AMOUNT OF ORDER	MONEY ORDER CHARGE+	
	Day	Overnight		Day	Overnight
$　　50.00 or less	$ 4.70	$ 3.95	$　　　　　$	$	$
50.01 -　　100.00	5.65	4.90	2,000.01 - 2,500.00	30.05	29.30
100.01 -　　300.00	7.90	7.15	2,500.01 - 3,000.00	34.50	33.75
300.01 -　　500.00	12.25	11.50	3,000.01 - 3,500.00	38.95	38.20
500.01 - 1,000.00	16.70	15.95	3,500.01 - 4,000.00	43.40	42.65
1,000.01 - 1,500.00	21.15	20.40	4,000.01 - 4,500.00	47.85	47.10
1,500.01 - 2,000.00	25.60	24.85	4,500.01 - 5,000.00	52.30	51.55

FOR EACH ADDITIONAL $500.00 OR FRACTION THEREOF OVER $5,000.00, ADD $4.45 TO THE APPLICABLE CHARGE SHOWN FOR A $5,000.00 DAY OR OVERNIGHT MONEY ORDER.

+ Rates quoted are for service requiring payee to call at telegraph office to receive payment. For messenger delivery of money order draft, add $3.00 per money order.

Courtesy Western Union Telegraph Company

PRESS FIRMLY—WRITE CLEARLY

western union　**Telegraphic Money Order**

Send the following Money Order subject to conditions below and on back hereof, which are hereby agreed to

SENDING DATA	CHECK	OFFICE	DATE AND FILING TIME	CLERKS INIT. AND ACCTG. INFORMATION	$ AMT.
					FEE
					TOLLS
	MOD └ ┴ ┘ 83 235 54=	↙DO NOT WRITE ABOVE THIS LINE↘		E TAX	
					TOTAL

PAY AMOUNT: _One hundred and -------------------00_ /100 DOLLARS　($100.00)　　=
　　　　　　　　　　　　　　　　　　　　　　　　　FIGURES　　　CAU OR VIG

TO: _Douglas Helm_　　　　　　　　　= TEST QUESTION _Birthday 6/1/45_　=

ADDRESS: _144 West King Street_　　CARE OF OR APT. NO. _____

CITY - STATE _Salisbury, Maryland 21801_　=SENDER'S NAME: _Jackson Company_　=
　　　　　　　　　　　(ZIP CODE)

DELIVER THE FOLLOWING MESSAGE WITH THE MONEY: _Advance on travel expenses for interview_

_____ _at Baltimore branch Monday, May 6._

　　　　　　　　　　　　　　　　　　　　　　　　　　　=MOD=

SENDER'S FULL NAME: _R. L. Jackson_　　_613 First Ave., Newberry, Mich. 49868　906-555-2897_
● Unless signed below the Telegraph Company is directed to　　ADDRESS　　　　　TELEPHONE NUMBER
pay this money order at my risk to such person as its paying
agent believes to be the above named payee, personal identification being waived. Foreign money orders excepted.　　　‖‖08323554‖‖ 66

Courtesy Western Union Telegraph Company

Personal Opinion Messages

At a special low cost, Personal Opinion Messages permit a sender to express her views on any matter of public interest to the President of the United States, the Vice President, a United States senator, or a member of the House of Representatives. Similar messages may be sent on an intrastate basis to the state governor, the lieutenant governor, or to any member of the state legislative body. Such messages are limited to 15 text words and may be sent only to the elected officials listed above.

INTERNATIONAL SERVICES

Telegrams for overseas destinations or for ships at sea are called international telegrams. They may be transmitted through Western Union to one of the five international record carriers operating in the United States—ITT World Communications, Inc.; RCA Global Communications, Inc.; TRT Telecommunications Corporation; Western Union International, Inc. (a separate company from Western Union); and the French Cable Company. These carriers transmit messages to the overseas destination or to the telegraph office that handles communications in the country of destination. Western Union exercises no control over either the international carriers or the foreign telegraph office in the country of destination. You can, when sending a telegram overseas through Western Union, specify which carrier you want them to use, if you have a preference. Also, you can place your message with any one of the international record carriers directly by phone, by Telex or TWX, or in person. Messages are transmitted by a variety of means—by cable, by radio, or by satellite.

Full-Rate International Telegrams

The fastest international service is the full-rate telegram. It is accepted at any time of the day or night and is transmitted immediately through the international record carrier. You may write it in ordinary language or in code. Any word not in code up to 15 letters is counted as one word; in code or cipher, any group of 5 or fewer letters or 5 or fewer figures is counted as one word. When counting the number of words, you must include the addressee's name, street address, city of destination, and your name.

Letter Telegrams

A less expensive international service is the letter telegram. Code is not permitted. These telegrams are accepted by Western Union and the carrier with the understanding that they generally will be delivered on the date following the day of filing. The symbol *LT*, meaning "Letter Telegram," must appear before the addressee's name and is charged as one word. The rate per word for a letter telegram is one-half that charged for the full-rate service. The minimum charge is for 22 words, including the LT symbol.

RCA
Global Telegram

Full Rate ☐ Letter Telegram ☐ Press ☐ (Full Rate unless otherwise marked). This telegram will be transmitted electronically by cable, radio, or satellite.

Sender's Name and Address___SCLBOOK_____Account Number___24Y-999___

All telegrams are accepted subject to the rates, rules, and regulations as set forth in the applicable tariff of RCA Global Communications, Inc. on file with the F.C.C.

To MCGRAWHILL   **Via**___RCA___
        LONDON (ENGLAND)   Insert "RCA"

        Large interest in new manual.   Advise shipping date.

                    SCLBOOK

(Over)

Courtesy RCA Global Communications, Inc.

RCA INTERNATIONAL CABLE RATES

In telegram rate listings, countries marked with a (■)
are reached by RCA's own telegraph circuits.
*Seven word minimum charge per message.

	*ORDINARY TELEGRAMS (FULL RATE)	LETTER TELEGRAMS			*ORDINARY TELEGRAMS (FULL RATE)	LETTER TELEGRAMS	
	Rate Per Word	22-Word Min.	Each Add'l. Word		Rate Per Word	22-Word Min.	Each Add'l. Word
Abu Dhabi	$0.34	$3.74	$0.17	■ Australia	.28	3.08	.14
Adelie Land	.34	3.74	.17	■ Austria	.265	2.92	.1325
Afghanistan	.34	3.74	.17	Azores	.265	2.92	.1325
Ajman	.34	3.74	.17	Bahama Islands	.23	2.53	.115
Albania	.265	2.92	.1325	Bahrain	.34	3.74	.17
■ Algeria	.34	3.74	.17	■ Bangladesh	.28	3.08	.14
Andorra	.265	2.92	.1325	■ Barbados	.23	2.53	.115
Angola	.34	3.74	.17	■ Belgium	.265	2.92	.1325
Antigua	.23	2.53	.115	Bermuda	.23	2.53	.115
■ Argentina	.31	3.41	.155	■ Bolivia	.31	3.41	.155
Aruba (Neth. Antilles)	.23	2.53	.115	Botswana	.28	3.08	.14
Ascension Island	.28	3.08	.14	■ Brazil	.31	3.41	.155

Note that while Central and South America and Hawaii fall within the category of international service, Mexico, Canada, and Alaska do not and generally are governed by the same rules and regulations that apply to the continental United States.

Registered Cable Code Address

To save on the cost of including the sender's name and address on an international telegram, an abbreviated or coded form for the name and address may be used. This is called a *registered cable code*. You can readily see how this works by examining the address of the McGraw-Hill Book Company, 1221 Avenue of the Americas, New York, NY. In counting, *McGraw-Hill* is one word, *Book* is one word, *Company* is one word, *1221* is one word; *Avenue, of, the, Americas, New, York,* and *NY* are each one word. The total address, therefore, adds up to eleven words. But with a registered cable code the address becomes *MCGRAWHILL NEWYORK*—two words. The result is a saving of nine words. A cable code address must be registered with the telegraph company at the point of destination. The arrangements are made through Western Union or one of the carriers.

International Money Orders

The rates for sending money orders vary, and you should ask the particular company you plan to use about these rates at the time of filing. Money orders can be sent to almost every country in the world.

ADDITIONAL WESTERN UNION SERVICES

An alert employee can save her boss much time, effort, and even concern by making use of the supplementary services offered by Western Union.

Confirmation Copy

A confirmation copy of a message you sent is supplied upon request at a small additional charge and is mailed to you within three to ten days. It is a computer printout of the message exactly as it was recorded and transmitted by the recording operator at a Western Union centralized telephone bureau at the time you phoned in your message.

Report of Delivery

Let the recording operator at Western Union know that you want a report of the delivery of the message by saying, "report delivery," right after you give the name of the addressee. The report comes back to you in the form of a collect message for which you pay.

Dealer Inquiry Service

If you want to locate a dealer in your community who carries a specific product or a product with a brand name, you can call Western Union's Operator 25 by dialing 800-851-3360, and she will give you that information. There is no charge to you for the call. The listed dealer or distributor pays for it.

Market and Opinion Survey Service

Western Union will conduct local, regional, and nationwide surveys covering any part of the country.

Telex-TWX

You may find that your office has arranged to buy or lease a Telex machine from Western Union to provide direct customer-to-customer communication. The sender simply dials the receiver's number and within a few seconds gets a connection so that two-way messages can be exchanged with other Telex subscribers anywhere in the United States, Canada, Mexico, and some eighty overseas countries. With the same Telex equipment, messages to nonsubscribers can be transmitted to a local telegraph office and then delivered as specified.

TWX equipment enables subscribers in Canada and the continental United States to communicate with each other. Like Telex, TWX can be used to transmit messages to nonsubscribers in Canada and the United States via a local telegraph office near the point of destination.

Both Telex and TWX provide communication 24 hours a day at special time-distance rates based on metered usage, which is measured in fractions of a minute called *pulses*.

Courtesy Western Union Telegraph Company

A Telex machine provides direct customer-to-customer communication service in seconds.

Tie Lines

Companies that have a large volume of incoming and outgoing telegrams make use of a tie-line arrangement which hooks up a transmitting machine in their offices to a Western Union office. Tie lines do not provide for subscriber-to-subscriber communication.

Custom Designed Systems

Western Union will also custom design a system to meet the particular needs of a business. A custom-designed system would involve combining various types of communication devices.

PREPARING TELEGRAPH MESSAGES

With an annual volume of more than 6 billion words to transmit speedily, Western Union has developed simple and efficient procedures for the preparation and dispatch of messages. If you are the sender of a written message, you must use the standard telegram form shown on page 106.

In an office it is usual to type an original and two carbons, which are distributed in this way:

Original to the telegraph office.
First carbon to the sender's files.
Second carbon to the addressee (by mail) to confirm the wire.

A message that is phoned in is typed by an operator and simultaneously recorded. To send it on its way, the operator presses a button which activates a transmitting device connected to a switching computer. You can speed the transmission of your message by having on hand the information she will ask you in this order:

1   From what number are you calling?
2   In what city are you located? What state?
3   What is the name of the person to whom your message is being sent? (You may be also asked whether the addressee has a phone number, whether your message is going to a company or organization, whether their office is equipped with a Telex or TWX machine or tie line equipment. By making use of such information, Western Union can save you as much as $3 per telegram.)
4   The street address, please?
5   The city? State? ZIP Code?
6   The message, please?
7   How do you want this signed?
8   May we bill this to your Western Union account? To your telephone? Do you have a Master Charge (or any other charge)?
9   In whose name is the charge issued?
10 The street address, please? City? State? ZIP Code?

COUNTING THE WORDS

To determine the cost of a telegram at the domestic rate, which applies to the continental United States, Alaska, Canada, and Mexico, follow the rules below for counting chargeable words:

☐ The name and address of the addressee and one signature are transmitted free. A business signature may include the sender's title, the name of the department, or the name of the company. There is a charge if the sender's address is included.

☐ Within the message any word found in the dictionary is counted as one word regardless of its length.

☐ Proper names are counted as chargeable words, according to the number of words and initials they contain. *Van der Gross* would be counted as three words, but *Vanderwater* would be counted as one.

☐ Two or more initials may be placed together and counted at the rate of one word for each five letters. *A. B. C. Manufacturing Company* would be counted as five words, but *A.B.C. Manufacturing Company* would be counted as three.

☐ Punctuation marks are not counted. Words such as *stop, comma, period,* and *quote* are counted as one word each and should not be used in place of punctuation marks.

☐ Abbreviations of single words count as full words.

☐ A common abbreviation without spaces between the letters, such as *OK, FOB,* or *COD,* is counted as one word if it does not exceed five characters.

☐ The symbols $, /, &, plus # (for either pounds or number), ' (indicating feet or minutes), and " (indicating inches or seconds) are considered chargeable characters. The symbols @, %, ¢, *, and ° cannot be transmitted in telegrams. The word for each of these symbols must be used instead. In messages going to Canada, the dollar sign ($), the ampersand (&), and the sign used for pounds or number (#) cannot be used.

In messages to places in the continental United States, Alaska, and Mexico, numbers and the symbols listed in the preceding paragraph are counted at the rate of one chargeable word for every five characters or less. In messages to Canada, numbers and the symbols listed previously (the ones that can be used) are counted as separate, chargeable words.

The following combinations of numbers, characters, and letters are examples of groups which are counted at the rate of one chargeable word for every five characters or less in the continental United States, Alaska, and Mexico.

	Characters	*Chargeable Words*
#7654	5	1
$100.00	6	2
10/23/73	8	2
AWB98765432	11	3
24'10"	6	2
245.67	5	1
432ABC	6	2

WRITING A TELEGRAM

When words cost money, it pays to be brief in expressing your thought. But be sure your message is clear.

☐ Avoid contractions and abbreviations.
☐ Spell out directions such as *east, west, southwest,* and so on.
☐ Never divide a word by a hyphen at the end of a line.
☐ Avoid ambiguous phrases such as: "Arriving on 2 p.m. train. Please meet me." Instead say: "Arriving 2pm Saturday, Union Station. Please meet Burlington train #16."
☐ Do not use salutations or complimentary closes.

PAYING FOR A TELEGRAM

Telegrams, Mailgrams, international messages, and most other services may be paid for in a number of ways:

1   In cash at the time the message is sent. Infrequent users generally pay this way.
2   Through a Western Union charge account. Payment is made on a monthly basis.
3   With credit cards. Western Union will bill the charges to selected credit card companies.
4   Through your telephone bill. Charges will be included in your phone bill.
5   By the addressee when you send a telegram "collect."

TIME DIFFERENCES TO CONSIDER

Because American business and government operations today are so worldwide, you will find it quite useful to learn about international as well as domestic time differences. You are probably reasonably familiar with time zones in the

TIME IN DIFFERENT CITIES WHEN IT IS 12 NOON, EASTERN STANDARD TIME, IN NEW YORK CITY

Same Day — Monday						
				Dublin	5 p.m.	Bombay	10:30 p.m.
Honolulu	7 a.m.	Berlin	6 p.m.	London	6 p.m.	Bangkok	12 midnight
Managua	11 a.m.	Paris	6 p.m.			
Caracas	12:30 p.m.	Rome	6 p.m.			
San Juan	1 p.m.	Cairo	7 p.m.	*Next Day — Tuesday*		
Buenos Aires	2 p.m.	Helsinki	7 p.m.	Manila	1 a.m.	Tokyo	2 a.m.
Rio de Janeiro	2 p.m.	Baghdad	8 p.m.	Saigon	1 a.m.	Brisbane	2 a.m.
Dakar	5 p.m.	Moscow	8 p.m.	Shanghai	1 a.m.	Sydney	3 a.m.

continental United States, but do you know that global time differences between some places amount to almost a day? Be sure to keep these time differences in mind when you send your message. Note in the table on page 116 what time it is in principal cities around the world when it is 12 noon, eastern standard time, in New York City.

This Telex terminal provides a link to Telex and TWX subscribers all over the world.

Courtesy Western Union International, Inc.

REVIEWING YOUR READING

1   Explain why the telegram may be a good form of communication to use in accepting offers, announcing price changes, tracing shipments, and replenishing depleted stocks.

2   Refer to the telegram illustrated on page 106. Demonstrate or explain how the word-count system is applied.

3   Explain why you might request a written confirmation of some telegrams that you receive by telephone.

4   Explain when you would use a Mailgram to send a message instead of a telegram.

5   Both domestic and international telegrams must include the addressee's name and address. Which telegram includes them without charge?

OFFICE ASSIGNMENTS

1 Here is a rough draft of a message which is to be sent as a regular telegram: "Expect to arrive at your office Wednesday morning at 9 o'clock. Prepared to close deal for 120 rolls of your Regal Pattern fabric at $90.79 a roll, FOB your plant or $101.80 delivered here."

    a Using the telegraph company rules on page 115, how many words do you count in the message?

    b How could you cut the length of the message without altering its meaning?

    c Type the telegram in its final form, and address it to Richard Hale & Company, 12 Althea Avenue, Charleston, South Carolina 29405, telephone 803-818-5296. Use the blank provided in your workbook, or copy the one shown on page 106. Assume that you are sending the wire from Joseph Allen, Stein Associates, 169 Banington Avenue, Decatur, Illinois 62526, telephone 217-555-2323, and that the message will be delivered by telephone. Use today's date.

2 Refer to the telegraph-rate data and tables on page 107.

    a How much will it cost to send a 23-word messenger-delivered telegram from Chicago, Illinois, to Fort Smith, Arkansas?

    b How much will it cost to send a 64-word telegram from Chicago, Illinois, to Tucson, Arizona? How much would you save by sending this message by overnight telegram instead?

3 **a** You have been asked to wire $100 by the fastest service to the boss's son who is at college. The following message should accompany the funds:

To: Mr. Joseph Marx
     University of Minnesota
     Minneapolis, Minnesota 55455

Nancy and Bill coming. Buy two more midfield seats for game. Forward registered mail.

Sender: Mr. V. Marx
         1414 Prairie Avenue
         Emporia, Kansas 66801   (Tel: 316-555-4128)

You, the sender, are to supply the son's birth date (12/12/53) to the telegraph company for purposes of positive identification. Use the blank supplied in the workbook, or prepare a blank like the one on page 109.

    b Refer to the table of message rates on page 107 and the table of money order rates on page 109 to answer the following questions about the money order sent by telegraph to Joseph Marx. How much will it cost to send the money and the accompanying message by delivery other than messenger? Will any money be saved if overnight service is used to send the money and message? If so, how much?

4 Assume that you are sending the following as a full-rate message from World Sales Corporation, located at 10 Tremont Street, Boston, Massachusetts 02108, to a supplier in Austria whose cable address is AMMOL.

a Using the blank in the workbook or copying the form on page 111, prepare an international cablegram with this message:

Ship Order 769 tonight Lufthansa Dulles marked Worthington 648,912. (signed) World

b Count the number of chargeable words in the message according to the special rules that apply to international telegraph service.

c Compute the cost of the message. Refer to the RCA international cable rates on page 111.

BUSINESS CASES AND PROBLEMS

In the Boss's Shoes   1   Your boss expects you to intercept or screen the incoming calls on his line. On busy days the telephone rings so often that you fall behind in your other work. You have politely hinted to the boss that he should answer his own calls, but he doesn't seem to get the point. What should you do?

2   A visitor with a long-standing, half-hour appointment is forced to wait while the boss receives a prolonged and unexpected long-distance telephone call. Should incoming long-distance calls always receive priority? Without endangering the firm's best interests, can a procedure be devised to handle these calls so that they do not frequently interrupt conferences and interviews?

3   Your boss has dictated an important message to be sent as a regular telegram. After completing the telegram blank, you realize that the message consists of 18 words rather than 15. Should you delay the message until your boss returns from lunch to discuss the deletion of three words? You know that your boss is ordinarily very economy-minded.

Your Human Relations   1   You are expecting to receive a call at 3 p.m. However, at 2:55 p.m. the boss summons you to his office to help him check some computations. The work may take at least an hour of your time. What should you do about your expected caller?

2 Your company has prohibited its office workers from making personal telephone calls. Late one afternoon a visitor, who has just left your supervisor's office, stops at your desk and says: "May I please use your telephone? I must call my wife before she leaves the house to meet me at the station and tell her I'll be late." Should you deny the man's request, explaining the company rule? Should you ask him to obtain your supervisor's permission? Or what?

3 You are the person to whom incoming telegrams are first delivered. On several occasions you have relayed urgent telegrams by telephone to the secretaries of company officials only to discover that they either have failed to deliver the messages to their bosses or have delivered them too late for the information to be used effectively. In each instance you feel that your own efficiency and veracity have been questioned. How can you protect yourself in the future without hurting other people's feelings?

What Would You Do If . . . ?   **1** You were working as a switchboard attendant and received a call from someone who didn't know to whom he should speak.

2 As a receptionist for Mr. Gardner, you receive a collect call from a Mr. Sweeney who wishes to talk to Mr. Gardner. You do not know anyone named Sweeney, and the operator is waiting for you to accept or refuse the charges.

3 Your boss asked you to send a telegram from the telegraph office on your way home. However, because you were delayed in your own office by some last-minute jobs, you found the telegraph office closed for the day when you finally got there.

What Does This Mean?   **1** All the technical advancements that now speed calls from place to place can be nullified by the thoughtlessness of a single person.

2 When you arrange for a conference call, be sure to allow for time-zone differences.

3 Use no more words than are needed to convey a message by telegraph, but do not sacrifice clarity for the sake of brevity.

Business in Your Area   **1** Which companies, institutions, or agencies in your community make the greatest use of the telephone? What kinds of activities are involved? Could these businesses be operated efficiently without telephone service?

2 Visit your local telephone company employment office and inquire about job opportunities for switchboard attendants in your town. Remember to ask about full- and part-time jobs in business as well as in the telephone company.

3 From a local business establishment find out how messages are transmitted from the firm to the telegraph office. Also determine the circumstances under which the firm normally uses a telegram in preference to a long-distance telephone call.

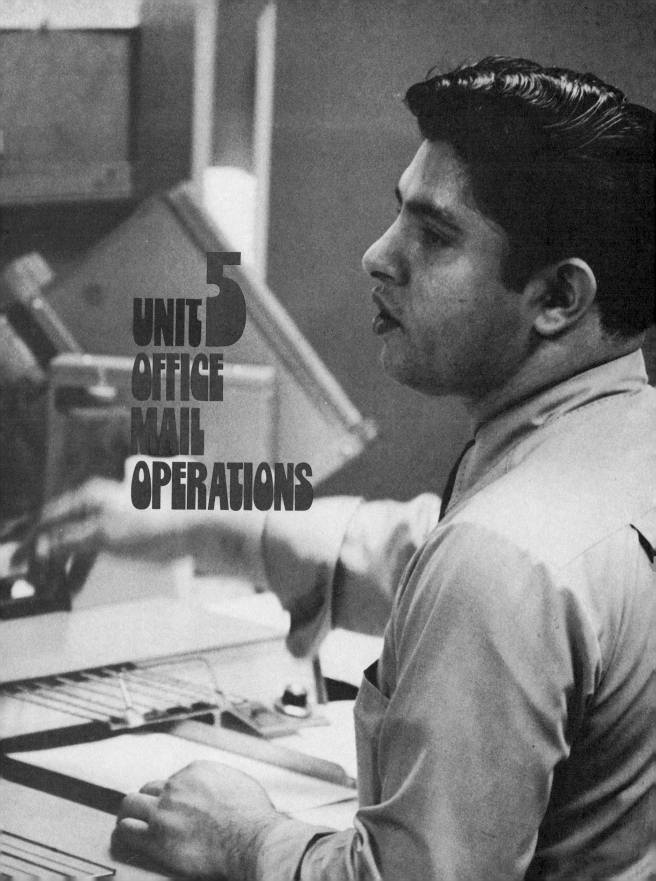

UNIT 5
OFFICE
MAIL
OPERATIONS

Incoming Mail

The day's activities in a business are often determined by the contents of the morning's mail. When you learn the procedures that your company follows in handling incoming mail, you will at the same time learn a great many things about its business.

Incoming mail contains new orders, instructions, inquiries, complaints, checks, estimates, reports, and many other types of messages that concern many departments. It also includes packages containing samples, supplies, catalogs, merchandise, repair parts, data cards, magnetic tapes, and countless other items. The sooner this mail is processed, the quicker it can be attended to by the appropriate person. Beginning office workers are frequently assigned jobs as clerks to help in the mail room during rush periods.

PROCESSING INCOMING MAIL

In many localities business concerns, stores, and professional offices receive at least two deliveries of mail a day from the post office. In addition to receiving regular postal service, some concerns pick up their mail by truck at frequent intervals throughout the day so that the work load resulting from the quantity of incoming mail will be distributed more evenly among office personnel. Some of the regular personnel assigned to incoming mail operations may be scheduled to start work before the rest of the staff so that the first load of mail can be fully processed and distributed to the different departments by the time the normal workday begins.

Opening Letter Mail

In a small business or professional office or store, you might open incoming mail with an ordinary letter opener. But opening letters by hand isn't practical in a large company where thousands of pieces of mail arrive in a single delivery. Volume mail operations call for the use of a mechanical letter opener, a device with a fine knife blade which trims off a thin strip of paper from one edge of the envelope. Since the strip trimmed off the envelope is so narrow, there's no danger of damaging the envelope's contents. All you do is place a handful of envelopes in a stack on the feed table so that one edge of each envelope is drawn by a belt or other feeding device against the cutting edge of the blade. The envelope is inserted against a stop, and the knife slices off the end of the envelope to make an opening.

Sorting Into Categories

Before the mail is opened, it is first sorted by clerks into two general categories: personal mail and nonpersonal mail.

Personal mail   This includes any communication addressed to a specific name or to a specific title. For example, a letter addressed to Mr. John Smith would be considered personal, as would a letter addressed to the advertising manager. Mail in this category is left unopened; it is transferred to the distribution end of the mail room and then delivered to the person to whom it is addressed.

Nonpersonal mail   This includes letters which are addressed to the company but not addressed to any specific individual or title. Such letters are opened by the mechanical letter opener. A mail clerk then unfolds the contents of the envelope and stamps them to show the time and date of arrival. Some companies discard the envelope if the address of the sender is clearly marked on the correspondence. Other companies, as a matter of routine, have all letters stapled to the envelopes in which they arrive. Once unfolded, stamped, and stapled to their accompanying envelopes, the opened letters are transferred to another mail clerk who reads each letter and determines to whom in the company the correspondence is to be delivered. To do this, the clerk often uses a sorting machine, which is really a sturdy file with separate compartments tabbed for company divisions or floors or any other breakdown the system calls for. In her sorting operation, the mail clerk routes letters to any one of the company's many departments, such as the sales department, the credit department, or the personnel department. When she has finished sorting a batch of mail, she transfers it to the distribution end of the mail room for delivery at the earliest possible time.

Handling Enclosures

If you are the mail clerk who first opens the mail, you generally follow a special procedure when handling nonpersonal letters containing enclosures such as money or any other item of value. The most common enclosures are checks, coins, bills, reports, certificates, forms, circulars, price lists, and diagrams. To avoid loss or separation of these items from their covering letter, follow these suggestions:

1   Inspect each envelope by passing it in front of an illuminated glass panel. By doing this, you can make sure that an enclosure is not overlooked.
2   Use staples, paper clips, or tape to secure enclosures to their accompanying letters. Put loose coins or small items in transparent envelopes so that they can be easily identified.
3   If you notice that an enclosure referred to in the correspondence is missing, recheck the envelope. If you can't find the enclosure, note on the correspondence the fact that it is missing.

Sorting Nonpersonal Mail

Clerks scan the text or the subject heading of each piece of mail in order to decide to whom it will be delivered. Next the mail is sorted according to the department, unit, or office to which it must be delivered.

Preliminary sorting   Routine preliminary sorting instructions might include any or all of the following steps:

1   Send cash or check remittances to the cashier. (The cashier takes the check or money and attaches a receipt to the customer's bill enclosure, showing the amount of payment received.)
2   Route orders to the sales department.
3   Send branch office payroll summaries to the payroll department.
4   Send letters of application to the personnel department.
5   Refer quotations and estimates to the purchasing department.

Sometimes an incoming letter covers more than one subject. For example, a letter might contain an order for merchandise and also request an explanation of an unidentified charge on a recent statement of account. If you have no photocopying device in the office, give the new business priority (the order for merchandise) and route the letter first to the sales department and then to the accounting department.

If you can photocopy the letter easily, send the original to the sales department and the copy to the accounting department. In this way the letter can be handled by the two different departments at the same time. Some concerns actually make photocopies of all documents received in the mail to avoid defacing the originals in subsequent processing or to guard against their possible loss.

Secondary sorting   In departments where correspondence is heavy, as it can be in the sales department, the mail placed in the general department slot

Courtesy Babcock & Wilcox Company

From a starting position as an incoming mail clerk, an energetic employee can advance to a supervisory position in which he is responsible for the expenditure of thousands of dollars.

in the first sorting may be sorted a second time so that it can be distributed more easily to specific individuals and sections within the department. In this re-sorting process, routine instructions such as the following may be issued:

1   Send salesmen's reports to the sales manager's office.
2   Send salesmen's expense reports to the assistant sales manager.
3   Send orders from retail customers to the retail sales section. Sort the different types of orders into separate batches; for instance, separate COD orders from credit card orders.
4   Send orders from wholesale customers to the wholesale sales section.
5   Route special orders and inquiries to the special service unit.
6   Refer complaints and requests for adjustments to the customer relations section.

Distributing Letter Mail

At regular intervals during the day, messengers clear the sorting racks and deliver the mail to the various departments. The messengers may use carts to help them carry large piles of sorted correspondence as they deliver the mail to baskets at receiving stations in each department.

Expediting Special Letters or Packages

Packages and letters arriving at the mail room by registered, certified, or insured mail, by special delivery, or by private messenger service require priority treat-ment because of the special urgency or the security measures involved in their mailing. The incoming mail supervisor first records the receipt of these letters and packages in a special record book or *log* as shown on pages 126–127. The item is promptly sent by special messenger to the person to whom it is addressed. If special messengers are not available, the mail room may phone the addressee and report to him the arrival of the special mail. Then the addressee either sends his own messenger to the mail room to claim the item or authorizes delivery to him in the next scheduled mail distribution. If the item is not ad-dressed to a specific person, the mail supervisor opens the envelope, scans the contents of the correspondence, and sends the letter or package to the proper person by special messenger.

Receiving Parcel Post

If there is only one mail room crew to handle both letters and parcels, letters are normally processed first with the exception of special items, such as regis-tered mail, perishable and fragile items, special delivery packages, and items listed on a special "Watch Out For" list, which receive immediate processing. Most companies refuse to accept registered or highly insured items which are received in poor condition. Those companies that do accept such items log their arrival in the supervisor's record book, noting the condition in which they were received.

SPECIAL MAIL LOG

Date	Time of Arrival	Via	Type of Item	From Name	Address
January 2	10:00 a.m.	PO	Insured Package	M. Cooley Assoc.	Hillsdale, Pa.
2	3:10 p.m.	PO	Special Delivery Package	King Supply	Laurel, Del.
3	9:08 a.m.	PO	Registered Letter	Hall Data Center	Bergen, N.Y.
3	11:19 a.m.	PO	Special Delivery Letter	Chicago Branch	
3	2:45 p.m.	Fleet	Delivered Package	J. R. Kline	New York, N.Y.
4	8:30 a.m.	PO	Certified Letter	R. Hise & Co.	Fayette, Maine

Sorting Parcel Post

Parcels are not usually opened in the mail room. They are sorted according to external clues and references and then dispatched to destinations within the company. Workers in a busy mail room of a manufacturing concern may follow these instructions for sorting procedures:

1 Route all parcels bearing purchase order number references on their address labels to the receiving department in the warehouse.
2 Forward other parcels to departments or persons shown on parcel labels.
3 Refer other parcels to supervisor for routing instructions.

REPORTING INCOMING VOLUME

In companies with large business operations, such as mail-order houses, banks, insurance companies, and certain retail stores with a large mail-order clientele, the volume of incoming mail is watched closely from hour to hour. Mail supervisors may be requested to telephone and report on this volume of mail to operations coordinators. In turn, these men alert the departments that will be next in line to receive the mail, so that sufficient manpower will be ready to handle the expected load of work. In this way customer needs can be met on a normal schedule even though the orders have been received on a very busy day. Some mail-order concerns promise to process and ship mail orders within 24 hours of the time the order was received. In order to give the best customer service, many offices make it a goal to acknowledge or to respond fully to a letter on the very day it is received. In the competitive business world, prompt service is vital, and speedy mail room operations are an absolute must.

REVIEWING YOUR READING

1 A business is located in an outlying area which receives only one late morning mail delivery a day from the post office. How can the firm arrange to distribute the incoming mail to personnel more evenly throughout the day in order to ease the work load?

To Name	Department	Condition	Notified		Comments
R. L. Scott	Accounting	wrapping torn	R. L. Scott	10:05 a.m.	Delivered to Mr. Scott by messenger, 10:30 a.m.
H. R. Brock	Advertising	OK	H. R. Brock	3:20 p.m.	Picked up by Brock's secretary, Helen Flagg, 3:30 p.m.
T. O. Whale	Data Processing	OK	T. O. Whale	9:15 a.m.	Delivered to T. O. Whale's secretary by messenger, 9:30 a.m.
	Payroll	OK	C. Dodge	11:45 a.m.	Delivered to C. Dodge by messenger, 11:55 a.m.
G. P. Byers	Purchasing	OK	G. P. Byers	3:05 p.m.	Delivered to Mr. Byers by messenger, 3:15 p.m.
G. E. Kettner	Legal	OK	G. E. Kettner	8:45 a.m.	Delivered on January 4, 9 a.m. cart.

2 Assume that the envelopes of incoming correspondence have already been sliced open by the mechanical letter opener. Demonstrate or explain how you would remove the contents and give special care to enclosures.

3 After the incoming letters have been opened and stamped with the date and time of their arrival, how would you, as mail clerk, determine to which department each item should be sent?

4 Assume that you are on duty in the mail room when a special delivery letter or parcel arrives. Outline the priority treatment that you give the item.

5 The notation "Your PO 6137 Dept 9: 9/16" appears on the shipping label of an incoming parcel. Does this information have any significance to you as a mail clerk? Explain.

OFFICE ASSIGNMENTS

1 You are assigned to the centralized incoming mail room unit operating in the department of Miscellaneous Office Services. The organization chart of your company is shown below.

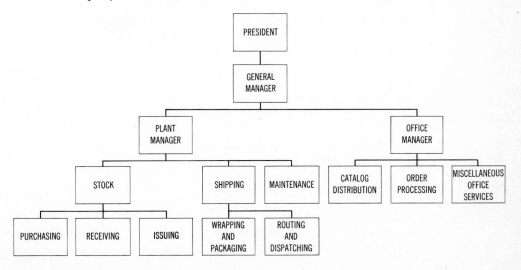

a In the preliminary sorting procedure, the incoming mail is separated in a sorting rack according to ten major departments or offices. Identify these departments by name. (If you are using the workbook, circle each department in the organization chart.)

b For which departments might secondary sorting be desirable? Name and circle the subdivisions recommended.

c If processing orders consists of accounting for payments received, order adjustments, billing, and so on, would the incoming orders need a secondary sorting? Explain with a diagram.

2 Your supervisor maintains a log for special letters and parcels similar to the one shown on pages 126–127 of the text. Follow this form as an example, and make a record of receipt of the following items.

Jan. 7. Registered letter from H. F. Grant, attorney, New York, New York, addressed to attention of E. Manning Bell, treasurer. Received 11 a.m., and notified Mr. Bell's office immediately. Picked up by Mr. Bell's secretary, W. Van Hook, at 11:15 a.m.

Jan. 8. At 3 p.m. received damaged parcel insured by U.S. Postal Service from Allen Manufacturing Company of Midland, Ohio, addressed to company with label reference to Purchase Order 61-71-8, Department 6. Delivered to K. L. Russo, manager of Department 6, by H. L. Klein, mail messenger, at 3:45 p.m. On Thursday, January 10, Mr. Klein notified the U.S. Postal Service and Allen Manufacturing Company of damage.

Jan. 10. Received special delivery letter from T. R. Sims Engineering Company, Duluth, Minnesota, at 9:30 a.m. At 9:35 notified office of Mr. H. L. Stone, president, to whom letter was addressed. Mr. Stone's secretary sent R. Kelly, special messenger, to pick up the item at 9:45 a.m.

Jan. 11. Received tropical fruit gift basket from REA Express at 10 a.m., addressed to E. W. Tate, plant manager, from K. L. Oyler, Marion, Pennsylvania. Called Mr. Tate's office at 10:10 a.m. Basket picked up by Mr. Tate in person at 4:45 p.m.

3 A special record book or log is a very useful source of information for future reference. For example, suppose you were asked to trace a registered letter, sent from the Hall Data Center and addressed to Mr. T. O. Whale, that was supposed to have arrived on January 2 or 3. Refer to the log illustrated on pages 126–127, and answer these questions:

a Has the letter arrived?
b When?
c What was the condition of the item upon arrival?
d Who was notified of its arrival?
e When was notification given?
f To whom was the item delivered?
g When was the item delivered?

4 In the preliminary sorting of incoming mail, Parson's mail room personnel routed the order shown on page 129 to the retail sales section. In a secondary

sorting procedure the item was classified as a payment-with-order rush item. Scan the order, and identify the clues that were noted in the sorting process.

a How would you know that the item was a retail order?

b How would you know that it was a payment-with-order transaction?

c How would you conclude that the order was ready for immediate processing?

d What is the purpose of each of the numbered parts of the order?

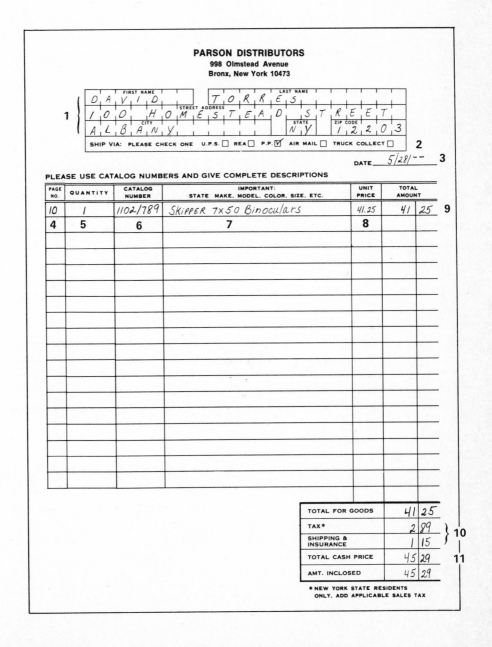

SECTION 11 Outgoing Mail

"Keep it moving!" is the motto of those who handle outgoing mail in a busy office. The outward movement of mail has to be a continuous effort from the opening hours to the closing of every workday. Sending frequent dispatches of mail to the post office during the day can minimize the work load at the end of the day not only for post office personnel but also for company mail room employees. Even a large mail room can become bogged down by a late afternoon rush of mail which can delay the dispatch of outgoing mail for hours.

PROCESSING OUTGOING MAIL

Since business wants to reach its customers and suppliers as quickly as possible, mail room operations must proceed at a smooth, steady rate. It's important that the office mail clerk do everything possible to speed the outward movement of mail.

Collecting Mail

In a large office the same messenger who distributes incoming mail also collects —at regular intervals—outgoing mail, so that there is a steady flow of mail all day long.

Sorting

As soon as the outgoing mail reaches the office mail department, a number of operations are performed so that the mail can be processed speedily. First, the outgoing mail is sorted. As a clerk assigned to outgoing mail duties, you may use baskets or sorting racks to subdivide the mail according to type or class, such as first-class mail (surface mail), airmail, combination mailings (letter and parcel mailed together), special service items, international mail, and parcel post.

Observing Priority Order

Mail rooms generally follow the order listed below in processing special service items, airmail, and first-class mail.

1 Registered
2 Insured Parcel Post
3 Certified
4 Special Delivery
5 Special Handling
6 Airmail
7 First-Class Mail

Folding and Inserting

If a letter has not been folded in the department where it originated (this might happen if you were given a batch of form letters to send out), you can fold the letter neatly and quickly by observing the following steps.

For large (No. 10) envelopes:

1 Place the letter flat on a table, face up. Fold up one-third of the bottom part of the letter.
2 Then fold down the top of the letter slightly less than one-third the letter length.
3 Insert the letter into the envelope so that the top one-third fold can be grasped when the letter is removed by the addressee.
4 Place any enclosures, which are not attached to the letter, inside the folds so that they will be drawn out of the envelope when the letter is removed.

For No. 10 window envelopes:

1 Place the letter flat on the table, face up. Fold up one-third of the bottom part of the letter.
2 Turn the folded letter face down, and make the second fold one-half the distance between the first fold and the top.

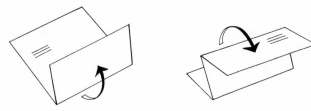

3 Insert the folded letter in the envelope, and check to see that the name and address typed on the letter line up with the window.
4 Adjust the location of the folds of the letter in the envelope to improve the alignment of the address with the window before proceeding to the next letter and envelope.

To help you align the address with the window, some firms have their forms, form letters, and regular letterheads designed with printed blocks in which the name and address are typed. As long as the typing falls within the block, the name and address will be visible through the window of the envelope. Many concerns print folding guides on the edge of the letterhead paper to help you align the folded letter in the address window of the envelope.

For small (No. 6¾) envelopes:

1 Place the letter on a table, face up. Fold the bottom half of the letter almost over the upper half, leaving ½ inch of the upper half of the letter exposed.
2 Fold the right side of the letter a little less than one-third its width.
3 Finally, fold the left side of the letter a little less than one-third its width.
4 Insert the folded letter in the envelope so that the addressee can grasp the upper right corner of the letter and unfold it in a quick and easy operation.

There are automatic folding devices that handle long runs of circulars and form letters.

Addressing

Unless window envelopes are used, a secretary or typist usually addresses an envelope as soon as she finishes typing the letter. However, if a typed envelope has been separated from its letter or mislaid, a mail clerk is usually expected to address a replacement rather than delay the mailing by waiting for the secretary to retype it.

The proper place for postage (stamps, meter stamps, or permit imprints) is in the upper right corner of the envelope. The return address of the sender is placed in the upper left corner, beginning on line 3, about ½ inch from the left edge of the envelope.

In general, the procedure for addressing an envelope is as follows:

☐ Use single spacing and blocked style.
☐ For a No. 10 envelope, start the address on line 14, about 4 inches from the left edge.
☐ For a No. 6¾ envelope or a postcard, start the address on line 12, about 2 inches from the left edge.
☐ When an address consists of four elements—the name of an individual; the company name; the street address; and the city, state, and ZIP Code—put each element on a separate line. The name of the individual goes on the first line, the company name on the second line, the street address on the third line, and the city, state, and ZIP Code on the fourth line. Leave one space between the state and the ZIP Code.
☐ Type an attention line or a notation such as *Personal* or *Confidential* or *Attention Sales Manager* on line 9 or at least three lines below the return address, and underline it. Begin each word with a capital.
☐ If a special mailing procedure is used, such as *SPECIAL DELIVERY* or *REGISTERED*, type the notation in all capitals in the upper right corner of the envelope, beginning on line 9. The notation should end about ½ inch from the right edge. Use a rubber stamp or sticker to indicate the notation on the other side of the envelope.
☐ Be consistent when you abbreviate state names. Whether you use the two-letter state abbreviations, recommended by the U.S. Postal Service, or the traditional abbreviations, be sure you use the same style abbreviation on the envelope that you use on the letter. (For state abbreviations, see page 134.)

Addressing for Automation

Because of a dramatic development in mail technology, there is an alternate way to address envelopes. The Optical Character Reader (OCR) is a device which reads and sorts mail automatically at a speed of 42,000 items per hour. Although it is now used in only a few post offices in the country, it will be in-

Morgan Brothers
Box 261
Mitchellville, Maryland 20716

Attention Sales Manager   REGISTERED

                        Mr. Henry Brown
                        Atlas Tools, Incorporated
                        1198 Albany Avenue S.
                        Chicago, Illinois 60612

Morgan Brothers
Box 261
Mitchellville, Maryland 20716

Attention Sales Manager   REGISTERED

                    Mr. Henry Brown
                    Atlas Tools, Incorporated
                    1198 Albany Avenue S.
                    Chicago, Illinois 60612

stalled in time in all major post offices in the United States. In order to benefit from the speed with which this device processes mail, you must address envelopes according to the directions given by the post office. This is because the scanning eye of the Reader is programmed to look for certain information on certain lines.

To address for OCR, use the two-letter, no-punctuation abbreviation for the state name. Also, if you are indicating a box number at a particular post office, write it before the name of the post office, like Box 220, Grand Central Station. If you are noting the number of a unit in a building, an apartment, a room, or a suite, type it on the same line as the street address, at the end of the line—never above, below, or in front.

If you are sending out a mass mailing or putting a mailing list on plates from which labels for envelopes are addressed mechanically, it may be advisable to follow the post office's recommendation that all punctuation be omitted and a format be followed in which the company name appears on the top line, and

STATE ABBREVIATIONS

	New	Old		New	Old
Alabama	AL	Ala.	Missouri	MO	Mo.
Alaska	AK	. . .	Montana	MT	Mont.
Arizona	AZ	Ariz.	Nebraska	NE	Nebr.
Arkansas	AR	Ark.	Nevada	NV	Nev.
California	CA	Calif.	New Hampshire	NH	N.H.
Canal Zone	CZ	C.Z.	New Jersey	NJ	N.J.
Colorado	CO	Colo.	New Mexico	NM	N. Mex.
Connecticut	CT	Conn.	New York	NY	N.Y.
Delaware	DE	Del.	North Carolina	NC	N.C.
District	DC	D.C.	North Dakota	ND	N. Dak.
of Columbia			Ohio	OH	. . .
Florida	FL	Fla.	Oklahoma	OK	Okla.
Georgia	GA	Ga.	Oregon	OR	Oreg.
Guam	GU	. . .	Pennsylvania	PA	Pa.
Hawaii	HI	. . .	Puerto Rico	PR	P.R.
Idaho	ID	. . .	Rhode Island	RI	R.I.
Illinois	IL	Ill.	South Carolina	SC	S.C.
Indiana	IN	Ind.	South Dakota	SD	S. Dak.
Iowa	IA	. . .	Tennessee	TN	Tenn.
Kansas	KS	Kans.	Texas	TX	Tex.
Kentucky	KY	Ky.	Utah	UT	. . .
Louisiana	LA	La.	Vermont	VT	Vt.
Maine	ME	. . .	Virgin Islands	VI	V.I.
Maryland	MD	Md.	Virginia	VA	Va.
Massachusetts	MA	Mass.	Washington	WA	Wash.
Michigan	MI	Mich.	West Virginia	WV	W. Va.
Minnesota	MN	Minn.	Wisconsin	WI	Wis.
Mississippi	MS	Miss.	Wyoming	WY	Wyo.

the name of the person addressed, the division, or department on the following line. Such an address would look like this:

General Window Shade Company
Mr C P Jones
1000 Maison Rd Room 4325
Detroit MI 48236

However, in ordinary correspondence it is quite acceptable to use the traditional form and include punctuation:

Mr. C. P. Jones
General Window Shade Company
1000 Maison Road, Room 4325
Detroit, Michigan 48236

In both cases the two important lines—the bottom line and the second line from the bottom—are in the same position, and that is where the scanning eye of the Reader looks first and where it expects to find the information that will send the correspondence to the correct street, city, state, and ZIP Code area.

USING THE ZIP CODE DIRECTORY

ZIP is the abbreviation for Zoning Improvement Plan, a system devised by the post office to speed up the processing of mail. Always use a ZIP Code on anything to be mailed. If you don't know the ZIP Code number, look it up in the *National ZIP Code Directory*, a book every mailing department should have. The directory can be ordered from the Superintendent of Documents, U.S. Government Printing Office, Washington, D.C. 20402. Old editions are replaced with new ones at no charge. The directory lists ZIP Codes for the United States and its possessions.

ZIP Code for Small Towns

The technique used to locate ZIP Codes in the directory is easy to learn. For example, you can find the ZIP Code for the following address in three steps:

Mr. Henry R. Butler
16 Oak Lane
Geneva, Alabama

1   ZIP Code information in the directory is arranged alphabetically by state. Turn to the Alabama section.
2   Locate the list of post offices at the front of the Alabama section that begins with the letter *G*.
3   Finally, within the *G* entries, find Geneva, which is in alphabetic order as shown below. The ZIP Code number is supplied at the right of the name of the post office.

Post Office	ZIP Code
Gastonburg	36743
Gaylesville	35973
Geneva	36340
Georgiana	36033

ZIP Code for Large Cities

Locating ZIP Codes for larger cities calls for a slightly different procedure. This time, suppose you are looking up the ZIP Code number for the following address:

Mrs. Elsa Foley
168 Duke Avenue
Birmingham, Alabama

1   Turn to the Alabama section of the directory.
2   Locate the entries that begin with the letter *B*.
3   Find the entry for Birmingham as follows:

Post Office	ZIP Code
Billingsley	36006
BIRMINGHAM (see appendix)	
Black	36314

The capital letters indicate that Birmingham is a large city having more than one postal delivery area with different ZIP Code numbers.

4 Consult the Birmingham section in the appendix that follows the regular listing. The city name and first three ZIP Code numbers appear at the head of the city listing in the appendix section. Note that the first three digits for Birmingham are 352. The last two digits vary according to the location within Birmingham.

5 Find the fourth and fifth digits under separate listings for Post Office Boxes; Rural Routes; Stations, Branches, and Units; Named Streets; and Numbered Streets. The entry for Duke Avenue under the heading Named Streets appears as follows:

Dugan Ave	14
Duke Ave	10
Dunbar Ave	14

This means that the complete ZIP Code number for the address is 35210.

ZIP Code for Very Large Cities

The directory simplifies the search for ZIP Code numbers in the appendix section for very large cities by supplying additional headings or groupings, such as Apartments, Hotels, Motels; Buildings; Government Offices; Hospitals; Universities and Colleges. Suppose you want to know the ZIP Code number for the following address:

Miss Helen Paige
Registrar of Deeds
Court House, Square
Huntsville, Alabama

1 Turn to the Alabama section of the directory.
2 Locate the entries that begin with the letter *H*.
3 Find the entry for Huntsville.
4 Consult the Huntsville section in the appendix, and note the first three digits of the ZIP Code for Huntsville — 358.
5 Find the fourth and fifth digits under the heading, Government Offices. Thus the entry *Court House, Square 01* signifies that the complete ZIP Code for the address is 35801.

Of course, if you recognize at once that Huntsville is a large city, you can actually skip steps 2 and 3, proceed directly to the Huntsville section in the Alabama appendix, and complete steps 4 and 5.

SPECIAL SERVICE NOTATIONS

Notations for special postal service, such as *Special Delivery, Special Handling,* and *Airmail,* should appear prominently on both sides of the envelope. Be careful about using special services excessively, because they can be costly and even wasteful. Use them wisely.

SEALING

You can seal envelope flaps individually with a sponge or a damp cloth, but when a firm has a large quantity of outgoing mail, automatic sealing machines are generally used to seal envelopes. The envelopes are stacked on the feed table with the flaps up and the flap folds to the rear. The envelopes are drawn to a moistener blade that wets the glue on the flaps. Now the envelopes fall onto a receiving tray where the weight of additional envelopes on top of the pile presses the flaps to the envelopes and completes the sealing.

WEIGHING

The amount of postage for a particular piece of mail depends, in part, upon how much it weighs. Postage scales vary in size from small desk models to large commercial ones. However, whatever the size, the postage scale is an important part of mailing equipment.

FACING, SORTING, BUNDLING, TRAYING, AND TYING

Postal authorities encourage business firms to face and rough-sort letter mail and to put it on trays before it is dispatched to the post office. *Facing* means arranging the envelopes on the trays so that all addresses face forward and read from left to right. The sorting procedure consists of dividing the letters into two groups: local mail and out-of-town mail. Mailing bands for labels are supplied free of charge by the post office, so that the faced and sorted mail can be bundled at the company office. This procedure helps the post office process the mail more quickly. In addition, postal regulations specify that certain classes of mail must be sorted, bundled, trayed, and labeled with the ZIP Code number. Packages must be securely tied to ensure safe transit; if they are heavy, they should be sealed with tape and reinforced with string.

STAMPING

You can stamp individual pieces of mail with regular postage stamps, but if you have large volumes of mail, you can speed up the stamping process by using a postage meter. One type of postage meter prints the proper amount of postage directly on the envelope at the same time it prints the postmark, date, and an advertising slogan. Still another model prints the required postage on gummed tape, making it very convenient for stamping parcel post packages and oddly shaped pieces.

The firm using a postage meter pays the post office in advance for the postage printed. To do this, the detachable meter is taken to the post office and set there for the amount of postage purchased. Every time the machine prints out postage, that amount is deducted from the original value set in the meter. When the postage amount runs low, the meter is reset at the post office after more postage is purchased. Should the postage amount become completely used up,

Courtesy Pitney Bowes

To get a 10 cent stamp, push the 1 button and the 0 bar; insert the envelope; then touch the trip lever.

an automatic locking device will prevent the meter from printing any more postage.

DISPATCHING LETTER MAIL

It is important that outgoing mail be dispatched promptly. A general clerk in a small office may send off the accumulated mail several times a day by way of the corner mailbox or the mail chute in the building where the office is located. In larger cities and in metropolitan areas, special letter collection boxes are provided on street corners. In the lobbies of large office buildings, there may be similar letter collection boxes or mailbag racks. These devices require that the sender perform a preliminary sorting and routing operation in order to save the post office time in its handling of the mail. Special delivery and airmail items are placed in a separate box or bag for priority attention. Mail for the immediate area is placed in a receptacle labeled "Local" or "City." Mail for other cities goes into a box or bag labeled "Out of Town."

The post office also employs other methods to speed mail service. ZIP Coded airmail letters deposited before 4 p.m. in "Airmail Only" collection points in a particular city are delivered the next day to principal cities within a 600-mile radius as well as many other cities to which there are convenient evening flights. The U.S. Postal Service is also experimenting with downtown-to-downtown service between 34 major cities in the United States. Under this plan letters or packages weighing up to 50 pounds, deposited at a designated post office or station by 5 p.m., are guaranteed to reach a specific station in the addressee's city the following day and be available for pickup by 10 a.m.

First-class metered mail made up of more than five letter-type pieces has to be bundled with addresses facing in one direction. Such metered mail may be mailed in the usual collection facilities at the post office shown in the meter postage stamp.

You can often expedite special outgoing rush items by taking them directly to the post office. Mail can also be taken directly to postal drops at railroad terminals, steamship piers, and airports for quick dispatch on the earliest available departures.

In larger concerns the company mail department usually sends mail to the post office at frequent and regular intervals throughout the day by truck and special messenger. In this way, mail gets to the post office faster and reaches its destination quicker.

As a customer service the post office will pick up first-class mail when there is a substantial volume of it. How many pieces make up that volume varies from city to city.

In a further effort to prevent the flooding of mail to the post offices at the end of the day, the U.S. Postal Service encourages people who have large volumes of mail to hold the late afternoon's low-priority mail until the next morning. Millions of bills, notices, receipts, and statements that fall into this category are mailed every day. When this material is received at the post office during the slow period between 8 a.m. and 2 p.m. (the post office prefers that it arrive before noon), it can receive far better attention and be dispatched more quickly.

HANDLING INTEROFFICE MAIL

In many businesses there is a large volume of internal mail that passes among the various departments, offices, and branches. Most of it does not even leave the building. In order to deal with interoffice mail efficiently, many procedures have been devised along the lines of the ones listed below.

1 Interoffice messages are prepared on special stationery known as interoffice memorandum forms. (See Section 14, pages 192–194.)

2 Interoffice memorandums may be dispatched without envelopes, especially if they contain no confidential information and if they are to be delivered to some office in the same geographic location.

3 When envelopes are required, informal and reusable ones can be used. These save time as well as money because no lengthy address is required.

4 If several pieces of interoffice mail are addressed to the same person at a distant branch, all the pieces can be assembled for dispatch in a single envelope. In this way, three single-page letters may travel in one envelope for as little as the price of one stamp.

5 Interoffice mail generally moves quickly. Interoffice items not enclosed in envelopes are date-stamped and routed at once according to the instructions on the heading as shown in the illustration. Interoffice mail enclosed in

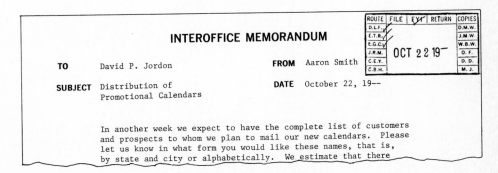

envelopes is promptly directed to the person or department indicated in the last entry in the address block of the envelope. In this case the receiver or receiving department notes the time and date of arrival on the correspondence.

HANDLING OUTGOING PARCELS

Merchandise and any other items that are to be sent by parcel post are usually packed and wrapped for shipment in the shipping department, as explained later in Unit 16. The items then reach the mail room by hand truck, mail chute, or conveyor.

Sorting

When the mail arrives at the mail room, it is sorted according to its classification: first-class mail, airmail, second-class mail, third-class mail, fourth-class mail, special service items, and international mail.

Addressing Parcels

All parcels are checked to see that shipping labels are glued or taped on one side of the package only. If labels are not used, all essential shipping data must be printed clearly and legibly on the outer wrapping.

Weighing Parcels

Parcels are weighed in order to determine the postal charge. Surface fourth-class mail, which travels by rail, truck, or ship, is subject to zone rates according to weight and distance, as shown in the table on page 146. Parcels weighing more than 9 ounces may be sent by air under the priority mail rates shown on page 145. First-class, second-class, and third-class parcels are subject to rates which will be described in the following section. Special service fees are charged in addition to regular postal charges.

International parcel post rates are shown on page 153. Parcel post service to foreign countries is subject to many special regulations depending upon weight, dimensions, packing, sealing, and customs declarations.

For the latest information, shippers should consult the *Postal Service Manual* or *Directory of International Mail,* which can be obtained from the Superintendent of Documents, U.S. Government Printing Office, Washington, D.C. 20402.

Dispatching Parcels

Concerns that have a large volume of outgoing parcels find it advantageous to send the parcels to the post office along with the frequently scheduled dispatches of letter mail. You can speed mail delivery if you know the local post office's schedule for moving out their mail to air, rail, and ship terminals. Also, if you have an exceptionally large volume of mail to send out, notify the postmaster in advance, so that he can arrange for it to be handled by the post office as efficiently as possible. If there is a large volume of mail to be dispatched, the postmaster will arrange to have it picked up at your office.

REVIEWING YOUR READING

1   Demonstrate the steps in folding and inserting an 8½- by 11-inch sheet of letterhead paper into a large No. 10 envelope.
2   Demonstrate the steps in folding and inserting an 8½- by 11-inch sheet of letterhead paper into a No. 6¾ envelope.
3   Demonstrate the steps in folding an actual letter prepared on an 8½- by 11-inch sheet of letterhead paper into a No. 10 window envelope.
4   Demonstrate proper placement of data by addressing a No. 6¾ envelope and a No. 10 envelope to Miss Joann Todd, 1401 Park Avenue, Hudson, Wisconsin 54016. The envelopes are to be sent airmail, special delivery.
5   Explain how to determine ZIP Code numbers for the following addresses:

   a   927 Main Street, Mercersburg, Pennsylvania
   b   1000 Broadway, New York, New York
   c   Drake Hotel, Chicago, Illinois

6   Obtain a schedule of outgoing mail dispatches from your local post office. Explain how this schedule might affect the internal collection and dispatch of a firm's mail.
7   Explain how outgoing interoffice mail can be processed for greater efficiency and economy.

OFFICE ASSIGNMENTS

1   Arrange and edit the following address data as though you were addressing an envelope for processing by optical scanning equipment.

   Medical Research Foundation
   Attention of Dr. Henry Jaffe
   202 Highbrook Avenue, Room 298
   West Nyack, New York 10994

   Identify each element in the address, and explain the reason for its particular order in the format.

2 In the *National ZIP Code Directory,* look up the ZIP Codes for the following addresses in St. Petersburg, Florida. Check your school library or local post office for a copy of the directory.

Example: Richard Miller
4100 Benson Avenue, N.
St. Petersburg, Florida 33713

a Bernard L. Fleming
2430 Catalonia Way, S.

b Leonard Fusby
Box 3614 Open Air Station

c Walter L. Bryson, Cashier
Florida National Bank

d Edward T. Alberts
1800 Americana Drive, N.E.

e C. C. Harrison
1723 Beach Drive, N.E.

f John E. Schaff
1642 Central Avenue

g Dr. Lawrence Kane, President
St. Petersburg Junior College

h Mr. R. A. Davies, Manager
Martha Washington Hotel

i Management Office
Ponce De Leon Apartments

j Oliver A. Olson
2752 Connecticut Avenue, N.E.

k Harry F. Garner
Box 20533 Gateway Mall Station

l Dr. Michael G. Layton
Suncoast Medical Clinic

m Louise Kinyon
379 Beach Avenue

n Henry DiMatteo
744 Crystal Drive

3 Prepare envelopes for the names and addresses used in Office Assignment 2. Then demonstrate the correct techniques for sealing, stamping, facing, and bundling outgoing letter mail.

4 Examine the reusable interoffice envelope shown below.

a Who was the last addressee?
b Where was he located?
c Who was the third addressee to receive this envelope?
d In which department did she work?
e What will have to be done so that the envelope can be used again?
f For your future reference make a list of the four typical instructions printed in the upper right corner of the interoffice envelope. Then demonstrate the meaning of each of these instructions.

INTER-COMPANY ENVELOPE
(FOR ALL INTER-OFFICE <u>AND</u> BRANCH OFFICE MAIL)

1. PLEASE WRITE LEGIBLY FULL NAME AND COMPLETE ADDRESS.
2. USE ONLY ONE CONSECUTIVE LINE AT A TIME.
3. CROSS OUT ALL PREVIOUS ADDRESSES.
4. USE ALL SPACES BEFORE DESTROYING ENVELOPE.

NAME	DEPT. OR BRANCH OFFICE	FLOOR	NAME	DEPT. OR BRANCH OFFICE	FLOOR
~~Jerry Orvis~~	~~Purchasing~~	~~26~~			
~~Jona Farrar~~	~~Library~~	~~18~~			
~~Barbara Lesser~~	~~Sales~~	~~34~~			
DAVID LaComBE	PERSONNEL	3			

SECTION 12 Postal Services

In the U.S. Postal Service some 680,000 postal employees are required in approximately 32,000 post offices, branches, and stations to handle over *39 billion* pieces of mail in a single year. Such figures make it clear that the cooperation of office mail room personnel is vital if the Postal Service is to move this tremendous volume of mail efficiently and speedily. You can be of invaluable help in this huge task if you learn about the basic postal services available and how to use them to the best advantage.

CLASSES OF MAIL

Since postal services and rates are determined by the class of mail involved, it's important that you get to know all you can about the four major classes.

First-Class Mail

Letters, single or double postcards, any communication with a personal message, such as a form letter with an insertion showing how much you owe on an account, and matter sealed or closed against inspection must bear postage for first-class mail.

Note that a postal card is a card bearing a printed postage stamp and is sold by the U.S. Postal Service. A postcard is an unofficial or private card to which postage may be applied in any manner—by stamp, meter, or permit.

First-class written matter includes the following types of material:

☐ Written or typed matter (including identical copies prepared by automatic typewriters) and manifold or carbon copies of such matter.
☐ Reproductions of written or typed matter.
☐ Autograph albums containing writing.
☐ Notebooks or blank books containing written or typed entries or stenographic or shorthand notes.
☐ Printed forms with blanks filled out in writing or with amounts due, signatures, or other writing—such as notices, certificates, receipts, and checks, either canceled or uncanceled.
☐ Printed price lists containing written figures changing individual items.
☐ Bills or statements of account produced by any photographic or mechanical process.
☐ Printed cards or letters bearing a written date which is not the date of the card, but a date which gives information as to when something will occur or has occurred.

FIRST CLASS

Kind of Mail	Rate
All first-class mail weighing 12 ounces or less except postal and post cards.	10¢ per ounce.
Over 12 ounces	Priority mail (heavy pieces) rates apply.
Single postal cards sold by the post office.	8¢ each.
Double postal cards sold by the post office.	16¢ (8¢ each half).
Single post cards	8¢ each.
Double post cards (reply portion of double post card does not have to bear postage when originally mailed).	16¢ (8¢ each half).
Business reply mail:	
Cards	10¢ each.
Other than cards:	
Weight not over 2 ounces.....	10¢ per ounce or fraction of an ounce plus 2¢ per piece.
Weight over 2 ounces........	10¢ per ounce or fraction of an ounce plus 6¢ per piece.
Over 12 ounces	Priority mail (heavy pieces) rates apply plus 6¢ per piece.

AIRMAIL

Weight	Kind of Mail	Rate
9 ounces or less.	Air postal or post cards.	11¢ each.
	Letters and packages.	13¢ an ounce.
	See Priority Mail (Heavy Pieces) Schedule for rates on pieces weighing more than 9 ounces.	
	Business reply:	
	Air cards	13¢ each.
	Airmail other than cards:	
	Weight not over 2 ounces.	13¢ an ounce, plus 2¢ per piece.
	Weight over 2 ounces.	13¢ an ounce, plus 6¢ per piece.
	Weight over 9 ounces.	Priority mail (heavy pieces) rates apply plus 6¢ per piece.

Courtesy United States Postal Service

☐ Printed cards or coupons having a signature attached (and are thus considered personal communications), such as a receipt or an order.

☐ Identical communications entirely in print, except the name of the sender, sent by several persons to the same addressee.

Sealed matter includes mail of any class wrapped in a way that prevents easy inspection, except sealed third- or fourth-class matter subject to postal inspection. Sealed third-class matter must be marked "Third-Class."

Postal rates are quoted "per ounce or fraction thereof." This means that any part of an ounce costs the same as a full ounce. A letter weighing $3\frac{1}{3}$ ounces costs the same as a letter weighing 4 ounces.

Although it is not categorized as first-class mail, airmail is included here because it is the fastest mail service, traveling by planes and by fast connecting surface carriers. Postage is computed at 13 cents an ounce for letters and packages and 11 cents each for air postal or postcards. Postage on other airmail items is shown above. Airmail items over 9 ounces in weight are covered by the priority mail (heavy pieces) rate table shown on page 145.

PRIORITY MAIL (HEAVY PIECES)

Weight over 9 ounces and not exceeding (Lbs.)	RATE						Weight over 9 ounces and not exceeding (Lbs.)	RATE					
	Local Zones 1, 2, and 3	Zone 4	Zone 5	Zone 6	Zone 7	Zone 8		Local Zones 1, 2, and 3	Zone 4	Zone 5	Zone 6	Zone 7	Zone 8
1 ...	$ 1.25	$ 1.25	$ 1.25	$ 1.30	$ 1.30	$ 1.30	21 ...	8.59	9.43	10.31	11.56	12.84	14.12
1.5 ..	1.50	1.54	1.60	1.68	1.75	1.82	22 ...	8.95	9.83	10.75	12.06	13.40	14.74
2 ...	1.75	1.83	1.95	2.06	2.20	2.34	23 ...	9.31	10.23	11.19	12.56	13.96	15.36
2.5 ..	1.93	2.03	2.17	2.31	2.48	2.65	24 ...	9.67	10.63	11.63	13.06	14.52	15.98
3 ...	2.11	2.23	2.39	2.56	2.76	2.96	25 ...	10.03	11.03	12.07	13.56	15.08	16.60
3.5 ..	2.29	2.43	2.61	2.81	3.04	3.27							
4 ...	2.47	2.63	2.83	3.06	3.32	3.58	26 ...	10.39	11.43	12.51	14.06	15.64	17.22
4.5 ..	2.65	2.83	3.05	3.31	3.60	3.89	27 ...	10.75	11.83	12.95	14.56	16.20	17.84
5 ...	2.83	3.03	3.27	3.56	3.88	4.20	28 ...	11.11	12.23	13.39	15.06	16.76	18.46
							29 ...	11.47	12.63	13.83	15.56	17.32	19.08
6 ...	3.19	3.43	3.71	4.06	4.44	4.82	30 ...	11.83	13.03	14.27	16.06	17.88	19.70
7 ...	3.55	3.83	4.15	4.56	5.00	5.44							
8 ...	3.91	4.23	4.59	5.06	5.56	6.06	31 ...	12.19	13.43	14.71	16.56	18.44	20.32
9 ...	4.27	4.63	5.03	5.56	6.12	6.68	32 ...	12.55	13.83	15.15	17.06	19.00	20.94
10 ...	4.63	5.03	5.47	6.06	6.68	7.30	33 ...	12.91	14.23	15.59	17.56	19.56	21.56
							34 ...	13.27	14.63	16.03	18.06	20.12	22.18
11 ...	4.99	5.43	5.91	6.56	7.24	7.92	35 ...	13.63	15.03	16.47	18.56	20.68	22.80
12 ...	5.35	5.83	6.35	7.06	7.80	8.54							
13 ...	5.71	6.23	6.79	7.56	8.36	9.16	36 ...	$13.99	$15.43	$16.91	$19.06	$21.24	$23.42
14 ...	6.07	6.63	7.23	8.06	8.92	9.78	37 ...	14.35	15.83	17.35	19.56	21.80	24.04
15 ...	6.43	7.03	7.67	8.56	9.48	10.40	38 ...	14.71	16.23	17.79	20.06	22.36	24.66
							39 ...	15.07	16.63	18.23	20.56	22.92	25.28
16 ...	6.79	7.43	8.11	9.06	10.04	11.02	40 ...	15.43	17.03	18.67	21.06	23.48	25.90
17 ...	7.15	7.83	8.55	9.56	10.60	11.64							
18 ...	7.51	8.23	8.99	10.06	11.16	12.26	41 ...	15.79	17.43	19.11	21.56	24.04	26.52
19 ...	7.87	8.63	9.43	10.56	11.72	12.88	42 ...	16.15	17.83	19.55	22.06	24.60	27.14
20 ...	8.23	9.03	9.87	11.06	12.28	13.50	43 ...	16.51	18.23	19.99	22.56	25.16	27.76

Courtesy United States Postal Service

Second-Class Mail

Newspapers, magazines, and other periodicals mailed by publishers have special, low postal rates that vary according to type of publication, type of copy, weight, and delivery distance. Copies of second-class publications mailed by private individuals cost 8 cents for the first 2 ounces and 2 cents for each additional ounce or fraction thereof. These publications can be mailed at the fourth-class rate, depending on which rate is lower.

Third-Class Mail

Circulars, books, catalogs, miscellaneous printed matter, and merchandise up to but not including 16 ounces in weight per piece are included in this group.

Items can be mailed by the single piece or in any quantity. The cost is 10 cents for the first 2 ounces, 6 cents for the next 2 ounces, and 8 cents for each additional 2 ounces or fraction thereof.

There is a special third-class bulk rate used for mailing not less than 200 identical pieces or not less than 50 pounds total weight. For current postal rates it is best to consult the postmaster.

Fourth-Class Mail

This class is more commonly known as parcel post and is used for merchandise, books, printed matter, and all other mailable material not included in first-, second-, or third-classes. Zone rates are applied according to weight of the material and the distance it is being sent. The chart below is an excerpt from the fourth-class rate section of the postal regulations.

With certain exceptions weight and size limits on parcels vary according to the size or class of the post office of origin and destination and, in some cases, according to the distance the parcel is being sent. In general, 70 pounds is the maximum weight limit for parcels being sent fourth-class mail. Manuscripts for books, articles for periodicals, and music are mailable at the special fourth-class rate.

FOURTH-CLASS (PARCEL POST) ZONE RATES

Weight—1 pound and not exceeding (pounds)	Local	1 and 2	3	4	5	6	7	8
2	$0.61	$0.72	$0.75	$ .83	$0.92	$1.02	$1.12	$1.21
3	.65	.78	.83	.92	1.04	1.18	1.32	1.45
4	.69	.84	.90	1.01	1.16	1.33	1.51	1.69
5	.73	.90	.98	1.10	1.28	1.49	1.71	1.93
6	.77	.96	1.05	1.19	1.40	1.64	1.90	2.17
7	.81	1.02	1.13	1.28	1.52	1.80	2.10	2.41
8	.85	1.08	1.20	1.37	1.64	1.95	2.29	2.65
9	.89	1.14	1.28	1.46	1.76	2.11	2.49	2.89
10	.93	1.20	1.35	1.55	1.88	2.26	2.68	3.13
11	.97	1.26	1.43	1.64	2.00	2.42	2.88	3.37
12	1.01	1.32	1.50	1.73	2.12	2.57	3.07	3.61
13	1.05	1.38	1.58	1.82	2.24	2.73	3.27	3.85
14	1.09	1.44	1.65	1.91	2.36	2.88	3.46	4.09
15	1.13	1.50	1.73	2.00	2.48	3.04	3.66	4.33

Weight—1 pound and not exceeding (pounds)	Local	1 and 2	3	4	5	6	7	8
16	1.17	1.56	1.80	2.09	2.60	3.19	3.85	4.57
17	1.21	1.62	1.88	2.18	2.72	3.35	4.05	4.81
18	1.25	1.68	1.95	2.27	2.84	3.50	4.24	5.05
19	1.29	1.74	2.03	2.36	2.96	3.66	4.44	5.29
20	1.33	1.80	2.10	2.45	3.08	3.81	4.63	5.53
21	1.37	1.86	2.18	2.54	3.20	3.97	4.83	5.77
22	1.41	1.92	2.25	2.63	3.32	4.12	5.02	6.01
23	1.45	1.98	2.33	2.72	3.44	4.28	5.22	6.25
24	1.49	2.04	2.40	2.81	3.56	4.43	5.41	6.49
25	1.53	2.10	2.48	2.90	3.68	4.59	5.61	6.73
26	1.57	2.16	2.55	2.99	3.80	4.74	5.80	6.97
27	1.61	2.22	2.63	3.08	3.92	4.90	6.00	7.21
28	1.65	2.28	2.70	3.17	4.04	5.05	6.19	7.45
29	1.69	2.34	2.78	3.26	4.16	5.21	6.39	7.69
30	1.73	2.40	2.85	3.35	4.28	5.36	6.58	7.93

Courtesy United States Postal Service

SPECIAL SERVICES

The post office sells stamped envelopes, postal cards, and stamps in several forms and denominations. The chart on page 147 does not include the several denominations of stamps canceled in advance of mailing for convenience in bulk mailings.

Special Delivery

Airmail certainly speeds a letter across long distances, but an airmail letter still has to wait at the post office of its destination to be picked up by the regular mail service. Airmail letters are usually delayed from reaching the addressee if they arrive at the post office in the late afternoon or during a weekend. However, a letter sent special delivery generally is delivered soon after it arrives at the post office of its destination. Special delivery service is available for all classes of mail; rates vary according to weight and class of material sent. (See page 149.)

STAMPS, ENVELOPES, AND POSTAL CARDS

ADHESIVE STAMPS AVAILABLE

Purpose	Form	Denomination and prices
Ordinary postage	Single or sheet	1, 2, 3, 4, 5, 6, 7, 8, 10, 12, 13, 14, 15, 16, 18, 20, 25, 30, 40, and 50 cents; $1 and $5.
	Book	10—10¢ $1.00 40—10¢ $4.00
	Coil of 100*	8 and 10 cents.
	Coils of 500 & 3,000	1, 2, 5, 6, 8 and 10 cents.
	Coils of 3,000	25 cents.
Airmail postage (for use on airmail only)	Single or sheet	9, 11, 13, 18, 21 and 26 cents.
	Book	10—13¢ $1.30
	Coils of 100,* 500 & 3,000	13 cents.
Special delivery	Single or sheet	60 cents. (Good only for special delivery fee.)

*Dispenser to hold coils of 100 stamps may be purchased for 5¢ additional.

ENVELOPES AVAILABLE

Kind	Denomination	Selling price each
		(Less than 500)
Regular	10¢	12¢
Airmail.......	13¢	15¢

POSTAL CARDS AVAILABLE

Kind	Selling price each
Single......................	8¢
Airmail single (use for airmail only)	11¢
Reply (8¢ each half)	16¢

Courtesy United States Postal Service

Combination Mailing

It is frequently advantageous to have a letter, bill, or other first-class communication mailed with its accompanying parcel. The communication and the parcel arrive together, and the recipient, after reading the written communication, knows immediately what the parcel contains and how to handle its contents.

Under special regulations dealing with combination mailings, letters accompanying parcels may be handled as follows:

1   The letter may be placed in a fully addressed envelope and attached to the address side of the parcel. It should be marked "First Class" and should carry first-class or airmail postage.
2   If it is practical, a letter may also be enclosed inside the parcel itself and placed on top of the contents. The presence of the letter must be indicated by the notation "First-Class Mail Enclosed" placed on the outside of the

wrapped package right below the postage area. The entire postage for the package consists of first-class postage for the letter plus fourth-class postage for the parcel.

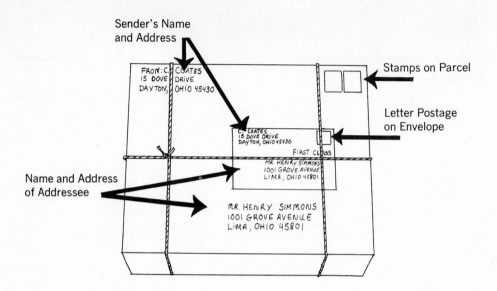

Certificate of Mailing

When the sender needs positive proof of mailing, he may secure a certificate of mailing from the post office upon payment of a fee of 5 cents for each piece of mail. This fee does not guarantee delivery, does not provide a receipt for delivery, and does not insure against loss, damage, or rifling.

Courtesy United States Postal Service

U.S. POSTAL SERVICE
CERTIFICATE OF MAILING

Affix 5¢ in postage and postmark.

Received From:
Parson Distributors
998 Olmstead Avenue
Bronx, New York 10473

One piece of ordinary mail addressed to:
Mr. Gerald W. Lesher
328 East Garfield Street
Shippensburg, Pennsylvania 17257

MAY BE USED FOR DOMESTIC AND INTERNATIONAL MAIL, DOES NOT PROVIDE FOR INSURANCE.   — POSTMASTER

Special Handling

Special handling service hastens the movement of third- and fourth-class mail. Parcels for which the special handling fee has been paid receive the most expeditious handling, dispatch, and transportation from both the post office from which it is mailed to the post office which receives it. Current fees, based on weight, are shown below.

SPECIAL DELIVERY
(Fees in addition to postage)

Class of Mail	Weight		
	Not more than 2 pounds	More than 2 pounds but not more than 10 pounds	More than 10 pound
First class, air, and priority mail	60¢	75¢	90¢
All other classes ..	80¢	90¢	1.05¢

SPECIAL HANDLING

THIRD- AND FOURTH-CLASS ONLY
(Fees in addition to postage)

Weight	Fee
Not more than 2 pounds	25¢
More than 2 pounds but not more than 10 pounds	35¢
More than 10 pounds	50¢

Courtesy United States Postal Service

Certified Mail (Domestic Only)

This relatively inexpensive service provides for a proof of mailing and a record of delivery by the post office. There is no protection against loss. The basic fee is 30 cents in addition to postage at the first-class rate.

Restricted delivery to a designated person only and return receipt service are available at extra cost.

Restricted delivery	$.50
Return receipt requested at time of mailing:	
Showing to whom and when delivered.	.15
Showing to whom, when, and address where delivered.	.35
Return receipt requested after mailing:	
Showing to whom and when delivered.	.25
Showing to whom, when, and address where delivered.	.45

Registered Mail

This service provides special protection for valuable mail such as money or securities which are considered negotiable, that is, securities which anyone can sell for cash. Registered mail furnishes evidence of delivery and provides for indemnity against loss. All registered mail, whatever its shape, packaging, or size, must go first-class or airmail. Registry fees are figured according to the valuation of the material shipped, with a minimum fee of 95 cents.

In general, it's easy to tell or find out what the value is of the merchandise you are mailing. However, you may frequently be puzzled about the value to be declared on business papers or certain stock certificates. It's best to ask. Some firms have standard instructions that you are told to follow when mailing items such as these. For example, many papers and documents which have no value in themselves but which would be difficult or time-consuming to duplicate are registered at the minimum post office valuation for the main purpose of assuring extra care and protection while they are in transit. For an extra fee you may request a receipt as evidence of delivery of registered mail. For still another fee you may request restricted delivery, which means that delivery may be made only to the person whose name appears on the address; no one else may sign for it and accept it.

Insured Mail

Third- and fourth-class mail includes merchandise and other material subject to damage and loss. Protection against these risks may be secured upon payment of an insurance fee based upon valuation, which cannot exceed $200.

REGISTRY FEES

Declared Value*		Fees	
		If Mailer Does Not Have Commercial or Other Insurance	If Mailer Has Commercial or Other Insurance
$ .01 to $ 100		$ .95	$ .95
100.01 to 200		1.25	1.25
200.01 to 400		1.55	1.55
400.01 to 600		1.85	1.85
600.01 to 800		2.15	2.15
800.01 to 1,000		2.45	2.45
1,000.01 to 2,000		2.75	$2.45 plus handling charge of 20 cents per $1,000 or fraction over first $1,000.
2,000.01 to 3,000		3.05	
3,000.01 to 4,000		3.35	
4,000.01 to 5,000		3.65	
5,000.01 to 6,000		3.95	
6,000.01 to 7,000		4.25	
7,000.01 to 8,000		4.55	
8,000.01 to 9,000		4.85	
9,000.01 to 10,000		5.15	
10,000.01 to 1,000,000		$5.15 plus 20 cents per $1,000 or fraction above $10,000.	
$1,000,000.01 to $15,000,000		$203.15 plus 15 cents per $1,000 or fraction above first $1,000,000.	$202.25 plus 15 cents per $1,000 or fraction above first $1,000,000.
Over $15,000,000		Additional charges may be applied, based on consideration of weight, space, and value.	

*Must be full value.

Restricted delivery and return receipt services are available for mail that is insured for over $15. The additional fees are the same as those mentioned previously for certified mail.

COD Service

The U.S. Postal Service offers a collect-on-delivery service for businessmen who ship merchandise orders not paid for in advance. The delivering carrier collects the amount due from the buyer before releasing the parcel. Fees cover insurance protection as well as the collection service. The charges—in addition to postage—vary according to the amount to be collected from the receiver and the insurance coverage on the material.

INSURANCE FEES	
Valuation	*Fee*
$ .01 to $ 15	$.20
15.01 to 50	.30
50.01 to 100	.40
100.01 to 150	.50
150.01 to 200	.60

COD FEES	
Collection Value	*Fee*
$ .01 to $ 10	$ .70
10.01 to 25	.80
25.01 to 50	.90
50.01 to 100	1.00
100.01 to 200	1.10

International Mail

Since World War II the volume of international and personal mail has increased steadily as a natural result of our nation's broader involvement in foreign trade, travel, aid programs, and countless special projects. Many concerns have established branch offices and factories abroad, and others have large foreign staffs constantly on the move in connection with buying and selling operations. For that reason questions about foreign mail services, rates, and regulations arise with growing frequency in more and more offices.

For information on international mailings, consult the *Postal Service Manual* and *Directory of International Mail*. Weight and dimension limitations as well as rates vary widely according to the destination of the material. In general, bear in mind that the domestic classes or categories of mail do not apply in international postal service. Instead, mail is divided into two basic categories: Postal Union items and parcel post. The Postal Union classification covers a wide range of items known as LC and AO mail. Note the chart on page 152.

LC mail These letters stand for letters and cards. The category consists of letters and cards, letter packages, and Aerograms—letter forms that become their own envelopes when folded.

LETTERS AND LETTER PACKAGES

Definition: Written or recorded communications having the character of actual and personal correspondence must be sent as letter mail. Unless prohibited by the country of destination, dutiable merchandise may be transmitted in packages prepaid at the letter rate of postage.

Weight limit: 4 pounds to all countries except Canada; Canada, 60 pounds.

Surface rates:

1 Canada and Mexico, 10 cents per ounce to 12 ounces; eighth zone priority rates apply for heavier weights.
2 Countries other than Canada and Mexico, 1 ounce, 18 cents; over 1 to 2 ounces, 31 cents; over 2 to 4 ounces, 41 cents; over 4 to 8 ounces, 92 cents; over 8 ounces to 1 pound, $1.74; over 1 to 2 pounds, $2.89; and over 2 to 4 pounds, $4.62.

Air rates for letters:

1 Canada and Mexico, 13 cents per ounce.
2 Central America, South America, the Caribbean islands, Bahamas, Bermuda, and St. Pierre and Miquelon, 21 cents per half ounce up to and including 2 ounces; 17 cents each additional half ounce or fraction thereof.
3 All other countries, 26 cents per half ounce up to and including 2 ounces; 21 cents each additional half ounce or fraction thereof.
4 Aerograms, which can be folded into the form of an envelope and sent by air to all countries, are available at post offices for 18 cents each.

AO mail   These letters stand for other articles. The category includes printed matter, matter for the blind, and small packets. Note the rates listed below.

AIRMAIL OTHER ARTICLES

1 Mexico, Central America, the Caribbean islands, Bahamas, Bermuda, and St. Pierre and Miquelon: 50 cents for the first 2 ounces and 13 cents for each additional 2 ounces.
2 South America, Europe (except Estonia, Latvia, Lithuania, and U.S.S.R.), and Mediterranean Africa: 60 cents for the first 2 ounces and 24 cents each additional 2 ounces.
3 Estonia, Latvia, Lithuania, U.S.S.R., Asia, the Pacific, and Africa (other than Mediterranean): 70 cents for the first 2 ounces and 35 cents for each additional 2 ounces.

Parcel post   Merchandise may be routed by surface or by air. The surface rates vary according to country (see Foreign Surface Parcel Post rates on page 153).

Since air transportation to distant countries is so much faster than surface travel, airmail service is frequently used in international mailings to send parcels as well as letters. See the Air Parcel Post Rates table on page 153.

AIRMAIL STATIONERY

Since postage on airmail letters is calculated by the half ounce, office clerks and secretaries are cautioned to be "weight conscious" in preparing and dispatching letters abroad. One popular way to save money is to use so-called airmail weight letterheads and envelopes. This lightweight stationery may look like or actually be onionskin paper. Despite its light weight, it is sufficiently durable for the purpose. Envelopes with a printed pattern on the inside are generally preferred with this type of stationery because they are difficult to see through. A two-page letter and envelope of this weight paper can be sent to Europe for 26 cents (if it is not more than 1/2 ounce), while the same message on regular stationery would cost 52 cents—a worthwhile savings of 50 percent, which could total to a savings of many dollars in the course of a year.

AIR PARCEL POST RATES

Country	First 4 Oz.	Each Additional 4 Oz. or Fraction
Afghanistan	$2.53	$0.96
Albania	2.68	.63
Algeria	2.18	.64
Andorra (Republic of)	2.25	.56
Argentina	1.98	.86
Ascension	. . . .	. . . .
Australia	2.11	.97
Austria	2.17	.59
Azores	1.57	.45
Bahamas	1.76	.21
Bahrain (State of)	1.95	.83
Bangladesh (People's Republic of)	2.79	.98
Barbados	1.53	.41
Belgium	1.94	.53
Belize	1.52	.38
Bermuda	1.42	.28
Bhutan	. . . . .	. . . .
Bolivia	1.99	.55

FOREIGN SURFACE PARCEL POST
Service Available

Parcel post service is available to most countries.

Rates
Surface rates: For Canada and Mexico, Central America, the Caribbean islands, Bahamas, Bermuda, and St. Pierre and Miquelon, $1.40 for 2 pounds or less and 40 cents for each additional pound or fraction. For all other countries, $1.55 for 2 pounds or less and 45 cents for each additional pound or fraction.

Air rates: See Air Parcel Post Rates table above.

REVIEWING YOUR READING

1 Cite six examples of written material used in business communications, besides letters and postcards, that must bear first-class postage.

2 If a letter weighs $3\frac{1}{2}$ ounces and the first-class postage rate is 10 cents per ounce, how much postage must be affixed to the envelope? Explain.

3 What amount of postage is required for domestic airmail on a $6\frac{1}{2}$-ounce first-class envelope? On a 10-ounce envelope being mailed to Zone 8?   ce

4 What service should be used to expedite delivery of a letter or parcel that might arrive at a destination city in the late afternoon or over a weekend? How is this special service obtained?

5 What service would you purchase to send a first-class letter when the boss says, "Be sure to get proof of delivery"?

6 What is the total cost of sending a 4-ounce envelope containing a covering letter and two $5,000 registered bond certificates (nonnegotiable) by registered airmail and of obtaining a receipt showing to whom and when it was delivered?

7 Compute the postage required to mail a 4-pound 8-ounce parcel insured for $150 to Zone 4.

8 How much would it cost to send a 4-pound uninsured parcel of merchandise from the United States to Belgium by surface parcel post? by airmail?

OFFICE ASSIGNMENTS

1 Here is a list of items to be mailed to various addresses. What class of surface mail applies in each case?

a Package (4 pounds)
b Postal card
c Circulars
d Carton (75 pounds)
e Typed letters
f Written report
g Merchandise sample (4 ounces)
h Double postcard
i Newspaper
j Seeds (12 ounces)

2 In the list of mailings below, the postage for each ounce or fraction of an ounce is 10 cents for first-class mail and 13 cents for airmail. Calculate the postage for each item.

a First-class mail, 10 ounces
b Airmail, $8\frac{1}{4}$ ounces
c First-class mail, $2\frac{1}{2}$ ounces
d Airmail, $1\frac{3}{4}$ ounces
e First-class mail, $12\frac{1}{2}$ ounces
f First-class mail, 2 ounces
g Airmail, 4 ounces
h First-class mail, $2\frac{1}{4}$ ounces
i First-class mail, $\frac{3}{4}$ ounce
j First-class mail, $8\frac{1}{2}$ ounces
k Airmail, $\frac{1}{2}$ ounce
l First-class mail, $14\frac{3}{4}$ ounces
m Airmail, $3\frac{3}{4}$ ounces
n First-class mail, $\frac{1}{2}$ pound
o First-class mail, $3\frac{1}{4}$ ounces

3 Using the mail rates specified in the text, compute the proper postage for the following items of surface mail.

   a A typed business letter, enclosed in a sealed envelope, weighing 2 ounces, to be sent special delivery to a neighboring state.

   b A 2-pound parcel, insured for minimum value, to be sent with special handling service to a town in Zone 4.

   c A 3-ounce first-class envelope, for which a receipt showing to whom, when, and address where delivered are required, to be sent to a nearby town. Receipt requested at time of mailing.

   d A 1½-ounce envelope of valuable papers to be registered for the minimum fee.

   e A 6-pound package to be sent to a local address COD for $15.

4 Airmail is being used with increased frequency. Compute the cost of airmail service for the following items:

   a A 7-ounce, sealed, first-class envelope.

   b A 3-pound package to be sent to a town in Zone 8.

   c A 2-ounce letter, registered for $50.

   d A 3-ounce envelope addressed special delivery to Washington, D.C., with certificate of mailing requested.

   e A 1½-ounce letter registered for minimum value, with return receipt requested at time of mailing to show to whom and when delivered.

5 Foreign mail operations are covered by special rates and regulations. Determine the correct postage for the following international items:

   a A 2½-ounce airmail letter to Austria.

   b A 2-pound merchandise airmail parcel to the Azores.

   c A 6-ounce airmail parcel (AO mail) to Bermuda.

   d A 3-ounce airmail letter to Argentina.

   e A 1½-ounce airmail letter to Australia.

UNIT 5

BUSINESS CASES AND PROBLEMS

In the Boss's Shoes   1 You have been requested by the mail room supervisor to take a two-week turn on the early shift (7:30 a.m. to 3:30 p.m.) in the mail room to where you have been recently assigned. Frankly, you feel that the schedule is going to upset to a great extent your regular routine, especially your social life. Should you refuse the assignment? Should you complain to the office manager? Should you request a transfer?

2 Among other duties you are in sole charge of all mailing operations in a small company. The firm has received a number of complaints from customers about delays in the delivery of letters and parcels. When the boss visits the mail room, you assure him that you are doing your best to get the mail out. However, you admit that there are some days when you do not have much time to handle the mail because you have to attend to other assignments. Consequently, some of the letters are not dispatched until the next day. If you know that things are not "going right," should you simply keep quiet until the boss discovers the trouble for himself?

3 As many as four or five separate shipments may be sent to certain large customers in a single day. Matching invoices are then sent separately in window envelopes from your mail room. Yesterday, the office manager inspected the outgoing invoice mail and discovered several cases in which more than one envelope was being sent to the same customer. He estimated that at least 90 cents might have been saved if you had consolidated all of the invoices going to the same customer in a single envelope. He was obviously being critical, and to defend yourself you said, "But nobody ever told me to do it that way." Was the boss justified in being concerned about unnecessary expense? Are you supposed to do just what you are told to do and no more?

Your Human Relations   1 A registered piece of mail was received several days ago, and you reported its arrival at that time to the mail room supervisor, so that he could record it in his log book. He instructed you to deliver it to the waiting executive and then to return to your normal duties. This morning upon checking the log regarding another matter you discover that the receipt of the registered letter was never recorded and that several entries have been made since that time. Should you call your supervisor's attention to the oversight? How? Or should you ignore this matter since it is not your direct responsibility?

2 You are a messenger making a scheduled 4:45 p.m. mail pickup in the accounting department. The chief accountant asks you to wait a minute while he puts the finishing touches on some reports that have to go out tonight. If you don't get back to the mail room promptly, you know that the rest of the mail on your cart may be delayed. Should you refuse the chief accountant's request? Explain what you would do or say.

3 In the few weeks that you have been employed in your new job, you have observed what you believe to be wasteful postage practices. Some of your co-workers never use a postal scale. They simply guess at the weight of an envelope and put the stamps on, allowing extra postage for an item if they aren't sure of its weight. At other times they request unnecessary costly services, such as air-mail and special delivery, on nonurgent items or on items being mailed over weekends. Should you tell them about the waste, or mind your own business?

What Would You Do If . . . ?   **1**   You open an envelope and time-stamp the enclosed letter. Then you realize that the item was personal, and a notation to that effect was clearly marked on the outside of the envelope.

2   You observe that a number of employees use company envelopes and letterheads for writing personal correspondence during lunch hour. Then in order to avoid paying for stamps, they place unstamped sealed letters in the outgoing mail basket for processing with company mail through the firm's postage meter.

3   You have worked overtime at the office until quite late to complete a report that you have promised to mail on your way home. After weighing the envelope and figuring the postage, you discover that you do not have enough stamps to cover the cost. The firm's stamps are locked in a safe for which you do not know the combination. The post office is closed at this hour, and there is no one else in the office who might lend you some stamps. Assume that no special services are required.

What Does This Mean?   **1**   Much of the day's activities in a business office are determined by what is in the morning's mail.

2   The less time you spend in handling the mail, the more time you save.

3   Office clerks and secretaries must be "weight conscious" in preparing and dispatching letters abroad.

Business in Your Area   **1**   Visit your post office and inquire about the job opportunities in the U.S. Postal Service. Find out how to apply for a postal job and what kinds of examinations are given to a prospective employee like yourself.

2   Mail-order houses, banks, insurance companies, and utilities are normally the largest mailers in the community. Visit one of these firms, and find out how their mail unit is equipped and how it operates. Also, ask about the job opportunities for young people in mail operations, including part-time openings during rush periods.

3   Visit your local postmaster and ask: **(a)** How many letters and parcels are received and dispatched during an average week of postal operations? **(b)** What are the best days and hours for dispatching large quantities of mail at the post office? **(c)** What are the ways (including preliminary sorting) in which business mailers can help postal workers to keep the mail moving?

UNIT 6
TYPING IN THE BUSINESS OFFICE

No single office machine is used more widely than the typewriter, and it would be safe to say that no office skill is more in demand than typing. As a good typist you will be called on to type many documents. Chief among these will be the business letter. How well you set up your business letter and how accurately you type it will reveal a great deal about you to your employer as well as to the letter's recipient. Yet, all it takes to become a typist of professional caliber is steady practice and experience.

THE IMPACT OF A BUSINESS LETTER

Attractive people draw second glances, and attractive letters get better attention. To be effective, a business letter must make a good first impression. The quality of the paper and the printing of the company's letterhead are of some importance, of course, but more important in creating that favorable first impression is the placement of a letter on the page and the accuracy and evenness of the typing. Correct typographical errors when you must — that's what erasers are for — but do so neatly and carefully so that the erasures barely can be seen. Set margins and choose the proper spacing for the parts of the letter that are appropriate for the particular letter you are writing.

COMPONENTS OF A BUSINESS LETTER

A business letter has the following standard parts, which are identified by number in the illustration on page 167.

Letterhead (1)   Body (5)
Date line (2)   Complimentary closing (6)
Inside address (3)   Signer's identification line (7)
Salutation (4)   Reference initials (8)

In addition, a business letter *may* contain some or all of the following:

Attention line   Carbon copy notation
Subject line   Blind carbon copy notation
Company signature line Postscript
Enclosure notation (9)

Letterhead

A company's printed letterhead always gives its name and address. It may also include the telephone number, a list of branch offices, the company's slogan, and similar information.

Date Line

Every business letter should be dated with the month, the day of the month, and the year. The correct way to type the date line is as follows: February 15, 19—. Never abbreviate the month or use *st, nd, d, rd,* or *th* after the day of the month. When you type the date, don't use just figures, such as 2/15/75 or 2-15-75.

Inside Address

The inside address may contain all of the following parts: the name and title of the person to whom the letter is addressed, the name of the addressee's company, the street address, the city and state, and the ZIP Code. For example:

Mr. J. E. Dent, President   Mr. William O. Smithson
Dent Trucking Company   570 Eastland Village Drive
1365 East Broad Street   Detroit, Michigan 48225
Columbus, Ohio 43205

The business title can be typed on the same line as the name of the addressee or on the same line as the company name. However, if you want to obtain a better balance, type the title on a line by itself.

Mr. Lyman Harrington
Director of Marketing
Metal Fabricating Corporation
295 Whit Avenue
Norfolk, Virginia 23503

If the letter is addressed to the company, use a three-line arrangement.

Beacon Auto Parts Company
649 Riverside Avenue
Princeton, Minnesota 55371

Avoid abbreviating names of streets, cities, and countries. However, the abbreviation of the state name is standard practice. You may use the traditional abbreviations, write out the state name in full if you prefer, or use the two-letter abbreviations authorized by the U.S. Postal Service. The two-letter abbreviations are typed in all capitals without periods or a space between the letters. (For the list of state abbreviations, see Section 11, page 134.)

Abbreviations are useful and can be used. However, it is more attractive to spell out the state name.

Always type the city, state, and ZIP Code on the last line of the address. Don't use a comma after the state name, whether it is abbreviated or written out. Instead, leave one space between the state name and the ZIP Code.

Attention Line

The attention line is really a part of the inside address. It consists of the word *Attention* followed by the name of a person or business title of a person or the name of a department within the company. Type the attention line between the inside address and the salutation, and leave one blank line space above and below it. You can display the attention line in many ways: capitals and small letters with all letters underscored or with no letters underscored or with just the word attention underscored or with just the name of the person or department underscored. Or you can type it in all capitals. The word Attention may or may not be followed by a colon, or the words *Attention of* may be used.

Victor Insurance Company	Victor Insurance Company
2115 Scenic Avenue	2115 Scenic Avenue
Los Angeles, California 90068	Los Angeles, California 90068
ATTENTION: SALES MANAGER	Attention Mr. Rimer
Gentlemen:	Gentlemen:

The attention line may be blocked at the left margin, indented the same amount of space as the paragraph, or centered on the page.

Salutation

The salutation is the opening greeting of the letter. It is always blocked at the left margin and has one blank line space above and below it. (The salutation is omitted in the simplified letter form. See model letter on page 171.)

In a salutation capitalize only the first word, names, and titles. It is important to use an appropriate salutation. In selecting one, consider both the position of the person being addressed and the general tone of the message. Approved forms of salutations include the following.

For a letter addressed to a firm:

Ladies (firm composed of women)	Gentlemen (firm composed of men or men and women)

For a letter addressed to a person:

Dear Mr. Brown	Dear Mrs. Brown
Dear Dr. Carter	Dear Miss Wyley
Dear Reverend Howerton	Dear Ms. Zader (marital status unknown)
Dear Sir (more formal)	Dear Madam (more formal)

You would use a formal salutation, such as *My dear Mr. Holmes,* for letters to persons whose positions command great respect or to government officials. If an addressee is a close personal or business friend, it is quite correct to use the very informal *Dear Bob* or *Dear Anne.*

Subject Line

The subject line may consist of the word *Subject* or the Latin term *Re* or *In Re,* followed by a notation that may be used in filing—a statement that gives the main point of the message or a similar reference. The subject line follows the salutation and is typed with one blank line space above and below it. It may be displayed by using all-capital letters or capitals and small letters that are underscored, and it may be blocked at the left margin, indented as the paragraphs, or centered on the page.

Body

The body of the letter is the message. Except in very short letters, the body is always single-spaced. If it is double-spaced, the paragraphs should be indented. Always leave one blank line space between the body and the salutation or the subject line. Avoid dividing words at the end of lines. If it is absolutely necessary to divide a word in order to maintain a fairly even right margin, check the dictionary for the correct word division. Try to have at least two paragraphs in each letter, and no matter how many paragraphs there are, keep them short.

Complimentary Closing

The complimentary closing follows the body of the letter and is typed on the second line below the last line of the body of the letter. Capitalize only the first word of the complimentary closing, and remember to use a form of closing that agrees with the formality or informality of the salutation.

The following are approved forms of complimentary closings.

To show great respect:

Respectfully yours	Yours respectfully
Very respectfully yours	Yours very respectfully

Formal (also used when the salutation is *Gentlemen* or *Dear Sir*):

Yours very truly	Very truly yours

Somewhat less formal (used when a name is in salutation, such as *Dear Mr. Jones*):

Sincerely yours	Yours sincerely
Yours very sincerely	Very sincerely yours

More personal and friendly:

Cordially yours	Yours cordially
Yours very cordially	Very cordially yours

Company Signature Line

The company signature is the name of the business firm. It may or may not be included at the end of a business letter. When it is, the name is typed in all-capital letters on the second line below the complimentary closing. For example:

Cordially yours,

THE WIDEWAYS PAVING COMPANY

Henry Ullman, Sales Manager

In order to look attractive, business letters must be typed accurately and evenly and placed correctly on the page.

Courtesy Breck

Signer's Identification Line

This line may consist either of the typed name of the one who signs the letter, the typed name and business title of the signer (in either a one-line or two-line arrangement), the business title of the signer, or the department of the signer. The signer's identification is usually typed on the fourth line below the company signature line or the complimentary closing, but also it may be typed on the third or the fifth line below either of the closing lines. For example:

Yours very truly,   Yours very truly,

                                      John A. Rynerson
H. B. Evans, President   Training Director

Since *Mr.* is the only courtesy title for men, it is not included with either the typed name or the written signature except when the first name cannot be easily identified as a man's.

Miss, Mrs., Ms., or no courtesy title is used for women, depending upon their personal preference. When it is part of the written signature, the courtesy title appears in parentheses; when the courtesy title is included in the typed name, it is not put in parentheses.

Reference Initials

The reference initials identify the signer of the letter and the typist. If the signer's name is typed in the signer's identification line, it is not necessary to repeat his initials in the reference line; however, if the signer wishes his initials to be used, they precede those of the typist. If the signer's name is *not* typed in the signer's identification line, his or her name may be typed in full in the reference line. Initials also can be used.

Reference initials are blocked at the left margin and typed preferably on the second line below the signer's identification line. If it is necessary to save space, type the reference initials on the same line as the signer's identification line. Here are some examples of different styles of reference initials:

ABS:RG   ABS:G   abs/g   A. B. Smith/rg   rdg   ABS/rg

Enclosures and Carbon Copy Notations

Indicate that an item is enclosed in the envelope with the letter by typing the word *Enclosure* (or *Enc.*) on the line below the reference initials. If there is more than one enclosure, type either *Enclosures* (or *Encs.*) and note the number of enclosures. The following are typical forms of enclosure notations:

Enclosure   Encs. 2   3 Enclosures   Enclosures:
                                                             1. Check
                                                             2. Money order

If carbon copies of the letter are to be sent to a person or persons other than the addressee, type a *cc* notation in either lower case or caps at the left margin on the line below the enclosure notation (if used) or on the line below the reference initials. *CC* may or may not be followed by a colon.

cc: Mr. John W. Craig   CC Mrs. Mary Walsh
                                   Mr. Barry Smith

If the addressee is not to know that a carbon copy is being sent to someone else, remove the original letter and then type a *bcc* (blind carbon copy) notation on the carbon copy (or copies). That notation is typed on line 6 at the left margin at the top of the carbon copy. BCC notations follow the same style as the cc notations.

bcc Mr. Fred C. Smith

Postscript

A postscript is an additional paragraph which is typed two lines below the cc notation or another preceding line. It is typed in the same style as the paragraphs in the letter—blocked or indented. A postscript may be used to express an afterthought or to give extra emphasis to a major point of the letter. It is generally indicated by *PS* or *P.S.*, with or without a colon.

LETTER PLACEMENT

White space has great value in written communications. Never crowd a letter just to get it on a single page. Copy is more inviting to read and easier to understand when it is framed with adequate margins. Decide whether the length of your letter warrants one or two pages, and place it accordingly on the sheet of paper. Note that pica type has ten spaces to the inch and elite type twelve. Check to see which typeface your machine has. All standard machines space vertically six lines to the inch.

One-Page Letter

The typical business letter is typed on 8½- by 11-inch bond letterhead paper and generally looks best if it is centered on the paper, with the printed letterhead at the top and white space at the bottom and side margins.

Letters vary in length, and you'll need skill, judgment, and experience in deciding where to position the letter. In order to get a balanced appearance, learn how to estimate the length of a letter to determine whether it is short, average, or long.

The body of a short letter consists of fewer than 100 words, while an average letter contains between 100 and 200 words. Add 20 words for every display line, that is, every line in addition to the message portion of the letter. You won't always need to count the words. In time, you'll get the knack of estimating the letter length.

Once you determine the length of the letter you are going to type, set the margin stops and allow proper spacing for the letter parts. An easy way to do this is to use the 4-5-6 placement plan. For a *short* letter of 100 words or less, make your typing line 4 inches long. That yields 40 characters of pica type and 48 characters of elite type, which can be rounded to 50. Depending on the kind of type your machine has, set the left and right margin stops so that there are either 40 or 50 character spaces between them. For an average letter of 100 to 200 words, make your line 5 inches long with a yield of 50 pica character spaces and 60 elite character spaces. Set your margin stops accordingly. And for a long letter of 200 words or for a letter of two pages, use a line 6 inches long with a yield of 60 pica character spaces or 72 elite character spaces, which, for convenience, can be rounded to 70. With your margins set, space to the correct starting position of your letter as follows:

Date: Start on the fifteenth line from the top of the page or three lines below the last line of the letterhead, whichever is lower.

Inside address: Start on the fifth line below the date.

Two-Page Letter

When a letter requires more than one page, type the second page (and any succeeding pages) on plain paper of the same quality and color as the first page with the letterhead. Use the same left and right margins that were used on the first page. Start the second-page heading on the seventh line (leaving a 1-inch margin) from the top. The heading should contain the name of the addressee, the page number, and the date. The following are acceptable forms for the heading:

Mr. William O. Manring   2   November 6, 19—

Mr. William O. Manring
Page 2
November 6, 19—

Begin the body of the letter three lines below the second-page heading. If you must divide a paragraph at the bottom of the first page, leave at least two lines on the first page and carry over at least two lines to the second page. Don't divide the last word on a page. Remember that the second page should always contain at least three lines of the body of the letter.

Short, Short Letter

If the letter to be typed consists of no more than a sentence or two, modify the 4-5-6 plan by double-spacing the letter and placing it on the sheet in the most attractive way. You'll get the knack of how to do this with experience. The process involves estimating the number of lines that the note will require, including all standard parts and spacing, and then centering the letter on the sheet.

LETTER PUNCTUATION FORMS

There are three forms of punctuation that you can select for use in business letters: *standard* (or *mixed*), *open*, and *close* (or *full*).

In the standard or mixed style of punctuation, a colon is used after the salutation, and a comma after the complimentary closing. In the open style no punctuation is used at the end of any line outside the body of the letter unless that line ends with an abbreviation. The close or full style (which is very seldom used) has punctuation marks after each line outside the body of the letter. The three punctuation forms are summarized here:

Letter Part	Standard (mixed)	Open	Close (full)
Date	May 10, 19—	May 10, 19—	May 10, 19—.
Inside address	Mr. W. S. Jones	Mr. W. S. Jones	Mr. W. S. Jones,
	Jones Brothers, Inc.	Jones Brothers, Inc.	Jones Brothers, Inc.,
	625 East 24 Street	625 East 24 Street	625 East 24 Street,
	Ames, Iowa 50010	Ames, Iowa 50010	Ames, Iowa 50010.
Salutation	Dear Mr. Jones:	Dear Mr. Jones	Dear Mr. Jones:
Complimentary closing	Yours very truly,	Yours very truly	Yours very truly,

LETTER STYLES

Several letter styles are used in business. Five of these letter styles are illustrated and explained on the pages that follow.

Blocked

In this letter style all lines begin at the left margin except the date and the closing line. The closing line begins at the center of the page, and the date may either begin at the center of the page or end at the right margin. Standard punctuation has been used in the model letter shown below.

FRIBURMON

1 CALCULATING MACHINE COMPANY

2232 FIFTH AVENUE, MILWAUKEE, WISCONSIN 53236

2 October 14, 19-- (Line 15)

3
Mr. Lee R. Kline, Manager (Line 20)
Griffin & Hartley, Inc.
5879 K Street
Sacramento, California 95819

4 Dear Mr. Kline:

The blocked form is the letter style most frequently used in business.

The date usually ends at or near the right margin. Use the backspace key to determine the point at which to start typing. The date can also begin at the center of the page or be placed at any point that results in an attractive alignment with some part of the printed letterhead.

5
In standard punctuation, no punctuation is used after the date or any line in the inside address except after a line that ends with an abbreviation, such as "Inc." A colon is placed after the salutation, and a comma after the complimentary closing.

Start the complimentary closing at the center of the paper. If a company signature is used, type it in all-capital letters on the second line below the complimentary closing.

The signer's identification is blocked four lines below the company signature or the complimentary closing if no company signature is used. The signer's title may be typed on the same line with his name. However, if his title is long, such as "General Manager" or "Supervisor, Media Merchandising Activities," it could be typed on the line below his name or broken and carried over to the second line. The word "Enclosures," in the reference notation shows that additional papers are being enclosed in the envelope.

6 Very sincerely yours,

Charles A. Gordon

7 Charles A. Gordon, Head
Adjustment Department

8 CAG:REM
9 Enclosures

Blocked

Full Blocked

This letter style is quite popular probably because it is so easy to type. All lines, including the date, begin at the left margin. Open punctuation is frequently used in the full-blocked letter.

COMPTON
INSURANCE AGENCY
33 Redding Road, Hartford, Connecticut 06114

February 2, 19--

Mr. Lloyd R. McConnell, Jr.
Director of Personnel
The Province Corporation
Market and Sansome Streets
San Francisco, California 94109

Dear Lloyd

In the full-blocked letter every line begins at the left margin. A full-blocked letter is never double-spaced.

If a typed company signature is part of the closing, it should be typed in all-capital letters two lines below the complimentary closing. If a company signature is not used, the signer's name and/or identification is typed four lines below the complimentary closing.

Note the form of the reference notations. Other accepted forms could, of course, be used with this letter style.

When letters are sent by other than regular mail, notations such as "Registered" and "Special Delivery" can be typed in small letters below the reference initials or the enclosure notation. This information can also be typed in all-capital letters two lines below the date line.

Sincerely yours

COMPTON INSURANCE AGENCY

Louis Allen
Service Office

Louis Allen/sun
Registered

Full blocked

Semiblocked

This letter style is the same as the blocked form except that the first line of each paragraph is indented. In the model letter shown below, standard punctuation has been used.

HYLE-McCANN
BALTIMORE, MARYLAND ▪ 21203

September 17, 19--

The Glenn Phillips Industrial
    Fabricating & Processing Company
1853 Third Avenue
New Orleans, Louisiana 70113

Attention of Mr. Graham

Gentlemen:

    The semiblocked form is like the blocked form except that in the semiblocked form the paragraphs are indented five spaces.

    The date usually ends at or near the right margin. Use the backspace key to determine the point at which to start typing. The date can also begin at the center of the page or be placed at any point that results in an attractive alignment with some part of the printed letterhead.

    The attention line can be positioned as shown here, that is, blocked at the left margin, or it can be centered. It may be written in all-capital letters. It is not necessary to use either a colon or the word "of" in the attention line.

    Since a letter having an attention line is addressed to a firm, the salutation used should be "Gentlemen" or, if appropriate, "Mesdames" or "Ladies" or "Ladies and Gentlemen."

    Some companies use only the typist's initials in the reference notation, as shown here, if the dictator's name is included in the signer's identification line. The notation "cc" indicates that a carbon copy is being sent to one or more persons, whose company name and address may also be included.

                                        Sincerely yours,

                                        R. C. Perry

                                        R. C. Perry, Sales Manager

obf
cc: Mr. Lewis

Semiblocked

Indented

This is a carry-over from penmanship practices of the past. The lines of the inside address and the closing are indented in steps of five spaces each. The date is typed at the right. The first line of each paragraph is indented. Below, close punctuation is shown. The indented style is rarely used in this country.

Reliable Products Company

512 Spring Street
Akron, Ohio 44304

March 8, 19--.

Miss Jane Grey,

    2831 Tall Oak Court,

        Kingsport, Tennessee 37663.

Dear Miss Grey:

    The indented style is one of the few that may be typed either single-spaced or double-spaced. The double-spaced form is convenient to use when you have a short letter that must be stretched.

    When you plan the placement of a double-spaced letter, you must remember that it will stretch out to twice its single-spaced length. This letter of 73 words, double-spaced, occupies as much space as would a single-spaced letter of 146 words.

                Cordially yours,

Irwin Sullivan
                  District Manager.

HIS/urs.

cc Mr. Wilson.

Indented

Simplified

The Administrative Management Society is interested in the improvement and simplification of letter writing. With the hope of speeding letter output and processing, it devised the simplified letter style. This is based on the time-saving and effort-saving full-blocked style with open punctuation. The subject

---

Towle Bros., Inc.

100 Fifth Avenue
New York, N.Y. 10011

March 6, 19--

Mr. Ted Benson
King Paper Products
1000 Kincaid Street
Eugene, Oregon 97401

THE SIMPLIFIED LETTER

You will be interested to know, Mr. Benson, that several years ago the Administrative Management Society (formerly NOMA) designed a new letter form called the simplified letter. This is a sample:

1 It uses the full-blocked form and open punctuation.

2 It contains no salutation or closing. (AMS believes such expressions to be meaningless.)

3 It displays a subject line in all capitals, which is preceded and followed by two blank lines. Note that the word subject is omitted.

4 It identifies the signer by an all-capital line that is preceded by at least four blank lines and followed by one--if further notations are used.

5 It seeks to maintain a brisk but friendly tone, partly by using the addressee's name at least in the first sentence.

Perhaps, Mr. Benson, as some say, this form does not really look like a business letter, but its efficiency suggests that this style is worth a trial, especially where output must be increased.

Ralph E. Jones

RALPH E. JONES, TRAINING CONSULTANT

---

line and signer's identification line are typed in all-capital letters. The subject line is typed with two blank lines above and below it. The salutation and the complimentary closing are omitted, and the reference initials are generally not used. In typing the simplified letter, follow the style on page 171.

FEDERAL GOVERNMENT AND ARMED SERVICES CORRESPONDENCE

When you complete your business training you may take a civil service position with the federal government, which is the largest single employer of clerical workers in the country. Or you may work in one of the armed services where efficient clerical workers are always in demand. The correspondence procedures of these organizations are somewhat different from general business procedures. Because of their huge size, correspondence procedures must be standardized to facilitate follow-up and distribution through many channels.

A Variety of Arrangements

Compare, for example, the illustrations on pages 173 and 174. They are typical of the arrangements that you can expect to find in government correspondence, although changes in format do occur from time to time. Also, there are minor variations in format within the many bureaus of the government and the different services.

Size   Most federal government and military correspondence is typed on stationery which measures 8 by 10½ inches, ½ inch less in both width and height than standard business correspondence stationery.

Number of copies   Each agency is very specific about how many copies to make and who is to get which copy. *It is important that you read the instructions issued in your office very carefully.*

Margins   Your instructions will indicate how much space to leave for side and bottom margins. Typed lines in government and armed services correspondence tend to run longer than they do in regular business correspondence.

Date   You can see from the illustration on page 173 that the federal government style is to write the date as it is written normally. The armed services, however, give the day of the month first, the month, and then the year. (Note the illustration on page 174.) Sometimes a date stamp appears below the typed date to indicate the actual day the correspondence was mailed.

Reference line   "Reply to the Attention of" or "In Reply Refer to" is often printed on the letterhead of the memorandum form. You are expected to fill in the proper information to enable the recipient of the letter to gather together related correspondence easily and quickly. Some departments prefer to type

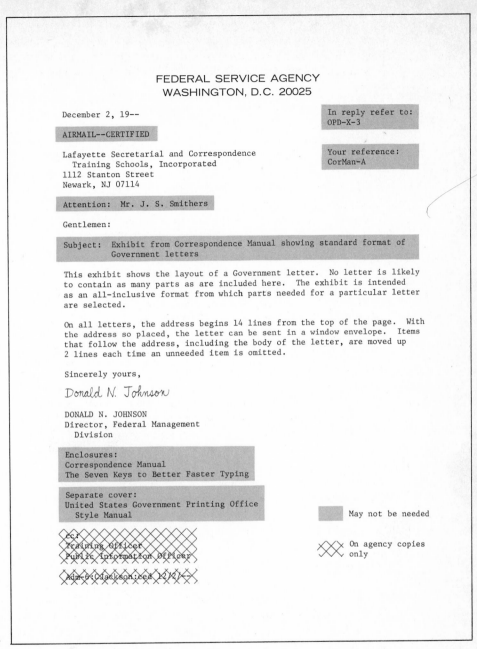

Federal government correspondence

the reference line at the right margin as shown in the illustration above; others type it at the left margin as shown in the illustration on page 174.

Signature and title   For quick identification the name of the signer in armed services letters is typed in all capitals. The title of the signer, though not in capitals, follows on the next line or on as many lines as it takes to write it out in

DEPARTMENT OF THE AIR FORCE
Headquarters United States Air Force
Washington, D.C. 20330

Reply to
Attn of: AFDASCB   20 Feb 19--

Subject: Photograph Required by AFR 36-93

    To: T/Sgt Edward Baker, AF13635187
         1001st Civil Engineers Group
         Andrews AFB
         Washington, D.C. 20330

         1. A screening of your personnel record indicates that your
         photograph is missing or does not satisfy the requirements of
         AFR 36-93.

         2. Request you report to the Photo Lab, Rm 1C356, Pentagon,
         between 0830 and 1130 on Tuesday, Wednesday, or Thursday for
         photographing. The authorized blue service uniform with coat
         including ALL authorized decorations, awards, and badges must
         be worn.

         3. If you are unable to report during the times listed above,
         call Code 11, Extension 52603, to arrange for scheduling. This
         letter is the authorization for the Photo Lab to photograph you.

         W. J. Goodson

         W. J. GOODSON, Major, USAF
         Chief, Unit Personnel Branch
         Directorate of Administrative Services

Armed services correspondence

full. That's because the man may move on to another job, but the title and position remain. By making the title clear, a point of reference is established for further correspondence. The position of the signature and title on the correspondence varies from bureau to bureau and from service to service. Also, in government correspondence the identification of the office, the writer, the typist, and the date of typing are noted on the duplicate copy of the correspondence.

Looking Through the Files

Aside from the special elements mentioned above, you will find that the style and format of government correspondence and armed services correspondence is similar to ordinary business correspondence. The smart thing to do on a new job is to look through the files and observe how letters and memorandums are arranged, how many copies are usually made of correspondence, where special instructions are placed, and anything else that will help you do a good job.

OTHER TYPING TECHNIQUES

The more familiar you become with your typewriter and what it can do, the more professional your letters will look. Make sure you take advantage of all the typing aids with which typewriters are equipped.

Addressing Envelopes

When addressing small envelopes ($6\frac{1}{2}$ by $3\frac{5}{8}$ inches), begin typing the address on line 12, 2 inches from the left edge. For large envelopes ($9\frac{1}{2}$ by $4\frac{1}{8}$ inches), begin typing the address on line 14, 4 inches from the left edge. Use a blocked arrangement and single spacing, regardless of the number of lines in the address.

If the return address is not printed on the envelope, type it in the upper left corner on line 3, $\frac{1}{2}$ inch from the left edge. Type any special notations, such as *Attention, Personal,* or *Please Forward,* on line 9, $\frac{1}{2}$ inch from the left edge, in capital and small letters, underscored. Type mailing notations, such as *SPECIAL DELIVERY, REGISTERED,* or *AIRMAIL* (although this is not necessary if airmail envelopes are used), in all capitals below the postage stamp on line 9 or 10. These notations should end $\frac{1}{2}$ to 1 inch from the right edge. (See illustrations on page 133.)

Making Carbon Copies

It is standard practice to make at least one carbon of every letter, so that you have a complete record of all correspondence in the files. When you prepare a carbon pack, consisting of an original sheet of paper with a letterhead, a sheet of carbon paper, and a second sheet of paper, follow these suggestions:

1   Put the carbon paper between the letterhead and the second sheet of paper, with the coated side of the carbon facing the second sheet. Use additional carbon paper and sheets of paper for every extra copy required.
2   When you insert several sheets into a typewriter at the same time, fold a sheet of paper over the top of the pack, so that the papers will align better. A large envelope also can be used for this purpose. The edges of the carbon pack nest in the crease and feed evenly into the machine.
3   When the carbon pack is in place, disengage the paper release lever, flatten out the papers, and then push back the paper release lever so that it holds the pack of papers firmly in place. Now you are ready to type.
4   After you have typed the letter and removed it from the typewriter, separate the carbon pack. You can speed up this process by choosing carbon paper from which the upper left and lower right corners have been clipped. Some

carbon papers are precut in this manner. If they aren't, allow the carbon to extend about ½ inch below the bottom of the letterhead sheet and second sheet (or sheets) when you arrange the carbons in the pack.

5   Remove the carbons by grasping the upper left corner of the pack with your left hand and by pulling the protruding ends of the carbons with your right. One motion is all it takes.

Making Corrections With Erasers

When you make an error, follow these rules to save time and to obtain the neatest results.

1   Move the carriage of your machine to one side so that erasure crumbs don't fall into the working parts of the machine. Such particles gum up the working mechanism and cause the type bars to stick. On Selectric typewriters move the type element.

2   Roll the paper up a few lines if the error is in the upper two-thirds of the sheet. Roll the paper down if the error is on the lower third of the sheet.

3   Use the correct eraser for the different copies — abrasive (ink) for the original and soft (pencil) for the carbon copies.

4   Make sure that the eraser is clean. A small piece of sandpaper or an emery board will help to clean and sharpen erasers.

5   Touch up lightly. Several light typing strokes are better for proper matching of ink than a single heavy blow.

6   If you have any doubts about the alignment or the location of the type, set the ribbon on stencil position and note where the uninked key impression falls.

7   When you erase carbon copies, be sure to place a stiff card on top of each sheet of carbon in order to protect the copies beneath from being smudged. Use the following procedure:

   a   Place the card between the original copy and the first sheet of carbon paper. Then make your erasure on the original.

   b   Place the card between the first carbon copy and the second sheet of carbon paper. Then make the erasure on the first carbon copy.

   c   Continue this procedure until all copies are erased.

A useful trick at the office is to staple the end of an emery board to the upper right corner of a 3- by 5-inch file card or to a pocket calendar of cardboard or plastic. The emery board serves as a handle to make it easier to get between the sheets in the pack.

Making Corrections With Correction Materials

In addition to erasers, there are other correction materials with which you should become familiar.

Chalk-back paper   Place the chalk-back paper over the error and retype the incorrect letters. As the keys strike, the chalk is transferred to the sheet of paper, concealing the original marks. The spaces are now clear for typing the correct letters.

Correction fluid   White correction fluid is used to paint over and to conceal the error. The correct version can be then typed on the whitened surface. This technique is especially useful when you are typing copy that will be photographed for offset reproduction.

Correction tape   White adhesive-backed tape is cut and applied to the paper to cover the error. Then the correct word or letter is typed on the clean surface of the tape. This is also an acceptable method of making corrections on copy that will be photocopied.

Self-correcting typewriter ribbon   The bottom half of this black ribbon is inked white. To correct an error, you backspace over the letters that are wrong and type those letters again with the white portion of the ribbon. The error is whited out, and you can proceed to type the correct letters.

REVIEWING YOUR READING

1   What is the purpose of the following letter parts **(a)** salutation, **(b)** subject line, and **(c)** reference initials?
2   What is the relationship between the salutation and the complimentary closing of a letter?
3   Explain the use of enclosure notations. What is meant by a blind carbon copy?
4   Why is a postscript sometimes used?
5   Why is the full-blocked letter style so easy to type?

OFFICE ASSIGNMENTS

1   Type an exact copy of the letter illustrated on page 167, using the blocked style and standard punctuation.
2   Type an exact copy of the letter illustrated on page 169, using the semi-blocked style and standard punctuation.
3   Your employer, Mr. William Blanford, sales manager for Compton Insurance Agency, writes a letter to a policyholder, Mr. Robert Baker, 614 Elm Street, Cedar Falls, Iowa 50613, concerning his policy number 2,065,358. Type the current date, inside address, salutation, and subject line for this correspondence. Leave 16 blank lines for the body. Then type the complimentary closing, company name, signer's name and title, and reference initials. Use blocked style and open punctuation.

4 The blocked letter to Mr. Keith H. Furtsch below contains ten hidden errors. Try to find all ten errors; then retype the letter, and make the corrections.

LEXINGTON SPORT SHOP
121 East Main Street
Lexington, Kentucky 40507

February 30, 19--

Mr. Keith H. Furtsch, President
All-America Sportswear, Incorporated
6000 Benson Garden Bulevard
Brockton, Masachusetts 02402

Dear Keith:

Here it is the last day of the month, and I am
just getting around to answering your letter of
the thirteenth. I apologize for the delay, Keith;
things have been extremely busy since January 1.

As you know, our board of directors are definitely
interested in proceeding with the merger plans.
The enclosed summary of our proposed stock transfer arrangments will provide your board of directors
with the information you have requested.

Please give my best regards to Mrs. Furtcsh. I
shall see you in Brockton on March 23.

                    Cordially,

                    W. D. Smyth

                    W. D. Smyth
                    President

CEB:WBS

---

5 Type the following letter on a plain sheet of paper, using the simplified letter style. Begin with a typed, centered letterhead for Towle Brothers, Inc., 100 Fifth Avenue, New York, N.Y. 10011. Make one carbon copy.

May 2, 19—, Mr. Robert M. Kahn, Manager, Corner Music Shop, Corwith, Iowa 50430. Your order March 25. (Paragraph) A duplicate shipment was made as soon as your letter arrived, Mr. Kahn. The parcel was sent air express, charges prepaid, to assure delivery first thing tomorrow morning. (Paragraph) Our records show that your original order was shipped by truck on April 1. The carrier has been asked to trace this shipment. Your account will be adjusted promptly. (Paragraph) Please tell your customer that we sincerely regret the delay and inconvenience. Thank you, Mr. Kahn, for writing so that we could get things straightened out. Thomas W. Jones, Sales Department.

6 Type the following letter for Francis Byrd, Colonel, USAF, Chief of Administration. Use today's date, and replay to the attention of HUSAF. The subject is Field Payroll for Armed Forces Joint Exercises. Address the letter to Commander, Charleston Naval Shipyard, U.S. Naval Base, Charleston, South Carolina 29408. 1. This office will coordinate military field payroll for future Armed Forces Joint Exercises. 2. Civilian payroll will remain the responsibility of the employing service during the exercises. Standard procedures will remain in effect for civilian field pay services.

SECTION 14 Specialized Typing Assignments

In addition to business letters, office typists also prepare other material such as tables, manuscripts, reports, legal documents, interoffice memorandums, financial statements, and press releases. This section outlines procedures to follow in handling such specialized typing assignments.

CENTERING

Headings for tables, charts, and special announcements are most attractively and effectively arranged when they are centered on the page or above the columns of text.

There are a number of quick ways to find the horizontal center of the sheet of paper on which a heading is to be placed. You can fold the sheet in half and make a slight crease at the top edge to indicate the center position. Or you can use a ruler and indicate the center at the top edge of the paper by a light pencil mark. The most efficient way to find the horizontal center is to select a scale number on your typewriter and use it as the centering point. The number 50 is a good centering point because it's easy to remember and will work for either elite or pica typewriters. Now fold a sheet of paper in half, and make a slight crease at the top to indicate the center of the paper. Unfold it, and insert it into the typewriter so that the crease appears at 50 on the scale. You can do this easily by using the paper release. Then adjust the paper guide so that it fits snugly against the left edge of the paper. Note where the paper guide is on the typewriter scale so that you can readily insert other sheets of the same width according to the centering point you select, in this case, 50.

Another way to determine the centering point of a sheet of paper is to observe the scale number at the left edge of the sheet and the scale number at the right edge of the sheet after you have inserted the paper. Add the two scale numbers, and divide the total by 2 to determine the centering point on the scale. For example, if the scale number at the left edge is 9 and the number at the right edge is 111, you add 9 and 111 to get 120. Now you divide 120 by 2, and you get 60 as the centering point.

TABULATION TECHNIQUES

When you must arrange material in table form, study the material and plan its arrangement before you start to type. A good table should be completely self-explanatory and as easy to read as a manuscript.

Horizontal Placement—Backspace Method

1 Clear the machine of all margin and tab stops.
2 Select the key item (the longest item) for each of the four columns in the table on page 181. They would be San Francisco, 11, 3, and Pct. (Sometimes the key item can be the column heading itself.)
3 Determine the number of blank spaces to be left between the columns. The average of six spaces is recommended, unless there is a special reason for leaving more or fewer spaces.
4 Starting at 50 (or at any other centering point), backspace to center the key items six spaces apart. To do this, backspace once for each pair of strokes in the combined key items of all columns. (Disregard any odd stroke.) If you are leaving six spaces between columns, backspace three times for each blank area between the columns (once for every two spaces). Set the left margin stop at this point.
5 Space over to the start of the second column by tapping the space bar once for each stroke in the key item of the first column and once for each of the six spaces between the columns. Set a tab stop at this point, which is the beginning of the second column (San Francisco123456).
6 Repeat the procedure given in step 5 for each of the columns until all the tab stops have been set.

Vertical Placement

1 Count the number of lines in the table, including the main heading, column headings, and the blank lines between the typed lines of the table. If the body of the table is to be single-spaced, leave two blank line spaces between the main heading and the column headings. Leave one blank line space between the column headings and the body of the table. If a subheading is

TOP EIGHT NFL TEAMS

December 17, 19--

Team	W	L	Pct.
Washington	11	3	786
Dallas	10	4	714
Green Bay	10	4	714
San Francisco	9	5	643
Detroit	8	6	571
New York	8	6	571
Atlanta	7	7	500
Minnesota	7	7	500

used, leave one blank line space between the subheading and the main heading; then leave two blank line spaces between the subheading and the column headings. The main heading should be typed in capitals, subheadings in capitals and small letters, and column heads in capital and small letters, underscored.

2 Subtract the number of lines needed from the number of lines available—66 on an 8½- by 11-inch sheet of paper. To illustrate, consider a table that measures 22 lines. If you subtract the number of lines needed for the table, 22, from the number of lines available on a full sheet, 66, you'll get the number of lines available for the top and bottom margins, 44.

3 Divide 44 by 2 to find the number of the line on which to start typing the table. In this case, begin typing the table on line 22. If there is a fraction in your answer, count the fraction as the next whole number (for example if your answer is 12½, count it as line 13).

Column Headings

In general, a table looks best if the column headings are centered over the columns, although this is not a rigid rule. A long column head should be broken into no more than two or three lines. To center a column heading over the column text, follow the steps below:

1 Subtract the number of strokes in the longest line in the column heading from the number of strokes in the longest line in the body of the column.

2 Divide the difference by 2 (drop any fraction) to find the number of spaces to indent the longest line in the column heading. Center the other lines in the column head in relation to the longest line. For instance, if the longest line in the column heading is the word *State*, which has 5 spaces, and the longest line in the column text is 14 spaces, subtract 5 from 14, which is 9. If you divide 9 by 2 (drop the fraction), you are left with 4, the number of spaces to indent to center the longest line in your column heading.

Although column headings are usually centered, you can align each line in the column heading at the left with the column text if **(a)** all the column headings are shorter than their column text and **(b)** the table is for informal or temporary use, such as a rough draft.

If the column headings are wider than the column, reverse the process described previously.

1 Subtract the strokes in the longest item in the column text from the number of strokes in the longest line in the column heading.

2 Divide the difference by 2 (drop any fraction) to find the number of spaces to indent the body of the column. For an example, see the head in the last column of the table on page 181.

PREPARATION OF OUTLINES

Before an author writes a long report, he may make an outline of what he wants to say in order to help him organize his ideas. The outline helps him arrange his thoughts in a logical order, show important relationships between his ideas, and develop each thought properly. Your employer may ask you to type such an outline.

Outlines are generally made up of key words or phrases. Major headings are assigned roman numerals (I, II, III); main subheadings are designated by capital letters in alphabetic order (A, B, C); and further subheadings are identified by arabic numerals (1, 2, 3), as shown in the illustration on page 183. Outlines can be subdivided further by using small letters of the alphabet (a, b, c).

WORKING FROM ROUGH DRAFT

You may be asked to type a rough draft of a letter or a report which a writer has written in a tentative form in order to get her ideas on paper. After looking it over, she will indicate corrections and changes on the rough draft by using proofreader's marks. These proofreader's marks are an abbreviated and standardized language used in printing and publishing in which corrections are expressed clearly and briefly. Some common proofreader's marks and their applications are shown on page 183. Look them over.

MANUSCRIPTS AND REPORTS

Since rough drafts of manuscripts and reports usually contain corrections and additions made by hand, you should observe the following points before beginning the typing assignment.

TYPING AN OUTLINE

I.   MARGINS

      A.   Set margin stops to center the longest line, allowing for the first roman numeral.
      B.   Center the outline vertically on the paper.

II.   INDENTIONS

      A.   Steps should be indented four spaces each.
          1.   Set several tab stops four spaces apart.
          2.   Indent similar parts in similar steps.
      B.   Guide letters or numbers precede the steps.
          1.   Follow the guide with a period.
          2.   Space twice after the period.
      C.   For roman numerals that take more than one space, use the margin release and backspace from the left margin stop.

III. SPACING

      A.   Leave two blank lines before (above) a roman numeral.
      B.   Leave one blank line after (below) a roman numeral.
      C.   Single-space all the other lines.

PROOFREADER'S MARKS

Mark in Margin	Meaning	Illustration of Mark in Copy
∧	Insert as indicated.	It is necessary, *to* know
- - - - - -	Dots under words mean to retain crossed-out material.	item is often, by mistake *stet*, overlooked
=	Straighten lines; line up.	To: // __All__ New Teachers
//	Line up; make even.	From: // Superintendent
no #	No paragraph here.	no # In any case, the
#	Make a paragraph here.	to help themselves. Some of
tr	Transpose as indicated.	the dialy charge
℘	Take out matter indicated.	Money is also used to
lc	Use lower case (small letter).	information in the Report
○	Write it out; spell it out.	The (Dr.) said that (2) or (3) were
◡	Close up; no space.	Shown in the foot note below
#	Add space.	that you will enjoy
[	Move to left.	[and the next day
]	Move to right.	] the afternoon mail came early
=	Capitalize.	this is the end

1   Read the material to be sure you understand all the changes.
2   See if you must follow a certain style or pattern.
3   Plan the heading arrangement in advance.
4   Find out what kind of paper to use and how many carbon copies to make.

Paper

Manuscripts are generally typed on 8½- by 11-inch bond paper of good quality, and carbon copies are usually prepared on onionskin paper. Type on only one side of the paper.

Margins and Spacing

Observe the following rules in arranging manuscripts.

1   Use double spacing.
2   Use a 6-inch typing line; this provides side margins of 1¼ inches. If the manuscript is to be bound at the left, move the paper and paper guide to the left ¼ inch so that you have 1½ inches for the left margin and 1 inch for the right. Remember that a 6-inch line of pica type amounts to 60 spaces and a 6-inch line of elite type is 72 spaces, which is rounded to 70.
3   Leave a 2-inch top margin on the first page. On succeeding pages leave a 1-inch top margin. On the second page of a book manuscript, type the heading (title) in all capitals on line 7 at the left margin and the page number at the right margin. (There is no page number on the first page.) Then leave two blank lines between this line and the body of the manuscript.
4   Leave 1 to 1½ inches for the bottom margin. Many typists use a ruled backing sheet as a visual guide for typing manuscripts that require several pages. This guide is placed between the top sheet and the first carbon; the heavy lines on the visual guide show through the original copy to serve as a guide. If you don't have a visual guide, make a very light pencil mark in the side margin of your paper about 1 inch up from the bottom. When you type, this mark will show you that you have reached a stopping point.
5   In general, leave two blank line spaces before and one blank line space after side headings. (When a side heading comes directly below a centered heading, leave only one blank line above the side heading.)

Heading Arrangements

Center the title, and type it in all-capital letters. If the title is short, you can spread it out by leaving either a half or a full space between each letter.

Center the author's name on the second line below the title. (If a subtitle is included in the heading, center it on the second line below the main title and then type the author's name on the second line below the subtitle.) On the third line below the author's name, begin typing the first line of the body of the manuscript.

Off-the-Line Items

In these times of technical research and development, you may work on manuscripts involving degree signs, footnote numbers, root signs, and chemical formulas.

Type superior (raised) numbers by turning the cylinder down a half line space and holding the cylinder knob as you type the symbol or number required, such as "180°" or "reported in 1972.[1]"

Make inferior (lowered) numbers by turning the cylinder up a half line space and holding the cylinder knob firmly while typing the special data, such as "H_2SO_4" for sulfuric acid.

Footnotes

Footnotes are used to indicate the source of a quotation or of an opinion mentioned in the body of the manuscript or to give supplementary information. The examples and the following directions will help you to type footnotes correctly.

1   Type a solid underscore line 2 inches long to separate the footnote from the body of the manuscript. This line goes one line below the last line of the text. Start the first footnote on the second line below the underscore line.

2   Number the footnotes so that they agree with the notations in the text. They should be numbered consecutively throughout the entire manuscript. The notations in the body of the manuscript are made with superior or raised numbers.

3   Type each footnote single-spaced, and leave a blank line space between footnotes.

4   Footnotes must appear on the same page as the notations to which they refer.

1. Edgar H. Schein and Diane W. Kommers, <u>Professional Education: Some New Directions</u>, McGraw-Hill Book Company, New York, 1972, p. 76.

2. Grant Venn, "Career Education: Not a Panacea," <u>Business Education Forum</u>, November, 1972, pp. 3-4.

Table of Contents

Long manuscripts may need a table of contents. Use an outline structure like the one shown in the illustration on page 186. The right column shows the page number where each division begins. To prepare a table of contents:

1   Center the title *Table of Contents* or *Contents* about 2 inches from the top of the page.

2 Use a 5-inch line.

3 Use leader lines (rows of periods) to bridge the space between the headings and the page numbers. Make open leader lines by striking alternately the period key and the space bar. Be sure the leaders are aligned vertically. To do this easily, note whether the last period in the first line of leaders falls on an odd or even number space on the scale. Make all your following leaders conform to that number. Sometimes you have to space twice at the start of a leader line to keep all the periods aligned.

4 Type the table of contents last, after the paging of the manuscript has been completed, and then verify the page references.

TABLE OF CONTENTS

Bibliography

The bibliography lists the sources of material used in preparing a manuscript or report. It also may include other reference matter relating to the subject. It is generally placed at the end of each chapter or at the end of the entire manuscript. Note the examples and the following directions.

1   Center or spread center the word *Bibliography* in all-capital letters. Leave two blank lines between that word and the first entry.

2   Arrange the names of the authors in alphabetic order with the last name first. If a book has more than one author, the name of the first author only is transposed. Start the first line of a reference at the left margin. Succeeding lines of the same reference are indented ten spaces.

3   Type each entry single-spaced, and leave one blank line space between each entry.

4   Underscore titles of books or magazines. When the bibliography is long and includes both books and magazine articles, they may be listed separately.

5   Enclose the titles of magazine articles in quotation marks.

```
                    B I B L I O G R A P H Y


Schein, Edgar H., and Diane W. Kommers, Professional Education:  Some
        New Directions, McGraw-Hill Book Company, New York, 1972.

Venn, Grant, "Career Education:  Not a Panacea," Business Education
        Forum, November, 1972, pp. 3-4.
```

PROOFREADING

Every good typist acquires the habit of proofreading carefully the material she types. You are expected to proofread letters and other short reports of a nontechnical nature that you type. It is advisable, however, to ask a co-worker to help you to proofread a manuscript, particularly if the manuscript contains numbers or other technical data. When two people proofread together, one reads the manuscript aloud from the original copy while the other follows the final copy. Since it is sometimes difficult to see your own mistakes, it is better to have the one who typed the material read while the helper listens and checks the final copy. You'll find the following suggestions helpful in proofreading aloud:

1   Read distinctly at an even pace, giving the proofreader time to make corrections.

2   Read all punctuation marks, capitals, paragraphs, and special symbols.

3   Spell out all proper names.

4   Read 3,562 as "three-comma-five-six-two," not as "three thousand five hundred sixty-two."

5   Read decimals as follows: "Point-oh-oh-nine-seven-two" for .00972.

In addition to checking the accuracy of the typing, keep the following points in mind during proofreading:

1   Technical arrangement

   a   Placement of letter on a sheet of paper in relation to the letterhead.

b Paragraphing.

c Arrangement of letter parts.

2 Technical content

a Accuracy of dates.

b Accuracy of the inside address as compared with the original source and with the address on the envelope.

c Agreement of salutation and inside address.

d Agreement of complimentary closing with tone of message and salutation.

3 Thought conveyance

a Complete sentences.

b No omissions or transposed letters, words, or phrases.

c Correct spelling and punctuation.

d Agreement of verb to subject and pronoun to antecedent.

e Acceptable phrase or word substitutions.

TYPING TIPS

Professionals in every trade make use of shortcuts which they develop after years of experience. You can save time and turn out a better typing job by taking advantage of these useful tips. Try them and see.

Using the Tab Key

Many typists set their tab stops to control the typewriter carriage movements when they are typing a chart or a table. However, they frequently overlook the fact that the tab mechanism can also be used to preset the position of the common parts of regular business letters. For instance, you can set a tab stop for the date line, the paragraph indents, the start of the complimentary closing, and the signer's identification line. Once you've set the tab stops, you don't have to count each space. With just a flick of the tab key you are in position and ready to type.

Minimizing Word Division

If you don't have to think about dividing words at the end of the line, you can get a lot more work done. Simplify your work by carrying long words over to the next line. This may cause the right margin to be slightly uneven at times, but you'll get extra speed from not having to think about word division.

Drawing Long Lines

The easiest way for you to make horizontal lines is to use the underscore key on the typewriter while the material is still in the machine. Horizontal lines can also be made by placing the point of a ball-point pen on the edge of the alignment scale and by moving the carriage across manually. You can rule vertical lines by placing your pen at a point on the alignment scale and by turning the cylinder. You can also rule horizontal and vertical lines by hand with a ruler, after you remove your paper from the typewriter. Just be sure to leave space for the rules.

Using Chain Feeding

You can speed up the work of addressing envelopes from a mailing list or typing addresses on cards by using a chain-feeding method.

When you chain feed from the *front:*

1 Type the first envelope; then roll it back so that about ½ inch of the top shows.
2 Insert the next envelope from the front with the address side facing you, and place the bottom edge of the envelope between the first envelope and the cylinder.
3 Turn the cylinder toward you to back out the first envelope, and then bring the second envelope into position.
4 Continue in this manner to feed the envelopes from the front until you finish. The completed envelopes will be stacked in the same order as they were typed.

When you chain feed from the *back:*

1 Insert the first envelope about halfway. Insert the second envelope between the first envelope and the cylinder.
2 Turn the cylinder away from you to bring the first envelope into position. This motion brings the second envelope part way into the machine.
3 Then address the first envelope. Insert the third envelope as you did the second.
4 Turn the cylinder to remove the first envelope; this brings the second envelope into place for typing.

You can use these chain-feeding methods for cards, form letters, enclosures, and record slips.

Typing Envelopes and Cards Simultaneously

Suppose you want to keep a record on a file card of the person to whom an envelope is being addressed. You can address the envelope and card with a single effort. Simply place a file card behind the envelope to be addressed. In front of the file card place a piece of carbon paper of the same size, with the shiny or carbon side facing the card. The address typed on the envelope is reproduced as a carbon copy on the file card.

Back-Feeding Bound Papers

If you are asked to type a correction on an inside page of a manuscript which is bound at the top margin, follow this procedure:

1   Put a sheet of paper into the typewriter in the usual way. Turn it up until the top edge extends about 1 inch above the alignment scale.
2   Insert the bottom of the page on which the correction is to be made between the sheet of paper and the front of the cylinder.
3   Hold the manuscript page carefully with one hand, and with the other turn the cylinder to the place where the correction is to be made.
4   Type the correction.

Typing Labels

Many labels come in rolls to simplify the job of feeding them into the typewriter. If you have to type small detached labels which can be hard to handle, back-feed them into the typewriter by turning the cylinder to bring the labels into position. You can also make a kind of pocket for the label in a lightweight card. Insert the card into the typewriter, and turn the cylinder until the pocket is visible. Then insert the label into the pocket, and turn the cylinder back until the label is in typing position.

Half Spacing

The technique of permitting the carriage to move only one-half space at a time is known as half spacing. You'll find this technique necessary when you have to correct an error which involves squeezing or spreading a word into a larger or smaller space than it requires. For example, you may want to change *to* to *too* or substitute *were* for *are*. Also, you may occasionally find use for the half-spacing technique when you want to even out the right margin.

The following are various methods you can use to half space:

1   On manual and electric typewriters that are equipped with a halfspace key, simply depress the key and hold it down as you type each letter of the word to be squeezed or spread.
2   On some manual machines you can half-space by depressing and holding down the space bar as you type each letter in the word.
3   On all manual machines you can half-space by depressing and holding down the backspace key about halfway as you type each letter in the word.
4   On both manual and electric typewriters you can half-space by lightly blocking the movement of the carriage after each stroke. To do this, depress and hold down the carriage release to permit the carriage to move to a position halfway between scale points. (Check the position of the print-point indicator.) Apply only enough pressure to prevent a full-space movement.

Filling In

To insert inside addresses and other data on form letters, you need a typewriter with a typeface that matches the size and style of the type on the printed form. Use extreme care in aligning what you type with the type on the form, and be sure to use a typewriter ribbon which matches the color of the type on the form. You can check the alignment by moving the ribbon control to stencil position and by observing where an uninked key impression falls. Another way to check alignment is to leave the ribbon control in normal position and very lightly strike over a period or comma in the body of the letter. If you strike over a period perfectly, you know that the alignment is correct.

Justifying the Right Margin

Some special articles or reports must be typed so that the lines of the right margin end evenly. This technique is called *justifying*. Use the following procedure when you must justify the right margin.

1 Choose the line length desired for the final copy.
2 Type the material in rough-draft form, making the lines end as nearly as possible at the desired place, as shown in the illustration.
3 Note at the end of each line the number of strokes required to make an even right margin. You may have to squeeze words (see Half Spacing, page 190) to shorten a line, or you may need to add extra spacing between words to lengthen a line. (It is easier to insert extra spacing in a line than to condense a line.)
4 Place a check mark after each word where extra spacing is to be inserted or where the word is to be squeezed. Avoid inserting extra spacing or squeezing words near the same point on consecutive lines.
5 Retype the material, adding a space or half space or subtracting a half space at each check mark.

FIRST DRAFT		JUSTIFIED COPY
If you✓are unable✓to take a✓trip	3	If you are unable to take a trip
around the world, the next best thing is	0	around the world, the next best thing is
to visit the import✓fair. This fair is	1	to visit the import fair. This fair is
a delight✓to the ear as well as the eye	1	a delight to the ear as well as the eye
with✓the music of Italian✓folk✓songs,	3	with the music of Italian folk songs,
German and✓Irish lullabies and even gay	1	German and Irish lullabies and even gay
Caribbean calypsos pervading the air.		Caribbean calypsos pervading the air.

TYPING LEGAL DOCUMENTS

If you work in a legal office or in the legal department of a company, you may be required to help prepare and to type legal documents. The most frequently used legal papers are affidavits, agreements, assignments, leases, mortgages, bills of sale, contracts, deeds, powers of attorney, and wills. Many of these documents are printed forms which can be purchased at stationery stores. You merely fill in the blanks on the forms with the proper information. If a printed form is not used, the entire document may be prepared on the typewriter. In this case the following suggestions should be helpful.

Wholly Typed Documents

☐ Use legal-size typing paper. Most legal paper is 8½ by 13 inches and has vertical ruled lines at the margins. Double ruled lines are usually 1½ inches from the left edge, and a single line is ½ inch from the right edge. (In many states regular 8½- by 11-inch paper is used.)

☐ Leave a top margin of 2 inches on the first page and a top margin of 1½ inches on following pages. Leave a bottom margin of at least 1 inch, and set margin stops one or two spaces inside the ruled lines.

☐ Use double spacing unless you are instructed otherwise.

☐ Indent paragraphs ten spaces.

☐ Center the page number at the bottom of the page, three lines below the text. End your typing 1½ inches from the bottom of the page so that the page number is 1 inch from the bottom.

☐ Be accurate. Erasures are not permitted on some important documents.

Printed Legal Forms

☐ Be sure the typing is aligned satisfactorily with the printing on the form.

☐ Type word insertions one space from the printed word on the form or center in the space provided. Type word completions as close to the root word as possible. The unused space may be filled with hyphens.

INTEROFFICE MEMORANDUMS

Interoffice memorandums are messages from one office or person within a company to another office or person within the same company. Such messages are frequently prepared on special interoffice stationery so that a formal letter does not have to be typed. Note the following about the interoffice memorandum illustrated on page 195.

☐ The heading contains places to type the name of the office or person or persons to whom the memorandum is addressed; the subject of the memoran-·dum; the name of the person or office who is sending the memorandum; and the date. The four heading items are aligned both horizontally and vertically.

☐ Set the left margin stop two or three spaces after the longest guide word in the left half of the printed heading (for example, after *Subject*). Set a tab stop

POWER OF ATTORNEY

KNOW ALL MEN BY THESE PRESENTS

      THAT I, George J. Ross, of the City of Cleveland, County of Cuya-
hoga, State of Ohio, have made, constituted and appointed, and by these presents do make, constitute and appoint my wife, Jane Wilson Ross, my true and
lawful attorney for me and in my name, place and stead to act as my agent in
the management of my property, real and personal, of whatsoever nature and
wheresoever situated, giving and granting unto my said attorney full power
and authority to do and perform all and every act and thing whatsoever requisite and necessary to be done in and about the premises, as fully, to all
intents and purposes, as I might or could do if personally present, with full
power of substitution and revocation, and hereby ratifying and confirming
all that my said attorney or his substitute shall lawfully do or cause to
be done by virtue hereof.

      IN WITNESS WHEREOF, I have hereunto set my hand and seal the
_2nd_ day of December, 19--.

                                    George J. Ross   (L.S.)

Sealed and delivered in the presence of

Earl J. Brownell   and   _Richard Suess_

State of Ohio   ) ss.:
County of Cuyahoga)

      BE IT KNOWN, that on the _2nd_ day of December, 19--, before me,
James J. Jason, a Notary Public in and for the State of Ohio, duly commis-
sioned and sworn, dwelling in the City of Cleveland, personally came and appeared George J. Ross, to me personally known, and known to me to be the
same person described in and who executed the within Power of Attorney, and
he acknowledged the within Power of Attorney to be his act and deed.

      IN TESTIMONY WHEREOF, I have hereunto subscribed my name and af-
fixed my seal of office, the day and year last above written.

                            James J. Jason
                            Notary Public

My commission expires December 31, 19--

A typed legal document. The bottom part, the _acknowledgment clause_, is usually typed single-spaced.

two or three spaces after the longest guide word in the right half of the printed heading (for example, after _From_). Set the right margin stop to leave a right margin equal to the left margin.

☐ The body of the memorandum begins three or four lines below the bottom line of the heading.

POWER OF ATTORNEY

Know all Men by these Presents: That I, George J. Ross, of the City of Cleveland, County of Cuyahoga, State of Ohio

have made, constituted and appointed, and by these presents do make, constitute and appoint my wife, Jane Wilson Ross——

my *true and lawful attorney* for me *and in* my *name, place and stead,* to act as my agent in the management of my property, real and personal, of whatsoever nature and wheresoever situated——

giving and granting unto my *said attorney* *full power and authority to do and perform all and every act and thing whatsoever requisite and necessary to be done in the premises; as fully, to all intents and purposes, as* I *might or could do if personally present, with full power of substitution and revocation, hereby ratifying and confirming all that* my *said attorney* *or* his *substitute* *shall lawfully do or cause to be done by virtue hereof.*

In witness whereof I *hereunto set* my *hand* *and seal*, *at* Cleveland this 2nd *day of* December *A. D. 19--.*

Signed and acknowledged in presence of

Earl J. Brownell

Richard Suess

George J. Ross   [Seal]

    [Seal]

    [Seal]

THE STATE OF OHIO
Cuyahoga *County* } *ss.*

Before me, a *Notary Public in and for said County, person-ally appeared the above named* George J. Ross who *acknowledged that* he *did sign and seal the foregoing instrument and that the same is* his *free act and deed.*

In testimony whereof *I have hereunto set my hand and official seal,* at Cleveland *this* 2nd *day of* December *A. D. 19--.*

James J. Jason *Notary Public*

My commission expires December 31, 19--

A printed legal form.

☐ Paragraphs are blocked or indented.
☐ A blank line space is left between paragraphs.
☐ The sender's initials are typed two lines below the body, aligned with the typed date at the top of the page.
☐ The typist's initials appear two lines below the sender's initials, blocked at the left margin.

FINANCIAL STATEMENTS

The owner of every business needs to have a picture of the overall financial condition of his enterprise. One report of great importance to him is the

Interoffice | *Memorandum* | BIRCH COMPANY

TO   All Male Employees   FROM   Ira M. Wilder

SUBJECT   Men's Softball Team   DATE   March 17, 19--

There will be a meeting at 5:10 p.m., Wednesday, March 19, to discuss plans for the 19-- season of the company-sponsored softball team. The meeting will be held in the Personnel Relations Office on the eighth floor. All members of last year's team who still hold uniforms should return them at this meeting.

For the benefit of interested parties, the company sponsors a softball team in the "Copyright League" of the Center Recreation Association of New York. Games are played in Central Park at 63rd Street at 5:30 p.m. or at 7:30 p.m. on weekday nights (after the start of daylight savings time).

If you are interested in playing but cannot attend the organization meeting, please write me a memo so signifying.

IMW

EH

balance sheet, illustrated on page 196, which shows the company's assets, liabilities, and net worth or owner's equity at a stated time. Another report of particular interest to the businessman and to the government is the statement of income and expense or simply the income statement. This report shows the net profit or loss for an accounting period of time, such as a month, a quarter, a half year, or a year. Before starting to work, check the company files for an established format to follow as a model for each kind of statement. Observe the following hints on how to arrange this material.

1   Enter the heading in capitals and small letters or in all capitals.
2   Type the money columns at the right, and leave two spaces between them. Be sure to align the dollar signs at top and bottom of the page.
3   Type a single rule to show addition or subtraction of numbers listed in the column.
4   Type a double rule under the final totals. To do this, type the first rule and then type the second rule, using the variable spacer to roll the paper up slightly.

PRESS RELEASES

Most firms are eager to create and to maintain a favorable impression with their customers and with the general public. For that reason they report important new company developments to newspapers, radio stations, and trade journals in the form of news releases. If the news is thought to be of sufficient interest to readers and if time and space permit, the news editor may include all or part of the story as a news item. News releases are prepared in a special style to make it easy for the editor to spot the who, what, when, where, how, and why of the story. A typical one is shown on page 197.

```
                        Elmhurst French Cleaners
                            Balance Sheet
                         December 31, 19--

                              ASSETS

Current Assets
      Cash in Bank                               $ 4,135
      Petty Cash                                     100
      Change Fund                                    150
      Investment in U.S. Treasury Securities         500
      Notes Receivable                             2,750
      Accounts Receivable Control                  6,250
      Merchandise Inventory                        1,625
      Total Current Assets                                    $15,510

Fixed Assets
      Plant Buildings and Equipment     $20,000
      Less Allowance for Depreciation     1,500   $18,500
      Store Equipment                   $ 4,800
      Less Allowance for Depreciation     2,100     2,700
      Delivery Equipment                $ 3,450
      Less Allowance for Depreciation     1,640     1,810
      Office Equipment                  $ 3,170
      Less Allowance for Depreciation     1,430     1,740
      Land                                          5,000
      Total Fixed Assets                                       29,750
Total Assets                                                  $45,260

                   LIABILITIES AND OWNER'S EQUITY

Current Liabilities
      Notes Payable                              $ 3,000
      Accounts Payable Control                     1,100
      Sales Taxes Payable                            235
      Employee Deductions:
        FICA Taxes                    $    198
        Income Taxes Withheld              440        638
      Total Current Liabilities                               $ 4,973

Long-Term Liabilities
      8% Mortgage Payable on Plant 19--                         15,000
Total Liabilities                                             $19,973

Owner's Equity
      Carter Investment, January 1, 19--         $19,946
      Net Profit for Year 19--          $12,541
      Less Withdrawals by Carter          7,200
      Net Increase in Investment in 19--           5,341
      Carter Investment, December 31, 19--                     25,287
Total Liabilities and Owner's Equity                         $45,260
```

REVIEWING YOUR READING

1   What is the most efficient way to find the centering point of your typewriter?
2   Explain the procedure to determine the vertical placement of a table on a page.
3   Explain the backspace method of figuring the horizontal placement of a table on a page.

```
                              Public Relations Department
                              Dexter Data Card Company
                              598 Broadway, N.
                              Dayton, Ohio 45407

      N E W S   R E L E A S E     Release:  At once

                              From:    Richard Sands
                                       513-555-3498


                   NEW SUPPLY PRODUCTION PLANT IN ARIZONA

          DAYTON, Ohio, Oct. 2--The Dexter Data Card Company announces pur-

      chase of a seven-acre site in Tucson, on which the company will build

      a new supply production plant.

          The new 50,000-square-foot facility is scheduled to be completed

      and in operation by the end of 19--.  It will employ approximately 55

      people.

          The plant will manufacture magnetic ledger cards used in bank

      automation systems, as well as other special forms for various types of

      business systems and machines.

          "The growing Southwest market and expanded business in the area

      has prompted our locating in the Tucson region," R. C. Allison, super-

      visor of supply manufacturing for the company, said.

          The new facility will be located on Avenue R East, facing State

      Highway 99.  It will be of modern design and a one-floor brick construc-

      tion.  (END)
```

4 What four steps should you take before beginning to type a finished manuscript from a rough draft?

5 What is a bibliography? In what part of a report is it placed?

6 Explain and be ready to demonstrate for the class the procedure to follow in chain feeding envelopes from the front of the typewriter.

7 What is meant by justifying the right margin?

OFFICE ASSIGNMENTS

1 Prepare a power of attorney in typed form (similar to the one shown on page 193) in which Thomas Arthur Hayne appoints his wife, Martha Taylor Hayne, as his attorney. The Haynes live in Lorain, Lorain County, Ohio. Use the current date and your name as notary public. Supply names for the two witnesses. Legal paper should be used if available. Make two carbon copies.

2 Prepare a table of contents from the following information. Type it on a full sheet of paper. Use leader lines. Use the illustration on page 186 as a model.

Contents: Section I, Beginning Your First Job, 1; Strictly Personal, 1; Telephone Techniques, 2; Typing Shortcuts, 3; You and Your Typewriter, 4; Questions to Ask Yourself, 5. Section II, Improving Your Skills, 7; Letters, 7; Typing Envelopes, 16; Folding Letters, 18; Memorandums, 19; Reports, 24; Report Binders, 30. Section III, Becoming an Expert, 32; Punctuation, 32; Writing Numbers, 36; Word Division, 38; Words to Forget, 39; Words That Sound Alike, 40; Abbreviations—General Rules, 43; Proofreading, 49. Section IV, Ordering Services and Stationery, 50; Stationery Items, 50; Requisitioning Stationery, 51; Petty Expense Voucher, 52; Stenographic and Copying Services, 53; Copying Service Cost Guide, 54; Transportation Request, 56.

3 Using the information below, type a balance sheet for the Barton Manufacturing Company. Use the illustration on page 196 as your model.

The Barton Manufacturing Company, Balance Sheet, December 31, 19—. Assets. Current Assets: Cash, $5,680.50; Notes Receivable, $10,220.00; Interest Receivable, $400.00; Accounts Receivable, $13,412.75; Merchandise Inventory, Department A, $4,200.00; Department B, $6,700.00; Department C, $5,200.00; Prepaid Advertising, $1,500.00; Prepaid Insurance, $1,200.00; Total Current Assets, $48,513.25. Fixed Assets: Office Equipment, $750.00; Building, $25,670.00; Land, $12,000.00; Total Fixed Assets, $38,420.00. Total Assets, $86,933.25. Liabilities and Owner's Equity. Current Liabilities: Notes Payable, $5,225.00; Interest Payable, $45.00; Accounts Payable, $8,200.00; Federal Insurance Contributions Taxes Payable, $120.50; Salaries Payable, $2,412.50; Total Current Liabilities, $16,003.00. Long-Term Liabilities: Mortgage Payable, $18,000.00. Total Liabilities, $34,003.00. Owner's Equity: Barton Investment, January 1, 19—, $42,000.00; Net Profit for Year 19—, $10,930.25; Barton Investment, December 31, 19—, $52,930.25. Total Liabilities and Owner's Equity, $86,933.25.

4 On a sheet of plain paper justify the right margin on the following two paragraphs, using a 50-space line:

Tables, charts, and special announcements often contain headings that should be centered on the page or above the column to achieve the most attractive arrangement.

There are a number of quick ways to find the center of the sheet on which a heading is to be placed. The typist can fold the sheet in half without creasing. A slight pinch at the top edge will indicate the center position. Or he can use a ruler and indicate the center at the top edge of the paper by a light pencil mark.

5   Review the procedures on page 187 for proofreading with a helper. Then team up with a classmate and proofread the original copy in the left column below against the final copy in the right column. You and your helper should each have a copy of the textbook or workbook. Since the original copy is assumed to be the correct one, the person reading the final copy should make changes in the workbook (or make notes of changes if the textbook is being used) on the final copy, so that the final copy conforms with the original.

ORIGINAL COPY

Sundry Sale Procedures

When an item other than merchandise is sold, a sundry sale invoice is given to the purchaser. If the purchaser pays cash, the invoice and copy are immediately stamped "paid."

The invoice copy is delivered to the chief accounting clerk who makes an entry in the general journal. For sundry credit sales the debit is to accounts receivable, and the credit is to the appropriate asset account. The invoice copy is filed, and it serves as the customer's account card or subsidiary ledger.

When the cashier receives the customer's check, he writes a remittance advice as the original record that cash was received.

The remittance advice is delivered to the chief accounting clerk, and an entry is made in the general journal. The debit is to cash, and the credit is to accounts receivable. The filed sundry sale invoice copy is stamped "paid" and is refiled with other paid sundry sale invoices.

FINAL COPY

Sunday Sale Procedures

When an other item than merchandise is sold, a sundry sale invoice is given to the purchaser. If the purchaser has cash, the invoice copy are imediately stamped paid.

The invoice copy is delivered the chief accountant clerk who make an entry in the general gournal. For credit sales the debit is to accounts receivable and the credit to the asset appropriate account. The invoice copy is filled, and it serve as the customer's account card or subsidary leger.

When the cashier receives the customer's check, he writes a remittance advice as the original record that cash received.

The remittance advise is delivered to the chief accounting clerk, and entry is made in the general journal. The debt is to cash, and the credit is to account receivable. The filed sundry sale invoice copy is stamped "paid", and it is refiled with other sundry sale invoices.

SECTION 15 Typing Equipment

In an age of specialization it's a good idea to acquire as much knowledge as you can about your particular job and the equipment you use for it. If you are a typist, you can extend your qualifications considerably by becoming familiar with the many kinds of typewriters in use and the special jobs they are equipped to do.

KINDS OF TYPEWRITERS

The descriptions that follow pertain primarily to typewriters, but note the references to other office machines that have a similar keyboard arrangement.

Manual Typewriters

Although more and more businesses are purchasing electric typewriters, manual typewriters are still used in many offices. And it's more than likely that at some time in your office career you will be expected to use a manual typewriter. Those offices changing from manual to electric typewriters do so gradually, not all at once. And some offices don't bother to buy electric typewriters because they don't have occasion to use them often enough during the day.

Electric Typewriters

Electric typewriters are made by all the major manufacturers of typewriters. An electric typewriter produces better-looking copy than a manual typewriter because the electrically propelled keys strike the paper with the same amount of force. This uniformity of type is important when you prepare master copies for duplication. You can also produce a large number of high-quality carbon copies by using the adjustment lever found on most machines to increase the pressure applied to the keys. Since you only have to touch the keys of the electric typewriter lightly, you'll find you can produce more copy in less time and with less effort.

The IBM Selectric typewriter is a little different from other electric models. The type element is about the size of a golf ball, and it rotates and strikes the paper as the keys are depressed. Since there are no type bars, the keys never jam. There is no carriage in the usual sense, because the top part of the machine does not move. Instead, the element carrier, which is hidden from view, moves the type element across the page as you press the keys. Extra type elements with different typefaces are available and can be substituted easily.

The IBM Correcting Selectric eliminates the need to erase errors on the original copy. When an error is made, the typist depresses a special backspace correction key and again strikes the key which made the error. A special correcting ribbon whites out the error, and the type element remains in position so that the correct character can be typed.

Portable Typewriters

Portable typewriters, both electric and manual, are a great convenience for people who have to carry their machine with them from place to place. They're ideal for personal use; and, of course, hundreds of thousands of students, businessmen, and sales representatives depend on them. Portables are smaller and lighter than standard machines and come in protective carrying cases.

Courtesy Sperry Remington Office Systems

Electric typewriters such as this one respond to the lightest touch.

Courtesy IBM

Interchangeable typefaces are a feature of this electric typewriter.

Automatic Typewriters

The automatic typewriter, sometimes referred to as a word-processing machine, produces an individually typed form letter from a master record, which can be a punched paper tape, a magnetic tape, or a magnetic card. The master record is prepared on a unit with a standard keyboard, and once it is inserted into the automatic typewriter, it directs every stroke and carriage movement of the machine. Special controls and stops on the master record permit different names, addresses, dates, and other common variables to be inserted on the form letters.

You can supervise several automatic typewriters at one time. All you do is insert the paper into the machine and supply the variable information at the proper point in each message. The machine takes care of the rest, producing accurate, uniform, top-quality copy with amazing speed. You can also type a rough draft on it, and what you type will be recorded simultaneously on magnetic tape. Then when the corrected rough draft is returned to you by your

Courtesy IBM

With this automatic typewriter a completely error-free letter can be produced repeatedly.

boss, you make only the indicated changes on the magnetic tape. Once you've done this, the machine takes over again and speedily and automatically turns out a perfect letter.

VariTyper

The VariTyper is a special kind of machine that provides many opportunities to improve the appearance of messages. Two different typefaces can be installed in the machine at the same time, and it can be easily fitted with some 600 different type styles, including italic, boldface, and large type for captions. In general, the VariTyper is used in offset reproduction for preparing the original copy known as a *master*, from which additional copies are made.

Another advantage of the VariTyper is that it can produce an even right margin. This procedure is called *justifying*. First the material is typed in the regular way with an uneven right margin. The operator then notes the amount of space that must be added to or subtracted from each line to make it end at a certain point. When she retypes the material, the operator sets a lever for the needed adjustment before she types each line. Then the machine adjusts the spacing as that line is typed.

Justowriter

The Justowriter also justifies the right margin, but with the use of a punched tape. The copy is typed once on the machine, producing a tape on which is recorded whether a typed line is too long or too short. When the tape is put on a reproducer unit, the machine automatically types the copy, justifying the margins.

Proportional Spacing Typewriters

The characters and letters on the proportional spacing typewriter do not all have the same width. Instead, each letter and character is given its natural amount of space, according to its width, and each is measured in terms of *units*. A *w* is four units, an *i* is two, an *m* is five, and so on. When it is effectively used, this typewriter can give your typed work the appearance of fine printing. Justifying is one of the outstanding features of the machine. As you type a line, you note how many units short or long a line is. When you type the copy a second time, you make use of a set of space bars to expand or contract the line to fit the space allotted. Even though everything must be typed twice, the machine with its carbon ribbon produces an attractive page particularly suited to photographic reproduction. IBM, Hermes, and Olivetti manufacture this type of machine.

Typewriter Keyboards on Other Office Machines

A great many other office machines have keyboards similar to the typewriter. Among the most widely used are accounting machines, billing machines, card-

	Ordinary Typing	Proportional Typing
	swim	swim
	sssss	sssss
	wwwww	wwwww
	iiiii	iiiii
	mmmmm	mmmmm

Courtesy IBM

This proportional spacing typewriter has characters and letters of different widths.

Courtesy IBM

Proportional spacing typewriter type compared with regular typewriter types.

punch machines, and teletypewriters. You can easily adapt your typing skills to them.

VARIATIONS IN TYPEWRITER TYPE AND STRUCTURE

Standard typewriters have uppercase and lowercase letters in either pica or elite type. On some newer models both pica and elite spacing are available. There are billing and accounting machines which print in capital letters only and special typewriters with oversize type used for preparing labels and name tags and for preparing special display and sight-saving work. By special order, typewriter manufacturers can replace any key with another, supply the alphabet of any language that can be reproduced in printed characters, and provide any one of a variety of typefaces. Extra long carriages can be ordered as well as heavier alternate cylinders (for jobs such as card typing and stencil typing) and special tabulators.

If a typewriter of any description is a tool with which you work often, explore all its possibilities with the supervisor of your department or with a representative of the typewriter company.

Courtesy Smith-Corona Division of SCM

A large assortment of changeable type is available to meet special typing needs.

REVIEWING YOUR READING

1 Why is it important for you to learn how to operate both manual and electric typewriters?
2 In what ways does the VariTyper improve the appearance of typed messages?

OFFICE ASSIGNMENT

List the numbers 1 through 12 on a sheet of paper. In order to sharpen your proofreading skill, compare each set of addresses in the list on pages 204–205. Addresses in the Original Document column are correct. If the two addresses are exactly alike, place a check mark by the corresponding number on the sheet of paper. If the addresses differ, correct the typed copy.

Original Document	*Typed Copy*
1 Mr. Woodrow Shivley 8436 Melrose Avenue Seattle, WA 98122	Mr. Woodrow Shivley 8436 Melrose Avenue Seattle, WA 98122
2 Mrs. Charles E. Baine 8277 Camelia Drive San Jose, CA 95120	Mrs. Charles E. Baine 8277 Camelot Drive San Jose, CA 91520
3 Mrs. Ross Mashburn 22 Turquoise Drive Cincinnati, OH 45230	Mrs. Ross Mashburn 22 Turquoise Drive Cincinnati, OH 45230
4 Mr. Kelly Hansbrough 10 Crest Drive Kalamazoo, MI 49008	Mr. Kelly Hansbough 10 Crest Drive Kalamazoo, MI 49008
5 Mr. Garnett Spaulding 1880 Lexington Drive Covington, KY 41018	Mr. Garnett Spaulding 1880 Lexington Drive Covington, KY 41018
6 Mr. Vernon Southerland 801 Weigner Road Troy, NY 12180	Mr. Vernon Sutherland 801 Weigner Road Troy, NY 12180
7 Mrs. Anne Meacham 209 Grandview Drive, S.E. Albuquerque, NM 87108	Mrs. Anne Meacham 209 Grandview Drive, S.E. Albuquerque, NM 81708
8 Mr. Benjamin Gibson 1803 Giraudo Place Aaronsburg, PA 16820	Mr. Benjamin Gibon 1803 Giraudo Place Aaronsburg, PA 16820

Original Document	*Typewritten Copy*
9 Mr. Clayton Brubaker 202 Estates Boulevard Aberdeen, SD 57401	Mr. Clayton Brubaker 220 Estes Boulevard Aberdeen, SD 57401
10 Mr. Allen Rothgeb 5705 Gridley Avenue Milwaukee, WI 53213	Mr. Allen Rothgeb 5705 Gridley Avenue Milwaukee, WI 52313
11 Miss Henrietta Strahley 3401 Redford Drive, S.E. Atlanta, GA 30315	Miss Henrietta Strahley 3401 Redford Drive S.E. Atlanta, GA 30315
12 Mr. Zachery Walthall 38 Mattos Drive Fremont, CA 94536	Mr. Zachery Walthall 38 Mattox Drive Fremont, CA 94536

UNIT 6

BUSINESS CASES AND PROBLEMS

In the Boss's Shoes   1   Your friend Doris complained, "Mary's boss requisitioned an electric typewriter for her, but my boss got me only a new manual machine. Some people get all the breaks."

Do you sympathize with Doris? Could her boss have had sound reasons for his action? Explain.

2   Sally wants to be promoted to the job of statistical typist. She can type very rapidly and accurately, but she doesn't use her head. For example, she will never check figures that seem wrong, nor will she follow a format precisely as directed. When you talk to Sally about these shortcomings, she always says that she'll try harder to please "next time," but no improvement seems to result.

If you were Sally's boss, how long would you wait for Sally to wake up before giving the job to someone else?

3   Some executives seem to operate at a steady, even pace. Others never seem to finish the day without a last-minute rush of some kind. Can rush jobs be avoided? What can employees do to prevent emergencies from arising or to minimize them?

Your Human Relations   1   Your boss is a perfectionist. He says, "Since every letter affects the customer's impression of the company, everything should be exactly right." His fussiness about erasing shadows and uneven stroking is quite annoying. Should you tell him how you feel? Ask for a transfer? Resign? Or what?

2 Your firm is very proud of its reputation and traditions. However, you think that the firm's old-fashioned methods of letter production are more inefficient and time-consuming than your boss realizes. Should you tell him what you think? Do you believe that you can convince him merely by telling him your opinion of the situation?

3 "I like to type, but I hate those tabulation jobs. I wish Mr. Price would give them to someone else and let me do just the letters and envelopes."

How far is Mr. Price supposed to go in considering your likes and dislikes? Who will do the work that "someone else" doesn't like to do?

4 You do a lot of typing from rough draft. Your boss's written notations, inserts, and corrections are difficult to read because of his almost illegible handwriting. Should you tell him to write more neatly and clearly? If so, how can you say this diplomatically? If not, what can be done to simplify your problem?

What Would You Do If . . . ? **1** The town and state name are typed in full on an address label, but there is not enough room to include the ZIP Code on the same line.

2 Your boss has refused your request for an electric typewriter to replace your old manual machine, which is beyond repair. He says you simply don't do enough typing in a day to justify the investment. What would you do?

What Does This Mean? **1** To be effective, a business letter must make a good first impression.

2 Your boss instructs you to have a legal paper notarized.

Business in Your Area **1** Obtain at least five envelopes that have been addressed to you or some member of your family. Compare the address on each envelope with the standards for addressing envelopes outlined on pages 132 and 175.

2 Do your local employers require applicants for office jobs to take skill tests for employment?

3 If so, what are the skill requirements for typing positions?

4 Which firms in your area have the most modern office facilities?

5 Are the most modern offices in your town equipped with more manual or more electric typewriters?

**UNIT 7
FILING**

16 Alphabetic Filing— Part 1

There's a simple, sensible reason for filing systematically—to make it possible to find what you want when you want it. But before you study filing, you must become familiar with the basic filing concepts.

BASIC FILING CONCEPTS

Three terms common to all filing systems are caption, unit, and indexing. It's important that you learn them.

A *caption* is the name or number used to identify a record for filing purposes. It may be the name of a person *(Helen S. Robinson)*, an organization *(the Henry Street Settlement)*, a place *(Montgomery, Alabama)*, a subject *(Office Furniture)*, or a number *(Purchase Order 17701)*. Every caption contains one or more units.

Each part of a name that is to be considered in filing is called a *unit*, and each unit has a number. In the name *Helen S. Robinson*, the last name, *Robinson*, is unit 1; the first name, *Helen*, is unit 2; and the middle initial, *S.*, is unit 3.

Indexing is the process of (1) selecting a caption under which a record is to be filed and then (2) determining the order in which the units are to be considered in filing.

For instance, you alphabetically index the name *Helen S. Robinson* when you decide that in order to find her name in the telephone directory, you will have to look under *R* and not *H*.

The most commonly used filing system and the one that's easiest to learn is *alphabetic filing*. This involves putting records in order in an *A* to *Z* sequence, according to the letters of the alphabet, and then indexing them for filing.

TRANSPOSITION OF NAMES

Rule 1: Transpose the units in the name of an individual in the following order: first, the surname (last name); second, the first name or first initial; third, the middle name or middle initial, if any.

Normal Order	Indexing Order
David Charles Blair	Blair, David Charles
John C. Blane	Blane, John C.
F. W. Davis	Davis, F. W.
J. Paul Smith	Smith, J. Paul
Mary Williams	Williams, Mary
R. Young	Young, R.

```
Blane, John C.
```

ALPHABETIC ORDER

Rule 2: Alphabetize names by comparing them unit by unit and letter by letter.

If all the letters in the first units are identical, compare the second units. If both the first and second units are identical, compare the third units, and so on.

First alphabetize by last names (unit 1). For example, in the illustration below *Blane*, beginning with the letter *B*, comes before *Jones*, beginning with the letter *J*; *Smith* follows *Jones* because *S* comes after *J*.

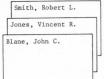

	Indexing Order
John C. Blane	Blane, John C.
Vincent R. Jones	Jones, Vincent R.
Robert L. Smith	Smith, Robert L.

If all the last names are the same, alphabetize the first names or first initials (unit 2).

	Indexing Order	
	Unit 1	*Unit 2*
James Blane	Blane	James
Jean Blane	Blane	Jean
Joanne Blane	Blane	Joanne

If all the last names and all the first names are the same, then alphabetize the middle names or middle initials (unit 3).

	Indexing Order		
	Unit 1	*Unit 2*	*Unit 3*
John C. Blane	Blane	John	C.
John K. Blane	Blane	John	K.
John R. Blane	Blane	John	R.

Remember, it is easier, faster, and more accurate to compare names unit by unit, starting with unit 1, the last name.

SURNAMES ALONE OR WITH INITIALS

Rule 3: File "nothing before something."

A last name alone comes before the same last name with a first name or first initial.

	Indexing Order	
	Unit 1	*Unit 2*
Jones	Jones	
J. Jones	Jones	J.

A last name with a first initial comes before the same last name with a complete first name beginning with the same letter as the initial.

	Indexing Order	
	Unit 1	*Unit 2*
Jones	Jones	
J. Jones	Jones	J.
Joseph Jones	Jones	Joseph

The name *Green* with nothing after the *n* comes before *Greene* with an *e* added on. *Holland* comes before *Hollandsworth*. *Lee* comes before *Leeds*. *Jean* comes before *Jeanette*. The reason is the same in every case: Nothing comes before something.

Indexing Order

	Unit 1	Unit 2	Unit 3
John Green	Green	John	
Alice Greene	Greene	Alice	
Wanda Holland	Holland	Wanda	
Martha Hollandsworth	Hollandsworth	Martha	
P. R. Lee	Lee	P.	R.
G. E. Leeds	Leeds	G.	E.
Jean L. Rucker	Rucker	Jean	L.
Jeanette A. Rucker	Rucker	Jeanette	A.

```
Greene, Alice
Green, John
```

SURNAME PREFIXES

Rule 4: Treat last-name prefixes as part of the last name.

Some last names include a prefix such as *D'*, *De*, *Del*, *Mac*, *Mc*, and *O'*. Sometimes these prefixes are connected to the main part of the name, sometimes they aren't. Sometimes they are written with a capital letter, other times they are written in lowercase. No matter how the prefix appears, treat it exactly as if it were part of the last name, never as a separate indexing unit. If an apostrophe is part of the prefix, ignore the apostrophe.

A name like *DeForrest*, *DuPont*, *LaRosa*, *O'Malley*, *Van Dresser* or any other name with a prefix won't give you a moment's pause if you remember the rule: Consider the last name and its prefix as one unit.

Indexing Order

	Unit 1	Unit 2	Unit 3
Richard C. Deering	Deering	Richard	C.
Arthur B. DeForrest	DeForrest	Arthur	B.
James T. Degraw	Degraw	James	T.
Peter DiNapoli	DiNapoli	Peter	
Mary L. Dione	Dione	Mary	L.
Edward O. Dumas	Dumas	Edward	O.
Samuel F. DuPont	DuPont	Samuel	F.
Jacob R. Dutro	Dutro	Jacob	R.

```
DuPont, Samuel F.
Dumas, Edward O.
```

```
Solomon, Karl
St. Clair, Ella
```

A special prefix to make a note of is *St.*, the abbreviation for *Saint*. Always treat this prefix as if it were spelled out, and consider it as a separate indexing unit unless it is part of the name of an individual.

The names in the following list are correctly indexed and alphabetized. The rules applying to each name are noted in the Rule column. See if you can explain how these rules have been applied.

Indexing Order

	Unit 1	Unit 2	Unit 3	Rule
Edward Lang	Lang	Edward		1, 2
James Lang	Lang	James		1, 2
Mark Lange	Lange	Mark		1, 2, 3
Mark C. Lange	Lange	Mark	C.	1, 2
Thomas R. LaPern	LaPern	Thomas	R.	1, 2, 4
John Larken	Larken	John		1, 2
Helen T. Larson	Larson	Helen	T.	1, 2
S. R. LaSala	LaSala	S.	R.	1, 2, 3, 4
Stephen T. LaSala	LaSala	Stephen	T.	1, 2, 4
Brigette Lawton	Lawton	Brigette		1, 2
Adam Leach	Leach	Adam		1, 2, 3
Adam A. Leach	Leach	Adam	A.	1, 2
Lee	Lee			2, 3
Dora Lee	Lee	Dora		1, 2, 3
Barbara Leech	Leech	Barbara		1, 2
O. Kenneth Leech	Leech	O.	Kenneth	1, 2, 3
Orville O. Leech	Leech	Orville	O.	1, 2
Ernest R. LePaige	LePaige	Ernest	R.	1, 2, 4
Arthur J. Lester	Lester	Arthur	J.	1, 2
Herbert S. Levine	Levine	Herbert	S.	1, 2

THE USES OF ALPHABETIC FILING

There are many ways you can use the alphabetic filing system in the office. You can arrange papers or letters by the writer's name; you can sort checks, cards, and lists of all kinds.

Some firms find it useful to set up address files with each card showing the name in two ways: (1) name transposed in indexing order on the top line to facilitate filing; (2) name in normal order, complete with the address, to make it easy to copy when envelopes and postal cards are being addressed.

You may be asked to prepare labels which are attached to the tabs of file folders. In the same manner described before, transpose the name of the individual—last name, first; first name or first initial, second; and middle name or middle initial, last. (The address may or may not be added.) Labels come in rolls and sheets so that they can be inserted easily into the typewriter. They also come in a variety of colors, which effectively divide files into sections.

```
Acker, Bruce T.
Mr. Bruce T. Acker
12 Main Street
Finly, Indiana 46129
```

```
Acker, Bruce T.
```

```
Acker, Bruce T.
12 Main Street
Finly, Ind. 46129
```

FINDING A NAME IN THE FILES

It's easy. Just review quickly the four rules you already know. Then follow these steps to locate the name you're looking for. Get the *complete* name if possible. This one is *Stephen T. LaSala*. Transpose it, and visualize it as *LaSala, Stephen T.* (Rule 1)

Locate the *L* section of the file or list you are looking through. Remind yourself that the prefix *La* in the name *LaSala* is considered as a part of the last name. (Rule 4)

Look for *LaSala* in the *L* section of the file. If you find more than one LaSala, compare the *second* indexing units and locate Stephen LaSala. If you find more than one Stephen LaSala, go to the third indexing units. (Rule 2)

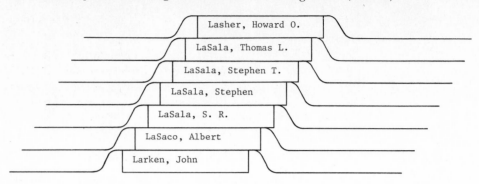

REVIEWING YOUR READING

1 What is the indexing order of individual names?
2 How is the distinction made between two separate names to be filed which have identical first and second indexing units?
3 What basic indexing principle is involved in the expression, "Nothing comes before something"? Explain.
4 How are last-name prefixes treated?

OFFICE ASSIGNMENTS

1 On a separate sheet of paper arrange three columns as shown below. In Column 1 list the ten names below. In Column 2 show how the names should be transposed for indexing. In Column 3 alphabetize the names.

Column 1   *Column 2*   *Column 3*
A. R. Blake
Arthur J. Block
Allen Blake
R. Allen Black
Charles Blackmore
Henry B. Blanco
O. Blake
E. A. Blank
James O. Bliven
Chester S. Blade

2 Each of the following ten lines contains three names in random order. Each name is identified by the letters *a, b,* or *c.* On a separate sheet of paper list

the numbers 1 to 10. Now for each number show the proper alphabetic order of the names on each line. Use the letters *a, b, c,* instead of names in order to save time.

Example: *(a)* Ellen Trout; *(b)* Basil Tripp; *(c)* Henry Trotta
Answer: *b, c, a*

1 *(a)* Ellen Trout; *(b)* Basil Tripp; *(c)* Henry Trotta
2 *(a)* Jerome Drew; *(b)* Ralph O. Drews; *(c)* Peter R. Drewes
3 *(a)* Harold A. Jacob; *(b)* Adam Jabow; *(c)* Samuel Jacobs
4 *(a)* William Ian; *(b)* William Iller; *(c)* Thomas Ilardi
5 *(a)* George King; *(b)* Roger Killip; *(c)* Lee Kirby
6 *(a)* William Dee; *(b)* Allen DeForrest; *(c)* Ruth DeAllessi
7 *(a)* Wilber Kurie; *(b)* Alice Knapp; *(c)* Roy Kolb
8 *(a)* A. Lockwood; *(b)* Locke; *(c)* Alan Locke
9 *(a)* James Coy; *(b)* Carl Coyle; *(c)* H. T. Clure
10 *(a)* Thomas M. Phillips; *(b)* T. M. Phillips; *(c)* T. Max Phillips

3 Type or write each of the following names in proper indexing order on a 5- by 3-inch card or slip of paper. Refer to the illustration on page 208 as an example. Also, record in the upper right corner of each card or slip the item number accompanying the names listed below.

1	Roger L. Marble	**6**	Timothy Manle
2	J. A. Maney	**7**	Joseph Marino
3	King D. Marratt	**8**	A. Turner Mann
4	Ellen Mahon	**9**	A. T. Mann
5	Frances R. Marino	**10**	Ted O. Mackay

a Arrange the cards or slips in alphabetic order.
b Make a list of the alphabetized names on a sheet of paper, and give it to your teacher.
c Retain the cards or slips so that you can use them again.

4 Type or write each of the following names in proper indexing order on a 5- by 3-inch card or slip of paper. Be sure to record the item number of each name in the upper right corner of each card or slip of paper.

11	Donald A. Manning	**16**	Leo S. Marano
12	Mary F. Mandel	**17**	Manne
13	King Douglas Marratt	**18**	Arthur T. Mann
14	George W. Moran	**19**	Fred C. Mante
15	Peter H. Macleod	**20**	Betty C. Markey

a Arrange the cards or slips in alphabetic order.
b Make a list of the alphabetized names on a sheet of paper, and give it to your teacher.
c Combine cards numbered 11 to 20 with cards numbered 1 to 10 (Office Assignment 3), and put them in alphabetic order.

d   Make a list of the 20 alphabetized names on a sheet of paper, and give it to your teacher.

e   Keep all the cards in alphabetic order for future use.

5   Most people know the alphabet perfectly when they're asked to repeat all the letters in sequence. A good file worker, however, can almost say the alphabet backward. You can develop speed and accuracy in learning to recognize which letters appear first in the alphabet by quizzing yourself when you read things such as street signs and headlines. Try it on a friend, and see who scores better.

Look at the list of paired letters below. On a separate sheet of paper, in exactly the same order as shown, write the letter that appears first in the alphabet in each of these pairs.

g-k	y-w	c-d	f-g	j-i
t-o	o-n	e-d	l-k	h-g
w-u	b-d	z-x	o-n	i-h
x-s	f-h	q-p	d-c	p-o
f-e	j-l	n-m	k-l	s-t
l-n	h-j	r-q	m-l	v-u
o-r	i-e	g-f	y-x	c-b
d-e	p-m	t-u	o-p	e-f
k-j	s-r	w-x	b-c	z-y
m-n	v-x	x-y	f-g	q-r

SECTION 17 Alphabetic Filing – Part 2

In addition to doing business with individuals, the company for which you work will have dealings with a great number and variety of other firms. So the next thing you will want to learn is how to file papers and documents according to the names of firms or organizations.

ORDER OF INDEXING UNITS IN FIRM NAMES

Rule 5: Index a firm name as it is written unless it includes the complete name of an individual.

If you are asked to make out cards for Wise Hardware Store and Whalen Cab Service. Your cards will look like the cards shown at the top of page 215.

Do you agree with the indexing order of the business firms listed below?

| | Indexing Order | | | |
	Unit 1	Unit 2	Unit 3	Unit 4
Western Foods Express	Western	Foods	Express	
Western Union Telegraph Company	Western	Union	Telegraph	Company
Whalen Cab Service	Whalen	Cab	Service	
Wild West Dude Ranch	Wild	West	Dude	Ranch
Wise Hardware Store	Wise	Hardware	Store	

Wise Hardware Store
Whalen Cab Service

INDIVIDUAL NAMES IN FIRM NAMES

Rule 6: If a firm name includes the surname and one or more other parts of the name of a person, transpose only the units in the name of the person.

Only the name of the individual is transposed. Everything else normally indexed in the firm name is indexed as it is written. If *Robert Lane* is the name of one of your accounts and if you also do business with a company called *Robert Lane Rentals*, you index each in the manner illustrated here.

| | Indexing Order | | | |
	Unit 1	Unit 2	Unit 3	Unit 4
Robert Lane	Lane	Robert		
Robert Lane Rentals	Lane	Robert	Rentals	
Robert T. Lane, Inc.	Lane	Robert	T.	Incorporated
Robert Lang Company	Lang	Robert	Company	
Robert Lange	Lange	Robert		

Lane, Robert, Rentals
Lane, Robert

THE ARTICLE *THE*

Rule 7: Disregard the article "the" as an indexing unit.

| | Indexing Order | | |
	Unit 1	Unit 2	Unit 3
Kenneth J. Salz	Salz	Kenneth	J.
Sam the Cook	Sam	Cook	
The Song Shop	Song	Shop	

Song Shop (The)
Sam (the) Cook

On file cards and file folders *the* is enclosed in parentheses and placed at the end of the name if it is the first word in the company name. Thus *The Song Shop* would appear as *Song Shop (The)*. If *the* appears in the middle of the name, as in *Sam the Cook*, enclose it in parentheses and leave it where it is.

HYPHENATED NAMES

Rule 8: Index hyphenated company names as separate units; index hyphenated surnames of individuals as one unit.

A hyphenated firm name often results from the formation of a partnership or from the union of two companies that were at one time separate. That's why you index each part of the hyphenated name as a separate unit.

Pitney Candy Shop

Pitney-Bowes, Inc.

Indexing Order

	Unit 1	Unit 2	Unit 3
Albert L. Pitney	Pitney	Albert	L.
Pitney-Bowes, Inc.	Pitney-	Bowes	Incorporated
Pitney Candy Shop	Pitney	Candy	Shop
Poly-Scientific Corp.	Poly-	Scientific	Corporation

A hyphenated individual name is the complete family name. Ignore the hyphen, and treat the two parts as one unit. In instances where the hyphenated name of an individual appears with nothing before or after it, as in *Kingsley-Jones*, index it as two units.

Kingsley-James, John, Associates, Inc.*

Kingsley, Mary E.

Indexing Order

	Unit 1	Unit 2	Unit 3	Unit 4
Robert Kincey	Kincey	Robert		
Kingsley-Jones	Kingsley-	Jones		
Kingsley-Jones Manufacturing Co.	Kingsley-	Jones	Manufacturing	Company
Mary E. Kingsley	Kingsley	Mary	E.	
John Kingsley-James Associates, Inc.	Kingsley-James	John	Associates	Incorporated
Henry J. Kingsley-Jones	Kingsley-Jones	Henry	J.	
Adam Kingslund	Kingslund	Adam		

ABBREVIATED NAMES

Rule 9: Index abbreviated words as if they were written out in full; index single letters that are not abbreviations as separate units.

Some well-known business firms are commonly identified by initials. Good examples are RCA for Radio Corporation of America and IBM for International Business Machines Corporation. Since you must index abbreviations such as these as if they were actually spelled out, be sure you know what the initials stand for.

Gibson, William

GMC

Indexing Order

	Unit 1	Unit 2	Unit 3
CTA	Chicago	Transit	Authority
GMC	General	Motors	Corporation
Wm. Gibson	Gibson	William	
Thompkins H. S.	Thompkins	High	School

*On account of the limitations of space, some captions in the marginal illustrations appear on two lines. It should be remembered, however, that there is enough room on an actual 3- by 5-inch card to type the caption on one line.

When the name of a concern consists of separate letters that are not actual abbreviations, treat each letter as a separate indexing unit. Remember to compare first unit by unit, then letter by letter.

Indexing Order

	Unit 1	Unit 2	Unit 3	Unit 4
ABC Cleaners	A	B	C	Cleaners
ABC Products	A	B	C	Products
AMA	American	Management	Association	
BBC	British	Broadcasting	Corporation	
CIT Corporation	C	I	T	Corporation
FJ Garage	F	J	Garage	
XYZ Company	X	Y	Z	Company

AMA

ABC Products

ABC Cleaners

You may index letters in a firm name as separate units on the assumption that the letters don't stand for any specific words. Later, you may discover that the letters really do stand for words. *FJ Garage*, you learn, is the *Ferguson and Jenkins Garage*. If the company, however, is commonly known as the *FJ Garage*, everything should be filed under that name, and a cross-reference notation should be made under *Ferguson and Jenkins Garage*. You'll learn how to cross-reference later on.

CONJUNCTIONS, PREPOSITIONS, AND FIRM ENDINGS

Rule 10: Disregard conjunctions and prepositions in indexing. Treat company name endings as separate indexing units as though they were written out in full.

On cards and folders show conjunctions and prepositions, such as *for, of, as, and, in, &,* and *or,* in parentheses in their regular order.

Words such as *Corporation, Company, Limited, Associates,* and so on are important because they not only are part of the legal name of the organization but also describe its structure.

Indexing Order

	Unit 1	Unit 2	Unit 3
B and J Co.	B	J	Company
Ruth Baker	Baker	Ruth	
Daughters of the American Revolution	Daughters	American	Revolution
Friends in the Village, Inc.	Friends	Village	Incorporated
Ward for Governor Headquarters	Ward	Governor	Headquarters

Baker, Ruth

B (and) J Co.

REVIEW OF THE FIRST TEN RULES

The following 20 names are correctly indexed and alphabetized and illustrate how the first ten rules are applied. The rules applying to each name are noted in the Rule column. See if you can explain how these rules are applied.

Indexing Order

	Unit 1	Unit 2	Unit 3	Unit 4	Rule
D and D Laundry	D	D	Laundry		2, 5, 9, 10
Roger Dahl, Inc.	Dahl	Roger	Incorporated		2, 6, 10
Robert Daley	Daley	Robert			1, 2
Dallow-Dawes Associates	Dallow-	Dawes	Associates		2, 5, 8
John T. Daly	Daly	John	T.		1, 2
T. F. Daly	Daly	T.	F.		1, 2, 3
Teresa Daly	Daly	Teresa			1, 2
Dan the Barber	Dan	Barber			2, 5, 7
Charles P. D'Andrea	D'Andrea	Charles	P.		1, 2, 4
Arthur Daniels H. S.	Daniels	Arthur	High	School	2, 6, 9
Dante Custom Tailor Shop	Dante	Custom	Tailor	Shop	2, 5
Daughters of Charity	Daughters	Charity			2, 5, 10
Davis	Davis				2, 3
Mary S. Davis	Davis	Mary	S.		1, 2, 3
James R. Davis-Parker	Davis-Parker	James	R.		1, 2, 8
Daviss-Powers Pump Corp.	Daviss-	Powers	Pump	Corporation	2, 5, 8, 10
Kingsley Dawes	Dawes	Kingsley			1, 2
Dawson Corporation	Dawson	Corporation			2, 5
Peter deBrum	deBrum	Peter			1, 2, 4
D.C. Transit Lines	District	Columbia	Transit	Lines	2, 5, 9, 10

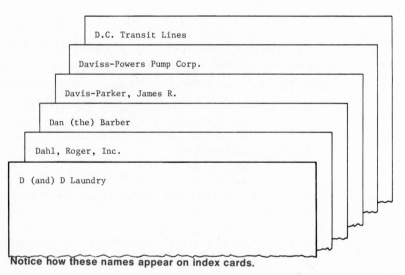

Notice how these names appear on index cards.

REVIEWING YOUR READING

1 How is the article *the* handled in indexing? Why? How would the article appear on a file folder label?

2 Why would the first indexing unit of McKensey-Clark Company be different from that of Roger McKensey-Clark?

3 How are abbreviated words in firm names handled in indexing?

4 How are conjunctions and prepositions handled in indexing?

5 Why aren't firm endings disregarded in indexing?

OFFICE ASSIGNMENTS

1 On a separate sheet of paper arrange two columns as shown here. In Column 1 list the ten names below. Then alphabetize them in Column 2.

Column 1   *Column 2*

1 Robert L. Pitts Company
2 Pete the Butcher
3 Donald Penna
4 Howard Pierce-Baker
5 Penn Central
6 Petro-Motive Corporation
7 James A. Philips
8 Pinto Riding Stables
9 Petrie of Pinewood, Inc.
10 Percy L. Pine

2 Each of the ten lines below contains three names in random order. On a separate sheet of paper list the numbers 1 to 10. Then to the right of the number, show the proper alphabetic order of the names on each line. Use the letters *a, b, c* instead of names in order to save time.

Example: *(a)* George King Stores; *(b)* Leon George; *(c)* Kingsley-Wood Co.
    Answer: *b, a, c*

1 *(a)* George King Stores; *(b)* Leon George; *(c)* Kingsley-Wood Co.
2 *(a)* The Art Shop; *(b)* Arthur the Tailor; *(c)* The P. Arlen Co.
3 *(a)* Joseph Logan; *(b)* A. R. Long; *(c)* Jean Long Shops, Inc.
4 *(a)* R. Lore; *(b)* P. R. Lord; *(c)* Susan Lowe
5 *(a)* Peter Larson; *(b)* John LaRosa; *(c)* Alan Larsen
6 *(a)* FDIC; *(b)* F & F Furniture Co.; *(c)* Fairview Lodge
7 *(a)* Leon Louis; *(b)* Leo Lewis; *(c)* St. Louis Terminal
8 *(a)* J. R. Moore; *(b)* J. S. Moore; *(c)* J. R. S. Moore
9 *(a)* Pat Mulleck; *(b)* Carol Mullen; *(c)* Robin Malhall
10 *(a)* Baker-Stoll Co.; *(b)* Baker of Quality; *(c)* Baker Street Pharmacy

3 Type or write each of the following names in proper indexing order on a 5- by 3-inch card or slip of paper. Also, record the item number in the upper right corner of each card or slip.

21 Manor Garden Apartments
22 Martino for Footwear
23 Leonard L. Mako
24 Terrance Maher Construction Company
25 Mansfield Record Company

26   Martin-Mallory Truckline
27   Michigan Central Railroad
28   Mariano Restaurants
29   Richard Mannix-Davis
30   Manor Garden Bootery

a   Arrange the cards or slips in alphabetic order.
b   Make a list of the alphabetized names on a sheet of paper, and give it to your teacher.
c   Combine cards 21 to 30 with cards 1 to 20 (from previous assignments), and put them in alphabetic order.
d   Using the numbers in the upper right corner of your 30 cards or slips of paper, list the item numbers (names not required) in correct alphabetic order as follows:

Alphabetic Order	Item No.
1	10
2	15
3	24

e   Give the list to your teacher, and keep the cards in alphabetic order for future use.

4   Type or write each of the following names in proper indexing order on a 5- by 3-inch card or slip of paper. Also, record the item number in the upper right corner.

31   Mather-Martin Supply Stores
32   R. T. Mayberry
33   Manuel T. Manus
34   Master Patterns Press
35   Manny for Fine Food
36   A. Dale Masters
37   Maria Marsden Cosmetics Corporation
38   Maya Dining Room
39   Richard T. May
40   Matteson Engineering, Incorporated

a   Arrange the cards or slips in alphabetic order.
b   Make a list of the ten alphabetized names on a sheet of paper, and give it to your teacher.
c   Combine cards 31 to 40 with cards 1 to 30 (from previous assignments), and put them in alphabetic order.
d   List the item numbers in correct alphabetic order as explained previously in Office Assignment 3.
e   Give the list to your teacher, and keep cards 1 to 40 in alphabetic order for future use.

5   Test yourself. See how fast you can identify the proper alphabetic sequence of the following pairs of file captions. On a separate sheet of paper write the caption in each pair that is first alphabetically.

Al-All	Ap-Ar	Bai-Bak	Au-Ay	Av-Aur
Alp-Am	At-Asi	Ban-Balm	Bar-Barr	Ad-Ae
Andr-Ang	Atl-Art	Adc-Ae	Alli-Alp	Ame-Alp
Art-Ard	Bae-Bad	Ami-Am	Abd-Aar	Ai-Adc

The indexing rules that apply to the names of individuals and business firms will cover most of the routine situations you will encounter on a job. However, there are bound to be some names that will make you pause now and then. The special rules in this section will tell you how to file these names with the same sureness and efficiency with which you handle the rest of your filing responsibilities.

ONE- OR TWO-WORD OPTIONS

Rule 11: Index as one unit any word that may be written as either one word or two words.

Some firm names include words which may be written as either one word or two words, such as *Interstate* or *Inter State* and *Northwest* or *North West.* Regardless of how they appear on the firm's correspondence, treat such words as one unit. If you are consistent in applying this rule, you'll avoid having to look in more than one location for such a name.

	Indexing Order		
	Unit 1	*Unit 2*	*Unit 3*
Northeast Airlines	Northeast	Airlines	
North East Travel Bureau	North East	Travel	Bureau
Northeastern Oil Company	Northeastern	Oil	Company
North West Harbor Club	North West	Harbor	Club
Northwestern Mills, Inc.	Northwestern	Mills	Incorporated

COMPOUND GEOGRAPHIC NAMES

Rule 12: Index compound geographic names as separate units except when the first part of the name is a foreign word.

Many business firm names contain the name of a town, river, or other geographic location. An example is Philadelphia Knitting Mills. When the geographic term is a single word, it is treated, as you would expect, as one unit.

	Indexing Order		
	Unit 1	*Unit 2*	*Unit 3*
Parker Supply Company	Parker	Supply	Company
Philadelphia Knitting Mills	Philadelphia	Knitting	Mills
Pillsbury Hotel	Pillsbury	Hotel	

If the compound name consists of two English words, treat each word as a separate unit.

Hudson River Day Line
Houston News Company

	Indexing Order			
	Unit 1	**Unit 2**	**Unit 3**	**Unit 4**
Houston News Company	Houston	News	Company	
Hudson River Day Line	Hudson	River	Day	Line
Lake Erie Transportation Company	Lake	Erie	Transportation	Company
Lakewood Dairy	Lakewood	Dairy		
New York Land Co.	New	York	Land	Company
Pikes Peak Service Station	Pikes	Peak	Service	Station

If the first part of a compound name is a foreign language word, consider the foreign word and the word following it as one indexing unit. Compound names of this sort include foreign words such as *Des, El, Los,* and *San,* as in *Des Moines, El Paso, Los Angeles, San Diego, San Francisco,* and *San Juan.*

Mille Lacs Resort
Millear Theater

	Indexing Order			
	Unit 1	**Unit 2**	**Unit 3**	**Unit 4**
Los Alamos Construction Company	Los Alamos	Construction	Company	
Los Angeles Terminal Corporation	Los Angeles	Terminal	Corporation	
Millear Theater	Millear	Theater		
Mille Lacs Resort	Mille Lacs	Resort		
New River Power Co.	New	River	Power	Company
St. Louis Waterways Co.	Saint	Louis	Waterways	Company

TITLES, DEGREES, AND SENIORITY TERMS

Rule 13: Do not consider titles and degrees as indexing units, but do treat seniority terms as indexing units.

Persons in certain professions are generally addressed by their titles, as in *Dr. Richard L. Brown, Dean Mary J. Knight, Reverend Henry B. Lake,* and *Senator Robert Simons.* On documents and correspondence some people prefer to write their names, followed with abbreviations of academic degrees, as in *Lyle M. Turner, M.D.,* and *Ronald H. Adams, Ph.D.* On file cards and folders titles and degrees are enclosed in parentheses and placed at the end of the name.

Turner, Lyle M. (M.D.)
Brown, Richard L. (Dr.)

	Indexing Order		
	Unit 1	**Unit 2**	**Unit 3**
Dr. Richard L. Brown	Brown	Richard	L.
Major James H. Carpenter	Carpenter	James	H.
Reverend Henry B. Lake	Lake	Henry	B.
Professor Peter M. Moran	Moran	Peter	M.
Lyle M. Turner, M.D.	Turner	Lyle	M.
Dean Edwin N. Victor	Victor	Edwin	N.

Note that there are two exceptions:

1 If used with one name only, a title *is* an indexing unit, *is not* enclosed in parentheses, and *is not* transposed. The most common examples of this exception occur in royalty and religious orders.

Queen Mary

Prince Albert

Indexing Order

	Unit 1	Unit 2
Prince Albert	Prince	Albert
Queen Mary	Queen	Mary
Sister Marie	Sister	Marie

2 If it is the first word in a firm name, a title *is* an indexing unit, *is not* enclosed in parentheses, and *is not* transposed. An example is *Dr. Pepper Bottling Company.*

Since seniority terms often distinguish names that are otherwise identical, they are always indexed as individual units. When numbers are used to indicate seniority, spell them out in full and alphabetize accordingly. *Jr.* is Junior, *Sr.* is Senior, *II* is Second, *III* is Third, and *IV* is Fourth.

Duncan, Paul, Jr.

Duncan, Paul

Indexing Order

	Unit 1	Unit 2	Unit 3
Paul Duncan	Duncan	Paul	
Paul Duncan, Jr.	Duncan	Paul	Junior
Paul Duncan, Sr.	Duncan	Paul	Senior
Paul Duncan, III	Duncan	Paul	Third

The following are abbreviations of commonly used titles and degrees:

Title		Degree	
Col.	(Colonel)	D.D.S.	(Doctor of Dental Science)
Dr.	(Doctor)	D.V.M.	(Doctor of Veterinary Medicine)
Hon.	(Honorable)	M.D.	(Doctor of Medicine)
Prof.	(Professor)	M.S.	(Master of Science)
Rev.	(Reverend)	Ph.D.	(Doctor of Philosophy)

POSSESSIVES

Rule 14: When a word ends with "apostrophe s," drop the "s" in indexing; when a word ends in "s apostrophe," retain the "s" because it is part of the word.

Occasionally you will come across a firm name such as *Lane's Super Service.* Actually, their name means a Super Service company belonging to a man named Lane. Since the way he spells his name does not change if the apostrophe and the *s* are dropped, you can disregard both in filing.

Indexing Order

	Unit 1	Unit 2	Unit 3
Audrey R. Lamb	Lamb	Audrey	R.
Lamb's Bookstore	Lamb	Bookstore	
Lane's Super Service	Lane	Super	Service
Thomas Allen Lane	Lane	Thomas	Allen

In a name like *The Pirates' Den*, disregard only the apostrophe, because the *s* is actually part of the original name.

Indexing Order

	Unit 1	Unit 2	Unit 3
Leon Vincent Perry	Perry	Leon	Vincent
June O. Persons	Persons	June	O.
The Pirate's Place	Pirate	Place	
The Pirates' Den	Pirates	Den	
Powell's Laundry	Powell	Laundry	

Pirates' Den (The)

Pirate's Place (The)

U.S. AND FOREIGN GOVERNMENT NAMES

Rule 15: Index U.S. federal government names under United States Government, then department name, then bureau or board name or any other subdivision.

Phrases such as *Department of, Bureau of,* and *Office of* are not considered indexing units and on file cards and folders are enclosed in parentheses and placed after the words with which they are used.

Even if the word *Government* or the words *United States* or *United States Government* are not part of the title of a federal agency, make your first three indexing units the words *United States Government*. For example, your first three indexing units for NASA (National Aeronautics and Space Administration) would be *United States Government*.

United States Steel Corp.

United States Government Treasury (Department)

Indexing Order

	Unit 1	Unit 2	Unit 3	Unit 4
Treasury Department	United	States	Government	Treasury

Foreign government names are indexed in much the same way U.S. federal government names are indexed: (1) by name of country, then (2) by name of agency.

Canadian Sales Co.

Canada (Dominion of) Defense (Department)

Indexing Order

	Unit 1	Unit 2	Unit 3
Dominion of Canada Defense Department	Canada	Defense	
Canadian Sales Company	Canadian	Sales	Company
Commonwealth of India, Education Department	India	Education	

NONFEDERAL POLITICAL DIVISIONS

Rule 16: Index names pertaining to states and other political divisions under the name of the political division; then the division classification (state, county, city, or town); and then under the name of the department, bureau, board, or other subdivision.

Thus, for indexing purposes, the name Chicago Fire Department becomes Chicago City Fire; Texas Highway Department becomes Texas State Highway.

One of the things to watch out for is that often the classification is not specifically given. You know that Texas is a state, but the name of the Texas Highway Department does not include the word state. In indexing you have to supply that information.

Indexing Order

	Unit 1	Unit 2	Unit 3	Unit 4
Street Department, City of Butte	Butte	City	Street	
Kansas State University	Kansas	State	University	
Newark Township, Community Center	Newark	Township	Community	Center
San Francisco Police Department	San Francisco	City	Police	
San Francisco College for Women	San Francisco	College	Women	

San Francisco College (for) Women

San Francisco City Police (Department)

NUMBERS

Rule 17: Index numbers in a name as though they were written out in words, and regard the whole number as one unit.

Express large numbers in the fewest possible words. For example, index *1205* as *twelve hundred five* (not *one thousand two hundred five*). This same rule applies to names of business firms which include numbers, such as *Keith's 7th Avenue Theater* and the *21 Club*. Spell out the numbers, and treat them as one indexing unit.

Indexing Order

	Unit 1	Unit 2	Unit 3	Unit 4
Keith's 7th Avenue Theater	Keith	Seventh	Avenue	Theater
Twenty Plus Society	Twenty	Plus	Society	
21 Club	Twenty-one	Club		
2100 East Boulevard Apartments	Twenty-one hundred	East	Boulevard	Apartments

Twenty-one Club

Twenty Plus Society

ADDRESSES

Rule 18: Consider addresses when names of individuals or firms are identical.

Index identical names first by name of individual or firm, then by name of city, then by name of state if cities are identical, then by name of street. If every indexing unit you check is identical, down to the very street, go on to the house or building number, working from the lowest to the highest number. These numbers are not spelled out because they will always be the last unit and can be treated numerically more easily.

Dave's Markets,
Chester, Pennsylvania

Dave's Markets,
Chester, Delaware

	Unit 1	Unit 2	Unit 3	Unit 4	Unit 5
Dave's Markets, Chester, Delaware	Dave	Markets	Chester	Delaware	
Dave's Markets, Chester, Pennsylvania	Dave	Markets	Chester	Pennsylvania	
Dave's Markets, Ruxton, Maryland	Dave	Markets	Ruxton		
Dave's Markets, Academy Street, Sheffield, Alabama	Dave	Markets	Sheffield	Alabama	Academy
Dave's Markets, Roberts Street, Sheffield, Alabama	Dave	Markets	Sheffield	Alabama	Roberts

BANK NAMES

Rule 19: Index bank names under the name of the city, then the name of the bank, and then the name of the state (when the city names and the bank names are identical).

The city name is indexed first because of the similarity of bank names all over the country. A First National Bank, for instance, can be found in almost any sizable city. Index by state names only when both the city names and the bank names are identical.

Columbus, American
National Bank

Cleveland, American
National Bank

Indexing Order

	Unit 1	Unit 2	Unit 3	Unit 4	Unit 5
American National Bank, Cleveland, Ohio	Cleveland	American	National	Bank	
American National Bank, Columbus, Ohio	Columbus	American	National	Bank	
First National Bank, Delta, Georgia	Delta	First	National	Bank	Georgia
First National Bank, Delta, Texas	Delta	First	National	Bank	Texas

MARRIED WOMEN'S NAMES

Rule 20: Use the legal name of a married woman in indexing.

The legal name of a married woman may be in either of two forms: (1) her own first name and maiden last name and her husband's last name; (2) her own first and middle names and her husband's last name.

Daniels, Helen
Virginia (Mrs.)

Daniels, Adam

On file cards and folders *Mrs.* is enclosed in parentheses and placed at the end of a name. The husband's first name and middle name or initial are enclosed in parentheses and placed on the line below the woman's legal name.

Thus Mrs. Adam Daniels' legal name may be Mrs. Helen Kane Daniels or Mrs. Helen Virginia Daniels. Either way distinguishes clearly between her name and her husband's.

Miss, Mrs., Ms., and *Mr.* are not considered indexing units and are noted on file cards only for addressing purposes. Since *Mrs.* indicates a married woman, the name following it is indexed according to the two alternatives for married women. *Ms.* indicates a wish to be addressed in just that manner and should be treated as a title, that is, not indexed but placed in parentheses at the end of the name.

REVIEW OF ALPHABETIC FILING RULES

The 20 indexing rules you have learned represent a complete system for indexing all kinds of names alphabetically. If you can identify the rules involved in each of the names on the list below, you'll have no trouble on your first filing job. Try it.

Indexing Order

	Unit 1	Unit 2	Unit 3	Unit 4	Rule
Lorna T. SaBelle	SaBelle	Lorna	T.		1, 2, 4
St. Paul Department Store	Saint	Paul	Department	Store	2, 9
Sampson's	Sampson				2, 14
Sister Scholastica	Sister	Scholastica			2, 13
16 Park Place Hotel	Sixteen	Park	Place	Hotel	2, 17
Department of Health, South Carolina	South	Carolina	State	Health	2, 12, 16
South Dakota State Police	South	Dakota	State	Police	2, 12, 16
South Haven Feed Store	South	Haven	Feed	Store	2, 12
South Side Stationery Store	South	Side	Stationery	Store	2, 5
James R. Southall	Southall	James	R.		1, 2
Mrs. Robert (Dora L.) Southerland	Southerland	Dora	L.		1, 2, 20
Southland Printing Corporation	Southland	Printing	Corporation		2, 10
S. P. Southwell, Ph.D.	Southwell	S.	P.		1, 2, 3, 13
Samuel R. Southwell	Southwell	Samuel	R.		1, 2
South West Motor Stages	South West	Motor	Stages		2, 11
Mrs. Stephen (Mary Smith) Stanley	Stanley	Mary	Smith		1, 2, 20
Steve's Appliances, Manchester, Vermont	Steve	Appliances	Manchester		2, 14, 18
Steve's Appliances, Stowe, Vermont	Steve	Appliances	Stowe		2, 14, 18
The Roger S. Stevens Co.	Stevens	Roger	S.	Company	2, 6, 7, 10
Henry R. Stone-Sims	Stone-Sims	Henry	R.		1, 2, 8
First National Bank, Sunbury, Pennsylvania	Sunbury	First	National	Bank	2, 19
Swiss Consulate at Chicago	Switzerland	Consulate	Chicago		2, 15, 18
Swiss Consulate at New York	Switzerland	Consulate	New	York	2, 15, 18

REVIEWING YOUR READING

1 For indexing purposes does it matter if a name is spelled Northeast or North East? What is the rule?

2 What is the difference in meaning between Pirate's and Pirates'? How would each name be treated in indexing?

3 What are the first three indexing units involved in filing correspondence from an agency of the U.S. federal government?

4 Identify the indexing units involved in a name such as 1215 Park Avenue Hotel.

5 How do you determine a married woman's legal name for indexing purposes? What constitutes her legal name?

OFFICE ASSIGNMENTS

1 On a separate sheet of paper, arrange two columns as shown here. In Column 1 list the ten names below. Then alphabetize them in Column 2.

Column 1	*Column 2*
1 Samuel L. Spencer, D.D.S.	
2 The Seamen's Home	
3 San Diego Loan Company	
4 Sidney A. Spruce, Incorporated	
5 17 South Main Apartments	
6 South West Motor Lines	
7 South Dakota Highway Department	
8 Steamboat Springs Hotel	
9 Sister Veronica	
10 Seattle Board of Education	

2 Each of the five groups below contains five names in random order. On a separate sheet of paper show the proper alphabetic order for each item in the group. Use letters *a, b, c, d, e* instead of names in order to save time.

Example: *a*   Brandon's Dairy
              b   Brother Barnabas
              c   Bryant Park Inn
              d   City of Bristol, Bureau of Buildings
              e   Baja Rio Steamboat Line
              Answer: *e, a, d, b, c*

1   *a*   100 Halstead Building
    b   Hall-Hallett Car Wash
    c   Haas' Restaurant
    d   Hamilton County Welfare Department
    e   James H. Fitz-Hall

2 *a* Maco's Cab Company
    b McDonald and Maguire, Attorneys
    c Mrs. Hazel McArdle Maker
    d Dr. Maxwell MacInnes
    e Mackay Parcel Service

3 *a* U.S. Treasury Department
    b Department of Health, Education, and Welfare
    c FBI
    d U.S. Justice Department
    e Director of Internal Revenue

4 *a* Tyler Drugs, Tyler, Texas
    b Tyler Drugs, Tucson, Arizona
    c Tyler Drugs, Twin Falls, Idaho
    d Tyler Drugs, Turnerville, New Mexico
    e Tyler Drugs, Tyrone, Pennsylvania

5 *a* Second District Clubhouse
    b 666 Club
    c Secor Lane Tailor
    d 7th Avenue Arcade Tailor
    e Sister Sophia

3 Type or write each of the following names in proper indexing order on a 5- by 3-inch card or slip of paper. Record the item number in the upper right corner of each card or slip of paper.

41 Mesa Verde Motel		**46** McArthur and MacLeod	
42 Massachusetts Turnpike Authority		**47** Mother's Fine Bread Company	
43 Midway Falls Resort		**48** Mayor Michael Maguire	
44 Midland City Planning Board		**49** Monsignor Martin McCarthy	
45 Mid West Truck Lines		**50** Midwestern Air Freight, Incorporated	

a Arrange the cards or slips in alphabetic order.
b Make a list of the alphabetized names on a sheet of paper, and give it to your teacher.
c Combine items 41 to 50 with items 1 to 40 (from previous assignments), and put them in alphabetic order.
d Using the numbers in the upper right corner of the cards or slips of paper, list the item numbers (names not required) in correct alphabetic order as follows:

Alphabetic Order	*Item No.*
1	10
2	15
3	48

e Give the list to your teacher, and keep the cards in alphabetic order for future use.

4 Type or write the following names in proper indexing order on a 5- by 3-inch card or slip of paper. Then record the item number in the upper right corner.

51 Margaret L. Matos
52 Principality of Monaco, Immigration Service
53 Middle Island Realty Company
54 James McCaffrey Travel Agency
55 Mike's Midtown Parking
56 Mrs. Robert (Mary McAvoy) Manning
57 Mayflower Laundry and Cleaners
58 Macbeth Players Company
59 Water Department, Town of Mayberry
60 Reverend Manuel R. Mannion

a Arrange the cards or slips in alphabetic order.
b Make a list of the ten alphabetized names on a sheet of paper, and give it to your teacher.
c Combine cards 51 to 60 with cards 1 to 50 (from previous assignments), and put them in alphabetic order.
d List the item numbers in correct alphabetic order as explained previously in Office Assignment 3.
e Give the list to your teacher, and keep all the cards in alphabetic order for future use.

5 List the following last names in alphabetic order on a separate sheet of paper:

Karzar   Kercher
Kircher   Kursheer
Karraker   Kirsher
Kerger   Karscher
Kirker   Kershaver
Kerriger   Karicker
Karcher   Karker
Kirscher   Kerschker

19 Subject, Numeric, Chronological, and Geographic Filing

"Let me have last week's sales report, please." "May I have the ecology file?" "Do we have any information on tax-sheltered annuities?"

These kinds of requests made by employers are very common. They need information of all kinds throughout the day in order to run their business efficiently, and they count on you to find this information. Note that all three of these requests have one special characteristic in common. They call for information about *things* rather than about people or businesses. Information like this is filed by subject in a system called *subject filing*—the organization of information by subject or topic.

Another series of requests from an employer might sound like this: "I need Policy 274-8007." "Please check this invoice against Purchase Order 34824." "Type this on form No. 8-26."

Material like this is filed by number in an effective system known as *numeric filing*.

Still another system of filing is used to deal with the fact that in every office there are important dates and deadlines to note and remember.

Your boss may say, "Please have the Minnesota and Wisconsin distributorship lists ready for my meeting on Friday." This type of information is filed according to the date on which action is to be taken. Filing according to date is called *chronological filing*.

And finally, the system of filing based on geographic location is called *geographic filing*. "We have a customer," your boss may say, "who is looking for an apartment in the Hickory Grove development." Information would be filed under geographic location, which in this case would be *Hickory Grove*.

Let's explore these four additional filing systems: subject filing, numeric filing, chronological filing, and geographic filing.

SUBJECT FILING

Some items are filed by subject instead of by an individual or company name. Subject categories may be activities, such as Purchasing or Selling; classifications, such as Office Furniture or Electric Tools; or products, such as Desks or Hammers. File the subject category just as you would file a regular name, and place the folder in alphabetic order in the general correspondence file along with the folders of individuals and companies. Your alphabetic file will then contain a mixture of names and subject items.

As the business grows and the number of subjects increases, you may want to divide large subject categories, such as office furniture, into smaller divisions, such as desks, chairs, file cabinets, and so on. This will make your filing easier and your files less cumbersome. If there are a great many items filed by subject category in the general correspondence file, the company may decide to set up a separate alphabetic subject file just for them.

Subject filing can be adapted to the operation of almost any organization such as a professional office, a retail store, a school, or a large business. The subject captions will vary, depending upon the nature of the organization. A file for a doctor's office might include the following subject captions:

Automobile	Inventory
Expense Record	Equipment
Rental Contract	Furniture
Contributions	Supplies
Correspondence (personal)	Investments
Drugs and Pharmaceuticals	Office Supplies and Expenses
Equipment	Personnel
Office	Professional Activities
Surgical	Meetings
Insurance	Memberships
Fire and Theft	Papers and Articles
Malpractice	Tax Reports and Records

On the other hand, the files maintained by the centralized office services unit of a large corporation might include subject captions like the following:

Budget	Messenger Service
Cash Control	Payroll Procedures
Contracts	Personnel Procedures
Credit and Collections	Postal Rules and Regulations
Emergency Procedures	Purchase Orders
Employee Ratings	Quotations
Equipment	Reports
Filing	Requisitions
Financial Statements	Standards
Forms and Records	Supplies
Handbooks	Telegrams
Interoffice Communications	Telephone Services
Job Descriptions	Transcribing Procedures

Filing Procedure

Papers to be filed by subject are indexed by your filing supervisor or a file clerk, according to a list of possible captions developed from a study of the company's operations. The papers are then sorted and stored in the files.

Files are arranged in a certain way to help make filing papers easy. Note the subject file illustrated on page 233. The caption on the tab to the far left is a primary guide. Primary guides help divide this subject file into alphabetic sections. Individual folders with their subject captions are filed alphabetically behind the guide. Behind the last subject folder in each alphabetic section there is a folder called the *miscellaneous folder*. This folder is used to hold single papers pertaining to some subject for which five pieces of correspondence have not yet accumulated. When five pieces for that particular subject do accumulate, the correspondence is taken out of the miscellaneous folder, assigned its own individual folder with its subject caption, and filed alphabetically among the individual folders in that alphabetic section.

Finding Techniques

Information can be found in two ways. Items that are used frequently may be requested by their specific names. If your boss asks for last week's safety report, you'd have no problem locating it promptly in a folder you have marked "Safety Reports."

However, not all requests are so specific. Someone in the purchasing department, for example, asks you, "Do we have any recent quotations on typewriter ribbons?" You think about where such information might be filed and decide to look under "Office Supplies," and there it is! If typewriter ribbons had been a frequently requested item, you might have found the information about them in their own separate individual folder. The point is that with subject filing you have to think in what subject category the information you are seeking might be located and perhaps look in more than one place for it.

When the paper volume grows too large for a main subject heading, you may want to break down the main heading into smaller divisions by using a subject and number division instead of just a subject division.

Subject-Number System

Subject Division Only	Subject-Number System	
Office Equipment	Office Equipment	600
Bookcases	Bookcases	601
Cabinets	Cabinets	602
Chairs	Chairs	603
Desks	Desks	604
Files	Files	605
Lights	Lights	606
Machines	Machines	607
Racks	Racks	608
Stands	Stands	609
Tables	Tables	610

An alphabetic subject file.

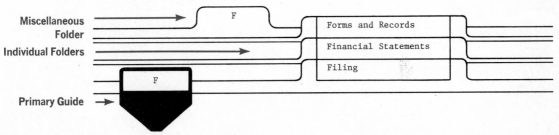

Miscellaneous Folder

Individual Folders

F

Forms and Records

Financial Statements

Filing

Primary Guide

F

You can further subdivide the subject-number system by using decimals.

Decimal-Numeric System

Office Equipment 600			
Machines	607		
Adding		607.1	
Calculating		607.2	
Duplicating		607.3	
Offset			607.31
Photocopy			607.32
Stencil			607.33
Folding		607.4	
Mailing		607.5	
Posting		607.6	
Sorting		607.7	
Tying		607.8	
Wrapping		607.9	

Government agencies are well known for their use of the decimal-numeric filing system.

NUMERIC FILING

In some businesses numbers are the logical basis for distinguishing one transaction or one customer from another. For instance, insurance companies issue numbered policies to new policyholders and then file their records according to policy number. Legal offices, engineering companies, social agencies, and public agencies that deal with thousands of people keep records according to account or case number.

Filing Procedure

The numeric filing system uses numeric rather than alphabetic breakdowns. It is customary to have a guide for approximately every ten to twenty file folders. *Guides* are signaling devices installed in file drawers and other types of file containers, such as tubs, which help you find and file papers quickly and easily. Guides act as signposts which designate the location of records behind the guide and up to the next guide and distribute the file folders evenly among the cabinet drawers. In addition, an alphabetic miscellaneous file is placed in front of the first file drawer. The miscellaneous file holds papers dealing with individuals and companies with whom the company only occasionally corresponds and for whom five pieces of correspondence have not yet accumulated. Note the illustration on page 235. To file correspondence to or from a new customer who will later be assigned a specific number, do the following:

1   Index and code the name under which the item is to be filed. When you *code* a record, you mark the correspondence with the caption selected for indexing. The caption can be either underlined or written in the upper right corner of the correspondence.

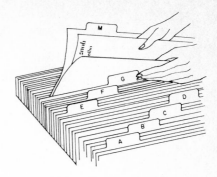

A main numeric file.

A miscellaneous alphabetic file.

2 Prepare an index card bearing the name or caption indexed and coded on the correspondence. Write the code letter *M* (for miscellaneous) on the card.

3 File the card in its proper alphabetic position in a card index.

4 File the paper or correspondence in alphabetic order in the miscellaneous file for new names, pending number assignments.

5 When five or more pieces of correspondence have accumulated for an individual, assign the name a number selected from the numeric file register and write the name alongside its assigned number in the register. The register contains the numbers which are assigned in sequence to each active correspondent.

6 Cross off the *M* code on the index card, and write the assigned code number in its place. Refile the card in its correct alphabetic position in the card index.

7 Prepare an individual file folder, label the top of the file folder with the individual's assigned number, and store in it all the papers withdrawn from the miscellaneous folder which pertain to that individual.

8 Place the new file folder in the main numeric file in its correct numeric position.

A numeric file register listing accounts with their assigned numbers.

As shown on this index card, the Benson Supply Company has been assigned the number 1633.

NUMBER	NAME	DATE
1633	Benson Supply Company	11/26/--
1634	A. G. Knowles, Inc.	11/26/--
1635	Norris, William A.	11/27/--
1636		
1637		

```
Benson Supply Company                          ✗  1633
403 Newton Road
Wilmington, Delaware 19810
```

To file material from a frequent correspondent, follow these steps:

1 Read the correspondence to find out what the customer's assigned number is.
2 If the number is not listed on the correspondence, find the name on its card in alphabetic order in the card index. The card will list the customer's file number.
3 Note the file number on the correspondence.
4 File the item in its appropriate file folder. To be sure you file the item correctly, compare the name on the correspondence with the name appearing on the material already in the folder.

Finding Techniques

You may be asked to find something in a numeric file either by number or by name.

By number: If you are asked to find a specific numbered folder, you can do this easily by going directly to the main numeric file and by pulling out the folder requested.

By name: You are asked for the A. B. Smith folder. You check the alphabetic card file, find the card for A. B. Smith, and note his assigned number listed on the card. Then you go to the numeric file, and pull out the right folder.

TERMINAL-DIGIT FILING SYSTEM

The efficiency of the consecutive-number system diminishes when the numbers get too large and cumbersome. Consequently, large companies whose files include thousands of names use a form of numeric filing called *terminal-digit filing*. The main advantage of this system is that it distributes the storing of records among several file drawers and overcomes crowded working conditions when many forms have to be filed by several file workers.

In the consecutive-number system numbers are read from left to right. In the terminal-digit system a number is broken down into pairs and read from right to left. For the number 156780, 80 is the terminal number and indicates the drawer number in which a folder is located, 67 indicates the folder number, and 15 indicates the sequence of the record in the folder. File guides help to pinpoint the exact location of the desired folder by subdividing the file folders numbered 00–99 by tens.

Filing Procedure

Like the procedure for regular numeric filing, the item to be filed is assigned a number from a numeric file register, and a record of its assigned number is kept in an alphabetic card index.

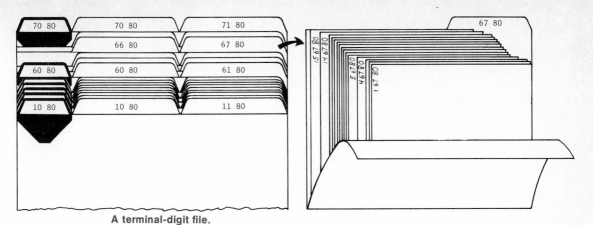

A terminal-digit file.

In a simple type of terminal-digit plan you take three steps to file an item numbered 156780:

1 Locate the drawer of the file cabinet containing the terminal digits (80).
2 Locate folder 67 by looking for the guide labeled with the number nearest to 67. It might be 60. Look at the folders behind the file guide until you come to the folder labeled 67.
3 Within the folder locate the position for the document you want to file according to its sequence number, which in this case is 15.

Finding Techniques

1 Determine the number of the material you want to locate either by looking at the correspondence itself or by consulting the alphabetic card file which shows a record of all correspondents and their assigned numbers.
2 Note the terminal digits in the number, and locate the drawer in which numbers ending in that terminal number are filed.
3 By using the file guides, locate the folder bearing the secondary pair of numbers (67) that appear to the left of the terminal digits (80).
4 Look for the document bearing the last pair of numbers (15) and filed in numeric sequence in the folder.

Variations in the Terminal-Digit Filing System

There is no one terminal-digit format. Depending upon their preferences and their needs, companies make use of various groupings. A number like 156780 might be grouped 15-67-80 in one system, 15-6780 in another, and 1567-80 in a third. Don't concern yourself about the variations. Just keep in mind that they occur and that there will always be someone who will explain that particular system to you. The important thing is to understand the principle of simplifying and grouping large numbers.

CHRONOLOGICAL FILING

The purpose of a chronological system is to keep track of things to make sure they are dealt with on time. Items requiring attention at some future date are filed by the date on which action is to be taken instead of by name or number. At the beginning of every workday, you or the secretary or administrative assistant pulls out all items marked for that date and places them on the boss's desk. This is a very important task and one which your boss counts on your performing.

You can keep your follow-up (chronological) file in front of a drawer in the regular files, in a tub file, a desk tray, or a desk-drawer file. Your file may consist of a guide for each month and one set of day guides numbered 1 through 31. The guide for the current month is kept in front and is followed by the set of day guides. The rest of the month guides are arranged behind the file for the current month in calendar order. It's a good idea to put a folder behind each month guide. Loose papers can be stored in these folders until the time comes when they must be distributed in the set of day guides.

A follow-up date is determined in various ways. In many instances, the item and the correspondence will specify a follow-up date. Sometimes the date is determined by company policy. Sometimes only the boss can decide on the follow-up date.

Filing Procedure

1 Determine the follow-up date, and note it on the item by writing, by underscoring, or by other means.
2 Place the item behind the correct month guide.
3 File the item behind the appropriate day guide if the follow-up is to be made in the current month. Otherwise, store it behind the appropriate month guide until that month becomes the current month.
4 At the beginning of every month, refile in the set of day guides the items originally filed behind the month guide.

Finding Techniques

Since your active follow-up file is numbered by the day of the month, it's simple for you to find the folder containing the items on which action is to be taken for that particular day. Some executives prefer to have follow-up items called to their attention several days before the deadline. This practice gives them time to assemble data, hold conferences, if necessary, and reach well-thought-out decisions. When you're in charge of the follow-up file, you should anticipate holidays, vacations, business trips, and other work interruptions. In this way an item scheduled for follow-up on a date that falls on a weekend can receive attention the day before. Another trick is to photocopy ahead of time any material in the follow-up file that might be needed for other purposes.

GEOGRAPHIC FILING

In some lines of business, especially in distribution, transportation, utilities, travel, and publishing, the geographic locations of customers and prospective customers and their activities is a primary concern. Individual identifications, such as the name, size of business, and so on, do not become important until their relationship to a location is first established. Typical questions such as these come up every day: "Who are our California representatives?" "What major warehouse points are nearby?" "Where are our principal markets in Illinois?" "How many subscribers do we have in Fairfield County?"

To locate and pinpoint the answers to these questions, a *geographic system* of filing is used. Here the items are filed according to major divisions, such as regions or states, then into smaller groupings such as counties, cities, towns, and perhaps even streets. Each geographic filing system is designed to meet the special requirements of the business.

The illustration below shows what a file drawer in a geographic system might look like. Notice that it has both state and city guides. Behind the state guide is a city guide, and behind the city guide are individual company folders in alphabetic order. Following the individual company folders, there is a city miscellaneous folder and a state miscellaneous folder for customers for whom five pieces of correspondence have not yet accumulated and who, therefore, do not warrant an individual folder.

Filing Procedure

1   Index and code the material in terms of the breakdown used in the particular system, that is, by region, state, city, or street.
2   Sort the items according to the major division, such as large geographic regions or states. Then sort them into subdivisions, such as cities or towns or even streets.

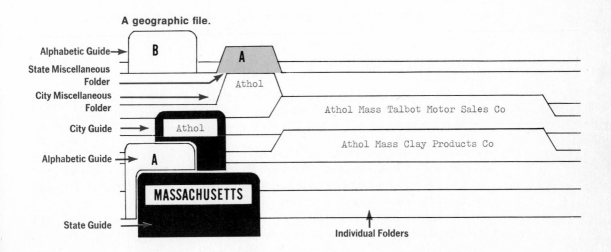

A geographic file.

3   File alphabetically those items for which there are individual folders.

4   Store alphabetically in the miscellaneous folder following the individual folders any items that do not yet warrant an individual folder. When five items accumulate for a single individual or company, put the items in an individual folder and file the folder in alphabetic order among the individual folders.

Finding Techniques

1   Determine what the major division is, such as a region or state. For example, if you are looking for correspondence pertaining to Clay Products Co. of Athol, Massachusetts, the first major division you would look under would be Massachusetts.

2   Then look behind the state guide to see if there is an individual city guide for Athol.

3   If there is a city guide for Athol, look behind it to see if there is an individual folder for Clay Products Co.

4   If there is, compare the name on the correspondence with the name on the material in the folder to be sure that you have the right folder. Then file your material in chronological order with latest date in front.

5   If at any step in narrowing the search from state to city to company, you can't find an individual guide or folder, look in the related miscellaneous folder. For example, if in step 2 you can't find an Athol guide, look directly in the state miscellaneous folder for Athol and then for the Clay Products Co. correspondence. Similarly, if in step 3 you do not find an individual folder for Clay Products Co. behind the city of Athol guide, look directly in the city of Athol miscellaneous folder.

Usually, placement and location of items can be worked out in a geographic filing system within two breakdowns: state and city or town. However, it is possible to come across firms and persons with identical names in the same city and state. When that happens, just make additional distinctions by using the name of the street and then the street number. (See Rule 18, Section 18, page 225.)

DELIVERING THE GOODS

The final test of any filing system is the rapidity with which material can be found when it is needed. You can "deliver the goods" consistently and promptly only if the filing system chosen is the one that meets your firm's special needs. Here are some important points to keep in mind:

☐ A firm that is growing in size should select a filing system that can grow with the business. Otherwise, the filing operations will bog down under a work load they were not designed to handle.

☐ A business that is expanding rapidly should try to choose a system that is easy to learn so that new recruits can catch on quickly and become productive workers in a short time.

☐ A filing system should be easy to operate in the daily routine. Some complex systems may cost more to run than they are worth in terms of what they offer a company. Sometimes the less complex and less costly system is quite adequate for a company's needs. This is an important decision to make when you consider that filing can represent as much as 20 percent of all the clerical duties in an office.

REVIEWING YOUR READING

1 List five captions that might be found in:

a A subject file
b A numeric file
c A geographic file

2 What types of businesses are likely to use numeric filing?
3 What is the difference between a miscellaneous folder and an individual folder?
4 How does terminal-digit filing distribute the filing traffic more easily?
5 What is meant by the term *follow-up date*? With what filing system is the expression used?
6 What types of businesses are likely to use geographic filing?
7 What is the final test of any filing system?

OFFICE ASSIGNMENTS

1 Listed below in scrambled order are several captions that might be found in a subject file in a wholesale grocery supply company. There are four major divisions, each having five subdivisions.

a Study the captions and decide which four are the major divisions.
b Then decide which five subdivisions belong to each division.
c On a separate sheet of paper list each division name in alphabetic order followed by each subdivision name in alphabetic order. Then assign a number to each caption, beginning with 200 for the first division and 210 for the first subdivision. The second division should be numbered 300, and so on.

Cereal	Pork	Oranges
Fish	Grocery	Poultry
Apples	Cake mix	Butter
Dairy	Cheese	Produce
Bread	Cold cuts	Candy
Meat	Bananas	Buttermilk
Lettuce	Ice cream	Beef
Milk	Pickles	Cabbage

2 Each rectangle in the illustration below represents the front of an invoice file drawer. The numbers on the front of each drawer represent the range of numbers found in the drawer.

	File A	*File B*	*File C*
Drawer 1	10 800 through 11 799	13 800 through 14 799	16 800 through 17 799
Drawer 2	11 800 through 12 799	14 800 through 15 799	17 800 through 18 799
Drawer 3	12 800 through 13 799	15 800 through 16 799	18 800 through 19 799

File the following invoices by indicating on a separate sheet of paper the file (A, B, or C) and the drawer (1, 2, or 3) in which invoices bearing the following numbers would be filed:

	File	Drawer
Example: 17921	C	2

a 10923   d 11800   g 15383   j 15977   m 18780
b 12151   e 17447   h 13896   k 12820   n 14653
c 16343   f 13414   i 19000   l 14114   o 11482

3 The following is an alphabetic listing of the district offices of an insurance company. The number in parentheses is the district number. Prepare a list of these offices showing how they would be arranged in a numeric file according to district office numbers from 1 to 20.

Allentown, PA (10)
Bakersfield, CA (2)
Bethlehem, PA (12)
Boise, ID (4)
Boston, MA (11)
Columbus, OH (20)
Davenport, IA (1)
Dayton, OH (7)
Denver, CO (16)
Des Moines, IA (19)
Easton, PA (9)
Elko, NV (6)
Ely, NV (14)
Eugene, OR (3)
Fort Wayne, IN (18)
Fresno, CA (15)
Grand Junction, CO (17)
Hartford, CT (8)
Honolulu, HI (13)
Kansas City, MO (5)

4 A nationwide sales organization has offices in the 50 cities shown below. Prepare a list of these offices as they would appear in a geographic file; first consider the state and then the city. Alphabetize the states as if they were spelled out in full.

1 Asheville, NC
2 Atlanta, GA
3 Bay City, MI
4 Birmingham, AL
5 Bristol, TN
6 Buffalo, NY
7 Cedar Rapids, IA
8 Charleston, WV

9	Charlotte, NC		**30**	Miami, FL
10	Chattanooga, TN		**31**	Midland, MI
11	Clearwater, FL		**32**	Minneapolis, MN
12	Corning, NY		**33**	Mobile, AL
13	Durham, NC		**34**	Muskegon, MI
14	Elmira, NY		**35**	New Orleans, LA
15	Flint, MI		**36**	Newport News, VA
16	Fort Lauderdale, FL		**37**	Norfolk, VA
17	Grand Rapids, MI		**38**	Portsmouth, VA
18	Greensboro, NC		**39**	Raleigh, NC
19	Hampton, VA		**40**	Richmond, VA
20	Harrisburg, PA		**41**	Rochester, NY
21	Hendersonville, NC		**42**	Saginaw, MI
22	High Point, NC		**43**	St. Paul, MN
23	Huntsville, AL		**44**	St. Petersburg, FL
24	Jacksonville, FL		**45**	San Francisco, CA
25	Johnson City, TN		**46**	Tampa, FL
26	Kingsport, TN		**47**	Warsaw, VA
27	Knoxville, TN		**48**	West Palm Beach, FL
28	Lansing, MI		**49**	Williamsport, PA
29	Memphis, TN		**50**	Winston-Salem, NC

5 Type or write each of the following names in proper indexing order on 5- by 3-inch cards or slips of paper. Record the item number in the upper right corner of each card or slip of paper.

61	M and D Home Builders		**66**	Walter E. Malone
62	Adolph Z. Mandell		**67**	Dept. of Docks, Mobile, Alabama
63	Missouri Stone Quarries, Inc.		**68**	The Marvel Process Cleaners
64	Marshall-Wells Store		**69**	Roger O. Mahoney Pharmacy
65	Monon Railroad		**70**	Maritime Coal Corporation

a Arrange the cards or slips in alphabetic order.

b Make a list of the alphabetized names on a sheet of paper, and give it to your teacher.

c Combine items 61 to 70 with items 1 to 60 (from previous assignments), and put them in alphabetic order.

d Using the numbers in the upper right corner of the cards or slips of paper, list the item numbers (names not required) in correct alphabetic order as follows:

Alphabetic Order	*Item No.*
1	61
2	58
3	10

e Give the list to your teacher, and retain all items in alphabetic order for future use.

SECTION 20 General Filing Procedures and Equipment

Anything that is written, typed, or printed on cards or papers (such as letters, business forms, records, reports, brochures, pamphlets, contracts, and memorandums) is likely to find its way into one kind of file or another. In order to store these communications in files and to be able to find them when you want them, you need to become familiar with filing procedures and equipment.

FILING PROCEDURES

There are seven basic steps in a typical filing routine: collecting, inspecting, indexing, cross-referencing, coding, sorting, and storing.

Collecting

The papers to be filed are deposited in an "In" basket and are picked up on a regular schedule by interoffice messengers who deliver them to a central filing unit.

Inspecting

Papers to be filed are first checked to see if they have a "release mark" on them. This process is called *inspecting*. A release mark, which is generally the initials of a person authorized to send material to the files, indicates that the transaction has been concluded and that the paper is ready to be filed. Any papers received without a release mark are returned to the supervisor of the unit from which they came.

Indexing

Once the release mark has been noted, the filing supervisor or a file clerk indexes the material to be filed. *Indexing* has been previously explained as the process of selecting the caption under which a record is to be filed and determining the proper order in which the units are to be considered in filing.

Cross-Referencing

Cross-referencing is a process designed to help locate a record that may be requested by a name or caption other than the caption under which the record is originally filed. To cross-reference, you underscore or write on the correspondence the alternate caption under which an item is to be filed. To indicate that it is a cross-reference caption, add an *X* either at the end of the line on which the alternate caption appears or after the written alternate caption.

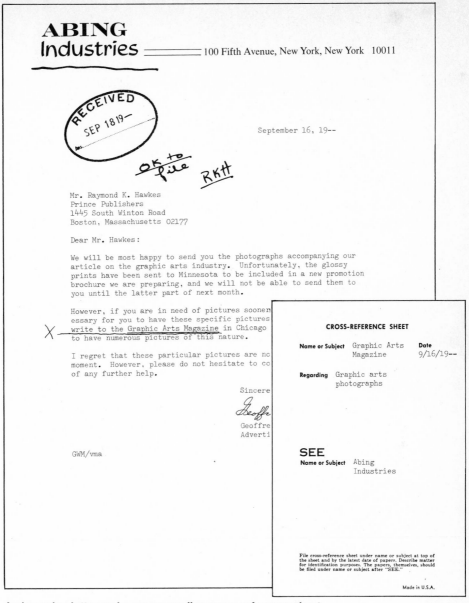

ABING
Industries ═══════ 100 Fifth Avenue, New York, New York 10011

RECEIVED SEP 18 19--

OK to File RKH

September 16, 19--

Mr. Raymond K. Hawkes
Prince Publishers
1445 South Winton Road
Boston, Massachusetts 02177

Dear Mr. Hawkes:

We will be most happy to send you the photographs accompanying our
article on the graphic arts industry. Unfortunately, the glossy
prints have been sent to Minnesota to be included in a new promotion
brochure we are preparing, and we will not be able to send them to
you until the latter part of next month.

However, if you are in need of pictures sooner
essary for you to have these specific pictures
X   write to the Graphic Arts Magazine in Chicago
to have numerous pictures of this nature.

I regret that these particular pictures are no
moment. However, please do not hesitate to co
of any further help.

Sincere

Geoffre
Adverti

GWM/vma

CROSS-REFERENCE SHEET

Name or Subject Graphic Arts   **Date**
                     Magazine   9/16/19--

Regarding Graphic arts
               photographs

SEE
Name or Subject Abing
                     Industries

File cross-reference sheet under name or subject at top of
the sheet and by the latest date of papers. Describe matter
for identification purposes. The papers, themselves, should
be filed under name or subject after "SEE."

Made in U.S.A.

An incoming letter and a corresponding cross-reference sheet.

A cross-reference sheet is prepared for the alternate caption. The original
material is filed under the caption by which you think it is most likely to be
requested. The cross-reference sheet is filed under the alternate caption and
directs you to the location of the original correspondence. In many offices
where photocopying equipment is available, copies of the original material
are made and filed in place of the cross-reference sheets. Time is saved
because the photocopy gives the same information as the original and thus
eliminates the need to backtrack to the location where the original copy is filed.

Coding

Once a record has been indexed, it is coded. *Coding* is the process of marking the correspondence with the caption selected in indexing and helps to guide the file clerk in putting away the item. The caption can be underlined with a colored pencil or written in colored pencil in the upper right corner of the correspondence if the name or caption does not appear anywhere on the record to be filed.

Sorting

Papers can be put away in the files any time after they have been coded. However, if you sort the papers into the divisions used in the file drawers, you can save time and footsteps by filing for a particular drawer or cabinet in a single trip. Rather than pile papers helter-skelter in a desk tray or a filing basket until you find time to file, sort the papers into broad categories as you receive them. Many types of sorters are available. Some are open file boxes with indexes, called *file tubs;* others are designed flat to rest on a desk or rack. The size of the sorter you use will depend on the volume of papers that need to be filed.

If you work in a small office and haven't a sorter, you can easily sort or organize alphabetically a pile of papers by the 2-3-4 system. This system operates well in a situation where you are frequently interrupted.

1   Divide the pile into *two* smaller piles or groups, *A–L* and *M–Z*, according to the first letter of the first indexing unit.
2   Divide each of the two piles into *three* groups, according to the first letter of the first indexing unit.

Pile 1	Pile 2
A–D	M–P
E–H	Q–T
I–L	U–Z

3   Arrange each of the six groups into *four* piles, according to the first letter of the first indexing unit. Then alphabetize the papers in each letter group in the normal manner. For filing, you can either combine all six groups in alphabetic order or file a section at a time as the opportunity presents itself.

Storing

File folders of varying designs and sizes are used to hold the papers to be filed. Some file folders open on three sides, some open just on top, and some have fasteners. Papers are stored in folders with the head of the letter to the *left*, so that the left edge of the paper rests on the bottom of the folder. In individual folders the paper bearing the most recent date is placed in the front of the folder. File folders are used in conjunction with dividers called

A ROUTINE FOR FILING

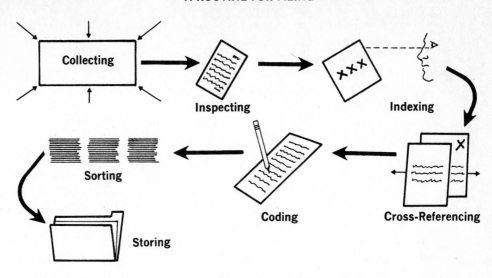

guides which, as their name suggests, guide the eye to a particular section of a file. Guides also help to keep order in a file because they are generally made of heavy cardboard or pressboard that is rigid enough to support the file folders vertically.

On all guides you will find projections or tabs that extend upward. These tabs are made in various widths known as *cuts*. When the tab occupies one-fifth of the space on the top edge of the guide, it is called a *one-fifth cut guide*. If it occupies one-third of the space, it is called a *one-third cut guide*. The tabs may appear in various places called *positions* along the top edge of the guide. Reading from left to right, one identifies tab positions by the place in which they occur. When a tab is one-fifth cut and placed at the extreme left of the upper edge, the guide is termed *one-fifth cut, first position*. Should the tab be one-third cut and placed in the center of the upper edge, the guide is termed *one-third cut, center position*. You can buy sets of guides with printed captions in a variety of sizes in any stationery store, or you can prepare your own guides and captions to meet the special requirements of your office.

CHARGE-OUT PROCEDURES

Besides the responsibility of caring for the firm's valuable papers while they are in the files, you also have the responsibility of charging out records removed from the files, making sure they are returned by the borrower, and locating any borrowed material promptly when it is requested. To do this efficiently, you need a charge-out system. Here is one that can help you do the job:

1 Ask the authorized person who requests papers or folders from the files to complete a requisition form. This gives you a written record of who the borrower is and what material he has borrowed. It includes the name

or the subject of the record, the date of the record, the signature or printed name of the borrower, the date on which the record was borrowed, and the date on which the record is to be followed up in order to ensure its return (the tickler date).

2   If the request is for one record rather than the entire folder of records, insert the filled-in requisition form in the pocket of a *substitution card*. This form, placed in the folder, indicates that a specific document has been removed from the folder and charged out to the individual noted. It is put in the exact place occupied by the paper removed.

3   If the request is for a whole file folder, put an *out guide* or an *out folder* in the file in place of the folder you are removing. The out folder has a pocket on the front of it into which you put a copy of the completed requisition form. You can then send the original folder to the person wishing to borrow it. When the borrowed folder is returned, the out folder and the copy of the requisition form are removed from the file drawer. If the borrowed folder is kept beyond the tickler date, the out folder serves as a reminder to you to follow up and to make sure the original folder is returned.

Some people prefer out folders instead of out guides because any new incoming records can be filed in the out folder while the original folder is out on loan.

THE TICKLER FILE

A *tickler file* is kept to organize information chronologically, so that you will be reminded of what has to be done on a given date. It is organized just like a follow-up file with a set of month guides and a set of day guides. When you charge out records, you place a duplicate of the substitution card (or a duplicate of the requisition form) in the tickler file behind the date on which the borrowed record or folder is to be returned. Each day you check to see what records are due, and if they have not been returned, you either extend the date of return or notify the borrower. If you receive a request for a record to be delivered at a future date, place that request behind the proper date in the tickler file and act on it at that time.

DISPOSAL OF OLD RECORDS

Business papers pile up month after month and year after year. They can't, and indeed they shouldn't, be kept indefinitely in the active files. They take up valuable space, and their importance diminishes with the passage of time. What do you do with them?

The disposal of records is generally handled according to a standard routine. Suppose you have a four-drawer file cabinet in which the top two drawers are used for the current year's correspondence and the two lower drawers hold correspondence for the previous year.

At the end of the calendar or fiscal year, the contents of the two top drawers (or the drawers themselves if they are interchangeable) are moved down

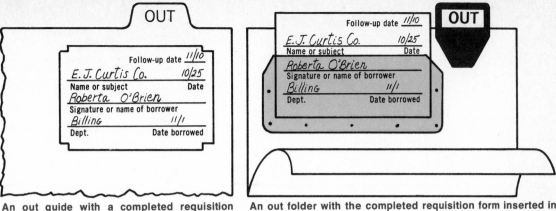

An out guide with a completed requisition form attached.

An out folder with the completed requisition form inserted in the pocket.

to the two lower drawers; the contents of the two lower drawers are either discarded or moved to the storage files. How long do they stay there? That depends on their importance. Usually, after a year the contents of the inactive files are examined to determine what records can be kept and what can be discarded. Records that are not confidential may simply be thrown away or, better yet, sold for scrap or delivered to a recycling center. Confidential records are often burned in incinerators or shredded in large machines or small "electric wastebaskets."

After consultation with others in your office, you may decide that certain records should be kept longer than usual. These records are either kept in transfer files near at hand or placed in permanent storage facilities in less valuable space, located in a remote place, such as a basement, warehouse, storeroom, or, in certain instances, a vault. Depending on the circumstances and the importance of their contents, the papers may be housed in cardboard cartons; in steel, steel and corrugated, or corrugated file drawers; in old file cabinets; or on open shelves.

When legal considerations permit, many firms use microfilm to record and to store essential records for long periods of time. This method greatly reduces the size of the records and the space they occupy. You can appreciate how advantageous this method is when you consider that the contents of one cabinet of film are equivalent to the contents of about 100 cabinets of original papers and documents. As a precaution against fire or other disasters, some firms have additional duplicate rolls of their microfilm records prepared and stored in different geographic locations.

An alternate to microfilm is microfiche, which is a miniature photographic reproduction of a document on a card instead of on a strip of film. A standard 6- by 4-inch microfiche card stores the images of 60 or more pages of records; two microfiche file drawers equivalent in size to a single standard file drawer can store the images of some 240,000 records. A special advantage of microfiche is that as little as a single card can be pulled out of the files easily for viewing or for dispatch to some other location at very little cost.

Old Records May Be:

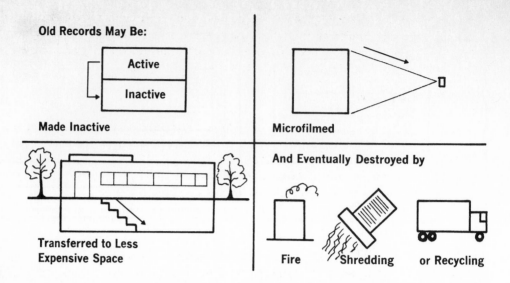

Made Inactive

Microfilmed

Transferred to Less Expensive Space

And Eventually Destroyed by

Fire   Shredding   or Recycling

Both microfilm and microfiche are read by means of reading machines, which project an enlarged image of the film or card on a screen. There are also machines that can print full-size copies of the photographed records in seconds.

FILING EQUIPMENT

The right equipment, the right tools, and the appropriate supplies mark the professional in every kind of job. Filing is no exception. The whole filing process operates more efficiently when you use the equipment that is specifically designed for it. As an office worker you probably will use some of this equipment every day. Also, you may be called on from time to time to make suggestions about the kind of equipment the company should purchase to improve filing efficiency. Consult current catalogs of equipment manufacturers for suggestions on new kinds of filing equipment. When you choose equip-

A 3M microfilm camera card stores information in miniature in the rectangle at the right. Cards can be sorted on data processing machines.

Each card in this microfiche file contains 60 miniature photographs.

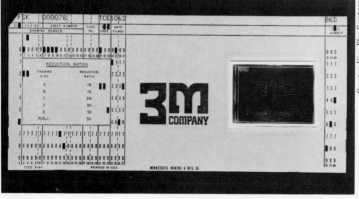

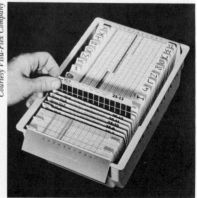

Courtesy 3M Microfilm Products Division

Courtesy Visu-Flex Company

ment, first consider its quality and usefulness rather than its price. Filing equipment is used for many years. Inexpensive equipment can prove to be expensive in the long run if it can't stand up under wear and tear or if it takes too much time and effort to use.

Cabinets

Correspondence is usually kept in vertical filing cabinets that have from one to six drawers. Two-drawer files are frequently used to stand near a desk or a table in the immediate work area. Three-drawer file units can be built into counter arrangements. Taller units are generally used in the main filing area because they make the best use of floor space.

Shelf Files

As the number of file cabinets increases, space, especially floor space, becomes a serious problem. You need room not only for the file cabinets but also for the file drawers, so that they can open freely without blocking office traffic. One solution is to make use of shelf-style filing equipment, which is available with and without doors.

Desk Files

Frequently used or confidential papers are often kept in a drawer file located in a one- or two-drawer desk or credenza.

Card Files

Card files are popular because they are so versatile. A secretary may use cards for addresses and telephone numbers; the advertising department frequently maintains its mailing list on cards. The credit department usually keeps a

The records in this open-shelf file are stored in suspended folders.

This type of open reference card file is available in many sizes.

Courtesy Robert P. Gillotte & Co., Inc.

Courtesy Tab Products Co.

quick-reference card system to speed up the work of approving sales on credit. Banks keep signature card files. And cards are used to keep records, such as inventories, receivables, payables, and fixed assets. Specially designed cabinets come in many sizes to hold these cards.

Rotary Wheels and Elevator Files

Card records that are used constantly can be reviewed more conveniently when they are housed in rotary wheels such as the one illustrated below. In an elevator file cards are filed in trays placed in revolving shelves or pans. You merely push a button to move the desired tray into reference position. The table ledge on the front of the elevator file provides a convenient working surface for writing, sorting cards, or resting trays.

Visible Files

Certain types of business data, such as telephone numbers, prices, and inventory balances, are made available instantly at your work station with fingertip convenience through the use of visible files. An important characteristic of all types of visible files is that key information on each record can be seen without handling when the record is in storage because the information is on a projecting edge. Depending upon the nature of the operation, data is recorded on strips, cards, or sheets. Strip-type visible files are kept in desk stands, on wall brackets, or on easel stands.

Other card records can be kept in flat, book form or in drawer cabinets. There is a special reference stand that is popular for use in pricing, for catalog sales, and for repair parts operations.

Courtesy Wheeldex, Inc.

The wheel file puts a large amount of information at a worker's fingertips.

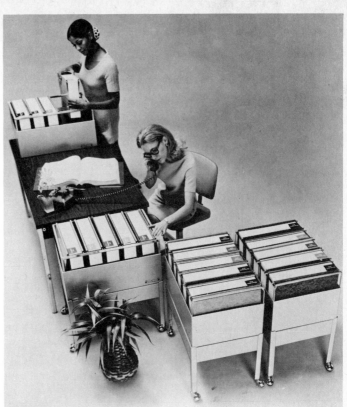

An open-top data printout rack.

Courtesy Wilson Jones Company

DATA PROCESSING MEDIA STORAGE

The rapid advance in data processing techniques in recent years has brought about a need for storage equipment for such data processing media as punched cards, punched tape, magnetic tape, and magnetic disk units.

It's important that the punched cards be filed so that their edges do not become bent or torn. Damaged cards can't be fed into the high-speed data processing machines. Also, it's important to keep them under pressure when they are in the files to prevent their warping.

Magnetic tapes and disk units should be stored near the computer with which they will be used and protected from dust or exposure to extreme temperatures. They should be handled carefully so that they are not dropped.

REVIEWING YOUR READING

1   List some of the kinds of records that are likely to be found in the files of a business office.
2   What is the purpose of inspecting papers before they are indexed for filing?

3   What are two reasons for performing the coding step in filing?

4   Give an example of a record that might be asked for by more than one name. What step should be followed before filing such a record?

5   How can the sorting step save time for the file worker?

6   How should a record be stored in a file folder?

7   How does the file worker keep track of records that have been borrowed from the files?

8   What are several ways in which records that are no longer needed can be disposed of?

9   In selecting filing equipment, which is more important to consider, cost or quality? State your reason.

10   What kind of filing equipment can be purchased to save a great deal of walking to and from the files?

11   What special filing precautions should be taken with punched cards?

OFFICE ASSIGNMENTS

1   a   Complete a requisition form in order to borrow the Felden Company correspondence, dated June 12, for your employer, Mr. Hugh Johnson of the sales department. Use July 7 for the date borrowed and July 17 for the follow-up date. If you do not have a workbook, make a form similar to the one on page 249.

    b   Fill out a cross-reference sheet for a letter (use last Friday's date) from a regular customer, the Whitford Supply Company of Buffalo, New York. The letter refers to a shipment of goods that was sent to Henry W. Stanley of Springfield, Virginia. If you do not have a workbook, make a form similar to the one on page 245.

2   Type or write the following names in proper indexing order on 5- by 3-inch cards or slips of paper. Then record the item number in the upper right corner of each card or slip.

71	Mallary	79	Male-Town, Inc.
72	Maggie's Kitchen	80	Maggi-Madsen Plumbing Supply
73	M. and O. Morgan, Inc.	81	Mac's Place
74	Main Stationery Shoppe	82	Marsh Brothers Instrument Company
75	Mason City Meat Packers		
76	James Marsh, D.D.S.	83	Main Street Garage
77	Mont Blanc Ski Club	84	Jacques Marsh and Sons
78	Mo. Pac. R.R.	85	Madison County Children's Court

    a   Arrange the cards or slips in alphabetic order.

    b   Make a list of the 15 alphabetized names on a sheet of paper, and give it to your teacher.

    c   Combine cards 71 to 85 with cards 1 to 70 (from previous assignments), and put them in alphabetic order.

d Using the numbers in the upper right corner of the cards or slips of paper, list the item numbers (names not required) in correct alphabetic order as follows:

Alphabetic Order	Item No.
1	61
2	81
3	58

e Give the list to your teacher, and retain all items in alphabetic order for future use.

3 List the captions below on a sheet of paper. Then write each name in proper alphabetic order beside the caption under which the name should be filed.

Captions	Names	
A	Bartlett	Apgar
Ad	Asteinya	Agee
Al	Allen	Alls
All	Barker	Alford
Am	Alley	Beecher
An	Amos	Alcorn
Ar	Adkins	Armstrong
As	Battle	Basham
Au	Alderman	Bain
B	Bailey	Angle
Bar	Adams	Absher
Barr	Austin	Aaron
Bas	Arrington	Anderson
Be	Ackerman	Akers
	Altizer	Atkinson

4 Type or write the following names in proper indexing order on 5- by 3-inch cards or slips of paper. Record the item number in the upper right corner of each card or slip.

86 Mahopac Kennels
87 Madison Drive-In Theater
88 Memorial Hospital
89 Medico, Inc.
90 Media Press
91 Metro Camera Shop
92 Max Maiaro
93 Medicine for Overseas Fund, Inc.
94 The Maples Hotel
95 Mount Hope Hospital
96 Merrett and Lynch

97 City Attorney, Madison, WI
98 McLean Avenue Delicatessen
99 Majestic Clothiers
100 Mercury Garage
101 Roger D. McAn
102 Moore's Coffee Shop, Albany, NY
103 Mrs. Agnes Meade
104 Methodist Church
105 Moore's Coffee Shop, Albany, GA

a Arrange the cards or slips in alphabetic order.

b Make a list of the 20 alphabetized names on a sheet of paper, and give it to your teacher.

c Combine items 86 to 105 with items 1 to 85 (from previous assignments) in alphabetic order.

d List the item numbers in correct alphabetic order as explained previously in Office Assignment 2.

e Give the list to your teacher, and keep all items in alphabetic order for future use.

5 Type or write the following names in proper indexing order on 5- by 3-inch cards or slips of paper. Record the item number in the upper right corner of each card or slip.

106 Gerald Midgley-Marks
107 Motel in the Sky
108 Meyer's Bookstore
109 Michael and Michael for Fashions
110 Morgan Woodwork Co.
111 R. Thomas Marks
112 Kingsley Marratt and Brothers
113 Mory's Mountain Inn
114 Gary V. Moran
115 Metropolitan Dairy
116 Morehead City Fisheries, Inc.
117 Minnesota Conservation Commission
118 Middleton Warehouse Corporation
119 Morris B. Meyers
120 Mrs. Georgette Moran
121 Master-Paterson Publishers
122 Mt. Hood Scenic Railroad
123 Herbert Miele
124 Anthony M. Mora
125 Middle Atlantic Oil Company
126 Moran Register Printing Company
127 Mike's Service Station
128 Manning Manufacturing Company
129 Mrs. Morgan's Flower Shop
130 Tax Assessor, Village of Midwood, NJ

a Arrange the cards or slips in alphabetic order.

b Make a list of the 25 alphabetized names on a sheet of paper, and give it to your teacher.

c Combine cards 106 to 130 with cards 1 to 105 (from previous assignments), and put them in alphabetic order.

d Make a complete list of the 130 items in correct alphabetic order as explained in Office Assignment 2.

e Retain all items for future use.

6 Finding records quickly and easily is the true test of filing efficiency.

a Locate the 25 names shown on page 257 among the 130 items in your alphabetic card file.

b Note the following information about each item on a separate sheet of paper:

Name	Item No.	Indexed As	Behind Name	In Front of No.
Max Maiaro	92	Maiaro, Max	Mahopac Kennels	74

1	A. Turner Mann	**14**	Kingsley Marratt and Brothers
2	Maya Dining Room	**15**	George W. Moran
3	Max Maiaro	**16**	Mid West Truck Lines
4	Mike's Midtown Parking	**17**	Master Patterns Press
5	Medico, Inc.	**18**	Richard Mannix-Davis
6	Mory's Mountain Inn	**19**	Mesa Verde Motel
7	The Maples Hotel	**20**	Mrs. Morgan's Flower Shop
8	Male-Town, Inc.	**21**	Midland City Planning Board
9	Roger D. McAn	**22**	Terrance Maher Construction Company
10	Martino for Footwear	**23**	Marshall-Wells Store
11	Maggi-Madsen Plumbing Supply	**24**	Mont Blanc Ski Club
12	Dept. of Docks, Mobile, Alabama	**25**	McLean Avenue Delicatessen
13	Michigan Central Railroad		

UNIT 7

BUSINESS CASES AND PROBLEMS

In the Boss's Shoes   1   "Yes, I know that I'm behind on the filing work. I was so busy last week straightening out the supply room and sorting last year's trade magazines that I let the filing go. I thought that I could take care of those papers anytime."

If you were the boss, what would you think of this explanation of why the filing was not up to date? If you do not think that the explanation is a good one, what should be done to prevent a similar situation in the future.

2   Delores has just been reprimanded. She says, "Why does the boss have to be so unreasonable? I handle thousands of papers every day. When I can't find just one single item that he wants, he acts as if I'd committed a crime. Does he think I'm perfect?" Explain why the file clerk is expected to have such a high standard of accuracy.

3   "Whenever I leave papers on the top of my desk overnight, the boss bawls me out in the morning. Why do the desks have to be so neat and clean at night anyway? That doesn't help to get the work done any faster."

Your friend Roy is obviously looking for sympathy. Do you agree with him? Is it unreasonable for a boss to expect his workers to put things away before going home? Do you think the boss might be concerned about something more than neatness in his "put it away" policy?

4   As a filing supervisor in charge of indexing and coding, you note that an increasing number of items require cross-referencing because they involve more than one subject or name. However, having to stop constantly to make cross-reference sheets is slowing down your overall performance. How can you make the most efficient use of your time? What suggestions would you make to the management for eliminating or simplifying your problem?

5   "I have to call you back, Mr. Wilkins. It will take me a few minutes to get the file; I'm not quite sure where it is." Does this sound like an efficient procedure for a firm that receives many telephone inquiries? What would you suggest?

Your Human Relations   **1**   Each time a file folder is returned to you by Miss Keene, the messenger in the executive office, the papers in the folder are out of order, upside down, and even badly creased from rough and careless handling. When you tactfully call her attention to the condition of the folder, she says, "That's your job, sister. I just get them and bring them back."

Should you report Miss Keene to her boss for her lack of cooperation? Should you let the matter drop? Or should you tell someone else about the trouble? Or what? Explain.

2   You are responsible for the files in a small professional office. The accountant and the secretary always ask you to get material for them from the files, and immediately after they finish with what they have borrowed, they return the material promptly. However, your employer goes to the files whether you are present or not and often fails to return what he borrows. When he puts material back in the files, he frequently places it in the wrong folder. What can you do or say to convince him that he should leave the filing to you?

3   "Miss Jensen, you're late again this morning," says the supervisor to Margaret Jensen, a filing clerk in a large insurance company. "This is the fifth time in two weeks that you've been late—from five minutes to twenty minutes. Let's talk this over. Just what is the cause of your lateness?"

Actually, Margaret has been arriving by 9 a.m., the starting time. But by the time she freshens up and combs her hair, it is often 9:10 or 9:15 before she arrives at her desk.

Margaret is about to say, "But I always arrive on time . . . ." However, she catches herself and pauses momentarily. What should she say?

4 "I'm sure that I sent those papers to the file. What did you do with them?" Suppose you are equally confident that you never saw the papers in question. Should you argue with your co-worker about it? Would your reaction be different if your accuser were a high-ranking executive?

5 "Sorry I couldn't get to those papers sooner. They were on the very bottom of the basket of work to be done." Is this an adequate excuse for delaying an urgent matter? What is wrong with saying, "Put it on the pile, and I'll get to it as soon as I can"?

6 "That filing department is after us again to return the Griffin file. It seems as though they want things back about two minutes after they lend them out." Is a filing department justified in close follow-up of borrowed materials? Why or why not? If you cannot return a borrowed folder when it is requested, what should you do?

7 "While I'm away, please set up a personal file to fit in the bottom drawer of my desk, so that I can keep the papers on current problems close at hand." Suppose your boss asked you to do this. Where would you begin. What would you include? What kinds of questions would you ask?

What Would You Do If . . . ? **1** You are asked to index an invoice from "Shorty" Miles, Plumbing and Repairing. Name the units in the order in which they would be considered for indexing.

2 The files in the small office where you are employed have all names beginning with *Mc* filed in a separate section after the letter *M*. Would you use this system? Or would you try to change the system or take some other action?

3 Your co-worker in the filing department suggests that you skip the coding step and file the paper before you forget the indexing caption you have decided to use. What are the arguments for and against this suggestion?

4 You are a file clerk in charge of a subject file, and requests for a certain folder are sometimes made under the title "Advertising Contracts" folder, but are more often made under the title, "Contracts" folder?

What Does This Mean? **1** Your office supervisor asks you to rough-sort a pile of unfiled papers.

2 A letter to be indexed is signed "Sr. Mary Beatrice."

3 A company name is abbreviated N. E. Lumber Prod. Mfg. Co., Ltd.

4 The words *Bowling—Building* are printed in the upper right corner of a page in the Yellow Pages section of a telephone directory.

5 A file cabinet bears a metal plate with the statement, "This file cabinet is unconditionally guaranteed against any operating failure for a period of five years."

Business in Your Area   **1**   Look in the telephone directory to see whether or not the rule concerning last-name prefixes is followed.

2   Look in the telephone directory to see whether or not the indexing rule concerning such names as AAA Travel Service is followed.

3   Search the Yellow Pages of the local telephone directory for an unusual firm name which you do not believe is covered by one of the 20 indexing rules. Bring the name to class and discuss the way in which you believe the name would most logically be indexed.

4   Determine from a local business the number of different methods of filing (alphabetic, subject, and so on) that are used by that firm. If possible, determine why each method is used.

5   Visit a local office supply dealer, and obtain the price of the least expensive and the most expensive four-drawer file cabinet. Then make a list which compares the features of each cabinet. Discuss in class the wide range of special features available for file cabinets.

UNIT 8.
COMPUTING AND DATA PROCESSING ACTIVITIES

SECTION 21 Adding and Calculating Machines

One of the most exciting developments in the business world has been the introduction of machines that perform at incredible speeds computations which at one time had to be done by hand. Today, adding and calculating machines are used widely to handle the tremendous volume of data generated by business. Consider for a minute the chain of computations involved when you purchase something at a department store:

☐ The store's buyer has already studied the purchasing and selling costs of the merchandise and has established a fair retail price.
☐ The advertising department has computed the cost of advertising the product.
☐ The salesman adds up your bill.
☐ The cashier records your payment and gives you change.
☐ The store stock clerk adjusts his inventory.
☐ The shipping clerk computes the postage or delivery charge.
☐ The deliveryman collects the balance due, if any.
☐ Later, the accounting clerk matches the payment received against the cost.
☐ The payroll clerk figures out how much each sales employee involved has earned.
☐ Finally, the government makes its claim for a share of the store's income.

These computations, once done by hand, are now performed quickly and accurately by machines.

When an employer decides to hire someone to run these expensive machines, you can be certain that he will choose carefully. If you have been taught how to use this equipment, you have an advantage because your employer will know that you will need only a minimal amount of training and that you will not likely damage expensive equipment by improper operation.

That's why it's smart to get what training you can in office machine operation. The skills you learn on a basic machine can be adapted easily to the various machines in a real office. On a new job no employer will expect you to be an expert on everything, but he'll know that if you have mastered the fundamentals of operating adding and calculating machines, you will soon become a very useful and productive employee.

Don't think that the trend toward office mechanization means fewer job opportunities for you. Fewer people are needed for certain clerical jobs because machines can handle much of this work quickly and accurately. However, the growing demand for goods and business services has greatly increased paper work. Offices still require a full force of workers plus machines to keep operations moving smoothly.

Adding and calculating machines are found wherever modern clerical operations are performed. They are used more than any other type of office machine except the typewriter. As a prospective office worker you should know what these machines look like, how they work, and how they are used in office operations. Note the illustrations of these machines on page 268.

Generally, each type of machine is manufactured by several different companies, and there will be slight differences between models, depending on the manufacturer. However, if you know how one type of machine operates, you can easily get to know how to handle other models. It is very much like learning how to drive one make of automobile and then, with just a few additional instructions, learning how to drive another.

The first machines you will learn about are sometimes known as listing machines because they list, or print, amounts and totals on a paper tape for inspection and reference. Many models are equipped also to produce a record in the form of a punched tape, which can be used further in the processing of data.

The two basic types of listing machines discussed here are called the *ten-key adding machine* and the *full-key adding machine*.

THE TEN-KEY ADDING MACHINE

Since most offices, large and small, have at least one ten-key adding machine, it is important that you learn how to operate one. You'll discover that the skill you develop in using the keyboard of this machine will help you operate most other kinds of office computing machines.

The ten-key adding machine is so named because its basic keyboard contains only ten numbered keys (1, 2, 3, 4, 5, 6, 7, 8, 9, and 0). It is designed for a touch system of fingering, which means that you look at the copy you are reading from rather than the keyboard when you enter the numbers in the machine. You will be able to operate this machine speedily and accurately once you have learned how to use the "base" or "home row" technique. This means that you return to the familiar home position as soon as you press any key.

How It Works

To add the numbers listed below on a ten-key adding machine, follow this procedure:

```
456
654
546
123
789
```

1 Clear the machine by depressing the Total key or bar. This step assures you that there are no figures left in the machine from previous computations. Some machines print a symbol such as *T*, *, or □ to indicate that the machine's registers or counters are empty.

2   Place your right hand in home position on the keyboard. Your index finger should rest on the 4 key, the second finger on the 5 key, and the third finger on the 6 key. Your thumb may rest lightly on the 0.

3   To enter 456, depress the 4, 5, and 6 keys in the same order as you would read the number (from left to right). Then depress the Plus bar with your little (fourth) finger. The amount is printed automatically on the paper tape. Remember throughout your computations that it is essential always to return to home position immediately after you press the Plus bar.

4   Enter 654 by depressing the 6, 5, 4 keys in that order. Then depress the Plus bar. The amount appears on the tape so that it can be checked or used for future reference.

5   Next enter 546 in the same manner, and then depress the Plus bar.

6   In order to enter 123, move your fingers one at a time from home position. This motion is similar to that used on a typewriter. Your index finger reaches down to depress the 1 and then returns to its home position, the second finger reaches down to enter the 2 and then returns to its home position, and the third finger moves down to enter the 3 and then returns to its home position. After you make the entry and depress the Plus bar, your hand should be back in home position ready to enter the next number.

```
    .0 0 T

   4 .5 6
   6 .5 4
   5 .4 6
   1 .2 3
   7 .8 9
 2 5 .6 8 T
```

7   Enter 789 by reaching up from home position. Your index finger depresses the 7, the second finger depresses the 8, and the third finger depresses the 9. Once again strike the Plus bar, and return your hand to home position.

8   Obtain a total of the amounts entered and listed by depressing the Total key. In this instance, the total should be 2,568. The letter *T* or some other symbol should be printed next to the total amount to identify it as a final figure.

Special Techniques

1   In order to subtract a number from the numbers being listed and added, enter the number to be subtracted on the keyboard in normal fashion and then depress the Minus key or bar (instead of the Plus bar).

2   Use your thumb to enter zeros and your little finger to operate the Plus bar, the Minus bar, and the Total key or bar.

3   If you enter a wrong figure and have not yet depressed the Plus or Minus bar, use the Correction key to clear the error from the registers.

4   If you discover an error after depressing the Plus or Minus bar, subtract or add the incorrect entry. Then enter the correct figures. For example, if you added 484 but should have added 187, enter and subtract 484 and then enter and add 187. Or if you entered and added a number twice, simply enter and subtract the number once.

5   Enter dollars and cents the same way you handle whole numbers. Most machines automatically print a decimal point between the second and third figures from the right, but some have a special function key that permits you to set the decimal point wherever you wish. If one of the figures you are adding is all dollars and no cents, enter zeros in the cents columns.

```
      .0 0  T

     1 .9 8
     1 .9 8
     1 .9 8
     1 .9 8
     1 .9 8
     1 .9 8
     1 .9 8
     1 .9 8
     1 .9 8
   1 7 .8 2  T
```

6 When you require a subtotal before the entire calculation is completed, depress the special Subtotal key.

7 You can complete simple multiplication problems on the machine by using the repeat addition process. To do this, use the Repeat key. For example, $45 \times 5 = 45 + 45 + 45 + 45 + 45$.

8 Use shortcuts in multiplying by employing the Minus key or bar. For example, 9 pairs of socks at $1.98 per pair could be multiplied by adding 1.98 nine times, as shown on the tape at the left. A shortcut in solving the same problem would be to subtract 1.98, the price for one pair of socks, from 19.80, the price for ten pairs, to obtain the price for nine pairs. Enter 1.98 on the keyboard, and depress the Minus bar. Enter 19.80, and depress the Plus bar. Then press the Total key. As you can see from the tape, this procedure takes less time than the repeat addition process.

Typical Applications

```
      .0 0  T

     1 .9 8  -
   1 9 .8 0
   1 7 .8 2  T
```

The ten-key adding machine is most suitable for problems involving figures with relatively few digits. It is most commonly used to list bills, receipts, small checks, service charges, and expense accounts. It is also used to total stock records for simple financial statements and to total small figures on reports. It is popular and widely used because its touch system permits the operator to enter amounts quickly and accurately and because one can be trained how to use it in a relatively short period of time.

THE FULL-KEY ADDING MACHINE

The full-key (sometimes called the full-keyboard or full-bank) adding machine has rows of keys numbered vertically from 1 to 9 as shown in the illustration on page 268. How many rows of numbers a model will have will depend upon its capacity. Each row represents an arithmetic column similar to the vertically ruled lines on ledger paper and other printed forms. The right-hand row is for values from 1 to 9; the second row from the right is for tens; the third row is for hundreds; and so on. It does not make use of the touch system. Instead you look at the keyboard as you register the figures, which are entered in exactly the same order as they are read. Through practice and experience you will be able to depress a number of keys simultaneously.

How It Works

An addition problem, such as the following, is a very simple task to complete on the full-key adding machine:

```
    34,567
    45,678
    12,345
    24,653
   -35,764
```

Here is the step-by-step procedure to follow:

1   Clear the machine registers by depressing the Total key or T bar. A symbol such as *T*, *, or □ will then appear on the tape to indicate that the registers contain no figures from previous computations.

2   Enter 34,567 on the right-hand side of the keyboard. Locate the figures as you read the number from left to right. Depress the 3 key in the fifth column from the right, then depress the 4 key in the fourth column, the 5 key in the third column, the 6 key in the second column, and the 7 key in the first column.

3   Check to see that you have depressed the right keys in the correct column locations.

4   Then depress the Plus bar to add and to print the amount on the paper tape.

5   Enter 45,678 on the keyboard in the same way as described previously.

6   Check to see that you have depressed the correct keys, and then depress the Plus bar.

7   Enter the remaining numbers in the same manner.

8   Obtain a total of the numbers listed by depressing the Total key. The sum of the numbers in this problem is 153,007. The letter *T* or another symbol will be printed on the tape next to the total to indicate that it is a final amount.

```
            .00 T

       3 4 5 .6 7
       4 5 6 .7 8
       1 2 3 .4 5
       2 4 6 .5 3
       3 5 7 .6 4
    1.5 3 0 .0 7 T
```

Special Techniques

1   You may subtract a figure that has been entered on the keyboard from the amounts previously recorded by depressing the Subtract or Minus bar (instead of the Plus bar).

2   Use the fingers that are closest to the numbers on the keys for entering the figures. The touch system is not used.

3   Once the keys are depressed, they will remain depressed until the Plus or Minus bar is operated. Before you do that, double-check the amount.

4   You need not depress a key to enter a zero. This is a considerable time-saver. To enter 8,000, for example, you have only to depress the 8 key in the thousand column (or the fourth column from the right). To enter 405, depress the 4 in the hundred (or third column from the right) and the five in the first column.

5   Depress adjacent keys, such as 22 or 333, simultaneously to save time.

6   If you depress a single wrong key, correct your mistake by depressing the correct figure in the same column. This action releases the key that was depressed by mistake.

7   If you have made a complicated error in depressing the keys, release the entire amount on the keyboard by operating the Clear key or Error key.

8   Correct an error that you discover after the Plus bar has been depressed by subtracting the incorrect entry and then adding the correct entry.

9   Enter dollars and cents by employing the same technique used to handle whole numbers. Most machines automatically print a decimal point between the second and third figures from the right.

10   Depress the Subtotal key to obtain an intermediate or running total before the end of the problem.

11   Multiply simple figures by the repeat addition process: $64 \times 4 = 64 + 64 + 64 + 64$.

Typical Applications

The full-key adding machine is most useful in listing large numbers, such as those found on bills or invoices; in totaling large cash accounts; in verifying payroll records; and in computing detailed sales data. It is used extensively in financial institutions where large numbers are common. An advantage of this machine is that the keys remain depressed and nothing is registered in the machine until the motor is activated. This gives you a chance to double-check the accuracy of the entry before the figure is picked up in the machine.

THE MECHANICAL PRINTING CALCULATOR

The number keyboard of this machine is similar to that of the ten-key adding machine. Like the ten-key adding machine, the calculator adds and subtracts and uses the touch system. The major difference between the two machines is that the printing calculator multiplies and divides automatically. Instead of having to repeat a figure a given number of times in order to multiply or divide, you depress a special function key, and the machine computes and prints the sum automatically.

How It Works

Let's consider two different problems that can be worked out on a Friden printing calculator.

Multiplication   To multiply 87 by 56:

```
         T
   8 7 ×
     5 6 =
 4 8. 7 2 T
```

1   Clear the machine by touching the Total bar.
2   Enter the amount to be multiplied, 87, on the keyboard.
3   Depress the Times (×) key.
4   Enter the multiplier, 56, on the keyboard.
5   Depress the Equals (=) key. The product, 4,872, is computed and printed automatically and is identified by the symbol T. You use the tape to check all factors in the problem.

Division   To divide 9,671 by 43:

1   Clear the machine by touching the Total bar.
2   Enter the amount to be divided, 9,671, on the keyboard.
3   Depress the Enter Dividend (÷) key. (This is the key that also has a "+" at the top and "subtotal" at the bottom.)
4   Enter the divisor, 43, on the keyboard.

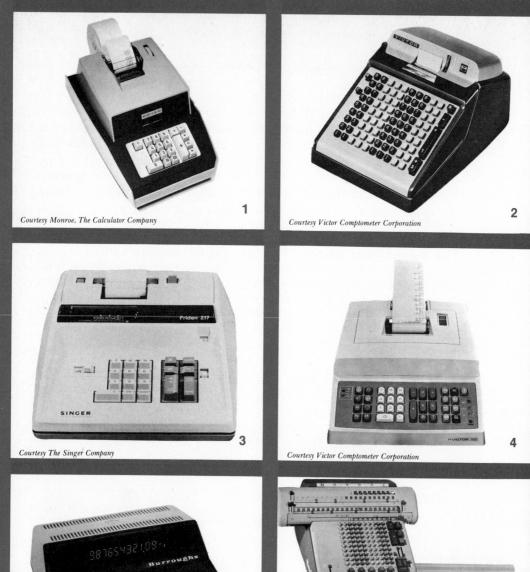

Courtesy Monroe, The Calculator Company   **1**

Courtesy Victor Comptometer Corporation   **2**

Courtesy The Singer Company   **3**

Courtesy Victor Comptometer Corporation   **4**

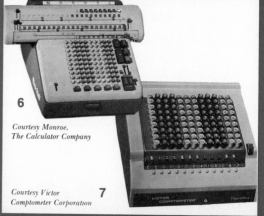

Courtesy Burroughs Corporation   **5**

6

*Courtesy Monroe,
The Calculator Company*

*Courtesy Victor
Comptometer Corporation*   **7**

1, Ten-key adding machine; 2, full-key adding machine; 3, mechanical printing calculator; 4, electronic printing calculator; 5, electronic display calculator; 6, rotary calculator; 7, key-driven calculator.

5 Depress the Equals (=) key. The quotient, 224, is computed and printed automatically and is identified by the symbol *Q*. The remainder, 39, is printed below the quotient and is identified by the symbol *T*.

```
          T
9 6. 7 1
    4 3 =
2. 2 4 Q
    3 9 T
```

Typical Applications

The mechanical printing calculator is best used when a printed tape is required and when the work involves all four basic mathematical processes: addition, subtraction, multiplication, and division. Invoices, inventories, vouchers, checks, and statements are only a few of the items that are computed and checked on the mechanical printing calculator.

THE ELECTRONIC PRINTING CALCULATOR

The electronic printing calculator offers the advantages of any electronic device: high speed, quiet operation, and ease of maintenance. The cost of electronic printing calculators is decreasing, and it is likely that within a few years they will almost entirely replace mechanical printing calculators. Electronic printing calculators compute and print the answers to multiplication and division problems, no matter how complicated, within split seconds with the decimal point properly positioned. Most of these machines have ten-key keyboards, which are operated by the touch system, and numerous special function keys. The capabilities of each model vary, depending on the features selected by the customer. Machines can provide data storage, round off numbers, and drop decimal extensions; they can provide automatic credit balancing and automatically repeat addition or subtraction. Several models can store a program for later use.

How It Works

To operate the machine, you enter the figures on the keyboard and depress the keys that tell the machine what to do. The calculator operates silently at virtually the speed of light and supplies the answer in a few milliseconds or less. Operating procedures vary slightly, depending upon the model. The step-by-step procedure for one make of machine, a Victor, is outlined below.

To multiply 12.345 by 1.29 on the electronic printing calculator, do the following:

1 Touch the Clear All $\left(\begin{smallmatrix} C \\ All \end{smallmatrix}\right)$ key to clear the machine.
2 Touch the 1 and 2 keys on the keyboard, touch the decimal (.) key, and then touch the 3, 4, and 5 keys.
3 Touch the Times (×) key.
4 Enter the multiplier, 1.29, on the keyboard. Remember to use the decimal key.
5 Touch the Equals (=) key. The product, 15.92505, is computed and printed almost instantaneously.

```
  0. 00 C *

12.345 X
  1 .29 =
15.92505
```

Typical Applications

In addition to its wide use in the fields of engineering and science, the electronic printing calculator is employed extensively in the business world to figure or check invoices, taxes, payrolls, inventories, and commissions.

THE ELECTRONIC DISPLAY CALCULATOR

The ten-key electronic display calculator operates by the touch system and is similar to the electronic printing calculator. Unlike the electronic printing calculator, however, the electronic display calculator has no paper tape or printing device. Instead, the numbers are "displayed" in lights on the face of the machine. Hundreds of different models have been developed in recent years in sizes that range from small, $2\frac{1}{2}$- by $3\frac{1}{2}$-inch models to large, typewriter-size models that perform elaborate statistical and scientific calculations. Smaller models which sell for less than $100 and even less than $50 are being purchased by housewives, traveling salesmen, and students. Some models are battery-operated, and many can be powered by either battery or electric outlet.

How It Works

Here is the step-by-step procedure for multiplying 12.345 by 1.29 on an electronic display calculator:

1 Touch the Clear (C) key to clear the machine.
2 Touch the 1 and 2 keys on the keyboard, then touch the Decimal (.) key, and then touch the 3, 4, and 5 keys.
3 Touch the Times (×) key.
4 Enter the multiplier, 1.29. Remember to use the Decimal key.
5 Touch the Plus Equals (+=) key. The product, 15.92505, is computed and displayed in the lighted tubes almost instantaneously.

Typical Applications

The electronic display calculator is used for any commercial application that does not require a printed tape, and for checking work previously done on a machine with printed tape. It is said that the machine is so flexible that only the operator's imagination limits its applications. Its flexibility permits it to be used for simple calculations as well as for advanced mathematical work and sophisticated statistical problems. Because it is lightweight and may be battery-operated, it is useful in field work such as construction, surveying, and outside sales.

THE ROTARY CALCULATOR AND THE KEY-DRIVEN CALCULATOR

It is important that you become familiar with these two types of machines, even though they are rapidly being replaced by the types of calculators discussed previously.

You can easily identify the rotary calculator because it is the only type of calculator which has a movable carriage at the top of the machine. It has a full-key arrangement and special keys for automatic multiplication and division. Computations appear on dials instead of on paper tape. This calculator is used for large computations in which printed records on tape are not important. For instance, a cost accountant may find it a very simple matter to figure to four decimal places the accurate cost of each item by using a rotary calculator. Other uses are for large tax calculations, engineering computations, estimates, budgets, complex discounts, and large amounts in billing.

The keyboard of a key-driven calculator resembles that of a full-key adding machine. There is a row of keys numbered vertically from 1 to 9 for each arithmetic column. When you depress a key, the figure is immediately picked up by the registers and is shown on the machine dials. As more figures are entered, the dials show the accumulated total.

It is not as simple to operate as the other calculators described; however, a trained operator can add, subtract, and multiply at a very fast rate by using a special touch system. The key-driven calculator is useful for the rapid computation of cash discounts, bills, time cards, inventories, stock records, sales taxes, and payroll deductions, as well as for double-checking previous calculations of all kinds.

REVIEWING YOUR READING

1 List the chain of computations involved in a purchase from a department store.
2 In addition to having technical skill, what should a machine operator know about office work?
3 Explain why people are still vital to office operation, regardless of the advances made in mechanization and automation.
4 In what sequence are keys depressed when entering amounts in the ten-key adding machines?
5 What functions will the mechanical printing calculator perform automatically that the ten-key adding machine will not?
6 Which calculators are used for double-checking invoice amounts, inventories, and similar calculations?
7 What types of machines produce printed tapes? What types show the answers only on dials?

OFFICE ASSIGNMENTS

1 Adding and calculating machines help to speed business computations. Nevertheless, if you know how to perform the calculations with paper and pencil, you have a better idea of the processes involved in mathematical computations and can select the best machine for the work.

Complete the following samples of common business calculations. Use the pencil and paper method first; then, if a suitable machine is available, use it to verify your accuracy.

Add.	$ 43.69 Register 1	Subtract.	$643.67 Sales
	64.08 Register 2		−486.79 Less cost of goods sold
	−5.67 Refunds		$_____ Gross profit
	22.64 Register 3	Multiply.	$ 45.50 List price
	$_____ Subtotal		×.27 Discount
	13.86 Cash fund		$_____ Amount of discount
	$_____ Total cash	Divide.	$64,920 (total sales) ÷
			24 (business days in
			month) = $_____
			(average sales per day)

Which machine would be best for performing each of these computations? Why?

2 Calculating inventory is an extremely important responsibility. Mistakes can mean delays in shipment and serious loss of business. Complete the extensions required to determine the value of the following partial inventory.

Quantity	Stock Number	Price	Amount
15	RH1079	$1.20	$_____
26	EA1374	.75	_____
12	MP1129	3.64	_____
18	AJ0657	1.42	_____
9	JC4471	.23	_____
		Total bin No. 10	$_____

Which machine would be best for making the original calculations? Which machine would be best for verifying inventory calculations like these? Why?

3 Some business computations involve very large figures. Verify the figuring for the first year, and then complete the calculations required for the second and third years.

	First Year	Second Year	Third Year
Current liabilities	$1,540,715	$2,717,506	$5,707,616
First mortgage bonds	2,000,000	2,000,000	2,000,000
5 percent debentures	3,256,800	3,069,600	2,882,400
Total liabilities	$6,797,515	$_____	$_____
Tangible net worth	$2,662,696	$2,590,666	$3,899,133
Ratio of total liabilities to tangible net worth (TL ÷ TNW)	255.3%	_____	_____

Which calculating machine would be best for this type of work? Explain your choice.

4 In the table below, each figure in the Amount column belongs in one of the Distribution columns, in accordance with the letter in the Classification column. The first two items have been classified. Classify the remainder of the items, and obtain the total for each column. The grand total of columns A, B, C, and D should equal the total of the Amount column.

Classification	Amount	Distribution			
		A	B	C	D
D	$19.98	$_____	$_____	$_____	$ 19.98
C	24.95	_____	_____	24.95	_____
B	32.85	_____	_____	_____	_____
B	11.67	_____	_____	_____	_____
A	31.19	_____	_____	_____	_____
C	40.07	_____	_____	_____	_____
C	18.76	_____	_____	_____	_____
D	23.62	_____	_____	_____	_____
B	44.87	_____	_____	_____	_____
A	20.08	_____	_____	_____	_____
D	44.00	_____	_____	_____	_____
B	24.66	_____	_____	_____	_____
A	18.70	_____	_____	_____	_____
D	39.76	_____	_____	_____	_____
C	34.50	_____	_____	_____	_____
A	46.32	_____	_____	_____	_____
Totals	$	$	$	$	$

5 Buying and selling merchandise involves a number of price calculations. One procedure, called extending, requires that the quantity be multiplied by the price to determine the total value of the goods. Complete the extensions required in the partial invoice shown below. The first line has been computed as an example. Double-check your work when you finish.

	Quantity	Description	Unit Price	Amount
	6	XA173	$ .25	$ 1.50
a	10	BT478	1.17	_____
b	39	RL064	.89	_____
c	23	KK282	1.66	_____
d	5	TM609	2.25	_____
e	8	BJ181	4.41	_____

6 Another common office computing problem involves the recording of amounts owed by customers, which are called *accounts receivable*. Here is a portion of a customer's charge account. Compute the balance amount on each line after adding the new sale or deducting the payment. The first two items have been completed as an example. Double-check your work when you finish.

	Date	Ref. No.	Sales	Payments	Balance
	Feb. 2	S 694	$21.00		$21.00
	Feb. 7	C027		$11.00	10.00
a	Feb. 8	S 743	16.00		_____
b	Feb. 12	S 811	7.50		_____
c	Feb. 15	C164		20.00	_____
d	Feb. 25	S 905	14.69		_____
e	Feb. 28	C256		13.50	_____

7 As soon as a shipment is made, the inventory record has to be adjusted. Hence, another office computing problem arises. Compute the balance on each line after adding the receipt of new stock and deducting shipments of stock. The first two items have been completed as an example. Double-check your work when you finish.

	Date	Ref. No.	In	Out	Balance
	Mar. 1	R1864	1,265		1,265
	Mar. 2	S469		325	940
a	Mar. 5	S635		590	_____
b	Mar. 11	R2843	923		_____
c	Mar. 14	S741		245	_____
d	Mar. 19	S1022		632	_____
e	Mar. 23	R3725	505		_____

8 At the end of a day's work, the salesman will be eager to find out how much commission he has earned. Compute the following summary of sales commissions. The first item has been completed as an example. Double-check your work when you finish.

	Type of Sale	Amount	Rate	Commission Earned
	Overcoats	$120.00	4%	$ 4.80
a	Rainwear	89.60	5%	_____
b	Shirts and Ties	57.10	8%	_____
c	Shoes	65.50	6%	_____
d	Suits	254.00	10%	_____
e	Sweaters	93.45	$7\frac{1}{2}\%$	_____
			Total $	_____

9 The office machine operator is frequently called upon to check an adding machine tape against figures on original documents. On a separate sheet of paper copy the two columns of figures below and make a third column for your answers. Compare each set of numbers to determine whether they are identical or different in any way. If the two amounts are identical, place a check mark in your Answer column. If the two numbers are different in any way, place an X in the Answer column, draw a horizontal line through the number in the Adding Machine Tape column, and rewrite the number to agree with the one in the Original Document column.

	Original Document	Adding Machine Tape	Answer
Example:	71.24	71.24	✔
		121.75	
Example:	121.75	~~121.45~~	X
1	92.86	98.86	
2	412.98	412.89	
3	1,427.64	1,427.64	
4	18.43	18.43	
5	16.40	1.64	
6	23.77	23.77	
7	121.21	122.12	
8	432.27	432.17	
9	44.40	44.00	
10	94.55	94.55	
11	166.83	166.83	
12	8,435.24	8,435.24	
13	990.09	9,900.90	
14	433.27	433.27	
15	14.86	18.46	
16	8.48	8.48	
17	23.96	23.96	
18	14.45	14.45	
19	221.77	221.79	
20	3,312.84	3,312.84	
21	42,196.43	42,196.43	
22	8,420.00	8,420.00	
23	6,716.99	6,617.99	
24	12,222.22	12.222.00	
25	3,417.88	3,417.88	
26	4,554.45	4,544.45	
27	82,600.00	82,060.00	
28	9,417.39	9,417.89	
29	2,432.08	2,438.02	
30	71,996.64	71,996.64	
31	14,770.08	14,700.08	
32	6,667.76	6,667.76	
33	32,085.76	32,086.76	
34	8,111.81	8,111.81	
35	19,198.43	19,198.43	
36	5,000.76	6,000.76	
37	70,824.95	70,842.95	
38	8,847.20	8,847.20	
39	96,664.72	90,664.72	
40	143,914.88	143,914.98	
41	84,635.27	84,635.27	
42	221,808.94	221,808.94	

The enormous growth in the volume of office operations has created a need for machines that can do more than just add and subtract rapidly. A desk calculator, such as the kind you studied in Section 21, can be used to figure the net amount of a paycheck, but it can't write the check and make the entry in the payroll journal. There are, however, advanced machines that can perform all these functions and many more.

In the same way that the touch-tone telephone has improved and enlarged communication, data processing has improved and enlarged American business operations. For example, one of the country's large banks processes 2 million checks each day. Processing each one by hand would be costly, if not impossible. However, by using data processing methods, this task becomes a routine operation.

Office data processing, sometimes referred to as office automation, is defined as the technique of performing automatically—either by special timesaving devices, punched-card machines, or electronic computers—such repetitive office tasks as recording, sorting, reading, calculating, and recopying.

KEYSORT DATA PROCESSING

In many clerical operations the elementary process of sorting can be a bottleneck. To speed up the procedure, a special system called *Keysort Data Processing* has been devised. Two vital components of this system are a hole-punched card and a needle-type selector.

Data regarding a transaction, an activity, or a situation is recorded in writing on a special card that has holes punched evenly along one or more edges. The marginal edges of the card are then divided into "fields," which are groups of punched holes. (The number of holes in a field will vary with the company and with the information it plans to sort.) The significance of each hole is determined by a prearranged code and location plan. Data is recorded in

A McBee product, courtesy of Litton ABS

Data is recorded by notching away the portion of the card between the hole and the edge of the card.

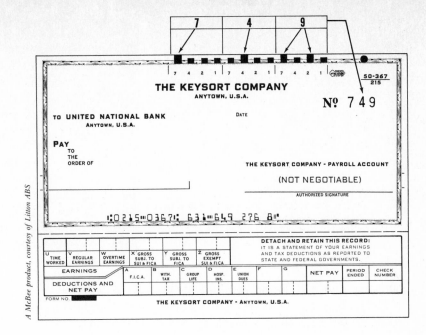

A McBee product, courtesy of Litton ABS

the margin of the card by notching in the correct holes in each field. The notching can be done by a hand punch or by an electrically powered keypunch machine, whose keyboard looks like an adding machine. The card is inserted in the machine, and the desired data is notched in the edge of the card.

The Keysort system is frequently used by companies to sort canceled checks. Before the checks are issued by the company, they are coded along the upper edge according to the printed check number. Notice that in the illustration of Check 749 there are three fields of punched holes, one field for each digit of the check number, and four holes in each field. These four holes have the values, from left to right, of 7, 4, 2, and 1. The units digit of the check number, 9, is coded by notching the 7 and 2 holes in the field at the right. The tens digit, 4, is coded by notching the 4 in the next field. The hundreds digit, 7, is coded by notching the 7 in the field at the left. It is possible to record numbers 1 to 14 by notching one or more of the four holes in a field. No hole is notched to record a zero.

Let us say that 300 coded Keysort checks have been issued, cleared through the bank, and returned to the issuing company with the monthly bank statement. By using the Keysort process, the issuing company puts the checks in numeric order so that it can learn what checks are still outstanding and reconcile its bank balance with the bank statement.

Keysorting is accomplished by using (1) a long sorting needle with a handle at one end and (2) an alignment block. The stack of cards or checks is aligned on the block, and the needle is inserted in the position being sorted. When the needle is lifted, the checks that have been notched in the position being sorted remain on the alignment block, and the checks that are unnotched in the position being sorted remain on the sorting needle.

When the sorting needle is inserted into one of the holes in this group of cards, the notched cards fall away and remain on the alignment block.

A McBee product, courtesy of Litton ABS

The 300 checks are arranged numerically by performing 12 sorts, one for each of the 12 holes at the top of the checks, beginning at the right and proceeding to the left. After each sort, the checks that remain in the alignment block are placed in back of the stack of checks. At the end of the last sort, the checks will be in exact numeric sequence. More sorts would be required, of course, if more than three digits were used in the numbering of the checks.

PEGBOARD DATA PROCESSING

Many clerical operations require that a name, an amount, or other data be written on two or more related records. Pegboard data processing saves the office worker time and energy because it has specially designed forms with carbon paper, which allow several related forms to be prepared in one writing, and a device known as a pegboard, which accurately aligns the forms.

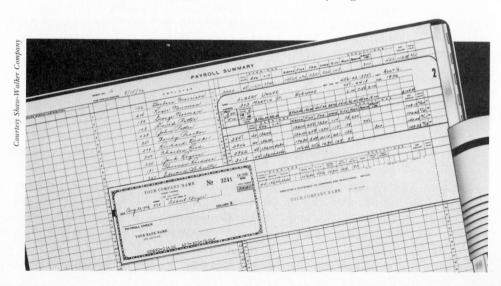

Courtesy Shaw-Walker Company

Pegboards are used in such office systems as accounts receivable, accounts payable, cash payments, and payroll. In a payroll system, for example, all of the following related records must be prepared from information found on the time cards: (1) payroll summary, (2) permanent employee earnings record, (3) employee's check, and (4) employee's notice of deductions. By using pegs that fit into holes on the forms or a clamp, the payroll clerk aligns all the payroll forms on the pegboard and fills them in simultaneously. Note the illustration on page 278.

PUNCHED-TAPE DATA PROCESSING

Although the Keysort system and the pegboard can save you a great deal of time, they are used for relatively few tasks because the forms they employ are usually not adapted to machine processing. Several types of machines are available, however, which not only produce printed records but also produce punched tape that can be read and processed very rapidly by machines.

The Flexowriter

The *Flexowriter* is an electric typewriter with tape-punching and tape-reading stations attached at the side. It is similar to the *Justowriter* described in Section 15. As you type, information is transferred onto a punched tape in coded form. For instance, if you want many copies of a form letter, you can type the form letter on the Flexowriter, which will produce the information on punched tape. This punched tape can then be fed through the reading station, and the form letter will be retyped automatically as many times as needed. Only the date, address, and salutation need to be typed manually.

The Computyper

The *Computyper* is a combination of an electric typewriter and an electric calculator with tape-punching and tape-reading stations. Used largely for typing invoices, it not only can produce a punched tape from typed information but also can perform calculations and record answers automatically on invoices and punched tape. The data on the tape can be transmitted by wire to distant warehouses and control centers.

PUNCHED-CARD DATA PROCESSING

A second type of record designed to be read and processed by machines is the punched card—a card containing small punched holes on its face. An advantage of the punched card over punched tape is that each card carries information about one unit—that is, about one product or one sale or one purchase or one payment or any other single unit designated when the system is set up. That is why it is commonly referred to as the *unit record card.* A further advantage of punched cards is that they can be grouped and regrouped for different auditing purposes and read rapidly by machine. Punched cards are also called *tab cards* because the data on them is tabulated on the printing machines.

Since one group of cards is to be used to produce several reports, a survey is made to determine what kind of information should be included on the cards. For example, if the punched cards are to be sales records, the cards must contain data such as the date of the sale, the amount of the sale, the name or account number of the customer, the department in which the sale occurred, the sales tax, and the sales-clerk number. Different reports, pertaining to accounts receivable, cash receipts, sales analysis, stock control, cost study, and sales tax computations, can be compiled from this information.

After the data needed for a sales record is identified, each kind of data is assigned to a particular field on the card. A *field* is simply one or more adjacent columns on a unit record card and contains one kind of data, such as the amount of a sale or the date. The card is then placed in a keypunch machine, and the data is recorded on the card in the form of punched holes. Since an IBM (International Business Machines) card has 80 vertical columns, it will hold up to 80 pieces of data, each represented by a letter, digit, or special character.

Once the card is punched, it may be placed in a separate verifier unit, or it may be verified on certain models of keypunch machines. The verifying operator enters on her keyboard the same data that was entered on the keypunch machine. This time no new holes are punched in the card because the function of verifying is only to check that the keypunching was done correctly. If an incorrect punch is discovered, a notch is made on the card at the top of the column in which the error appears.

These punched cards are useful only if they can be arranged in different groupings. Thus, if a daily sales report must be compiled, all sales cards having sales for that day must be identified and grouped together. The arranging or sorting is done on a *sorter* unit. This equipment not only selects all the sales

An IBM punched card.

Courtesy IBM

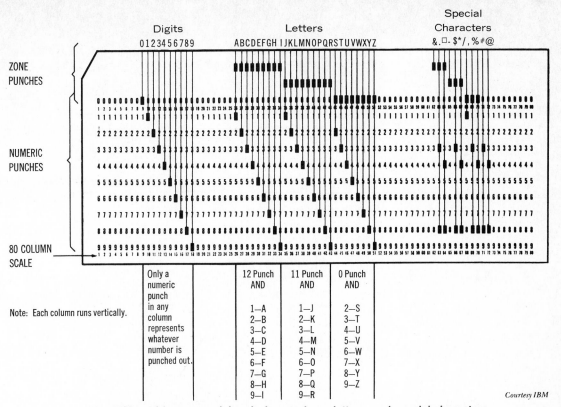

The IBM card has a special code for numbers, letters, and special characters.

items out of a mixed stack of cards (a process called *grouping* or *segregating)* but also arranges them alphabetically or numerically (a process called *sequencing*). Sales cards, for instance, may be sequenced by invoice number if such an arrangement is desired for reporting purposes.

The sorter operates by examining one column of data at a time. If the day's invoice numbers ranged from 001 to 500, the sales cards would be passed through the sorter three times (one time for each digit) in order to arrange them in numeric sequence. An illustration showing how cards are sorted is shown on page 282.

Cards that have been grouped and sequenced may be fed into an accounting machine, also called a tabulating machine, for the preparation of a printed report. For example, the punched cards containing sales data are read by the machine, which selects and prints information, one line at a time, on a columnar report form. When all entries are listed on the report, the machine adds the dollar columns and prints a total, which might be the total sales for the day. A wired control panel tells the accounting machine what to do.

APPLICATIONS OF DATA PROCESSING

The basic punched-card operations just described are used for such laborious clerical routines as analysis, statistical tabulation, and posting.

HOW IBM CARDS ARE SORTED

1. Cards to be sorted on columns 1 (left) and 2 (right) are placed in hopper of sorting machine.

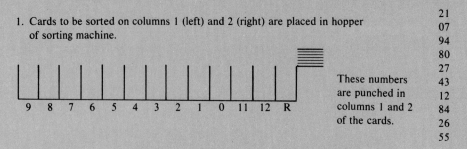

These numbers are punched in columns 1 and 2 of the cards.

21
07
94
80
27
43
12
84
26
55

2. Column selector is set on column 2; machine start button is depressed.

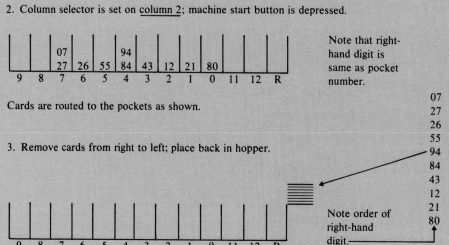

Note that right-hand digit is same as pocket number.

Cards are routed to the pockets as shown.

07
27
26
55
94
84
43
12
21
80

3. Remove cards from right to left; place back in hopper.

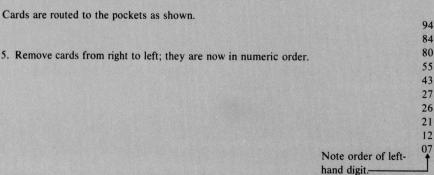

Note order of right-hand digit.

4. Column selector is set on column 1 (left); machine start button is depressed.

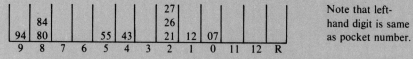

Note that left-hand digit is same as pocket number.

Cards are routed to the pockets as shown.

94
84
80
55
43
27
26
21
12
07

5. Remove cards from right to left; they are now in numeric order.

Note order of left-hand digit.

Analysis

Sorting and re-sorting operations help to analyze, select, and classify data.

Statistical Tabulation

The accounting machine that summarizes data in a printed report can actually list information in prearranged tabular form much faster than a competent statistical typist.

Posting

The clerical process of posting is often made more efficient by the use of a unit record system. Certain traditional records may not be kept in the usual ledger form at all. Instead, a record of what a customer owes may consist of a collection of punched cards for unpaid charges. When a complete record of unpaid charges is required — possibly for end-of-month billing — the accounting machine quickly prints, lists, and totals the cards on a statement form.

Reproducing

Extra copies of data can be made at every step of a punched-card operation. A reproducing unit can make an extra set of punched cards automatically from the original, verified set. Extra copies of reports and summaries can be prepared by running cards through the accounting machine a second time or by preparing an offset master or a fluid process master of the first copy of the report.

Mark Sensing

The reproducing unit also has the capacity to sense pencil marks on cards and to translate these marks into punched holes on the same cards. For instance, the reproducing unit can translate the pencil recordings of electric meter readings, made by an employee of a utilities company.

Conversion

Converter units are used to transfer data from one form to another. For example, data on punched cards can be converted to punched tape and vice versa. Data on prepunched sales tags can be transferred to regular punched cards for stock control purposes.

MAGNETIC INK CHARACTER RECOGNITION (MICR)

In the past several years devices have been developed that can read printed or typed words and numbers. Thus it is not necessary to code data in the form of punched holes before it can be processed by machines. The printed or typed words can be read by both machines and people.

In the MICR system numbers are printed in magnetic ink along the bottom edge of checks. Special machines recognize the magnetic characters and perform sorting operations at very high speeds.

OPTICAL SCANNING

In this system characters are printed in ordinary ink rather than magnetic ink and are read by machines by a beam of light. Some cash registers and adding machines print numbers on tapes in a special type style that the machine can read. Oil company credit cards imprint a special code on the sales ticket so that it can be read by optical scanning machines. Some machines can read special typewriter type styles, and others can read hand lettering.

Because of the new advances made by technology, you can expect that some day business machines will be developed that will accept instructions and data directly from your spoken voice.

COMPUTER DATA PROCESSING

After they had improved techniques for recording and reading information, business equipment manufacturers devised complex and high-speed devices known as *electronic data processing systems*, or *electronic computers*, for processing and storing vast quantities of data.

Electronic computer systems combine many of the operations, previously explained, into one operation that requires a minimum of human assistance. However, as clever as a computer is, it is not a genie. It will not perform unless it has a program. A *program* is a series of detailed instructions that are fed into a computer before the operation begins.

Electronic computers have a device that reads magnetic tape, punched paper tape, or punched cards. This device is known as the *input unit*, and it is used to read the program as well as the data into the computer.

The *processing unit* of a computer contains three parts. The *internal storage unit* stores the program and temporarily stores the data being acted upon, the *arithmetic unit* performs various calculations, and the *control unit* determines the actions of every part of the system.

Every computer has an *output unit* which provides results of computations or lists of information in various forms, such as paper, cards, and magnetic tape. A *printing unit*, for instance, lists on paper at an extremely high speed the results of computer operations; a *punching unit* punches data onto cards; a *tape unit* transcribes data onto magnetic tape; a *visual display unit* pictures data in the form of words, numbers, charts, graphs, and illustrations on a television type of picture tube; and an *audio-response unit* provides, from a prerecorded vocabulary, spoken answers to questions that have been made by special input devices.

Parts of an Electronic Computer System

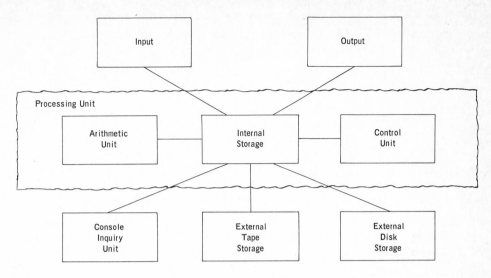

Adapted from PRINCIPLES OF PROGRAMMING, Section 2, IBM Personal Study Program.

Because the internal storage unit of computers is generally limited in size, many computers have external storage units. Data may be externally stored on magnetic tape that is available on a 10½-inch diameter reel with either 1,200 or 2,400 feet of tape. A single 2,400-foot tape, ½ inch in width, can be used to record as many as 14 million characters. The tape reels are placed on special magnetic tape units that are wired to the processing unit.

Data may also be stored externally on *random access disk storage units,* which permit access to data in nonsequential order and at irregular intervals of time. Each unit has a capacity to record up to 20 million characters. Disk units are more expensive than tape units; however, data can be located in disk units in much less time than it can be located in tape units.

A *console inquiry unit,* which looks like a typewriter, can be used to give special instructions to computers and to receive automatically typed results. Many computer systems do not have the console inquiry unit because it is not essential for all operations. Other systems have inquiry units which are located far from the computer and are connected to it by telephone lines. These inquiry systems, used by airlines and other firms, are known as *on-line real-time* systems: they are on the direct line of communications with the computer, and inquiries are answered immediately—in real time as opposed to delayed time.

A COMPARISON OF DATA PROCESSING METHODS

The methods, machines, and equipment discussed in this unit can be used to perform many different operations. Look at the office assignment on page 288 and see by means of flowcharts how it can be performed by different methods.

1 MANUAL METHOD

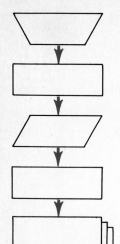

STEP 1 ACTIVATE
Handwrite sales ticket

STEP 2 PROCESS
Figure total of sale
manually

STEP 3 MANUAL
Deliver ticket copy to
office

STEP 4 PROCESS
Journalize in sales journal
by hand

STEP 5 PROCESS
Post to customer's account
by hand

STEP 6 PROCESS
Figure and record balance
of account manually

STEP 7 FILE
File sales ticket copy

STEP 8 DOCUMENT
Prepare statement from
account at end of month
manually

STEP 9 TERMINAL
Mail statement

2 A SMALL BUSINESS MACHINE METHOD

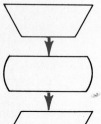

STEP 1 ACTIVATE
Handwrite sales ticket

STEP 2 MACHINE
Total sale on calculator

STEP 3 MANUAL
Deliver ticket copy to
office

STEP 4 MACHINE
Journalize in sales journal
by typewriter

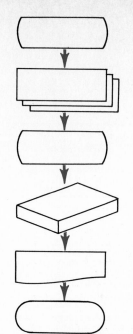

STEP 5 PROCESS
Post to customer's account
by hand

STEP 6 MACHINE
Figure balance by machine,
record manually

STEP 7 FILE
File sales ticket copy

STEP 8 DOCUMENT
Photocopy account at end
of month

STEP 9 TERMINAL
Mail photocopy of account
statement

3 A PEGBOARD METHOD

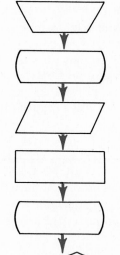

STEP 1 ACTIVATE
Handwrite sales ticket

STEP 2 MACHINE
Total sale on calculator

STEP 3 MANUAL
Deliver ticket copy to
office

STEP 4 PROCESS
Journalize in sales journal,
post to customer's account,
and prepare statement all in
one handwriting on pegboard

STEP 5 MACHINE
Figure balance by machine

STEP 6 FILE
File sales ticket copy

STEP 7 TERMINAL
Mail statement at end of
month

4 A POSTING MACHINE METHOD

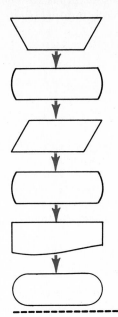

STEP 1 ACTIVATE
Prepare sales ticket by hand and by imprint plate

STEP 2 MACHINE
Total sale on cash register

STEP 3 MANUAL
Deliver ticket copy to office

STEP 4 MACHINE
Journalize in sales journal, post to customer's account, figure balance, and prepare statement in one machine operation on posting machine

STEP 5 DOCUMENT
Microfilm sales ticket copy

STEP 6 TERMINAL
Mail statement at end of month

---

5 A PUNCHED-CARD METHOD

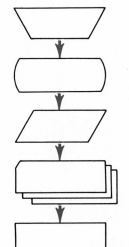

STEP 1 ACTIVATE
Prepare sales ticket by hand and by imprint plate

STEP 2 MACHINE
Total sale on cash register

STEP 3 MANUAL
Deliver ticket copy to office

STEP 4 PUNCHED CARD
Prepare punched card for each ticket

STEP 5 PROCESS
Use cards to journalize in sales journal, post to customer's account, and prepare statement*

*CARDS CAN BE REUSED TO PREPARE:
1. SALES ANALYSIS
2. COMMISSION REPORT
3. INVENTORY REPORT
4. OTHER SALES REPORTS

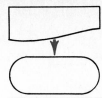

STEP 6 DOCUMENT
Microfilm sales ticket copy

STEP 7 TERMINAL
Mail statement at end of month

---

6 AN ELECTRONIC COMPUTER METHOD

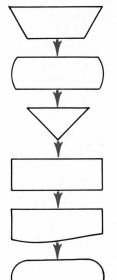

STEP 1 ACTIVATE
Prepare sales ticket on special mark-sensing form by hand and by imprint plate

STEP 2 MACHINE
Total sale on cash register

STEP 3 STORAGE
Place sales ticket into mark-sense reader attached to computer

STEP 4 PROCESS
Computer journalizes, posts, and prints out statements when needed*

STEP 5 DOCUMENT
Microfilm sales ticket copy

STEP 6 TERMINAL
Mail statement at end of month

*DATA FED TO COMPUTER CAN ALSO BE USED FOR:
1. SALES ANALYSIS
2. COMMISSION REPORT
3. INVENTORY REPORT
4. OTHER SALES REPORTS

---

7 AN ON-LINE REAL-TIME METHOD

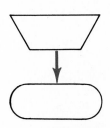

STEP 1 ACTIVATE
Punch sales data into machines linked to computers which immediately charge sale against customer's independent service account and debit firm's cash accounts*

STEP 2 TERMINAL
Credit service mails statement to customer; customer makes payment to credit service

*DATA FED TO COMPUTER CAN ALSO BE USED FOR:
1. SALES ANALYSIS
2. COMMISSION REPORT
3. INVENTORY REPORT
4. OTHER SALES REPORTS

The Job: Post a Sales Ticket; Mail a Monthly Statement

This office assignment involves crediting a sales ticket to an individual customer's account and mailing a statement to him at the end of the month. Illustrated on pages 286–287 are flowcharts showing how the assignment can be completed by any of seven methods: (1) by hand, (2) with a small business machine, (3) with a pegboard, (4) with a posting machine, (5) with punched cards, (6) with an electronic computer, (7) with an on-line real-time computer.

GLOSSARY OF COMPUTER DATA PROCESSING TERMS

Arithmetic unit Performs calculations.

Audio-response unit Provides spoken answers.

Computer Device for processing and storing a vast quantity of data electronically.

Console inquiry unit Types instructions to computers and receives typed results.

Control unit Determines the actions of the system.

Input unit Reads the program and the data into the computer.

Internal storage unit Stores the program and data until needed.

Mark sensing The translation of pencil marks on cards to punched holes on the same cards.

MICR Magnetic Ink Character Recognition—a system by which characters and numbers are read by machines.

On-line real-time system Direct telephone connections to a computer stationed elsewhere for immediate response.

Optical scanning The reading of characters and numbers printed in ordinary ink by means of a beam of light.

Output unit Provides computation results or lists of information in a variety of forms.

Printing unit Lists results of computer operations on paper.

Processing unit Consists of an internal storage unit, an arithmetic unit, and a control unit.

Program A set of detailed instructions fed into the computer before operation begins.

Punched tape Tape that can be read and processed rapidly by machine.

Punching unit Punches data onto cards.

Random access disk storage unit Permits access to data in nonsequential order and at irregular intervals of time.

Tab card A punched card containing one unit of information which can be tabulated on a printing machine.

Tape unit Transcribes data onto magnetic tape.

Visual display unit Pictures data on a television type of picture tube.

REVIEWING YOUR READING

1 What items are needed for the Keysort operation?
2 Describe the system of sorting cards by means of Keysort.
3 What are two ways in which an office worker can perform more efficiently by using the pegboard system?
4 What is the advantage of having information coded on punched tape instead of having it written on a sheet of paper?
5 How is data first recorded and verified in the punched-card system?

6 How does the sorting operation enable the accounting machine to prepare several different kinds of reports from the same deck of cards?

7 What is the difference between MICR and optical scanning?

8 Name several forms of computer input and computer output.

9 What are the parts of the processing unit of a computer?

OFFICE ASSIGNMENTS

1 Draw the first ten columns of six IBM cards, or use the cards in your workbook. "Punch" the department numbers, amounts of sales, and salesclerk numbers listed below into the six cards by blacking out with a pencil the numbers to be punched. Use columns 1 to 3 for the department number, columns 4 to 8 for the amount of sales, and columns 9 and 10 for the salesclerk number. Be sure that all department numbers end on column 3, all sale amounts on column 8, and all salesclerk numbers on column 10.

	Department No. (Columns 1 to 3)	Amount of Sales (Columns 4 to 8)	Salesclerk No. (Columns 9 and 10)
a	212	124.21	12
b	146	200.70	46
c	073	29.95	09
d	320	114.26	30
e	063	4.50	15
f	108	13.75	27

2 Draw two sets of sorting machine pockets like the ones illustrated on page 282. Study the illustration.

a At the right is a list of numbers that have been punched in columns 1 (left) and 2 (right) of IBM cards. Show how they would be arranged in pockets after the first sort (column 2) by writing the numbers in the pockets. The first (bottom) card number is written in the correct pocket below as an example.

20
11
35
17
22
18
26
17
34
30
15
36
29
18
23
21
39
33
14
32

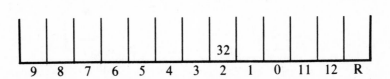

9 8 7 6 5 4 3 2 1 0 11 12 R

b List the numbers of the cards in the order in which they will appear after they are removed from the sorter.

c Show how the cards in the list you prepared will be arranged in pockets after the second sort (column 1). Write the numbers in the second set of pockets.

d List the numbers of the cards in the order in which they will appear after they are removed from the sorter. Check to see that the numbers are in correct sequence. If they are not, study the illustration on page 282 and perform steps *a* through *d* again.

3 An IBM card used for mailing list control purposes is shown on page 280. The customer's name, address, and account number appear at the top of the card, and the information is represented by punched holes below.

Review the explanation of card punching on pages 279–281 to interpret the holes in the card. Explain how and where punches would be made for a customer named George W. Browne instead of Robert A. Jamison. Assume that all other details remain the same.

4 Data processing, like any other specialized field, has a vocabulary all its own. Define or use each of the following ten terms in a sentence. Then review the section, and add five other new technical terms to the list, supplying a definition or illustrative sentence for each.

punched tape	tab card	internal storage	MICR	input
computer	output	mark sensing	optical scanning	program

5 The monthly electric bill illustrated below was prepared on IBM tabulating equipment. Identify five clerical functions involved in processing such bills, and indicate which steps may be mechanized by the use of data processing equipment.

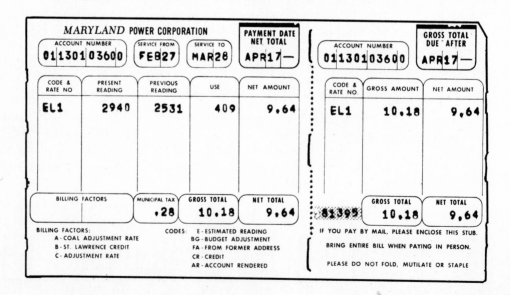

UNIT 8

BUSINESS CASES AND PROBLEMS

In the Boss's Shoes   1   "I've been keeping those stock records by hand for years. You gave me raises and often told me what a fine job I was doing. Now it looks as though my work wasn't good enough after all because next month you are supposed to install machines. Well, I don't want any part of this machine business, and that's final."

As a supervisor, what can you say or do to placate this older employee? What do you think is the employer's responsibility with regard to the rights and feelings of employees when procedures are mechanized?

2   Carlos works fast and can turn out more work than anyone else in the department. However, he is careless and frequently sends out cards and bills with errors on them. Although you have asked Carlos to try to be more careful, you can see that he has not improved. He seems to think that he is entitled to special consideration because he works so rapidly. Does Carlos have a valid excuse, or should a really competent person be both speedy and accurate?

3   Rita asked her boss, "As the operator of that new machine, I handle the work formerly done by three clerks. If you are saving all this money, why isn't my salary two or three times what it was before the change? It doesn't seem fair to me." If you were Rita's boss, how would you explain why her salary isn't as large as she seems to expect?

Your Human Relations   1   "Hey, Joe, will you help me sort these cards? I should have done them an hour ago, but I had to run an errand for Mr. Klein." Why should Joe help you? Doesn't he have his own work to do? If you were in Joe's place, would you be willing to do someone else's work just because he asked you? Should you have told Mr. Klein about the cards?

2   "Why does it always happen to me?" wails Blanche when she realizes that she is out of supplies halfway through a job. Extra supplies will not be obtainable for several hours. As Blanche's friend and co-worker, what friendly advice can you give her about her working habits? What might you do to help her out in the meantime?

3   "Mr. King was angry because I didn't type out that report properly. They didn't teach me to do anything like that in school. What does he expect from a beginner?" Is it reasonable to expect the school to teach you everything that you will ever need to know? If you encounter a new assignment and if you don't know what to do, how can you easily find out?

4 "Look at the terrific bargain I just found at a shoe outlet store." Sally proceeds excitedly to unwrap a parcel on your desk. You are already far behind in your work and simply cannot spare time to show enthusiasm over her new shoes and wait while she tries them on for your benefit. What can you say without hurting her feelings?

5 "If the boss looks for me, tell him I went to the stockroom." You know that Bill plans to sneak out for a late breakfast. What should you say if the boss actually does inquire. What should you say to Bill when he asks you to "cover up" for him?

6 "How do you like it?" Mabel expects you to admire her new outfit, but the truth is that it is totally unbecoming as well as unbusinesslike. What do you say?

What Would You Do If ... ? 1 Your supervisor tells you to finish some computations for him, but he leaves before you can ask him which machine you should use. What would you do?

2 You are asked to sort by hand a stack of 1,000 cards that are coded for Keysort?

3 You hear a rumor that the operations in the office in which you work will be automated within two years. What would you do?

What Does This Mean? 1 Your friend says that he has been promoted to a job in the front office.

2 An employee's manual says that workers who are asked to work extra hours in emergencies may ask for "compensatory time off."

3 A want ad for an office job says, "Training in data processing peripheral equipment required."

Business in Your Area 1 List some of the businesses or industries in your area in which data processing has been applied to office operations. Then describe the nature of each application. (Find as many different applications as you can.)

2 What local office has the reputation for being the nicest place to work? Why?

3 What are the opportunities for part-time office employment while you are still in school? What are the opportunities for employment after you have completed your training?

4 Do any offices operate on more than a normal day shift?

UNIT **9**
PREPARING
MULTIPLE
COPIES

23 Fluid Duplicating

"Paper work explosion" is the term used to describe the enormous increase in communications material produced by industry and institutions. Office workers would be completely overwhelmed with extra work were it not for the remarkable duplicating processes and material at their disposal. Copies that once took hours to produce are turned out today in seconds.

Although you may not become a full-time operator of duplicating equipment, you should still know something about the different kinds of duplicators and how they are most suitably used. If you know this, you'll be able to turn out the number of copies you need, on the right quality of paper, in the shortest amount of time, with the least effort.

BASIC FACTORS IN DUPLICATING

Here, as in every instance, using the right tool makes the job easier and yields more professional results. If your office has a variety of duplicating machines, you'll find it a great advantage to know which one to use. The duplicator you choose will depend upon the particular characteristics of the individual job.

Number of Copies

The number of copies needed may range from a few bulletins to be distributed to a small sales force to thousands of financial reports to be sent annually to stockholders in a large corporation. You will want to figure out as accurately as possible how many copies are needed for a particular job. By doing this, you'll not only avoid wasting paper but also eliminate the headache of wondering what to do with the extra copies that take up storage space. Also, since paper is made from wood, you extend the life of a tree every time you avoid wasting paper.

Characteristics of Material

Written or typed items are not the only kinds of material that are duplicated. Tables, charts, diagrams, sketches, drawings, photographs, forms, and information of all kinds can also be reproduced; however, not all duplicating machines can handle every type of copying problem.

Color

Color adds considerably to the appeal of duplicated copies. A number of duplicators permit the use of color, but operating procedures vary a great deal among machines. Tinted paper can sometimes be used to liven up the appearance of material done in standard black ink.

Size of Copy

Certain duplicators are made to handle primarily the standard, 8½- by 11-inch paper or legal-size, 8½- by 13-inch paper. Some duplicators can take the larger sheets of paper that some business reports, forms, and charts require.

Type of Paper

Sometimes the duplicating method that you use will depend on the quality of the paper needed for the finished copies. Some methods require specially finished papers.

Number of Sides

Most of the time, copy is reproduced only on one side of the sheet of paper. Sometimes, however, copy can be reproduced more economically if both sides of the sheet of paper are used. Items such as bulletins and pamphlets are duplicated in this way. For such jobs there are special duplicating processes that can produce copy on both sides of the paper more efficiently than others.

Quality Desired

Make sure you know to whom the duplicated copies are going. If you are repro-ducing a sales letter, you want to be sure that the letter is neat and legible so that it will create a favorable impression on the customer. But for routine office operations you are likely not to place as much importance on the appearance of the copy as long as it can be read without any difficulty. Different processes produce different qualities of work. An expert office worker makes her decision on the basis of the quality of work desired.

Speed

Duplicating methods are meant to speed up operations and deliver copies as fast as they are needed. When calculating the time required to complete a job, include time for the preparation of the message and the production of copies. First the message must be prepared for copying. Preparation may involve simply writing out or typing the message, or it may involve a more complex and technical makeup problem. Then copies must be run off. Certain common devices produce only a few copies a minute, while others produce from 75 to 100 copies in the same amount of time. Still other devices operate like small printing presses and turn out thousands of copies an hour.

Dependability

Speedy service to customers is important, and business cannot waste time purchasing duplicators that need frequent and involved repairs. You will want to use a dependable machine that is easy to clean and adjust so that work can be turned out on schedule.

Cost

While the cost for reproducing each individual copy is relatively inexpensive, the paper cost for the huge quantities of copies produced in an office adds up to a very considerable amount. Cost is always a factor in any job. It is up to you to determine which duplicating process yields the most satisfactory job at a reasonable cost.

DUPLICATING PROCESSES

Once the requirements of a job have been identified, the next step is to select the process that will be the best one to use. There are at least seven basic processes available for making duplicate copies of material in the office.

1	Hand copying	5	Stencil duplicating
2	Repeated typing	6	Offset duplicating
3	Use of carbon paper	7	Photocopying
4	Fluid duplicating		

You have already been introduced to the first three methods listed in previous units. In this unit you will become acquainted with the other four processes of office duplicating.

FLUID DUPLICATING

One of the oldest techniques for making duplicate copies is the fluid method, which is based upon the use of aniline dye. You can recognize something that has been reproduced by means of fluid duplicating by the characteristic purple color of the copy. Copy can be reproduced in other colors as well. The process gets its name from the chemical solvent used to produce copies. You may also hear it referred to as the chemical method, the direct method, the liquid method, or the spirit method.

Fluid duplicating is a good process to use when a limited number of low-cost copies are required quickly without special concern for artistic appearance or

Courtesy A. B. Dick Company, Inc.

The electric fluid duplicator permits short runs to be made economically and speedily.

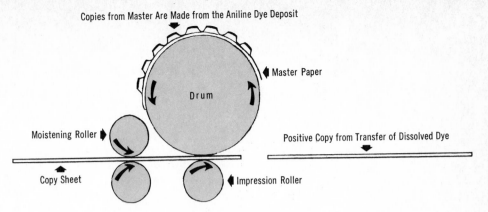

Copies from Master Are Made from the Aniline Dye Deposit

Drum

Master Paper

Moistening Roller

Positive Copy from Transfer of Dissolved Dye

Copy Sheet

Impression Roller

paper quality. Typical examples of its use are hasty bulletins and notices, orders, instructions, announcements, and reminders. Schools use the fluid process for tests and student handouts. Billing operations make use of it when several copies are required. With this process corrections, additions, and deletions can be made with ease. It is versatile, and after a typed master sheet is used to run off a number of copies, it may be filed for future use.

A negative master is required in this process. To obtain it, a sheet of aniline dye-coated carbon paper is placed behind a master sheet with the coated side of the carbon facing the *back* of the master. The message is then put on the *front* side of the master. You can prepare the message on a typewriter, a teletype machine, a computer with a printout device, or a photocopying machine. You can also draw, write, or rule the message by hand. When the message is put on the face of the master sheet, it appears on the opposite side of the master in reverse. This is the negative master. With this negative side facing up, the master is placed on the drum of the duplicator. As the drum revolves, moistened paper is fed into the machine and pressed against the negative image. The fluid on the paper dissolves a small quantity of the dye, and the message image is transferred, like a rubber stamp action, to the paper in positive form.

Operating the Fluid Duplicator

The number of copies a duplicator will produce varies according to the machine model, but as a rule of thumb you can expect to get up to 300 copies from a single master.

Check the solvent supply   The fluid process uses an alcohol-based mixture as a solvent. After removing the machine cover, check the fluid tank to be certain that there is enough of the chemical mixture to do the job.

Prime the wick   Fluid is drawn from the tank to a wick or a roller assembly by gravity or by pump action. The wick or rollers then spread the liquid evenly over the rubber moisture roller. On some models the flow of the duplicator fluid has to be initiated by manual pumping, a process known as *priming*. Operators of electric machines frequently prime by opening the fluid feed and running plain paper through the machine. Priming saturates the wick and dampens the moisture rollers so that the machine is ready to make copies as soon as the first sheet of paper is fed into it.

Make adjustments   The number of copies that can be made from one master depends upon the moisture on the duplicating paper and the amount of pressure exerted in squeezing the paper against the master. For example, on long runs it is wise to conserve the ink or dye by using as little moisture and pressure as possible. The amount of fluid and the pressure exerted can be regulated through adjustable settings at the beginning of the run and gradually increased as the job progresses in order to keep the copy at the desired brightness or density.

Attach the master sheet   Open the paper clamps, and insert the end of the master on the drum with the negative side up. The master can be moved from side to side, and its length can be adjusted to center the copy properly. When the master is in the proper position, lock it in place by closing the clamps.

Run off copies   Place the blank paper on the feed table, and adjust the side guides and feed rollers. Then use the crank handle or motor to rotate the drum and feed the paper into the machine.

Obtain approval   Check your copies closely as they come out of the machine, and show the first good copy to your supervisor for acceptance.

Complete the run   On a manual machine use a brisk, even stroke of the crank to obtain the best results. If you have an electric machine, set the control for automatic operation. Watch the finished copy to see if you need to adjust the fluid or pressure settings. Many machines are equipped with a counting device that keeps a running count of the copies made.

Tidy up   When the run is completed, open the clamps and remove the master. If all the dye on the master has not been used up, you may carefully file the

Courtesy A. B. Dick Company, Inc.

The master should be carefully aligned when it is attached to the drum of the fluid duplicator.

master so that it may be used again. Turn off the fluid feed, release the pressure setting, and wipe up any lint, dust, or spots of dye. Don't forget to put the cover back on the machine.

Special Techniques and Materials

Shortcuts help to simplify the process of preparing a fluid master.

Preprinted master   To save time, fluid process masters are often preprinted in a printing press in the form of letterheads, sales invoices, interoffice memo-randums, bulletins, and other routine business papers. Variable data are then added to these forms as the need arises.

Continuous master units   Continuous printed master units are available for use with tabulating and communications equipment. These forms, like invoice copies, come in an unbroken series of zigzag packs with control hole punching on the edge of the set for accurate, continuous feeding.

Guide printed masters   Guidelines and form rulings that will not reproduce can be printed on the face of the master to guide a typist or writer in positioning and aligning copy.

Reflex masters   The original of a message that is to be reproduced by means of fluid duplicating can be transferred to a duplicating master in less than four seconds by using a thermal office duplicator. In this process the master sheet and transfer sheet are placed over the original, the pack is placed in a carrier, and the unit is passed through the duplicator to obtain an exact and inexpensive negative reproduction on the master sheet. It does not matter whether the original is printed, typed, drawn, or written as long as the image can be re-produced by the thermal principle of photocopying, which uses heat as the medium of transference.

Blockouts   Masters that have been run for a particular distribution can be altered and rerun for different purposes. For example, you may prepare a master containing both retail and wholesale prices. Afterward, you can make additional copies that will show only retail prices. You do this by masking the wholesale data with tape or by actually cutting out the section of the master that is not needed.

Of course, you can also do the reverse; you can add copy to a previously typed master.

Centering   To position a message in the vertical center of the page, begin typing as close to the top of the fluid master sheet as possible. When you finish, fold the bottom edge of the master sheet up to the bottom of the typed copy. Then insert the folded edge into the clamps on the drum with the negative side of the master outside as usual. The copies will be produced with equal margins above and below.

Corrections   Locate the error in the negative image. Use a correction blade to remove most of the carbon deposit from the master sheet. Clean up the last traces of carbon with an eraser or a correction pencil. Cut a strip of unused carbon, and place it over the point of the error with the shiny side facing the master sheet. Return to typing position, and type the correction. Don't forget to remove the strip of carbon as soon as you have made the correction.

Supplies for Fluid Duplicators

It may be that you will be responsible for setting up supply reserves and even for ordering supplies. Or you may be involved with only a part of the process, perhaps with preparing the copy. In any case, it is well for you to know what is used in the fluid duplicating process and what alternates certain materials offer.

Masters   Ready-made master sets consisting of a master sheet and the carbon sheet that have been already assembled in a pack are normally used. The two sheets are separated by a thin tissue that must be removed before the set is inserted into the typewriter or before any drawing or writing is done on the face of the master sheet when the master copy is being prepared. A master set is shown at the top of page 301.

Duplicating paper   Fluid process copy paper has a smooth, hard surface which helps to hold the dye on the surface of the copy sheet. This produces sharp copies with a minimum of ink.

Ink   With colored carbons you can make copies in various colors. Purple is the strongest dye and gives the greatest number of copies per single master sheet. Blue, red, and green are next in strength, in that order. All these colors can be duplicated from the same single master sheet. While you are preparing the master sheet, you can add different colors by inserting a carbon of the color desired for that particular part of the copy. Azograph fluid masters produce

Courtesy A. B. Dick Company, Inc.

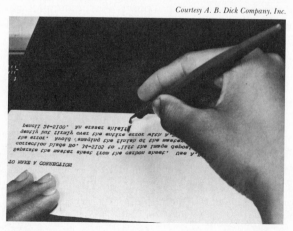

When an error is made, the correction blade is used to scrape the carbon deposit from the back of the master.

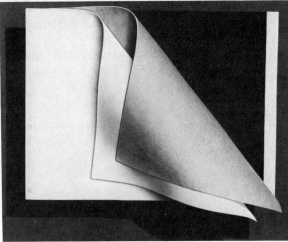

A ready-made, assembled fluid master set. A tissue, or slip sheet, separates the master sheet and the carbon sheet.

Courtesy A. B. Dick Company, Inc.

special blue copies free of the purple stain and smudging that are normally associated with the fluid process.

Other supplies   Tracing paper, a ruler, and a hard black lead pencil or a ball-point pen are useful when illustrations are being prepared. Cleaning cloths and brushes help to keep the machine in good running order. You can get a special hand cleaner which dissolves the purple aniline dye. You'll also need a correction pencil, a correction blade, an eraser, and a roll of correction tape.

REVIEWING YOUR READING

1   Explain the two factors that affect the time required for a duplicating job.
2   If the cost for reproducing each individual copy is relatively inexpensive, why does the cost of paper receive so much attention?
3   Explain how a master for the fluid process is prepared on the typewriter.
4   What is the function of the solvent in the fluid duplicator?
5   Why is a smoothly finished paper used for fluid duplicating?
6   If all the dye on the master has not been used up after a run, what can be done with the fluid master?
7   What colors other than purple are available for preparing a fluid master?

OFFICE ASSIGNMENTS

1   Prepare a fluid master of the instructions for Operating the Fluid Duplicator on pages 297–299. Make a first draft on typing paper. Follow all other suggestions for completing the master. After obtaining your teacher's approval, make copies on the duplicator.
2   Repeat Office Assignment 1, but this time type the material sideways on the master so that the typed lines are parallel to the long edge of the master.

3 Fluid duplicators permit reproduction of messages in color. Below is an announcement of price reductions. If color supplies are available, prepare a master so that the sale prices are in red, the capitalized headings are in another color, and the rest of the copy is printed in regular purple ink. After obtaining your teacher's approval, make copies of this sale notice.

PARTIAL LIST OF EXTRAORDINARY VALUES
RESERVED FOR PRIVATE CLEARANCE
Friday, December 28, Through Saturday, January 5

Sofas, Chairs, Etc.

	Regular	Sale
Luxury Lounge Chair	$ 269.00	$ 169.00
Pillowback Club Chair	255.00	169.00
Hand-Tufted Lounge Chair	299.00	199.00
Contemporary Sofa, Hand-Finished Walnut Frame	475.00	299.50
Lawson Sofa, Foam Rubber Cushions	389.00	299.00
Contemporary Lounge Chair	249.00	175.00

Bedrooms

6 Pc. Contemporary Bedroom Suite by Drexel	999.00	719.00
6 Pc. French Provincial Bedroom Suite	899.00	649.00
6 Pc. Italian Provincial Bedroom Suite	900.00	669.00
6 Pc. Provincial Bedroom Suite by Kindel	1,550.00	1,229.00
6 Pc. Provincial Bedroom Suite by Fancher	1,500.00	1,099.00

Dining Furniture

5 Pc. French Provincial Group	299.00	249.00
5 Pc. Italian Provincial Group	299.00	249.00
9 Pc. Provincial Dining Suite by Fancher	1,686.00	950.00
9 Pc. Regency Dining Suite, Custom-Made	1,608.00	950.00

Tables and Occasional Pieces

Lamp Table by Widdicomb	99.00	44.00
Italian Provincial Lamp Table	149.00	50.00
End Table by Drexel	155.00	127.50
Contemporary Lamp Table	167.50	135.00
Italian Provincial Step Table	169.00	135.00
3-Drawer Chest, Hand-Finished Butternut	295.00	240.00
French Provincial Step Table	109.00	55.00
French Provincial Lamp Table	129.00	65.00
Bookcase-Record Cabinet, Hand-Finished Butternut	169.00	130.00
Commode, Hand-Finished Cherry Wood	279.00	199.00

Carpet Shop
Truly fantastic savings on all the very newest broadloom fashions!

Custom Draperies
Draperies and bedspreads made to your order at our lowest prices in years!

4 Find a simple line drawing or illustration (from a newspaper or magazine) that is suitable for tracing. Trace the picture, and then transfer it to the master using a ball-point pen and a fluid master set. Obtain your teacher's approval, and then run off copies of the illustration.

5 Fluid duplicators are frequently used to turn out inexpensive notices and bulletins. Prepare a layout for the following lost and found announcement to be inserted in the mailboxes of a club's resident guests. (Use 8½- by 5½-inch paper.) When the layout is approved, prepare a master and run off copies of the notice.

Lost and Found Department. The following articles are at the desk in the main lobby. Will the owners please call and claim them: 1 small black hand-bag; 2 black lace scarves; 1 white stole; 2 pairs of sunglasses — 1 with gold rims, 1 with brown rims; 3 pairs of glasses with silver rims; 1 pair of small-size glasses with red rims; several pairs of earrings. Howard P. Price, Manager.

SECTION 24 Stencil Duplicating

The stencil, or mimeograph, process is a popular method of duplicating because it can quickly and easily reproduce different kinds of material on inexpensive duplicating paper. When it is properly prepared, the appearance of well-run mimeograph copy is quite adequate to meet most routine needs.

THE PRINCIPLE OF STENCIL DUPLICATING

The stencil consists of tough, porous tissue paper covered with a thin coat of wax- or plastic-like material. Messages or other images are cut into the stencil

A modern electric stencil duplicator.

Courtesy A. B. Dick Company, Inc.

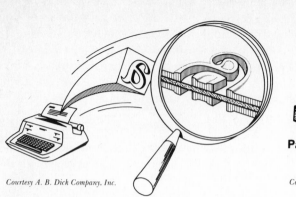

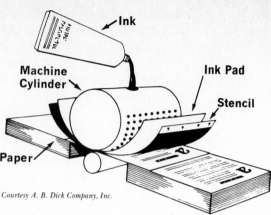

Courtesy A. B. Dick Company, Inc.

Courtesy A. B. Dick Company, Inc.

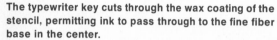

The typewriter key cuts through the wax coating of the stencil, permitting ink to pass through to the fine fiber base in the center.

The ink in the machine cylinder flows through the ink pad and passes through the cuts in the stencil onto the copy paper.

mechanically by a typewriter, tabulator, computer, or teleprinter. Writing, drawing, ruling, and lettering can also be cut into the stencil with a hand instrument called a *stylus*. The typewriter type bars or the stylus pushes aside or cuts through the wax so that the message appears on the tissue. The stencil itself serves as the master copy.

After the stencil is cut, it is placed face down on an ink pad, which has been stretched over part of the outer surface of the cylinder, or drum. With every revolution of the cylinder a clean sheet of paper is inserted into the machine from the feed table. The impression roller presses the paper against the stencil, and ink is forced through the cuts in the stencil, leaving a duplicate impression on the paper. Once it has received the impression, the paper drops into a receiving tray. Ink dries quickly on mimeograph paper because this type of paper absorbs liquid rapidly.

Preparing Copy

Fast results are important, but quality is important too. It pays to take a few extra minutes to prepare your copy carefully because a well-prepared job will produce many fine copies on the first run and many more copies on reruns. Follow these steps in preparing copy for stencil duplicating.

Plan your layout   Make a rough layout of the material so that it is spaced and arranged correctly. This procedure is referred to as preparing the dummy copy. Try different kinds and sizes of headings and illustrations that you plan to include. Scissors and paste will help you change things around until you have the arrangement you want.

Get approval   When you have prepared the copy to your satisfaction, take it to your supervisor for approval.

Prepare your equipment   The best layout in the world will not produce good results if you use the wrong tools or poor equipment. Be sure to clean the type bars or element of your typewriter thoroughly with a cleaning brush. Disengage the ribbon. Position your paper bail rollers at the extreme right and left so that they do not touch the stencil. Place the dummy copy where you can follow it easily. Before you start, assemble the proper tools and supplies that you will need for illustrations, if your job includes them.

Position your copy   Guidelines and marks are printed on the stencil to help you position the copy as desired. If you understand the stencil guide marks, you can quickly position your copy on the stencil sheet. The top edge paper guide-line, located ½ inch above the broken line, indicates the duplicating limit. The typewriter line spaces are shown in the side margins—six lines to the inch. If you start typing at line 1, you will automatically have a ½-inch top margin on your duplicated copy; if you start typing at line 7, you will have a 1½-inch top margin, and so on.

The side margins are also indicated on the stencil. The distance from the outside edge of the stencil to the limitation line is approximately ⅝ inch. If you type from duplicating limit to duplicating limit across the stencil, you will have a ⅝-inch margin on each side of an 8½-inch-wide sheet of paper.

Use the typewriter character scales located at the top and bottom of the stencil to help you position your copy. They are marked for pica (10 characters to the inch) and elite (12 characters to the inch) as well as in inches.

Note the warning numbers which show you how many lines can be typed before you reach the bottom boundary line for the size of paper you plan to use.

Use suitable typing techniques   When you cut a stencil on a manual type-writer, use a firm, even touch against a medium-hard cylinder to produce the best results. Insert a cushion sheet behind the stencil to soften the impression of the type bar. You may need to strike capitals and other keys with large type surfaces, such as *m*, *g*, and *w*, a little harder than you need to strike the others. Strike punctuation marks rather lightly. On an electric typewriter, set the

Courtesy A. B. Dick Company, Inc.

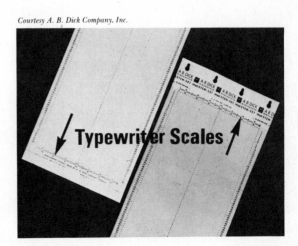

Positioning of copy is greatly simplified when the typewriter scales
are used.

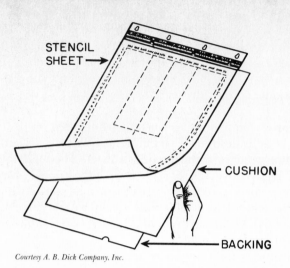

STENCIL
SHEET →

← CUSHION

← BACKING

A stencil assembly. Sometimes a plastic typing film is placed over the stencil sheet to produce darker impressions and to keep the stencil wax off the typeface.

Courtesy A. B. Dick Company, Inc.

pressure regulator at a position that will produce a good cut on all typed characters.

Make corrections   If you make an error, you can use correction fluid to cover it. Apply the fluid sparingly, directly on the mistake, and let the fluid dry. Some stencil directions suggest burnishing corrections. This means that before you apply the correction fluid, you rub the error gently with a blunt instrument (the curved end of a paper clip will do) to close the old cuts. If you are using a plastic typing film which is designed to keep wax off the type bars, be sure to peel the film back from the stencil before you make the correction.

Follow drawing procedures   For pictures and diagrams set up the stencil on an illuminated drawing board, such as a mimeoscope. Place a plastic writing plate under the stencil to provide a clean, smooth cutting surface. Place your layout under the writing plate so that it can serve as a pattern to follow. The light under the glass makes the image on the layout show up so that you can trace it with a smooth and rounded stylus, as shown at the top of page 307. Use bold, deliberate strokes that will cut through the wax.

Courtesy A. B. Dick Company, Inc.

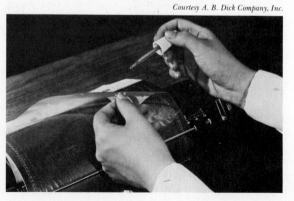

The plastic typing film must be peeled back before a correction is made on the face of the stencil.

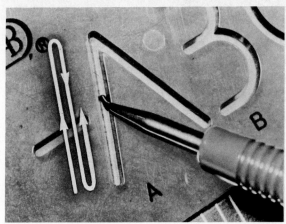

The stylus and lettering guide are used to make professional-looking characters on stencils.

Courtesy A. B. Dick Company, Inc.

Proofread   The time to check your copy carefully is before removing it from the typewriter or the mimeoscope. By doing this, you can make corrections or additions easily without disturbing the alignment.

Operating the Duplicator

Although specific directions vary slightly for different models, most duplicators can, in general, be operated by following the steps listed here.

Uncover the machine   When it is not in use, the machine should be covered to keep out dust and dirt. When you are ready to use the machine, remove the cover, and either fold it up or tuck it neatly into a convenient space or a storage cabinet where it will be out of the way while you are working.

Release the brake   When you are ready to run off copies on the machine, release the brake so that the cylinder and the ink within it can revolve freely. This lock, or brake, is designed to hold the cylinder properly while it is not in use.

Remove the protective strip   When the duplicator is not in use, the wet surface of the ink pad is covered with a protective cover, which is a nonabsorbent paper strip. In addition to keeping out dust and dirt, this cover prevents ink from dripping and keeps the pad moist and fresh. The cover is removed by releasing the clamps, and it should be saved so that it can be reused.

Attach the stencil   Place the stencil face down on the ink pad or screen. Insert the "tab end" first, remove the backing sheet, and then stretch the rest of the stencil over the pad or screen. Be sure that it is straight and smooth. This procedure is illustrated at the top of page 308.

Put the paper on the feed table   Place the duplicating paper on the feed table, and adjust the side guides to the proper width and position. Paper has a tendency to curl in one direction and feeds best when placed on the table with the

Both photos courtesy A. B. Dick Company, Inc.

The stencil is attached to the cylinder of the machine facedown.

The backing sheet is removed after the stencil has been attached to the cylinder of the duplicator.

curl down and the grain of the curl going from the top to the bottom of the sheet. This is referred to as "the grain going the long way." Read the label on the package of mimeograph paper to see which side should be up.

Make a trial run   Rotate the operating crank or wheel to obtain a few copies, and check them for any noticeable shortcomings such as these:

☐ Dark areas, with the spots appearing in the same position on each copy, are caused by too much ink. The excess will gather in some areas, and the paper will tend to stick to the cylinder when copies are being run off.

☐ Spotty copies, with the spots appearing in different positions on each copy, are caused by an impression roller in poor condition.

☐ Uniformly poor copies, that is, copies that are too light in certain areas, are the result of too little ink or an improperly cut stencil.

☐ Indistinct copies, with the light areas appearing in the same position on each copy, are caused by an ink pad in poor condition (matted down). To correct this, change the ink pad.

☐ Copy becomes gradually light on the high side of the cylinder as the ink supply in the pad becomes exhausted. This will occur if the duplicator is not level or if ink seeps out from the low side of the cylinder.

☐ Generally poor copies can result from ink residue in the cylinder diaphragm. When the cylinder diaphragm openings become clogged, the cylinder needs to be cleaned thoroughly.

☐ A condition called *setoff* occurs when the ink on the top sheet of paper in the receiving tray doesn't dry before the next sheet falls into the tray. This causes ink spots to appear on the back of every sheet. You can reduce setoff by using fast-drying ink, absorbent paper, and a slower operating speed.

Make adjustments   Trial copies are just what the name indicates. If they are not acceptable, you can generally make adjustments so that the rest of the copies will be satisfactory.

Make another trial run   If you find it necessary to adjust the machine, make another trial run.

Get approval   When you are satisfied with the appearance of the adjusted copy, show it to your supervisor for final approval.

Set the counting device   The counter on the side of the machine keeps track of the number of copies that you make. In some models it stops the paper feed when the desired number of copies has been reached. This useful device saves you the bother of counting every sheet and prevents the waste that results from producing too many copies.

Keep watch   Once the copy is adjusted and approved and the counting device set, you are ready to go ahead. Whether you have a hand-operated or an electric machine, remember to keep an eye on the quality of the work being produced. If inking or other adjustments are needed, attend to them immediately so that you can turn out high-quality copies.

Tidy up   Clean as you go, and when the job is finished, clean up any lint, dust, ink spots, or other soil. Remove the stencil, and place it between the folds of some old newspaper. Replace the protective cover. Set the brake, and cover the machine.

If there is no reason to keep the stencil, leave it between the sheets of newspaper, fold it up, and drop it into the wastebasket. If the stencil is to be saved for another run, flatten it and store it in a stencil file folder which is made of paper that absorbs the ink from the stencil. You can also blot stencils dry with newspaper and hang them vertically in a stencil file case.

SPECIAL TECHNIQUES

Duplicator manufacturers and skilled operators have perfected a number of techniques for getting more and better work done by the stencil duplicating process.

Die-Impressed Stencils

You can buy stencils with a letterhead, a ruled form, or a routine message already precut. All you have to do is to insert the variable data, such as date, price, or other specifications.

Form-Topped Stencils

If the copy is to be duplicated on preprinted forms, it must be aligned properly on the forms. You can get stencils with special guidelines printed on them to help you position the message.

Electronic Stencils

Ready-to-use plastic stencils can be prepared electronically from an original layout, which may consist of line work, headlines, typed copy, ruled forms, written signatures or messages, and even photographs pasted on a paper. This paper version is then turned over to a stencil supplier who makes it into a ready-to-use plastic stencil. This service provides a quick and easy way of obtaining special effects in the final copy.

Copy Blockouts

There are times when you may want to duplicate a certain number of copies from the complete stencil and an additional number of copies of only portions of the stencil. This can be done easily and quickly.

Run the copies of the complete stencil first. If a vertical column is to be blocked out, place a strip of very lightweight, smooth paper or a strip of carbon paper over the area to be eliminated. Keep it in position by making sure that it is held securely by the stencil head clamp.

If a portion is to be blocked out in a horizontal position on the stencil, depend on the adhesive action of the ink to hold the strip in place. Run the copies rather slowly, and watch the copies as they fall into the receiving tray to be sure that the blockout strip remains in the correct position. Replace the strip if it becomes saturated with ink.

When the blockout strip is removed, you can again run the complete stencil. Remove and discard the blockout strip before the stencil is filed.

You can permanently block out copy by using strips of gummed paper or paper which is gummed along one edge. The strip should be large enough to cover the unwanted portion of the copy.

Postal Card Stencils

The correct position on a stencil for a postal card message is indicated by pre-printed guidelines on the stencil. The message must be placed at the top of the stencil and centered so that the long sides of the card parallel the length of the stencil sheet. To do this, insert the stencil sideways into the typewriter to give you a longer typing line. Unless you have an extra wide carriage, you'll find the stencil easier to manage if you cut it off at line 45. Here are other useful tips.

Layout Prepare your layout carefully, and make sure that the message does not extend beyond the boundary lines or guidelines.

Verifying Double-check your layout by placing it directly under the stencil sheet.

Positioning To aid in positioning, place a dot of correction fluid on the stencil wherever key words or features are to begin.

Cushion sheet Insert the cushion sheet with the shiny side up between the stencil sheet and the backing.

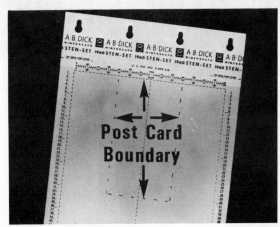

To position a postal card message on a stencil, center the message with the long sides of the card parallel to the length of the stencil.

Courtesy A. B. Dick Company, Inc.

Stencil pocket   Often a stencil can be inserted into a typewriter more easily if it is put into a pocket. To make a pocket, fold an 8½- by 11-inch sheet of paper lengthwise, insert the left side of the stencil into the pocket, and roll both into the typewriter.

Alignment   Turn the typewriter cylinder until you can remove the folded paper. Then align the stencil according to its guidelines.

Typing guides   Locate the first dot of correction fluid that you placed as a guide, and begin to type.

Proofreading   Always proofread your stencil before removing it from the typewriter.

Preparing the cylinder   If your stencil is short, place an 8½- by 11-inch sheet of paper over the bottom of the ink pad so that the stencil overlaps the paper at least ¾ inch.

Installing and duplicating   Install the stencil, and run off the required number of copies.

COLOR WORK

Since color plays a big part in attracting customers' attention, it is important to know how to use it in duplicating processes.

Preparing the Cylinder

When you are color duplicating with equipment having a closed drum or cylinder—such as the A. B. Dick Mimeograph—remove the black ink pad and apply a protective cover or a sheet of wax paper directly over the perforated portion of the cylinder. Then place a clean ink pad over the fresh protective cover, and proceed to spot the various colored inks as required for multicolor reproduction. If the color areas are too close together, make separate stencils for each color. Each color will then have to be run separately through the machine.

Preparing the Copy

If you do color work on the silk-screen-type duplicators—such as the Rex-Rotary, Gestetner, or the Roneo—you must change the ink rollers and the silk screen. You can do this in a few minutes with a little training. Again, color work on these machines requires a separate stencil for each color, and each color requires a separate run. A three-color job means that each of the three colors must be run off separately.

You can order insets containing various drawings from stencil supply houses. Once you decide where you want to place the inset on the stencil, cut a "window" at this point and glue the inset into position.

SUPPLIES FOR STENCIL DUPLICATING

A well-stocked mimeograph duplicating unit should have an adequate supply of stencils, duplicating paper, ink, ink pads, cleaning materials, drawing supplies, protective covers, and file folders.

Stencils

Stencils are available in various sizes, weights, and colors. Most stencils measure 8½ by 11 inches (standard letter size) or 8½ by 13 inches (legal size). Stencils are manufactured in several different weights or grades. Small, quick jobs requiring a few copies need only an inexpensive stencil. Large jobs, involving tables and illustrations, should be set up on a stencil of the best quality. Typewritten copy can be read more easily on light-colored stencils (yellow or white) that are combined with a dark cushion sheet. The dark blue or dark green colors reduce glare on the illuminated drawing board and allow the light to show through the areas where the stencil is cut. Still other stencils are manufactured with a plastic typing film on top of the wax stencil surface. Typing through the film produces a broader and darker printed impression and reduces the possibility of cutting out the centers of such letters as o, d, b, p, and so on. The film also keeps the stencil wax from clogging the typefaces of the machine.

Paper

A rough-surface absorbent paper is used for stencil duplicating. It comes in a variety of weights. The 16-pound paper is the type most commonly used for single-sided jobs; that is, jobs in which copy is being reproduced on only one side of the paper. Since this type of paper is not too strong, 20-pound paper is recommended when it is expected that the copy will be handled a great deal or when a two-sided duplicating job is required.

Duplicating paper comes in a variety of colors so that it can contrast or harmonize with the ink. Use it to get interesting, colorful effects in office communications and business press releases.

Inks

Duplicating ink comes in many colors besides the usual black. It is also possible to obtain inks with special quick-drying qualities for high-speed operations. This is particularly desirable when both sides of the paper are to be used. Some duplicators require liquid ink, others use paste ink that comes in a tube.

Drawing Supplies

When you use a mimeoscope, or illuminated drawing board, you need extra writing plates, styluses, lettering guides, and screen plates. The styluses come in different points (balls, wheels, and so on) to produce varied line effects.

Even if you are not an expert letterer, you can get fine results by using lettering guides. Use these guides or patterns to trace a wide variety of letter styles and sizes for headings and special effects.

Because solid black areas don't reproduce satisfactorily, screen plates are used to produce a shaded background effect.

Cleaning Materials

Keep cleaning cloths, brushes, and solvents on hand so that the duplicating is neat and tidy from start to finish. Improve your skills (and become more valuable as an employee) by knowing how to care for the machine in use, change the ink pad, remove the cylinder, clean the impression roller, and oil the machine. So that you don't create problems for the next user, leave the machine the way you'd like to find it—clean and in good working order.

COMMON OFFICE APPLICATIONS

The stencil duplicator is used for such jobs as notices, price lists, forms, special instructions, form letters, announcements, inexpensive sales literature, conference reports, tables, and simple charts. You may find that early in your work experience you'll be asked to prepare stencils or operate duplicating machines. If you are skilled and knowledgeable about stencil duplicating, your work will be varied and interesting.

REVIEWING YOUR READING

1   Explain why it pays to spend a few extra minutes to prepare your copy carefully.
2   What is the meaning of the expression "preparing the dummy copy"?
3   How can you obtain best results when cutting a stencil on the typewriter?
4   Outline the steps involved in operating the mimeograph.

OFFICE ASSIGNMENTS

1 Prepare a stencil to duplicate the first five pointers in Preparing Copy on pages 304–306 of this text. Follow the usual procedure of planning the layout on a sheet of typing paper first. As you type each point, make a mental check to determine whether you are following the suggestions. After the stencil has been typed, attach it to the duplicator cylinder. Complete a trial run, and obtain your teacher's approval of the trial copies. Then run off finished copies of the job.

2 Repeat Office Assignment 1, except this time type the material sideways on the stencil so that the lines of writing parallel the long edge of the stencil.

3 Obtain a simple line drawing or illustration (from a newspaper or magazine) that is suitable for tracing on an illuminated drawing board. Transfer the picture to the stencil, using such tools as styluses, screen plates, and lettering guides. After the stencil has been cut, attach it to the duplicator. Complete a trial run, obtain your teacher's approval of the trial copies, and then run off finished copies of the job.

4 Many business office forms are prepared by the stencil process of duplication. A typical example is shown below. Make a preliminary layout of this copy to fit on 8½- by 5½-inch paper. Then proceed to type the stencil. Type the form twice on the stencil—once on the top half and once on the bottom half. Run off finished copies of the form on 8½- by 11-inch paper, and then cut the paper to 8½- by 5½-inch size.

```
                      REQUEST FOR VACATION PAY

                                            Date_____

Name_____ Payroll #_____    Bi-weekly

                                            Payroll    Monthly
Company_____ Department_____
                                                      Weekly


I am leaving for_____weeks vacation at the close of business on_____
                                                                   (date)

I would like to be paid for these weeks before leaving.


    Payroll Department Record:                _____
                                               (Employee's Signature)

    _____

    _____              _____
                                             (Department Head Approval)
    _____
                               IMPORTANT:  Omitting your payroll number
                                           may delay your check.
```

5 At the top of page 315 are some notes covering a special announcement. Prepare a dummy copy for an 8½- by 11-inch mimeographed message to be sent to all employees. Try several layouts. Include a suitable but simple cartoon or illustration. After your teacher approves the layout, prepare the stencil and make a number of copies.

Games, prizes, refreshments

Brumpus Brubaker's Six will
   provide the music until 1 a.m.

New Year's party and dance

All employees invited

Contests

Company cafeteria—8:30 p.m.,
   Monday, December 31

Noisemakers

Food

SECTION 25 Offset and Photocopy Duplicating

The offset process gets its name from the fact that the master plate used does not print directly on the copy paper. Instead, it transfers the image to a rubber-blanketed cylinder. It is the cylinder that comes into contact with the paper and prints, or offsets, the image.

   You can understand the principle involved in offset printing if you first examine another printing process known as *letterpress.* When printing was first developed, it was in the form of letterpress. The simplest example of this type of printing is a typewriter. Look at any key. You will see that the letter of the alphabet on the key is raised up from the base. When you type, that raised portion of the letter comes into contact with the inked ribbon and literally presses the ink onto the paper. Hence the process is called letterpress. It is a two-dimensional method: the raised area is one dimension, and the base is the other dimension.

THE PRINCIPLE OF OFFSET DUPLICATING

Offset is described as a *planographic process;* that is, it has only one dimension. To obtain an image, it makes use of the principle that oil and water do not mix. In this case an oil-based ink is attracted to and adheres to an oil-based image on a moist plate. Any part of the plate that does not have an oil-based image attracts no ink. No ink, no picture.

Courtesy A. B. Dick Company, Inc.

When the master is correctly typed and operating procedures are carefully performed, the offset duplicator can produce excellent copies.

The advantage of using offset in commercial printing is that the master plates employed in the process are much lighter in weight and can be prepared more quickly than those used in letterpress. Today the offset process has the widest range of uses of any of the modern office duplicating methods. It offers all-around usefulness, quantity output, and quality copy and requires only a small amount of preparation for average jobs. It is an efficient process to use for very short runs or for runs producing many thousands of copies. Copy for the master plate can be preprinted and can include material such as photographs and diagrams. The copy may be typed, drawn, written, or ruled.

Two types of offset masters in general use are the direct-image and pre-sensitized master.

Direct-Image Masters

The inexpensive direct-image paper master is a popular choice for everyday office purposes when short runs of average-quality copies are required. There are several types of masters.

Manually prepared masters   The master is prepared on a typewriter equipped with a special carbon ribbon. Copy can also be written, drawn, or ruled by using special inks. You can achieve shading effects with manufacturer-approved crayons. Forms and other copy can be traced and transferred to the master by using a ball-point pen and special carbon paper. The special oil-based ink forms an ink-retaining image on the surface of the master which is coated with a moisture-holding substance.

Preprinted masters   You can sometimes eliminate part of the work that is involved in preparing the masters by using preprinted master forms. All you have to do is to insert the variable copy on the preprinted form. For example, a short-form insurance contract might be preprinted on a direct-image master. You complete the contract by filling in dates, names of the parties, policy number, and so on, and then make the number of copies required.

Copier prepared masters   Modern photocopy machines permit a direct-image offset master to be prepared as a photocopy of the original. With little or no effort a typist or clerk can prepare a master by using many methods—xerography (uses powder), thermography (uses heat), dye transfer, and facsimile.

Presensitized Masters

Sometimes the copy to be duplicated consists of many fine details, such as photographs, screening effects, or technical diagrams. It may be a paste-up, which might include phototype, typed copy, and even written work. Copy of such an involved nature is transferred photographically from the original paste-up to an offset master. The master is presensitized; that is, it consists of an aluminum, paper, or plastic sheet which has been coated with a layer of

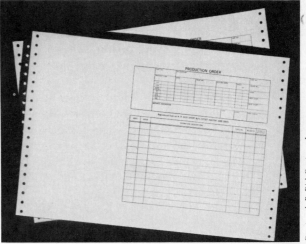

Courtesy A. B. Dick Company, Inc.

Direct-image masters, like the one shown at the left, are available with or without pinholes at the ends. The type of offset duplicating machine determines which style to use. On the preprinted offset masters shown above, only the variable copy needs to be typed.

material that is sensitive to light. The process of preparing this presensitized master includes three basic steps.

Burning   The image of the original is transferred to the master by photography and can be reproduced in the same size, an enlarged size, or a reduced size.

☐ The master surface corresponding to the copy area of the original is exposed to a strong light and hardens to become an insoluble ink-retaining image.
☐ The unexposed master surface corresponding to the clear area of the original remains unchanged.

Developing   The master is washed with chemicals to remove the soluble material from the unexposed clear surface.

Drying   The master is washed with water and dried so that it can be installed on the offset duplicator.

OPERATION OF THE OFFSET DUPLICATOR

On the illustration on page 318 a paper or metal master plate containing an oil-based (sometimes called a grease-based) image is fastened on the master cylinder of the machine (3). The master is moistened by a moistening roller (2). (The moistening agent consists of distilled water mixed with a repellent solution.) The oil-based image on the master repels the water, but the clear portion of the master attracts the water and is coated by it.

As the master cylinder revolves, the ink roller (1) rolls over the surface of the master. The oil-based image attracts a coating of oil-based ink, while the water on the clear portion of the master repels the ink. As the master cylinder (3) revolves further, it turns the rubber-blanketed cylinder (4). This cylinder picks up the ink image from the master. This image is a negative, or mirror, image.

As the machine revolves, copy paper (5) is fed into the machine between the rubber-blanketed cylinder (4) and the impression cylinder (6). The copy paper pressed against the negative inked image on the rubber blanket picks up the impression, or image. This time the copy is a positive image of the negative image on the rubber blanket. The whole process is repeated when the copy falls into the paper receiving tray and another sheet of copy paper is fed into the machine.

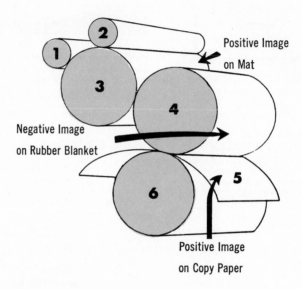

Positive Image on Mat

Negative Image on Rubber Blanket

Positive Image on Copy Paper

PREPARING THE OFFSET MASTER

The offset master, like a mirror, reproduces only the exact image produced on its surface. It is important then that the copy on the master be styled and set up correctly and look as much like the original as possible. To get the best results, keep these points in mind when preparing the offset master.

Advance Planning

Unless you've done the job many times, prepare a rough draft before you type the master to get the best layout and placement of copy. If the job involves an illustration, caption, or other special effects, prepare a paste-up or dummy of the material so that you can try out different ideas. Remember to position the copy correctly on the master so that you don't have to make adjustments later.

Typing Techniques

Since most of your routine jobs will be typed on direct-image masters, you should observe the following suggestions:

1 Clean the typewriter keys frequently.
2 Use an approved carbon ribbon for the sharpest copy.
3 Use a nonreproducing pencil to make guidelines on the master, if needed.
4 Align the master carefully before you start to type.
5 If you use an electric typewriter, set the pressure control low enough so the characters print clearly but do not emboss, or make dents in, the master.
6 If you use a manual typewriter, type with an even touch that is light enough to avoid embossing the master.
7 Correct any errors with a soft rubber eraser, and take care not to damage the surface of the master.
8 When you put the typed master back in the typewriter, cover the text with a tissue sheet to prevent smudging.
9 Hold the master by its edges to avoid making fingerprints on the surface.

Drawing Techniques

Illustrations, diagrams, and charts may be traced on the offset master in the same way as they are traced on the mimeograph stencil. Merely place the illustration you want to trace on the illuminated drawing board, and position the paper offset master over the illustration. The light under the glass will outline the image through the master for tracing. You can fill in solid areas on the master with a duplicating pencil or ink.

Use of Cold Composition

Now that new processes, improved supplies, and better equipment are available, you can practically operate a printshop in your office with the offset duplicator playing a second role as the firm's private printing press.

Copy that was once set or composed in metal type by printers can now be composed in the office with the aid of special typewriters, a drawing table, a glue pot, and skilled help. You can prepare a price list involving three or four different typefaces and sizes on the IBM Selectric or the VariTyper, which have changeable typefaces. With special typefaces you can create many functional and attractive effects. The Justowriter produces a justified or straight right margin similar to the margins found in book pages and newspaper columns. Other typewriters are available that provide proportional spacing. A sophisticated piece of equipment called a *phototypesetter* produces display type of various styles and sizes by a photographic process. The letters and special characters, which are typed at the keyboard, come out of the machine on a special photographic paper. This output is then used in the preparation of a master.

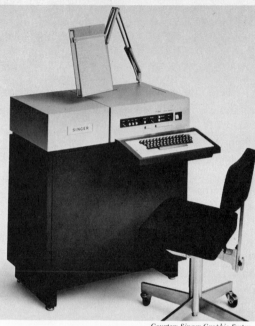

Courtesy Singer Graphic Systems

This attractive, compact phototype-setter can produce five different type styles in ten sizes each.

A makeup specialist plans a job and then prepares each section of the material with the type style, type size, and features meant to produce the desired effect. Large captions and sections calling for unusual type can be assembled using pads of preprinted letters with adhesive backing called *phototype*. (Prestype and Zip-a-Tone are among the popular brand names.) Words can be created by pasting down one letter at a time. Illustrations or rulings can be drawn or picked up from previously printed sources. Special screen effects, symbols, and borders can be purchased and preprinted on transparent sheets with adhesive on the reverse side. When the various components are assembled, they are laid out on the dummy sheet and pasted down. Screens are positioned where indicated.

The final copy is then photographically transferred to a presensitized master as previously explained. The whole job is produced quickly and at a fraction of the cost of traditional printing methods. (Incidentally, new employees who are mechanically inclined and have a flair for layout work are often assigned to the office printshop.)

Proofreading

Proofreading is important if you want to produce accurate, professional work. It is more effective when it is done by two persons. One person reads to the other who checks the original copy. It is better to have the original copy checked by someone other than the person who typed the original copy on the master. This is because the person who has prepared the master has had so much contact with the copy that he or she may tend to overlook some errors. A person seeing copy for the first time is more likely to spot them immediately.

Getting Approval

Show all direct-image masters to your supervisor for suggestions and approval before you install them on the duplicator. Have all dummy copy prepared for transfer to presensitized plates approved before the photographic work begins.

OPERATING THE OFFSET DUPLICATOR

Although specific operating steps may vary slightly with different models, most offset duplicators can, in general, be operated by following the procedure listed below.

1   Uncover the duplicator. Fold the cover carefully, and put it in a place provided for it in the storage cabinet.
2   Place the ink in the ink fountain. Ink comes in a tube or a can.
3   Turn on the duplicator to distribute the ink on the roller.
4   Turn off the duplicator, and fill the water fountain with a solution of repellent and distilled water.
5   Turn on the duplicator for at least six to eight revolutions to distribute the water.
6   If necessary, adjust the ink roller.
7   Place the offset master on the master cylinder, and secure it with clamps.

The offset master is attached to the cylinder faceup.

Courtesy A. B. Dick Company, Inc.

8   Use a small cotton pad to moisten the surface of the master with a special initial moistening or etching solution.
9   Place the copy paper in the feed tray, and lower the feeder arm. Copy sheets will feed better if they are placed in the tray with the curl of the paper down and the grain going the long way.
10   Turn on the duplicator.

11   Engage the moistening roller. Allow the machine to revolve about six to eight times and then engage the ink roller.

12   Engage the master cylinder with the rubber-blanketed cylinder. Allow the machine to revolve about six times so that the rubber blanket becomes inked with the image on the mat.

13   Start feeding the paper.

14   After a few copies have been duplicated, take one from the receiving tray and inspect it to see if any adjustments are necessary.

15   Show the adjusted copy to your supervisor for approval.

16   When you have produced the required number of copies, take the following steps to turn off the machine:

   a   Disengage the paper-feed mechanism.
   b   Disengage the master cylinder from the rubber-blanketed cylinder.
   c   Disengage the ink roller from the master cylinder, and allow the machine to feed about eight sheets.
   d   Turn off the motor switch.

17   Prepare the master for storage by moistening it with a preservative solution. Make certain to cover the entire surface edge to edge. (You can eliminate this step, if the master is to be discarded.)

18   Remove the master from the master cylinder.

COLOR IN OFFSET

Most work duplicated by offset is printed in black ink on white paper, but there are times when special color effects are desirable. A special announcement or bulletin will generally attract more attention if it has a strategic dash of color in the right places. The preparation of a color job calls for special care.

☐ Plan the job in advance.
☐ Separate colored areas as much as possible.
☐ Identify colored areas.
☐ Make a master for each color.
☐ Align masters so that the printing registers perfectly.
☐ Proofread all masters.
☐ Run the master containing the copy to be printed in black on the duplicator first.
☐ Clean the rollers, fountains, and rubber blanket before a new color of ink is applied.
☐ Examine the first copies in each run to check the position or the register of each color.

OFFSET SUPPLIES

It's a good idea to keep a checklist of the supplies you need for offset duplicating if you prepare material for offset often.

Masters

Offset masters come in different sizes, but the most popular size is the one that will duplicate 8½- by 13-inch sheets. Smaller masters are more economical to use when half-size or smaller forms are to be duplicated. Masters come in different grades depending upon the number of copies that will be duplicated.

Paper

A wide variety of paper can be used, but the best results are obtained from paper that is specially made offset duplicating stock.

Other Supplies

You will need writing media consisting of reproducing pencils (oil-based), reproducing ink, nonreproducing pencils for drawing guidelines, and carbon ribbons for the typewriter. Moistening and preservative solutions usually come in quart bottles. Duplicating inks come in a wide variety of colors. Cleaning supplies such as cotton pads, cleaning cloths, and cleaning solution are also needed.

PHOTOCOPY PROCESSES

Photocopy duplicating is totally different from the duplicating techniques you've learned about so far, which require that you prepare an intermediate copy, such as a fluid master, a stencil, or an offset master. Photocopy processes reproduce documents and papers *directly*, complete with original marks, notations, and signatures. Some photocopy machines will actually reproduce in color. These machines are fast, efficient, and relatively economical, when used to produce one copy or a small number of copies. Here are three photocopy processes that you may encounter.

Diazo

The diazo process uses a dye that is produced by combining two chemicals, a diazonium salt (diazo) and a coupler (an agent which enables two chemicals to mix that normally do not mix). In a chemical action which is precipitated by exposure to ultraviolet light rays, dye is formed and takes on the outlines and shape of the copy.

Diazo process photocopying equipment is manufactured by Charles Bruning Company, GAF Corporation, and others.

Electrostatic

This is a dry process of making duplicate copies. The technique is based on the law of physics which states that opposite electric charges attract each other. In one process called *xerography*, the printed areas on an original are projected by lenses to the surface of an electrically charged plate. In the *direct electrostatic method*, the printed areas are projected to copy paper instead of a charged plate. The areas on the copy paper or the plate that correspond to the printed areas of the original retain the electric charge. Black powder with an opposite charge is then fused to paper by heat, thereby printing the copy.

The advantage of the electrostatic method is that it can be used to prepare offset masters on paper or metal plates. It can also turn out masters for use on the fluid duplicator as well as translucent copies for the diazo process. The electrostatic method can reproduce photographs, drawings, sketches, and forms in addition to typed and written copy.

Equipment is manufactured by Addressograph-Multigraph Corporation, Apeco Corporation, Charles Bruning, A. B. Dick, GAF, IBM, Olivetti, SCM, Xerox, and others.

Thermal

This process utilizes heat to create an image or copy. Infrared light rays pass through a copy sheet to the original. When the light rays hit a blank area on the original, they are absorbed by the paper, causing no reaction on the corresponding copy sheet. However, when the light rays hit an area on the original that has an image, they cause the corresponding area on the copy sheet to turn black and thereby print the image.

The original in the thermal process must be made with carbon-based ink or pencil, because the image made by some inks can't be reproduced.

Copies printed by the thermal method usually appear as blue-black on buff-colored paper. However, because of many improved products, sturdier and more attractive copies are now available.

The thermal process not only duplicates copies speedily and easily but also produces direct-image offset masters in a two-step process: (1) original to inter-

Courtesy Addressograph-Multigraph Corporation

An electrostatic copier.

This thermal copying machine can even make transparencies that are used in overhead projectors.

Courtesy 3M Company

mediate and (2) intermediate to master. The thermal process also can produce fluid masters and mimeograph stencils.

Finally, a thermal copying machine is handy for preparing transparencies used as visual aids in training and conference sessions.

REVIEWING YOUR READING

1 In offset duplicating how can part of the work involved in preparing masters be eliminated?
2 What are the steps involved in preparing an offset master from a presensitized plate?
3 What basic principle is applied in the process of offset duplicating?
4 Why is water used in the operation of an offset duplicator?
5 What is the function of the rubber-blanketed cylinder in an offset duplicator?
6 Why is alignment of copy on offset masters especially important when more than one color is being used?
7 Compare the diazo, electrostatic, and thermal photocopy methods.

OFFICE ASSIGNMENTS

1 On a direct-image offset master, type the list of typing techniques that appears on page 319. Provide an appropriate heading, and center the copy on the master for duplication on 8½- by 11-inch paper. If an offset duplicator is available, run off copies of the list.

2   On a direct-image offset master, trace an illustration, diagram, or chart of your choice on an illuminated drawing board. If an offset duplicator is available, run off copies of the tracing.

3   Using an IBM Selectric typewriter and at least two typing elements with different typefaces, type the procedures for operating the offset duplicator listed on pages 321–322. Type the copy on a plain sheet of paper as if you were preparing a draft preliminary to making a final master. You are to decide ahead of time on an appropriate heading and which parts of the copy are to be typed with each typeface.

4   On three plain sheets of paper, type the procedures listed on pages 321–322 for operating the offset duplicator as if they were to be run in three colors. Decide which portions of the copy are to be reproduced in each color, and then type on each sheet the copy for one color. Be sure to align the copy properly. To check alignment, place the three typed sheets together and hold them up to a light.

5   Using letters of various sizes and typefaces and illustrations clipped from magazines, your typewriter, and glue, prepare a paste-up of an advertisement of some event that is to take place in your school.

BUSINESS CASES AND PROBLEMS

In the Boss's Shoes   1 "But I didn't know that you wanted the copies made on green paper, Mr. Puryear," said Carmella, after she had finished a big job on the stencil duplicator. "I took over the job when Ruby was sent home ill an hour ago. Nobody told me about your special instructions."

How could Ruby's supervisor avoid such mix-ups even in emergencies? What should Carmella have done before she took over the job after Ruby had gone home?

2   It was the peak of the firm's busiest season. Julio had put in a hard day's work but still had a pile of papers on his desk waiting for his attention. In desperation he said: "My basket is always full of new bulletins and announcements. Why doesn't somebody stop this flood of duplicated paper? Who has time to read half of it anyhow?" What can management do to keep everyone informed without increasing the amount of paper needed to carry messages?

3   A valuable and experienced office employee, Mrs. Auner of Futronics Corporation, has become proud of her expert work in preparing stencils and in operating the stencil duplicator. The office manager wants to install an offset duplicator and do away with the stencil duplicator because of an increased work load. Considering Mrs. Auner's value to the company and the importance of her morale, how should the office manager proceed to make the change?

Your Human Relations 1 You are assigned to run off several offset masters while your boss is away from the office for a half hour. You are unable to get the machine to start because of a faulty electric outlet. How would you spend the 30 minutes until your boss returns?

2 It is now ten minutes before closing time. The boss gave orders to have a special bulletin fluid-duplicated and mailed today. As you are folding the first copy into an envelope, you notice a glaring typographic error. Should you patch the master and rerun the copies? (The dye on the master is rather worn, and the patch will show, even if you can make enough copies.) Or should you recut the master, and stay as late as necessary to get the job done right?

3 One morning your boss says to you, "Please run this memorandum off on regular mimeograph paper, and make 150 copies." When you get ready to run the job, you find that there is no mimeograph paper in the supply cabinet and that you will have to walk to the main stockroom in the next building to get some. There is, however, a ream of expensive bond paper in your supply cabinet. From past experience you know that mimeograph ink reproduces satisfactorily on bond paper. It seems such a chore to walk to the next building for paper when you have a supply right in front of you. What should you do?

4 Your employer asks you to obtain offset materials from the supply room for an important duplicating job that is to be started the first thing the next morning. Just as you arrive at the supply room, the supply clerk is leaving. As he locks the door, he says rather bluntly, "I am sorry, but it is closing time." You note that there are actually 15 minutes until closing time. You know that if you have to wait at the supply room the next morning, the job will be delayed. What should you say to the supply clerk, and in what tone of voice should you say it?

5 Emil Mack, Alfredo Jones, and John Wills work together in the duplicating unit of the Jefferson National Insurance Company. They went to high school together, obtained their jobs at the same time, and have been close friends ever since. Today, a new employee, Julio Cruz, reports to work in their unit. Julio had also gone to the same high school as Emil, Al, and John, but since he had been two years behind them, he did not know the other boys very well. At lunch time Julio does not seem to know what to do. Emil, Al, and John, on their way to their usual eating place, pass Julio just as he is reaching for his coat. If you were one of this trio of close friends, would you suggest inviting Julio to lunch? Why?

6 It is now 4:30 p.m., and your boss is fuming with impatience to see that a special report is duplicated and ready to be mailed before 5 p.m. Actually, you received the material from the duplicating unit an hour ago, but you had to send it back because the copies were full of ink blots and smears. A few moments ago you telephoned the duplicating unit to ask them to hurry the job, but you were told to "keep your shirt on." You don't want to blame the duplicating unit, but you don't want the boss to think that the delay is your fault. What should you do?

What Would You Do If . . . ? **1** You have just received an assignment in which you will be preparing offset masters and running off the required number of copies. Your boss expects high-quality work, but you notice that the equipment is dirty and that the supplies are few and disorganized.

2 The counting device on your stencil duplicator is out of order. The duplicator operates too fast for you to count the copies as they drop into the receiving tray.

3 Your supply of preprinted interoffice memorandum masters is exhausted, and you must send a special announcement to the field staff at once. The boss says that he doesn't want you to use regular bond interoffice letterhead paper to do the job. What would you do?

What Does This Mean? **1** The offset process probably has more uses than any of the other modern office duplicating processes.

2 The machine operator's manual says that proper care of the equipment will prevent downtime.

Business in Your Area **1** How many large offices in your area have full-time duplicating machine operators?

2 How many offices have offset duplicators in your area? How many have their offset jobs done by outside printshops?

3 How many printshops are listed in your local telephone directory?

4 How do restaurants in your community duplicate their daily menus?

UNIT 10
DICTATION SYSTEMS

SECTION 26 Equipment and Procedures

Once you learn how to speed up business communications through the use of form letters, standard replies, and other timesaving techniques, you can relieve your boss of a lot of the routine letterwriting. By doing this, you will give your boss more time to concentrate on the more complex communications that need special attention. To save time, your boss may sometimes use dictating equipment of one kind or another.

There's no way of knowing what kind of dictation system you'll find in the office in which you'll eventually work, but you won't have trouble operating any of these systems once you know generally what types there are and how they work. All of them, whatever their design, include two components: a dictation unit and a transcription unit.

THE DICTATION UNIT

Some dictation units require that the dictator operate push buttons to start, stop, record, or play back the dictation; others are more sophisticated, and all that the dictator needs to do is to pick up a telephone, dial a special code number to a word processing center, and dictate to a machine at the other end. In both cases the receiving unit picks up the dictator's voice by way of a microphone or a receiver and records the message on a plastic belt or magnetic tape.

When the dictating machine is right at hand, the dictator makes corrections on the recording in two ways, depending on whether the machine employed uses a tape or plastic belt.

1 If the dictation is recorded on magnetic tape, the dictator returns to the place where the error was made on the tape and dictates the correct version in the same place. The new dictation wipes out the old, and all that the transcriber hears is the last dictation.

2 If the dictation is recorded on a plastic belt, the dictator plays back the dictation until he locates the place where the error was made. He notes that spot on an indication slip. (Many models provide the dictator with an *indication slip*, or index slip, on which he notes the length of the letter, corrections, and any additional special instructions.) Then the dictator returns to the clear section of the sound track and dictates the correct copy. Guided by the indication slip notation, the transcriber skips the part that is incorrect and types only the correct version. On some newer machines, a circular disk takes the place of an indication slip. When he wants to indicate corrections or special instructions, the dictator presses a button which causes a mark to appear on the circular disk on the front of the transcriber's machine. These marks tell the transcriber that there are special instructions on the tape, and she listens to them before she begins to type.

In some systems the typist receives the related correspondence so that she can refer to it in case she has any questions about the material to be transcribed. However, in other systems she may be guided entirely by the instructions recorded on the tape or belt.

When the recording portion of the machine is part of a word processing center in another section of the building or someplace other than where the dictator is located, the dictator dictates his corrections verbally. The transcribing typist makes the corrections on the rough draft that she prepares.

If she prepares a rough draft, the typist may use a special typewriter which produces the copy on paper and at the same time records it on a special magnetic tape. To correct an error, she erases the typed copy, back spaces, presses the correction key, and types over the wrong letters or words. The correction key eliminates the old letters or words from the tape and allows the new ones to be substituted. This version, called a *draft*, goes to the dictator for review, changes, or corrections. It is then returned to the word processing center, where changes, if any, are made. Now, in a final step, the corrected, error-free magnetic tape is processed on a special machine which automatically and at great speed types out the letter in its final form, complete, correct, and ready for signature.

Types of Dictation Systems

Single combination dictation-transcription units These units suffice for small offices and wherever there is a limited amount of correspondence. They offer the convenience and efficiency that the machine dictation system offers without the added expense of a two-machine unit. An executive can share the machine with a secretary or typist without too much bother because the machine is lightweight and easily moved from one desk to another.

Modified combination dictation-transcription units These devices are equipped with a separate telephone-like instrument for recording and a special control unit for transcribing. This arrangement permits the dictator and the transcriber to share the basic unit without having to move it from place to place. If you are transcribing, you can begin seconds after your boss begins dictating.

Separate dictation and transcription units Separate units are particularly convenient for executives who have a large daily volume of correspondence to dictate. These compact units are usually placed on a desk or tabletop. The boss has a unit and can dictate whenever it is convenient; you, the transcriber, have another unit and can type whenever you're ready. Separate dictation and transcription units are shown in use at the top of page 332.

Selective recorder networks With this system, dictation can be recorded on units that are centrally located elsewhere in the building. The dictator speaks into a special phone on the desk to record the correspondence, and a member of the transcription pool that is part of the network transcribes it.

Both photos courtesy Lanier Business Products

Separate desk-top dictation unit.

Separate transcription unit.

Telephone hookups With these devices an executive's desk telephone can be turned into a dictating unit. Simply by calling an extension code number, which is connected to a central battery of recorders, the dictator can telephone from his office or from outside of the building.

Portable dictation units These units enable dictators to record their memorandums, instructions, ideas, and correspondence wherever they happen to be — in the office, on the road, or at home. The dictation is recorded on magnetic tape cassettes that are compatible with the regular office dictation equipment. These cassettes are sent by mail or messenger to the company word processing center.

Dictation handled this way is transcribed quickly. Very often, in fact, the dictated correspondence is in the hands of those to whom it was addressed before the dictator has returned from an out-of-town trip.

In a selective recorder network, dictation "phoned in" is transcribed in an efficient word processing center.

Both photos courtesy Dictaphone Corporation

With a telephone hookup device, the dictator can dial an assigned telephone extension from any location and be connected to the transcribing unit.

This portable dictating unit enables the dictator to record wherever he happens to be.

Getting Ready to Dictate

In order to dictate effectively, you must know how to compose a good business letter. If you ever have to dictate, follow the tips on letter writing listed below. (These same tips are presented in more complete form in Section 30, "Composing Business Letters and Memorandums.")

1 Understand the limits of your authority and responsibility.
2 Make sure you understand all company policies and procedures relating to the subject of the letter.
3 Know where to find the facts you need about the customer as well as your company and its products or services.
4 Be sure to examine all related documents, notes, instructions, and references.
5 If you are not exactly sure about what to do, look in the files for samples of previous correspondence relating to similar situations.
6 If you still have doubts, ask your supervisor to clarify things for you. Make a note of any directions or suggestions for future use.
7 Be sure to plan what you are going to say before you start dictating your message.
8 Each time you respond to a new situation, make a photocopy of the inquiry and your reply for future reference. If you have some ideas for improvement, be sure to note them for the next time.

Before you start, get acquainted with the controls of the recording unit you are going to use so that when you start to dictate you can concentrate on what you want to say and not on the operation of the unit.

Give the transcriber a break! If the system you are using doesn't provide her with the related correspondence or an indication slip, do the following to help her execute a better job:

1 Identify yourself by name, title, and unit or department.
2 Indicate the type of work that you are dictating—letter, memo, proposal, report, and so on, and the stationery and format that should be used.

3   Specify the number of carbon copies you want made and to whom they are to be sent, and indicate whether or not blind carbon copies are to be made.

4   Spell out the name and address of the addressee, including the ZIP Code.

5   Spell out any unusual names or terms used in the text of your letter, and indicate special capitalizations, underlining, or tabulation.

6   Dictate when a new paragraph begins and punctuation such as a colon or a semicolon.

7   Repeat complicated code names, stock numbers, or any other items that might be difficult to understand the first time.

8   Supply special instructions at or before the place where they apply. For example, if quotation marks (") are required, tell the typist to use an open quotation mark before you dictate the quoted material, and then tell her when the quote is ended, with the words "close quote."

9   Indicate enclosures, if any.

10   Dictate how you want the signer's identification line typed, giving name, title, and department.

THE TRANSCRIPTION UNIT

This unit is compact enough to rest on a desk top or worktable. Earphones or speakers are used for listening. Foot or hand controls are used to start, stop, or play back the recording. On some models you can adjust the speed of the tape; you can adjust the volume on all models.

The mechanical aspects of transcribing are really quite simple, and you will learn very quickly how to operate the machine. After you learn how to operate it, you'll need to practice a lot on the machine so that you'll become proficient in using it. You'll also need skills and the ability to perform certain fundamental operations. Look them over:

☐ Be able to type proficiently.
☐ Know how to spell, punctuate, and divide words correctly.
☐ Know how to apply common rules of grammar.
☐ Be able to listen carefully.
☐ Be able to follow directions.
☐ Be able to recognize the difference between the dictated material and the instructions given to you as the transcriber.

Word Processing Centers

Mechanical dictation systems are frequently set up in what are called *word processing centers*. These are compact transcribing centers organized to handle large volumes of dictated material in the quickest fashion possible. In addition to transcribing dictated correspondence, they also transcribe lengthy speeches and speech rehearsals, interviews, conversations, agreements, memorandums, case histories, inventory data, survey reports, sales call reports, job instructions, directions for completing forms, and convention proceedings. Word processing centers record and transcribe this material inexpensively. A dictator can record from any location—from his desk, from an automobile, from a train or plane, or from a manufacturing plant.

The Transcribing Pool Operation

The supervisor of the transcribing pool directs and coordinates the work of the transcribing machine operators. She assigns work to individual workers, gives special instructions, answers questions, verifies the quality and the amount of work performed, and trains beginners to become productive workers as quickly as possible. Your skill and efficiency in handling transcription procedures affects the quality and the amount of work you produce. As a transcriber you may be paid on the basis of output—the number of words or letters of mailable quality turned out—and it is obvious that the more skillfully you handle transcription assignments, the larger your paycheck will be.

Normal Transcription Routine

Although there are many models of transcribing machines on the market, most models can, in general, be operated by following the procedures listed below. If the list seems long, just bear in mind that many of the steps are once-a-day operations and that others are so elementary that you'll soon be doing them almost without thinking.

1   Make sure that the unit is connected to an electric outlet.
2   Attach the accessories (headset and so on) to the unit.
3   Place the recording (and the indication slip, if any) on the machine.
4   Depress the "Play" or "Start" button.
5   *Listen to special instructions.*
6   Adjust the volume and tuning mechanism.
7   Adjust the hearing device and the foot or hand controls for greater comfort.
8   Review special instructions and corrections.
9   *Estimate letter length.*
10 Prepare the typewriter; set margin stops and tabs, select the stationery with the correct letterhead, and make a carbon pack.
11 *Proceed to transcribe.*
12 Proofread before removing the letter from the machine.
13 When all letters on the recording have been transcribed, remove the recording and indication slip.
14 Turn off the machine, disconnect it from the outlet, and replace the cover.
15 *Prepare the letters for the boss's signature, or send the draft to the boss for any changes, additions, or corrections.*

Special Transcribing Considerations

Four of the operating steps listed on page 335 were put in italics so that you would focus your attention on them. They are explained further here.

Special instructions If the dictator has no person-to-person contact with you, the transcriber, he must dictate all special instructions regarding his correspondence. In doing this he may tell you which are rush items or ask you to use special stationery for a particular letter. Other instructions may concern the number of copies required, the persons to whom copies should be sent, and the method of distributing or dispatching the finished work. He may also tell you how he wants material, such as tables or lists, set up in the body of the letter.

Letter length To save time, many large firms using dictation equipment adopt a standard line length and a fixed starting point for all letters. This eliminates placement problems for you if you are the typist. Most companies also adopt a particular letter and punctuation style to be used for all typed letters. If your employer has not standardized transcription operations to this extent, here is what to do:

1 Consult your office manual to see what letter style has been used for a particular department.
2 To determine the letter length, note the distance on the measuring scale between the starting and ending marks on the indication slip, if one is provided. In addition to corrections and special instructions, the indication slip can also show the letter's length. The dictator marks where the letter begins and ends on the measuring scale.
3 Interpret the scale distance according to the manufacturer's suggested formula. For example, on one make of machine each scale division represents approximately 60 words of dictation at an average speed of 100 words a minute.
4 Consult a letter-placement table in your office manual (or see pages 164–166), and set the margins required.

Transcribing After a little practice you will be able to coordinate your typing skill with the voice instructions and dictation. The machine transcribing cycle consists of four steps: starting, listening, stopping, and typing. At first you will be able to listen to and to remember only a few words or phrases at a time. Gradually your memory span will increase, and you will be able to retain longer thought units, such as clauses and even short sentences. When you become expert and accustomed to the dictator's style and the trade terminology, you will be able to pick up and retain dictation fast enough to keep your typewriter moving continuously. To do that, deliberately pace your transcription so that it trails about one sentence behind the dictation. In this way you can anticipate problems of spelling, punctuation, capitalization, and paragraphing. If you can't hear any part of the dictation clearly, use the backspace or repeat mechanism so that you can listen to it again.

Preparing letters for signature The firm's office manual will usually instruct you on how to arrange the finished letters so that they may be returned to the dictator, who will sign and mail the correspondence and file the carbon copies. The folder of transcribed correspondence may be returned to the dictator by messenger. It's a good idea to arrange the letters and their carbon copies in the folder in the order in which they were dictated. Place urgent messages on top if you have not already forwarded them by special messenger.

Each individual letter actually involves an original, enclosures if any, an envelope, previous correspondence, and carbon copies. It is best to put the original with enclosures attached, on top of all previous correspondence and all related papers. This puts the papers in a convenient order so that the dictator can use them for reference, if necessary. The envelope is placed face up with the flap over the top of the letter and enclosures. Carbon copies usually come last and are placed underneath the other papers.

Transcribing Problems

Unusual words Good dictators usually spell out difficult words or tell the operator where to look for the correct spelling in the related correspondence. Frequently, supervisors of transcription pools prepare special lists of trade terms used in the company's industry. These lists may be distributed to new transcribers during their orientation and training sessions.

Punctuation Dictators sometimes prefer to supply punctuation to the operator, especially when technical data is being recorded. However, if you think that some of the dictator's punctuation instructions are wrong, consult a reference book or ask your supervisor for the correct form. Sometimes a change in punctuation may affect the meaning of a sentence. In this case you may have to consult the dictator to be sure that your use of punctuation is correct. Of course, you are responsible for any punctuation the dictator doesn't give but which the material requires.

Errors in grammar Your boss relies on you to correct any errors in grammar that might have been inadvertently dictated. Most errors of this kind are minor, but if the error is major, that is, if it necessitates your making a major correction, consult your supervisor before making the change.

Similar sounding words When you first begin to transcribe, you may hesitate when you encounter a word in the dictation that might from its sound be spelled in several different ways. For example, is the word *know* or *no; tale* or *tail; to, too,* or *two?* Usually you can find a clue in the context of the letter to guide you in the choice of the correct word. After you become more experienced and more familiar with the dictator's vocabulary, you'll find yourself typing the correct word without the slightest pause in your normal typing rhythm.

Errors in content The wonderful thing about acquiring experience is that you grow more sure of yourself and more confident as you learn about what is going on. When you have acquired such experience, you may one day discover in the dictated material an error of fact, such as a name, date, price, quantity, or invoice number. First check to be sure your information is correct. Then correct the mistake in your transcription. As a courtesy, attach a note to the finished letter, explaining the change you made.

If you find an obvious mistake in the dictation but have no way of checking the data, report the mistake to your supervisor.

Material omitted from dictation Some dictators expect the operator to look up and fill in details such as addresses, file numbers, invoice details, and so on. Although this is normally not good dictating practice, be prepared to fill in the gaps when you can. You may find some of the data in the accompanying correspondence, some of it in the files, or some in special reference books in the office.

SPECIAL APPLICATIONS

In some specialized operations, such as insurance investigations, the dictator may not record a letter at all. Instead, the dictator may give the transcriber all the pertinent facts so that she may complete a form letter or report form that covers the situation.

REVIEWING YOUR READING

1 Demonstrate or explain how dictation systems can increase a firm's efficiency in handling a heavy volume of written communications.
2 Cite specific ways in which the dictator can simplify the transcriber's job.
3 Name several skills that an efficient transcriber should have. Do you now possess these skills? How can you develop them?
4 Giving careful attention to special instructions is a critical part of the machine transcription routine. Supply examples of the kinds of special instructions that might be given by the dictator.
5 Expert transcribers pace their transcription to trail about one sentence behind the dictation. Explain the purpose of this technique.
6 If errors in content or in grammar are encountered in transcription, what corrective measures should the typist attempt to do herself? When should she consult her supervisor?

OFFICE ASSIGNMENTS

1 When a dictating unit is used, the dictation includes special instructions and corrections as well as the correspondence itself. You should become accustomed to office-style dictation. Here is the way it sounds. Instructions are arranged on the left, and the text of the letter is shown on the right. Type this letter in mailable form on letterhead stationery.

Instructions	Dictation

Instructions

Letter number one goes to

That is B-E-A-V-E-R.

By the way, send this airmail.

Colon

Paragraph

Spelled H-O-L-L-Y

Make that office training
instead of commercial training.

Colon

Indent and list each position.
Put number of vacancies in
parentheses after the job title.

Paragraph

(You supply company signature,
dictator's name and title, and
reference initials.)

Dictation

Beaver Employment Agency

2463 Tower Avenue, Waterville,
Maine 04901

Gentlemen

Our new branch office at Waterville
will open for business on July 1.

Mr. James Holly

estimates that he will require
12 office workers to staff this
operation. Experienced personnel
will be needed for the key positions
of chief accountant, secretary to
Mr. Holly, and file supervisor.
Beginners with commercial training

in high school or in private business
school are eligible to apply
for the other vacancies as follows

Receptionist 1, mail clerks 2, file
clerks 2, messenger 1, clerk-typists
2, order clerk 1.

Please instruct any qualified
applicants to telephone Mr. Holly
at 207-626-2000 for an appointment.

Yours truly

2 Your teacher will give office-style dictation to be transcribed directly at your typewriter. Wait until the teacher pauses at the end of a phrase or sentence before you start typing.

3 If transcribing units are available, transcribe letters on the recordings assigned by the teacher. Check your letters carefully. They should be in mailable form before being handed to the teacher.

If transcribing equipment is not available, type the following unarranged material in the form of a publicity release similar to the sample on page 197.

From Public Information Office, Orange County Junior College, Middletown, New York 10940. From William Andrews, Supervisor of Public Information, Orange County Junior College, 914-555-2758. Release at once. WORKSHOP IN SPEECH AND VOICE IMPROVEMENT. (Paragraph) Middletown, N. Y., Sept. 7—A workshop in speech and voice improvement will be offered by the College's Evening Division next semester. (Paragraph) Registration will be held December 20 from 6:30 to 8:30 p.m. at the South Building, 270 East Water Street. Fee is $13 for residents of Orange County and $26 for nonresidents. The course will run for ten weeks beginning January 11, at the South Building from 7 to 9 p.m. (Paragraph) To allow for individual attention, groups will be limited to nine, according to Dr. Henry O. Smith, Dean of Continuing Education. (Paragraph) The objective of the course is to provide all persons enrolled with an opportunity to acquire more precise speech and better voice quality. (Paragraph) Each member of the group will be given a speech analysis and practical exercises for his particular problem, such as omitting endings of words, substituting sounds, slurring words, and using regional speech variations. (Paragraph) Tape recorders will be used to familiarize each member with his own speech or voice production, to make each member more conscious of the spoken word and speech sounds, and to chart progress in improvement. (END)

4 Your boss, Mr. A. B. Stouffer, has recorded the following message on his dictating unit. Prepare the reminder as directed.

"Operator, prepare the following reminder to me in triplicate. The original should be placed in my personal file marked for follow-up on the twentieth; the first carbon goes to Robert Wells, my Administrative Assistant, and the second carbon goes to the central file. The message is, 'Prepare final recommendations on budget due in home office on the twenty-fifth. Wells will provide tentative figures and last year's data.'"

5 Some employers who use dictating equipment dictate letters and other materials without indicating punctuation, capitalization, or paragraphs. From the copy below prepare a blocked business letter. Supply the correct punctuation and capitalization and begin new paragraphs where they appear to be needed. Also supply company signature, dictator's name and title, and reference initials.

This letter is to mr dante friento 241 cambria avenue hartford connecticut 06111 dear mr friento we have received your application for employment and your data sheet it will be a pleasure to talk with you at 9 a.m. on january 16 after the interview we will ask that you take two routine written tests that will last for about an hour each a brief description of the tests is enclosed please have your physician complete the enclosed medical history statement form 623 and mail it directly to me in the attached envelope it will be helpful if you can take care of this in time for us to receive the form by january 16 sincerely yours

UNIT 10

BUSINESS CASES AND PROBLEMS

In the Boss's Shoes   Your boss has just announced that a network dictation system will be installed in the office within a few weeks. The new equipment is intended to increase the growing firm's efficiency by handling routine correspondence as quickly and as inexpensively as possible. You are not eager to see the change. You feel that you are going to lose the personal satisfaction that you have always derived from being an indispensable administrative assistant called upon to perform a variety of duties, such as composing letters, taking shorthand, routine filing, and recordkeeping. Should you complain to your boss? Refuse the readjustment of your duties? Or quit?

Your Human Relations   A high-ranking executive in your office frequently uses dictation equipment. However, many times he does not indicate the number of carbon copies required for his letters and does not spell out the addressees' names and addresses on the tape while he is recording or on an indication slip. Since you have no access to related correspondence, you find that these omissions cut down on your output as a transcriber. You must stop and call your supervisor each time additional information is needed. Your supervisor is reluctant to tell the dictator about these omissions. Should you tell him yourself?

What Would You Do If . . .?   You are unable to hear large portions of the dictation on the cassette that you have been given to transcribe. The dictator may not have spoken loudly and clearly enough, or his dictation unit might not have been functioning properly.

What Does This Mean?   You are transcribing a speech given by a government official. You come to a point in the speech where the government official tells the audience, "Now this is strictly off the record."

Business in Your Area   Consult whatever references are necessary to answer the following questions.

1   Do many large offices in your town use dictation systems?
2   For what kinds of correspondence is the equipment used?
3   What is the average pay of a transcribing machine operator?

UNIT **11**
PERSONAL
EFFICIENCY

27 Working Methods and Habits

One of the most valuable assets a new employee can bring to a job is judgment. Judgment, for the most part, is a combination of experience and common sense and involves recognizing priorities, asking when you don't know, and applying what you do know. To have judgment, you must have competence in the skills your job requires. And when we talk about personal efficiency, we're really talking about the results of using your competence and judgment. The more you demonstrate your abilities in both these areas, the more you qualify as an employee to be considered for promotion.

WORKING METHODS

Time and motion study engineering sounds complicated, but all it means is that a trained person figures out the way to do a given job with the least effort and the greatest results. A company asks you to follow certain office procedures developed by time and motion study engineers because it has evidence that these procedures can save you time and effort.

Sometimes you're left to work out your own procedure which can be as efficient as one designed by a professional. If that happens, keep these principles in mind.*

☐ All materials and tools should be located within easy reach.
☐ Equipment and materials should be organized in advance and placed in the order and at the spot required for efficient operation.
☐ The sequence of operations should be devised so that work can be performed with rhythmic motions.
☐ Motions should be as simple as possible to reduce fatigue. Common motions in order of increasing energy required are:

1 Finger motions.
2 Finger and wrist motions.
3 Finger, wrist, and lower arm motions.
4 Finger, wrist, lower arm, and upper arm motions.
5 Finger, wrist, lower arm, upper arm, and body motions.

☐ The work load should be divided as equally as possible between the two hands.
☐ Motions of both hands should take place at the same time.
☐ Crisscrossing arm motions should be avoided.
☐ Any pauses or hesitations should be analyzed, and the causes should be removed, if possible.

*Allen H. Mogensen, *Common Sense Applied to Time and Motion Study*, McGraw-Hill Book Company, New York, 1932.

WORKING HABITS

To say that neatness is a trait to cultivate sounds a bit prissy, but there's more to this advice than meets the eye. The fact is that by working neatly, you can avoid many unpleasant problems. First you must make the effort to follow good working habits. Then through repetition and time these habits will become automatic. Here are some useful tips:

1   Use clean type, clean paper, and a well-inked ribbon when you type.
2   Make sure your hands are clean and free of ink smudges.
3   Work carefully when you assemble and staple enclosures, when you fold papers, and when you seal and stamp envelopes.
4   Keep your desk and the machines you use in good working order.

The result of this kind of neatness is that you produce work that is professional, that attracts favorable attention, and that commands respect for both you and your firm.

Accuracy

Business competition is intense, and errors are rarely tolerated. A secretary or clerk who types a bid to read $45.23 a unit when it should be $54.23 a unit can agitate even the most understanding boss. The financial loss could be immense. Worse still, it could cost you your job. It would be better for you to acquire the reputation that any data, figures, promises, or guarantees handled by you can be counted on as being completely accurate. Top that off with presenting your material in clean, unmistakable form, and you're inevitably in line for bigger things.

Proofreading

After you have finished any business assignment, double-check your work to be on the safe side.

1   Always proofread every page before it is removed from the typewriter.
2   Read slowly for sense as well as for grammar, spelling, and punctuation.
3   Read the page again to check on fine details, such as word division, footnote data, spacing, and special effects.
4   If the material that you typed is very technical, ask a second person to check the finished work while you read from the original.
5   Correct any error while the paper is still in the machine. If extensive corrections are required, retype the material.

Care of Materials

At present prices an individually dictated and typed letter costs over $4 to produce. A set of supplies such as the one listed on page 356 costs up to $50. This explains why an employer depends on you not to waste supplies or redo work on paper unnecessarily. When many people and large quantities of supplies are involved, the loss from unnecessary waste can be staggering.

Time Consciousness

In the business world, time is money. So many activities in an office function on deadlines. Mail must be dispatched promptly, appointments made for specific hours, conferences planned, trips arranged, telephone calls placed, payrolls computed, taxes paid, receipts deposited, and deliveries completed—all according to schedules. You must know exactly what to do during your working day and when to do it. Others depend on you to be consistent and reliable.

Improvement of Performance

After you have been on a new job for a while and are familiar with the company's work methods and equipment, you should try to evaluate how you are spending your work time and whether there is room for improvement.

You can get so engrossed in what you are doing on your job that you concentrate only on getting it done and fail to think about ways of doing it better. Start evaluating your work by keeping an informal time record for a typical week. Then with a summary of your activities before you, consider how you can improve on accomplishing each one by using these guidelines.

Planning ahead   Do you plan ahead of time and then try to work according to that schedule? When you plan ahead, you must take into consideration what others expect you to do as well as the things that you want to do. It begins with an understanding of your boss's responsibilities and the duties that he delegates to you and includes company policies and procedures relating to the work to be done. You plan ahead in order to organize your work. In this way you can complete your assignments on time with perhaps a small margin of time to spare.

You will plan ahead more effectively if you identify long-range objectives first and then pinpoint short-term goals, which are to be completed at designated time intervals or dates along the way. For example, meeting the monthly deadline is the ultimate objective for the publisher of a monthly magazine. In order to meet that final deadline, however, manuscripts must be edited by a certain date, advertising copy must be ready at still another date, and illustrations must be prepared and available at even a third date.

Avoiding interruptions   Is your efficiency hampered by a lot of interruptions that could be eliminated? Interruptions that stop you from using your time to the greatest advantage are usually caused by unexpected visitors, insistent telephones, chatty colleagues, and special business and personal problems or events that seem to demand immediate attention. (Personal interruptions are a special category, of course, and should be kept to a minimum as much as possible.) To protect yourself from interruptions, ask yourself these questions: Do you always have to answer the telephone, or can a co-worker or subordinate respond when you need to concentrate on what you are doing? If you must answer, can you cut the conversation short with a courteous but firm offer to call back later after you have finished an important job? Can you suggest that callers telephone at certain hours of the working day when the interruptions will be less troublesome?

You can also plan strategy for dealing with unexpected callers. Have the receptionist announce them in a way that permits you to avoid seeing them if you are too busy. If you are obliged to see them, go to the reception area and chat right there very briefly as though you were on your way to an important conference. (Once callers get to your desk or office, it is more difficult to control the length of time that you must spend with them.)

Another way to avoid interruptions is to use a simple appointment pad and limit your commitments so that they do not take too much time out of any single day. If possible, set appointments when you can best spare the time. Be fully prepared with the necessary facts and figures needed for the appointment so that your meeting does not take any longer than necessary.

Getting complete information Do you always obtain complete information and instructions before starting an assignment? If you know exactly what you are supposed to do, how you are supposed to do it, and what materials you are to use, you have the best possible chance to turn in an excellent performance. Many office assignments are routine and repetitive in nature, but you still must be able to master them completely if you are going to be able to fill in for someone else when requested. Keep in touch. Procedures can change without your knowing. And remember that you can easily forget routines and details if you don't use them very often.

Stay alert to changes and new developments. Watch for and read instruction sheets, bulletins, and manuals concerning methods and procedures. Be an unobtrusive but good listener when changes are either forthcoming or in progress. Be observant of what is going on about you, especially of anything that seems new and different. In addition, keep in close touch with your boss. Ask questions when you really don't know or aren't sure of something.

Keep a record of any new information that you pick up, and file it in a place where it will be readily accessible for speedy reference in the future. It's valuable only if you can find it when you need it.

Recognizing priorities Are you mindful of priorities and do you do the most important jobs first? If you're not sure about priorities, ask your boss what he wants done first. An office is a busy place because there are many procedures involving paper work that must be done in a given amount of time. Today's customers expect prompt if not immediate service, and a successful firm has to see that they get what they want.

As a beginner, under the demanding pressure of office operations, you may feel that the fairest way to treat customers is to process their orders strictly in order of receipt. This procedure may be the easiest because it allows you to take things as they come without having to consider exceptions. However, your boss may have other ideas—and with good reason.

For instance, the boss would probably favor your processing a larger order over a smaller order. Why? A big order produces a substantial profit, while the small order may actually produce little or no profit. The boss might also prefer that you process the order of a new customer before you process the order of an old customer. Why? It is important for the boss to make a favorable first impression on the new customer. In time you will be able to make some of these decisions yourself, but when you begin work at a new job or for a new boss, find out the relative importance of things, that is, *which* absolutely come first at all costs, *which* come second, and so on down the line. You may not agree with the order of the preferences, but you will be expected to perform your work in accordance with that order. If you are ever in doubt about a preference, ask the boss. If your boss is not present and if the matter cannot wait, try to find out how a similar case was handled before. The person who handled your job before you might be able to tell you how it was done.

Priorities are tricky, but you will soon learn how the boss thinks and the reasons for thinking that way. Eventually, you'll be able to predict many of the preferences. As you gain more experience, you may feel that the established priorities need to be reevaluated. Discuss your ideas with the boss before making changes or experimenting on your own. If your suggestions are found to be perfectly valid, your changes may be authorized. But until they are authorized, do the work the way you are asked to do it.

Processing in batches   Have you tried accumulating certain routine papers for an hour or two so that you can process them in batches rather than one at a time?

For example, suppose your workbasket of incoming papers to be processed included, in mixed order, 14 orders to be acknowledged, 17 invoices to be verified, 8 orders to be priced, 4 price lists to be changed and duplicated, 20 inquiry coupons from which mailing list cards are to be made, and 8 expense accounts to be typed. If you processed this work in order of receipt, you would obtain an order acknowledgment form and type it. Then using a calculating machine on a nearby table, you would verify the computations on an invoice. After verifying the invoice and sending it on its way, you would assemble the catalogs needed to price one of the new orders. Having done this, you would clear the working area, obtain new supplies, and prepare a stencil incorporating the new price changes. After this you would go down the hall to the duplicating room to make the necessary copies. After returning to your work station, you would tackle the next task, which would be the preparation of an expense account.

It is easy to see that if you use the order-of-receipt procedure, you might be forced to make 14 trips to the supply cabinet to get 14 order acknowledgment forms. Similarly, you might take 17 trips to the calculating machine, assemble and put away the catalogs 8 times, make 4 trips to the duplicating room, and so on. The way to eliminate this wasted motion is to batch the work into tasks of similar nature. For example, gather all 14 of the orders to be acknowledged into a single batch or pile, and prepare all of the acknowledgments at one time.

Then gather the 17 invoices into one pile, make one trip to the calculating machine, and complete all verifications in the single trip.

The batching technique allows you to perform more efficiently because you can concentrate on one type of task at a time. In short, no matter how varied the assignments may be, examine the tasks to be done in each one and identify those tasks that require similar information, supplies, equipment, and work layout. Devise a batching system of your own that will permit you to work more intelligently.

Allowing for emergencies   Do you allow any leeway for emergencies in your schedule? Do you anticipate work loads caused by vacations and holidays? Usually when you develop a plan or schedule for your work, you try to visualize a normal day's work and you probably assume that the working situation will remain more or less stable. However, emergency situations arise in office operations as often as they do everywhere else. In fact, since the office is a control center for many different kinds of activities, it receives alarm signals from any unit that is experiencing a serious difficulty or crisis.

An emergency situation usually demands immediate attention, regardless of what the normal order of priorities is. As an office worker you have to learn to take emergencies in stride. Don't let them cause you to panic, and don't feel frustrated. Your boss knows that you didn't cause the situation, but expects that you, as a member of the team, will help to straighten things out. One way you can minimize the personal impact of an emergency situation is to provide an extra margin of time in your schedule. Then if normal operations have to be suspended briefly, there will be enough time in the working period to take care of the emergency situation. Later, you can go back to your normal activities. If you can't handle the emergency and the regular work load within the workday, tell your supervisor. She may assign other clerks to help you, she may pitch in and help you herself, she may ask you to work overtime, or she may give you permission to defer other work until the next day. If the boss isn't around, give first priority to the emergency problem and then go on to the assignment that would normally have the highest priority rating.

Vacations and holidays are also factors that can lead to extra work loads. Some firms stagger vacation schedules so that there are no critical gaps in the working force to slow down the normal rate and volume of the work flow. They also *cross-train* their employees, which means that they train people for other jobs so that they can substitute for absentee employees. Sometimes the employee is trained for the job that is higher up on the promotion ladder. Cross-training, therefore, can also serve as preparation for promotion as well as an emergency staffing technique.

Coordinating output   Do you release your output at the same time that the mail is collected or the next operating unit takes over?

Doing your own job speedily and well is very commendable. But go a step beyond, and anticipate what is coming next. It won't do very much good, for instance, to rush through a letter for the boss just before closing time only to discover that the mail room is closed for the day or that the last collection at the corner mailbox has been made. To avoid that kind of frustration, get to know the inflow and outflow schedules of other departments of the company and develop one of your own that coincides with theirs. Discuss your schedule with your supervisor. She may have some helpful suggestions or preferences, or she may want to talk to other supervisors about your schedule in order to improve the flow of work in general.

Keeping in touch   Do you know how to reach your boss at all times? Does your boss always know where you are and what you are doing? The television stereotype of a boss working diligently in a private office with the secretary on guard outside the door is misleading. In this fast-moving world many bosses, a large part of the time, are not in their offices and not even in the building. They travel to supervise field staffs, to visit clients, to scout for new business, to visit factories, and so on. Even the boss who isn't out of town may not be in the office for very long each day. Modern management activities include meetings, conferences, training sessions, discussion groups, research operations, and so on, as well as the traditional business lunch with a prospective customer from out of town or a quick visit to a local customer. When you add to the list the boss's occasional visit to the broker, lawyer, or banker, you'll soon realize that keeping track of him is a continuing responsibility. The problem is compounded by the fact that he is usually so completely immersed in his own activities that he fails to tell his staff where he is going. However, the same boss can become very annoyed if he doesn't find you waiting for him on his return to his office, no matter how long he has been away.

You can solve this problem of keeping track of your boss through communication and cooperation. Tell the boss, tactfully of course, why it is important for you and the staff to know where he is at all times. If he minimizes the problem, cite actual cases to illustrate how much confusion occurs when he is needed

An efficient secretary knows where her boss is at all times.

and can't be located. Point out that you feel foolish when you have to say in response to repeated inquiries that you don't know where the boss is and cannot say when he'll be back. A phone number or simple message avoids embarrassment for all.

But remember the other side of the problem. Your boss should also know or have a way of finding out where the staff is during regular office hours. When it is necessary for you to leave your desk, alert someone to answer the telephone and take messages in your absence. Also leave a telephone number where you can be reached in the meantime. If you are going to the duplicating department, for example, supply the extension number where you can be located if necessary.

Following up   Do you follow up your own work to be sure that whatever action you initiated has actually been taken? Size has its advantages and its limitations in business operations. Large organizations can handle a tremendous volume of sales in a variety of products with impressive speed and efficiency. However, in such massive operations customer relations tend to be on a rather impersonal basis. If something goes wrong, an individual customer can encounter a great deal of delay because of the red tape involved in rectifying a situation.

Suppose your boss receives a complaint from a customer and, after investigating it, promises to have a refund check sent to him. The customer is pleased to have reached the right person, your boss, and to have been assured of a prompt and fair settlement, but the matter may drag on for a long time yet. Why? Because there are likely to be many steps to go through before the promised check is issued and sent. Any mix-up along the way can delay or fail to bring about the promised settlement.

To eliminate or minimize this danger, make use of a technique called *follow-up*. For instance, before you pass along a paper to the accounting department to have the refund check issued, make a photocopy of the paper and place it in a chronological, or follow-up, file. When the follow-up date arrives, the photocopy in the file will remind you to see if the proper action has been taken and if the check has been issued. If you find that no action has been taken or that the response is taking too long, call the situation to your boss's attention.

Using specialized help   Do you conserve your own time by letting others that have specialized training help you? Do you leave your busy desk to take a rush letter to the post office when messengers are available to do the job? Are you one of those persons who says, "The only way I can be sure that a job is done properly is to do it *all* myself"?

Even though this statement indicates a zealous and commendable desire to get things done right, doing everything yourself results in misplaced energy and an uneconomic use of manpower. A competent, properly instructed messenger can take a letter to the post office as well as you. If there is any concern about his performance, the messenger's supervisor can record the messenger's departure and arrival times. The supervisor can even have the messenger obtain a certificate of mailing receipt. There really is no reason to worry about getting the letter to the post office and mailed.

Nevertheless, some people want to do everything for themselves perhaps because it makes them feel or sound more important. Some cannot explain to others what has to be done. A few decline to delegate work to others for fear that they may learn to do their job and, possibly, become a threat to their job security. But a greater threat to job security is failure to use your time to the firm's greatest advantage. When a $3.50-an-hour secretary is performing the work of a $2-an-hour messenger, the firm is being shortchanged $1.50 an hour. The way to prove your personal superiority is to do those tasks that you *alone* can do faster and better than anyone else.

The best equipment in the world is of no help unless you use it. If the boss has made it available, it is because he wants to save your time for something else. In the same way if helpers are available, give them whatever part of your work load they are competent to handle. If you have some doubts about their competency, help them learn the skills that are needed to perform the job. In this way everyone benefits—you, the helpers, and the company.

Avoiding wasted motion   Do you know enough about your company to find out what you need to know without a lot of wasted motions? In a very small office it's easy to figure out who is responsible for what duties. Sometimes only the clerk-stenographer and the sole owner constitute the entire office staff. However, as the company grows and responsibilities become scattered, it becomes more difficult to know who is supposed to do what. The problem is compounded with every expansion and reshuffling of assignments.

Every office worker should have or should try to develop a broad picture of the scope of office operations and the sequence of the work flow. With such knowledge it becomes easier to trace missing data, to locate bottlenecks, to audit prior operations, to expedite special items, and to obtain advice.

For example, suppose the boss receives a complaint from a customer about a shipment being late and asks you to see what happened to the customer's order. If you are familiar with the way an order is processed, you will know where to start checking and what questions to ask. When was the order received? When did the order pass through the invoicing unit? When was the order shipped? How was the order shipped? Did the carrier report any delivery problems? When did the shipment reach the customer's receiving department? Who signed for the shipment? Was any shortage or damage reported upon delivery or since that time? When you report back to the boss with *all* the answers, he will be able to reply promptly to the customer and initiate any corrective action. Knowledge of the company operations helps you to do a good detective job. Your findings save your boss time and help him to mend fences with the customer as quickly as possible.

Studying better ways   Do you consciously try to find better ways of doing assigned tasks? Have you made any suggestions lately? Business is constantly looking for better ways to operate because it is always eager to reduce costs, overcome manpower shortages, give faster service, achieve greater accuracy, develop better controls, and speed up communications. Every year large companies spend thousands of dollars to improve their office systems and adapt new ideas to their particular needs. Improved procedures are described in company manuals, and job instruction sheets are prepared for newcomers in order to help them learn their jobs more easily. These improvements often represent a big investment of time and money, and you are expected to comply with these recommended rules and procedures. Indeed, you are often evaluated as a worker on the basis of how fully you do comply with these rules.

At the same time industry recognizes that the many improved procedures that have revolutionized many office activities have come about as the result of systematic observation of normal working conditions, research, and experimentation. Contributions have also been made by employees who have had practical experience on the job. Their everyday activities enable them to note firsthand what works well and what does not. They can see how methods stand up under the pressure of both normal and rush working conditions. They can see where the rough spots in the work flow are, and they can make helpful suggestions on how to eliminate them. That's why you'll find that your boss is usually receptive to suggestions for improvement. He may not have the authority to adopt any one of them on the spot, but he'll pass it along and see that it receives proper consideration. Don't be pushy about proposing a better way to do a particular job, but don't be hesitant about expressing your ideas either. Write up a description of your proposal, and let your boss study it. Many concerns give bonuses to employees for suggestions that are adopted.

PERSONAL EFFICIENCY DEFINED

The list of guidelines and suggestions above can definitely help you become more efficient, but the list isn't complete by any means. Job situations vary, and so do the people who deal with them. Personal efficiency is really the product of skills, knowledge, experience, attitude, human relations, and constructive supervision applied to situations where you have at your disposal the most modern tools, equipment, materials, policies, and methods.

WORKING AREA ORGANIZATION

A sea of untidy desks in a busy office cuts down on everyone's efficiency, including your own. Have a system for keeping your papers, folders, and anything else you work with in order. Here are some tips given by George Terry, a nationally known office operations expert:*

☐ Work on one task at a time, and finish it before starting another. Abstain from trying to do several tasks at the same time.
☐ Keep your desk free from excess papers and supplies, and have only the items that you need on your desk.
☐ Strive to keep the work moving over the desk. Take action on each paper coming to the desk as quickly as possible.
☐ Adopt a convenient, standardized arrangement for papers and supplies in desk drawers.

*George R. Terry, *Office Management and Control*, Richard D. Irwin, Inc., Homewood, Ill., 1952, pp. 200–201. Used by permission.

FURNISHINGS AND OFFICE EQUIPMENT

Almost any job can be done better with the right tools and a suitable place to use them. This is true whether you're hanging a shelf, fixing a flat tire, or baking a cake. It's also true in an office. The furnishings and office equipment are designed to help you do your work efficiently in an attractive environment.

You'll find it useful to know something about those furnishings and the equipment and materials commonly in use.

Desks

Never underestimate the importance of a desk with a full working surface. Most desks have the typewriter on a platform or on an extended unit to the left or right. However, on some desks the typewriter is attached to a platform that can be folded down and hidden from view when the machine is not in use.

A popular general utility desk has a typewriter shelf that fits into a drawer space on either the right or left side. Extended from the desk, the shelf provides a comfortable typing surface and does not interfere with the working or storage areas. If desired, the shelf can be removed in minutes, and the drawer reinserted in its place.

Your desk drawers can serve as a miniature stockroom, providing that you know what they contain and have arranged the material contained in them systematically. Having on hand what you need when you want it can save you many hours of needless searching for something you can't find.

Typewriter Stands

You can get additional work space with an extended typewriter stand or wing that is fitted to either the right or left pedestal of the desk. This L-shaped device is popular because you don't have to move anything when you are ready to type. Instead, you have a large, uncluttered desk area and extra drawer space in which to keep your supplies and reference material in an organized way. You'll discover that having frequently used files right at hand can save you lots of time and trouble.

Sometimes office workers who don't have much typing to do prefer a typewriter stand that has wheels. This stand can be pushed to a corner until needed, allowing all desk drawers and files to become more accessible.

Posture Chairs

A comfortable chair is very important if you have the kind of job where you spend long periods of time seated at a desk. For maximum comfort, you should be able to adjust your chair so that your body weight is properly distributed and so that the components of the chair conform to your shape and size. When your chair is adjusted properly, you'll sit with better posture and work more comfortably. There are several adjustments that you can easily make to the seat and back of posture chairs:

Raise or lower the seat and back adjustment to fit your height. Determine the correct height for you by sitting well back in the chair with both feet flat on the floor. Adjust the height so that there is support but no pressure on your feet. The proper chair height for the average person is somewhere near 17 inches from the floor.

Raise or lower the chair back so that the backrest pad fits you at the proper height.

Use the pivot adjustment at the back to change the angle of the backrest pad and to provide correct distribution of your weight.

Move the entire back frame forward or backward, depending on whether you are slender or stout.

Use the tension or balance tilt adjustment to give you back support throughout the tilting range of the chair.

Copyholders

If you are a good typist, you know that you have to concentrate on what you are doing to get good results. A copy typist or a statistical typist in particular must watch every detail of the material closely, one line at a time. To help you do this, there are copyholders, which are devices that hold copy in a convenient position. There are two main types available.

The Direct View Copyholder stands behind the typewriter and permits you to look directly in front as you type.

The Side View Copyholder has an easel design and is placed at either side of the typewriter.

Many copyholders have a very useful attachment that underlines the copy by dropping down a line at a time so that your eyes are directed to the line you are typing. This helps you to type more quickly and accurately.

Tables

If you aren't required to type very often in your office assignment, you may find that you can work more efficiently at a table than at a desk. The larger working surface is handy for sorting, gathering, and stacking papers and is also excellent for manual recordkeeping, proofreading, clipping, cutting, pasting, stamping, marking, and a thousand and one other operations.

Special Purpose Equipment

Some offices are equipped with tables, racks, cabinets, stands, and consoles that are specially designed for the specific work of the department. For example, incoming mail units have racks with pigeonholes to speed sorting mail; an accounts receivable unit may have special carts, shelves, and containers for the ledger cards. Much of this special purpose equipment is produced by office equipment manufacturers, but very often it is homemade by a company's own maintenance staff because the manufactured items available aren't adaptable to the particular needs of that office.

OFFICE SUPPLIES

You'll perform your job more efficiently when you see to it that your desk is well stocked with the supplies you need.

Paper

Business firms use many kinds of paper, including plain bond, letterhead stock, manifold, second sheets, and duplicating paper for multiple copies. Generally, a good quality bond paper is chosen for company letterheads. Paper is identified by weight, among other things, and for letterhead stationery the most popular are the 20- and 24-pound weight. Plain bond paper of the same quality and weight is used for the second and succeeding pages of a letter.

It is customary to use a thin paper known as *manifold* to make carbon copies. Some companies prefer a glazed manifold called *onionskin* for their carbon copies; others prefer an inexpensive tinted paper.

The paper used for certain kinds of duplicating such as mimeographing is quite different from letterhead stock. Paper used for duplicating is soft and porous enough to permit the ink used to penetrate it and dry quickly.

Carbon Paper and Carbon Film

These are used to make copies when just a few are needed. The weight of the paper determines how many acceptable copies you can make. Heavy carbon is suitable for one or two copies; medium weight carbon paper yields from two to five copies; thin, lightweight carbon paper with a hard finish is best for five to seven copies. Carbon film uses a plastic backing instead of a paper one and is, therefore, more durable though it is initially more expensive. Many offices prefer to use timesaving "snap-out" carbon packs which have sheets of carbon paper in between copy sheets.

Typewriter Ribbons

A ribbon can make a lot of difference in the appearance of typed work. Many kinds of ribbons are available and are made mostly of cotton, silk, or nylon. It's a good idea to consider the advantages of each. Nylon ribbons are more expensive than cotton ones, but they last longer and, therefore, may be more economical in the long run. The type bars do not have to be cleaned as frequently if nylon and silk ribbons are used instead of the cheaper grades of cotton ribbons.

Carbon ribbons require a special spool attachment on your typewriter. They produce sharper impressions than fabric ribbons and are highly desirable for the preparation of master copies for offset duplicating or for any work that is to be photographed. The reason for this is that the carbon ribbon moves the full width of a character each time you strike a key, and a fresh, unused portion of the ribbon becomes available for each successive character. Carbon ribbons are not reusable.

If you are using a cloth ribbon, change it as soon as your typed work begins to look gray and unattractive. After all, if your typing is good, it doesn't take any extra effort to give your boss letters that are clean and crisp.

Erasers and Correction Materials

Finally, consider the many different types of erasers available. They do their best job when you use the right one for a given job. An abrasive kind is better for erasing on hard-surface bond paper. On carbon copies use soft, nonabrasive ones. Popular designs include the circular typewriter eraser with a brush attachment and the rectangular block type with a slanted cut at the ends to give a sharper edge. Another popular one is the pencil-shaped eraser with a wooden casing which you sharpen like a pencil.

There are times when it is best to correct an error by using an eraser. But very often, especially when you are going to duplicate what you have typed, you can get excellent results with a correction sheet coated with a white, waxy substance. When the error is retyped, the wax is transferred to the paper where it covers the original mistake. The correct version can then be typed on the newly whitened surface. Typing errors may also be corrected by using correction tape, which is placed over the error.

Basic Supplies

Your progress can be slowed up if you run out of office supplies right in the middle of a job. Figure out what you'll need in advance, and get enough supplies before you start to work. Check over this inventory list of basic supplies that you are likely to require:

Ball-point and/or felt-tipped pens
Carbon paper sheets or packs
Cellophane tape and dispenser
Copyholder
Correction fluid or tape
Date stamp and pad
Desk calendar
Dictionary
Dustcloth
Envelopes
Erasers
Erasing shield
Good paper for second and
    succeeding pages of a letter
Index cards
Interoffice stationery
Letter opener

Machine oil
Memo pads
Onionskin paper for copies
Paper clips
Pencil sharpener
Pencils
Pertinent reference books
Plain low-quality paper for drafts
Razor blades
Requisition forms
Rubber bands
Rubber cement
Ruler
Scissors
Stapling machine and staples
Telephone message forms
Thumbtacks

TYPEWRITER CARE

Equipment that works well makes life easier for you. Therefore, it is to your advantage to keep what you use in good running order. Your typewriter takes a lot of pounding day in and day out. Here are some hints for keeping it running at peak efficiency:

1   Just before you leave the office each day:

   a   Clean ink and dirt from the type bars with a bristle brush.
   b   Clean other parts of the machine with a long-handle brush.
   c   Clean underneath the machine with a cloth or brush.
   d   Move the carriage to center position for safety.
   e   Cover the typewriter.

2   Periodically (at least once a month or when needed):

   a   Wipe the cylinder with a clean cloth dampened with alcohol.
   b   Oil carriage rails and other parts of the machine as recommended by the manufacturer.
   c   Check the condition of the ribbon. If it needs to be changed, replace it, following the manufacturer's directions carefully.

REVIEWING YOUR READING

1   As a beginning office worker what information would you need to know concerning your general daily performance? Where would you get this information?
2   Demonstrate or explain how general information about your job assignment should be kept for future reference.
3   If your boss asked you to look into a complaint received from an established customer regarding a late shipment, what kind of information about the company's operations would help you to check on the customer's order?
4   What are the elements that add up to personal efficiency?

OFFICE ASSIGNMENTS

1   Type the list of supplies on page 356 on a sheet of paper 4¼ by 5½ inches. When you report for work on your first job, take this list along. It will be a handy way to check to see if you have the supplies you need each morning.

2   **a**   A daily routine for the care of your typewriter is outlined above. On an 8½- by 11-inch sheet of paper type a copy of this routine. Then paste it inside the front cover of your workbook (if you are using one), tape it to your desk, or post it on a bulletin board near your work area.
   b   List three things which you should do to your typewriter periodically in order to keep it in good working condition.

Courtesy Acme Visible Records, Inc.

3 The employees at the work station illustrated above are responding to tele-phone inquiries requesting inventory balances and unit prices. How does the work layout reflect the application of the efficiency ideas of Terry and Mogensen with regard to **(a)** economy of motions? **(b)** division of work load? **(c)** location of tools and equipment? **(d)** orderly arrangement of papers and supplies? **(e)** reduction in fatigue?

4 Study the efficiency guidelines presented in this section. Then:

   a Cite cases in which human relations are a vital element in improving the performance of an employee. Explain.

   b Point out instances in which constructive supervision might help to improve the performance of someone new on the job. Explain.

   c Explain how practical, on-the-job experience contributes to an employee's efficiency.

   d Explain why observing company policies can help you improve your efficiency.

   e Identify situations in which an employee's ingenuity can be an important contribution. Explain.

5 You may find that the guidelines presented in the text to improve personal efficiency will not always apply perfectly to a specific job situation. In this case you'll have to modify and adapt the guidelines to fit the given situation. Why not see if you can apply some of your judgment and ingenuity to the following problems.

   a Despite your best efforts, you cannot organize your work so that all of your assignments can be completed adequately and on time. There is just too much work and too little time. What would you do?

b You have worked hard to reduce interruptions, but new workers constantly come to you for instructions and suggestions about their work. In fact, you overheard your boss say to a new recruit: "I'm sure it won't take long for you to catch on, but if you have any questions, ask Mary. She knows more about the work than any of us!" Obviously, you'll never overcome your problem with interruptions if your supervisor persists in sending people to see you. What should you do?

c Your boss seems to have no pattern of priorities. Whatever is uppermost in his mind at the moment gets his attention first. You are never sure what to do first and dislike having to ask each time a new batch of work comes along. What can you do to help clarify the priorities that apply to your own work?

d What can you do in the 30 minutes after the final 4:30 p.m. mail pickup that will help you to get off to a head start on your work the next day? Is there anything you should be doing to help your boss prepare for tomorrow's activities?

e Your boss is not inclined to delegate assignments or responsibilities to you that you are capable of undertaking. As a result, your boss is overworked and always behind schedule. In fact, some of the work gets buried under other papers and is delayed for an inexcusable length of time. Is there anything you can or should do to improve the situation?

SECTION 28 Resources to Know

No matter how structured and defined your job is, you'll find that sometimes you'll have special assignments to handle. Sometimes you'll be given specific information for your assignment; other times you'll have to exercise initiative and research the information yourself. You'll do the job more quickly and productively if you have some idea of where to go to find the information you are looking for.

The list that follows includes some of the resources used most frequently by office workers. Many of the publications may already be in your possession. Other publications may be in your company library. Still others can be found in your public library. When you can, look through these publications to get a general idea of what information they include. The more familiar you are with such resource material, the more quickly and authoritatively you can come up with answers.

ACCOUNTING PRINCIPLES AND PROCEDURES

Federal Tax Handbook, Prentice-Hall, Inc., Englewood Cliffs, N.J.
Handbook for Auditors, McGraw-Hill Book Company, New York.
Handbook of Modern Accounting, McGraw-Hill Book Company, New York.

Income Tax Regulations, Commerce Clearing House, Inc., New York.
The Journal of Accountancy, American Institute of Certified Public Accountants, New York.

ADDRESSES AND TELEPHONE NUMBERS

City directories. Some cities have a directory of residents that gives their occupations and certain other information as well as addresses.
Congressional Directory, U.S. Government Printing Office, Washington.
Telephone directories—regular and classified.

BANKS AND BANKING

The American Institute of Banking offers many publications to serve the specialized needs of bank personnel. Other important sources of related information are bank research departments, trade associations, and government agencies.

BIBLIOGRAPHIES

Applied Science & Technology Index, The H. W. Wilson Company, New York.
Books in Print, R. R. Bowker Company, New York.
Business Periodical Index, The H. W. Wilson Company, New York.
The New York Times Index, The New York Times Company, New York.
Readers' Guide to Periodical Literature, The H. W. Wilson Company, New York.

BIOGRAPHIES

Current Biography, The H. W. Wilson Company, New York.
The New York Times Biographical Edition, The New York Times Company, New York.
The New York Times Obituaries Index, The New York Times Company, New York.
The New York Times Oral History Program, Microfilming Corporation of America, Glen Rock, N.J.
Webster's Biographical Dictionary, G. & C. Merriam Company, Springfield, Mass.
Who's Who in America, Marquis—Who's Who, Inc., Chicago.
Who's Who in Finance and Industry, Marquis—Who's Who, Inc., Chicago.

BUSINESS—GENERAL

Ayer Directory of Publications, N. W. Ayer & Son, Inc., Philadelphia.
Business Management Handbook, McGraw-Hill Book Company, New York.
Business Week (magazine), McGraw-Hill Publishing Company, New York.
Dun's Review (magazine), Dun and Bradstreet Publications, Inc., New York.
Fortune (magazine), Time, Inc., Chicago.
Harvard Business Review (magazine), Harvard Graduate School of Business Administration, Boston.

Journal of Business (magazine), The University of Chicago Press, Chicago.
The Journal of Commerce (newspaper), Eric Ridder, Sr., New York.
The Kiplinger Washington Letter, Kiplinger Washington Editors, Inc., Washington.
The New York Times (newspaper), The New York Times Company, New York.
Standard Rate and Data Services (provides advertising rates and circulation figures), Standard Rate and Data Services, Inc., Skokie, Ill.
Thomas Register of American Manufacturers, Thomas Publishing Company, Inc., New York.
Wall Street Journal (newspaper), Dow Jones & Co., Inc., New York.

COMMUNITY AND GOVERNMENT RELATIONS

Congressional Quarterly Guide to Current American Government, Congressional Quarterly, Inc., Washington.

COMPANY ACCOUNTING SYSTEMS

Company accounting manuals. Some firms supply manuals, which include charts of accounts, flowcharts, description of procedures, and format of reports.

COMPANY ORGANIZATION

Company manuals. These set forth the structure of company, identify divisions and personnel and levels of authority.

COMPUTATION TABLES

Standard tables. These are available in trade stationery and office supply houses.

CREDIT AND FINANCE

Barrons National Business & Financial Weekly, Dow Jones & Co., Inc., New York.
Dun & Bradstreet Reference Book, Dun and Bradstreet Publications, Inc., New York.
Moody's Banks and Finance Manual and *Moody's Industrial Manual*, Moody's Investors Service, Inc., New York.
Standard & Poor's Corporation Records, Standard & Poor's Corporation, McGraw-Hill, Inc., New York.
United States Government Organization Manual, U.S. Government Printing Office, Washington.

FREIGHT

Bullinger's Postal and Shippers Guide for the United States and Canada, Bullinger's Guides, Inc., Westwood, N.J.
Leonard's Guide and Service (available on a rental basis only), G. R. Leonard & Company, New York.

Leonard's Guide for Parcel Post, Express, Railroad, Motor Rates, and Routing, G. R. Leonard & Company, New York.

National Highway and Airway Carriers and Routes, National Highway Carriers Directory, Inc., Chicago.

National Motor Freight Classification, American Trucking Association, Washington.

Rand McNally World Atlas, Rand McNally & Company, Chicago.

GENERAL INFORMATION

Guide to Reference Books, American Library Association, Chicago.

Information Please Almanac, Atlas and Yearbook, Simon & Schuster, Inc., New York.

Statistical Abstract of the United States, U.S. Government Printing Office, Washington.

The World Almanac and Book of Facts, Doubleday & Company, Inc., Garden City, N.Y.

GRAMMAR AND STYLE

Business English and Communication, Stewart et al., Gregg Division, McGraw-Hill Book Company, New York.

A Manual of Style, The University of Chicago Press, Chicago.

Reference Manual for Stenographers and Typists, Gavin and Sabin, Gregg Division, McGraw-Hill Book Company, New York.

Standard Handbook for Secretaries, Hutchinson, Gregg Division, McGraw-Hill Book Company, New York.

MACHINE OPERATIONS

Manufacturers manuals. These are instruction manuals with data on operation, maintenance, parts, and supplementary supplies.

POSTAL DATA

Directory of International Mail, U.S. Government Printing Office, Washington.

Directory of Post Offices, U.S. Government Printing Office, Washington.

National ZIP Code Directory, U.S. Government Printing Office, Washington.

Postal Service Manual, U.S. Government Printing Office, Washington.

SALES

Companies issue material which consists of catalogs, price lists, and special announcements.

TRADE AND INDUSTRY NEWS

This type of material pertains to and is issued by members of a given trade, or industry. For example, people involved with administrative services might use the following reference material:

Administrative Management (magazine), Geyer-McAllister Publications, New York.
Office Administration Handbook, The Dartnell Corporation, Chicago.
Records Management Quarterly, American Records Management Association, Chicago.

TRAVEL

Hotel & Motel Red Book, American Hotel & Motel Association, New York.
Official Airline Guide, American Aviation Publishers, Inc., Washington.
Official Guide of the Railways, National Railway Publication Company, New York.

VOCABULARY—GENERAL

The American Heritage Dictionary of the English Language, American Heritage Publishing Co., Inc., New York.
Funk & Wagnalls New Standard Dictionary of the English Language, Funk & Wagnalls, Inc., New York.
Roget's International Thesaurus, Thomas Y. Crowell Company, New York.
10,000 Legal Words, Kurtz et al., Gregg Division, McGraw-Hill Book Company, New York.
10,000 Medical Words, Byers, Gregg Division, McGraw-Hill Book Company, New York.
20,000 Words, Leslie, Gregg Division, McGraw-Hill Book Company, New York.
Webster's New Collegiate Dictionary, 8th ed., G. & C. Merriam Company, Springfield, Mass.
Webster's Third New International Dictionary, G. & C. Merriam Company, Springfield, Mass.

VOCABULARY—TECHNICAL

Black's Law Dictionary, West Publishing Company, St. Paul, Minn.
Blakiston's New Gould Medical Dictionary, McGraw-Hill Book Company, New York.
Dictionary for Accountants, Prentice-Hall, Inc., Englewood Cliffs, N.J.
Dictionary of Arts and Artists, Penguin Books, Inc., Baltimore.
Dorland's Illustrated Medical Dictionary, W. B. Saunders Company, Philadelphia.
Hackh's Chemical Dictionary, McGraw-Hill Book Company, New York.
Webster's Geographical Dictionary, G. & C. Merriam Company, Springfield, Mass.

REVIEWING YOUR READING

1   Some reference books are supplied to individual workers; other books have to be shared. Wouldn't it be easier if everyone were completely equipped with all the references he could possibly need? Explain.
2   How does a knowledge of resource materials help you perform efficiently in your position?

OFFICE ASSIGNMENTS

1   Here is an entry taken from *Webster's New Collegiate Dictionary*, eighth edition, a popular reference book for secretaries, stenographers, and typists. Study the illustration, and answer the following questions:

busi·ness \'biz-nəs, -nəz\ *n, often attrib* **1** *archaic* : purposeful activity : BUSYNESS **2 a** : ROLE, FUNCTION <how the human mind went about its ~ of learning —H. A. Overstreet> **b** : an immediate task or objective : MISSION <what is your ~ here at this hour> **c** : a particular field of endeavor <the best in the ~> **3 a** : a usu. commercial or mercantile activity engaged in as a means of livelihood : TRADE, LINE <in the ~ of supplying emergency services to industry> **b** : a commercial or sometimes an industrial enterprise <sold his ~ and retired>; *also* : such enterprises <~ seldom acts as a unit> **c** : usu. economic dealings : PATRONAGE <ready to take his ~ elsewhere unless service improved> **4** : AFFAIR, MATTER <a strange ~> **5** : movement or action (as lighting a cigarette) by an actor intended esp. to establish atmosphere, reveal character or explain a situation — called also *stage business* **6 a** : personal concern <none of your ~> **b** : RIGHT <you have no ~ hitting her> **7 a** : serious activity requiring time and effort and usu. the avoidance of distractions <immediately got down to ~> **b** : maximum effort **8 a** : a damaging assault **b** : a rebuke or tongue-lashing : a hard time **c** : DOUBLE CROSS
syn BUSINESS, COMMERCE, INDUSTRY, TRADE, TRAFFIC *shared meaning element* : activity concerned with the supplying and distribution of commodities

By permission. From Webster's New Collegiate Dictionary © 1974 by G. & C. Merriam Co., Publishers of the Merriam-Webster Dictionaries.

a   What part of speech is this word?
b   Which meanings are most frequently employed in business communications?
c   What does *syn* mean? List several that have been supplied.

2   Consult a city directory in your area in order to answer the questions listed below. If a city directory is not available in your community, consult the regular telephone directory.

a   Your boss wants to write to the county assessor. How will the letter be addressed?
b   You are told to mail a check in payment of county taxes to the county treasurer. Who is he, and how will you address the envelope?
c   You are asked to telephone the office of the county superintendent of schools. Who is he, and what is his telephone number?
d   You want to inquire about the availability of temporary extra help for the holiday season. Which public office will you call? What is the telephone number?

3   Your boss wants to know the names of the ten largest companies in *Fortune's* list of the top 500 business firms in the country. How will you locate the information? What are the names and addresses of the companies?

4   Your boss wants to know if there is a nonstop flight from Atlanta to Baltimore on Saturday afternoon. Because there is no travel agent or airline ticket office in your town, you consult the official airline guide shown at the top of page 365.

Leave	Arrive	Flight	Stops or Via	Meals F Y/YL	Remarks	Leave	Arrive	Flight	Stops or Via	Meals F Y/YL	Remarks
Atlanta, Ga. to:				Reservations: 435-1111	Air Freight: 432-4281	**Antigua, West Indies**—F $181 Y $146					
						11 30a	5 33p	961/775	San Juan	M- M-	
Acapulco, Mexico—F $159 Y $124						**Aruba, Netherlands Antilles**—F $219 Y $172					
12 15p	1 40p	919	NONSTOP	M M	Sa Su	11 30a	6 40p	961	Two-stop	M M	
Akron/Canton, Ohio—F $67 Y $51						**Baltimore, Md.**—F $68 Y $53 YN $41					
3 25p	7 20p	336/300	Pittsburgh	- - - -		9 30a	10 55a	138	NONSTOP	- -	
Allentown/Bethlehem/Easton, Pa.—F $81 Y $62						3 10p	4 41p	134	NONSTOP	S S	
12 35p	3 26p	146	One-stop	M M		6 39p	8 12p	132	NONSTOP	M M	
3 15p	7 29p	380/176	Washington	S- S-	Ex Sa Su	10 05p	11 27p	126	NONSTOP	- -	NC
3 15p	7 29p	136/176	Washington	- - - -	Sa Su	**Barbados, West Indies**—F $244 Y $192					
						11 30a	5 38p	961/947	San Juan	MS MS	

•• Operates daily except Saturday.   △ Operates daily except Sunday.   Light face (9:30) indicates A.M. Bold face **(9:30)** indicates P.M.

Courtesy Eastern Air Lines Incorporated

UNIT 11

BUSINESS CASES AND PROBLEMS

In the Boss's Shoes   As a general typist in the sales department you are expected to confirm the spelling and accuracy of the names and addresses of prospective customers before mailing promotional literature to them. Your boss has also asked you to insert current prices and stock numbers in letters responding to requests for bids. This prevents you from being as productive as you would like to be. Should you tactfully suggest to the boss that he provide all of the information in the first place so that you can concentrate on your typing?

Your Human Relations   A worker who occupies a desk nearby is constantly borrowing your desk reference materials and usually fails to return them. He seems to have mislaid his own set of these items a long time ago. Should you continue to let him impose upon you indefinitely? If not, should you ask him to end this practice?

What Would You Do If . . . ?   Your supervisor tells you that you have completed your probationary employment period satisfactorily and are soon to be assigned to a position as a general typist in the office of the company's weekly newspaper. Should you order some special reference books on editing and publishing operations so that you will be fully equipped when you report for work?

What Does This Mean?   Each clerical worker must know where to find the specialized information that his full- or part-time job or assignment requires.

Business in Your Area   Visit some offices in your community to find out what kinds of reference materials are used by various clerical workers. Select different types and sizes of businesses such as a bank, a public utility, a government agency, a department store, and a lawyer's office.

UNIT 12
BUSINESS
WRITING

SECTION 29 Handling Correspondence

Since millions of letters and written communications are exchanged each year in the process of doing business, you will want to know about the most current methods for handling business correspondence.

TYPES OF BUSINESS LETTERS

As a beginning clerical worker, you will probably be handling correspondence that has already been written rather than originating the correspondence yourself. You will receive written instructions on how to perform your work—instructions which may be in the form of an office procedures manual. You will also receive announcements, bulletins, reports, and special messages about new company procedures. Once you are assigned to work in mail, filing, duplicating, sales, or purchasing operations, you will be directly involved in the communications process. You will soon learn that virtually every phase of business activity is controlled or expedited by the written word. In a single day's work you may see one or more of these types of business letters:

- *Sales letters* sell goods or services.
- *Public relations letters* build up a firm's reputation or prestige.
- *Inquiry letters* request information such as prices and delivery dates on goods and services.
- *Order letters* order merchandise or services.
- *Acknowledgment letters* acknowledge receipt of orders or inquiries.
- *Credit letters* obtain credit information about prospective customers in order to grant credit to them.
- *Referral letters* refer inquiries to the correct person for attention.
- *Thank-you letters* thank customers and others for their patronage or favors.
- *Adjustment letters* adjust errors or settle misunderstandings between buyers and sellers.
- *Collection letters* request payment of accounts when overdue.
- *Employment letters* are applications for employment or invite an applicant to call for an interview.

ROUTINE REPLIES

As you become more experienced in office procedures, you may be assigned increased responsibilities in connection with correspondence. A typist is often called on to help speed up replies to routine, repetitive correspondence involving inquiries and orders. In such a procedure the supervisor reads or scans each incoming inquiry, then makes a notation on the letter telling the typist the name or code number of the form reply to use.

Form Letters

Information covering routine situations and answers to common inquiries can be quickly and efficiently handled by form letters. If the Acme Data Processing Center wants to invite a large number of prospective customers to a special demonstration, a letter, such as the one illustrated here, is composed and duplicated on an offset or other type of office duplicator. Then a skilled typist, work-

---

Acme Data Processing Center

2418 Center Avenue
St. Louis, Missouri 63136

June 11, 19--

Mr. Gregory H. Lewis
Business Manager
B-Z Machines, Inc.
407 St. Paul Street
Newark, New Jersey 07110

Dear Mr. Lewis:

You are cordially invited to join me at the National Machine Accountants Association conference June 19-21 to see the first public demonstration of our B260 punched-card computer system. We have arranged for special press demonstrations beginning at 11 a.m. on June 19, two hours before the scheduled opening of the conference, in the Washington Room of the Statler Hilton in New York.

If you should find it more convenient, we would be happy to have you join us at the same hour on either Wednesday or Thursday of that week. If you drop by the Washington Room for the demonstration, we then can move to our hospitality suite in the hotel for discussions away from the busy atmosphere of the exhibit area.

If your plans will allow, we also would appreciate having you as our guest for lunch on whichever of the three days you find it most convenient to drop by. Although we have planned no formal presentation, we think that we have some significant things to say about the role of the manufacturer in bringing electronic data processing results to the businessman at a price he can afford.

Please advise me if you can plan to attend by returning the enclosed postcard.

Sincerely,

Ken T. Bement

Ken T. Bement
Vice President, Marketing

KTB:mm
Enclosure

ing from a mailing list or card file, fills in the date, inside address, and personal salutation. She is very careful to match these items and other fill-ins with the type size used for the rest of the letter. If the body of the letter is in elite type, she uses elite for the fill-ins; if the body is in pica type, she uses pica for the fill-ins. The more personal the letter looks, the better impression it makes on the customer.

By using form letters, the company can send the customer a quick notice at the lowest possible cost and in a fraction of the time required to process an individually typed letter. Form letters can even look more personal when they are individually signed.

Sometimes it is very important that a letter appear to be individually typed. In order to do this and to avoid having to type each letter separately, you can use an automatic typewriter. Messages can easily be prepared on paper tape, magnetic tape, or a card, depending on the kind of machine used. You insert the individual letterhead in the machine, type in the date, inside address, and salutation, and then let the machine do the rest. Guided by the tape or card, the machine automatically types the body of the letter, the complimentary closing, the writer's identification, reference initials, and the enclosure notation. It looks exactly like an individually typed letter because it *is* individually typed. The time for the whole job from start to finish is approximately two minutes.

Form Paragraphs

Sometimes a routine reply will have to be adapted to a particular situation. You can do this easily by combining or rearranging several form paragraphs. Simply type the paragraphs in the sequence in which your supervisor has numbered them.

When an automatic typewriter unit is available, the standard paragraphs can be stored on a tape. You set the selector device to pick out the paragraphs desired, and the machine types them automatically in the proper sequence.

Courtesy Royal Typewriter Company

When the selector device is set, this automatic typewriter types only the paragraphs designated by the operator.

Form Postcards

With form postcards you can immediately dispatch brief and standardized replies. As a rule the text of the message is designed so that the variable data can be filled in on the form. Sometimes a rubber stamp can be used to supply the variable information, such as an expected delivery date. Postcards eliminate the need for envelopes, simplify certain mailing operations, and save on postage.

Check Sheets and Cards

The check sheet or card is another method of handling large amounts of correspondence quickly and economically. A number of stock answers to common questions are listed on a single sheet. The statement that answers a customer's question is checked on the sheet. The customer notes the checked statement and simply ignores the unchecked ones.

Printed Messages

Sometimes when thousands of similar messages have to be sent out, the date, address, and salutation fill-ins are eliminated. In such cases a standard printed notice or message is used to save money and time. It may be printed on regular letterhead paper, on postcards, or on odd-sized memorandum sheets. The primary objective is to deliver the message. It is assumed that the recipient will not object to the absence of a personalized address as long as she finds out what she wants to know as quickly as possible.

Reply Blanks

In addition to using low-cost techniques to respond to his customer, the business-man employs easy ways in which the customer can reply to him.

For example, postage-paid reply cards are designed so that the customer has to spend as little time as possible responding to the correspondence. Sometimes

---

PARSON DISTRIBUTORS
998 Olmstead Avenue
Bronx, New York 10473

Dear Customer:

Your recently placed catalog order is as follows:

☐ _____ No Longer Available.

☑ _____ Out of Stock until

___ *5/17/—* ___ . If you would like to reorder this
merchandise, please call customer service, 555-5142,
on the date the merchandise can be reordered.

Catalog Department

A check card communicates information quickly and efficiently.

```
┌─────────────────────────────────────────────────────────────┐
│           OCCUPATIONAL OUTLOOK HANDBOOK REPRINTS              │
│              FOR JOBS DISCUSSED IN THIS PAMPHLET              │
```

Employment Outlook for	Bulletin No.	Price (each)	How Many	Total Cost
Dental Hygienist, Dental Assistant	1650-8	15¢	____	____
Registered Nurse	1650-9	15¢	____	____
Medical Laboratory Worker	1650-16	10¢	____	____
Radiologic Technologist	1650-17	10¢	____	____
Engineering and Science Technician, Draftsman	1650-27	15¢	____	____
Commercial Artist, Interior Designer and Decorator	1650-30	15¢	____	____
Forestry Aid	1650-31	15¢	____	____
Library Technician	1650-36	15¢	____	____
Actor, Actress, Dancer, Musician, Singer	1650-39	15¢	____	____
Surveyor	1650-46	10¢	____	____
Television and Radio Service Technician	1650-89	10¢	____	____
Occupational Outlook Handbook	1650	$6.25	____	____
		TOTAL COST		____

A customer can easily complete this printed order blank.

Enclosed find $_____ (check, money order made payable to Superintendent of Documents, Washington, D.C.   20402)

U. S. Government Printing Office

all he has to do is to sign the card and drop it into the nearest mailbox. The information on the card explains what the customer wants.

The familiar order blank is another way of helping the customer to complete his order quickly and clearly. It is designed to minimize the possibility of the customer's forgetting to indicate the quantity, color, size, or some other information, regarding his order. Space is provided on the blank for each of these important details. When the completed form arrives at the supplier's office, it can be processed speedily because procedures have been devised to handle each item of information on the form and every member of the office staff knows where to look on the order form for what he needs to know.

REVIEWING YOUR READING

1 Demonstrate how a skilled typist can make a form letter look more personal.
2 Explain or demonstrate why a form postcard message is more efficient to use than a regular form letter.
3 Compare a form paragraph message and a printed message in terms of efficiency, cost, and personal touch.
4 Obtain three or more samples of reply blanks or mail-order forms that are used by business in your area. Explain or demonstrate how the customer is supposed to complete them.
5 Assume that the customer reply blanks, discussed in question 4, have been completed and sent to the suppliers. Explain or demonstrate how orders in the form of reply blanks can be processed by suppliers more efficiently than orders in the form of letters.

OFFICE ASSIGNMENTS

1 Assume that you have received the following stencil-duplicated form letter. Evaluate it as a model of a quick, inexpensive, adequate, and attractive reply to your request for a catalog, a price list, and discount information.

WESTERN SYSTEMS CORP. 484 Market Street, San Francisco, California 94111

Dear Customer:

Thank you for your interest in our products. So that we may serve you more promptly, we are replying to your communication in this manner. The volume of mail we receive would make a prompt reply impossible if we adhered to the procedure of typing a formal reply.

☑ Literature enclosed.

☐ Enclosed order form lists Photo-Vu reels and packets available.

☐ Use the enclosed order form to order merchandise direct from Western Systems Corp. Please list the name of your Photo-Vu dealer.

☐ Please enclose remittance with order. We do not make COD shipments. Postage is prepaid.

☐ The item about which you inquired has been discontinued by Western Systems Corp.

☐ The price of the item about which you inquired is $_____.

☐ Photo-Vu reels cannot be produced from negatives, prints, or 35mm transparencies.

☐ Send 25 cents for complete Slide Catalog, which lists the foreign subjects available and the individual subjects included in each sleeve. Sample slide included.

☑ *Sorry, no special school discount.* _____

_____

_____

Western Systems Corp.
Consumer Photo Division

2 Explain how the message in the form letter illustrated in Office Assignment 1 could have been made more personal. Type the letter in a more personal form, and note how long it takes you to revise and retype the letter.

3 Assume that you have just received the following offset-duplicated form letter. Evaluate it as a quick, informative, inexpensive, efficient, and attractive response to your request for an estimate of repairs.

CAMERA SALES CORPORATION OF AMERICA
EASTERN REGIONAL OFFICE
113 Hudson Street
New York, New York 10013
212-555-3090

NAME: *Dr. Emily Pratt*   DATE: *1/11/—*

ADDRESS: *305 East 15 Street*   OUR NO.: *21550*

New York, New York 10003   CUSTOMER'S NO.: _____

Dear Customer:

We are in receipt of your Model *TR-368* which you sent to us for an estimate.

The charges required to restore your unit(s) to proper working condition are as follows:

PARTS $ _____   R E M A R K S

LABOR   *5.00*

TAX   *.35*

SHIPPING   *1.50*

TOTAL $ *6.85*

If you would like us to proceed with this repair, please sign and return this form to CAMERA SALES CORPORATION OF AMERICA at the above address, together with your remittance (check or money order; no cash, please).

IMPORTANT: If we do not hear from you within the next three weeks, your merchandise will be returned, unrepaired, freight collect.

Thank you for your cooperation.

Sincerely,

Judy L. Judson

Judy L. Judson

CUSTOMER'S COMMENT OR INSTRUCTION: _____

_____

IN ORDER TO CLAIM WARRANTY, PLEASE REMIT ORIGINAL SALES RECEIPT.

( ) Check this box if you have a charge account with us and if you wish to be billed.

YOUR SIGNATURE _____

NOTE: When your merchandise is ready, you will receive a postcard in the mail. All repairs take approximately ten working days.

---

4 Prepare an improved version of the form letter shown in Office Assignment 3. On the reverse side of your completed work indicate why you considered each major change to be desirable.

30 Composing Business Letters and Memorandums

Although a large percentage of business correspondence involves form letters, every mail delivery contains letters that require individual replies. As you progress in your job, you may have to write some of these letters. By that time, however, you will have worked on routine form letters and will have been exposed to many different kinds of business communications. By then you will also know a good deal about the company's policies and procedures.

ANSWERING INQUIRIES

You will be assigned to answer more complex inquiries when you have demonstrated competence in handling the mail. This assignment could mean a promotion and a raise as well as a chance to show your judgment and initiative.

When the opportunity comes, keep these tips in mind:

1 Understand exactly the limits of your authority and responsibility.
2 Make sure you understand all company policies and procedures relating to the subject of the letter.
3 Know where to find the facts you need about the customer as well as your company and its products or services.
4 Be sure to examine all related documents, notes, instructions, and references.
5 If you are not exactly sure about what to do, look in the files for samples of previous correspondence relating to similar situations.
6 If you still have any doubts, ask your supervisor to clarify things for you. Make a note of any directions or suggestions for future use.
7 Plan what you are going to write before you start writing. If necessary, prepare a rough draft of the message, edit it, and then type the final copy.
8 Each time you finish a new assignment, make a photocopy of the inquiry and your reply for future reference. Be sure to note any ideas for improvement for the next time.

ORGANIZING YOUR IDEAS

Many writers find that it's an excellent idea to outline their ideas before they begin to write. This enables them to organize their thoughts better and also helps them to see the subject as a whole and to understand the relative importance of points to be made. The outline's headings and subheadings (which you learned to arrange in Section 14) represent the key ideas in the sentences and paragraphs that make up the letter. Outlines need not be formal or elaborate. They take only a small amount of time to prepare and help you turn out superior communications.

For example, an outline for the simple request letter illustrated on page 377 might be prepared as follows:

1   Request a copy of the "Paper Selection Guide."
2   Refer to *The Business Executive*, October.
3   Enclose a self-addressed, stamped envelope.

EFFECTIVE LETTER QUALITIES

As you read, sort, classify, or perform any process dealing with business letters, you will note that some letters are easier than others to handle or to understand. The really effective letters—the ones that get the point across more readily—come from writers who know how to write a good business letter. Here are some tips:

☐ *Be brief.* Say what needs to be said and then stop.
☐ *Be complete.* Include all information the recipient needs to know so that he understands what he is supposed to do.
☐ *Be clear.* Say what you want to say in a simple and direct way.
☐ *Be accurate.* Give correct facts and figures. Use correct spelling, punctuation, and grammar according to an accepted style.
☐ *Be courteous.* Show good manners by being considerate and helpful in your letter. These qualities are as important in letters as they are in speech.

GUIDE LETTERS

Some firms supply correspondence trainees with guide letters or model letters to follow. However, you do not copy these letters word for word as you do with form letters. Guide letters are to show you how similar situations were successfully handled in the past. You then make your own adaptation of the guide to fit the situation at hand.

Some office correspondence manuals suggest that you present your ideas in a specified order. A sales letter, for instance, might follow the paragraph order shown here:

1   Attract the prospect's attention.
2   Stimulate his interest.
3   Arouse his desire for the product.
4   Move the prospect to take action.

Sometimes you are given just an informal checklist of ideas and suggestions to follow from which you can adapt your own letter to suit the particular circumstances. The point is that when you're writing individual letters, you should have some format to guide you.

PLANNING A LETTER

If you must write letters and have no guides to follow, use the newspaper reporter's approach. Study the situation, and identify the essential elements: *what, when, where, who, why,* and *how.* Once you know what you want to say, figure out how you want to say it. How do you start? What do you say next? Then after that? And finally, how do you close?

Still another approach to creative writing suggests that the writer visualize the situation. Let's say you want to compose an appropriate thank-you letter. First think about how you would thank the individual if you were to walk into his office, in person. You might say: "Good morning, Mr. Jones. Thank you for sending the new price list so promptly. It reached me the very next day. I certainly appreciate your cooperation." Or ask yourself how you would say thank you on the telephone. Perhaps you'd say: "Good morning, Mr. Jones, this is Helen Mack of Parson Distributors. I called to thank you for sending the new price list so promptly. It reached me the very next day. I certainly appreciate your cooperation." Does it sound very much the same? Of course it does because it is the same situation, and you are simply using a few well-chosen words to say thank you promptly and courteously. Once you visualize the situation, all you have to do is put the words down on paper.

Dear Mr. Jones:

Thank you for sending the new price list so promptly. It reached me the very next morning. I certainly appreciate your cooperation.

Cordially yours,

Not much different, is it?

KINDS OF BUSINESS LETTERS

As a junior correspondent you'll be expected to answer many different kinds of letters. Here are some typical examples.

Acknowledgment Letter

An acknowledgment letter is written to show courtesy, to avoid misunderstanding, and to provide a record. It should clearly indicate *what* is being acknowledged, and it should *thank* the other party for what he has done. The letter should also indicate whether any *further action* is to be taken. Try to make your acknowledgment express sincere interest, and if it is appropriate, express your desire to help.

Suppose Mr. Smith, an engineering consultant, has just submitted a special laboratory report. Your boss directs you to acknowledge the receipt of the report in his behalf and to tell Mr. Smith that he will receive more instructions in a few days. Your boss wants a little time to study the findings very carefully. Bearing these various facts in mind and using the reporter's approach or the visualization method, you may produce a letter like this:

Dear Mr. Smith:

Your laboratory report of November 7 was received today. Thank you for sending it. Your prompt service exceeded our most optimistic hopes. In a few days, after we have studied your findings, you will receive further instructions.

Sincerely yours,

Compare this draft with the description of what a letter of acknowledgment should be. Notice that the first sentence specifically states *what* is being acknowledged (the laboratory report); the second and third sentences express appreciation and *thanks* for the unusually fast service; and the last sentence indicates the *further action* to be taken.

Evaluating your work in this way helps you to check to see that your letter does a *complete* job. If the message you propose to write doesn't meet the requirements of an acknowledgment letter, modify it or rewrite it until it does. Many people make several drafts before they produce the letter that does the job right.

Request Letter

All letters have similar characteristics, but a characteristic — or rather a requirement — of a request letter is that it be *brief, complete,* and *tactful.*

> Gentlemen:
>
> Please send me a copy of your "Paper Selection Guide" as advertised in the October issue of *The Business Executive.*
>
> A stamped, self-addressed envelope is enclosed for your convenience.
>
> Sincerely yours,

The reply to a request letter should include answers to *all* the questions asked. In some instances it should furnish other important information even if it is not asked for. Use an opening that acknowledges the request letter in order to establish a rapport or to provide the recipient with a point of reference.

> Dear Mr. Daly:
>
> Our brochure, entitled "Paper Selection Guide," is being sent to you with our compliments. Your copy should reach you in a few days.
>
> Thank you for your interest, and please write again if we can be of any further help.
>
> Cordially yours,

Referral Letter

A referral letter acknowledges receipt of the original message and explains why the matter is being referred to someone else for attention. It should certainly mention if there will be any possible delay in the final reply. For example, the reply will be delayed if the person to whom the original letter is being referred is absent from the office. In particular, a referral letter should make the recipient feel that the additional attention which his inquiry will receive will more than compensate for the slightest delay caused by the referral.

> Dear Mr. Brown:
>
> Thank you for your letter of November 25, in which you requested instructions for the installation of your Model XB-6 air conditioner.

Recent modifications in design have made it necessary to print new instruction sheets which have not yet reached this office. Therefore, your request has been relayed by wire to our home office for attention by Mr. Olson, Chief of Customer Services.

You may expect to hear directly from Mr. Olson within a few days.

                                        Sincerely yours,

Thank-You Letter

Such letters identify the service or favor that has been done, indicate the writer's appreciation, and if appropriate, state a willingness to be of equal service. It should convey sincere gratitude and in some cases include a personal touch. Needless to say, a thank-you letter should be sent promptly.

Dear Ralph:

Thank you for your permission to quote from your article in the October issue of *Economic Outlook*. It contains the best discussion of business cycles that our technical staff has read.

As you know, we expect to use excerpts from this article in preparing our quarterly report to the stockholders. We shall send you a copy of the report when it is finished. It may prove helpful in connection with your latest special research project.

                                        Sincerely yours,

Follow-Up Letter

Many letters are written to keep the recipients up to date on developments in a given area. They are not necessarily direct replies to inquiries. Several weeks earlier a customer's order may have been acknowledged but remains unfilled. As a courtesy the follow-up letter reports the latest estimated delivery date so that the customer will not be kept wondering.

Gentlemen:

You may expect to receive the goods on your Order 649 of June 3 within the next five days.

New stock has arrived at our distribution center and orders are already being filled. Your shipment will be packed in time for dispatch by motor freight on Friday afternoon, July 12. The carrier has promised delivery the following morning in time for weekend sales promotion.

Thank you for waiting so patiently.

                                        Sincerely yours,

Order Letter

Like the request letter an order letter should include a simple request and then a detailed description of the items required, including quantity, price, catalog number, name, and special characteristics such as color, size, and so on. The order letter should also indicate accurately shipping instructions, terms, or discount. When the order letter is concise, complete, and accurate, it simplifies clerical procedures tremendously all along the way.

Gentlemen:

Please ship the following merchandise at once via Rogers Express on 2/10 net 30 day terms, FOB your plant.

6	X174 Motor units, ½ horsepower	@ $40
14	A6B1 Cabinets, yellow, brass trim	@ $25
	less 40 percent trade discount	

This equipment is for a special job. Make no substitutions, please.

Thank you.

Sincerely yours,

INTEROFFICE MEMORANDUMS

All of the business writing situations discussed so far in this unit have involved communications between the company and an outside party. Actually, many business letters are exchanged between employees or between units of the same company. These written messages are called interoffice memorandums and cover situations or problems similar to those previously discussed. For example, the sales manager may send a letter of inquiry to the chief engineer. The latter then acknowledges the inquiry and supplies the answer and any other necessary information. As in all business correspondence, interoffice memorandums should be courteous, efficient, clear, and accurate. In fact, routine interoffice messages may be prepared on the typewriter in the same way as regular correspondence. However, it is common practice to use interoffice memorandum forms which are designed for dispatch within the company only.

Interoffice memorandums are efficient to use because:

1   They use a simplified heading rather than the typical inside address and salutation used in outside correspondence.
2   The subject of the memorandum is listed in the heading so that the recipient can easily identify, scan, and route the material.
3   The introductory and closing paragraphs that are used in outside correspondence are eliminated.
4   A simple, individual signature (some firms use only initials) is used in place of a complimentary closing, corporate name, and so on.
5   They are generally printed on inexpensive stationery and are also available in ready-made carbon packs which help you save time.
6   These forms are adaptable for mass distribution when they are prepared as fluid, stencil, or offset masters.

Interoffice memorandums are distributed by messenger or by conveyor, chute, or tube systems. In most instances the written interoffice memorandum is better than verbal instruction. It provides a written record which prevents any misunderstanding of orders or instructions and is a reminder to the addressee who is temporarily absent.

REVIEWING YOUR READING

1 Explain why a writer needs to understand the limits of his authority, company policies and procedures, and facts about the company before he can compose business letters.

2 How and where could a correspondent gather facts in order to answer an inquiry about a delayed or lost shipment?

3 Demonstrate or explain how you would outline a letter acknowledging receipt of a customer's order for $100 worth of goods accompanied by his check for $50 in partial payment. The merchandise will be shipped in five days by bus package express as requested. The balance of the amount due is payable thirty days after shipment.

4 Demonstrate or explain how you would use the visualization method to compose a letter to an allergy-minded customer who has asked some technical questions about the ingredients of a hand cream sold by your company. Tell him that his inquiry has been referred to the firm's chief chemist at the factory and that a full reply may be expected within ten days.

5 Demonstrate or explain how you would use the reporter's approach to compose a follow-up letter to Mr. John L. Rogers, a customer. The central air-conditioning unit ordered for his new house in Hillside Estates is on its way from the factory via motor freight and will be installed within a week or ten days. The exact date and time for installation will be set by telephone. You will phone the customer when the unit reaches your warehouse.

OFFICE ASSIGNMENTS

In the following assignments you are a typist in the imaginary firm of Reliable Products Company, 512 Spring Street, Akron, Ohio 44304. Your employer is David R. Buckland, who is in charge of the office services department. Mr. Buckland prefers that you use the full-blocked letter style with open punctuation.

1 *Request letter.* Mr. Buckland found the following magazine advertisement and has asked you to write a letter requesting the bulletin.

BB Post, a quarterly bulletin of postal information and items of human interest about mailing, is available on request from Browne-Bowes, Inc. The publication is illustrated and contains six pages. Write to the Editor, *BB Post*, P.O. Box 741, Stafford, Ohio 43786.

2 *Acknowledgment letter.* Mr. Buckland has been out of town for a few days, but he will be back next Tuesday. Today you received a letter from John R. Fulton, Office Manager of the Whitcomb Supply Company, 821 Spring Street, Jackson, Michigan 49202. Accompanying the letter was a copy of the

Whitcomb Supply Company's Office Procedures Manual. Acknowledge receipt of the letter and the manual.

3   *Referral letter.* Mr. Buckland has received a letter from George A. Mooney of the Miller Equipment Company, 608 Linwood Avenue, N.W., Canton, Ohio 44708, requesting credit information concerning Robert Carter of 88 Marlowe Avenue, Akron, Ohio 44313. Mr. Edwin A. Parrish of the home office in Cleveland, Ohio 44115 (100 Midland Building) has charge of credit information. Write a letter telling Mr. Mooney that you are referring his letter to Mr. Parrish.

4   *Order letter.* Mr. Buckland asks you to write a letter ordering the following:

1 doz.	No. 2074	Adding machine tape 2½" roll	@ $2.37 per dozen
6 qrs.	No. 2251	Stencils, 8½" × 11" mimeograph	@ $2.80 per quire
6 boxes	No. 2091	Carbon paper, typewriter 8½" × 11" black 7 lb.	@ $ .94 per box

Order from the Martin Supply Company, 490 Sanford Avenue, Akron, Ohio 44305. Ask them to send the materials by parcel post.

5   *Letter in Reply to a Request.* Mr. Buckland has received a letter from Mr. Samuel Hill, General Manager, Stylecraft Wood Products, Inc., 1610 Lake Avenue, Hillsdale, Pennsylvania 15746, requesting the size, color, price, and delivery information on your line of metal folding tables. Tell him that you are sending a catalog under separate cover. Refer him to pages 10 to 12 for size and color data and to page 36 for delivery information. Mention that you are enclosing a current price list with your letter. Also tell him that some larger tables will be added to your line within the next two months. Inform him that you will send him a brochure describing the new items as soon as it is off the press.

UNIT 12

BUSINESS CASES AND PROBLEMS

In the Boss's Shoes   1   Peggy, the new typist, is trying hard to please. The letters that she completes are flawless, but she doesn't get much work done. You notice that her wastebasket is always full of letterheads and carbon packs that she has discarded because of mistakes.

As Peggy's supervisor should you continue to ignore this waste of time and materials? How do you correct her without discouraging her?

2 When you report to the correspondence unit for the first time, the supervisor asks you to let him have a copy of each letter that you write. He explains that he wants to keep track of everything that is going on, and he also wants to be able to make some helpful suggestions to you from time to time. This request takes you by surprise. In fact, you wonder if the boss has some reservations about your ability to do a good job. What should you do or say?

Your Human Relations 1 "Sure, you can use Jo's typewriter. She won't mind. Just move her papers to one side and make yourself at home. She keeps her supplies in the top drawer."

Does Jo's bighearted office neighbor have the right to invite someone else to use Jo's equipment and supplies when she is absent from her desk? If you were Jo, would you like it?

2 In your efforts to find out all the facts before responding to an inquiry, you have had to make many demands upon the centralized filing unit for documents, notes, and papers. You detect a feeling of increasing impatience toward you because you are taking up so much of their time. Should you abandon your search for the facts in the future? Or should you remind the filing personnel that they are being paid to find what you need?

What Would You Do If . . . ? 1 You notice that there is no check or other mark on a checklist type of response letter that your supervisor asked you to mail right away. He has left for lunch, saying that he might not be back for the rest of the afternoon.

2 You have made several drafts of a letter in reply to an involved inquiry, and the message still doesn't sound right. Should you mail your best effort and hope that everything will work out all right?

What Does This Mean? 1 There is no phase of business activity that is not controlled or expedited by the written word.

2 An opening that acknowledges a request might be appropriate in certain cases to establish a rapport or point of reference.

Business in Your Area 1 Ask your postmaster for the names and addresses of local firms or organizations that frequently mail form letters for selling or informational purposes. Then visit one of these firms to find out how their letters are planned, prepared, filled in, and mailed.

2 Office management trainees, junior supervisors, secretaries, and correspondents are frequently encouraged and sometimes required to participate in special training courses for the improvement of correspondence procedures. These courses may be offered on company premises during office hours, after hours, or at local schools in the evening. Some courses are even taken by mail. Find out how the largest local employers train their personnel in basic or more advanced correspondence procedures.

UNIT 13
CASH
CONTROL
SYSTEMS

31 Handling Incoming Funds

Many customers are permitted to charge their purchases and to pay their bills at the end of each month. Other customers pay cash with every order. Since the daily receipts of a business may total thousands of dollars, special provisions must be made for handling these funds accurately and safely.

Every sale and every purchase involves a payment of some kind. As a cashier it is your responsibility to handle the cash that constantly flows into and out of the business—an important responsibility since the company's success may well depend upon the safety and efficiency of the cash control procedures. To be a good cashier you have to be attentive to detail, check your work carefully before you turn it over to your co-workers and supervisors, and be completely trustworthy when you handle the money of others. First let's consider incoming funds, that is, money that flows into the company.

COUNTING

When money in the form of coins or bills is turned over to you, the first thing to do is to count it.

1 Make sure that your tabletop or desk top is clear so that the money will not get mixed with other papers or receipts.
2 Sort bills and coins into piles according to denominations.
3 Count each pile of bills first, and then count the coins. Record the amounts on a tally slip.
4 Verify the total of the tally slip by adding the amounts on a calculating machine with a tape. Then check the amounts on the tape against those on the tally slip.
5 Even if the tally amount agrees with the amount of the order, count the money once again for extra safety.
6 If there is any discrepancy, count the money again. If a shortage or excess is then confirmed, notify your supervisor or tell the customer if he is paying in person.

EXAMINING

Before placing bills or coins in the cash drawer, examine them to see if they are badly torn, damaged, foreign, or counterfeit. Torn and damaged bills can be repaired with cellophane tape. Report foreign and counterfeit bills and coins to your unit supervisor.

The U.S. Secret Service offers this advice to the person who receives counterfeit money:

☐ Do not return it.
☐ Telephone the police at once.

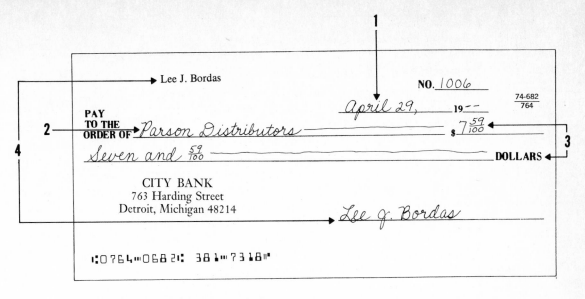

☐ Use some pretext to delay the passer.

☐ Avoid argument; if necessary, say that the police will handle the matter.

☐ If the passer leaves, write down a description of him. If possible, write down the license number of his car.

If you are handling incoming funds in the form of a check, compare the amount shown on the check with the total amount of the order, invoice, or accompanying statement. Also, examine the check to make sure that it meets the following requirements, which are keyed to the illustration above.

1 Dated with current date.
2 Properly made payable to your company with the name written in full and spelled correctly.
3 Accurately drawn with the figures indicating the same amount as the written amount.
4 Properly and legibly signed by the maker.

GIVING A RECEIPT

Most customers who pay by check will not ask for a receipt—their canceled check is their receipt. However, those who pay in cash will naturally want a receipt in case proof of their having paid their bill is needed later on. Remember these points when completing a receipt form such as the one illustrated on page 386.

1 Fill in the receipt blank as carefully as you would write a check.
2 Be sure to record accurately and legibly the date, the amount, and a description of what the payment is for.
3 Use a pen to write the receipt because ink is less likely to fade than pencil marks and is much more difficult to alter.
4 Make a carbon copy of the receipt, and check to see that all information on the receipt has been recorded on the copy.

No. 3247   May 7,   19 —

RECEIVED FROM _Brenda Hale_

Twenty-nine and $\frac{95}{100}$ _____ DOLLARS

FOR _Office supplies_

$ 29.95

                                    WWD

MAKING CHANGE

A customer who pays in cash does not usually give the exact amount owed. For instance, a customer may offer a $20 bill in payment of a balance of $17.29. After examining the bill, do the following:

1 Place the bill on the counter, on the cash register shelf, or on some other visible surface out of the customer's reach and away from your other currency.
2 Say "That is $17.29 out of $20" to prevent any misunderstanding about the amount received or the amount owed.
3 Count the change for the customer from the lowest to the highest denomination.

    Say: $17.30 (giving him one cent)
        17.40 (giving one dime)
        17.50 (giving one dime)
        18.00 (giving a half-dollar or two quarters)
        19.00 (giving one dollar)
        20.00 (giving one dollar)

4 Thank the customer, and make sure that he picks up all his change.
5 Put the $20 bill in your cash drawer.

Some cash registers are equipped to figure the amount of change for you. After entering the amount of the sale, you record in the machine the amount received from the customer—this amount is referred to as the *amount tendered*. The machine subtracts the amount of the sale from the amount tendered and shows the amount of change in its display window. In this case it is considered proper procedure to count the change displayed from the highest to the lowest denomination.

For example, if a customer offers a $20 bill in payment of a balance of $17.29, he will receive $2.71 in change, which will be shown in the display window of the register. Count the change for the customer, beginning with the largest denomination.

Say: $1.00 (giving one dollar)
   2.00 (giving one dollar)
   2.50 (giving a half-dollar or two quarters)
   2.70 (giving two dimes)
   2.71 (giving one cent)

Special change-making machines for coins are available to many cashiers. The coins are placed in slots in the machine, buttons are depressed for the amount of change to be given, and the change slides down a chute to a receiving tray which is within the reach of the customer. It is important that you depress the correct buttons; otherwise, the customer may receive the wrong change.

DEDUCTING CASH DISCOUNTS

When a charge customer pays her bill within ten days instead of waiting until the end of the month, many companies allow her to deduct a cash discount, such as 2 percent, from the amount of the invoice. This is usually written as 2/10 on the bill.

If your examination of the customer's remittance indicates that a discount was taken, you must verify three points:

1 Was the customer entitled to a discount according to the terms of the sale? Some firms have standard terms for all credit customers. Other firms may have different types of discount. Be sure you know your company's policy.
2 If the customer was entitled to the cash discount, did she pay within the stated period? For example, a customer who bought merchandise on May 10 for $320 under the terms 2/10, net 30 must send in her check on or before May 20 (May 10 plus ten days) to be eligible for the 2 percent cash discount. Many concerns make an extra allowance when the last date for taking the discount falls on a holiday or on another nonbusiness day.
3 If the customer is entitled to a discount and made her payment within the discount period, did she compute the discount and the net payment amount correctly? In the example given in step 2, a bill of $320 would be settled on May 20 with a check for $313.60.

$$\begin{array}{ll}
\$320.00 & \text{Gross amount} \\
\times .02 & \text{Rate of discount} \\
\hline
\$6.4000 & \text{Discount}
\end{array}
\qquad
\begin{array}{ll}
\$320.00 & \text{Gross amount} \\
-6.40 & \text{Discount} \\
\hline
\$313.60 & \text{Net payment}
\end{array}$$

Another method of checking is to deduct the rate of discount from 100 percent and then multiply the result by the gross amount to obtain the net figure directly.

$$100\% - 2\% = 98\%$$

$$\begin{array}{l}
\$320.00 \\
\times .98 \\
\hline
256000 \\
288000 \\
\hline
\$313.6000 \quad \text{Net payment}
\end{array}$$

CASH RECEIPTS JOURNAL							
DATE	ACCOUNT CREDITED	EXPLANATION	POST. REF.	GENERAL LEDGER CREDIT	ACCOUNTS RECEIVABLE CREDIT	SALES DISCOUNT DEBIT	NET CASH DEBIT
19— Apr. 5	D. L. Hooper	Invoice 2426, 4/1			249 80	5 00	244 80
5	Zader Company	Balance of account			50 77		50 77
5	Sales	Cash sales for day		59 95			59 95

RECORDING

The amount that you have received must then be recorded so that the customer's account will be properly credited. Note that the cash receipts journal above provides a place to record the following:

☐ Date and customer's name or general receipts category.
☐ Explanation of transaction.
☐ Gross amount, classified by source, such as payment from a customer:
    1 Receipts from cash sales (General Ledger Credit).
    2 Receipts from customers with charge accounts (Accounts Receivable Credit).
☐ Sales discount taken, if any.
☐ Net cash received.

Thus the record on the top line covers the receipt on April 5 of a check for $244.80 from D. L. Hooper to cover payment due on Invoice 2426 of April 1, less $5.00 discount. The amount of money actually received, $244.80, is entered under Net Cash Debit; the amount of the discount, $5.00, is entered under Sales Discount Debit; and the total of the money received plus the discount, $249.80, is entered under Accounts Receivable Credit. Because the customer was given a $5.00 discount, he received credit for paying $249.80 even though his check was for only $244.80.

The record on the second line covers the receipt on April 5 of a check for $50.77 from the Zader Company to pay the balance due on that account without a discount. Note that the amount of the check received, $50.77, is entered under Net Cash Debit, and because there was no discount, the same amount is entered under Accounts Receivable Credit. Because the customer received no discount, he was given credit for the exact amount of his payment.

The record on the third line lists the total cash sales for the day. This amount is recorded in the General Ledger Credit column.

CASHING CHECKS

Observe these important precautions if you are authorized to cash checks:

1 Know the person who is cashing the check. If you do not, ask for foolproof identification and note any key data on the reverse side of the check. You may need this information for future reference.

2　Have the payee, the person cashing the check, endorse it in your presence.

3　Compare the signature on the back of the check with the signature on the identification.

4　Compare that signature with the name of the payee on the check.

5　Make sure the check bears a current or very recent date.

6　Be sure that the payee's name is complete and legible.

7　Make sure that the amount of the check written in words is the same as the amount shown in figures.

8　Watch out for alterations, erasures, or irregularities.

9　Check any recent police or Better Business Bureau warnings that you may have handy.

10　Count the money very carefully from the highest denomination to the lowest.

11　Place the check in the cash drawer.

12　Return the customer's identification.

RETAINING CUSTODY

Once you have received incoming funds, you are held personally responsible for their safety. Never leave bills, coins, or checks around loose. Keep them under lock and key in your cash drawer until you release them for deposit. If, for a special authorized reason, you turn over any cash to another employee or to your supervisor, always ask for a receipt to protect yourself. At the end of each business day be sure that any funds you have on hand are placed in the vault for overnight storage.

PROVING CASH

Cashiers are usually required to complete daily cash reports or proofs at the time that the money is put away for the night. The cash-drawer count and proof-of-cash form illustrated on page 390 is prepared as follows:

1　Enter the cash register number and date at the top of the form.

2　Enter the number and amount of each denomination of coin and currency in the drawer.

3　Enter the number and total amount of checks in the drawer.

4　Total the coin, currency, and checks on the Total Cash in Drawer line.

5　Add cash paid out to determine total cash.

6　Subtract the change in the drawer at the beginning of the day to determine the cash received during that day.

7　Enter the cash register reading. It should agree with your count. If your count is less than the register reading, the cash is "short." If your count is more than the register reading, the cash is "over." If the cash proves, that is, if your count is the same as the register reading, enter "00.00" on the last line and check the Cash Proved block.

8　If cash is short or over, recount the cash and refigure the cash-drawer count. If the cash still does not prove, enter the amount of cash short or over on the last line and check either the Cash Short or Cash Over block.

CASH-DRAWER COUNT
AND PROOF-OF-CASH
CASH REGISTER ___6___ DATE _May 4, 19—_

Quantity	Denomination	Amount	
78	Pennies		78
42	Nickels	2	10
66	Dimes	6	60
50	Quarters	12	50
18	Half-dollars	9	00
112	$1 Bills	112	00
30	$5 Bills	150	00
22	$10 Bills	220	00
14	$20 Bills	280	00
3	Checks	1 87	50
	Total Cash in Drawer	980	48
	Plus Cash Paid Out	13	00
	Total Cash	993	48
	Less Change	50	00
	Cash Received, Actual Count	943	48
	Cash Received, Register Record	943	48

Cash ☑ Proved Cash ☐ Short Cash ☐ Over   Amount Short/Over 00 | 00

MAKING DEPOSITS

In many firms it is standard practice to deposit all receipts daily just before bank-closing time so that the amount of funds carried over to the next day are kept to a minimum. If there have been unexpectedly heavy receipts after the day's deposit has been made, the supervisor may arrange for another deposit through the use of the bank's night depository service.

Your daily bank deposit is prepared by listing the cash and other items on a form called a *deposit slip*. If only a few checks are to be deposited, each check is listed separately on this slip. However, if there are a large number of checks, an adding machine tape listing the checks is attached to the slip and only the total is shown on the deposit slip, as in the example shown at the top of page 391. If large amounts of coins and currency are to be deposited, they should first be wrapped by denomination in standard coin and currency wrappers, which are supplied by the bank. Money can be counted and handled rapidly and accurately when it is wrapped in this way.

When the bank teller receives your deposit, he will verify the completeness of your listing, count the coins and bills, examine the endorsements on the checks, and confirm the accuracy of your addition. Then he will issue a receipt, which is your proof that you have deposited the company's funds.

Deposited In **NATIONAL BANK AND TRUST CO.**
Carlsbad, New Mexico 88220

	Dollars	Cents
Currency	24	00
Coin	8	75
Checks	6,250	37
TOTAL	6,283	12

Date *September 22, 19—*

Deposit to
Account of MESA DEVELOPMENT, INC.

SILVER CREEK ROAD

CARLSBAD, NM 88220

This deposit accepted under and subject to the
provisions of the Uniform Commercial Code.

⑆ 1122 ⑈ 0088 ⑆ 821 ⑈ 5246 ⑈

ENDORSING

When a company deposits its checks, the bank in which it deposits its checks credits the depositor's account and then collects the amount of each check from the bank on which each check was drawn. The bank's right to collect that money on behalf of the depositing company is granted when the depositor *endorses* the check, that is, when he signs his name on the back of the check. There are several types of endorsements that you should know about.

Sometimes you may receive payment in the form of a check, such as a paycheck, that has been made payable to the customer. When the customer endorses the check, he transfers his right to cash that check to your company. The endorsement may take the form of a blank endorsement or a full endorsement. The *blank endorsement* is frequently used when the customer passes a check across the counter while paying in person. The *full endorsement* is much safer for transmission by mail or messenger because it specifies who has the right to cash that check. A third type, the *restrictive endorsement,* is used when the check is to be deposited in the bank. Endorsements are illustrated below.

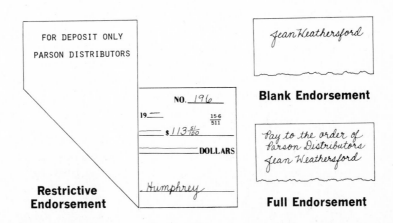

FOR DEPOSIT ONLY
PARSON DISTRIBUTORS

NO. *196*

19 ___   15-6
                   511

___ $ *113 51/100*

_____ **DOLLARS**

Humphrey

**Restrictive
Endorsement**

Jean Weathersford

Blank Endorsement

*Pay to the order of
Parson Distributors
Jean Weathersford*

Full Endorsement

REVIEWING YOUR READING

1 Name several personal characteristics that a cashier should possess.
2 List the steps to be observed when counting money.
3 What steps should be included in the complete examination of a check received with a mail order?
4 Outline the procedure for making change for a cash sale.
5 What precautions should you take if you are cashing a check for someone?
6 What is the meaning of "cash short" and "cash over"?
7 Explain the procedure for preparing the daily bank deposit.
8 Name three types of endorsement. What is the special purpose of each?

OFFICE ASSIGNMENTS

1 Ten sales and amounts tendered are listed below. You are to determine how to count change to the customer. Use a chart with headings as shown in the example to report your answers. Remember to use the smallest possible number of each denomination.

Example: Amount of Sale $2.50   Amount Tendered $5.00

Amount of Sale	Amount Tendered	Say	Giving	Say	Giving	Say	Giving
$2.50	$5.00	$3.00	50¢	$4.00	$1.00	$5.00	$1.00

Amount of Sale	Amount Tendered
$38.75	$40.00
.79	1.00
3.80	5.00
9.45	10.00
12.95	15.00
1.89	2.00
8.65	10.00
48.74	50.00
3.10	3.50
19.30	20.00

2 Assume that you are using a machine that figures the amount of change to be given by subtracting the amount of sale from the amount tendered. Use a chart with headings as shown in the example on page 393 to record the number of each denomination to be given for each of the ten amounts of change listed. Remember to use the smallest possible number of each denomination.

Example:

Amount of Change **$27.73**

Change	Number of Each Denomination to Be Given							
	$10	*$5*	*$1*	*50¢*	*25¢*	*10¢*	*5¢*	*1¢*
$27.73	2	1	2	1	0	2	0	3

Amount of Change	*Amount of Change*
$15.09	$16.42
8.14	5.37
1.46	6.91
11.38	31.88
22.90	.79

3 Assume that you are a cashier in charge of incoming funds. Show how you would enter the following receipts on June 21, 19—in a cash receipts journal similar to the one illustrated on page 388.

a Check for $100 from Vallco, Ltd., to pay last month's balance in full.

b Check for $196 from BOA Corporation to cover Invoice 609, dated June 15, for $200, less 2 percent discount for payment within discount period.

c Cashier's check for $55 from Chin Chien to cover past-due Invoice 448, dated May 2, in full.

d Check from Creative Styling Corporation to cover Invoice 597, dated June 14, for $350, less 2 percent cash discount.

e Cash amount for $10 paid by Nancye Plesha to apply to her account.

f Check from Perry and Washington, Inc., to cover Invoice 638, dated June 16, for $180, less 2 percent cash discount.

4 From the information given below, prepare a cash-drawer count and proof of cash on a form similar to the one shown on page 390. Use the current date.

The cash drawer contains 62 pennies, 30 nickels, 38 dimes, 18 quarters, 7 half-dollars, 25 $1 bills, 12 $5 bills, 8 $10 bills, 3 $20 bills, and checks for $16.50 and $8.45. According to records in the drawer, the following amounts were paid out during the day: $6 for a refund, $2.48 for a COD package, and $5.98 for returned merchandise. The cash in the drawer at the beginning of the day was $45. Cash received according to the register reading is $233.33.

5 Complete a deposit slip, like the one on page 391, dated October 22, 19—, for the Steel-Frame Corporation, Johns Road, Carlsbad, New Mexico 88220. List each check separately. Here are the cash receipts for the day:

15 $ 1.00 bills	$ 49.71 check
7 5.00 bills	4.62 check
3 10.00 bills	1,029.62 check
12.39 coin	496.31 check
	5.97 check

SECTION 32 Handling Outgoing Funds

Every business must purchase supplies and equipment to replenish its stock from which customers' orders are filled. This means that every business office has bills that must be paid. Another important job for the office cashier is to pay these bills when they are due. This is accomplished efficiently by using systematic procedures.

GETTING AUTHORIZATION

As a disbursing cashier you make payments only when you are authorized to do so. Every request for payment to a supplier must be approved by one or more responsible executives of the company. Generally, these are the purchasing agent and the treasurer. Look for their signatures on the invoice or voucher. The invoice illustrated below has been approved for payment by the notation OK-E. King in the upper right corner. If any signatures are missing, return the form to your supervisor for further clearance.

VERIFYING

Even though a request for payment, such as an invoice, has already passed through many hands, check every computation on the invoice to be absolutely certain that you pay only the correct amount. Your verifying the computations again is an added safety measure which protects your employer's funds.

PALMER MANUFACTURERS
800 Lakewood Avenue
Chicago, Illinois 60651

OK- E. King

Invoice No. 85334

Sold To Martindale Dairy
290 Pioneer Road
Evanston, Illinois 60201

Date February 23, 19--
Ship Via Parcel Post
Terms n/30

Ship To Same

QUANTITY	STOCK NO.	DESCRIPTION	UNIT PRICE	TOTAL
1	B-10	Culture for Buttermilk	5.20	5.20
1	B-11	Culture for Buttermilk	5.20	5.20
		TOTAL		10.40

394

DISBURSING BY CHECK

All routine payments are made by checks drawn on bank balances made up of daily receipts. Since checks represent orders to pay out the firm's money, you should take special care in writing or typing them. The illustration above is keyed to the following instructions for writing checks.

1 Complete the check stub before you write the check itself.
2 Write on the check the date on which it is actually written.
3 Spell out accurately, completely, and legibly the name of the firm or person to whom payment is being made. Fill in blank space with dashes (if you are typing the check) or a wavy line (if you are writing it) to prevent alteration.
4 Write the amount in clear, unmistakable numerals as close to the dollar sign as possible. If you are writing the check, express the cents in the form of a fraction. Use standard alignment and spacing when the check is typed.
5 Write out the amount in words on the next line. Use the word *and* to separate the dollars from the cents. The cents are generally expressed in the form of a fraction on this line whether the check is written or typed. Fill in the blank space to prevent alteration.
6 Make certain the check is completed with an authorized signature.
7 Record the purpose of the check on the check itself.

USING VOUCHER CHECKS

It is common practice for large concerns to use voucher checks to pay their bills. The voucher section of the check represents an explanation of the nature and amount of the payment and can be detached and filed by the payee for future reference. Sometimes the voucher section appears on the face of the check itself, usually on the left side as shown in the following illustration. Payroll

White Swan Dairy

2485 Swan Lake Road
Bluebonnet, Texas 77045

CHECK NO. 458

March 1 19 --

35-79
1130

CHECK IN PAYMENT OF THE FOLLOWING DESCRIPTION		
Invoice 3847		
DATE	AMOUNT	
3/1/--	275	00
LESS DISCOUNT	--	
LESS OTHER DEDUCTIONS	--	
NET AMOUNT	275	00

PAY Two hundred seventy-five and 00/100-- DOLLARS $ 275.00

TO THE ORDER OF

Texland Chemical Corporation
811 Dallas Avenue
Houston, Texas 77002

FIRST NATIONAL BANK
Houston, Texas 77036

C. Ned Bollinger
AUTHORIZED SIGNATURE

⑃1130⑃0079⑃682⑃015⑃003⑃

checks usually have a detachable stub, which the employee keeps as a record of her earnings and deductions. This type of voucher check is illustrated in Section 43 on the bottom of page 491.

RECORDING

After you write the check, record the payment in the cash payments journal. The routine to follow is similar in many respects to the one used for recording cash receipts. The cash payments journal provides space to record:

☐ Date.
☐ Payee's name or expense category.
☐ Explanation of payment.
☐ Check number.
☐ Gross amount of payment, classified by purpose, such as:

  1 Payment of expense to a firm with whom you do not have a charge account (General Ledger Debit).
  2 Payment of expense to a firm with whom you have an account (Accounts Payable Debit).

☐ Purchase discount taken for payment within discount period.
☐ Net cash paid.

The illustration on page 397 shows a payment made on February 14 to Aerobic Systems, Inc., an account payable, by Check 2047 to pay their Invoice 1199 of February 2 for $4,264. The Purchases Discount Credit column shows that no discount was given. The second entry in the illustrated cash payments journal is for a payment on February 15 to Western Paper Company for office supplies in the amount of $147.50 for which no discount was given. Because you do not have a charge account with this firm, the amount of the debit is recorded in the General Ledger Debit column. Notice that the expense category is recorded in the Account Debited column, and the firm name is recorded in the Explanation column. The third entry is for a payment made on February 15

					GENERAL LEDGER DEBIT	ACCOUNTS PAYABLE DEBIT	PURCHASES DISCOUNT CREDIT	NET CASH CREDIT
		CASH PAYMENTS JOURNAL						Page 12
DATE	ACCOUNT DEBITED	EXPLANATION	CHECK NO.	POST. REF.	GENERAL LEDGER DEBIT	ACCOUNTS PAYABLE DEBIT	PURCHASES DISCOUNT CREDIT	NET CASH CREDIT
19— Feb. 14	Aerobic Systems, Inc.	Invoice 1199, 2/2	2047			4264 00		4264 00
15	Office supplies	Western Paper Company	2048		147 50			147 50
15	Triangle Equipment Co	Invoice 7435, 2/6	2049			2000 00	40 00	1960 00

to Triangle Equipment Company, an account payable, by Check 2049 to pay their Invoice 7435 of February 6 in the amount of $2,000, less a 2 percent discount. The amount owed, $2,000, is recorded under Accounts Payable Debit; the amount of the discount, $40, is recorded under Purchases Discount Credit; and the amount actually paid, $1,960, is recorded under Net Cash Credit.

In some small- and medium-sized offices, the pegboard accounting system (see page 278) is used so that the check, voucher, and cash payments journal can be prepared in one writing.

Of course, in large offices where a great many payments have to be made each day, an accounting machine or some other data processing device is used to prepare the check, voucher, and cash payments journal in a single operation.

REVIEWING YOUR READING

1   Why must you check for authorization before making payments?
2   List seven details which require special care in the writing of checks.
3   What is the purpose of the voucher section of a voucher check?

OFFICE ASSIGNMENTS

1   As a cashier in charge of writing checks for Laurel Park Water System, use check stubs and checks to do the following. Either use the forms provided in the workbook, or copy the forms presented on page 395.

   a   Record a balance of $3,965.36 at the top of the first check stub.
   b   Record a deposit made on March 4 of $76.24.
   c   Write a check to the United Chemical Company dated March 5 in the amount of $225.75 for treatment chemicals. Remember to fill out the check stub first, then type or write the check. Because you are not authorized to sign the checks, leave the signature space blank.
   d   Record a deposit made on March 5 of $362.27 and another deposit made on March 6 of $80.00.
   e   Write a check to the County Health Department dated March 7 in the amount of $25 for inspection fee.
   f   Write a check to Long's Pump Service dated March 7 in the amount of $1,475 for pump repairs. Your final balance should be $2,758.12. If it is not, carefully recheck your work.

2 As a cashier for Erwin Wholesale Company, record the following transactions in a cash payments journal similar to the one illustrated on page 397. Begin with Check 2050, and continue in numeric order.

Feb. 18 Paid Invoice 2620 of February 4 for $307.25 to Carter's Ink Company (account payable). There is no discount.

18 Paid Invoice 18-422 of February 4 for $100, less 2 percent discount, to Ross's Exxon (account payable).

19 Paid Paper Products, Inc. $35.42 for office supplies. Use the General Ledger Debit column because this is not an account payable.

19 Paid News Messenger $635 for advertising. Use the General Ledger Debit column.

19 Paid Invoice 949 of February 5 for $832 to Fuller-Stephens Corporation (account payable). There is no discount.

20 Paid Invoice 24-332 of February 5 for $750, less 3 percent discount, to Donaldson Company (account payable).

20 Paid Invoice 7749-2 of February 6 for $39.86, less 1 percent discount, to World News (account payable).

SECTION 33 Reconciling the Bank Statement

Depositing and issuing checks daily can add up to a great deal of banking activity in a month's time. It is vital that the bank's records and the depositor's records of the in-and-out cash flow be absolutely accurate.

At the end of the month the bank furnishes a statement showing the amounts deposited by your company and the checks drawn against your employer's account during the period. This report gives the cashier unit an opportunity to verify the accuracy of its own calculations—a very important safety measure. As an employee assigned to cashier duty, you will be doing your share of the verification work. Don't be alarmed if you see at first that the bank figures do not agree with the company's records. There are reasons for this situation, and there is a recognized procedure to account for the difference.

CHECKING CHARGES

On your bank statement you will find that in addition to the amounts deducted for canceled checks, there may also be amounts deducted for special items. One such item might be a special service performed by the bank, such as complying with your request to stop payment on a check. Your bank statement will then include a charge slip for this special service. Another item might be a monthly service fee imposed by the bank to cover the expense of handling your checking account. The amount of the charge usually depends upon the balance of the

PEOPLE'S BANK
Rutland, Vermont 05701

LAUREL PARK WATER SYSTEM
BOX 770
RUTLAND, VT. 05701

ACCOUNT NUMBER   703-813-5201

PERIOD ENDING   01-31-

Checks	Checks	Deposits	Date	Balance
125.50			01-02	2,266.10
53.60	321.60		01-03	1,890.90
596.73			01-05	1,294.17
4,000.00		8,621.50	01-08	5,915.67
150.00	2,575.00		01-09	3,190.67
23.81			01-14	3,166.86
1,300.00			01-17	1,866.86
.82SC			01-20	1,866.04
932.68		3,921.60	01-27	4,854.96
307.97	13.03		01-31	4,533.96

Beginning Balance	Total Amount of Deposits	Total Amount of Checks Paid	Total Charges	Ending Balance
2,391.60	12,543.10	10,399.92	.82	4,533.96

Number of Deposits Made	Number of Checks Paid	Number of Other Charges
2	12	

Codes: CC Certified Check   OD Overdrawn
        DM Debit Memorandum   RI Returned Item
        EC Error Correction   SC Service Charge

Please examine this statement upon receipt and report at once if you find any difference. If no error is reported in ten days, the account will be considered correct. All items are subject to final payment.

account, the number of checks paid, and the number of items deposited. The amount deducted for the monthly service fee appears on the bank statement (it does not appear on a separate slip) and is usually accompanied by the notation *SC* which stands for service charge.

To reconcile your bank statement, first examine the canceled checks and any charge slips that accompany the bank statement. All checks should bear the signature of a company official who is authorized to sign them. And every check should be endorsed by the person or firm to whom it was made payable. The endorsement proves that the payee received the check.

Treat bank fees as expenses paid during the period just as if a check had actually been written to the bank to cover them. Make an entry in the cash payments journal to record the special bank charges.

CHECKING DEPOSITS

On the statement verify the amounts listed as deposits during the month. Check these amounts against your deposit slip receipts and your entries in the cash receipts journal.

When you are checking your deposit slips against the amounts credited on the bank statement, you may discover that some deposits are not listed by the bank. Make a special note of such items. These omissions are called *uncredited deposits;* they occur when you make a deposit shortly after the statement was prepared by the bank. Uncredited deposits occur frequently when deposits are made by mail, by armored car, or by the night deposit chute. Such deposits will appear on the next statement.

DETERMINING OUTSTANDING CHECKS

Not all checks issued by the cashier during the month will be listed on the bank statement. For instance, some checks must travel long distances by mail; other checks may not be deposited promptly by the payees. If the bank statement shows a larger balance than the cashier's books indicate, it is because the bank has not received all the checks and charged them to the company's account. These checks, called *outstanding checks,* represent unsettled obligations, and your company needs to have a complete record of them at the end of each accounting period. To determine which checks are outstanding:

1 Arrange canceled checks in numeric order.
2 Put a check mark next to the check number on the stub of each returned check.
3 Note that the stubs without check marks have checks that are outstanding.

COMPUTING THE CORRECT BALANCE

Once you have verified the bank statement and identified uncredited deposits and outstanding checks, confirm the fact that your checkbook balance agrees with the bank statement balance by completing a reconciliation statement.

The word *reconcile* means to bring two different things into agreement. You will note on the reconciliation statement illustrated on page 401 that the bank statement balance differs from the cashier's or checkbook balance on the top line; however, the figures are the same on the bottom line after a series of adjustments have been made. On one side you add the uncredited deposits to the bank figure and then subtract the amount of the outstanding checks. On the other side your checkbook figures are adjusted to cover bank service charges not known until the statement is actually received.

Most banks provide a reconciliation form, such as the one illustrated on page 401, on the reverse side of the monthly statement. This arrangement helps the customer reconcile his bank statement easily and allows him to keep all pertinent figures together for quick future reference.

The final step in reconciling the bank statement is to subtract service charges, if any, from the checkbook balance shown on the checkbook stub.

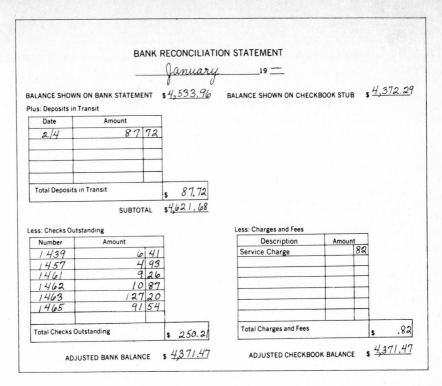

BANK RECONCILIATION STATEMENT

January 19 —

BALANCE SHOWN ON BANK STATEMENT $ 4,533.96   BALANCE SHOWN ON CHECKBOOK STUB $ 4,372.29

Plus: Deposits in Transit

Date	Amount
2/4	87 72
Total Deposits in Transit	$ 87.72

SUBTOTAL $ 4,621.68

Less: Checks Outstanding

Number	Amount
1439	6 41
1457	4 93
1461	9 26
1462	10 87
1463	127 20
1465	91 54
Total Checks Outstanding	$ 250.21

Less: Charges and Fees

Description	Amount
Service Charge	82
Total Charges and Fees	$ .82

ADJUSTED BANK BALANCE $ 4,371.47   ADJUSTED CHECKBOOK BALANCE $ 4,371.47

Once you have reconciled the bank statement and know that your records are correct, you are ready to proceed with the transactions for the next period.

REVIEWING YOUR READING

1 Why does the company's record of cash seldom agree with the bank statement record?
2 What is the procedure for determining which checks are outstanding at the end of the month?
3 Why might deposits made by a company fail to be listed on the current bank statement? What are these deposits called?

OFFICE ASSIGNMENTS

1 Use the form in your workbook to prepare a bank reconciliation statement for Danco Studios for the month of January. If you are not using a workbook, copy the form shown above. The balance shown on the bank statement is $13,824.08. The following deposits were made but do not appear on the statement: February 4, $85; February 5, $371.24; February 6, $2,600. The following checks were found to be outstanding: 421, $72.50; 427, $110.05; 429, $5; 430, $3,000; 431, $14.50; 432, $81.21. The checkbook balance is $13,600.06. A service charge of $3 is shown on the statement.

2   Prepare a bank reconciliation statement for Mackey Electronics for the month of June. Use the form in your workbook, or copy the form illustrated on page 401. The bank statement shows a balance of $72,217.18. An examination of the statement reveals that there are four uncredited deposits: July 2, $21,550; July 3, $14,772.28; July 6, $32,345.50; July 7, $4,200. The following checks were found to be outstanding: 7112, $850; 7120, $31.09; 7125, $24,000; 7127, $7,242.80; 7128, $3.07; 7129, $550.72; 7130, $2,600. The checkbook balance is $109,807.28. There is no service charge.

SECTION 34 Special Cashiering Activities

The cashiering procedures that you learned in Sections 31 to 33 will take care of most routine transactions. However, like so many other office activities, cashiering has its share of special operating problems. The experienced cashier can handle a special cash situation with the same speed and efficiency with which he handles his regular duties. He knows exactly what to do and does it accurately.

REFUNDS AND ALLOWANCES

Many businesses issue regular checks to customers for refunds and allowances on items such as damaged, lost, or defective merchandise. If the refund check does not have an explanatory voucher, a brief form letter is usually sent along with the check to tell the customer what action was taken.

However, in many stores a customer can obtain a cash refund upon request. She gets an authorization slip for the refund from a unit supervisor or claim adjuster and presents it to the cashier for payment. If you are the cashier making the refund, observe the following precautions:

1   Examine the slip to see that it is genuine and complete. Make sure that it bears an authorized signature.
2   Request identification from the customer to make sure that the money is being paid to the right person.
3   Ask the customer to sign a receipt for the money.
4   Collect all related documents that are to be attached to the authorization slip for future reference.
5   Count out the cash.
6   Put the authorization slip and any essential documents in the cash drawer.

CREDIT CARD PROCEDURE

When the card is presented, examine it to determine if the card number is listed on the current cancellation bulletin, if the card has been altered in any way, or if the card has expired.

Record of Charge

Fill out a thorough record of the purchase by following these suggestions:

1   Make sure that you fill out the correct form since each credit card plan has its own record of charge.
2   Record the cardholder's name and account number on the record of charge; use an imprinting device, if available.
3   Complete the record of charge, including the amount of the purchase, taxes, extras (such as a delivery fee), and total.
4   Have the customer sign on the signature line.
5   Compare the signature on the record of charge with the signature on the credit card.
6   Return the credit card to the customer along with a carbon copy of the record of charge.
7   Retain all the other copies of the charge slip for further processing.

The record of charge, which is sometimes referred to as a sales draft, may look like the one shown in the illustration below.

Summary of Charges

At least once each week the cashier, who has accepted credit card charges for merchandise, forwards the charges to the credit company for reimbursement. To do this, take the following steps:

1   Sort the original copies of the record of charge according to plan or company; then total each group.
2   Complete a summary form for each credit card company. This form shows the amount due from each company. A summary slip may appear like the one on page 404.
3   Have the supervisor sign the summary form.

A completed record of charge form.

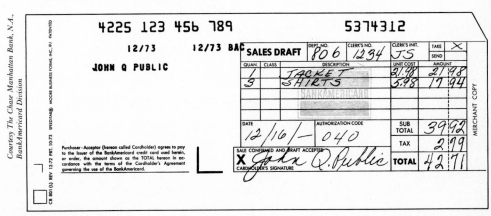

Courtesy The Chase Manhattan Bank, N.A., BankAmericard Division

80 SUMMARY MAIL-IN SLIP 2

59 12345 000 1

YOUR STORE
123 MAIN ST
NEW YORK N Y 10000

CHASE MANHATTAN BANKAMERICARD ®

SUMMARY SLIP

Attach adding machine tape to Bank Copy when more than one sales slip is enclosed. **97**

x *Ralph Conklin*
MERCHANT SIGNATURE

MERCHANT COPY

Date 2/14/—

ITEM	NO. SLIPS	AMOUNT
Total Sales	35	462 71
LESS: Total Credits	2	36 03
NET AMOUNT		426 68

® Service Mark Owned and Licensed by BankAmerica Service Corporation 1972

A completed summary of record of charge forms.

4 Send the original of the summary form and the original copies of the record of charge to each credit card company.
5 Retain the carbon of the summary form and the carbon copies of the record of charge for reference.

Some companies find it more convenient to be reimbursed for their credit card sales through banks. Instead of sending the charge slips to the credit card company, the depositing company sends the original copy of each charge slip and the summary to the bank authorized to handle the charges of a particular credit card company.

USING A PRICE CHART

Cashiers in movie theaters, amusement parks, and other similar enterprises often use a price chart to assist them in determining the total amount of a sale. For example, if a customer asks you, the cashier, for three adults' tickets at $1.25 each and four children's tickets at $.75 each, you can quickly determine the total amount of the sale by looking in the proper column and row of the price chart. Thus the price chart enables the cashier to give rapid service.

The price chart on page 405 was prepared by a cashier who sells adults' and children's tickets for $1.25 and $.75 each. The amount for three adults' tickets and four children's, $6.75, is found under the No. 3 column in the No. 4 row.

HANDLING CHECKS

Checks have varied functions and can often be used in ways other than as payment for services or merchandise.

Certified Checks

In certain types of transactions, such as those involving real estate transfers or formal bids in business, a cashier's firm may be required to pay by certified

CASHIER'S PRICE CHART

	No.	0	1	2	Adults 3	4	5	6
	0	—	$1.25	$2.50	$3.75	$5.00	$ 6.25	$ 7.50
	1	$ .75	2.00	3.25	4.50	5.75	7.00	8.25
Children	2	1.50	2.75	4.00	5.25	6.50	7.75	9.00
	3	2.25	3.50	4.75	6.00	7.25	8.50	9.75
	4	3.00	4.25	5.50	6.75	8.00	9.25	10.50
	5	3.75	5.00	6.25	7.50	8.75	10.00	11.25
	6	4.50	5.75	7.00	8.25	9.50	10.75	12.00

check. Requesting a certified check assures the payee that the amount specified on the check will be paid by the bank. Here is the procedure:

1 The cashier completes a regular check following the normal routine.
2 The check is sent to the bank for certification.
3 The bank verifies the payer's account to see that the balance is sufficient to cover the check. Funds equal to the amount of the check are immediately set aside for its payment.
4 The bank teller stamps the check with the word *certified* and returns it to the cashier or company messenger.
5 The check is ready for dispatch to the payee.

Forwarded Funds

Traveling executives and salesmen frequently ask the cashier to send their expense and salary checks to forwarding addresses, such as their home or bank address. To send a check to a forwarding address:

1 Confirm that the address is correct by consulting the salesman's secretary or supervisor to see if there have been any last-minute changes in itinerary that may effect a change in the forwarding address. If so, correct the address.
2 Note special instructions on the outside of the envelope, such as "Please Hold for Arrival."
3 Mail by the fastest service so that the check reaches the post office of destination early in the day.
4 Complete a mail deposit slip if the check is to be deposited for the traveler, and send it to his bank by the fastest mail service.

Stop-Payment Orders

Occasionally, the writer of a check will request the bank to stop payment on a check after it has been issued and sent to the payee. This can happen if:

REQUEST TO STOP PAYMENT OF CHECK

December 2, 19—
DATE

TO: NORTHEAST BANK
     WATERVILLE, MAINE 04901

PLEASE **STOP PAYMENT** OF A CHECK DRAWN BY THE UNDERSIGNED,
DESCRIBED BELOW:

AMOUNT $ *16.00*   No. *1481*   DATED *December 1, 19—*

PAYABLE TO *Warren G. Lambert, Jr.*

The undersigned agrees to hold the above bank harmless for said amount and to indemnify
it against loss, expenses and costs incurred by reason of its refusal to pay the above
described check. The undersigned further agrees not to hold the bank responsible should
the check be paid through inadvertance, accident or oversight. Under provisions of the
Uniform Commercial Code, Sec. 4-403, this request shall automatically expire and become
null and void six months from date, unless revoked or released before that time, or
extended or renewed for additional periods of not more than six months.

TIME RECEIVED_____   *Paul F. Kelley*
                                     SIGNATURE OF DEPOSITOR

---

1 The check has apparently been lost in the mail or mislaid in handling.
2 The check has fallen into unauthorized hands.
3 A gross error is discovered resulting in a serious overpayment.
4 A fraud is discovered in connection with the claim for payment.

To stop payment, promptly telephone the bank, request that payment be
stopped, and supply a complete description of the check. Since an unauthorized
person might conceivably make such a call, the bank requires that the payer
fill out and file with them a formal stop-payment order, like the one shown
above, to protect the bank from any legal claims arising from their refusal to
cash the check. If the check has already been returned to the payer's bank,
payment cannot be stopped. A fee is charged by the bank for the stop-payment
service.

A request to stop payment on a check has many legal aspects, and you should
make such a request only in an emergency and when you are authorized to
do so.

HANDLING PETTY CASH

Every office has some minor expenses that must be paid in cash. Transportation
expenses for messengers is a typical example. To meet these needs, a special
fund known as a petty cash fund is set aside and turned over to a cashier or
another office employee. If you are in charge of this cash, place the money in
a special cashbox or locked drawer in order to separate it from your other
cashiering funds.

An employee who needs cash to pay small expenses in connection with
company business completes a petty cash voucher. The voucher, which may
look like the one shown at the top of page 407, is then approved by his supervisor
and presented to you for payment.

```
┌─────────────────────────────────────────────────────┐
│  No. 36              Amount $ 2.50                    │
│                                                       │
│              PETTY CASH VOUCHER                       │
│                                                       │
│                       Date May 2, 19—                 │
│                                                       │
│  Paid to  J. Wilson                                   │
│                                                       │
│  For  Taxi fare                                       │
│                                                       │
│  Charge to  Delivery expense                          │
│                                                       │
│                                                       │
│                                                       │
│  Approved by WWD       Received by J. Wilson          │
└─────────────────────────────────────────────────────┘
```

In turn, you observe the following procedures:

1 Examine the voucher to determine if it is filled out completely, has a current date, and is authorized.
2 Request identification if you are not personally acquainted with the employee who is asking for the cash.
3 Obtain a receipt for the money. This is usually done by having the employee receiving the cash sign his name in the receipt section of the voucher.
4 Count out the cash.
5 Place the voucher in the cashbox or locked drawer for safekeeping.
6 Make a record of the payment in a petty cash book. A page from such a book is illustrated below.

At any time you should be able to produce cash or authorized vouchers equal to the original amount of the fund. Prove this cash balance daily, usually just before closing time when the cashbox may be placed in a safe or vault overnight.

When the cash fund runs low—this may occur every one or two weeks—replenish the fund by following these steps:

1 Draw a single line under all money columns in the petty cash book, and total the columns.
2 Draw a double line under the Distribution of Payments columns.

PETTY CASH BOOK   Page 5

| PETTY CASH FUND | | DATE | EXPLANATION | VOU. NO. | DISTRIBUTION OF PAYMENTS | | | |
RECEIVED	PAID OUT				ADVERTISING EXPENSE	DELIVERY EXPENSE	MISC. EXPENSES	OFFICE EXPENSE
50 00	26 05	19— may 1	Brought forward			5 00	8 50		12 55
	2 50	2	Taxi fare, J. Wilson	36		2 50		
	7 80	2	Angel's Florist, flowers	37			7 80	
	5 00	3	FBLA, Program ad	38	5 00			
	2 72	4	REA Express collect	39		2 72		
	1 85	5	Master Printers, labels	40				1 85
	3 00	5	Ace Truck Lines, collect	41		3 00		
50 00	48 92		Totals		10 00	16 72	7 80	14 40
	1 08	5	Cash on hand					
50 00	50 00							
1 08		5	Cash on hand					
48 92		8	Replenish fund, check 412					

3 Add the amount of cash on hand to the Paid Out column. The sum should be the same as the amount in the Received column. Draw a double line under the Received and Paid Out columns.
4 Record the amount of cash on hand in the Received column.
5 Request a reimbursement check to restore the fund to its original balance.
6 Cash the reimbursement check, and place the money in the petty cash box.
7 Record the amount received in the Received column of the petty cash book.

Since the petty cash fund is relatively small, a cashier is not expected to cash checks and should never make cash loans or short-term advances to fellow employees.

REVIEWING YOUR READING

1 Explain the precautions to be observed by a cashier when she is making a cash refund.
2 Outline the cashiering routine when a credit card is presented instead of cash payment.
3 Describe four pointers that are important when dispatching checks to traveling executives and sales personnel.
4 How is payment stopped on a check that has been written and sent to the payee?
5 How would a messenger obtain taxi fare from the cashier in charge of the petty cash fund?
6 How is the petty cash fund replenished?

OFFICE ASSIGNMENTS

1 Complete a credit card record of charge. Use the form supplied in your workbook, or copy the form shown on page 403. Your clerk number is 249, and your department is 2B. The customer is purchasing one English bicycle priced at $85. The tax on this item is $3.40, and there is an assembly charge of $5.50. Use the current date and 214 for the authorization code. The customer will take the merchandise.
2 Refer to the price chart on page 405. See how rapidly you can find the total amount to be charged for the following ticket sales. Record your answers on a sheet of paper.

a 2 adults, 1 child	f 4 adults, 3 children	
b 4 children	g 2 adults, 5 children	
c 3 adults, 3 children	h 1 adult, 4 children	
d 5 adults	i 3 adults, 1 child	
e 1 adult, 2 children	j 5 adults, 4 children	

3 Study the price chart on page 405. Then prepare a similar price chart for the following prices: adults, $2, children, $1.25.

4 a As the cashier in charge of petty cash, record the following transactions in a petty cash book similar to the one shown on page 407.

July 15 Opened petty cash fund with $175.

16 Petty Cash Voucher 1, paid $14.60 to REA Express on collect package (delivery expense).

17 Petty Cash Voucher 2, paid $4.65 to John Kingsley, messenger, for taxi fare (delivery expense).

18 Petty Cash Voucher 3, paid $35 to Kee Stationery Company for typewriter repair (office expense).

19 Petty Cash Voucher 4, paid 30 cents to mailman for postage due (miscellaneous expense).

19 Petty Cash Voucher 5, paid $2.80 to John Kingsley, messenger, for taxi fare (delivery expense).

22 Petty Cash Voucher 6, paid $10 to WFBL for program advertisement (advertising expense).

22 Petty Cash Voucher 7, paid $17.50 to Wilker Stationers for paper and supplies (office expense).

24 Petty Cash Voucher 8, paid $10 to Master Printers, Inc., for labels (office expense).

25 Petty Cash Voucher 9, paid Ace Truck Lines for collect shipping charges, $65.62 (delivery expense).

26 Petty Cash Voucher 10, paid $3.50 to John Kingsley, messenger, for taxi fare (delivery expense).

b Since your cash on hand is running low, total the transactions listed in your petty cash book and request a reimbursement check. Record the amount of the check in the book, restoring the cash fund to its original balance. Use 420 as the check number.

UNIT 13

BUSINESS CASES AND PROBLEMS

In the Boss's Shoes   1 During rush periods when there is so much to do, you often wonder why the firm bothers to give trading stamps or to honor credit cards. You feel that it would be much simpler and quicker to do business on a straight cash basis. While this procedure might simplify matters for the cashier, do you think that these extra services should still be provided?

2 When you first went to work in the cashier unit, you secretly resented the bonding company's investigation of your personal background. You also feel that the boss's policy of rotating assignments in the unit is further evidence of his suspicious nature. In fact, you wonder why he keeps you if he doesn't trust you. Could the boss have less obvious reasons for his procedures?

Your Human Relations **1** As a store cashier you receive a $20 bill from a customer in payment for a purchase. The bill bears a serial number known to be counterfeit. You do not know the customer, and you do not want to create an embarrassing situation. What should you do?

2 One of the firm's regular customers has presented an expired credit card to cover his bill. He is with a party of friends, and you do not know how to explain matters to him without causing him embarrassment. Since the bill is quite high, you hesitate to take a chance; yet you realize that the man may not have the required cash with him. What should you do?

3 The signature of the purchasing agent is missing from a voucher that is presented to you for payment. As disbursing cashier, you have been instructed to return such vouchers to your supervisor for clearance. However, your supervisor is away for the afternoon, and the cash discount privilege will expire today. Since this is a routine purchase from a regular supplier, should you issue the check anyway and let your supervisor complete the formalities tomorrow morning? Should you hold all papers and take no action until your supervisor returns? Or what?

4 A co-worker has asked you, as the custodian of the petty cash fund, to extend him an overnight loan of $5 for a special emergency. He offers to sign an IOU and promises faithfully to return the money as soon as the office opens the next morning. You are convinced that the emergency is genuine, but you know that the loan would violate the rule against unauthorized payments. What should you do?

What Would You Do If . . .? **1** You are a cashier and have used proper procedures in making change to a customer. A half hour later the customer returns and says to you, "You have shortchanged me by $5."

2 You discover in preparing a bank reconciliation statement that your bank has recorded a $10 deposit to your account by mistake.

What Does This Mean? **1** Your employer asks you to make a bank deposit to the payroll account rather than to the regular checking account.

2 When a credit card is presented, it should be examined to determine if the number is on the current cancellation bulletin. Explain.

3 Have the person cashing the check endorse it in your presence. Explain.

Business in Your Area **1** Visit a supermarket in your area. Observe the cashier at work, and see if he uses the procedures outlined in this unit in counting change to the customer. Make note of any variations from these procedures, and give a report of these variations in class.

2 Determine from a local bank exactly how the monthly service charge on checking accounts is figured.

UNIT **14**
SALES
AND
ACCOUNTS
RECEIVABLE
SYSTEMS

SECTION 35 Sales Operations

Probably no two systems for controlling sales operations are exactly alike. There are systems for the sale of services, such as insurance; systems for the sale of merchandise, such as automobiles; and systems for the sale of used equipment, such as a used adding machine. Sales systems are used in retail, wholesale, and manufacturing firms. Sales are made by mail order, by telephone, and in person. A firm as small as a service station and as large as an automobile manufacturer has systems and procedures for selling goods and services. Whatever their size or nature, all businesses have a system for handling accounts receivable, which means collecting the money for the sales made on credit.

SALES OFFICE ACTIVITIES

Next to the sales force itself, the sales office has more direct contact with the customers than any other unit of the company. Every transaction can either add to or subtract from a customer's impression of the company's quality of service. The efficiency of the sales office is a big factor in maintaining the goodwill of the customer. There are several selling activities that are common to most organizations, regardless of their size or their major service.

1 *Contacting Customers.* Definite procedures are established for communicating information to the customer about the goods or services that are for sale.
2 *Receiving Orders.* This is the heart of the sales system and involves a procedure for accepting, verifying, and pricing orders and checking credit.
3 *Billing.* Procedures are established for preparing an invoice for each order shipped.
4 *Handling Accounts Receivable.* An accounting procedure is established to ensure that money due on charge accounts is received on time, in the proper amount, and with the correct discount and that receipts are credited to the proper account. This activity will be discussed in Section 36.

CONTACTING CUSTOMERS

In order to make a sale, salesmen contact customers by mail, by telephone, or in person. But once the salesman has made the sale, he must be backed up by efficient office personnel who fill the order, bill the customer, and charge the correct amount to the customer's account.

Customer Contact by Mail

Most of the firm's daily incoming and outgoing mail consists of sales correspondence. The following are a number of reasons why customers may write to a supplier or manufacturer:

☐ To obtain catalogs and current price lists.

☐ To ask questions about a product or service.

☐ To ask for special advice.

☐ To find out the name of a local dealer or to request a salesman to call.

☐ To place an order.

Requests for catalogs and sales literature should receive prompt attention. Form letters and postcards are frequently used to acknowledge such requests. Questions about products and requests for advice are usually referred to skilled correspondents for individual attention. A routine inquiry for the name of a local dealer generally necessitates two letters—one giving the data to the prospective customer and another notifying the dealer about the customer's interest. The firm's own salesmen are notified about sales prospects by sending them notices of inquiries made by customers.

Inquiries from customers are highly valued because they can lead to future sales. However, an order from a customer represents an actual sale and calls for immediate attention. You will learn about procedures for handling orders later in this section.

Customer Contact by Telephone

Customers who are in a special hurry to obtain information or to place an order will telephone the sales office. When you take an order over the telephone, first say some cordial words to the customer to establish a friendly relationship. Then proceed to record the details of the customer's order, such as:

☐ Name of the firm.

☐ Order number.

☐ Address to which the invoice is to be sent.

☐ Address to which the order is to be shipped.

☐ Name of the person placing the order.

☐ Merchandise wanted, including stock numbers, colors, sizes, and quantities.

☐ Delivery date.

☐ Special shipping instructions.

☐ Customer's telephone number in case more information is needed later.

Customer Contact in Person

Sometimes a field salesman will make an appointment with a prospective buyer at the company showroom in order to give him a personal demonstration of the company's products. This happens when large purchases with special requirements are involved in the sale. If the prospect calls at the showroom without an appointment and the salesman in charge is not on hand, ask the customer if you can help him and perhaps offer to take his order. The visitor may have spoken to a salesman earlier and may know already what he wants to purchase. On the other hand, he may still have some questions, which you can help to answer. The information or demonstration that you provide may convince him to place his order now so that he can receive the shipment promptly.

RECEIVING ORDERS

Getting a customer's order is very important, but no sale is complete until the customer obtains his goods and is fully satisfied with the service he has received. Procedures have been designed so that orders can be taken, speedily and efficiently.

Taking the Order

Special order forms, on which the customer's purchase is recorded, are generally used both by the field force and by those in the sales office. These forms provide spaces for recording all the necessary facts regarding the order and organize these facts so that the order can be processed quickly. In order to keep writing on the form to a minimum, some order forms contain a preprinted list of all current stock items. The customer merely has to check off the desired items on the form. Fill in order forms completely and legibly, and make sure that each form includes the customer's signature and the customer's purchase order number.

Verifying the Order

Neither the vendor nor the customer profits from a misunderstanding about an order. Carefully recheck the order—whether it is large or small—to see that it is accurate.

- If the customer is on the telephone, read the order back to him and then send him a confirmation copy immediately by mail.
- If the order arrives by telegram or mail, check every word of the original communication. If there are any questions, write, telephone, or wire immediately for clarification.
- If the customer gives his order in person, go over it with him and give him a copy of it.

Pricing the Order

Once you are sure that the items shown on the order are exactly what the customer wants, find out how much these items cost. Prices can be found by consulting the current price list. When a unit price is found:

1 Enter the unit price in the proper column on the order form.
2 Then multiply the number of units ordered by the unit price, and show the amount in the amount column.
3 When you have priced and multiplied all the items, add up the figures in the amount column to determine the total.
4 If prices shown in the price list are regular retail prices and the customer is entitled to a trade discount, deduct the amount of the discount from the gross amount.
5 Record the difference as the net payment to the trade customer.

Clearing for Credit

After you have totaled the amount of money on a customer's order, ask the credit department, "Can we extend credit terms on this order?"

Established customer   The record of an established customer, found in the accounts receivable ledger, tells the credit department whether or not there is any risk involved in extending credit to him. If the customer has always paid his bills on time, his order is approved at once, and open account terms, such as 2/10 EOM, are noted on the invoice.

A 2/10 EOM notation allows the customer to deduct a 2 percent discount from the total amount of his order if he pays the bill within ten days after the end of the month. (*EOM* are the initials for end of month.) Terms can also be stated 2/10 Prox. (*Prox.* stands for *proximo,* which means in the next month.)

If the customer's record of past payments is not satisfactory, shipment of the new order is usually deferred and he is asked to do one or more of the following:

☐ Clear up the outstanding debts.
☐ Send cash to cover the current order.
☐ Send a deposit, and authorize a COD (cash on delivery) shipment of the balance.

These requests are generally made by correspondence, and individually typed standard form letters are used for this purpose. Matters of extreme urgency may be handled by telephone or telegraph.

New customer   If the order is from a new customer, the credit department consults other sources for information in order to determine his credit rating. One likely source is the *Dun & Bradstreet Reference Book of Manufacturers.* If the prospective customer has a good credit rating, the credit department will probably give its approval right away. If the new account is not listed in the reference book, the local credit bureau or bank may be asked for a credit report. Business references may also be contacted.

BILLING

An order form can serve as a rough work sheet on which various sales office personnel can record essential data, fill in missing details, make adjustments, note substitutions, and complete calculations. After all vital facts have been assembled and credit clearance has been given, a bill, or invoice, is prepared.

Invoices generally have several carbon copies. The standard invoice pack for your firm might consist of an original, which is mailed to the customer, and five carbon copies, which are distributed to the following:

☐ Stock clerk.
☐ Shipping room.
☐ Accounts receivable department or unit.
☐ General files.
☐ Salesman in order to notify him that an order is being shipped to his territory.

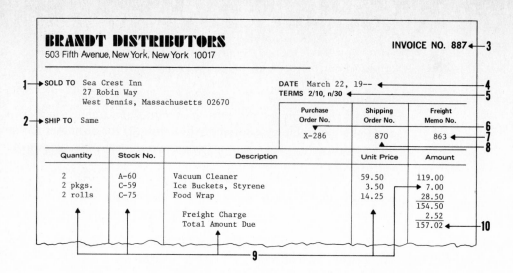

The typical invoice provides space for the following information which is keyed to the illustration above.

1 Customer's name and billing address.
2 Address to which the order is to be shipped.
3 Invoice number.
4 Date of the invoice.
5 Terms of sale.
6 Customer's purchase order number.
7 Your company's freight memorandum number.
8 Your company's shipping order number.
9 Quantity, stock number, description, unit price, and amount of each item ordered.
10 Total amount of the order, including taxes and shipping charges, if any.

Preparing Invoices

There are many kinds of equipment available which help you to prepare invoices more quickly.

The typewriter The ordinary typewriter can be used to prepare bills quickly, clearly, and uniformly.

The typewriter-calculator combination The typewriter-calculator combination offers the ease and speed of a typewriter along with the accuracy of a calculator. With this machine the billing clerk can type the written data and then use the special computing keys to figure the totals.

The adding machine adaptation The ten-key or full-key adding machine is used by businesses that issue simple invoices on which little data is printed. A service bill, such as a rent bill, is an example of a simple invoice because it needs only a few variable facts and symbols inserted in the blank spaces. The name, address, and date are preprinted.

The cash register adaptation   A billing machine has been developed which makes use of the many features of the cash register. The register is essentially a full-key adding machine with a cash drawer. It prints the sales figures on a sales slip. The cash register adaptation eliminates the cash drawer and expands the keyboard to include keys with special symbols. Information is printed on the invoice or statement when it is inserted in a special slot. The cash register adaptation is used for simple, preprinted invoices on which only a few variable facts need be inserted in the spaces provided.

Computer systems   For large billing operations invoices may be prepared from punched cards, punched tape, or magnetic tape used with an electronic computer system. Standard data, such as customer's name, address, terms, item description, discount, and so on, are recorded on cards or tapes which are filed or stored until needed. The computer system combines these prepunched or prerecorded units of data with variable data, such as quantity and order number, and prints this combined information on the invoice. In addition, the computer produces a tape or card which can be used for sales analysis or for customer account records.

The photocopy technique   Many small offices, such as those of physicians and pharmacists, prepare monthly bills, called *statements of account*, simply by making a photocopy of the customer's account card. The account card has the customer's name and address typed at the top, and the photocopy of the card needs only to be folded and mailed to the customer in a window envelope.

Checking the Invoice

By the time an invoice is prepared, a number of clerical operations, representing the efforts of possibly six or more persons, have been performed on the order. To guard against mistakes, check the invoice against the order form and against other related papers. This is the last opportunity to make sure that the invoice is absolutely correct before the shipment is sent.

When you are checking an invoice, verify each data block or each item individually. For example, confirm that the customer's name, address, and ZIP Code are correct by referring to the customer's order or letterhead. To avoid loss or delay of the shipment, check the address to be sure that you have listed a town with a popular name, such as Centerville or Riverside, with the appropriate state. Also check to see that any shipping charges have been calculated correctly.

Filling the Order

Once the invoice has been verified, the order can be released for shipment. The stockroom copies and shipping copies of the invoice are removed from the original pack and are sent to the respective units for action. The stock clerk issues the items from the inventory shown in his stock records, and the shipping department uses its copy to check to see that the order is complete before it is packed. The lower part of this invoice copy may serve as a packing slip which goes inside the parcel. The upper part of the invoice copy may be glued to the outside of the package as a shipping label.

REVIEWING YOUR READING

1   Outline the major activities of the sales office.
2   What details should you note when you take an order by telephone?
3   Why should a salesclerk take the time to verify that the order is correct? How should he do it?
4   Describe the procedure involved in clearing an order for credit.
5   Why do invoices have several copies? List the people and departments who might receive copies of the invoice, including the original.
6   At what point in the procedure does the invoice get checked? Explain what is done in this operation and why.

OFFICE ASSIGNMENTS

1   As a biller in the order section, you have been asked to complete Invoice 888 covering the following sale. If possible, make five extra carbon copies of the invoice. Either use the form provided in your workbook, or follow the style shown on page 416. Use the current date.

Sold to: Robert F. Buckley, Inc.
          6937 Avon Road
          Canby, Minnesota 56220
Ship to: Same
Terms: 2/10, n/30
Purchase Order: 41323
Shipping Order: 871
Freight Memorandum: 864
Items Ordered: 8   16439 Adapters   @ $ 1.25
                12   4965 Washers   @   .10
                 1   63881 C Screen   @   .60
                 3   11745 Fans   @   5.95
                 3   14709 Assemblies   @ 40.00
Freight Charge: $6.50

2   As a biller in the mail-order section, you have been asked to prepare an invoice for the following mail order dated March 12 and received on March 15.

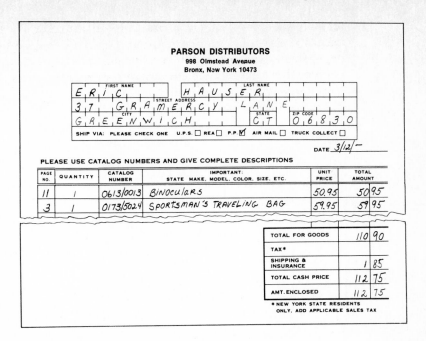

PARSON DISTRIBUTORS
998 Olmstead Avenue
Bronx, New York 10473

FIRST NAME: ERIC   LAST NAME: HAUSER
STREET ADDRESS: 37 GRAMERCY LANE
CITY: GREENWICH   STATE: CT   ZIP CODE: 06830

SHIP VIA: PLEASE CHECK ONE   U.P.S. ☐ REA ☐ P.P. ☑ AIR MAIL ☐ TRUCK COLLECT ☐

DATE 3/12/—

PLEASE USE CATALOG NUMBERS AND GIVE COMPLETE DESCRIPTIONS

PAGE NO.	QUANTITY	CATALOG NUMBER	IMPORTANT: STATE MAKE, MODEL, COLOR, SIZE, ETC.	UNIT PRICE	TOTAL AMOUNT
11	1	0613/0013	Binoculars	50.95	50 95
3	1	0173/5024	Sportsman's Traveling Bag	59.95	59 95

TOTAL FOR GOODS	110 90
TAX*	
SHIPPING & INSURANCE	1 85
TOTAL CASH PRICE	112 75
AMT. ENCLOSED	112 75

* NEW YORK STATE RESIDENTS ONLY, ADD APPLICABLE SALES TAX

Assume that the prices and postage are right and that the shipment was sent parcel post on the day the order was received. Complete Invoice 9746. Either use the form in your workbook, or prepare one similar to the one shown below. For terms use $112.75, Cash With Order. Make four carbons if supplies are available.

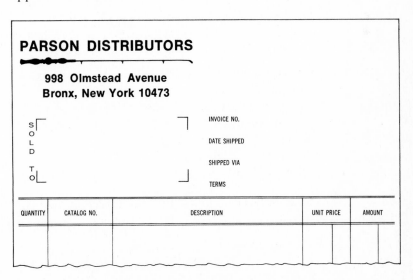

PARSON DISTRIBUTORS

998 Olmstead Avenue
Bronx, New York 10473

SOLD TO ⌐   ⌐   INVOICE NO.

                              DATE SHIPPED

                              SHIPPED VIA

          ⌞   ⌞   TERMS

QUANTITY	CATALOG NO.	DESCRIPTION	UNIT PRICE	AMOUNT

3   A customer, Jeffrey Wahl of 65 Irving Street, Dover, Delaware 19901, has telephoned requesting the following merchandise: 2 X4691 base assemblies, net price per unit, $12.25; and 10 Y3486 fans, net price per unit, $7.12. His order number is 649. He has asked that the merchandise be shipped

immediately via REA Express. Using the form in your workbook, complete Invoice 36-461 covering the sale. If you are not using the workbook, copy the form below. Use the current date for the invoice, date received, and date shipped. Compute the amount of the discount, and record the figure in the Amount of Discount box. Enter the word *Telephone* in the Salesman box. Prepare three carbons if supplies are available.

INVOICE

Towle Bros., Inc.

100 Fifth Avenue
New York, N.Y. 10011

Sold to

Invoice No.

Date

Salesman	Your Order No.	Date Received	Date Shipped	Shipped By	2% discount for payment in ten days.
					Amount of discount

Quantity	Stock No.	Description	Unit Price	Extension

36 Handling Accounts Receivable

The sales operation is considered to end when the goods that have been ordered are shipped. At this point the amount the customer will pay for the order becomes an account receivable, and definite procedures are followed to ensure that all money owed to the company is received and credited to the proper account.

DISTRIBUTING INVOICE COPIES

The shipping room and the stockroom receive their copies of the invoice. Then:

1 The accounts receivable section charges the customer's account with the amount shown on its copy of the invoice.
2 Another copy of the invoice is attached to the original order, and both are sent to the general file for future reference.
3 The original copy of the invoice is mailed to the customer so that he will know that shipment has been made and how much it will cost.
4 The remaining carbon is sent to the salesman in the field, informing him that the shipment has been sent.

RECORDING SALES

The accounts receivable section of the sales office receives a copy of every invoice issued. Data from the invoice is entered in the sales journal. The illustration below shows how you would record the invoice on page 416 to Sea Crest Inn in the sales journal.

	SALES JOURNAL				Page 6
DATE	INVOICE NO.	ACCOUNT DEBITED	TERMS	POST. REF.	AMOUNT
19— Mar. 22	887	Sea Crest Inn	2/10, n/30		157 02

Then working from the sales journal, you would charge the total of each sale to the individual customer's accounts receivable record. The account card for Sea Crest Inn is shown below with the total amount of the invoice, $157.02, posted as a charge. The notation *SJ6* in the Post. Ref. column means that the information on the account card was taken from page 6 of the sales journal.

NAME *Sea Crest Inn*							
ADDRESS *27 Robin Way, West Dennis, Massachusetts 02670*							
DATE 19—		POST. REF.	CHARGES	DATE 19___		POST. REF.	CREDITS
Mar. 22	Invoice 887	SJ6	157 02				

USING POSTING MACHINES

Because of the tremendous volume of sales, the process of charging or posting the amount to the customer's account is frequently done by machine or computer. The machine produces accurate and legible copy and relieves the office worker of having to compute a new balance each time.

PREPARING MONTHLY STATEMENTS

Not every customer will pay his account each time he receives a single invoice. If he buys frequently from your company, the customer may prefer to accumulate all the invoices for a month and pay them with one check. A monthly statement which summarizes all amounts owed can be issued to customers like these. It serves as a convenient and tactful reminder of their debts. The monthly statement is also helpful to customers whose balances may not be due immediately or to customers who do not choose to take advantage of discounts by paying their bills early. They use the statement to compare their own records with those of your company. This helps to check the accuracy of both records and prevents misunderstanding when payment is made.

USING CYCLE BILLING

Most firms send out monthly statements of account to their customers at the end of the calendar month. Yet an increasing number of concerns are using the cycle billing system to spread the clerical work load over a wider period.

Statements are mailed to different groups of customers at stated intervals over a one- or two-month period. For example, statements might be sent out to customers whose last names begin with *A*, *B*, and *C* on the first of the month, to customers whose last names begin with *D*, *E*, and *F* on the fifth of the month. By the end of the month all statements have been sent, and the cycle begins again.

POSTING DIRECTLY TO CUSTOMER RECORDS

The journal-to-ledger account method, described previously, is the conventional procedure used to post charges and credits to customers' accounts in small- and medium-size offices. In larger operations amounts may be posted to customers' accounts directly from invoice copies or payment vouchers. The papers from which the postings are made are then permanently filed, frequently in binders, for future reference. They are used in place of the sales journal as a record of the company's transactions. Obviously, time is saved by eliminating the journal.

BYPASSING LEDGERS

In an effort to achieve further efficiency in handling a large volume of sales transactions, some businesses eliminate both the journal record and the accounts receivable ledger records of sales. Here is how it works:

1 Copies of sales invoices are filed under the customer's name.
2 When payments are received, the related invoice is removed from the file, marked "Paid," and placed in a Paid file.
3 Credit memorandums for merchandise returned or damaged are also placed in the customer's file as they are issued.
4 At the end of the billing period, the customer's file contains all unpaid invoices and credit memorandums that have not been applied to his account.
5 All outstanding amounts due are listed on a statement of account.
6 Photocopies of all invoices and credits are attached to the customer's statement.
7 The statement and photocopies are mailed to the customer and the copy of the statement is retained in the file until payment is made.

In this procedure the record of the customer's account is actually maintained by a simple filing operation. You can see that the filing must be done with absolute accuracy and that papers must be filed immediately upon receipt.

REVIEWING YOUR READING

1   What record does the accounts receivable office use to record sales information in the sales journal?
2   What record is used to post sales data to individual customer accounts?
3   Why does the accounts receivable section receive a copy of every invoice issued?
4   What are the advantages of posting sales to customers' accounts by machine or computer?

OFFICE ASSIGNMENTS

1   Record the following sales transactions in a sales journal. If you are not using the workbook, copy the form on page 421.
   a   May 1; Invoice 1277 for $4,236.43 to Brown and Company; 2121 Page Drive, Centerville, Ohio 45459; 2/10, n/30.
   b   May 2; Invoice 1278 for $2,497.21 to Roger and Bacon Company; 29 Bono Avenue, Trenton, New Jersey 08612; 2/10, n/30.
   c   May 3; Invoice 1279 for $3,188.37 to K. B. Morre, Inc.; 67 La Valle Avenue, Biloxi, Mississippi 39530; 2/10, n/30.
   d   May 3; Invoice 1280 for $2,885.40 to Armstrong & Sons; 121–123 Johns Street, Sedalia, Missouri 65301; 2/10, n/30.
   e   May 3; Invoice 1281 for $1,953.47 to Drake Supply Company; 21 Mesa Drive, Chico, California 95926; 2/10, n/30.
2   On individual account records post the transactions made previously in the sales journal. Use SJ7 as the post reference on the account records. Then place a check mark in the Post. Ref. column on the sales journal to show that you posted each transaction. If you are not using the workbook, copy the account card illustrated on page 421.

UNIT 14

BUSINESS CASES AND PROBLEMS

In the Boss's Shoes   1   An old and valued retail store customer threatens to take his business to another firm unless he gets a bigger discount on his purchases. Your firm has always been generous in providing special services for this account. However, the customer is actually getting the same discount that all retail store customers receive, including some stores that give you much more business. How can your company keep this customer without changing its discount policy?

Your Human Relations   **1**   You are a salesclerk assigned to the showroom. A very domineering customer refuses to allow you to serve him. In a very loud voice he demands to have the manager wait on him. The boss is visible in the rear office where he is trying to complete some reports in order to meet important deadlines. He has told you: "I don't care who comes in this afternoon. Just see that I am not interrupted." What are you going to say to this customer? Can you handle the situation without losing his order?

2   Your job is to take telephone orders from local trade customers. One wholesale firm calls you almost daily to place a rush order for supplies. You have always done your best to handle their business efficiently. However, you have never actually provided any special service that would not be freely granted to other customers. During the holiday season the manager of the wholesale firm sends an expensive gift to you at your home. The enclosed card expresses sincere appreciation for your helpfulness. Should you accept the gift? Should you tell your boss about it? Could you return it without offending the customer?

What Would You Do If . . . ?   It is your job to check all incoming payments to determine whether or not customers have taken the correct discount on the invoices they have received. Upon comparing one remittance with the related invoice, you determine that the customer, Katherine Wilson, has taken a 2 percent discount amounting to $6.50. However, Ms. Wilson's payment was made one day past the allowed discount period. You know that Ms. Wilson is one of the company's best customers. Should you allow the discount, or not? If so, what will you do if the next time this customer takes a discount two, three, or four days past the discount period? If not, how do you propose to maintain the goodwill of Ms. Wilson?

What Does This Mean?   **1**   A store advertises that it provides the following credit services for its customers: regular charge accounts, revolving credit plans, and layaway.

2   Purchasing and inventory systems exist only to support the sales effort. Explain.

Business in Your Area   Make a study of at least three invoices that you or your family have received. Report the following to the class: **(1)** how the bills were prepared (written, typed, photocopied, on a punched card, and so on), **(2)** any terms that appear on the bills, **(3)** instructions for making the remittance, and **(4)** any other information about the bills that you believe would be of interest to the class.

UNIT 15
INVENTORY AND STOCK CONTROL SYSTEMS

The goods that a business receives in its warehouse or shop are called *inventory* or *stock*. An inventory and stock system keeps track of what stock is on hand and indicates what must be reordered and when. Such systems are also referred to as merchandise control systems.

BENEFITS OF AN INVENTORY AND STOCK SYSTEM

An inventory and stock system enables the businessman to have a minimum amount of his money tied up in inventory. For example, let us say that the owner of Star Hardware has a good inventory system and that the owner of Keystone Hardware, a store of the same size, does not. Star Hardware can carry a smaller amount of stock than Keystone Hardware and still do as much business because the owner of Star Hardware knows where everything is and doesn't have stock left over which must be sold at a loss.

The system also indicates what stock must be reordered in order to replace the stock that was sold. By using the system, a businessman can be fairly sure that he will always have the items his customers want—when they want them. He can maintain a balanced assortment of goods and give his customers an attractive range of choices.

Inventory and stock systems can also help the businessman to plan for the future. By studying the stock figures, he can observe trends in demand for certain items and adjust his future purchases accordingly. The figures also give him a factual basis for purchasing the following year's stock.

Finally, a well-managed inventory system enables the proprietor of a business to reduce stock shrinkage, that is, reduce the loss of stock due to theft, damage, shop wear, or other causes.

NECESSARY RECORDS

To operate an inventory and stock system, it is necessary to maintain several important kinds of records which must be kept complete and accurate so that the businessman can interpret them correctly. If the records are incorrect and the businessman makes decisions based upon them, the company can lose a good deal of money. This unit presents the basic information and records needed to maintain inventory control in most businesses. Remember, however, that inventory and stock systems differ from company to company.

INVENTORY COUNT AND REPORT OF ITEM SALES

Probably the most important items of information required for an inventory and stock system are the number of each item of inventory in stock (inventory count) and the number of each item sold (item sales). There are two basic methods for obtaining these two items of information: (1) the stock counting system and (2) the continuous inventory system.

Stock Counting System

This system is used in stores where the average price of each item is relatively low. For instance, it is used by retail stores that sell items which are considered staples, or items constantly in demand and continually being reordered, such as housewares and china. There are five basic steps to follow in a stock counting system:

1 At the beginning of a designated time period, such as a week, make a physical count of each item in stock and record the information on a tally sheet or inventory list.
2 From a copy of the receiving report, which is discussed in Section 40, record the items received on the inventory list.
3 Add the beginning inventory to receipts to determine items available for sale.
4 At the beginning of the next time period make another physical count of each item in stock.
5 Determine the number of each item sold by subtracting the ending inventory count from items available for sale.

Suppose that a hardware store manager makes a physical count of his inventory on October 1 and finds that he has 24 garden rakes in stock. He records the number 24 in the Beginning Inventory column next to the item garden rakes on his tally sheet (see the illustration below). On October 15 he receives a shipment of 36 garden rakes. The number 36 is recorded in the Receipts column. On November 1 the manager makes another count of his inventory; this time he has 12 garden rakes in stock and writes 12 in the Ending Inventory column. In order to determine the number of items sold, he adds the beginning inventory, 24, to the receipts, 36, and writes the total, 60, in the Available for Sale column. Then by subtracting the ending inventory, 12, from items available for sale, 60, he gets the number of items sold, 48, which is written in the Items Sold column.

STAR HARDWARE

Inventory Tally Sheet

October 19 —

Item	Beginning Inventory	Receipts				Available for Sale	Ending Inventory	Items Sold
		Date	No.	Date	No.			
Garden rakes	24	10/15	36			60	12	48

Continuous Inventory System

This system is used in places where the average price of each item is relatively high and where current fashion information, such as color, style, and size, is important. This system, which is also referred to as a *perpetual* inventory system, involves eight basic steps.

1   When a new item of stock is ordered, prepare an inventory record card for the item from a copy of the purchase order. An inventory record card is shown below. It includes:

INVENTORY RECORD CARD *(Front)*					
Description *Dress*			Style No. *432*		
Vendor Name *Kingston Co.*			Vendor No. *174*		
Cost Price *$12.50*			Retail Price *$21.95*		
Department *Ladies Fashions*			Period *April–June 19–*		
Date	Ordered	Received	Sold	Sales This Period	Available
19–					
April 1	*24*				

a   *Description.* The name of the item ordered.
b   *Vendor Name.* The name of the company from whom the item was ordered.
c   *Cost Price.* The amount of money that will be paid to the vendor for one item.
d   *Department.* The department in the store that will sell the item.
e   *Style Number.* The number which the vendor uses to identify the item.
f   *Vendor Number.* The number which the store uses to identify the vendor.
g   *Retail Price.* The price that will be charged to the customer for one item.
h   *Period.* The length of time this inventory card will be used before the balance number of items in stock is carried forward to a new card.

Then fill in the body of the card. Enter the date in the Date column and the number of items ordered in the Ordered column. A separate inventory record card is prepared for each style number listed on the purchase order.

2   A receiving report tells you that an item of stock has been received by the company. Post the information listed on the report to the inventory record card. Enter the date the items were received in the Date column, the number of items received in the Received column, and the number available in the Available column. Note the illustration at the top of page 429.

Date	Ordered	Received	Sold	Sales This Period	Available
19— April 1	24				
7		24			24

3 On the back of the inventory record card, show the size and color break-down, if any, of the items received. This information is obtained from the receiving report. Record the number for each size and color by using vertical marks. The number 3, for example, is recorded as ///.

INVENTORY RECORD CARD *(Back)*											
Size / Color	8	10	12	14	16						
White	/	//	///	/	/						
Blue	/	//	///	//							
Green	/	//	//	//	/						

4 Each day record sales as decreases in inventory on the inventory record card. The posting may be done from copies of sales slips which are forwarded daily (by salesclerks) to the inventory control clerk or from stubs which are detached from the goods at the time of sale and later forwarded to the inventory control clerk. In some large firms the stubs which are detached at the time of sale contain punched holes which can be read by machines. Sales lists are then printed by a data processing machine, and sales are posted to inventory cards by using the information from the sales lists. Enter the date in the Date column, the number of items sold in the Sold column and in the Sales This Period column, and the difference between previous items available and the items sold in the Available column as shown below. In some large firms the inventory record itself is prepared by computer.

Date	Ordered	Received	Sold	Sales This Period	Available
19— April 1	24				
7		24			24
9			6	6	18

5 On the back of the inventory record card cross off the items sold. The size and color information can be found on the sales slip or stub.

	Size Color	8	10	12	14	16							
White		/	X/	X//	/	/							
Blue		/	//	X//	X/								
Green		X	//	//	//	X							

INVENTORY RECORD CARD *(Back)*

6 Keep a running balance of sales to date and items on hand as additional items are reported sold. The two illustrations below show how the front and back of the inventory record card appear after two more selling days. Check to see if the number of items on hand on the front of the card is the same as the number of uncrossed marks on the back.

Date		Ordered	Received	Sold	Sales This Period	Available
19— April	1	24				
	7		24			24
	9			6	6	18
	11			3	9	15
	12			4	13	11

	Size Color	8	10	12	14	16							
White		X	X/	XX/	/	/							
Blue		X	X/	X//	X/								
Green		X	X/	X/	X/	X							

INVENTORY RECORD CARD *(Back)*

7 The store buyers will check the inventory records daily to determine which items need to be reordered, which need to be marked down or reduced in selling price, and which need to be discontinued. The inventory record cards must contain current, accurate information at all times.

8 At the end of the period for which the inventory record card is kept, a physical inventory, or count, is taken of each item in stock. The figure in the Available column is adjusted on the inventory card, if necessary, to reflect actual physical inventory.

RETURNS

Customers often return merchandise for exchange or credit, and it is important that such merchandise be entered as additions to inventory. A record of the kinds of items that are returned can help the store's buyers to decide what goods to purchase and, perhaps, what goods not to purchase.

In some systems, when a customer returns merchandise, the salesclerk sends a copy of a credit memo or return memo to the stock control office. In a continuous inventory system the credit memo is posted to the inventory record card under the column headed Sold, but the number entered is either encircled or written in red to show that it represents an addition to, rather than a subtraction from, stock. Note on the inventory record below that one item was returned on April 13. The number 1, encircled, is written in the Sold column. The sales to date figure is decreased by one, and the number available is increased by one.

The return is also indicated on the back of the inventory record card by the encircling of the item returned as shown in the illustration below.

Date	Ordered	Received	Sold	Sales This Period	Available
April 19—	1	24			
	7		24		24
	9			6	6	18
	11			3	9	15
	12			4	13	11
	13			①	12	12

INVENTORY RECORD CARD *(Back)*									
Color \ Size	8	10	12	14	16				
White	⊗	X/	XX/	/	/				
Blue	X	X/	X//	X/					
Green	X	X/	X/	X/	X				

REVIEWING YOUR READING

1 Name several reasons for having an inventory and stock system.
2 Compare the stock counting system and the continuous inventory system.
3 Information for the entries made on the inventory record card in a continuous inventory system is obtained from what records?
4 Describe the procedure for recording returns on an inventory record card.

OFFICE ASSIGNMENTS

1 As an employee in the accessories department of Northside Automobile Supply Company, you have been asked to keep an inventory record for March for various categories of items. You are to use the stock counting system. On an inventory tally sheet, record the transactions listed below. If you are not using the workbook, copy the form illustrated on page 427.

   a On March 1 you take inventory and count the following number of items for each category: 27 tachometers, 8 car vacuum cleaners, 6 cartop carriers, 13 litter baskets, 2 clothes rods, 6 door mirrors, 15 vanity mirrors, 19 auto compasses, 4 protective flaps, and 7 steering wheel covers.

   b March 7: Received 6 clothes rods.
   c March 9: Received 12 steering wheel covers.
   d March 12: Received 5 car vacuum cleaners.
   e March 14: Received 18 door mirrors.
   f March 18: Received 12 protective flaps.
   g March 21: Received 36 cartop carriers.
   h March 27: Received 36 tachometers.
   i March 27: Received 12 clothes rods.
   j March 29: Received 24 litter baskets.
   k March 29: Received 6 vanity mirrors.
   l On March 30 you take inventory and count the following number of items for each category: 23 tachometers, 6 car vacuum cleaners, 18 cartop carriers, 27 litter baskets, 7 clothes rods, 9 door mirrors, 11 vanity mirrors, 4 auto compasses, 4 protective flaps, and 6 steering wheel covers. Complete the inventory tally sheet, figuring the number of each item available for sale and the number of each item sold.

2 As a clerk in the inventory control section of a department store, you have been instructed to keep inventory records for several items of stock for the month of May for the ladies' fashions department. Using three inventory record cards (front and back), show how you would enter information for three of the items of stock by recording the transactions listed below. If you are not using the workbook, copy the forms illustrated on pages 428–429.

a   On May 2 you receive a copy of a purchase order dated May 1 to Mary Ann Fashions, Inc., vendor number 221. The order is for the three items for which you are to keep three inventory record cards:

1   18 dresses, style 422; cost price, $10.50; retail price, $19.95.
2   24 dresses, style 424; cost price, $14.50; retail price, $27.95.
3   12 dresses, style 426; cost price, $18.50; retail price, $35.95.

b   On May 10 copies of three receiving reports dated May 9 are delivered.

1   Received 18 dresses, style 422, as follows:

	8	*10*	*12*	*14*	*16*
Red	1	1	2	1	1
Yellow	1	1	2	1	1
Tangerine	1	1	2	1	1

2   Received 24 dresses, style 424, as follows:

	8	*10*	*12*	*14*	*16*
Tan	1	2	3	2	
Gray	1	2	2	2	
White	1	2	3	2	1

3   Received 12 dresses, style 426, as follows:

	8	*10*	*12*	*14*	*16*
Green	1	1	3	1	
Blue		2	2	1	1

c   You receive the following information on sales and returns during the month:

May 11   Sold one size 12 tan dress, style 424; sold one size 16 blue dress, style 426.

13   Sold one size 10 tangerine dress, style 422.

14   Sold one size 12 gray dress, style 424; sold one size 12 white dress, style 424.

15   Sold one size 14 tan dress, style 424; sold one size 10 red dress, style 422.

16   One size 10 tangerine dress, style 422, was returned.

17   Sold one size 12 yellow dress, style 422; sold one size 12 green dress, style 426; sold one size 10 gray dress, style 424.

18   Sold one size 12 tan dress, style 424; sold one size 8 white dress, style 424.

20   Sold one size 8 red dress, style 422; sold one size 14 gray dress, style 424.

21   Sold one size 10 blue dress, style 426.

22   Sold one size 12 gray dress, style 424; sold one size 12 green dress, style 426; sold one size 16 yellow dress, style 422.

SECTION 38 Inventory Reports

Inventory reports help the owners and executives of a business make important decisions on product selection, pricing, and the quantity of items to keep in stock.

TAKING PHYSICAL INVENTORY

As a check on the continuous inventory system and as a basis for preparing reports for the accounting department, most merchandising businesses count their stock at least once a year or preferably more often. The instructions outlined below represent the inventory procedures followed by a large automobile-supply chain store. They include most of the important steps in taking physical inventory. Keep in mind, however, that inventory procedures vary a great deal from company to company.

1 The week before the actual count:

    a Take out of the regular stock all merchandise not in condition to sell at full price—items that are shopworn, defective, or incomplete. Sell these items at clearance prices before inventory, if possible.

    b Check all bins, shelves, drawers, tables, and storeroom stock to see that all merchandise is in the right place. Items carrying the same stock number may be overlooked during the physical count if they are in more than one place.

    c Count any stock kept in reserve in a storeroom one or two days before you count the stock on the retail floor. Before counting, fill all bins, tables, and so on, so that withdrawals from reserve stock and recounting can be kept to a minimum.

2 What to count:

    a All merchandise in the store:

        (1) In bins and shelves and anywhere reserve stock is kept.
        (2) On display windows, on the sales floor, and in the service room.
        (3) Reserve stock in the storeroom.

    b Merchandise on demonstration in customers' homes, cars, and so on.
    c New incoming merchandise in transit that has already been paid for.

3 How to count:

    a In counting reserve stock in the storeroom, use a card or tag similar to the one shown at the left to record the count of each stock number. Leave the tag in plain sight in the bin. Change the count if any merchandise is removed from or added to the reserve stock. Add the reserve stock count to the retail floor count when it is completed.

b In counting the retail floor, service room, and window stock:

   (1) Complete the count preferably between selling days when the store is closed to customers.

   (2) List the items in stock on a tally sheet similar to the one shown below. The Total Quantity is written in as a total of the Assembly of Count after the count has been completed. Each block under the Assembly of Count is for five marks; each mark represents one item.

Inventory of _Caldwell Auto Supply Company_

Date _June 30, 19 –_   Counted by _GRH_   Checked by _WWD_

Product Class _Davis Nylon tube type tire_

Item	Stock No.	Unit Cost	Assembly of Count				Total Quantity	Cost Value	
6.70 x 15, black	ZAC5351	13.23 ea.	//				2	26	46
7.10 x 15, black	ZAC5352	14.93 ea.	₩₩	/			6	89	58
7.60 x 15, black	ZAC5353	16.60 ea.	////				4	66	40
6.70 x 15, white/black	ZAC5451	15.76 ea.	//				2	31	52
7.10 x 15, white/black	ZAC5452	17.36 ea.	//				2	34	72
7.60 x 15, white/black	ZAC5453	18.79 ea.	//				2	37	58
			Subtotal, this product class					286	26

   (3) Work in pairs, if possible, to get a faster, more accurate count. One person calls the stock numbers and count, and the other person records the count on the tally sheet. If the items are easy to count, the counting and recording may be done by just one person. In either case, recounts will be made by supervisory or other personnel to double-check the first count.

4 Totaling the figures:

   a Find the cost value of each stock number by multiplying the number of items counted times the unit cost.

   b Add the amounts for each item to get the total cost of the inventory on hand.

   c Add the total cost of the inventory on hand to the cost of items on demonstration and the cost of items in transit that have been paid for.

   d Have the amounts, extensions, and totals spot-checked by a responsible store official.

SHRINKAGE INFORMATION

Losses of stock due to theft, damage, shop wear, or other causes are referred to as *shrinkage*. Because such losses are not reported as sales, the book inventory, or the inventory shown on the inventory record card, is larger than the actual physical count of the inventory. Therefore, you can get shrinkage information by comparing the book inventory with the physical inventory.

ORDER-DELIVERY TIME

In order to determine when to order goods, you must know how much time it will take the merchandise to arrive from the date the order is mailed until the day it is actually received. Businessmen rely on records of past transactions to determine order-delivery time. Under the stock counting system, order-delivery time is figured by subtracting the date of the purchase order from the date of the related receiving report. For example:

Receiving report dated 3/15/—
                   (March 15)   3   15
Purchase order dated 3/3/—
                   (March 3)   −3   3
                                    0   12
Order-delivery time = 12 days

The following is an example of a purchase order and a receiving report that are dated in different months:

Receiving report dated 3/18/—(March 18)
Purchase order dated 2/16/—(February 16)
Days left in February (28 − 16)   12
Plus days in March   18
Order-delivery time   30 days

A similar procedure for figuring order-delivery time is followed in the continuous inventory system. However, the dates of the orders and receipts on the inventory record cards are used instead of the dates on the purchase orders and the receiving reports. In the illustration on page 428 the order-delivery time of the 24 dresses ordered on April 1 can quickly be determined to be six days.

Since order-delivery time often varies with the season of the year, it is important to keep records of past years in order to predict order-delivery time in the future. Above all, remember that the reasons for figuring order-delivery time are (1) to prevent ordering items too soon, causing overstock conditions; and (2) to prevent ordering items too late, causing out-of-stock conditions.

Manufacturers of certain products, such as ladies hosiery, place reminder cards in the cartons of goods they sell. The salesclerk is reminded that it is time to reorder a particular item when in the course of making a sale he comes to that card.

MAXIMUM-MINIMUM LIMITS

In many inventory operations the management of the business establishes a maximum and a minimum number of items to be kept in stock for each product the business sells or uses. A hardware store manager may set 15 as the maximum number of tile knives to be kept in stock and 8 as the minimum number.

Because of the time delay caused by order-delivery time, the inventory clerk may not wait to reorder until only 8 tile knives remain in stock. He reorders, perhaps, when 10 tile knives remain in stock so that the number on hand will not fall below 8 during the order-delivery period. The point at which items are reordered in order to keep a certain minimum number of the item on hand is called the *reorder point.*

DOLLAR SALES AND PROFIT

If you keep inventory records, you are often asked to provide information on dollar sales and profit for each item or group of items in inventory. Because the amounts obtained are figured from inventory records, the sales and profit figures are considered to be close estimates rather than exact amounts. Overall business sales and profits are determined by accountants from information entered in cash registers, from sales slips, and from other original records.

Even though the sales and profit figures obtained from inventory records may not be exact, they can be extremely helpful to the buyer or other person responsible for deciding what to buy, how much to charge, what to put on sale, what to advertise, and what to discontinue selling.

Four frequently asked questions about dollar sales and profit and how they are answered are outlined as follows.

Dollar Volume of Sales

How much money was received by the business for an item during a certain period of time? To answer this question, multiply the unit selling price (the price of one item) times the number of items sold.

What was the dollar volume of men's style 80 shirts during May?

Unit selling price × Items sold = Dollar volume of sales
$10   ×   60   = $600

Cost of Items Sold

How much money was spent by the business to purchase the items sold during a certain period of time? To answer, multiply the unit cost times the number of items sold.

The cost of men's style 80 shirts during May is figured here:

Unit cost × Items sold = Cost of items sold
$6   ×   60   = $360

Gross Profit in Dollars

How much more money was received on the sale of an item than was spent on its purchase? To answer, subtract the cost of items sold from the dollar volume of sales.

Dollar volume of sales	$600
Less cost of items sold	−360
Gross profit	$240

Gross Profit Percentage

What was the percentage of profit on an item when dollar volume of sales was compared to gross profit? (This does not include operating costs of the business.) To answer, divide the dollar volume of sales into the gross profit.

The gross profit percentage on men's style 80 shirts sold during May is calculated as follows:

$$\text{Dollar volume of sales }\overline{\smash{)}\text{Gross profit}}$$

$$600\,\overline{\smash{)}240.00} = .40 = 40\%$$

Gross profit percentage $= 40\%$

STOCK TURNOVER

A retail or wholesale businessman has a certain amount of his money (capital) invested in his merchandise, or stock. How much he makes on that investment depends upon how often he can sell the merchandise and reinvest the capital in more merchandise. If a business sells its products and reinvests the capital in more merchandise four times during the year, making a 5 percent profit each time, it makes a 20 percent profit for that year. If the merchandise had "turned" only three times, that is, sold out only three times, the business would have made only a 15 percent profit.

You may be called upon to figure turnover rates for various items, for classes of items, or for all merchandise. The object is to increase stock turnover in order to increase profit. The businessman needs to know the items for which turnover is low so that he can take corrective action.

Stock turnover may be figured in several ways. One of the more popular methods is to divide the cost of goods sold by the average inventory at cost:

1   Figure cost of goods sold as follows:

Inventory at cost, beginning of year	$ 50,000
Plus purchases of merchandise during year	160,000
Cost of merchandise available for sale	$210,000
Less inventory at cost, end of year	40,000
Cost of goods sold	$170,000

2   Figure average inventory as follows:

Inventory at cost, January 1	$ 50,000
Inventory at cost, April 1	45,000
Inventory at cost, July 1	55,000
Inventory at cost, October 1	60,000
Inventory at cost, December 31	40,000
Total	5)$250,000
Divide by 5 to obtain average =	$ 50,000

3   Figure turnover rate according to this formula:

$$\text{Turnover rate} = \frac{\text{Cost of goods sold during the year}}{\text{Average inventory at cost}}$$

$$\text{Turnover rate} = \frac{\$170,000}{\$50,000} = 3.4$$

A turnover rate of 3.4 would be considered very good (high) for a jewelry store but very poor (low) for a grocery store. Therefore, the turnover rate must be compared with the averages for other businesses of the same type to determine whether or not it is satisfactory.

REVIEWING YOUR READING

1 What steps should be taken in preparation for a physical inventory?
2 What merchandise is counted when a physical inventory is taken?
3 Why should a businessman know the order-delivery time for the merchandise he sells?
4 Knowing sales and profit figures will help a businessman to make what kinds of decisions?
5 Explain why a high turnover rate is more desirable to a businessman than a low turnover rate.
6 Why might book inventory be larger than physical inventory in a business?

OFFICE ASSIGNMENTS

1 Below is a section of an inventory tally sheet which has been partially filled in. On a separate sheet of paper determine the total quantity for each item, the cost value for each item, and the subtotal for the product class.

ITEM	STOCK NO.	UNIT COST	ASSEMBLY OF COUNT				TOTAL QUANTITY	COST VALUE	
Juvenile, right	G5539	.31 ea.	ⅢⅡ	ⅢⅡ	ⅢⅡ	/			
Juvenile, left	G5540	.31 ea.	ⅢⅡ	ⅢⅡ	ⅢⅡ	//			
Men's, right thread	G5541	.33 ea.	ⅢⅡ	ⅢⅡ	///				
Men's, left thread	G5542	.33 ea.	ⅢⅡ	ⅢⅡ	ⅢⅡ				
Ladies', right	G5546	.32 ea.	ⅢⅡ	////					
Ladies', left	G5547	.32 ea.	ⅢⅡ	ⅢⅡ	/				
Subtotal, this product class									

2 Determine the order-delivery time from the following purchase order and receiving report dates.

	Date of Purchase Order	Date of Receiving Report
a	June 3	June 18
b	November 20	December 3
c	April 9	April 27
d	August 22	September 4

3 For each of the following sets of information, determine **(a)** dollar volume of sales, **(b)** cost of items sold, **(c)** gross profit in dollars, and **(d)** gross profit percentage:

a Men's style 70 shirts: selling price, $8; unit cost, $5; items sold, 85.
b Men's style 90 shirts: selling price, $12; unit cost, $7.50; items sold, 50.
c Ladies' style 121 coats: selling price, $50; unit cost, $30; items sold, 25.

UNIT 15

BUSINESS CASES AND PROBLEMS

In the Boss's Shoes A physical inventory for Graham Hardware for the month of May reveals a count of 43 penknives in stock. The inventory record card for penknives shows a balance of 68. If you were the boss, what action would you take?

Your Human Relations 1 You and another worker have been assigned as a team to count stock in a certain section of a department store during the evening when the store is closed to customers. After you have completed the count, your co-worker says, "Let's each take one of these cassette tapes; the supervisor won't know the difference." Would you report this incident to the supervisor?

2 You are an inventory clerk assigned to the job of posting receipts and sales to inventory record cards and have received a stack of sales slip copies to be posted. As you begin your work, you notice that the numbers and words on the copies are extremely difficult to read. Would you do the best you could without saying anything? Would you try to do something about the situation? If so, what would you do?

What Would You Do If . . . ? You are recording the count during a physical inventory from information called to you by a sales worker. It is obvious that your co-worker is counting very hastily and inaccurately.

What Does This Mean? 1 A prospective employer tells you that his store specializes in staple dry goods.

2 A good inventory system will enable a businessman to study trends in demand and adjust his future purchases according to these trends. Explain.

Business in Your Area Determine how often two or three businesses in your area take a physical inventory of the merchandise they sell.

UNIT 16
SHIPPING SYSTEMS AND PROCEDURES

No order is complete until the customer receives his merchandise in good condition, at the appointed time, and at the appropriate place. Getting the merchandise to the customer is one of the most important functions of business. Thousands of railroads, motor carriers, airlines, pipelines, express companies, steamship lines, and freight forwarders are needed to assemble and ship the millions of tons of material sent all over the world. The nation's annual freight bill is in the billions.

MOVEMENT OF GOODS TO SHIPPING AREA

There are three basic phases involved in the operation of a typical shipping department. The first phase is the movement of goods to the shipping area. The items on the order move to the shipping area by way of conveyor, overhead carrier, chute, platform truck, skid, or tractor trailer. Several important procedures follow.

Inspection of Goods

When the items arrive in the shipping area, they receive a final examination to see if they show any evidence of damage or deterioration. Unsalable items are replaced immediately so that the customer will be completely satisfied.

Verification of Goods

The items received from the stockroom are also compared with the items listed on the shipping copy of the invoice shown below. This procedure is a precaution against shipping the wrong merchandise or shipping more or less than the number specified in the order.

B. J. Dawson Company
1100 Torrence Street
Waco, Texas 76705

Invoice No. **A-2504**
Date June 7, 19--
Terms 2/10, n/30
Order No. or Date May 18, 19--
Shipped Via Parcel Post

Sold To Mr. Matthew Polk
1919 Glorietta Street
San Antonio, Texas 78202

Ship To Same

Quantity	Stock No.	Description	Unit Price	Amount
1	012	Electric Drill Total		

Inspection of Papers

When the order has been assembled completely and correctly, the shipping room personnel are ready to finish the job. Shipping instructions are supplied on the invoice copy. (In some systems these instructions appear on the shipping order.) Labels are prepared and attached to the other papers, such as the *bill of lading* (which gives complete shipping information to the freight carrier). The shipping supervisor or his clerk checks to see that all shipping instructions have been supplied.

PREPARATION OF GOODS FOR SHIPMENT

The second phase in the operation of a shipping department is the preparation of goods for shipment. Losses due to faulty packing amount to millions of dollars annually. In parcel post service alone over a million broken or improperly prepared parcels that cannot be identified reach the dead-letter office every year.

Packing

Good packing means arranging and protecting goods to ensure their safe transit and arrival. It usually begins with the selection of the proper carton to serve as an outside container. The greater the distance that the shipment has to travel, the more handling it gets. The container not only has to be big and strong enough to hold the contents but also has to resist the weight of other packages stacked on top of it. Cartons made of corrugated, solid fiberboard or of kraft board are commonly used.

- ☐ Containers should be strong enough to retain and protect their contents in normal handling.
- ☐ The shipping container should allow enough space to hold the goods plus the cushioning matter placed inside the carton.
- ☐ Cushioning matter should be put in place by the packer after a carton or container has been selected. Excelsior, flexible corrugated fiberboard, felt, cellulose, cotton, shredded paper, and tissue paper are frequently used as cushioning materials.
- ☐ If a single item is shipped, sufficient cushioning material should be placed on all sides of the item to protect it from external impact.
- ☐ If two or more items are shipped in the same carton, the cushioning material should also protect the items from damaging one another.
- ☐ Fragile items should be individually cushioned.
- ☐ Heavy and lightweight items should not be packed together in the same container or compartment.
- ☐ Heavy items should be securely braced to prevent movement of the items in transit and should be packed in a strong exterior container.

The next step in packing is to seal the carton securely so that it stays closed in transit.

Wrapping

If the items are not being packed in a carton, they are wrapped in a soft package that is usually delivered by hand, parcel post, or package service. Wrapping paper should be of good quality kraft stock. Parcels may be tied, taped, or both. The cord used for tying a package should be strong and knotted at several intersecting points to prevent its loosening in transit. It's important to remember that the parcel may be picked up by the cord in the course of handling.

Tying

There are two basic methods used to tie parcels and packages. The single-string tie is designed for light packages.

1   Take the end of the string in your right hand.
2   Draw the string around the package the long way.
3   Cross the string, and take it once around the short way.
4   Tie a double square knot on the edge of the package.

The double-string tie is used on heavy parcels that require extra support.

1   Take the end of the string in your right hand; draw the string around the package twice the long way.
2   Cross and draw the string around the package the short way twice, looping the string at each intersection.
3   Tuck the short end of the string under the four strings crossing in the center.
4   Tie a double square knot and cut.

**Single-String Tie
Step 1**

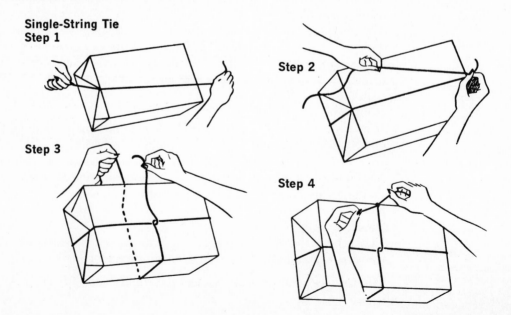

Step 2

Step 3

Step 4

Marking

Labels for addressing shipments are generally prepared as part of the invoicing operation. The label may be made separately from a file of address plates, or the upper portion of the shipping copy of the invoice may be torn off to serve the purpose. Address data may be printed on large or odd-size parcels, cartons, or crates with lumber pencil, marking pen, or stencil and brush. Most shipping authorities recommend that an extra copy of the invoice be placed inside the carton in case the outside address label or markings become defaced.

Parcels and cartons containing delicate articles should be marked "Fragile." Products that decay quickly should be marked "Perishable." Special service instructions such as "Special Handling," "Do Not Drop," and "This Side Up" should be prominently displayed, if required. Some customers also request suppliers to mark the purchase order number and the date on all shipments.

A first-class letter may accompany a parcel and may be either attached to the outside of the package or included inside. If the letter is on the outside of the package, it merely requires first-class letter postage. If it is inside the package, a notation must appear on the outside saying "First-Class Mail Enclosed," and first-class letter postage must be added to the parcel's postage. (See Section 12, page 147, concerning combination mailings.)

Weighing

The weight of the shipment is an important factor in deciding how to send it and in computing the cost of the transportation. Modern shipping departments are equipped with many sizes and types of scales.

Some desk and tabletop models are especially designed for weighing light packages. Floor scales take care of heavier shipments. Some special weighing equipment can weigh a truckload of material at a time. For most surface transportation any fraction of a pound is counted as an extra full pound in calculating charges.

METHODS OF SHIPMENT

The third phase in the operation of a shipping department is the selection of the carrier and the dispatch of goods. Sometimes the customer will specify the method of shipment in his order. On the other hand, there will be times when you may have to decide how the merchandise must be shipped. If you do, consider the following:

☐ Size and weight of the shipment.
☐ Nature of its contents.
☐ Urgency of the delivery.
☐ Location of the customer.
☐ Cost of the service.
☐ Special packing, handling, and collection problems.

Businesses in most localities have a number of shipping services at their disposal.

Messenger Service

Many small, light shipments can be delivered economically by messenger to addresses in the immediate vicinity. Service is direct and fast and normally requires no special packing. Messenger service is usually priced at an hourly rate.

Parcel Delivery Service

Shipments of every size, from a necktie to a suite of furniture, can be shipped by a parcel delivery service in most metropolitan areas. The pickup and delivery are performed on schedule. Delivery is frequently made the next day. Normal packing is usually required. COD (cash on delivery) service is generally available, and charges vary according to the weight of the package and the distance it is traveling.

The best-known parcel delivery service is the United Parcel Service (UPS). The shipper pays a small weekly service charge to have the UPS driver make a daily pickup call, regardless of whether or not any parcels are to be sent. In comparison to the rates of other parcel delivery services, UPS usually has the lowest rates available, which include insurance up to $100 for each package. No single parcel may exceed 50 pounds or 108 inches in length and girth combined, and not more than 100 pounds of parcels may be sent to one consignee in a single day. UPS, known for a long time as a consolidated package delivery service operating in large cities and suburban areas, also acts as an interstate carrier which links the Pacific states of Washington, Oregon, and California with 28 states and the District of Columbia in the eastern half of the United States.

Parcel Post

Shipments can be sent to any part of the country and to many foreign countries by mail. Charges vary according to weight and distance. Parcels must be taken to the post office for dispatch. Insurance, special delivery, receipt for delivery, and COD services are available at extra cost. Parcels sent parcel post travel by surface carriers such as trains and trucks, unless they are sent by air at higher rates (see the table for priority mail, Section 12, page 145).

Bus Package Express

Many passenger bus lines carry parcels on regularly scheduled runs. Same-day delivery service is usually available to points up to 300 miles away, and overnight delivery is available up to 500 miles away. One bus company carried 40 million packages in a single year and served 40,000 communities.

Packages must not exceed 100 pounds in weight; 141 inches in length, width, and height combined; or 60 inches in the longest single measurement. Normal packing is required, and each parcel must bear a shipper's label showing the name and address of the shipper and the addressee. It is also helpful to include the shipper's telephone number. Rates vary according to size, weight, and distance. Insurance protection up to $50 is included. This service is especially popular in suburban and rural areas where mail delivery and train stops are less frequent.

REA Express

This service combines truck and train facilities to speed parcels, baggage, pets, and a variety of other cargo. It is especially useful when the parcels being sent require speedy delivery or careful handling. Pickup and delivery service is included in the charges as well as a minimum insurance protection. Rates are based on weight, distance, and type of items shipped. COD service is available.

Air Express

Air-express service is offered by REA Express to all cities served by scheduled airlines. Rates include pickup and delivery service. If there is no direct air service to the consignee's town, air-express service will fly the shipment to the nearest airport and then transport it by rail and truck service the rest of the way. Air express is one of the most expensive shipping services available and should be used only after the other alternatives have been carefully considered.

Air Freight

Air freight is used for heavy top-priority cargoes of every description from Paris fashions to race horses. Shippers can charter whole planes or can ship a single carton or box. Such freight is picked up at the shipper's warehouse and taken to the airport by the freight company or its agent. At the end of the flight the merchandise is either picked up by the customer or, by arrangement, delivered by the freight company's truck to the customer's door (called *store-door* delivery). Air-freight rates, based on weight, distance, and type and value of merchandise, tend to be less expensive per pound than the rates for air parcel post and air express. In certain businesses the high transportation cost is offset by the competitive advantages of offering speedy service, having fewer distribution points, and having to invest a smaller amount of money in inventory because of the speed with which it can be replaced.

Truck

Trucklines operate in practically every town and hamlet in the country and carry 75 percent of the total tonnage moved in America's commerce. These carriers handle both bulk commodities, such as oil and grain, and finished merchandise. Solid trailer loads of goods can be shipped from factory to store without handling en route. Small shipments are consolidated at terminals for movement over main lines. The loads are sorted on arrival at the distribution point for delivery by smaller truck to final destination. Under average highway conditions, trucks can deliver parcels the following morning to points 300 miles away. Normal packing is required for truck transport; however, certain shortcuts can be taken when whole truckloads are shipped. Rates are moderate—usually lower than REA Express but somewhat higher than the rates for railroad freight on manufactured articles. The exact cost varies with the type of goods, weight, and distance. COD service is normally available.

Common carriers   These carriers offer their services to the general public. Consolidated Freightways and PIE Transport, Inc., are well-known trucking lines in this category.

Contract carriers   These perform delivery services for one shipper or a limited number of shippers. Contract carriers are usually local companies.

Private carriers   The shipper becomes a private carrier if he transports his own goods in vehicles that he owns or rents for the purpose.

Railroad

The railroads are the shipper's mainstay for handling bulk commodities that must travel fairly long distances and for moving heavier manufactured goods at a reasonable cost. To ease the loading and unloading of merchandise, large shippers usually have a railroad siding that runs to their warehouse. Freight can be shipped in carload lots (CL) or less-than-carload lots (LCL). Freight shipments must be well packed for safe transit. Rates vary according to weight, distance, and type of merchandise. In general, rates on LCL manufactured articles are fairly close to those offered by regular trucking companies. Because of the physical problem of assembling long trains and getting the movement started, railroads cannot generally offer the same overnight service as trucks. However, on longer hauls freight, traveling on some of the more efficient railroads, moves at a relatively good speed. As a rule COD collections on freight shipments have to be handled through banks.

Recently, railroads have entered into lively competition with trucks for such cargoes as new automobiles, container units, and trailer-van shipments (piggyback service). The illustration here shows how the combination of rail and truck services simplifies shipping operations.

Courtesy Penn Central Transportation Company

A Piggypacker lowers a highway trailer on a piggyback flatcar, where it is quickly secured for the trip.

Freight Forwarder

Freight forwarders handle freight that is to travel by rail, motor, or air. They consolidate smaller shipments into larger shipments that can be moved at lower rates and offer free pickup and delivery services by way of their own trucks or trucks operated by their agents. The Acme Fast Freight, Inc., National Carloading Corporation, and Universal Carloading and Distributing Company are some of the better-known firms in the field.

Ship

An amazing volume of goods is transported every year by ship in domestic as well as in international trade. The domestic trade moves along the coasts and inland waterways and consists principally of bulk commodities. The slow movement is offset by the low cost. International trade includes all types of goods, both bulk and manufactured. Fast liners carry the high-value, high-priority fashion, novelty, and finished goods. Slower ships carry the less glamorous cargoes. Unscheduled tramp ships and chartered vessels will transport literally anything by the boatload between any two ports. Movement of goods by ship involves extra packing precautions, including crating, casing, and strapping. Larger shipments can be packed in trailers or sturdy container units for movement without rehandling. When shipped by boat, merchandise has to be protected from the elements and theft as well as from rough handling. Although the rates are reasonable, service is slow and schedules to certain points are quite limited.

SHIPPER'S REFERENCE BOOKS

The shipping department keeps a record of customer's special instructions regarding the method of shipment. Even in the absence of special instructions, a record is kept of routes and carriers used for previous shipments to frequent customers. By referring to this record, you can quickly decide how to route and dispatch shipments to the same address the next time.

When merchandise is to be delivered to a new customer, the traffic manager or shipping clerk determines the types of service available to the destination where the goods are to be sent. There are several guidebooks that provide such vital data as the exact post office of the community, the carriers serving the location, and special routing information. Please see Section 28 under the headings "Freight," "Postal Data," and "Travel" for listings of these reference books.

If a shipment is to be sent by truck, the *National Highway and Airway Carriers and Routes* is the logical guidebook to use. Suppose that you are a shipping clerk for an El Paso, Texas, cotton goods manufacturer and you have to route a shipment to Pawtucket, Rhode Island.

1 Consult the routing section of the directory, which is arranged by state and city of destination. In this case you would look for *Rhode Island, Pawtucket.*

2 Under Pawtucket look for a Texas-based carrier with terminal facilities in that city. Note that it is *Tex. 19 TIME-DC.*

3 Then look in the Alphabetical Index of Carriers to find a description of the nature and scope of the carrier's operations. Observe that T.I.M.E.-DC, Inc. has terminal facilities in El Paso. Write down the address and telephone number: *7179 Industrial Blvd., El Paso, Texas 79915,* Tel. *915-778-8321.*

4 Call T.I.M.E.'s El Paso terminal, and arrange for a pickup.

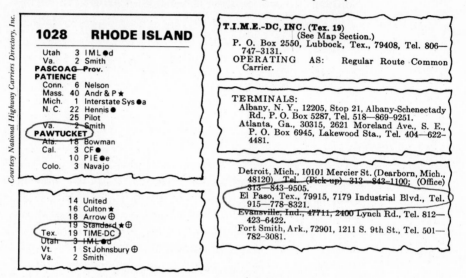

A shipping clerk must bear in mind that truckers are not always authorized to carry every type of commodity offered for delivery. Therefore, upon identifying T.I.M.E. as a company with terminal facilities in Pawtucket, you might refer to the Classified Index of Carriers by States and Cities to find the types of commodities that T.I.M.E. carries. Under Texas, Lubbock (home office), the entry reads *T.I.M.E.-DC, Inc.—12a, 13.*

A look at the Classification Index reveals that T.I.M.E. carries (12a) *Furniture, New, (Crated)* and (13) *General Commodities.* Cotton goods would be included in the latter category. After you determine that T.I.M.E. is authorized to carry your commodity, proceed with step 4 and telephone the carrier.

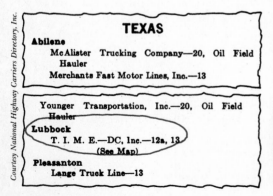

CLASSIFICATION INDEX

9—Farm Products
10—Fish
11—Food Products
12—Fruits
12a—Furniture, New (Crated).
12b—Furniture, New (Uncrated).
13—General Commodities
14—Glass Products

26—Petroleum and Petroleum Products
26a—Pipe and Pipeline Commodities
27—Rigging
28—Roofing Material
29—Rubber
30—Scrap Iron

PREPARATION OF SHIPPING PAPERS

Once the shipping clerk or traffic manager selects the shipping service that he is going to use, he completes the related papers, such as shipping labels and bills of lading, so that the shipment can begin its journey. Here are some examples of typical procedures.

Messenger Service

To save time, messenger service may be arranged by telephone. The dispatcher in the office of the messenger service fills out a delivery ticket, on which he records the essential details about the errand. A copy of this ticket is given to the messenger assigned to the call. The ticket tells him all that he needs to know.

United Parcel Service

The shipping clerk prepares a list of the parcels being sent on a particular day on a Pickup Record, a form supplied by the carrier. For example, a shipment to Centre TV, 1500 Brentwood Avenue, Baltimore, Maryland 21202, weighing 9 pounds is entered in the Pickup Record, illustrated on the top of page 452, as follows:

1 *Sales Memo.* Invoice number (if any) obtained from the notation on shipping label.
2 *Name.* Customer's name is taken from the shipping label.
3 Street number and street name.
4 City.
5 State.
6 ZIP Code.
7 Weight and destination zone.

   a The weight of the parcel is copied from the notation previously made in the shipping number area stamped above the shipping label. Note that the shipping label illustrated on page 452 indicates that the parcel weighs 9 pounds.

   b The destination zone is determined by referring to the UPS Zone Chart, also illustrated on page 452.

      (1) The Zone Chart uses the first three numbers of the destination's ZIP Code. This would be 212 in the case of the Baltimore address whose ZIP Code is 21202.

      (2) ZIP Code 212 falls within the range of numbers on line 200–218 on the Zone Chart.

      (3) The UPS destination zone number is 3.

      (4) The parcel's weight, 9, appears in the Zone 3 column of the Pickup Record.

A United Parcel Service pickup record.

Courtesy United Parcel Service

A shipping label.

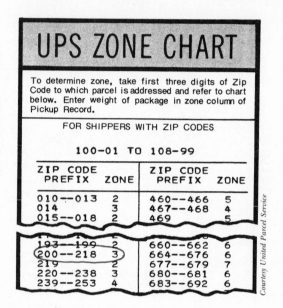

A UPS Zone Chart.

Courtesy United Parcel Service

REA Express

Receipts from different express services are kept in separate books in the shipping department. They are kept for prepaid and collect shipments. When the express driver calls to pick up a shipment, he completes the receipt record. Part of the receipt is affixed to the package for identification. Other parts provide a record for the carrier and a receipt for the shipper. Larger shippers also keep a record or register of items dispatched at the same time.

Truck or Rail Freight

A bill of lading is completed for each freight shipment moving by rail, truck, or ship. The form provides space for the shipper to supply a full description of the shipment and to give basic shipping instructions, such as routing, to the carrier. Weight data should be as accurate as possible. The rate, if given, refers to rate per hundred pounds as set forth in official freight rate tariffs. Unless the shipper indicates that freight charges are to be prepaid, the carrier assumes that the charges are to be collected when the goods are delivered. A business with a satisfactory credit rating is given a short credit period after shipment in which to pay charges. Railroads commonly allow from 48 to 120 hours as a credit period; trucklines may allow as much as a 7-day credit period. In another section of the form the carrier acknowledges receipt of the goods.

The original of the bill of lading is usually sent to the customer. The second copy, or shipping order, is kept by the carrier, and the third copy, called the memorandum, is retained by the shipper. A bill of lading is shown below.

(Uniform Domestic Straight Bill of Lading, adopted by Carriers in Official, Southern, Western and Illinois Classification territories, March 15, 1922, as amended August 1, 1930, June 15, 1941, September 21, 1944, January 9, 1948, and July 14, 1949.)   F. D. 3500

UNIFORM STRAIGHT BILL OF LADING — Original — Not Negotiable   PRINTED IN U.S.A.

RECEIVED, subject to the classifications and tariffs in effect on the date of the issue of this Bill of Lading, the property described below, in apparent good order, except as noted (contents and condition of contents of packages unknown), marked, consigned, and destined as indicated below, which said company (the word company being understood throughout this contract as meaning any person or corporation in possession of the property under the contract) agrees to carry to its usual place of delivery at said destination, if on its own road or its own water line, otherwise to deliver to another carrier on the route to said destination. It is mutually agreed, as to each carrier of all or any of said property over all or any portion of said route to destination, and as to each party at any time interested in all or any of said property, that every service to be performed hereunder shall be subject to all the conditions not prohibited by law, whether printed or written, herein contained, including the conditions on back hereof, which are hereby agreed to by the shipper and accepted for himself and his assigns.

622   PENN CENTRAL TRANSPORTATION COMPANY   622   **1**

GEORGE P. BAKER, RICHARD C. BOND, JERVIS
LANGDON, JR. AND WILLARD WIRTZ, TRUSTEES

CAR INITIAL	CAR NUMBER							LENGTH/CAPACITY OF CAR		WEIGHT IN TONS		WAYBILL DATE	WAYBILL NO.
L/E	LEN	TY	TRAILER INITIALS / NUMBER	&	L/E	LEN	TY	TRAILER INITIALS / NUMBER	&	ORDERED	FURNISHED	GROSS	TARE		

STOP THIS CAR

		FOR	**CONSIGNEE AND ADDRESS AT STOP**
AT			Grove Corporation
AT		FOR	101 Albion Road
AT		FOR	Cleveland, Ohio 44120

	ORIGIN	STATE
	New York	New York

SHIPPER   FULL NAME OF SHIPPER

Transportation, Inc.

BILL OF LADING DATE	BILL OF LADING NO.	INVOICE NO.	CUSTOMER NO.	WHEN SHIPPER IN THE UNITED STATES EXECUTES NO-RECOURSE CLAUSE OF SECT. 7 OF BILL OF LADING CHECK (x) →		WEIGHED AT
9/28/--		A-1035		YES		GROSS

CONSIGNEE AND ADDRESS

Grove Corporation

	DESTINATION	STATE OF	COUNTY OF	RECEIVED $_____ TO APPLY AS PREPAYMENT OF CHARGES ON THE PROPERTY DESCRIBED HEREON	TARE
	Cleveland	Ohio			

ROUTE (FOR SHIPPER'S USE ONLY)

Penn Central, Norfolk and Western

DELIVERY CARRIER
Norfolk and Western

ALLOWANCE

AGENT OR CASHIER

PER

NET

Subject to Section 7 of Conditions, if the shipment is to be delivered to the consignee without recourse on the consignor, the consignor shall sign the following statement: The carrier shall not make delivery of this shipment without payment of freight and all other lawful charges.
Signature of Consignor

Note—Where the rate is dependent upon value, shippers are required to state specifically in writing the agreed or declared value of the property. The agreed or declared value of the property is hereby specifically stated by the shipper to be not exceeding   PER

*If the shipment moves between two ports by a carrier by water, the law requires that the bill of lading shall state whether it is "carrier's or shipper's weight."

(THE SIGNATURE HERE ACKNOWLEDGES ONLY THE AMOUNT PREPAID)

CHARGES ADVANCED

$

IF CHARGES ARE TO BE PREPAID WRITE OR STAMP HERE:

'TO BE PREPAID'

To Be Prepaid

SHIPPERS SPECIAL INSTRUCTIONS (INCLUDE ICING. VENTILATION. HEATING. MILLING. WEIGHING. ETC.)

NO. PKGS.	DESCRIPTION OF ARTICLES, SPECIAL MARKS AND EXCEPTIONS	COMMODITY CODE NO.	*	WEIGHT (SUBJECT TO COR.)	RATE	FREIGHT	ADVANCES	PREPAID
100	Crates Lighting Fixtures, Fluorescent			6350 lbs.				

SHIPPER   Transportation, Inc.   PER   AGENT

PERMANENT POST OFFICE ADDRESS OF SHIPPER   Box 216, New York, New York 10040   PER

Air Freight

The forms that must be completed when you ship by air-express or air-freight service vary with the carrier or agent. One airline's priority air parcel service can be arranged at any airport ticket counter 30 minutes prior to scheduled flight time. An "Airbill" or invoice–bill of lading is prepared on the spot by the ticket agent, and the sender pays for the service in cash, by check, or by credit card. The sender then telephones the addressee and tells him the Airbill number, flight number, and time of arrival. The parcel can be picked up at the airlines baggage office in the destination airport within 30 minutes after the flight arrives.

Miscellaneous Shipments

Not all outgoing shipments involve merchandise for sale. For example, a branch office may have requested a ream of letterheads from the home office. A clerk in the stationery supply room will complete a general shipping order form which tells the shipping department how to handle the shipment.

DISPATCHING

Customers appreciate having their merchandise shipped to them as quickly as possible. Dispatching may be accomplished by using one of the following three methods:

1 Some carriers, such as the local parcel delivery service and REA Express, may call to pick up shipments on a daily or on a more frequently scheduled basis.
2 Certain carriers may have to be notified before they call. These may include trucklines, air-freight forwarders, and individual store-door pickup services.
3 In other cases the shipper must send the parcel to the receiving point to arrange for such services as parcel post, air parcel post, or bus package express.

Since timing is important, the shipping department maintains detailed pickup schedules of the carriers that it frequently uses. Alternate procedures for emergency, after hours, or holiday shipments are worked out in advance. A complete file of carriers' telephone numbers is used to speed arrangements and to obtain answers to last minute questions.

OTHER SHIPPING FUNCTIONS

The shipping department's job may not be over even after a shipment has been turned over to a carrier.

Reporting Prepaid Shipping Charges

If the terms of sale merchandise are FOB seller's warehouse, the buyer must pay the delivery expense. However, in the case of parcel post shipments, the postage is paid at the time and place of mailing. The seller recoups his outlay for postage by instructing his shipping department to tell the billing department how much postage to add to the invoice that will be charged to the customer's account. In dispatching freight shipments, the seller can normally arrange for the buyer to pay the delivery expense by specifying "charges collect" on the bill of lading. However, if there is no carrier's office or representative to accept payment at the destination, the shipper will pay the delivery costs at the time of dispatch and then add the charges to the buyer's invoice. This procedure is followed with parcel post.

Expediting

If the shipment is an emergency order, the shipping department will be asked to see that the goods move with all possible speed. This special follow-through process is called *expediting*. The shipping room supervisor telephones the carrier and makes a special request that the urgent shipment be attended to as quickly as possible. From day to day the movement of the goods is checked to see that delivery deadlines are being met.

Tracing

The performance records of the post office and of other shipping services are truly remarkable. These services succeed in handling millions of shipments every year with relatively few mishaps. However, delays and lost shipments do occur and can greatly upset a customer's plans. Consequently, the shipping department must be on its toes all the time. At the first sign that all is not going well with a shipment, it must try to trace the movement of the missing goods.

If the missing merchandise has been shipped parcel post, a tracer form is completed and filed at the post office right away. If a truck or freight shipment has apparently gone astray, another type of tracer is filed. (See the forms on page 456.)

If a shipment can't be found after a reasonable period of time, the shipper or customer files a claim with the carrier for reimbursement of the loss. Note the form on page 457. (The post office is liable only for loss of insured and registered parcels.) In the meantime, the shipper usually sends off a duplicate shipment to meet the customer's needs.

Auditing

The carrier's invoice for transportation service is called a *freight bill*. Charges on freight bills are carefully checked to be sure that there are no overcharges. Freight bills should be audited before payment is made, but because the credit terms for freight delivery are quite short, the audit is sometimes made after payment. The auditor checks the bills against all available evidence, especially against the bill of lading, weight readings, and tariff schedules. If he has a sharp eye, he can save the firm a great deal of money. Claims for refunds based on overcharges can be expedited by the use of a standard form. There are three common causes of overcharges:

1   The wrong and higher rate may be applied to the type of goods shipped.
2   An incorrect excessive weight may be applied to the correct rate.
3   An error in the description on the bill of lading or a misunderstanding about the description given results in an incorrect classification for pricing.

PS Form 1510   U.S. POSTAL SERVICE
Original—Part I   Post Office at *WATERTOWN, NEW YORK*
ADDRESSEE: ZIP Code *12601*   Date *MAY 24, 19—*
Please state in the spaces below whether the article described on Part II has been delivered to you and then return both parts of this form in the enclosed OFFICIAL SELF-ADDRESSED ENVELOPE WHICH REQUIRES NO POSTAGE. Your response will help to improve the postal service.
                                            POSTMASTER.
REPLY OF ADDRESSEE (Check one):   ( ) REFUSED.
My records show that the article was: (✓) NOT RECEIVED. ( ) RECEIVED.
If any contents missing, list them: ....
....
.... Value of missing articles, $...........
MAY 18, 19—   *Mary R. McNulty*
(Date of reply)   (Signature of addressee or agent)

PS Form 1510—Original—Part II   Date *MAY 10, 19—*
INQUIRY FOR THE LOSS OR RIFLING OF MAIL MATTER
( ) Letter   Registered No. .... ( ) Special Delivery
(✓) Parcel *4th* Certified No. .... ( ) Special Handling
    (Class)   Insured No. *7798*...................... ( ) Airmail
                 (Insert "Unnumbered" if minimum fee)
( ) Ordinary. COD No............... Amount due sender $..........
Envelope: ( ) Long. ( ) Short. ( ) Business reply (Postage to be paid by addressee.)
Complaint *LOSS* Date mailed *APRIL 11* 19— *2 P.M. MONDAY*
(Loss or rifling)   (Mo.)   (Date)   (Yr.) (Hr.) (Day of week)
Mailed at *CHAMPLAIN* *1st* *NEW YORK* *12919*
          (Post Office) (Class) (State)   (ZIP Code)
Where deposited *MAIN POST OFFICE*
              (Main office, station, branch, or location of collection box)
Contents (describe fully) and value *CRYSTAL SALAD BOWL, ROUND,*
12 INCHES IN DIAMETER, $24.95
                                              (Fold here)
Sender: Addressee:
MRS. FLORENCE JONES   *MISS MARY R. McNULTY*
(Name)   (Name)
945 MAIN STREET   *21 LAKE STREET*
(St. or P.O. Box or Rural Route No.)   (St. or P.O. Box or Rural Route No.)
CHAMPLAIN, N.Y. 12919   *WATERTOWN, N.Y. 13601*
(City) (State) (ZIP Code)   (City) (State) (ZIP Code)

PS Form 1510—Original—Part III
POSTMASTER, OFFICE OF ADDRESS: Date *MARCH 12, 19—*
Please show disposition of the above-described article.
          CHAMPLAIN, N.Y.   *12919*
          (Postmaster at mailing office)   (ZIP Code)
REPLY:
Date *MAY 18* , 19—. Has addressee received article? *NO*
                                            (Yes or No)
(If there is a record of delivery, show delivery date................. ;
If delivered to firm, state accepting employee's name ....
If not intact, what was missing? .... ;
If COD, give MO Nos. ...., Amts. ...., date ....)
If undelivered and on hand, state reason ....
If received but not delivered and not on hand, state disposition ....
          R. M. Russo   *13601*
          (Postmaster at address office)   (ZIP Code)
PS FORM 1510

The sender fills out Part II of this tracing form for packages sent parcel post. Part I is filled out by the addressee, and Part III by the post office of destination.

This tracing form notifies the carrier that a freight shipment has been lost.

Towle Bros., Inc.

100 Fifth Avenue
New York, N.Y. 10011

                                    DATE *June 10, 19—*

Freight Department
Hudson Central R.R.
350 Lexington Avenue
New York, New York 10017

Gentlemen:

SUBJECT *Lost Shipment – Utica, New York*

    Our customer has informed us that the shipment described below has not reached its destination.

CARRIER *H.C.*

CARRIER PRO. NO. *46-840-02*

DATE OF SHIPMENT *May 5, 19—*

SHIPPER'S NO. *21801*

CUSTOMER'S PURCHASE ORDER NO. *239*

CARTONS *12*   WEIGHT *500*

CONSIGNED TO *Valley Sports Shop*
            121 Genesee Street
            Utica, New York 13501

ANSWER NEEDED BY *6/20* VIA PHONE ✓ MAIL ____ WIRE ____
                (date)   (SWinburne 9-1700)
    Please investigate as soon as possible. If the goods were actually delivered, please supply photocopy of delivery receipt.

                                    Robert Kline
                                    Traffic Manager

Standard Form for Presentation of Loss and Damage Claims

Approved by the Interstate Commerce Commission; Freight Claim Division, American Railway Association;
National Industrial Traffic League, and the National Association of Railway Commissioners.

Mr. H. Frankel, Claims Agent   Muncie, Indiana 47302   L-251
(Name of person to whom claim is presented)   (Address of claimant)   (Claimant's Number)§

Great Western R.R.   June 21, 19--
(Name of carrier)   (Date)   (Carrier's Number)

Box 33, Denver, Colo. 80936
(Address)

This claim for $ 169.75 is made against the carrier named above by Kramer's Furniture, Inc.
(Amount of claim)   (Name of claimant)
for damage in connection with the following described shipments:
(Loss or damage)
Description of shipment 6 Crates of Office Furniture
Name and address of consignor (shipper) Kramer's Furniture, Inc., 8 Eaton Ave., Muncie, Ind. 47302
Shipped from Muncie, Indiana ; To Great Falls, Montana
(City, town or station)   (City, town or station)
Final Destination Great Falls, Montana ; Routed via Great Western R.R.
(City, town or station)
Bill of Lading issued by Great Western R.R. Co.; Date of Bill of Lading May 15, 19--
Paid Freight Bill (Pro) Number 71-619 ; Original Car Number and Initial
Name and address of consignee (whom shipped to) Dover Construction Co., Box 3001, Great Falls, Mont.
                                                                                    59103
If shipment reconsigned en route, state particulars:

DETAILED STATEMENT SHOWING HOW AMOUNT CLAIMED IS DETERMINED.

(Number and description of articles, nature and extent of loss or damage, invoice price of articles, amount of claim, etc.)

One executive desk, new, total loss in fire at Great Falls Freight Depot at delivered invoice price.	$169.75
TOTAL AMOUNT CLAIMED	

IN ADDITION TO THE INFORMATION GIVEN ABOVE, THE FOLLOWING DOCUMENTS ARE SUBMITTED IN SUPPORT OF THIS CLAIM.*

(X) 1. Original bill of lading, if not previously surrendered to carrier.
(X) 2. Original paid freight (expense) bill.
(X) 3. Original invoice or certified copy.
(   ) 4. Other particulars obtainable in proof of loss or damage claimed.

Statement of Station Agent, Great Falls.

REMARKS:

The foregoing statement of facts is hereby certified to as correct:

KRAMER'S FURNITURE, INC.

James Costa , Manager
(Signature of claimant)

§ Claimant should assign to each claim a number, inserting same in the space provided at the upper hand corner of this form. Reference should be made thereto in all correspondence pertaining to this claim.
* Claimants will please place check (x) before such of the documents mentioned as have been attached, and explain under "Remarks" the absence of any of the documents called for in connection with this claim.   When for any reason it is impossible for claimant to produce original bill of lading, or paid freight bill, claimant should indemnify carrier or carriers against duplicate claim, supported by original documents.

Courtesy The Traffic Service Corp., Washington, D.C.

Keeping Records

Every shipping or traffic department requires competent clerical help to keep its records and reports, such as the following, in order:

1   Reference books in which supplements must be inserted and changes posted.
2   Contracts and agreements with carriers which must be safely filed for future reference.
3   Memorandum copies of bills of lading and other shipping receipts.
4   Records of amounts owed to shippers for services and amounts due from shippers on claims on loss, damage, and overcharges.
5   Routing records to aid in the quick selection of carriers for shipments to regular clients.
6   Other records of cash due and received on COD shipments and of petty cash outlays for shipments dispatched by irregular carriers.
7   Personnel records, especially if the working force is working under an incentive payment plan.
8   Insurance records covering shipments that required protection in excess of the limits assumed by the carrier.
9   Up-to-date comprehensive correspondence files.
10 Periodic performance reports for higher management.
11 Budgets to assist in planning future operations.

Arranging Transportation

In larger firms the shipping operations are part of a large function called traffic, which refers to *inbound* and *outbound* movements of all kinds. The traffic department not only makes arrangements for the operation of delivery trucks, car pools, and corporate planes but may also arrange for other company transportation needs.

1   Personal effects of employees transferred from one location to another.
2   Machinery, equipment, and furniture requisitioned from one office or plant and sent to another.
3   Company personnel, usually executives journeying by rail, boat, or air to all parts of the world. Service may also include making hotel and car rental reservations.

REVIEWING YOUR READING

1   Demonstrate or explain how to wrap a fragile object for shipment by parcel post from your home to a point several hundred miles away.
2   Demonstrate or explain the use of the double-string tie to reinforce the parcel that you packed and wrapped for question 1 above.
3   Could the parcel that you prepared for question 1 above be sent by any other means? What factors would you consider in selecting any alternate shipping service?
4   Demonstrate or explain the use of the guidebook *National Highway and Airway Carriers and Routes* mentioned in your text.

OFFICE ASSIGNMENTS

1 Complete a pickup record for the following shipments by Parson Distributors, 998 Olmstead Avenue, Bronx, New York 10473; shipper's number 1-23-459; via United Parcel Service. Use the current date. If you are not using the workbook, copy the form illustrated on page 452.

    a 11-pound 2-ounce parcel containing items covered by Invoice 1247 to John Jones Company, 478 Atlantic Avenue, Hastings, New York 13076.

    b 15-pound package addressed to Joe Smith, Inc., 500 West Lake Street, Cooperstown, New York 13326, relating to Invoice 1249. The amount of $12.98 is to be collected upon delivery.

    c 9-pound parcel to Frank & Co., 222 Jackson Avenue, Buffalo, New York 14218, covered by Invoice 1263. The amount of $9.90 is to be collected on delivery.

    d 7-pound carton to Jones and Smith, 111 Hartford Street, Berlin, Pennsylvania 15530, covered by Invoice 1270.

    Use the following partial UPS Zone Chart to find the proper destination zone.

ZIP Code Prefix	Zone
128–136	3
137–139	2
140–149	3
150–154	4
155	3

2 Complete the bill of lading required for the following shipment by way of the Penn Central and Norfolk and Western railroads. If you are not using the workbook, copy the form illustrated on page 453.

Consignee: Name and address:	Displays, Incorporated 18 Valley View Road, S.E. Roanoke, Virginia 24014
Shipper:	Farber Suppliers 29 Manhattan Avenue New York, New York 10025
Bill of lading date:	Use current date
Invoice number:	17-412
Route:	Penn Central, Norfolk and Western
Delivery carrier:	Norfolk and Western
Charges:	To be prepaid.
Shipper's special instructions:	Stand right side up as indicated. Use no hooks.

3 crates display cases, wood, knocked down (KD) @ 200 pounds
1 carton hardware for above   @ 30 pounds

3   A trucker's claim representative completed the following inspection report after a visit to a consignee who had reported damage in shipment discovered after delivery.

Courtesy American Trucking Associations, Inc.

INSPECTION REPORT OF LOSS OR DAMAGE DISCOVERED AFTER DELIVERY

TERMINAL Dallas, Texas _____ **Date** January 27, _____ **19** -- **Report Number** 49618

Shipper Wholesale Sport Supplies _____ **Address** 90 Broadway, Yonkers, N.Y. 10706

Consignee Southwest Sport Center _____ **Address** 412 Elm Street, Dallas, Tex. 75202

F/B No. _____ **Prepaid** ☒ **Collect** ☐   **Date Consignee requested inspection** January 25, 19--

Date of Billing January 20, **19** -- **Date Delivered** Jan.18, **19** -- **Loss or Damage** Damage   **Could loss or damage have been noticed at time of delivery?** _____

Date Unpacked January 25, **19** -- **Date of Call** Jan.25, **19** --   **Were goods unpacked before the inspection was made?** Yes **Were containers and packing available?** Yes

What evidence was there of pilferage before delivery? None

Was there sufficient space in package to contain missing goods? ---- **What material occupied the remaining space?** ----

Did comparison of check with invoice or weighing package, verify loss ---- **If released valuation, show weight of articles damaged or short** 60 lbs.

Kind of Container Carton (Carton, Box, Crate, etc.) **New or Old** Old   **Wired** ☐ **Corded** ☐ **Strapped** ☐ **Nailed** ☐ **Sealed** ☒

Box Maker's Gross Weight Limit 100 **Gross Weight of Loaded Carton** 100 **If Carton Were Flaps Glued?** No **Were Seams or Edges Split?** Yes

How were goods packed? Newspaper for wrapping and cushioning.

Do you consider adequately packed or protected? No **What condition of container or contents indicated loss or damage occurred with carrier?** No external damage visible, but broken glass fragments found in wrappings.

To prevent comparable damage in the future, how in your judgment should they have been packed or prepared for shipment Glass shades should be packed separately from metal lamp body. Excelsior or plastic bubble cushioning needed around shades instead of crumpled newspaper. Fragile notation should appear more prominently on all sides of carton. New and stronger cartons needed. Carton flaps should be sealed.

Did shipment have prior transportation? No **If so, is merchandise still packed in original container?** Yes **Original point of shipment** Yonkers, N.Y.

No. of Articles	Describe fully nature and extent of loss or damage	Actual Value
24	Lanterns, kerosine (6 glass shades broken) plus	$15.00
	transportation of replacements.	6.00
	(If necessary use additional sheet)	

Will there be salvage? No **What disposition will be made of the salvage?** None

Consignee Southwest Sport Center _____ **Carrier** _____

By *D. Himes* _____ **By** _____
                                                          Inspector

EXECUTION OF THIS REPORT DOES NOT CONSTITUTE LEGAL FILING OF CLAIM IN WRITING.

This report is merely a statement of facts and not an acknowledgement of Carrier's liability. When presenting claims for loss and damage, attach the following documents:

1. This Inspection Report
2. Original Paid Freight Bill
3. Original Bill of Lading

4. Original Invoice or an exact certified copy showing all discounts
5. Your Bill showing nature and amount of claim
6. Shipper's and Consignee's Concealed Loss and Damage Forms

Assuming that the report is accurate, with whom do you think the fault lies? Explain. What action must be taken to remedy the situation? By whom?

4   Complete Part II of a postal service tracer Form 1510 to locate a missing parcel post shipment. Either use the form provided in your workbook, or copy the form on page 456.

Date:	June 8, 19–
Shipper:	Sands Electronics, Inc.
	111 Roff Way
	Reno, Nevada 89501
Addressee:	Henry Lake
	2259 Oro Valley Drive
	Tucson, Arizona 85704
Date and time mailed:	May 10, 19–; 3 p.m.; Friday.
Mailed at:	Main post office (first class), Reno, Nevada 89504.
Description:	Fourth-class parcel, special handling required. Insured number 16098 containing one cassette tape recorder, valued at $60.

5   Complete a claim for damage in shipment as follows. Either use the form in your workbook, or copy the illustration on page 457.

A claim for $75 is made against Union Pacific Railroad, 1416 Dodge Street, Omaha, Nebraska 68179, by Ross-Brock and Company (claimant number L-435), 129 Cedar Street, Omaha, Nebraska 68108. One of the four crates of office tables was in damaged condition upon delivery to the consignee, Peake's Office Supply Company, Box 101, Denver, Colorado 80201. One side and one end of a crate were badly damaged; the corner assembly of the table was splintered; side supports were broken; the top was dented and scratched. The item was considered to be beyond repair. The crates were shipped from Omaha, Nebraska, to Denver, Colorado, via Union Pacific Railroad, which issued the bill of lading on August 25, 19--. The shipment was covered by Waybill (freight bill) No. 648,933,121. The original bill of lading, the freight bill, and the invoice are submitted in support of the claim made on September 30, 19--, and presented to the claims agent, E. A. Marshall. Sign your name as manager of Ross-Brock and Company.

UNIT16

BUSINESS CASES AND PROBLEMS

In the Boss's Shoes   Your firm pays all shipping costs on customers' orders. You have just packed a small order amounting to $11.25 worth of goods. The shipping papers call for shipment by air express which will cost $5 or $6. Should you dispatch the parcel as specified, or should you ask more questions?

Your Human Relations   In the absence of the shipping room supervisor, you answer a telephone call from an irate customer complaining that his recent order was late again. You have heard the caller complain to the supervisor before. The reason for the delay is because the carrier moves very slowly en route. However, the customer refuses to change to another carrier because the one he specifies is the cheapest. Should you tell the customer that the problem is his own fault? Or what else would you say?

What Would You Do If . . . ?   A telephone-order customer has specified that he wants a certain carrier to deliver his order. From past experience you know that this line gives poor service and is very unreliable in handling claims. As shipping clerk should you change the routing? Should you telephone the customer and tell him the facts? Should you notify the sales office that took the order? Or should you do nothing and let the customer take his chances?

What Does This Mean?   A trucking company in San Francisco advertises second-morning delivery of shipments to Seattle.

Business in Your Area   Find out what shipping services are available to businessmen in your community. Explain the methods of dispatch normally used with each of the services available.

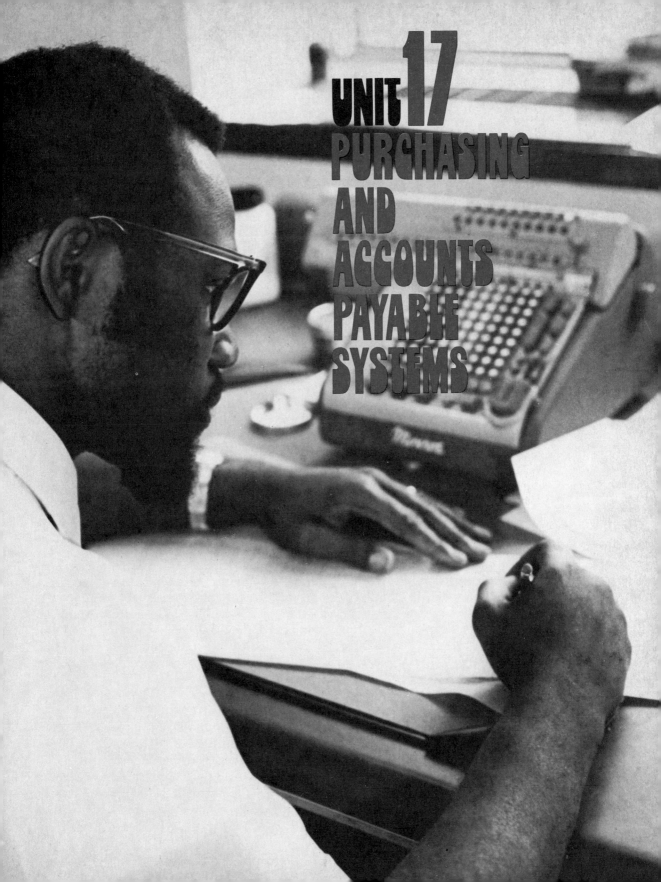

UNIT 17

PURCHASING AND ACCOUNTS PAYABLE SYSTEMS

SECTION 40 Purchasing Activities

It's important to have a good purchasing system because the efficiency with which merchandise is bought has a direct impact on the sales of the business and on the eventual profit that is earned. Purchasing systems and procedures vary greatly among businesses, but certain activities are common to all.

The purchase of raw materials for manufacture, merchandise for resale, equipment, supplies, or utilities for use in the business itself involves a number of activities common to most organizations regardless of their size, product lines, or services.

Budgeting. A plan for purchasing items is called a *budget.*

Requesting. A request for goods or services, in which the needs of individuals in the organization are made known to those responsible for purchasing, is called a *requisition.*

Ordering. A firm orders what it needs from suppliers by issuing a form called a *purchase order.*

Receiving. The process involving accepting and counting items, checking for any defects, putting the items in stock, and if the merchandise is to be resold, pricing and marking them for the customer. The receiving report form is used by many firms to record which items ordered have arrived.

Handling Accounts Payable. Payments made for items purchased by the business are called *accounts payable.* This topic is discussed in Section 41.

BUDGETING

The amount of money that is budgeted for purchases depends upon several factors. Previous sales and trends in consumer demand give the businessman a basis for predicting future sales and, therefore, future purchases. Inventory, or stock on hand, influences the purchasing budget because if a large stock of goods is on hand, fewer purchases are necessary. Cash available to the company also has an influence on the planned purchases. For example, large-scale purchases cannot be budgeted if cash to pay for the items cannot be readily obtained. Three important kinds of purchasing budgets are discussed below.

Materials Budget

Manufacturing companies draw up sales and production budgets and then on the basis of these two budgets prepare a materials budget, which is the list of planned purchases. The materials budget may include three parts, or schedules. As shown on page 465, Schedule 1 is the budgeted number for four items to be purchased that are necessary for the manufacture of trays. Notice that Schedule 1 takes into account the beginning and ending inventories of each

INDUSTRIAL TRAY COMPANY
Materials Budget
Year Ending December 31, 19—

Schedule 1: Unit Schedule of Purchases

	Material Number			
	SM-2 (in ft.)	LF-6 (in sets)	MS-1 (in sets)	PV-2 (in gal.)
Quantity required per tray	6	4	12	1/30
Total quantity required for 60,000 trays	360,000	240,000	720,000	2,000
Budgeted ending inventory of raw materials, December 31	22,000	16,000	40,000	100
Total budgeted requirements	382,000	256,000	760,000	2,100
Beginning inventory of raw materials, January 1	20,000	16,000	50,000	150
Total budgeted purchases	362,000	240,000	710,000	1,950

Schedule 2: Dollar Schedule of Purchases

Material	Budgeted Purchases	Unit Cost	Total Cost
SM-2	362,000 feet	$ .50 per foot	$181,000
LF-6	240,000 sets	.10 per set	24,000
MS-1	710,000 sets	.01 per set	7,100
PV-2	1,950 gal.	4.00 per gal.	7,800
Total			$219,900

Schedule 3: Budgeted Materials Usage

Material	Scheduled Usage	Unit Cost	Total Cost
SM-2	360,000 feet	$ .50 per foot	$180,000
LF-6	240,000 sets	.10 per set	24,000
MS-1	720,000 sets	.01 per set	7,200
PV-2	2,000 gal.	4.00 per gal.	8,000
Total			$219,200

SOURCE: Brock, Palmer, and Archer, *Cost Accounting, Theory and Practice,* 2d ed., McGraw-Hill Book Company, New York, 1971, p. 227.

of the four items. Schedule 2 consists of the cost of the purchases budgeted in Schedule 1. Schedule 3 shows the cost of the materials that are actually to be used; the amounts to be used may differ from the materials purchased because of plans to increase or decrease inventory levels.

Open-to-Buy Report

Merchandising companies, such as department stores, budget their purchases on a form known as an *open-to-buy report.* Usually each department is responsible

OPEN-TO-BUY REPORT
From August 19-- to January 19--

Sales Plan	Aug.	Sept.	Oct.	Nov.	Dec.	Jan.	Total
Last year sales	3.1	9.5	20.7	21.3	36.4	14.6	105.6
Plan for this year	3.4	9.8	20.2	21.0	30.5	13.5	98.4
Actual for this year	3.4	9.7	20.3				
Purchases Plan							
Last year purchases	5.1	7.2	8.0	19.6	6.4	12.5	58.8
Plan for this year	5.3	7.0	7.8	17.4	5.9	14.8	58.2
Actual for this year	5.3	7.0	7.6				
Open to buy	52.9	45.9	38.3				

R. Gallahan   *W. A. Bondurant*   *Men's Shoes*

Buyer   Merchandise Manager   Department

for preparing its own budget, which is based upon past and projected sales and inventory levels. Because of the rapid changes in consumer demand for particular items, the open-to-buy report is a plan for spending money rather than a plan for purchasing specific items. Each department's budget must be approved by the top officers of the company. Their approval is based upon such factors as plans for expansion, changes in competition, sales promotion plans, and the cash position of the firm. After the department's budget has been approved, the merchandising manager and his department heads, who are known as buyers, decide which items are to be purchased. A highly simplified open-to-buy report is illustrated above. All figures on the report are in thousands of dollars, that is, 3.1 means $3,100. Note that actual sales and purchases for this year have been posted through the month of October. The amount that is open to buy is figured by subtracting actual purchases from the total planned purchases, 58.2 ($58,200). Consequently, as purchases are made and subtracted from the total planned purchases, the amount remaining open-to-buy decreases.

Departmental Operating Budget

A third type of budget, the departmental operating budget, is used by medium- to large-size companies to allocate funds for equipment, supplies, utilities, salaries, and other internal expenses to the various departments of a company. Items of expense are listed along with their budgeted amounts. Whenever a department officer wishes to buy something for his department, he consults the departmental operating budget to see if funds have been allocated for that purpose.

Remember that no purchase can be made in a firm or institution unless money has been budgeted for purchase of that particular type of item. Every item used in a business from a paper clip to a steam generator costs money and affects the profits of the enterprise. A budget is essential in planning all purchases. It assures the company that money is being spent wisely.

REQUESTING

Individuals in an organization can report their needs to those responsible for purchasing in several ways. Some of the procedures to follow in reporting these needs are outlined below.

Stockroom Requisition

A worker who needs any materials completes a stockroom, or stores, requisition form. The requisition illustrated below includes spaces to record:

- Where the requisition is to be sent.
- Which department is requesting the materials.
- To whom and where the materials are to be delivered.
- The description and quantity of the materials needed.
- Who authorized the request.

In describing what he wants, the worker may refer to a standard parts list which can be included in a company procedures manual or indicated in work order sheets. Obviously, the more exact the description is, the easier it is for the supply personnel to understand precisely what is required.

Requisitions are usually prepared with several carbon copies and are usually distributed in the following manner:

SOUTHEAST TECHNOLOGICAL UNIVERSITY

STORES REQUISITION

TO _____ Central _____ STORES

FOR_____ VTE Division _____ DEPARTMENT

DELIVER TO____ Joan Randall, 2082 Derring Hall _____   DATE   February 19, 19--

CATALOG NO.	CATALOG DESCRIPTION (NAME, TYPE, SIZE, COLOR, ETC.)	√	ORDER QUANTITY	UNIT		
7450 00 016	Ribbon, typewriter, black, nylon,					
	9/16" x 18 yd., 12 per box		5	Box		

AUTHORIZED SIGNATURE _Jacob Klopman_ _____   RECEIVED BY _____

1 Original and one carbon to the stockroom.
2 One carbon to the authorizing supervisor for budget control.
3 One carbon retained by the requisitioning employee.

Issuing Stock

The properly authorized requisition passes through channels to the stockroom. Upon its arrival, the stockroom personnel check their records to see if the required material is on hand. The stockroom must keep careful records of stock balances because hundreds of items are handled every day and memory alone would not be sufficient to keep track of things. If stock were allowed to run out without being replenished, a serious work stoppage might occur. Therefore, for maximum protection a record is kept on every item in stock.

If the stock records indicate that the material required is available, a stock clerk locates the material in the storage area, counts out the exact quantity, and sends it along to the waiting employee. The original requisition remains in the stockroom so that stock records can be adjusted. The carbon copy is attached to the supplies ordered and identifies both the goods and the person to whom the goods are to be delivered.

Request for Purchase

When the stock of a standard supply item runs low, the stockroom sends a requisition to the purchasing office, asking them to order more of this item. This formal request for supplies is prepared on a special form.

If the stockroom receives a request for a nonstock item, it may forward the original requisition to the purchasing office. The requisition will carry a rubber stamp notation, such as "Nonstock Order Direct," indicating that immediate action should be taken on this order. The stockroom then retains the carbon copy of the requisition for follow-up purposes.

ORDERING

Once they receive a purchase requisition, the purchasing office first locates sources from which the material can be obtained. The files may provide names and addresses of former suppliers or firms that have solicited business in the past. Larger purchasing departments may have a complete, up-to-date collection of suppliers' catalogs and price lists which they use for comparative purposes. If there are not enough names of suppliers or price quotations on file, an index such as *Thomas Register of American Manufacturers* can be consulted.

Most routine purchasing decisions can be made from data on hand. The supplier is selected, and a purchase order is issued.

Issuing the Purchase Order

After the best buy has been selected, a formal purchase order is completed. This form should be filled out with care and double-checked for accuracy

```
                        ARTEX, INC.
                     123 Providence Street
                   Newark, New Jersey 07105
                                          PURCHASE ORDER NO. D6915
    TO  Monarch Paper Company                         DATE  April 20, 19--
        364 First Street                           SHIP TO  Artex, Inc. Warehouse
        Boise, Idaho 83760                                   900 Rosedale Avenue
                                                             East Orange, N.J. 07013
```

Date Wanted May 5, 19--		Ship Via Freight, FOB Boise		
Quantity	**Stock No.**	**Description**	**Unit Price**	**Amount**
3,000	351B	Reams, mimeograph paper, white, 8½" x 11", 16 lb.	1.10	3,300.00

R. J. Black

Purchasing Agent

before it is signed and mailed. The purchase order must be completed and checked carefully because it is a legal contract binding the company to pay for the items listed on the order. The firm can suffer severe financial losses if the quantity, description, or price is recorded incorrectly.

The purchase order form illustrated above indicates:

☐ Purchase order number.
☐ Date.
☐ Supplier's name and address.
☐ Place of delivery and date wanted.
☐ Shipping instructions.
☐ Description of material ordered, including quantity, stock number, description, unit price, and total amount.
☐ Signature of purchasing agent.

A purchase order has a number of carbon copies which are distributed as follows:

1 The original order is sent to the supplier.
2 One carbon is retained by the purchasing department for follow-up purposes.
3 One carbon is sent to the receiving department notifying them that the shipment is expected.
4 One carbon is sent to the stockroom telling them that their request has received attention.
5 One carbon is kept for the general files.

Following Up on the Order

Suppose you ordered a carload of steel for delivery on Friday, November 22, for use in factory production which is scheduled to start on Monday, November 25. Would it make good sense to wait until Friday night or Monday morning to see if the supplies arrived? What confusion there would be if the purchaser discovered at the last minute that the supplier bungled the order and could not meet his schedule.

Therefore, another important job for the purchasing office is to see that no delays in delivery occur to halt production. This is accomplished by being in constant communication with the supplier. By using mail, telephone, and telegraph service and even personal visits, the purchasing office checks to see that the suppliers meet the expected delivery date. Even after a supplier has shipped the goods, the purchasing staff, utilizing the services of the traffic or shipping department, keeps track of the progress of the shipment while it is in transit. In this way the company protects itself. Mistakes can be caught before the consequences become serious, and factory schedules can be changed if breakdowns in the supply line occur.

RECEIVING

When the shipment arrives, it is unpacked and checked by the receiving unit. A detailed record called a *receiving report* is completed and sent to the purchasing office; the goods are set aside until instructions are received.

The receiving report illustrated on page 471 shows:

☐ Date of receipt.
☐ Name and address of shipper.
☐ Purchase order number and requisition number.
☐ Shipper's packing slip number.
☐ Method of shipment (express, parcel post, freight, truck) and identification numbers.
☐ Amount of transportation charges paid.
☐ Description of contents, including quantity received, quantity accepted, quantity rejected, and description.
☐ Delivery instructions.
☐ Signature of receiving clerk.

Verifying Receiving Reports

As soon as the receiving report reaches the purchasing office, the files are checked to find the shipper's invoice and a copy of the original purchase order. All documents are then studied item by item to make sure the goods received and invoiced are exactly as ordered. The following control checks are applied:

1 Were the goods actually ordered?
2 Were the goods received in satisfactory condition?

```
┌────────────────────────────────────────────────────────────────────────┐
│                              RECEIVING                                   │
│                            ARTEX, INC.                                   │
│                         123 Providence Street                            │
│                        Newark, New Jersey 07105                          │
│                                                                          │
│   RECEIVING                                                              │
│   REPORT                                                 R  14124        │
│   RECEIVED FROM                    ADDRESS              DATE RECEIVED     │
│   Monarch Paper Company    Boise, Idaho                 5/4/—            │
│   PURCHASED FROM                   ADDRESS             PURCHASE ORDER NO. │
│   Above                                                 D6915            │
│   RECEIVED VIA                    TRANSPORTATION  PREPAID COLLECT  PURCH. REQUISITION NO.│
│   EXPRESS□ P.P.□ FREIGHT☑ TRUCK□ LOCAL□  CHARGES 67.93      ✓     498   4/7/—│
│   CAR INITIALS & NO.   WAYBILL NO.   BILL OF LADING NO.  PACKING SLIP NO.  CHARGE NO.│
│   N-64193                                               8431             │
│   DELIVER TO                   ACCEPTED BY            RECEIVED BY         │
│   Stationery Stores                                  K. L. Eddy          │
│   QUANTITY   QUANTITY   QUANTITY          DESCRIPTION                     │
│   RECEIVED   ACCEPTED   REJECTED                                         │
│    150        150              Cartons mimeograph paper, 8½"x11",        │
│                                white, 16 lb., 20 reams per carton        │
│                                                                          │
│                                                                          │
│                          INSPECTION RECORD                               │
│   RETURN TO VENDOR  REWORK   ACCEPTED   INSPECTOR'S SIGNATURE  DATE INSPECTED│
│                                                                          │
│   F-1003                                                                 │
└────────────────────────────────────────────────────────────────────────┘
```

3   Does the quantity received agree with the number originally ordered and the quantity listed on the shipper's invoice?

4   Is the price charged the same or less than the one indicated on the purchase order?

5   Do the goods that have been received meet the needed specifications?

6   Are the freight charges, discounts, and other allowances in agreement with the purchase order?

7   Is the shipper's invoice calculated correctly?

Pricing and Marking

Goods which are to be displayed for sale in a business must be tagged or marked in some way so that the customer and sales personnel will know the selling price of each item. A marking clerk stamps or tags each item with the selling price that the buyer has written on one copy of the purchase order.

Goods Transferred to Stock

When the verification has been completed, instructions are issued to the receiving unit to deliver the shipment to the stockroom or sales floor. Then the stockroom or sales personnel place the materials in the proper storage or display area.

REVIEWING YOUR READING

1   What are the major activities involved in purchasing?
2   What factors may determine the amount of money budgeted for purchases?
3   Name and describe the purpose of three kinds of purchasing budgets.
4   How does the purchasing office locate the best buy available?

5 Why should the purchasing office follow up on the orders that it sends to suppliers?

6 What information must be verified when the receiving report, purchase order, and shipper's invoice are compared?

OFFICE ASSIGNMENTS

1 As assistant buyer in the men's shoes department of the Catalina Mall Department Store, you have been asked to prepare an open-to-buy report for the buyer's signature and for the merchandise manager's approval. Use the illustration on page 466 as a model, and prepare the report using the following amounts for the period August through January of the current year. Report all amounts of money in thousands of dollars, rounded to one decimal place, and figure the totals.

Last year sales, August through January: $6,238; $19,019; $41,300; $42,695; $72,481; $29,019.

Sales plan for this year, August through January: $6,800; $19,100; $40,500; $42,100; $61,000; $26,600.

Last year purchases, August through January: $10,057; $14,419; $16,009; $38,995; $12,835; $25,050.

Purchase plan for this year, August through January: $10,600; $14,000; $15,600; $35,800; $11,400; $29,300.

2 Using the open-to-buy report which you prepared in Office Assignment 1 (you may assume it was approved), post the following actual sales and actual purchases for this year in thousands of dollars, rounded to one decimal place. Figure the amount that remains open-to-buy each month before proceeding to the next month. Total the actual sales and purchases.

August: sales, $6,828; purchases, $10,627.
September: sales, $19,273; purchases, $14,525.
October: sales, $40,301; purchases, $14,982.
November: sales, $43,287; purchases, $36,118.
December: sales, $60,450; purchases, $10,887.
January: sales, $26,572; purchases, $29,450.

3 As purchasing clerk for Heritage Manufacturing Company, it is your job to prepare purchase orders. Complete an order similar to the one shown on page 469 (or use the one provided in your workbook) to obtain the following parts from the Bristol Machine Company, 8610 Grand Avenue, Emporia, Kansas 66801:

7	X-1-4367-A	Gears	@ $14.77
1	X-3-1854-F	Switch	@ 6.95

Your firm's purchase order number is 17,691, dated May 1, 19—. Request shipment by air express, charges collect. Prepare papers for the signature of Helene Vickery, who is the purchasing agent. Specify delivery on May 6, 19—, to 111 Bloomfield Avenue, Newark, N.J. 07104.

4　Complete a receiving report, similar to the one shown on page 471, covering a shipment that has just arrived from a supplier, Baskin-Schofield, Inc., 684 Market Street, Dover, Delaware 19901. Include the following data: Our Purchase Order K6892; arrived by freight on April 25, 19—; supplier's Invoice (Charge No.) 49-268, dated April 19, 19—; merchandise includes ten cartons, each containing six individually boxed Model l6A Regal Steam Irons; Packing Slip No. 8421; transportation charges paid by the receiver, $15.60; merchandise inspected by T.A.H., found to be in good condition, and transferred to stores on day following receipt. Sign your initials as receiving clerk.

SECTION 41 Handling Accounts Payable

A system for the payment of purchases on account is known as an *accounts payable system*. Once a supplier has complied with his part of the purchase agreement, he expects to be paid when the amount of his invoice is due. A procedure must be established to ensure that the items received are paid for on time and that the proper amount is paid, including the correct discount, in accordance with acceptable accounting standards.

THE PURCHASE INVOICE

The *purchase invoice*, or bill from the supplier, is the primary document used as a record of an accounts payable transaction.

Assembling the Data

The process of paying the purchase invoice begins in the purchase office. A special form or voucher is prepared representing a formal request for a check to be issued. The following related papers are attached to this form, which is illustrated at the bottom of page 476.

☐ Original purchase requisition
☐ Purchase order
☐ Purchase invoice
☐ Receiving report
☐ Stockroom receipt

All papers are then examined by the purchasing agent. Once the purchasing agent approves:

	PURCHASES JOURNAL					Page 7
DATE	**ACCOUNT CREDITED**	**INVOICE**		**TERMS**	**POST. REF.**	**AMOUNT**
		NO.	**DATE**			
19— July 3	TransAmerica Steel Company	3933	7/1	net 30 days		8000 00

1 The request for payment is passed to the cashier unit, where a check will be issued for payment on the due date.
2 The accounting unit is then notified of the payment so that the supplier's account may be credited.

Buying on Credit

The privilege of buying on credit is best retained by establishing a reputation for paying promptly. To earn that reputation for your company, you must keep a careful record of the firm's debts to each supplier so that when payment is due, routine procedures will speed the money on its way.

Recording Purchases

The supplier's invoice, after it is received and approved, serves as the basis for an entry in the purchases journal. For example, you would record a bill from the TransAmerica Steel Company for $8,000 as illustrated above.

The next step in the accounting process is to credit each item listed in the purchases journal to the proper supplier's account as shown below.

Many offices use accounting machines to help speed up the process of posting information to creditors' accounts.

ACCOUNTS PAYABLE LEDGER

NAME TransAmerica Steel Company

ADDRESS Naugatuck, Connecticut 06770

DATE	REFERENCE	INVOICES	DEDUCTIONS	BALANCE
BALANCE FORWARDED				.00
Jul 3 PJ7 3933		8,000.00		8,000.00

```
                      ACCOUNTS PAYABLE LEDGER

          NAME  TransAmerica Steel Company

          ADDRESS  Naugatuck, Connecticut 06770
```

DATE	REFERENCE	INVOICES	DEDUCTIONS	BALANCE
BALANCE FORWARDED				.00
Jul 3	PJ7 3933	8,000.00		8,000.00
Jul 12	PRA7 948		100.00	7,900.00

Recording Adjustments

If a part of the TransAmerica order were found to be defective, a complaint would be made to the supplier. When the buyer's claim was approved, Trans-America would issue a credit memorandum for the value of, perhaps, $100 of defective goods.

As the accounting clerk in charge of suppliers' accounts, or accounts payable, you would record TransAmerica's credit memorandum as a deduction from your company's obligation. After this information is posted, the TransAmerica account would appear as shown above.

Recording Payments to Suppliers

In accordance with the terms shown on the bill, the net balance owed to Trans-America becomes due 30 days after the date of purchase. At this time the cashier unit is authorized to issue a check for settlement of the bill.

The disbursing cashier records the payment in the cash payments journal. The accounting clerk in charge of accounts payable then uses the entries in the cash payments journal as a guide for posting information to individual suppliers' accounts. After the payment of $7,900 is posted, the TransAmerica account appears as shown at the top of page 476.

Cash Discount on Purchases

The record in the purchases journal on page 474 indicates that net terms are applied to the purchase from the TransAmerica Steel Company. In other words, the entire amount or balance is payable when due. However, as discussed in Section 31, some suppliers allow a cash discount to encourage prompt payment. For example, if the arrangements with TransAmerica include terms of 2/10, net 30 days, a 2 percent discount can be deducted for payment on or before July 10 (within ten days of the date of the invoice). Instead of paying the full $7,900, the customer pays the account in full for $7,742.

ACCOUNTS PAYABLE LEDGER

NAME TransAmerica Steel Company

ADDRESS Naugatuck, Connecticut 06770

DATE	REFERENCE	INVOICES	DEDUCTIONS	BALANCE
BALANCE FORWARDED				.00
Jul 3 PJ7 3933		8,000.00		8,000.00
Jul 12 PRA7 948			100.00	7,900.00
Jul 29 CP7 7411			7,900.00	.00

$7,900   Gross amount
−158   2 percent cash discount
$7,742   Net payment if made within 10 days

When purchases run into thousands or even millions of dollars a year, cash discounts can result in a substantial saving. Everyone connected with purchasing and accounts payable should be alert to all discount opportunities.

1 Papers should be processed quickly so that the authorization for payment is completed before the discount period expires.

2 The request for a check should indicate the amount of discount so that the cashier can verify the amount to be paid. An example is illustrated below.

3 The cashier should double-check all terms and computations.

4 The amount of the cash discount is noted in the Purchases Discount Credit column of the cash payments journal at the time that the payment is recorded.

REQUEST FOR CHECK

NO. 4960

PAYABLE TO *Monarch Paper Company*   DATE *May 10*   19—

ITEM	ACCOUNT AFFECTED	AMOUNT
Their Invoice 8431, May 1, 19—		
$1,710.00, less 2% discount of		
$34.20	19-211	1,675 80

MAIL ☐ WILL CALL ☐ WAITING ☐   PREPARED BY *C.H.W.*   APPROVED BY *R.J.B.*   CHECK NO. 49081

DELIVER TO

Charles R. Hadley Co. Pathfinders   —   Printed in U.S.A.   Reg. U.S. Pat. Off. Standard Check Request Form C572
Los Angeles, San Francisco, New York, Chicago

THE VOUCHER SYSTEM

Large businesses may find that keeping separate account records for individual suppliers requires too many manual operations. The voucher system is designed to keep track of the accounts payable without using individual creditors' accounts. Here is how the system works.

Preparation of the Voucher

When a supplier's invoice has been fully checked and verified, a voucher is prepared. The complete and approved voucher form represents an authorization to pay when due.

Vouchers are frequently prepared on carbon packs.

1 The original is the basic document used for recording the amount due in a voucher register.
2 A carbon goes to an alphabetic file according to the creditor's name.
3 A carbon is placed numerically in a master file of vouchers issued.

Record of the Voucher

The approved voucher may be processed in one of several ways:

1 The voucher may be recorded in a voucher register (resembling a purchases journal) and then filed until the date payment is due.
2 The voucher may be filed until the due date and then recorded in a voucher register.
3 The voucher may be filed until the due date and then recorded in a special cash payments journal.

Payment of the Voucher

On the due date a check is issued for the net amount due. The payment is recorded in the cash payments journal or in the check register.

The voucher system uses a chronological (by date) filing procedure which eliminates the need for keeping individual creditors' accounts. The supporting master voucher file, creditor file, and voucher register entry provide an adequate margin of protection against any one record being lost or mislaid. The voucher system works especially well when a company buys items infrequently from many different suppliers.

REVIEWING YOUR READING

1 What information is recorded in the purchases journal?
2 How is the buyer's account adjusted when damaged merchandise is received from the supplier?

3   Outline the recording procedure involved in the payment of a supplier's bill when conventional creditors' accounts are maintained.

4   Contrast the voucher system with the separate account record system of keeping track of obligations to suppliers.

OFFICE ASSIGNMENTS

1   Record the following purchases on page 8 of a purchases journal similar to the one illustrated on page 474. Use the current date.

July 2   Received Invoice 6272 dated June 28 from Weller-Baker Chemical Company for $650. Terms, net 30 days.

3   Received Invoice 74828 dated June 28 from Klopman Filter Corporation for $1,250. Terms, net 30 days.

3   Received Invoice 242 dated July 1 from Anderson Engineering Company for $985. Terms, net 30 days.

4   Received Invoice 77-224 dated July 1 from Ilex Landscaping Company for $355. Terms, 2/10, n/30.

4   Received Invoice 6307 dated July 2 from Weller-Baker Chemical Company for $80. Terms, net 30 days.

5   Received Invoice 74913 dated July 4 from Klopman Filter Corporation for $3,200. Terms, 1/10, n/30.

2   Using accounts payable ledger forms similar to the one illustrated on page 474, post the above entries in the purchases journal to the individual suppliers accounts. Use PJ8 as the posting reference. Beginning balances are as follows:

Weller-Baker Chemical Company	$1,250.00
Klopman Filter Corporation	0
Anderson Engineering Company	317.00
Ilex Landscaping Company	112.00

Use your city, state, and ZIP Code for the addresses. After each item has been posted, place a check mark in the Post Ref. column of the purchases journal to show that the posting is complete for that item.

3   Assume that the invoice from Baskin-Schofield, Inc. (Account R1963), covering merchandise received in Office Assignment 4 in Section 40, has been checked for accuracy. Now before the discount period elapses, it is your job to prepare a formal request for payment of the amount due, $270, less 2 percent discount. See the illustration at the bottom of page 476 as a sample, and prepare one like it if you are not using a workbook. Date the request April 26, 19—, and make this request number 469.

Then make out a voucher check as though you were the clerk in the accounting department who had received the request for payment. When you have completed the voucher check, be sure to add the number of the check issued to the above Request for Check form. Either use the form in your workbook or copy the one illustrated at the top of page 479.

ARTEX, INC.
123 Providence Street
Newark, New Jersey 07105

Check No. **2075**   55-103 / 212

_____ 19 ___

Pay To
The Order Of _____ $ _____

_____ Dollars

CITY NATIONAL BANK
Newark, New Jersey 07105

_____
Authorized Signature

⑈0 2 ⑈2 ⑈0 ⑈0 3⑈0 7⑈ 40 6 ⑈68 9 7⑈

- -

ARTEX, INC.   Detach and retain for your records.

Date	Invoice No.	Invoice Date	Total Amount Due	Discount	Net Amount Paid

UNIT 17

BUSINESS CASES AND PROBLEMS

In the Boss's Shoes   You find that a parts supplier has shipped some parts that are not as good a quality as your order specified. The supplier has admitted his mistake and is willing to send you what you want. The problem is that the better-quality parts will not be available for a week. If you have to wait this length of time, your production line must be halted, sales orders will be delayed, and factory employees will be out of work for a few days.

Should you go ahead and use some inferior parts in order to continue production until the right ones reach you? If you use the inferior parts, should you tell your customer, reduce the price, or make some other adjustment? Or should you stop production and wait? What would you do? How could the trouble possibly have been avoided?

Your Human Relations   1   When Adele first came to work at your office several months ago, you did everything possible to help her get started in her job and to furnish any materials that she needed. However, she appears to be the kind of person who can never learn to organize her work or to have enough supplies on hand to finish her job. The result is that Adele is constantly leaning on you for help, and you are frequently forced to neglect some of your own work to assist her with things that she should be able to do herself. After a very busy day in which Adele has been her usual helpless self, the boss reprimands you for failing to get some of your own work done on time.

Should you take the reprimand and forget it? Should you tell Adele that she must do her own work from now on? Should you tell the boss about Adele? What would you do?

2 As a new employee, you are most grateful for the help that your co-workers have given you. However, you notice that when the boss is away on business, practically everyone loafs until he gets back. If the boss takes a late lunch hour, it is the same story. You do not think that this is the right thing to do, but almost everyone does it; the single exception is a girl named Ruby who is shunned by her fellow workers because she is very difficult to get along with and because she does not hesitate to boast that she does more work than any two people put together. Since you would like to be accepted by the group, should you go along with them and take it easy when they do? Should you join forces with Ruby and run the risk of losing the approval of the group? Or is there a compromise position that you can take?

What Would You Do If . . . ? You request three companies to submit prices for a purchase that your employer plans to make, but only one of the suppliers submits an offer.

What Does This Mean? **1** A vendor's invoice bears the following terms: 2/10 EOM with anticipation.

2 A knowledge of purchasing systems is important because efficiency in buying items may have a great effect on the sales of the business and on the eventual profit that is earned. Explain.

Business in Your Area Select a specific brand of an item of merchandise, and visit at least two stores that carry this item. If possible, one of the visits should be to a large discount store and the other to a small neighborhood shop. Locate the item in each store, and make a comparison of the prices charged. Is price the only factor to be considered in choosing a supplier?

UNIT **18**
PAYROLL
SYSTEMS

SECTION 42 Assembling Payroll Data

It is important that a company payroll system operate efficiently so that employees can be paid on time and in the correct amount of money every payday. However, a payroll system is also important to the company. It helps a company maintain accurate accounting records and keeps track of certain payroll information that must be reported to the federal and state government.

BASIS OF PAYMENT

Most office workers are paid a fixed sum as a weekly salary which is based upon a five-day workweek not exceeding 40 hours. You may earn time and a half ($1\frac{1}{2}$ times the hourly wage rate) for overtime beyond 40 hours and double time for work on Sundays and holidays.

The executives of a business also receive a regular salary; sometimes they are paid weekly but frequently by month. Executives are not eligible for overtime wages, but in many cases they receive an annual bonus if their unit performance level and business conditions justify it.

Factory employees are usually paid on an hourly basis. Each job carries a fixed hourly rate of pay. Beyond the first 40 hours, factory workers receive time and a half for overtime and frequently double time for work on Sundays and holidays. Some factory workers are paid according to the number of items they complete. This plan is known as *piecework wages*. Salesmen are frequently paid according to the dollar value of their sales. These payments are called *sales commissions*.

RECORDS OF TIME WORKED

Keeping track of the hours worked by several hundred employees can be a very complicated task unless a definite system is used.

You may be asked to note in an attendance register the time worked by factory workers who record their time worked on individual weekly time cards. When an employee reports to work in the morning, he removes his card from the "Out" rack, inserts it in a time clock which records the time of his arrival, and then places his card in the "In" rack. When he leaves for lunch he punches out and places his card in the Out rack. When he returns from lunch, he punches in and places his card in the In rack. At the end of the week the card shows a day-by-day record of the time the worker has spent on the job.

Some large business establishments use data processing equipment to record the number of hours worked by employees. Each employee has a numbered identification badge which he wears to work. The badge contains punched holes corresponding to the badge number. When the employee arrives at work, he inserts his badge into a machine that senses the punched holes and automatically records both the number and the time of arrival on a punched card. At the end of the week the punched cards are used to process the payroll.

FIGURING HOURS WORKED

As a payroll clerk one of your jobs may be to figure the total hours worked by each person during the workweek. Here is how you do it:

1   Compute and record the regular hours worked each day in accordance with the normal work schedule.
2   Compute and record extra or overtime hours worked beyond the normal schedule.
3   Determine total regular hours and total overtime hours worked during the week.
   Some time clocks print the time in black ink whenever the employee punches in or out within a few minutes of the scheduled time and in red ink at all other times. When the payroll clerk receives a card that has all the times recorded on it in black ink, he simply credits the employee for working the number of hours in the normal work schedule. No computations are necessary. However, when the payroll clerk receives a card having one or more entries in red ink, he must compute the number of hours worked.
   Many time clocks used for payroll purposes print the hours from 1 p.m. to midnight as 13 to 24 instead of 1 to 12. If a 24-hour clock is used, it is less likely that a morning (a.m.) hour will be confused with an afternoon (p.m.) hour or vice versa. You'll find that you can figure hours worked faster when you use a 24-hour clock. See for yourself. With a regular 12-hour clock, you would have to calculate the number of hours worked between 8 a.m. and 5 p.m. like this:

   12:00 minus 8:00 = 4 hours
   Plus 5:00   = 5 hours
   Total   = 9 hours

However, you can solve the same problem in one step by using the 24-hour clock because 5 p.m. is recorded as 17:00.

   17:00 minus 8:00 = 9 hours

Some payroll clocks go a step further and divide an hour into 100 units instead of 60 minutes. Dividing an hour into 100 units makes calculations easier. Suppose, for example, that you want to figure the amount of money an employee has earned for working from 8:30 a.m. to 12:15 p.m. at $3 an hour. Using the 60-minute hour, you solve it this way:

1   Change 12:15 to 11:75 so that 8:30 can be subtracted from it.
2   Subtract the beginning time from the ending time:

   11:75
   −8:30
   ─────
    3:45

3   Change 3:45 to 3¾, or 3.75, so that it can be multiplied by the rate of pay.

4 Multiply time worked by rate of pay:

$$\begin{array}{r} 3.75 \\ \times\,\$3 \\ \hline \$11.25 = \text{pay} \end{array}$$

With the 100-unit hour, 8:30 a.m. is recorded as 8.50 and 12:15 as 12.25. Notice that this method involves only two steps.

1 Subtract the beginning time from the ending time:

$$\begin{array}{r} 12.25 \\ -8.50 \\ \hline 3.75 \end{array}$$

2 Multiply time worked by rate of pay:

$$\begin{array}{r} 3.75 \\ \times\,\$3 \\ \hline \$11.25 = \text{pay} \end{array}$$

FIGURING GROSS PAY

A worker's gross pay is determined by multiplying the hours worked by the proper hourly rate. Of course, in the typical factory operation, rates of pay vary, depending on the different levels of skill, responsibility, and experience. The payroll clerk finds a worker's current pay rate by referring to the unit's record or file of rate assignments and adjustments. For example, the file would indicate that Margaret Bashaw, whose time card is illustrated on page 485, is employed at a current wage rate of $3.60 an hour.

Once you know the hours worked and the pay rate you can compute the gross pay for a worker by using either one of two commonly used methods. In the first (total hours) method:

1 Add the total regular hours to the total overtime hours to determine the total number of hours worked.
2 Compute the amount of regular earnings by multiplying the total hours worked by the regular rate.
3 Compute the amount of the overtime by multiplying the overtime hours by the overtime excess rate or premium which is 50 percent of the regular rate.

For Margaret Bashaw this computation would be:

$$\begin{array}{lll} 44 \text{ total hours worked} & @\ \$3.60 = & \$158.40 \\ 4 \text{ overtime hours worked} & @\ \ 1.80 = & \underline{7.20} \\ & & \$165.60 \end{array}$$

In the second method you compute gross pay by calculating the overtime separately from the regular hours. This is the method shown on the time card illustrated on page 485.

1 Multiply the number of regular hours by the regular hourly rate.
2 Multiply the number of overtime hours worked by 1½ times the regular rate.

```
┌─────────────────────────────────────────────────────────────┐
│  NAME  Margaret Bashaw              NO. 317                   │
│                                                               │
│              WEEK ENDING Jan. 20, 19--                        │
│  DEDUCTIONS    RATE       HOURS   EARNINGS                    │
│  INC. TAX $___  REG. $3.60   40   $ 144.00                    │
│  F.I.C.A.  $___ O.T. $5.40    4   $ 21.60                     │
│  _____ $___              ___  $___                           │
│  _____ $___              ___  $___                           │
│  _____ $___  TOTAL HOURS  44  TOTAL                          │
│  MISC.  $___                   EARNINGS $165.60               │
│                                TOTAL                          │
│                                DEDUCTIONS $___                │
│                                NET PAY  $___                  │
├───────────────────────────────┬───────────────────────────────┤
│           REGULAR             │         OVERTIME              │
│ HRS.│  IN  │ OUT  │  IN  │ OUT │   IN   │  OUT  │ HRS.         │
│  8  │M 725 │M 1202│M 1230│M 404│        │       │              │
│  8  │TU 727│TU 1131│TU 1200│TU 405│     │       │              │
│  8  │W 722 │W 1145│W 1215│W 402│        │       │              │
│  8  │TH 730│TH 1130│TH 1159│TH 407│TH 430│TH 834│  4           │
│  8  │F 723 │F 1133│F 1155│F 404│        │       │              │
│     │      │      │      │     │        │       │              │
│ 40  │      │      │      │     │        │       │  4           │
├───────────────────────────────────────────────────────────────┤
│  PAY BASIS $3.60      PER hour                                │
└───────────────────────────────────────────────────────────────┘
```

Margaret Bashaw's earnings are computed like this:

40 regular hours worked   @ $3.60 = $144.00
4 overtime hours worked   @   5.40 =   21.60
                                      $165.60

DEDUCTIONS

First a worker's gross pay is calculated. Then the deductions required by law or requested by the worker are computed. The following are typical deductions.

Income Tax Withheld

The federal law (as well as the laws of several states) requires that those who receive their income in the form of salaries and wages pay income tax. On each paycheck, a certain amount of taxes is deducted from the gross amount earned each week. You can find out the exact amount of the tax to withhold for an employee by referring to a printed table of deductions like the one on page 486. The tax to be paid varies with the amount earned, the marital status, and the number of withholding allowances claimed. You would find the tax to be withheld for Margaret Bashaw, who we are assuming claims two allowances, on the

					And the number of withholding allowances claimed is—							
And the wages are—		0	1	2	3	4	5	6	7	8	9	10 or more
At least	But less than											
						The amount of income tax to be withheld shall be—						
$100	$105	$14.10	$11.80	$9.50	$7.20	$4.90	$2.80	$.80	$0	$0	$0	$0
105	110	14.90	12.60	10.30	8.00	5.70	3.50	1.50	0	0	0	0
110	115	15.70	13.40	11.10	8.80	6.50	4.20	2.20	.10	0	0	0
115	120	16.50	14.20	11.90	9.60	7.30	5.00	2.90	.80	0	0	0
120	125	17.30	15.00	12.70	10.40	8.10	5.80	3.60	1.50	0	0	0
125	130	18.10	15.80	13.50	11.20	8.90	6.60	4.30	2.20	.20	0	0
130	135	18.90	16.60	14.30	12.00	9.70	7.40	5.10	2.90	.90	0	0
135	140	19.70	17.40	15.10	12.80	10.50	8.20	5.90	3.60	1.60	0	0
140	145	20.50	18.20	15.90	13.60	11.30	9.00	6.70	4.40	2.30	.30	0
145	150	21.30	19.00	16.70	14.40	12.10	9.80	7.50	5.20	3.00	1.00	0
150	160	22.50	20.20	17.90	15.60	13.30	11.00	8.70	6.40	4.10	2.00	0
160	170	24.10	21.80	19.50	17.20	14.90	12.60	10.30	8.00	5.70	3.40	1.40
170	180	26.00	23.40	21.10	18.80	16.50	14.20	11.90	9.60	7.30	5.00	2.80
180	190	28.00	25.20	22.70	20.40	18.10	15.80	13.50	11.20	8.90	6.60	4.30
190	200	30.00	27.20	24.30	22.00	19.70	17.40	15.10	12.80	10.50	8.20	5.90

MARRIED Persons — WEEKLY Payroll Period

$160 to $170 line ($165.60 was her gross pay) under the column for two allowances. The tax is shown as $19.50, and you would note it in the Deductions section of the time card shown on page 487. Income tax withholding is often abbreviated ITW on payroll records and forms.

Social Security Taxes

The federal social security and medicare laws require an employer to collect a tax of 5.85 percent on the first $13,200 of wages paid to each worker every year. Increases in the cost of living can cause the $13,200 base to increase each year. After 1977 the 5.85 percent rate will gradually increase. This amount, called the *Federal Insurance Contributions Act/Medicare* deduction, or FICA/Medicare, represents the employee's contribution toward the benefits provided for him by law for retired or elderly persons and dependents, and covers old age, survivors, disability, and hospital insurance.

You can determine Margaret Bashaw's FICA tax deduction by looking it up in a table, figuring it by machine, or calculating it as follows:

Gross wages subject to tax	$165.60
Multiplied by tax rate (5.85 percent)	.0585
	82800
	132480
	82800
Total and point off six decimal points	$9.687600
Round off to	$9.69

$9.69 = worker's FICA/Medicare deduction

The FICA/Medicare deduction is also recorded in the Deductions section of the time card, shown on page 487.

Payroll Savings Plan

Some employees have joined the Payroll Savings Plan sponsored by the United States Treasury. A worker asks the company to set aside a fixed sum from every

```
┌─────────────────────────────────────────────────────────┐
│  NAME Margaret Bashaw              NO. 317                │
│                                                           │
│              WEEK ENDING Jan. 20, 19--                    │
│ ┌───────────┬──────────────┬─────────┬─────────────────┐ │
│ │DEDUCTIONS │    RATE      │  HOURS  │   EARNINGS       │ │
│ │INC.TAX $19.50│REG. $3.60 │   40    │ $144.00          │ │
│ │F.I.C.A. $9.69│O.T. $5.40 │    4    │ $21.60           │ │
│ │ Sav.  $5.00 │            │         │ $                │ │
│ │ Ins.  $3.50 │            │         │ $                │ │
│ │       $     │TOTAL HOURS │   44    │TOTAL EARNINGS $165.60 │
│ │MISC.  $     │            │         │TOTAL DEDUCTIONS $39.69 │
│ │             │            │         │NET PAY $127.91   │ │
│ ├─────────────┴────────────┼─────────┴─────────────────┤ │
│ │         REGULAR          │         OVERTIME          │ │
│ │HRS. │ IN │OUT│ IN │OUT   │ IN │OUT│ HRS.             │ │
└─────────────────────────────────────────────────────────┘
```

paycheck for the purchase of United States savings bonds. When her savings accumulate to equal the full purchase price of the bond, she receives her bond certificate. The Deductions section of Margaret Bashaw's time card, illustrated above, lists a $5 deduction for savings.

Sickness and Accident Insurance Premium

Workers are usually eligible to buy insurance at greatly reduced rates so that they will be protected from the risks of illness and accident. An employee who wants this protection has his employer deduct the weekly premiums from his paycheck. There are generally separate rates for single persons, married persons, and married persons with dependent children. The Deductions section of Margaret Bashaw's time card lists a $3.50 deduction for insurance.

COMPUTING NET PAY

The net wages actually paid to a worker is the amount that remains after all deductions are taken away from the gross pay. Look at the computations made on Margaret Bashaw's time card shown above.

REVIEWING YOUR READING

1 Explain the purpose and use of the weekly time card in a payroll system.
2 Explain why the 24-hour clock is advantageous in figuring employees' pay.
3 Describe the two common methods used for computing the gross wages for a worker who is paid on an hourly basis.
4 How does the payroll clerk figure the amount to be deducted from an employee's gross pay?
5 What is the current rate of the Federal Insurance Contributions Act Medicare deduction?
6 How is the worker's net pay computed?

OFFICE ASSIGNMENTS

1 a Enter the following in-and-out record for Louis Perazzoli, employee number 324, during the week ending April 12. Either use the form in your workbook, or copy the time card illustrated on page 485.

Mon.   in 7:45 out 12:01 in 12:59 out 5:05
Tues.   in 7:58 out 12:03 in 12:55 out 5:00
Wed.   in 7:40 out 12:05 in 1:00   out 5:01
Thurs. in 7:57 out 12:00 in 12:56 out 5:00
Fri.   in 7:56 out 12:03 in 12:55 out 5:05

b Compute the hours worked, disregarding the odd minutes before and after normal opening and closing time. The regular hours are from 8 a.m. to 12 noon and from 1 to 5 p.m.

2 Use the time card from Office Assignment 1 as the basis for computing Louis Perazzoli's earnings. Assume that he earns $3.40 an hour, is subject to a 5.85 percent FICA/Medicare deduction, and has $10 deducted for savings bonds. Using the table on page 486, look up Mr. Perazzoli's income tax withholding as a married taxpayer claiming two withholding allowances. Record your computations on the time card, and retain the card for future use.

SECTION 43 Preparing the Payroll

As you learned in Section 42, the time card is used to assemble the basic information needed to pay employees. Before an employee can be paid, however, you must record the data on the time card to other records needed by the federal government and used for accounting purposes.

THE EMPLOYEE EARNINGS RECORD

A separate earnings record is kept for each person on the payroll so that each employee can prepare his annual income tax report required by the federal government. Information from each employee's time card is posted to his earnings record. As shown at the top of page 489, the heading contains the employee's name and other important information about her that is needed by employees in the payroll office. The body of the earnings record includes columns for the pay period, hours worked, regular earnings, overtime earnings, and total earnings, or gross pay. The amount of gross pay earned during the year is accumulated in the Year-to-Date Earnings column. When this figure exceeds $13,200 during any one year, the payroll clerk stops making the FICA deduction, which is made only on the first $13,200 earned by an employee during the year. A column is also provided for each deduction made from the employee's pay, such as income tax, FICA, and other deductions.

EMPLOYEE EARNINGS RECORD FOR YEAR 19——

Name _Bashaw, Margaret_
Address _12 Booth Drive_
Newark, New Jersey 07110
Telephone No. _201-555-1612_
Date of Birth _January 31, 1953_
Rate _$3.60 per hour_

Employee No. _317_
Social Security No. _101-69-4693_
Marital Status _Married_
Withholding Allowances _2_
Position _Cashier_
Date Employed _March 4, 1972_

| DATE | | HOURS | EARNINGS | | | DEDUCTIONS | | | | | | NET PAY | YEAR-TO-DATE EARNINGS |
PERIOD ENDING	PAID		REGULAR	OVERTIME	TOTAL	INCOME TAX	FICA TAX	PAYROLL SAVINGS	INSURANCE	MISC.	TOTAL		
1/6	1/9	40	144 00		144 00	15 90	8 42	5 00	3 50		32 82	111 18	144 00
1/13	1/16	40	144 00		144 00	15 90	8 42	5 00	3 50		32 82	111 18	288 00
1/20	1/23	44	144 00	21 60	165 60	19 50	9 69	5 00	3 50		37 69	127 91	453 60

THE PAYROLL REGISTER

The data on the time card and the earnings record for each employee are summarized on a special form called a *payroll register*, or *payroll journal*. One line is assigned to each name on the payroll. The figures relating to an individual's pay are entered in the proper columns from left to right across the form.

When all the names and amounts have been recorded, the columns are totaled and checked for accuracy. Sections of the payroll register can be audited against the employee's earnings record. For example, the week's total of earnings on the earnings record must equal the week's total of earnings on the payroll register. Then the totals of the various columns are posted to the General Ledger accounts. The total of the Net Pay Amount column indicates the amount of money that must be transferred from the General Cash account to the Payroll Cash account in order to cover the checks to be drawn or to cover the requisition for cash for the pay envelopes. Note that Margaret Bashaw's name appears on the first line of the payroll register shown below.

PAYROLL REGISTER   _page 23_

For the Week Beginning _January 14,_ 19 ——   and Ending _January 20,_ 19 ——   Paid _____ 19 ____

NO.	NAME	MARITAL STATUS	ALLOW.	HOURS	REGULAR	OVERTIME	TOTAL	INCOME TAX	FICA TAX	PAYROLL SAVINGS	INSURANCE	MISC.	TOTAL	AMOUNT	CK. NO.
317	Margaret Bashaw	M	2	44	144 00	21 60	165 60	19 50	9 69	5 00	3 50		37 69	127 91	
318	A. L. Rice	M	4	40	174 00		174 00	16 50	10 18		3 50		30 18	143 82	
319	Ralph Knox	S	1	40	160 00		160 00	26 60	9 36		3 50		39 46	120 54	
320	J. J. Brooke	M	3	40	136 00		136 00	12 80	7 96		3 50		24 26	111 74	
321	H. R. Moore	S	1	48	132 00	39 60	171 60	28 70	10 04	5 00	3 50		47 24	124 36	
322	A. H. Prentice	M	3	40	194 00		194 00	22 00	11 35		3 50		36 85	157 15	
323	W. A. Kingsley	M	5	46	160 00	36 00	196 00	17 40	11 47		3 50		32 37	163 63	

DISBURSING THE PAYROLL

Once his net pay has been computed, an employee is paid in cash or by check.

Payment in Cash

Payment in actual cash is one method of settling the worker's account for the pay period. In this plan you count out the net pay in bills and coins and then insert them in the worker's pay envelope. On the outside of the envelope, you show the details of the payroll computations so that the worker may check the amount enclosed.

You can speed up the process of counting money by using the largest denominations of bills and coins. For instance, the best way to make up the sum of $127.91 is to use:

Six $20 bills =	$120.00
One $5 bill =	5.00
Two $1 bills =	2.00
One half-dollar =	.50
One quarter =	.25
One dime =	.10
One nickel =	.05
One penny =	.01
	$127.91 (14 pieces)

You can note the bills and coins needed to pay each worker on a cash breakdown sheet, a section of which is shown below. If you total the columns of this sheet and enter them on a cash requisition form, you can order the cash from the bank in the exact denominations you want. A completed cash requisition form is shown at the top of page 491.

Payment by Check

Many companies prefer to pay by check. There are many advantages both to the employer and the employee in using this system. Paying by check not only

Cash Breakdown Sheet

Employee Number	Net Wages		$20	$10	$5	$1	50¢	25¢	10¢	5¢	1¢
						Bills and Change Required					
317	127	91	6		1	2	1	1	1	1	1
318	143	82	7			3	1	1		1	2
319	120	54	6				1				4

	Cash Requisition			

By _Artex, Inc._

Date _January 23,_ 19 _—_

Number	Denomination	Amount	
74	Twenties	1,480	00
9	Tens	90	00
6	Fives	30	00
31	Ones	31	00
12	Halves	6	00
17	Quarters	4	25
20	Dimes	2	00
18	Nickels		90
71	Pennies		71
	Total	1,644	86

eliminates the need for handling and counting cash, but also lessens the risk of loss. The payroll clerk doesn't have to worry about a miscount, workers don't suffer from the accidental loss of envelopes, and there is less chance of theft.

There are two parts to the paycheck. The stub, or voucher, provides a space to show the worker how her gross wages were computed, what deductions were made, and what remains as her net pay. The voucher should be torn off the check by the employee and kept as a personal record. The other part of the form is the check itself. Margaret Bashaw's paycheck is shown below.

1/20/--	44	144.00	21.60	165.60	19.50	9.69	5.00	3.50		37.69	127.91
Period Ending	Hours Worked	Regular	Overtime	Total	Income Tax	FICA	Savings	Ins.	Misc.	Total	Amount Net Pay
			Earnings				Deductions				

Employees Pay Statement
Detach and retain for your records.

- -

ARTEX, INC.
123 Providence Street
Newark, New Jersey 07105

Payroll Check No. **430** $\frac{55\text{-}103}{212}$

Jan. 23, 19 --

**Pay To
The Order Of** Margaret Bashaw--- $ 127.91

One hundred twenty seven and 91/100--- Dollars

CITY NATIONAL BANK
Newark, New Jersey 07105

G. Robert Mason
Authorized Signature

⑆0212⑈0103⑉07⑈406 16897⑈

Distributing the Pay

On payday the workers receive their checks or pay envelopes from a clerk at the pay window of the payroll office or from a special messenger or paymaster who distributes the checks or envelopes at the various work stations in the office. In some large payroll operations proper identification is asked for before a check or envelope is handed over to the employee, and employees carry badges or cards which identify them. The pay of absentees is placed in safekeeping until they return to work, when they can claim their money at the payroll office.

Payment by Direct Deposit

Many employees prefer that their pay be deposited directly in the bank where they have their checking accounts. Large businesses frequently make such deposits for them. To do this, the company sends the bank notices of earnings and deductions for each employee who wishes to have his pay deposited in a particular bank. However, instead of sending separate checks for each employee, the company totals the deposits being sent to one bank and sends one check to cover the whole group. The bank credits each employee's account and mails him both the notice of earnings and deductions and a deposit receipt.

MECHANICAL PAYROLL AIDS

Ingenuity in design has produced a variety of materials and machines that make the payroll process manageable and efficient.

Payroll Posting Machines

When there are hundreds of people on a company payroll, checks may be prepared on a payroll posting machine. With this device the payroll register, the paycheck, and an individual earnings record are completed in one operation by using carbon inserts.

Data Processing Machines

In larger operations payroll data in the form of punched cards or tape are fed into data processing machines which calculate gross pay, deductions, and net pay. They also print the payroll journal, the earnings record, and the employee's paycheck and voucher. However, these functions can be performed by the machines only after they have been carefully programmed, or instructed, by someone who understands all of the details of a payroll system.

Addressograph Plates

Another way to save time in processing the payroll is to prepare checks and forms in advance. This can be done by using addressograph plates containing each employee's name, clock number, and social security number.

Check Protector

The amount on a check can be protected from alteration by a device called a *protector*. This machine raises or presses a pattern onto the paper when the amount is written. Once this has been done, the amount cannot be changed without some obvious damage.

Check Signer

Even the laborious problem of signing hundreds of checks has been eliminated by the use of machinery. The signature of the company treasurer can be reproduced on a metal plate. When this is installed in a check-signing device, the official signature is produced on the checks as quickly as they are fed into the machine. It can be operated simply by pressing a button or motor bar.

TAX AND INFORMATION RECORDS AND RETURNS

Getting the workers paid on time is only one phase of modern payroll accounting. Under federal and state legislation an employer is also responsible for:

☐ Making payments to the government of money withheld from each employee.
☐ Paying his share of payroll taxes due.
☐ Filing periodic report forms.
☐ Maintaining payroll records.

The following are among the records and returns required.

Employee's Withholding Allowance Certificate, Form W-4

Each employee completes a Form W-4 when he is hired so that the employer will have an official record of the number of allowances he or she claims. The employee files a revised certificate when any change of status occurs. The Form W-4 for Margaret Bashaw is shown below.

Federal Tax Deposit, Form 501

This form is completed by the employer and accompanies deposits of income taxes withheld plus employer's and employee's FICA taxes. Deposits are made in a Federal Reserve bank or in a commercial bank designated as an official depository.

Employer's Quarterly Federal Tax Return, Form 941

This report summarizes income and social security taxes relating to a three-month period (quarter of a year). It also provides a listing of all employees and the amount of their earnings during the quarter.

Employee's Annual Federal Unemployment Tax Return, Form 940

Employers are required to determine and report the amount of tax payable under the Federal Unemployment Insurance Law.

Wage and Tax Statement, Form W-2

This form is used to report the gross earnings and amounts withheld for *each* employee.

Transmittal of Wage and Tax Statements, Form W-3

This form is used to summarize and transmit the W-2 forms when they are mailed to the Internal Revenue Service.

REVIEWING YOUR READING

1   How can you speed up the process of counting money when you are preparing a cash payroll?
2   Why is it advantageous for an employer to pay his employees by check? Why is it advantageous for an employee to receive his pay by check?
3   How are machines used to speed up payroll work in large- and medium-size offices?
4   What is the purpose of the individual employee earnings record?

OFFICE ASSIGNMENTS

1   Use the payroll register form in your workbook, or copy the one illustrated on page 489. Then from the time card completed in Office Assignment 2 in Section 42, enter the data for paying Louis Perazzoli. Also enter the information regarding these three other employees, look up the income tax

withholding in the table on page 486, complete the computations, and total. Use page 33 as the page number of the payroll register.

Abraham Kramer, employee number 325, regular rate $4.25 per hour. Monday worked 8 hours; Tuesday, 8 hours; Wednesday, 0 hours; Thursday, 8 hours; Friday, 9 hours. Subject to a 5.85 percent FICA/Medicare deduction; married; four withholding allowances; insurance, $3.

Adam Link, employee number 326, regular rate $3.85 per hour. Monday worked 9 hours; Tuesday, 8 hours; Wednesday, 8 hours; Thursday, 8 hours; Friday, 9 hours. Subject to a 5.85 percent FICA/Medicare deduction; married; two withholding allowances; insurance, $3; savings bonds, $5.

Ray Winthrop, employee number 327, regular rate $4 per hour. Monday worked 7 hours; Tuesday, 8 hours; Wednesday, 9 hours; Thursday, 7 hours; Friday, 8 hours. Subject to a 5.85 percent FICA/Medicare deduction; married; six withholding allowances; insurance, $3.

2   Use the four payroll checks and vouchers in your workbook, or make copies of the one illustrated on page 491. Then refer to the payroll register that you prepared for Office Assignment 1. Assume that this payroll was to be paid by check. Complete a check and voucher for each employee, and sign your name as the authorized signature. Date the checks April 15. Then note each check number in the Ck. No. column of the payroll register. When you finish the checks, enter the date the employees were paid (April 15) on the top part of the payroll register.

3   Use the cash breakdown sheet and cash requisition in your workbook, or make a copy of the forms illustrated on pages 490 and 491, respectively. Then refer to the payroll register that you prepared for Office Assignment 1. Assume that this payroll was to be paid in cash. Complete the cash breakdown sheet and the cash requisition.

UNIT 18

BUSINESS CASES AND PROBLEMS

In the Boss's Shoes   Carl is an ambitious and capable young man. He has worked for his present employer since graduation from high school six months ago. He has just asked the boss for a raise. Carl has pointed out that he is doing the same work as Jones and should, therefore, get the same pay. Carl's boss admits that he is doing good work but points out that Jones has worked for the firm faithfully for ten years. is married, and has a number of children to support. Should the boss consider experience, length of service, and financial needs in determining wages? What do you think?

Your Human Relations 1 As a clerk in the payroll unit, you are typing a confidential report of proposed salary increases which will become effective in a few weeks. Your friends are eager to find out if they are among the fortunate ones. One friend in particular is seriously considering another job because it offers more money. She is on the list for a salary increase, but she won't be told for at least ten days. She says that she is going to make up her mind about the other job offer before the end of the week. Without revealing confidential information, is there something that you might do to help your company retain a good worker and keep your friend from making a rash move?

2 "Sure, I know that salary information is supposed to be kept secret. But I've been a friend of yours for a long time, and I've done you a lot of favors. I've got a right to know whether Joe is getting a bigger raise than I am. If you were half the friend you say that you are, you'd tell me."

Is it right for your friend to recall past favors he has done for you in an effort to get you to tell him secret information? Should your friend try to understand your position? Is he right in evaluating your friendship on this basis?

What Would You Do If . . . ? An employee of the business for which you work as a payroll clerk asks you to change an "out" time on his time card from 3 p.m. to 5 p.m. because he has been asked to run an errand in town for his supervisor before he goes home that day.

What Does This Mean? 1 A newspaper advertisement for office help includes the following notation: HSG LT BKG.

2 Varying levels of skill, responsibility, and experience call for a number of different rates of pay in the typical factory operation. Explain.

Business in Your Area Compare the beginning rates of pay that appear in the classified ads section of the local newspaper for various jobs. What relationships are there between the salaries offered and the skill, responsibility, and experience required for each job?

UNIT 19
GETTING THE JOB YOU WANT

Nichols Building

PULL

EMPLOYMENT OFFICE

SECTION 44 Choosing Your Career

Once you have had a chance to study and compare different types of office work, you'll be in a better position to think in terms of a particular job. No decision you make needs to be a permanent one, of course, but that first decision can be a big one. To help you pinpoint your goal, ask yourself some questions like these:

☐ Does the job deal with the kind of work I like to do?
☐ Can I qualify?
☐ What does it offer for the future?
☐ Do I think well of the company?
☐ Are the working conditions satisfactory?
☐ What special benefits does the company provide?

When you have narrowed down the field, you can begin job hunting with at least a general idea of the type of work you'd like to do.

LOCATING JOB OPENINGS

Thousands of high school graduates will be looking for jobs soon after graduation. Beat the rush by starting early and planning ahead.

Cover All Sources

Businessmen use many sources to help them find the type of office worker they need. These sources include school guidance and placement offices, cooperative business training programs, public and private employment agencies, classified ads in newspapers, recommendations of present employees, personal contacts, and waiting lists. It's important that you know the sources or channels through which business recruits so that you can let these sources know that you are looking for a job. Broadcast the word that you are job hunting by registering at offices and agencies, making personal calls, and talking to friends and relatives.

Use Letters of Application

Use letters of application when you can't visit the office or agency personally. You can write a letter in reply to a classified ad or write to a particular company with the hope that an opening may exist. In either case, your letter will be much more effective if it is original and distinctive. Make it reflect you and what you are just as a telephone call or a personal visit might. Include in your letter:

☐ An attention-getting or informative opening.
☐ A description of the kind of work for which you are applying.

☐ A statement showing why you are sure that you qualify for the job.

☐ A résumé, or data sheet, that gives details about your personal history, education, experience and achievements.

☐ A polite request for an interview, indicating when you are available and how you can be contacted.

Note how each of these ideas is included in the sample letter and the résumé on page 500.

If clerical work is to be your speciality, be sure that the letter you send out represents your very best work. Type it, of course. Be sure that it has no mistakes or noticeable erasures. Use a good grade of white paper and a fairly dark ribbon; type with an even touch. Make the letter reflect your knowledge of grammar, punctuation, and spelling. Be sure to use the complete and correct name and address of the person to whom you are writing. Proofread the letter carefully, preferably with the help of someone else. See that the envelope is sealed and bears the proper postage.

PREPARING FOR YOUR INTERVIEW

The following are a few things you should do before you have your job interview. Take these suggestions seriously because they can make the difference as to whether you get the job or not.

Find Out About the Company

Seek out as much information as you can about the company in which you are interested. You will probably feel more secure and gain more experience in a firm that has a good reputation in your community or city. On the other hand, if you have learned that a company has a high rate of employee turnover and heard unfavorable comments about its policies and products, you should investigate it further before you go for an interview and accept a job offer. Talk to friends who work in the company you are interested in. Their opinions will give you more insight into the organization of the company and the position you are applying for.

You should also be interested in the benefits a company offers. Does the company offer health and insurance plans, retirement benefits, and recreational activities? These are very important considerations, and you should keep them in mind when you weigh the advantages and disadvantages of the job you are considering.

Find Out About the Interviewer

Sometimes someone in your school guidance department is familiar with the person who will be interviewing you. Find out what you can about the interviewer—what kind of person he is, what kind of questions he is likely to ask, what qualifications he considers to be important, and so on. It is useful to know about an individual's pet peeves or preferences and to be alert to them.

31 Dover Parkway
Pleasantville, Pennsylvania 16341
August 19, 19--

Mr. Harold Walters
Personnel Department
Raylon, Incorporated
Erie, Pennsylvania 19013

Dear Mr. Walters:

When your office building opens here in October, you will want
at least a skeleton crew of trained, experienced clerical workers
ready to go to work. This is why I am writing to offer my services as a billing clerk.

My business training started at Pleasantville High School, where
I graduated four years ago. After that, I also took an additional
nine months of training at Pittsfield Business College, graduating
with honors in 19--. Since that time I have had three years of
diversified office experience, including considerable work in
sales-order procedures and billing. I received special in-service
training in punched-tape billing techniques about a year ago and
have been assigned to that work ever since.

May I please have an interview as soon as your employment office
is ready? My complete personal history is included in the attached
sheet. You may prefer to save time by telephoning instead of
writing. My telephone number is 717-555-1076. Please call between
3:30 and 5:30 in the afternoon.

                    Sincerely,

                    Nancy Parker

                    Nancy Parker

Enclosure

RÉSUMÉ

Nancy Parker

31 Dover Parkway

Pleasantville, Pennsylvania 16341

Telephone: 717-555-1076

Physical Data

   Age - 22 years
   Height - 5'4"
   Weight - 112
   Health - Excellent
   Marital status - Single
   Place of birth - Dayton, Ohio

Education

   Graduated from Pleasantville High School, 19--, with business
      diploma.
   Graduated from Pittsfield Business College in 19--, completing
      general office program with honors.
   In-service training course in punched-tape billing techniques
      completed at Pleasantville Adult Evening Vocational Center,
      19--.

Experience

   Two summers as clerk and cashier in office of Morris Hotel in
      Pleasantville.
   Full-time work as sales clerk in Western State Dairy; transferred
      to billing clerk after one year.
   Moved to better job with Columbia Wholesale Hardware Company in
      January, 19-- where presently employed as head billing clerk.

References (Listed with permission)

   Mr. Harvey Jenkins, Placement Director
   Pleasantville High School
   Pleasantville, Pennsylvania 16341

   Mrs. Wanda Horton
   Pittsfield Business College
   Pittsfield, Pennsylvania 16340

   Mrs. Alice Barnes, Supervisor
   Billing and Order Section, Columbia Wholesale Hardware
   Pleasantville, Pennsylvania 16341

In large companies, of course, you may not be able to find out anything about the person who will be interviewing you because most big firms have four or five people who do this work. The best thing you can do is to review your qualifications, have confidence in your abilities, and relax.

Be Prepared to Answer Questions

After he has made a fair amount of small talk to put you at ease, the interviewer will probably begin to ask you many questions about yourself and your skills. He may ask why you feel you could make a contribution to the company, and he will look for a truthful and confident answer. A certain amount of modesty should temper your reply, of course, but don't be too modest. An employer is more impressed with an applicant who projects a belief in his qualifications than one who is so unassuming about them that he appears unqualified.

Study the questions on page 498. Make sure you can answer them all without any hesitation. Give yourself some practice by saying the answers aloud, or arrange with a friend or a member of your family to ask you the questions just as if you were being interviewed.

Check Your Appearance

The first impression is a very important one. (Think of your reaction to someone when you meet him for the first time.) Without a doubt, the way you look when you are having an interview is much more important than the way you look when you are with friends or family. They can forgive an occasional sloppy look because they know you well and have seen you when you have looked your best. But an interviewer knows very little about you. If your appearance isn't up to par, he will assume that you never look any different and never give attention to the way you look. Some interviewers even relate appearance to work habits and attitudes and conclude that a person who is not concerned about his appearance is not likely to be concerned about his work.

Give particular attention to what you wear when you go for your interview. Keep in mind that you're going to a business appointment, not a party. You needn't look like an undertaker, but dress conservatively. If you are a man, wear a tie, polish your shoes, and wear socks that stay up. Since women today wear an interesting variety of clothes, it's difficult to describe exactly what to wear. Avoid, however, very fussy clothes and dresses that are either too short or too long. If possible, find out what the standard dress is in the company you're visiting. If you can't find out, at least avoid extremes. And for that first interview, don't wear slacks. Later on, when you know more about the company, you can feel free to dress tastefully in the accepted mode.

No one, of course, needs to remind you how important it is to pay daily attention to your personal hygiene. It is essential that you take a bath or shower daily, use a deodorant, and have hair that is groomed and teeth and nails that are clean.

Remember Your Posture

Think for a minute of the people *you* consider attractive. Are they attractive just because they are pretty or handsome or because of a certain way they carry themselves? Posture contributes a great deal to the image you project, and every good actor or actress will testify to this. No matter how carefully you choose your clothes, you will never look your best in them if you stand with your stomach out and your shoulders hunched. Also, you're not likely to convince anyone that you care about getting or holding a job if you sit slumped in a chair with your feet sprawled and your head resting on your chin. It's worthwhile to practice sitting and standing correctly. See what it does for your own self-image.

APPLYING FOR THE JOB

After you have prepared yourself for your interview by following the suggestions above, you'll probably find that you are able to look your best and do your best because you feel much more assured. Here are some pointers to bear in mind when you have the actual interview.

Get There Bright and Early

To be *bright* means to be awake and alert. Get plenty of sleep the night before because you will probably have to take some tests as a normal part of the interviewing process. Set your alarm clock early enough to allow yourself time to bathe, dress, and have a good breakfast. Also be sure you have enough time to get where you are going without having to rush.

Fill Out Forms Neatly and Completely

Just about every employment office and personnel department requires that you complete an application form, even if you have a résumé, or data sheet, about your personal history. That application form is generally used to screen out the least desirable candidates right away. It is then examined by the interviewer and sometimes by the person who is to be your immediate supervisor. Needless to say, if you intend to work as a trained clerical worker, you should certainly fill out your form neatly, legibly, and completely. A prospective employer looking at a job application cannot fail to draw some conclusions about you from how well or how poorly you fill out the form. A properly filled-out application form appears on page 503.

Bring Necessary Papers

Some jobs call for an applicant to supply a license, health certificate, working papers, proof of age, proof of citizenship, or military records. Sometimes no decision regarding hiring can be made without these papers. Spare yourself unnecessary delay (and show how organized and businesslike you are) by having all relevant papers with you on your first visit.

SELLING YOURSELF

Up to this point, your record, your qualifications, and your test performances have spoken for you. Now at the personal interview you must do the rest. Your words and your actions will determine the company's decision about hiring you. How can you be sure that it will be a favorable decision? Perhaps these suggestions on what to do when you are escorted to the interviewer's office will help.

Acknowledge Your Introduction

When the receptionist or messenger presents you to the interviewer, repeat his name in your greeting like, "How do you do, Mr. Kelly." Don't say just "Hi" or "Hello!" Act as though it is really a pleasure to make his acquaintance. You will no doubt be asked to have a seat. The interviewer will probably tell you where to put any belongings (such as books, papers, or a coat) that you happen to have with you. If he doesn't, wait a couple of minutes before you put them down on your own, and be sure to put them out of the way of his desk.

UNIVERSAL DRUG CORPORATION

APPLICATION FOR EMPLOYMENT

PLEASE PRINT REQUIRED INFORMATION AND SIGN FORM WHEN COMPLETED.

MR. ~~MISS~~ ~~MRS.~~ (CROSS OUT TWO) _Donavan_ (LAST NAME) _James_ (FIRST NAME) _Ross_ (MIDDLE NAME) SOCIAL SECURITY NO. _501-12-4485_ DATE _June 12, 19-_

ADDRESS _1835 Pine_ (STREET) _Weston_ (CITY) _Maine_ (STATE) _04494_ TELEPHONE NO. _(207)555-9184_ OWN ☐ MESSAGE ☒

PREVIOUS ADDRESS _____ MAIDEN NAME OR FORMER NAME _____

IN CASE OF EMERGENCY, NOTIFY _Mr. Harold Donavan 1835 Pine Weston, Maine 04494_

TYPE OF WORK DESIRED _Accounting_

REFERRED BY _M.R. Mills_ (NAME)

HEIGHT _6'1"_ WEIGHT _190_

LENGTH OF TIME RESIDED IN LOCALITY _All My Life_

CHECK ONE: SINGLE ☒ MAR☐ DIV.☐ WID☐ SEP.☐

NO. OF DEPENDENTS FULL _1_ PARTIAL __

AMERICAN CITIZEN _yes_

HAVE YOU BEEN INCAPACITATED DUE TO ILLNESS IN THE PAST YEAR? _No_

IF SO, HOW LONG? _____

HAVE YOU ANY CHRONIC AILMENT OR DEFECTS IN SIGHT, HEARING, LIMBS, ETC.? _No_

GRAMMAR SCHOOL _Weston Public_ (NAME OF SCHOOL) _Weston, Me._ (CITY) (STATE)
NO. OF YEARS ATTENDED _8_ DATE LEFT _19-_

HIGH SCHOOL _Weston Public_ (NAME OF SCHOOL) _Weston, Me._ (CITY) (STATE)
NO. OF YEARS ATTENDED _4_ DATE LEFT _19-_

COLLEGE _Sinclair College_ (NAME OF SCHOOL) _Brunswick, Me._ (CITY) (STATE)
NO. OF YEARS ATTENDED _4_ DATE LEFT _19-_

NAME ANY SPECIAL TRAINING OR COURSES _____

HAVE YOU EVER WORKED FOR UNIVERSAL DRUG CORP. _No_

IF SO, WHEN _____ WHERE _____

DO YOU KNOW ANY UNIVERSAL EMPLOYEES? _yes_ IF SO, WHOM? _J.R. Thomas_

DO YOU HAVE ANY RELATIVES WORKING FOR THIS CO.? _No_ IF SO, STATE NAMES _____

IF EMPLOYED BY US, WOULD YOU BE HOLDING ANOTHER JOB AT THE SAME TIME? _No_ IF SO, HOW MANY HOURS PER WEEK _____

WOULD YOU WORK FOR UNIVERSAL DRUG CORP. IN ANOTHER TOWN? _yes_

CHECK WORK IN WHICH YOU HAVE HAD EXPERIENCE

☑ TYPING ☐ SHORTHAND
☑ INVOICING ☑ BOOKKEEPING
☑ PAY ROLL ☐ SELLING
☐ STOCKROOM

WHAT LINES DID YOU SELL? _____

CHECK MACHINES YOU KNOW HOW TO USE

☑ TYPEWRITER ☑ ADDING MACHINE
☑ CALCULATOR ☐ DICTAPHONE
☑ KEY PUNCH ☑ COMPTOMETER
☑ MIMEOGRAPH ☐ SWITCHBOARD

OTHER MACHINES _____

LAST THREE EMPLOYERS:

NAME OF COMPANY _Smith Wholesale_ POSITION _Accounting Clerk_ SALARY _$1.90/hr_ DATE EMPLOYED _19-_ DATE LEFT _19-_
COMPLETE ADDRESS _205 Park Lane Weston, Maine 04494_ REASON FOR LEAVING _To enter college_

NAME OF COMPANY _____ POSITION _____ SALARY _____ DATE EMPLOYED _____ DATE LEFT _____
COMPLETE ADDRESS _____ REASON FOR LEAVING _____

NAME OF COMPANY _____ POSITION _____ SALARY _____ DATE EMPLOYED _____ DATE LEFT _____
COMPLETE ADDRESS _____ REASON FOR LEAVING _____

PERSONAL REFERENCES (GIVE THREE OTHER THAN RELATIVES):

NAME _Dr. Harvey Dawson_ COMPLETE ADDRESS _955 Mill Road Weston, Maine 04494_
NAME _Mr. Frank Morton_ COMPLETE ADDRESS _816 Dover Drive Weston, Maine 04494_
NAME _Mr. F.L. Johnson_ COMPLETE ADDRESS _199 Harris Brunswick, Maine 04011_

I UNDERSTAND THAT ALL PERSONS EMPLOYED BY THE UNIVERSAL DRUG CORPORATION AFTER JULY 1, 19— ARE REQUIRED TO JOIN ITS RETIREMENT PLAN WHEN ELIGIBLE.
I HEREBY AFFIRM THE TRUTH OF THE ABOVE STATEMENTS.

James R. Donavan
SIGNATURE

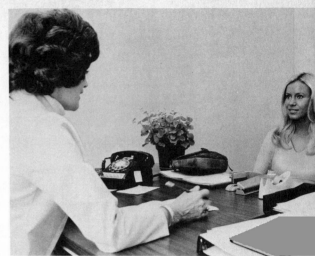

The interviewer reviewing your job skills is at the same time influenced by the way you speak, dress, and sit.

Courtesy Allied Chemical Corporation

Look at the Interviewer

His job is to evaluate you as a future employee. Sit quietly, and look at him directly as you answer his questions. Don't let your eyes wander when you are listening to him. This appears rude—though you don't intend it to be—and it gives the impression that you are bored and disinterested.

Keep Cool and Calm

Of course, you're nervous. You have a lot at stake, and this is a new experience for you. The interviewer knows how you feel, and he makes allowances for it. Try to keep from getting too high-strung so that you can look, act, and speak your best.

Speak Distinctly

It is very important how you speak and what you say at your interview. If you mumble your answer, your interviewer may have to ask you to repeat it. Make sure you're clearly understood.

Avoid Exaggeration

Bluffing seldom works on an experienced interviewer, and even if you think you have fooled him, the truth has a way of coming out sooner or later. State your case truthfully and confidently. If you believe in your qualifications, there is little need for exaggeration. Just give a sincere, straightforward answer.

Stress Your Abilities

In a competitive situation you have to convince the interviewer that you stand out over the other applicants. To do this, you must highlight your special talents. Mention each of your qualifications and skills that will help you do the job well.

Don't be afraid to stress these selling points more than once. If you're modest but enthusiastic when you talk about your capabilities, you will surely make a good impression.

Explain Your Plan to Improve Your Skills

Any prospective boss attempts to appraise an applicant in terms of the position's immediate and long-range needs. Your boss will be favorably impressed if you indicate to him that you have been thinking ahead and have plans to continue your education. Make it a point to follow through on your commitment to learn more about your job. Interviewers are accustomed to hearing glib promises about what an applicant intends to do. They look for employees who deliver.

Accept Competition Graciously

A prospective employer, who wants to select the best person available for a given job, will—as he should—interview a number of people before he makes a decision on one. If he puts you off until he sees the others, don't be discouraged. He'll remember you if you have sold yourself.

References

A company will check your references if it is considering you for a position. Checking references may be done by mail, by telephone, or by personal visit and has several objectives:

- ☐ To confirm the personal data furnished by you.
- ☐ To verify your statements concerning performance, experience, reason for leaving previous job, and so on.
- ☐ To evaluate your honesty and trustworthiness for bonding purposes.

FOLLOWING UP ON YOUR APPLICATION

While you're waiting to hear whether you have been hired or not, take several steps to demonstrate your interest in the company and the job.

Write a Thank-You Note

Drop the interviewer a nice thank-you note within a day or two after the interview.

Pay a Return Visit

If you don't hear from the company about the job within a week or ten days (or whatever the period of time the interviewer specified), visit the personnel office again, tell the interviewer that you are still interested, and if you can, supply any additional facts that will help your cause. You will be respected for your perseverance, and your visit may speed up some steps in the personnel routine. Make your visit brief, but as long as the position is open, keep letting them know that you are available and interested.

Check by Telephone

Some companies conduct preliminary interviews by phone rather than in person. In response to your written application, they will ask you to telephone. Make a careful note of the date, time, and name of the person to call, including his number and extension. Also, note any other information that you think you will need. Make sure to keep that telephone appointment just as you would keep an appointment for a personal interview. Use your best telephone technique. It is an opportunity to repeat or summarize your special qualifications or add some helpful information that you may have omitted on your application.

If an interviewer says that he will call you, make sure he knows when you will be at home to receive his call. If you have to be away from the phone at that time (and try *not* to be), have some competent person take the message for you.

HANDLING THE JOB

There's a wonderful satisfaction in learning that out of a large group of applicants you have been chosen for a particular job. And you have good reason to feel proud because your being chosen is proof that your abilities and the way you handled yourself at your interview stood the test.

Start Off on a Positive Note

Acknowledge the job offer and confirm any instructions that you are given about when and where to report for work. Thank those who encouraged and helped you—friends, relatives, teachers, and anyone else. Draw up plans for your personal development. It is never too early to make your job a stepping-stone to more responsible positions. Ask yourself, "Where do I want to go from here, and what am I going to do about it?"

Get Off on the Right Foot

There's nothing like starting off on the right foot and making the most of your chances. Here are some useful tips.

Report on time   Find out ahead of time about transportation facilities to your place of work. If necessary, make a trial run to see what the waiting time is for the train, bus, or whatever transportation you will be making use of. You will have enough to deal with the first day of work without having to get lost and arrive nervous and breathless.

Report fit and alert   Get plenty of sleep the night before. Allow yourself time for bathing and proper grooming. And have a substantial breakfast. You'll need plenty of energy to carry you through the day.

Remember names   You'll be meeting many new people. Try to learn their names. Be imaginative in figuring out ways to remember who the different people are. Make name and word associations. Write names down the way they sound until you get a chance to check on the right spelling. Keep your own "Who's Who," and make notes that help you remember who they are. A person always appreciates your using his name when he is greeted by you. This is sort of an indirect compliment. If you doubt it, see how you feel the next time a management person greets *you* by name.

Thank those who help you   A fellow worker takes time away from his job to answer your questions or to give you a helpful hint about some aspect of your new job. His help is well worth a "thank you."

Buckle down to business   Allowances will be made for you for a short time because you are new and are trying to learn your job, but you will be expected to learn how to do your new work better and faster each day so that you measure up to your co-workers. Until you do, they have to carry your share of the job.

Watch closely   On a new job you need to learn where to go for materials, how to arrange your work, the routines to observe, and all the things that enable you to become a member of a productive team. There's no better way to do this than to keep your eyes and ears open.

Find out where you fit   Besides knowing about your own job and the duties involved, make it your business to know what happens to the work before it reaches you and after it leaves you. If you understand your part in the work flow, you can often solve some problems immediately.

Ask questions   No new employee understands everything the first time, and you won't either. Wait until your teacher has finished talking or until she asks you if you have any questions. Then ask about points that aren't clear. Don't say that you understand if you don't. You'll find it a distinct advantage to know the reasons why you perform a task a certain way.

Take notes   Many things will be happening the first day, and you'll never be able to remember all of them. Take notes. Whenever possible, use sketches and diagrams to guide you. Don't be afraid to help yourself.

Try it out   After you have been shown some method or technique or procedure, ask if you may try it out yourself. This is a good chance to see whether you fully understand the instructions because someone will be there on hand to guide you. If you find that you are hesitating when you perform some of the steps, ask for help and suggestions. Take particular note of any special tips that are mentioned and of the order in which an operation is performed.

Use common sense   Maturity is a difficult thing to define, but one of its characteristics is the ability to use judgment, that is, to have a sense of proportion. There's a difference between a sensible question and an irrelevant one or one that is very simple to find the answer to. You can demonstrate your maturity by trying to handle the simple problems yourself. By doing this, you don't have to interrupt your co-workers unnecessarily and you show them that you know how to use your head.

Follow the rules   Once you're hired for a specific job in office operations, learn the job the boss's way and keep doing it that way as well as you can. Suggestions on a job are welcomed by business; indeed, suggestions often yield cash bonuses to those who make them. But don't make suggestions on your first day. Wait until your experience and skill are established and recognized. When that happens, your suggestions will be seriously considered.

Go easy on privileges   Many offices offer employees special privileges such as time for coffee breaks. Be fair, and take only your fair share.

Wait for cues   As a newcomer you're likely to be anxious to make a good impression, to have everyone like you, and to learn everything about the job as soon as possible. But some things take time. Don't force yourself aggressively on your new co-workers. Let them make the first move. They'll do this as soon as they conclude that you are worth knowing better. The same rule applies to your work situation. Don't try to take over the show and antagonize others by playing the role of the eager beaver. There will be plenty of time for you to prove what you can do after you have learned the ropes.

PROVING YOUR WORTH

Your supervisor can be a good friend. She is eager to plan and complete your training because your doing well reflects favorably on her. So you have a great deal to gain by working with her. The questions you ask guide her in spotting your special difficulties. Your attention to her suggestions and your efforts to act on them ultimately speed your progress. By working with her, you can learn your job better and faster. You can and will grow confident as you get to understand the job you are doing. In time, the competence you develop will not only earn you the respect of those with whom you work, but also make you eligible for the better positions available. Keep in mind that your desire to get ahead is matched by your employer's need to find and develop employees that can be counted on to become important assets in the operation of the business.

REVIEWING YOUR READING

1   List six questions that may help a student to pinpoint her personal job goal.
2   Explain what should be included in a letter of application.
3   Why is it a good idea to find out about a firm before going for an interview or before accepting a job?
4   Why should an applicant for a clerical position make a special effort to complete the application form neatly and accurately?

5 What can you do at the interview to help sell yourself?

6 What is the best way to win out over the competition in job hunting?

7 Describe three methods for following up on your application.

8 Explain why the beginner should go easy on privileges.

OFFICE ASSIGNMENTS

1 Prepare a résumé for yourself, using the format illustrated on page 500.

2 Consult the classified section of a local newspaper, and find an advertisement for clerical work that would interest you. Write a letter of application for the job. Be sure to cover the pointers mentioned on page 498 and 499. Use the résumé prepared for Office Assignment 1 as an enclosure.

3 Assume that you were interviewed for the job for which you wrote the letter of application in Office Assignment 2. Mr. Ely Porter, personnel manager of the Waverly Equipment Company, seemed favorably impressed, but he told you that he planned to interview several other applicants before deciding on whom to hire. Mr. Porter said that it would probably take about two weeks to decide. Write a letter to Mr. Porter thanking him for the interview. Mention any additional facts that may help your chances.

4 Your supervisor will watch you carefully your first few weeks on the job in order to determine what type of person you are. He will ask himself questions as he observes you in action. For instance, with respect to loyalty the supervisor might ask himself, "Does this new worker gossip about trade secrets?" Think of a question that the supervisor might use to weigh your performance under each of the following headings:

a Loyalty	**c** Initiative	**e** Tact	**g** Promptness
b Courtesy	**d** Honesty	**f** Cooperation	**h** Judgment

5 You have received the following letter from the office manager in the payroll department of a company that has received your application for office employment:

Dear _____:

Your application for office employment has been brought to my attention by our personnel department.

An opening exists in our payroll department, and I would like to discuss the position with you in the near future.

I will be in the office all next week, and I shall be glad to see you any afternoon.

Sincerely yours,

James R. Brooks
Office Manager

Type a reply letter, using the name and address of a local company and the current date.

UNIT 19

BUSINESS CASES AND PROBLEMS

In the Boss's Shoes   Charlotte has received several months of special training as an understudy to replace her unit supervisor who will be retiring shortly. Charlotte's boss now learns that Charlotte has applied for a job in another company where there is an immediate vacancy for someone with her background and experience. Does Charlotte have any moral obligation to the firm that trained her? If you were Charlotte's boss, how would you feel about this?

Your Human Relations   1   Your supervisor, Mrs. Griggs, is a very busy woman who does not know how to delegate work. She has told you to do nothing without her prior approval. The result is that you find yourself wasting hours just waiting for her to authorize small details that you could easily handle. You are willing to follow orders, but Mrs. Griggs has recently become critical about the time it takes you to get a job done.

Should you speak right up and tell Mrs. Griggs that the delay is all her fault? Should you overlook the criticism because you know that Mrs. Griggs is under great pressure and strain? Should you try to help Mrs. Griggs by handling small details without waiting for the approval that she has demanded? Or is there something else that you might try?

2   After working for the firm for about six months, a new clerk remarked:

"This place is the limit. As soon as you learn how to do a job properly, you are transferred to something else. The boss says that this makes you more valuable to the firm. Why should I care? I don't plan to work forever."

What is your opinion of this attitude? If a friend of yours made this remark, what would you say in reply?

What Would You Do If . . . ?   An interviewer asks you what you think the company can expect of you as a worker.

What Does This Mean?   1   An interviewer tells you that you will be paid an hourly wage plus a bonus.

2   If a company has a high rate of employee turnover, you would be wise to investigate the company further before going for an interview. Explain.

Business in Your Area   Follow the procedures outlined in this unit and your teacher's suggestions in obtaining and in participating in an interview (either real or simulated) for office employment in your area. Report on the details of the interview in class.

APPENDIX

MATHEMATICS

A Addition Facts Since clerical work often involves mathematics, you need to be sure that your skill with numbers is built on a solid foundation. There are 36 combinations of simple numbers that frequently cause hesitation, if not mistakes. Mentally, or on a separate sheet of paper, complete the test below as quickly as you can. If any combinations cause you to pause before reaching an answer, note the numbers involved and give them some intensive study later on.

1 9	**2** 8	**3** 6	**4** 7	**5** 5	**6** 9	**7** 7	**8** 8	**9** 5
+9	+3	+9	+9	+8	+4	+8	+6	+9

10 7	**11** 5	**12** 9	**13** 7	**14** 8	**15** 6	**16** 8	**17** 5	**18** 9
+6	+7	+2	+5	+8	+8	+5	+6	+6

19 4	**20** 9	**21** 3	**22** 8	**23** 6	**24** 9	**25** 7	**26** 8	**27** 8
+9	+5	+8	+4	+5	+7	+4	+9	+7

28 2	**29** 4	**30** 7	**31** 8	**32** 9	**33** 6	**34** 3	**35** 6	**36** 9
+9	+7	+7	+4	+3	+7	+9	+6	+8

B Addition Drill Even office workers who know their basic addition combinations find themselves slowing down when they encounter figures in the tens and beyond. Speed up your skill in mental addition by practicing the problems below.

1 3	**2** 13	**3** 23	**4** 33	**5** 43
+9	+9	+9	+9	+9

6 5	**7** 15	**8** 35	**9** 55	**10** 65
+8	+8	+8	+8	+8

11 7	**12** 27	**13** 37	**14** 17	**15** 77
+6	+6	+6	+6	+6

C Checking Addition "Check and double-check" is a standard operating rule in the office. Check your answer to an addition problem by adding in the opposite direction. If you added downward the first time, add upward the second time.

```
  69                         69   (311) Check (upward)
 145                        145
  97                         97
 ---                        ---
 311  First answer (downward)   311
```

Now add and double-check the following problems:

1 83	**2** 298	**3** $7.75	**4** $ 6.25	**5** $19.73
291	145	2.69	12.48	43.58
47	63	4.08	9.83	30.26
				64.20

D Addition and Subtraction Facts As shown here, each combination of two one-figure numbers generally yields two addition facts and two subtraction facts.

$$\begin{array}{r} 5 \\ +3 \\ \hline 8 \end{array} \qquad \begin{array}{r} 3 \\ +5 \\ \hline 8 \end{array} \qquad \begin{array}{r} 8 \\ -5 \\ \hline 3 \end{array} \qquad \begin{array}{r} 8 \\ -3 \\ \hline 5 \end{array}$$

Figure out the two addition facts and two subtraction facts that are related to the following combinations:

1 9 8   **2** 7 6   **3** 8 6   **4** 9 5   **5** 8 7

Why not make up additional drills yourself to get further practice?

E Borrowing in Subtraction One of the easiest methods of subtraction is the take-away borrow method. In the problem

$$\begin{array}{r} 634 \\ -358 \end{array}$$

you would start with the units column and say:

8 from 14= 6; then
5 from 12= 7; and
3 from 5= 2; or 276, which is the answer.

The 14 was obtained by combining the original 4 units with 1 of the 3 tens. The 12 was obtained, in similar fashion, by combining the remaining 2 tens with 1 of the 6 hundreds. The final operation was the subtraction of the original 3 from the remaining 5 hundreds. Practice this method in solving the following subtraction problems:

1 864 − 476   **2** 321 − 265   **3** 445 − 159   **4** 705 − 486   **5** 633 − 547

F Checking Subtraction The accuracy of your answer to a subtraction problem may be verified by addition. After the normal subtraction process, add the subtrahend and remainder together and compare your answer with the minuend.

Subtraction		*Verification*	
145	Minuend	97	Subtrahend
Less 97	Subtrahend	Plus 48	Remainder
48	Remainder	145	Answer = Minuend

Now complete the following subtraction problems, and verify your answers by the addition process.

1 487 − 294   **2** 667 − 408   **3** $14.69 − 10.84   **4** 1,809 − 1,573   **5** $175.37 − 68.43

G Multiplication Facts There are 81 basic multiplication facts from 1×1 to 9×9. Thirty-six of these facts cause difficulties for many young people. These facts are shown below in mixed order. You should be able to give each answer without hesitation. Do the test as quickly as you can to detect your weak spots.

1	3	2	6	3	4	4	8	5	3	6	9	7	7	8	6	9	3
	$\times 3$		$\times 3$		$\times 4$		$\times 4$		$\times 4$		$\times 6$		$\times 4$		$\times 6$		$\times 9$

10	7	11	9	12	8	13	6	14	8	15	8	16	7	17	3	18	4
	$\times 3$		$\times 4$		$\times 6$		$\times 9$		$\times 8$		$\times 7$		$\times 9$		$\times 6$		$\times 7$

19	9	20	6	21	4	22	7	23	9	24	6	25	8	26	4	27	6
	$\times 3$		$\times 8$		$\times 3$		$\times 7$		$\times 7$		$\times 4$		$\times 9$		$\times 8$		$\times 7$

28	3	29	4	30	9	31	3	32	9	33	7	34	4	35	8	36	7
	$\times 8$		$\times 6$		$\times 8$		$\times 7$		$\times 9$		$\times 6$		$\times 9$		$\times 3$		$\times 8$

H Multiplying Numbers of Two or More Digits When you multiply 376 by 234, you are actually multiplying 376 by 200, by 30, and by 4. Each operation is performed separately; then all the partial products are added together.

Example:

$$
\begin{array}{r}
376 \\
\times 234 \\
\hline
1504 \\
11280 \\
75200 \\
\hline
87{,}984
\end{array}
$$

     1504 ($376 \times \quad 4$)
  11280 ($376 \times \quad 30$)
  75200 (376×200)
  87,984 (376×234) Answer

Multiply the following figures, and then verify your accuracy by repeating your calculations in the manner described above.

1	268	2	369	3	407	4	1,987	5	2,258
	$\times 125$		$\times 284$		$\times 362$		$\times 426$		$\times 1{,}463$

I Checking Multiplication Repeating calculations is one way of verifying accuracy. However, a checking process that involves different number combinations is more reliable. Multiplication may be checked by reversing the factors in the problem and multiplying the original multiplier by the multiplicand.

    376 Original multiplicand
 $\times 234$ Original multiplier
 87,984 Product

The problem might be reversed for verification as follows:

    234 Original multiplier now multiplicand
 $\times 376$ Original multiplicand now multiplier
  1404
 16380
 70200
 87,984 Proof

Verify your answers to the following problems by reversing the factors:

1	2	3	4	5
48	185	632	907	1,092
$\times 23$	$\times 67$	$\times 314$	$\times 465$	$\times 236$

J **Division Facts** There are 81 combinations or mathematical facts that you should know in order to perform division easily. Thirty-six of these facts are a little tricky to master. They are shown here in mixed order. You should be able to give each answer without hesitation. Run through this test as quickly as you can to detect the facts about which you are not sure.

1 $3\overline{)9}$	2 $3\overline{)18}$	3 $4\overline{)16}$	4 $4\overline{)32}$	5 $4\overline{)12}$	6 $6\overline{)54}$
7 $4\overline{)28}$	8 $6\overline{)36}$	9 $9\overline{)27}$	10 $3\overline{)21}$	11 $4\overline{)36}$	12 $6\overline{)48}$
13 $9\overline{)54}$	14 $8\overline{)64}$	15 $7\overline{)56}$	16 $9\overline{)63}$	17 $6\overline{)18}$	18 $7\overline{)28}$
19 $3\overline{)27}$	20 $8\overline{)48}$	21 $3\overline{)12}$	22 $7\overline{)49}$	23 $7\overline{)63}$	24 $4\overline{)24}$
25 $9\overline{)72}$	26 $8\overline{)32}$	27 $7\overline{)42}$	28 $8\overline{)24}$	29 $6\overline{)24}$	30 $8\overline{)72}$
31 $7\overline{)21}$	32 $9\overline{)81}$	33 $6\overline{)42}$	34 $9\overline{)36}$	35 $3\overline{)24}$	36 $8\overline{)56}$

K **One-Figure Divisors** Division enables you to determine how many of one figure there are in another. For example, how many 8s are there in 72? Some answers are readily recalled from your knowledge of basic division facts. However, answers to problems involving amounts larger than 100 are more difficult to determine without a written solution. For instance, how many 7s are there in 861? Work from left to right, applying basic division facts to one figure at a time.

1 Since there is only one 7 in 8, subtract 7 from 8 and bring down a remainder of 1.

$$
\begin{array}{r}
1 \\
7\overline{)861} \\
7 \\
\hline
1
\end{array}
$$

2 Since there are only two 7s in 16 (the remainder, 1, combined with the next figure to be divided, 6), subtract 14 from 16 and bring down the remainder, 2.

$$
\begin{array}{r}
12 \\
7\overline{)861} \\
7 \\
\hline
16 \\
14 \\
\hline
2
\end{array}
$$

3 Note that there are three 7s in 21 and that there is no remainder. The answer to the problem is 123.

$$
\begin{array}{r}
123 \\
7\overline{)861} \\
7 \\
\hline
16 \\
14 \\
\hline
21 \\
21 \\
\hline
\end{array}
$$

Now complete the following division problems:

1 5)895   2 4)648   3 6)792   4 7)947   5 9)1,269

L Two-Figure Divisors Ending in Zero   Performing division with a two-figure divisor ending in zero is easy once you have mastered your division facts and the technique for one-figure divisors. Here is what you do to divide 8,560 *by* 40:

1 Set up the figures for division.

$$40)\overline{8,560}$$

2 Think how many 40s there are in 85. Comparing 40 and 85 is like comparing 4 and 8, and the answer is obviously 2. Subtract 80 (40 × 2) and bring down the remainder, 5.

$$\begin{array}{r} 2 \\ 40)\overline{8,560} \\ 8\ 0 \\ \hline 5 \end{array}$$

3 Estimate the number of 40s in 56. The answer is 1. Subtract 40 and bring down the remainder, 16.

$$\begin{array}{r} 21 \\ 40)\overline{8,560} \\ 8\ 0 \\ \hline 56 \\ 40 \\ \hline 16 \end{array}$$

4 Estimate the number of 40s in 160 (obviously, the same as the number of 4s in 16). The answer is 4. Subtract and obtain a zero remainder.

$$\begin{array}{r} 214 \\ 40)\overline{8,560} \\ 8\ 0 \\ \hline 56 \\ 40 \\ \hline 160 \\ 160 \\ \hline \end{array}$$

The final answer to the problem is 214.

Now complete the following division problems using the technique outlined:

1 30)960   2 20)2,860   3 50)7,350   4 70)7,840   5 80)10,400

M Division by Other Two-Figure Divisors   When you wanted to divide 40 into 160, it was easy to see that there were four 40s in 160 by recalling that there were four 4s in 16. However, when the divisor does not end in zero, as in 168 divided by 42, you might expect the computation to be more difficult because you do not know the multiples of 42. You can figure quickly in this situation by estimating.

For estimating purposes, divisors ending in 1, 2, 3, or 4 should be rounded downward, and those ending in 5, 6, 7, 8, or 9 should be rounded upward. For instance, in dividing 168 by 42, think how many 40s (42 rounded downward) there are in 168.

The rounding process permits you to make your estimates much faster because the figures you are thinking about are much simpler to manage. Now complete the following division problems using the rounding technique as required:

1 21)861   **2** 54)1,134   **3** 45)1,620   **4** 67)2,278   **5** 88)27,280

N   Checking Division   Since division problems usually involve a considerable amount of figuring, it pays to be extra careful. Double-check your answer by multiplying it by the divisor. The result (with any remainder added) should equal the original dividend. For example, the solution to $1,247 \div 43$

$$
\begin{array}{r}
29 \quad \text{Quotient} \\
\text{Divisor} \quad 43\overline{)1,247} \quad \text{Dividend} \\
\underline{86} \\
387 \\
\underline{387}
\end{array}
$$

may be checked by multiplying as follows:

$$
\begin{array}{r}
29 \quad \text{Quotient} \\
\underline{\times 43} \quad \text{Divisor} \\
87 \\
\underline{1160} \\
1,247 \quad \text{Proof}
\end{array}
$$

Now complete the following division problems, and then check them by the multiplication process:

1 47)3,055   **2** 53)4,664   **3** 65)8,125   **4** 27)23,247   **5** 35)11,340

O   Checking Division With a Remainder   When a division problem yields an answer that includes a remainder, the solution is checked by:

1 Multiplying the quotient by the divisor.
2 Adding the remainder.
3 Comparing the answer with the original dividend.

For example,

$$
\begin{array}{r}
279 \\
23\overline{)6,438} \\
\underline{4\ 6} \\
1\ 83 \\
\underline{1\ 61} \\
228 \\
\underline{207} \\
21
\end{array}
$$

may be checked by:

$$
\begin{array}{r}
279 \quad \text{Quotient} \\
\underline{\times 23} \quad \text{Divisor} \\
837 \\
\underline{558} \\
6,417 \\
\underline{+21} \quad \text{Remainder} \\
6,438 \quad \text{Original dividend}
\end{array}
$$

Now complete the following division problems, and check them by using the above procedure:

1 9)4,362   **2** 26)4,825   **3** 17)5,462   **4** 31)2,467   **5** 42)80,652

GRAMMAR

A Simple Sentences   A simple sentence conveys a complete thought. Two elements must be present in a complete thought: (1) a *subject* (person, place, or thing); and (2) a *predicate*, which tells what the subject does or what is done to the subject or what state of being the subject is.

> **Example:**   "*The girl* is in class today." In this sentence, *the girl* is the subject, and *is* is the predicate.

Identify the subject and the predicate in the first sentence below. In sentences 2, 3, 4, and 5, supply any missing elements required to make a sentence (a complete thought). Then indicate whether the word that you supply is a subject or a predicate.

1   The railroad delivered the shipment.
2   A special bulletin.
3   was late again.
4   to Max and me.
5   Order merchandise by number.

B   If a simple sentence conveys a complete thought, which of the following expressions are complete thoughts? How could you change the incomplete thoughts into simple sentences?

1   John parked his car in the garage
2   the typewriter
3   on the counter
4   was given me
5   she is taller than he

C Nouns   The name of a person, place, object, idea, quality, or activity is called a *noun*.

> **Example:**   The *park* opened early. (*Park* is a noun naming a place.)

How many nouns can you identify in the following sentences? Tell what they name, such as person, place, and so on.

1   The motor stopped when the switch was turned off.
2   Those men are preparing to go home.
3   The bus arrived at the station.
4   Dependability is a valuable asset.
5   That policy is realistic and pleases the customers.

D Verbs   Previously, you learned that every sentence contains a predicate. The predicate is always a verb. Active verbs are used to indicate some action by the subject—that is, they tell what the subject does. Identify the active verbs in the following expressions.

1   Henry laughed.
2   The train arrived.
3   Order a new mahogany desk and chair.
4   Jane wrote the report.
5   The boss telephoned.

E   Some of the active verbs that are used as predicates require an object to complete their meaning. These verbs are called *transitive* verbs because they need an object (a person or thing) that receives the action of the subject.

> **Example:**   The clerk counted the *change*. (*Change* is the direct object of the verb *counted*, telling *what* the clerk counted.)

Identify the transitive verbs and their direct objects in the following sentences:

1   The customer read the price tag.
2   The store announced a special sale.
3   Richard opened the parcel.
4   The cashier endorsed the check.
5   Mr. King approved the bill.

F   Verbs that require no object to complete their meaning are called *intransitive* verbs because the action stops with the verb.

> **Example:**   The profits *dropped* from the previous high level. (*The profits dropped* is itself complete in meaning.)

Certain sentences below contain transitive verbs; others contain intransitive verbs. Identify the type of verb used in each.

1   The records disappeared from the vault.
2   A clerk checks every bill before payment.
3   The manager prepared the operating instructions.
4   The train screeched to a halt.
5   All the employees attended the conferences.

G   Some intransitive verbs show state of being, not action. These verbs are often called *linking verbs* because they link the subject to a *predicate nominative* (a word that renames the subject) or *predicate adjective* (a word that modifies the subject).

> **Example:**   Miss Martin is our new *teacher*. (*Teacher* is the predicate nominative renaming the subject *Miss Martin*.)
> Paul was very *enthusiastic*. (*Enthusiastic* is the predicate adjective modifying the subject *Paul*.)

Certain sentences at the top of page 520 contain active verbs; others contain intransitive verbs; and still others use state-of-being verbs. Identify the type of verb used in these sentences.

1 Henry was here yesterday.
2 The president resigned from his post.
3 The receptionist greeted the caller.
4 He is leaving right away.
5 Double-checking one's accuracy is important.

H When the subject performs the action, the verb is in the active voice. However, when the subject is acted upon, the verb is in the passive voice.

> **Example:** The directors *examined* the report. (Transitive, active)
> The report *was examined* by the directors. (Transitive, passive)

The following sentences contain transitive verbs (T), intransitive verbs (I), and state-of-being verbs (B). Some of the transitive verbs are in the active voice (A); others are in the passive voice (P). Identify the type of verb and, in the case of transitive verbs, identify the voice being used by means of the code letters supplied.

1 The man is being treated by the doctor.
2 The machine broke down yesterday.
3 Henry answers his mail promptly.
4 Florence was promoted yesterday.
5 Our customers demand the best of service.

I A verb must agree with its subject in number and person. If only one person is involved (I, he, the postman), a singular form of the verb is used.

> **Example:** I am ready.

If more than one person is involved (we, they, the postmen), a plural form of the verb is required. (A plural verb is always used after *you*, even when *you* is singular, referring to only one person.)

> **Example:** We are ready. You are ready.

Examine the following sentences to see that the verb agrees with the subject. Supply the correct verb form if you discover any instances where the verb does not agree with its subject.

1 He went out to lunch.
2 They does a good job.
3 Each of the men are to speak.
4 There is four reports missing.
5 The management are undecided.

J Verb forms vary according to the person or persons involved in the action. When the speaker or writer performs the action, the first person form of the verb is used.

> **Example:** I am studying. We are studying.

When the one spoken to is performing the action, the second person form of the verb is used.

> **Example:** You are studying.

When other persons or agencies perform the action (he, she, it, they, the boss, and so on), the third person form is used.

> **Example:** He is studying. They are studying.

Copy each of the following sentences on a sheet of paper. Study them carefully. Then draw a single line under the complete subject. Draw a double line under the complete predicate. Identify the person of the verb being used.

1 The postman collected the postage due.
2 Richard, the unit file clerk, expects a raise.
3 As beginners eager to get ahead, you must keep informed about the new procedures.
4 I went out to eat. What did you do?
5 We shopped during our lunch hour.

K Verb forms are changed to indicate the time of the action involved. The commonest time forms, or tenses, are the present, past, and future.

The present tense of the verb is used to indicate an action that is taking place or a continuous condition. The past tense relates to something that took place or that existed at a definite time in the past. The future tense expresses action that will take place or a condition that will exist in the future.

> **Example:** He *drives* carefully in traffic. (Present)
> He *drove* carefully over the icy roads last winter. (Past)
> He *will drive* carefully when he gets his license. (Future)

Identify the verbs in the following sentences, and indicate whether they represent present, past, or future tense:

1 Mike telephoned yesterday.
2 The conference will start next month.
3 He buys cautiously.
4 No one is working now.
5 He overlooked a vital fact.

L As stated previously, the present tense is used to indicate action actually taking place at the time.

> **Example:** Jerry *practices* every day. (Present)

However, if the action began in the past and was completed at some indefinite time before the present, the present perfect tense is used. This consists of *has* or *have* and the past participle. The past participle is usually formed by adding *d* or *ed* to the infinitive.

> **Example:** Jerry *has practiced* this speech for months. (Present perfect)

Identify the verbs in the following sentences, and indicate whether they express the present, past, future, or present perfect tense.

1 She has done her homework.
2 Harry wrote for the money.
3 Our future expansion will amaze you.
4 Tom talks convincingly.
5 The customer refused the allowance.

M Previously, you learned that the past tense of the verb is used in connection with an action that took place or existed at a definite time in the past.

 Example: He *finished* the job yesterday. (Past)

However, if the action began in the past and was completed in the past before something else happened, the past perfect tense is used. The past perfect tense consists of *had* and the past participle.

 Example: He *had finished* the job before the contract expired. (Past perfect)

Study the following sentences carefully. Identify the verb(s), and indicate the tense used—present, past, future, present perfect, or past perfect:

1 Vicki left early yesterday.
2 Jameson has now completed the shipment.
3 The clerk tallies all cash receipts.
4 She had rushed into the office just before the boss appeared.
5 He will study during his leave of absence.

N You have already learned that the future tense is used in connection with an action that will take place in the future. The future perfect tense is used to express an action that will be completed before a certain time in the future. The future perfect tense is made up of *shall have* or *will have* and the past participle.

 Example: You *will have done* the job before that time.

Study the following sentences carefully. Identify the verb(s), and indicate the tense used—present, past, future, present perfect, past perfect, or future perfect.

1 He returned unexpectedly.
2 We will have finished our work before the boss returns from lunch.
3 I have recorded all the facts that have come to light.
4 He always shares the credit with his assistants.
5 William will leave first.

O The future tense is used when a person may wish to convey intention or determination rather than simple futurity. Simple futurity with which you have dealt so far was expressed by using *shall* with the first person singular or plural (I shall go, we shall go, and so on) and *will* with the second and third persons (you will arrive, he will finish, and so on).

Intention or determination in the future is expressed by reversing the use of *shall* and *will. Will* is used with the first person, and *shall* with the second and third persons.

Example: I *will* begin. We *will* go.
You *shall find out* for yourself.
He *shall* win. They *shall pay* in full.

Identify the verbs in the sentences below. Then indicate whether they express simple futurity or determination.

1   I will return as promised.
2   They will meet us at the gate.
3   In any event, the firm shall stand behind its guarantee.
4   You will soon see the new building.
5   When shall I call again?

P   A verb form ending in *ing* and used as a noun is called a *gerund.*

Example: *Driving* is hard work. (*Driving* is the subject of the sentence.)
They considered *moving* away. (*Moving* is the object of the verb *considered.*)
He can save time by *doing* the job himself. (*Doing* is the object of the preposition *by.*)

Identify the gerunds in the following sentences. Then explain how they are used in the sentences (for example, as subject, object of the verb, and so on).

1   Planning ahead saves worry.
2   He is deficient in reading.
3   They enjoy telling about their trip.
4   Talking and doing are two different things.
5   He prefers walking in mild weather.

Q   Capitals   The first word of a sentence always begins with a capital letter. A word in the body of the sentence that is used as the official name of a particular person, place, or thing (called a *proper noun*) is also written with a capital letter.

Example: *The* store is open today. (*The* is the first word in the sentence.)
John went to *Chicago.* (*John* is a proper noun relating to a particular person and also the first word in the sentence. *Chicago* is a proper noun relating to a particular place.)

Identify the proper nouns in the sentences below. Then rewrite the sentences, using the correct capitalization.

1   she bought it at the king department store.
2   roger said that his favorite hotel was the ritz in st. louis.
3   the visitor was henry hart, representing the otis supply company.
4   the smith foundation was established by thomas smith of centerville.
5   tell anna hooper in the sales department that mr. french will call back later.

R Pronouns   Pronouns are used in place of nouns. Personal pronouns are selected according to the noun form, or person, they stand in place of.

I, we: for the first person (the speaker)
You: for the second person (the person or persons spoken to)
He, she, it, they: for the third person (the person or persons spoken about)

> **Example:**   Mr. and Mrs. Edwards arrived late last night. *They* had a long, hard journey. (*They* is used in place of *Mr. and Mrs. Edwards.*)

How many personal pronouns can you identify in the following sentences? Indicate the person of each pronoun that you find.

1 They were in a big hurry to leave.
2 Have you had many job offers lately?
3 How do the Berrys expect me to finish when they keep interrupting me?
4 She is going with her family. They will all travel by plane.
5 You have all heard the news. We are as surprised as you.

S   Pronouns change form according to their use in the sentence. The form taken is referred to as the *case* of the pronoun. A pronoun used as a subject is in the nominative case, and one used as a predicate nominative (after the verb *to be*) is also in the nominative case.

> **Example:**   *He* spoke clearly. (*He* is the subject.)
> It is *he.* (*He* is the predicate nominative.)

A pronoun used as the object of a transitive verb, a preposition, or an infinitive is in the objective case.

> **Example:**   He called *him.* (*Him* is object of the verb *called.*)
> I went to see *him.* (*Him* is object of the infinitive *to see.*)

Pronouns in the possessive case express ownership.

> **Example:**   *My* book is lost.
> That car is *theirs.*

How many personal pronouns can you find in the following sentences? Tell the case of each pronoun that you find.

1 He took his car to the garage.
2 Hers is the green coat.
3 Give it to me, please.
4 Have you seen them?
5 Were you the lucky one? No, it was he.

T Adjectives   Adjectives are words used to modify nouns and pronouns. They describe or tell something about the word they modify.

> **Example:**   The *old* typewriter needed repairs. (*Old* is an adjective which describes or identifies *typewriter.*)

How many adjectives can you identify in the sentences below? Indicate which word is modified in each case.

1   The angry customer walked out.
2   This is the last chance to buy.
3   The stock was bought at a low price.
4   The heavy truck struck the white fence.
5   Use lined paper to make detailed notes.

U It is important that you be aware of the exact meaning of certain adjectives.

Little, less: refer to size or bulk.
Few, fewer: refer to number or quantity.
Farther, farthest: relate to measurable distance.
Further, furthest: relate to intangible distance or degree.
Latter: refers to order of position.
Later: relates to time.

Use each of the above adjectives in an original sentence to illustrate your understanding of their correct usage.

V Adverbs An adverb is a word used to modify a verb, an adjective, or another adverb. It usually tells *why, when, where, in what manner,* or *to what extent.*

Example: He walked *quickly.* (*Quickly* modifies the verb *walked.*)
He walked *very* quickly. (*Very* modifies the adverb *quickly.*)
I was *extremely* tired. (*Extremely* modifies the adjective *tired.*)

How many adverbs can you identify in the sentences below? Indicate the word that is modified in each case.

1   We felt very sad.
2   They drove too fast for safety.
3   He looked worried.
4   I spoke carefully.
5   You have done unbelievably well.

W Adjectives and adverbs are frequently used to make comparisons. If two items are compared, the comparative degree is used. If three or more items are involved, the superlative degree is used.

The comparative degree of many common one- and two-syllable words is formed by adding *er* to the original form of the word, or positive degree.

Example: He ran *faster* than Bob.

The superlative degree of many common one- and two-syllable words is formed by adding *est* to the original, or positive degree.

Example: She is the *youngest* of the four children.

Supply the correct form of the adjective or adverb to complete the following comparisons:

1   Bob, John, and Tom are the (tall).
2   I am the (slow) one in the class.
3   Robert is the (old) of the two.
4   Of all the cakes, this one is the (tasty).
5   The design of this machine is the (simple) that I have ever seen.

X   The comparative degree of certain adjectives and adverbs that have two or more syllables is formed by adding *more* or *less* to the original form of the word.

> **Example:**   He is *more* lenient than I.
> She is *less* flustered than Dora.

The superlative degree of certain adjectives and adverbs having two or more syllables is formed by adding *most* or *least* to the original.

> **Example:**   It is the *least* important fact.
> You are the *most* beautiful of the candidates.

Complete sentences 1 to 3 that follow by supplying the correct forms for the comparative or superlative degree. Complete sentences 4 and 5 by using negative comparisons in the comparative or superlative degree.

1   He is the (observant) of the two.
2   This paper is the one that is the (widely read) in the entire area.
3   Who is (quick) than he is?
4   Can anyone be (versatile) than I?
5   Of the two, this model is (flexible) in operation.

Y   Some adjectives and adverbs have irregular forms for comparative and superlative degrees.

Positive	*Comparative*	*Superlative*
many	more	most
little	less	least
bad	worse	worst

Use the comparative or superlative of each of these words in the kind of sentence that might appear in a business letter.

Z   Prepositions   A preposition such as *to, at, by, for, in, into, of, with,* and *between* connects a noun or pronoun with some other word in a sentence.

> **Example:**   He went *with* his friends. (*With* is the preposition connecting the noun *friends* with the verb *went.*)
> Give the map *to* the teacher. (*To* connects *teacher* and *map.*)
> I divided it *between* us. (*Between* connects *it* and *us.*)

Identify the prepositions in the following sentences. Then explain what words are being connected by each preposition.

1 We waited at the shopping center.
2 His telephone call to the station saved time.
3 Here is an order for five tickets.
4 I should be finished by five o'clock.
5 What is your opinion of the report?

PUNCTUATION

A Period   The period is used at the end of a sentence that makes a statement or expresses a command. Periods are also used to indicate common abbreviations. Copy the following sentences, using periods correctly in each.

   Example: Mr. Hall lives here.

1 The mail is late this morning
2 The first delivery arrived at 6 am today
3 Joe sorted the letters Bob took charge of the parcels
4 The COD package was addressed to Mr C R King of Huntsville
5 Ship the order fob Lansing no later than Jan 10

B Comma   The comma serves to separate words in a series (for example: desks, chairs, and tables) and to separate parts of a sentence that might result in confusion if run together (for example: Below, the man was struggling for his life.). Copy the following sentences, using commas correctly in each.

1 Please bring me all the books records and reports.
2 Inside the men were working.
3 A pencil some paper and an eraser are all that I need.
4 Birthdays anniversaries and holidays are special occasions.
5 Beyond the typewriters clattered.

C   A sentence may contain a word or an expression that is independent of the main thought. Such parenthetical words or expressions are set off by commas.

   Example: It is risky, *therefore*, to tackle the job alone. (*Therefore* is a parenthetical word.)

Copy the following sentences, using a comma or commas to set off the parenthetical words or expressions.

1 John suspected however that the facts were incomplete.
2 Consequently the case was referred to a higher court.
3 Therefore only one conclusion is possible.
4 As you can readily see the problem is not an easy one.
5 The rumor so he heard came from a reliable source.

D   Brevity is important in business writing. However, there are occasions when a word or phrase needs further explanation. A noun or noun phrase that identifies another noun or pronoun that immediately precedes it is called an *appositive*. Commas are used to set off most appositives from the rest of the sentence.

Example: Roger, *the leader of the group*, made all arrangements. (*The leader of the group* is an appositive identifying the noun *Roger*.)

Copy the following sentences, using commas to set off the appositives.

1   The speaker a well-known expert explained the new process.
2   Chicago a great transportation center is a popular place for conventions.
3   The new office building the tallest in the city attracted many comments.
4   Monday March 17 is St. Patrick's Day.
5   Give this message to Mr. Healy head of the department.

E   Question Mark   A question mark is used at the end of a sentence that asks a question.

Example: Did Robert telephone?

Copy the following sentences, and supply the correct punctuation. (Use a period, comma, or question mark, if necessary.)

1   When do you plan to return
2   Do you live very far away
3   That isn't too far in a fast plane
4   Shall I reserve a room for Friday night
5   Why people go there is more than I can understand

F   Semicolon   The semicolon is used to separate items in a series when the items already contain commas.

Example: We have fully equipped branches in Troy, New York; Denver, Colorado; and Seattle, Washington.

Copy the following sentences, and supply the correct punctuation (period, comma, question mark, or semicolon.)

1   The salesman went to Lorain Ohio Chicago Illinois and Madison Wisconsin
2   The parcel contained pens pencils and erasers
3   Obviously there is only one answer to the problem
4   Richard the new messenger reported to work on Monday
5   Would you prefer to visit Los Angeles or San Diego California

G   When two complete thoughts joined in a single sentence are linked by a transitional expression, such as *otherwise, for example, namely, that is, therefore*, and *furthermore*, a semicolon is used before the expression and a comma afterward.

Example: The invention was a success; *therefore*, the firm decided to expand its research activities.

No comma is needed after one-syllable transitional expressions like *hence*, *then*, and *thus*.

Example: Business was bad; *hence* the shops closed early.

Copy the following sentences, and supply the correct punctuation.

1 Thunder shattered the silence then the rains came
2 The account has been closed furthermore we shall have to sue to collect the balance we owe

H   Colon   A colon is used to indicate that additional information is to follow. It is commonly used after the salutation of a letter.

Example: Dear Mr. Jones:

The colon is also used after such expressions as *the following* or *as follows*.

Example: Employees on vacation this week include the following: Josephine, Vicky, Susan, Chris, and Mel.

Copy the following sentences, and supply the correct punctuation.

1 The new service centers are located in the following cities Chicago Seattle Mobile and Richmond
2 Jenkins the chief accountant is expected at 4 p m
3 Who approved this order for repair parts supplies and tools
4 Today is the deadline hence a decision must be made right away
5 Gentlemen Please ship our Order 647 at once

I   The colon is used to separate the figures for hours and minutes.

Example: 6:30 a.m.   11:24 p.m.

Copy the following sentences, and supply the correct punctuation.

1 Marie agreed to work until 830 p m Friday
2 Have you made your reservations yet
3 The entertainment will consist of singing dancing and storytelling
4 The bus schedule includes the following afternoon departures 245 335 425 and 538
5 Reply immediately on the enclosed card otherwise your share will be assigned to someone else

J   Exclamation Point and Dash   The exclamation point and the dash are marks of punctuation that require special care because excessive use robs them of their effectiveness.

Use the exclamation point at the end of a sentence (or an expression that stands for a sentence) only to show emotion or strong feeling.

Example: What a wonderful surprise!
Congratulations! It was an excellent job!

Use the dash in place of commas to set off a parenthetical element that requires special emphasis.

Example: I believe—but I could be wrong—that the case is settled.

Copy the following sentences, and supply the correct punctuation.

1   Let us know what you decide and we hope you will approve so that we can proceed
2   Have you heard from Mrs Roberts since she called at 915 yesterday
3   The following items were missing one desk six staplers and three chairs
4   The local expert Kenneth Hykes will therefore be asked to analyze the sample
5   Oh my Are you sick too That makes seven people absent

K   The dash is used before words such as *these*, *they*, and *all* when these words stand as subjects summarizing a preceding list of details.

Example: Filing, typewriting, computing—all are valuable skills in office work. (*All* stands as the subject summarizing a preceding list of details.)

Copy the following sentences, and supply the correct punctuation.

1   The office hours are from 9 to 11 a m on Tuesdays Thursdays and Saturdays
2   Teenagers newlyweds retired persons these are all important markets
3   Rogers the manager was too busy to come
4   Have you had your vacation yet
5   The order came too late therefore we refused to accept it

L   Hyphen   The hyphen is used in place of the word *to* in writing numbers and dates in continuous sequence and certain other compound expressions.

Example: The regulation appeared on pages 16–21.
One change occurred during the period 1937–1939.
A Chicago-Dallas flight leaves the airport at noon.

Copy the following sentences, and supply the correct punctuation.

1   During the years 1967 1973 he worked as a reporter
2   The New Orleans Memphis bus was overdue
3   A successful campaign takes money time and careful planning
4   Where were you at 6 30 last night
5   Thompson manager of the Oakland office was transferred to San Diego on June 30 1973

M   Parentheses   Parentheses are used in business writing to enclose explanatory data or remarks that are independent of the main thought of the sentence.

Example: The article appeared in the March 15 issue of *Time* (see page 24).
Josephine paid the bill ($4.98) when the parcel was delivered.

Copy the following sentences, and supply the correct punctuation.

1   In the previous edition 1974 the illustration was more distinct
2   Mrs Roy Smith formerly Jean Grant joined the club last week
3   The remittance $25 covered registration fee and tuition
4   What is the flying time on the Atlanta-Cincinnati route
5   Keith who served as chairman called the meeting to order

N   Parentheses are used around letters or numbers identifying items that are listed in a sentence.

    Example: Bulk mailing must be (1) faced, (2) sorted, and (3) tied before mailing.

Copy the following sentences, and supply the correct punctuation.

1   The two factors that make a big difference are a money and b talent
2   Oh no Don't tell me that the 6 10 bus is late again
3   Don't forget to complete each step in sequence 1 opening 2 reading 3 sorting and 4 distributing
4   I heard later however that the permit was canceled
5   The Dec 31 reports from Chicago Illinois and Dubuque Iowa arrived yesterday at 9 45 am

INDEX